A Documen

Communism

A Documentary History of

Communism and the World

From Revolution to Collapse

THIRD EDITION

Edited, with introduction, notes,
and original translations by

Robert V. Daniels

University of Vermont
Published by University Press of New England
Hanover and London

University of Vermont
Published by University Press of New England, Hanover, NH 03755
© 1994 by the Trustees of the University of Vermont
All rights reserved
Printed in the United States of America   5   4   3   2   1
CIP data appear at the end of the book

Contents

Preface (1960 Edition)

It would naturally be impossible in one volume of documentary materials to cover a subject as broad and complex as Communism from every point of view. The careful description of political institutions, events and everyday life as they have proceeded over the years under Communism would require whole shelves of source materials. The present work has been deliberately focused on the subject of Communist thought and doctrine, for reason of its commanding importance, its relative uniformity within the Communist scheme of things, and the appropriateness of the documentary approach to its elucidation. We will be primarily concerned with the evolution of top-level guiding ideas, policies and intentions among the Communists. Statements of deviators of all sorts are included along with the official line of those in power—we may regard anyone who claims descent from Lenin as equally meriting the label "Communist." Through the pronouncements of its leading figures, both those who have ruled and those who have fallen from grace, we may arrive at a reasonably approximate picture of what Communism actually is, historically considered.

The problems of selecting materials for a purpose such as this never permit a fully satisfactory solution. I have attempted a fair digest and representative choice of statements expressing all the main concepts and currents in Communism. Many readers, however, will find that their areas of interest are underrepresented. This failing is the price that must be paid in an effort to survey the entire Communist movement in one documentary volume, and meet the needs of the student, the general reader, and the scholar who is not a specialist in this field.

The present work would never have materialized without the assistance of the many people who helped in its preparation or who paved the way with their own studies. I am indebted to the many publishers who kindly permitted me to reprint selections of previously translated material (individually acknowledged under each item). Certain documentary collections which have been particularly helpful deserve special mention—the pioneering *Documentary History of Chinese Communism*, by Conrad Brandt, Benjamin Schwartz and John K. Fairbank (Harvard University Press, 1952); the *Materials for the Study of the Soviet System*, by James H. Meisel and Edward S. Kozera (The George Wahr Publishing Co., Ann Arbor, Michigan, 1950), which brings together a wide selection of previously translated Soviet documents; the documentary compilations prepared by the Legislative Reference Service of the Library of Congress; the various collections of Soviet documents published by the Stanford University Press; and the English editions of the selected works of Lenin and Stalin, published by the Foreign Languages Publishing House in Moscow. The Harvard University Library has kindly permitted me to include my translations from a number of hitherto unpublished documents in the Trotsky Archive. For suggestions regarding documents on Far Eastern Communism I am indebted to Professor George T. Little, and to him and Professor Lewis S. Feuer I am grateful for many helpful criticisms. To Mr. Nathan Glazer I wish to express my appreciation for initially encouraging me to undertake this project, and for his editorial assistance since that time. Mrs. Joyce McLaughlin of the InterLibrary Loan Department of the University of Vermont Library rendered me invaluable service in locating and obtaining many scarce but important publications. The vast work of transcribing and assembling the documentary materials was ably done by Mrs. Madeline Chaplin, Mrs. Jean Falls, Mrs. Phyllis Reservitz, Mrs. Roberta Stetson, and my wife, Alice Daniels.

Preface (Revised Edition)

Since the publication of the original edition of this work more than two decades ago the subject of Communism has expanded in years, in territory and in complexity. In the present revision I have endeavored to respond to these changes by abridging the pre-1960 material of the first edition and adding new selections to reflect recent developments in the various Communist parties both inside and outside the Soviet Union. To facilitate the interest of users in focusing either on internal Soviet history or on the evolution of Soviet foreign policy and Communist movements outside the USSR, the new edition has been organized into two volumes, each devoted to one of these aspects of Communism and proceeding chronologically. Both the original material and the post-1960 additions have been divided accordingly, and the portion of the 1960 introduction pertaining to external issues has been placed in this volume.

With the increasing scope and diversity of the subject of Communism it has become more difficult than ever to achieve a totally satisfactory and representative selection of documents within a reasonable compass. To comply with spatial limitations, items in the original edition have been culled where their retrospective importance is not crucial in mapping the development of the Communist movement. A few new pre-1960 items have been added. Post-1960 material has been selected with emphasis on illustrating the main internal developments in the Soviet Union, the most significant events in Soviet foreign relations and the chief variants among Communist movements outside the Soviet Union. As in the original edition, statements representing the views of dissenters within Communist countries are included together with the official views of the leadership. Though many points of particular interest inevitably remain unrepresented, I hope the reader will find that the overall usefulness of this collection has been substantially enhanced.

For their support in the initiation of this revised edition I am indebted to Mr. Thomas McFarland, Director of the University Press of New England, Professor Henry Steffens of the Editorial Board of the Press, and Dean Robert Lawson of the Graduate College of the University of Vermont. In the compilation of new material for this edition I have been greatly aided by the vast resources of Soviet documentation made available since the 1950's by the *Current Digest of the Soviet Press* and its companion series, *Current Soviet Policies.* My colleague Professor Peter Seybolt has been of great assistance with his advice about developments in Chinese Communism. Mrs. Carolyn Perry has provided expert and tireless support in the preparation of the revised manuscript. Mrs. Penni Bearden, Mrs. Susan Lacy, and Mrs. Claire Sheppard have also given me able assistance.

Chinese names have been rendered in the familiar Wade-Giles romanization, as in the 1960 edition, up to the official changeover in 1979; thereafter the new Pin-Yin system is followed with bracketed references to Wade-Giles where necessary to avoid confusion.

Preface (1994 Edition)

This third, revised and updated edition of *A Documentary History of Communism* coincides with the amazing collapse of Communist rule in the Soviet Union. It follows the fall of Communist governments in Eastern Europe and the virtual demise of the international Communist movement, except for the People's Republic of China and a few other outposts of old-style Communism in the Far East and in Cuba whose days may be numbered. Thus the story of Communism as a world-wide phenomenon is now essentially closed, and there will be no need for further revisions of this work.

While this new edition reflects the startling developments in the Communist world since the advent of reform under Mikhail Gorbachev in 1985, I have found no need to make other major changes either of concept or of content. Communism has become history, but that history is still a living background to post-Communist life. In fact, the historical understanding of Communism has become all the more important with the tendency since the collapse of the Soviet Union, among outsiders as well as among Russians and the other ex-Soviet peoples, to regard the entire Communist experience from 1917 to 1991 as an undifferentiated nightmare, better forgotten than studied. This attitude threatens to create a new historical "black hole" that could swallow up the true record as indiscriminately as the Communists themselves did. The post-Communist world can only be understood as Communism left it, as the end-product of a complex evolution, where professions of reality and claims of achievement, recorded in these documents, squared less and less with the actual course of affairs.

The events in the Communist world since 1985 are enormously complicated, and the wealth of documentation on the opening up and then the collapse of most Soviet client states and movements creates an embarrassment of riches. This is the more difficult to deal with because the format of the present work demands ruthless selection and condensation of the most important and representative materials to document key developments in the various branches of the Communist movement. No doubt the work invites more dissatisfaction over the selections from the post-1985 period, but this is inescapable given the complex and variegated nature of the developments that have to be included within it. For the earlier periods I have substituted a few more cogent documents and have condensed others to improve readability and keep the volume within manageable size.

This story closes with the dissolution of the Soviet Union, following the effective suppression of the CPSU. These events, coming after Soviet abandonment of all Communist satellite countries and parties, put an end to the Communist movement as the world has known it, leaving only anachronistic Communist outposts far from the old Soviet heartland. Their fates will be determined individually; the history of Communism as a unified global phenomenon has come to an end.

For their help in initiating and executing this final revision of the second volume of *A Documentary History of Communism* I am indebted once again to Thomas McFarland of UPNE, and also to the Documents division of the University of Vermont Library and to Mrs. Diann Varricchione, who processed the new portions of the manuscript.

Introduction

*The Evolution of the Communist Mind—
In the World*

World Revolution or Imperialist Expansion

The commanding importance of the subject of Communism is due to the international character of the movement. Up to this point we have dealt with the movement entirely as a Russian phenomenon, because its actual origins were Russian and the critical stages of its evolution were intimately shaped by Russian circumstances. From the time of its initial success in Russia, however, the movement has had an increasingly important impact on the rest of the world, in two principal ways: the power exercised by Communism in Russia as the ruling movement in a large country, and the doctrinally-inspired, Russia-oriented Communist revolutionary movements which have appeared almost everywhere else in the world.

These two lines of influence suggest the basic duality which has characterized international Communism. In part it is an international revolutionary movement ostensibly animated by Marx's vision of the world dictatorship of the proletariat. On the other hand, most of the time and in most places it has been firmly under the control of the rulers of Soviet Russia, who have not hesitated to employ the movement, in the short run at least, as an instrument for promoting the power and security of that particular state. There has been a definite trend from the first of these aspects to the second—from primitive revolutionary enthusiasm to calculated manipulation, with the power of the Russian state as a primary criterion. However, the old doctrine still contributes the basic sense of hostility toward the non-Communist world, which sometimes approaches the intensity of religious war.

World revolution, according to Marxism, was not a deliberate policy or duty (as many anxious opponents of the Communists imagine it to be), but merely a prediction of what the development of international capitalism supposedly made inevitable. For a person who does not accept the Marxian philosophy of history there is no particular reason for regarding the world-wide success of Communism as inevitable or even possible. For one brief moment—the time of the controversy in 1918 over peace with Germany or revolutionary war—the Russian Communists were at the point of direct action to help the inevitable along, but Lenin's cautious counsel of preserving power in one country prevailed. Had the Trotskyists been victorious in the 1920's, with their stress on the importance of world revolution for the realization of the socialist plan in Russia, it is conceivable that the issue could have arisen again, but Stalin's ideological tour de force of "socialism in one country" eliminated all theoretical grounds for risking the security of the regime in Russia in order to advance the fortunes of the revolution abroad.

From 1918 to 1935, insofar as Russian national security was not risked, the

Soviet leaders encouraged and assisted various Communist revolutionary movements abroad—notably in Germany and China—without questioning the identity of interest between Soviet Russia and the foreign revolutionaries. However, with the change of line to collective security and the "popular front" in 1935, the Soviet leadership temporarily suspended the revolutionary drive in international Communism. From 1935 to 1939 and from 1941 to 1946 or 1947 the Communists in most places coöperated with liberal and socialist groups, and made a highly successful appeal as a party aiming at democratic reform and resistance to fascism, rather than the one party proletarian dictatorship. During this period the Communists were distinguished only by the typical Leninist party organization and the unquestioning subservience to Russia which had been implanted in the international movement during the 1920's. A particularly dramatic demonstration of Communist preoccupation with the security of the Soviet state came with the Nazi-Soviet pact in 1939, which was concluded at the cost of a severe shock to Communist loyalties the world over.

The history of international Communism since World War II has been governed by a complicated interaction between Communist-oriented revolutionary emotion in many countries and the aggressive and unscrupulous pursuit of power politics and national security by the Soviet Union, which has used the non-Russian Communist movements as much as possible as an instrument of this policy. Where Communism has come to power outside Russia it has been through direct Russian imposition (as in most of Eastern Europe) or through guerrilla warfare conducted by the Communists against both enemy occupation forces and domestic rivals (as in Yugoslavia and China). No purely internal and independent Communist revolution has ever been accomplished since the short-lived Hungarian Soviet Republic of 1919.

The vague Marxist conviction survives that eventually the Communist movement will inevitably triumph everywhere. Khrushchev plays this theme with great pride, but the very notion of inevitability absolves the Soviet leaders from the obligation to take any risks to which they do not feel emotionally inclined. The main theoretical source of their anxiety is the fear that the capitalist powers, seeing the ground slipping from under their feet, might resort to force in order to check the presumed historical trend toward communism. Non-Communists who do not believe this is the trend need have little to fear unless the Russians are provoked or tempted into preventive war by threats or weakness on the part of the anti-Communist powers.

The Export of Communism—Eastern Europe

The establishment of Communist governments in the Soviet Union's satellite states of Eastern Europe represents the outstanding Russian success in the employment of Communism as an instrument of power politics. Everywhere that Soviet occupation regimes were in control—Poland, Rumania, Bulgaria, Hungary, East Germany—Communist Party dictatorships were installed in power with direct Russian backing and pressure, under the cover of the ostensibly democratic coalition governments established in the region when the Nazis collapsed in 1944–45. In these cases there was no significant popular revolutionary movement, and the Communists did not use a revolutionary appeal in driving for power; they preferred to work behind the scenes, penetrating (with the aid of Soviet leverage) the police and military organizations of the respective countries, and gradually constricting the opportunity for genuine legal opposition to their rule. By the end of 1947 the process was complete, though the dummy forms of multi-party coalition have survived to the present.

In marked contrast to this pattern in East Central Europe, the Communists came to power in Yugoslavia and Albania and scored their near-victory in Greece as active revolutionaries, waging guerrilla war simultaneously against the German and Italian occupying forces and against the native representatives of the status quo. When World War II ended, Communist Party rule was firmly established in Yugoslavia and Albania, without any appreciable Russian help.

Czechoslovakia stands somewhat apart, as the case where the Communist assumption of power most nearly resembled the original Bolshevik revolution in Russia. A large popular minority, animated not so much by revolutionary feeling as by reform aims and pro-Russian, anti-Nazi sentiment, had backed the Communists since the end of World War II; the Communist leader Gottwald was prime minister of a democratically functioning government. At the opportune moment, in February, 1948, the Communists precipitated a cabinet crisis; wielding the revolutionary force of a workers' militia and the threat of Russian intervention, they secured the support necessary for a parliamentary majority and overawed the opposition into nonresistance. Once they were in undisputed control of the government, it was an easy matter for the Communists to suppress the opposition altogether and proceed with the establishment of totalitarian controls.

The experience of Communism in Eastern Europe has been particularly stressful because of the telescoped imposition of Soviet political development, under close Russian control and strictly subordinated to considerations of Russian national power. Within the short span of years from 1945 to 1950, Eastern Europe experienced military defeat or occupation, Communist maneuvering for power, the distribution of estates to the peasants, the nationalization of industry, the establishment of one-party dictatorship, the creation of totalitarian police controls and censorship, the beginnings of collectivization of the peasants, the establishment of Communist industrial discipline, the pursuit of heavy-industry construction programs at the expense of national belt-tightening, and purge trials within the Communist parties themselves—developments which were spread over two decades in Russia. These rapid changes were brought about mainly at Russian behest, to cement Communist control over the satellite countries and to facilitate Soviet economic exploitation of the region.

Despite the traditional Communist antagonism toward imperialism, Soviet Russia suffered neither moral nor economic impediments to the exploitation of regions under its control. Under the state capitalism of the USSR such exploitation of the "colonies" eased the problem of capital accumulation without constituting the threat to the level of employment which it would mean in an ordinary capitalist economy. The terms of "international proletarian solidarity" in which the Russians cloaked their operations might be regarded as a rationalization on a par with the "white man's burden."

The main problem in Eastern Europe, from the Russian standpoint, was to maintain control over the local Communists in the face of increasingly apparent divergence between Communist aims in each country and the economic and strategic interest of the Russians. All of the Communist leaders in Eastern Europe had risen in the movement by accepting Russian authority and the disciplined duty of supporting the interests of the Soviet state. Most of them, moreover, owed their acquisition and tenure of political power to the backing which the Russians gave the Communist Party in each country. Yugoslavia is the outstanding exception, where Tito assumed power independently as the leader of a successful revolutionary and resistance movement. Outside of Yugoslavia it is certain that no Communist government could survive in Eastern Europe without Russian backing.

Despite their obligations to the Russians, most East-European Communist leaders found themselves in conflict between what their own ambitions or the interests of their respective countries called for, and the requirements of the Russians. The Russians, declining to rely solely on the doctrinal loyalty of their East-European comrades, moved swiftly to establish more reliable controls over the satellites by infiltrating Russian agents directly into their police and military organizations. With all the lines of influence at the Russians' disposal it was easy in most cases for them to shake up any satellite leadership which was too independent-minded, and assure an unquestioning response to Moscow's demands.

Under these circumstances of Russian control there could be no independent development of doctrine or policy by the East European Communists. They were compelled to conform to the Soviet model of forced industrialization and total organizational control, although in the more developed and sophisticated countries like Czechoslovakia and Poland less utility and more discontent were inherent in these steps. Communist doctrine in its finished Soviet form as an elaborately fraudulent but rigorously enforced rationalization of the modernizing dictatorship was made the rule. It remained only for Soviet propagandists to demonstrate scholastically how Eastern Europe remained at a lower level of the dictatorship of the proletariat than the Soviet Union, in the form of the so-called "People's Democracies."

All of the most important events in Eastern Europe since 1948 have centered around the understandable tendency of local Communist leaders to resist Russian domination—i.e., the movement of "national communism." The basic consideration in national communism is simply the distribution of power within the Communist movement—shall the national regimes dictate in their own right or serve merely as agents of Moscow? The basic features of Communism as developed in Russia—the party dictatorship, the quasi-capitalist economic function, and the rigid rationalizing doctrine—are for the most part carried over into national communism. However, the national Communists have characteristically tried to alleviate popular discontent by asserting national independence, suspending collectivization of the peasants, and scaling down industrial ambitions to permit a somewhat freer and more abundant economic life to the citizenry. In the economic caution which they combine with the party dictatorship the national Communist tendency in Eastern Europe is comparable to the Russian right-wing Communist faction led by Bukharin in the late 1920's. Beyond this, save for a modicum of uneasy cultural freedom, national communism has not yielded.

The initial success of national communism in Yugoslavia is easily understandable in terms of geography and the historical background. This was the satellite most defensible and most accessible to the non-Communist world, and at the same time one where the Communists had come to power without decisive Russian assistance. By inclination Tito was a thoroughly orthodox Communist, Stalin's most successful pupil in Eastern Europe, but his emulation of Stalin proceeded so far that he would brook no challenge to his own authority, not even from Stalin himself. When Russian efforts to penetrate the Yugoslav army and police assumed dangerous proportions by 1948, Tito undertook both protests and counter-measures. The Soviet reply was to expel Yugoslavia from the community of Communist states. This showed that in Stalin's eyes genuine Communism could not exist without unquestioning subordination to Soviet Russia. Here was the final step in the identification of the Communist movement and Russian national power.

The essence of Yugoslav Communism since the break in 1948 has been the effort to justify national independence from Moscow while at the same time maintaining firm Communist rule at home. The direct justification for independence has been sought by asserting the necessity for every country to approach socialism in its own way and at its own time. In effect, the revolution is not regarded as an international process at all, but a strictly national one (the logical extension of "socialism in one country"). The Yugoslavs have also sought to defend themselves against Russian denunciations by pointing to the internal imperfections of Communism in Russia, and correcting such defects in their own regime. The Soviet Union was especially criticized for allowing bureaucratic distortions of socialism, while the Yugoslavs, looking back in the Soviet past, rediscovered the old revolutionary ideal of decentralized administration carried out by the populace. This theory was then actually put into practice in Yugoslavia through administrative decentralization and workers' councils, although Tito and the Communist Party leaders keep firm political supervision over the country as a whole.

The Yugoslav antibureaucratic line has not been without danger to its users. Anyone following the argument consistently would find that in large measure the Yugoslav system conformed to the basically bureaucratic transformation of the Communist movement which had come about in the Soviet Union. One leading Yugoslav Communist—Milovan Djilas—actually did pursue this argument, which brought him to the rejection of the Communist dictatorship altogether (and to his prosecution and conviction by the Yugoslav government for treasonable activities).

Immediately after Tito's break with Moscow, signs of the national-communist tendency appeared almost everywhere in Eastern Europe. It was a natural reaction against foreign domination and the rigors of the economic policies demanded by Soviet interests. Severe shake-ups were undertaken in 1948 and 1949 to eliminate national-communist sentiment: in Poland, the Communist secretary-general Gomulka was ousted and then jailed, while in Hungary and Bulgaria deputy premiers Rajk and Kostov, respectively, were executed after show trials were staged. Similar purges characterized the other satellites, and the intensive development of heavy industry and agricultural collectivization were then pushed throughout the entire Soviet-dominated region.

The death of Stalin in 1953 opened the way for gestures of leniency in East European Communism. By 1956 the East Europeans were pressing their opportunity ambitiously, and one of the most severe crises in the history of Communism was the result. The Polish Communists brought Gomulka back to power despite Soviet threats, and under Gomulka's leadership the worst excesses of satellite economic policy and police controls were checked. The clock in Poland was turned back to a compromise similar to Russia's NEP, with the abandonment of collective farms, the restoration of considerable intellectual freedom outside the political sphere, and the end of arbitrary police terror, though the characteristic discipline of the Communist Party and its dominant position in the state were emphatically retained, together with subservience to Russia in matters of foreign policy. Poland has become the least totalitarian of any Communist country.

For a brief moment Hungary promised to outdo the Poles by far in the revision of Communism. Popular agitation for reform in October, 1956, developed into a nation-wide insurrectionary movement so powerful that the Communist government saw its only course of survival in endorsing the revolution and acceding to its demands. The moderate-minded Communist ex-premier Imre Nagy was recalled to his post. In a rapid series of decrees Nagy in effect proclaimed the end of the Communist system in Hungary, abolishing its police controls and economic rigors, ending the political monopoly of the Communist Party, and renouncing ties with the Soviet bloc. The Nagy government was thus returning to the form of coalition regime which had prevailed in Eastern Europe between the end of World War II and the establishment of the Communist dictatorships. This course was rudely interrupted, however, by the intervention of Soviet troops (who were already present in Hungary under the terms of the Communist alliance and who had briefly fought the revolution in its initial stages). Early in November, 1956, Soviet forces overthrew the Nagy government and installed a new regime, headed by János Kádár, made up of those Hungarian Communists who preferred to serve as Soviet puppets and maintain the Communist Party dictatorship. Hungary was thus brought forcibly back into line with the majority of the satellites, though all of them henceforth enjoyed considerably more lenient economic conditions without any more direct Soviet exploitation.

National communism is now a reality, in different forms, in two countries (Poland with more internal freedom and Yugoslavia with unimpaired national sovereignty), while it is an ever-present potential in the rest of Eastern Europe. Discipline over the Communist bloc (not counting Yugoslavia) is still maintained by the Soviet Union under the theoretical guise of "proletarian internationalism." The Western threat to Communist rule as such is made the most of to keep the European Communists firmly committed to the Soviet alliance, whatever propensity for independent action they might have.

China and Asian Communism

In contrast to Eastern Europe, Communism in Asia is to a far lesser degree a direct Russian imposition. The movement in China grew independently and came to power basically under its own power. Moreover, Communism has proved to be more appropriate to the problems of the East; it conforms to conditions and traditions rather than defying them.

The Communist appeal in the East has nothing to do with the Marxian analysis of history or the dictatorship of the proletariat. Whereas Communism has had its main appeal in the West under its old proletarian guise, the East has responded to the more straightforward attraction of actual Soviet aims and methods. Communism captures the imagination of many Eastern intellectuals and semi-intellectuals and appeals to them as a new way of life, a new discipline, that will enable their country to pursue the goals of industrialization and national power, and thus to compete with the hitherto dominant West on equal terms. Communism comes to the East as the ideology, program and instrument of anti-Western westernization.

One of the distinctive characteristics of Communism in China was its complete divorce from the industrial working class during most of the years before its assumption of power. While the movement did have some worker participation just after its establishment in the early 1920's, it was primarily the expression of radically-minded intellectuals, and in alliance with Chiang Kai-shek helped bring the Nationalist Party to power. Then, hard-pressed by their erstwhile ally, the Communists at the initiative of Mao Tse-tung shifted the focus of their operations to the peasantry. The Communist Party became a major political force in China as a disciplined party of intellectuals mobilizing the peasants in order to wage war and revolution.

With respect to the strongly centralized party and its leading role in the revolution the Chinese Communists were following closely in the footsteps of Lenin. In their dogmatic adherence to Marxist doctrine and the rigorous enforcement of the official doctrinal justification of each policy measure, the Chinese were quick pupils of Stalin. But where the Russian Revolution could at least in part be described as a working-class affair, this presumed foundation of the Marxist dictatorship was quite lacking in China. The Chinese Communist revolution actually proceeded much more in conformity with the pre-Marxist doctrines of the Russian "populists," who called for a peasant revolution led by a determined party of intellectuals. Maoism, coming to terms with these circumstances, is the ultimate extension of the philosophical changes which Lenin had begun to introduce in Marx.

In the absence of working-class participation, the Chinese Communists could claim Marxist legitimacy only by insisting that the party was proletarian in "spirit," i.e., in its discipline and revolutionary single-mindedness. Implicitly this reasoning transferred the essence of revolution from the realm of social classes to the realm of thought. In actuality, apart from the liquidation of landlords, there has been comparatively little clear-cut class struggle in the Chinese revolution. The choice was rather one between systems of moral authority; anyone accepting Communist authority and discipline could be absorbed into the movement, and from the very beginning of their rule the Communists have readily taken middle-class elements into collaboration with them if these conditions were met. The tasks of maintaining doctrinal discipline on the basis of Marxist orthodoxy, however, were all the more demanding—hence the unique Chinese development of indoctrination and "brain washing."

In the nature of its policies once power was consolidated, Chinese Communism represents the logical extension of Leninism-Stalinism in yet another respect—the use of totalitarian political controls to effect a cultural transformation and carry out the industrial revolution with the utmost rapidity. With the exception of a few areas developed by foreign capital, Chinese Communism began with no industrial base at all, whereas Russia was appreciably industrialized at the time of the revolution (though very unevenly and to a low per capita degree). With the adoption of the military commune system China is striving toward the ultimate in the bureaucratic direction of individual energy toward the compelling national goal of industrial power.

Communism as both the goal and the instrument of building national power through industrialization naturally exercises a powerful fascination for the self-conscious minority of would-be revolutionary nationalist leaders throughout Asia and the underdeveloped regions of the world generally. As such it is the end-product of centuries of European political, economic and cultural domination of the world. Long stagnant or subservient peoples have been discovering new energies, thanks to the impact of Western influence upon them. Their emotional reaction is to bite the hand that has culturally fed them, and turn to a movement which emulates Western ways at the same time that it expresses the anti-Western resentment of the former underdog. Communism is admirably suited to satisfy these desires, and its potential for expansion in this part of the world is by no means exhausted.

An alternative to Communism can be observed in the one-party nationalist reform movements which have appeared at various times in China, the Near East, and at present in West Africa. These movements have the same political and emotional function as Communism in such regions, though they have not ordinarily displayed the requisite drive and discipline. The main difference is that they are free of Communism's two great burdens of irrelevance—doctrinaire commitment to Marxist ideology, and the obligations of loyalty to Moscow.

The Meaning of Communism

There are two important characteristics of the Communist movement which are rarely understood and are responsible for most of the widespread confusion on the subject (among both opponents and sympathizers). One of these is the relation between theory and practice. The other is the course of evolution which the practice itself has followed.

It is rare indeed that a doctrinaire movement, whether of religion or politics or whatever, has kept strictly to the literal dictates of its principles. Life never turns out as the founder of a doctrine expects. Historically speaking, the function of a doctrine is to give reinforcement and cohesiveness to a social emotion, which emotion may or may not be logically consistent with the doctrine to which it becomes attached. The outcome of the movement is the result of interaction between its central emotion and the circumstances of life in which it finds itself, with all the innumerable complications of chance. Such an interaction, as we have noted, underlay the basic changes which have taken place in Communism over the years. This is natural, and it would be readily intelligible were it not for the unnatural stance which Communism maintains toward its original doctrine. The doctrine is still invested with absolute validity, and made to square with the actual flow of life by a clumsy process of scholastic reinterpretation. The truth of the doctrine as officially interpreted is then enjoined upon the faithful with all the force at the command of the Communist state. Thus refashioned according to the needs or preferences of the leader, the doctrine loses all long-term guiding significance. It serves two purposes only: to maintain mental discipline in the totalitarian state, and to perpetuate the sense of basic enmity between people and countries who subscribe to the doctrine, and those who do not.

In the evolving policies and institutions of Communism which the doctrine is made to justify there is much more than the chaos of zigs and zags which some observers see. To be sure, Communist decision-making is highly pragmatic—tactical rather than philosophical—but the contours of social reality confer a definite shape upon the movement as it maneuvers from one turning point to the next.

Essentially the history of the Communist movement has been one of progressive adaptation to the problems of modernization and national regeneration of under-developed countries whose traditional cultural equilibrium was upset by European influence. By the time the movement crystallized firmly, its essential meaning had changed so much that the propositions of its prophets had become quite irrelevant. The Western, international, post-industrial, anarchistic, proletarian revolution had become the Eastern, national, industrializing, totalitarian, middle-class-intellectual revolution. Two movements could scarcely be less similar, yet this is the situation in which the Communist faithful feel compelled to maintain the complete Marxist orthodoxy of their ideas and their system. The madness of this dogmatism is death to the free individual or the creative mind.

There are four basic attributes which define the Communist movement as it exists today. Its structural core is the Leninist concept of the party, a disciplined, hierarchical organization serving either to spearhead a revolutionary movement or to rule the Communist state. Its dynamic urge is the drive to industrialize, to over-come backwardness and fashion the sinews of national power by systematic exhor-tation and compulsion imposed on the population through the party. Its mentality is the ideology of Marxism as officially interpreted—the obligatory rationalization of the party's policies enforced by totalitarian thought controls. Its international orientation is unquestioning loyalty to Soviet Russia as the initiator, sustainer, and doctrinal authority of the movement, together with uncompromising hostility toward the liberalism and capitalism associated with the "imperialism" of the major Western powers. (In the one case—Yugoslavia—where this no longer holds, it was nonetheless true at the time the Communist system took shape there.) Taken together, these four features necessarily indicate the Communist movement and nothing but the Communist movement. They are the necessary and sufficient counts in a definition of Communism.

The Communist movement, thus defined, did not come into being because of some law of historical inevitability. It is the product of a complicated interaction of circumstances, human intentions and historical accidents (particularly the events of the Russian Revolution). It has spread and gained strength because it has adapted itself to the resolution of widespread and serious social problems and weaknesses. If it is not the only solution to these ills, it has often been the most vigorous alter-native. It enjoys today the prospect of gaining still more ground, on more than one continent. One might wonder, however, about the implications which success itself might have for the Communist movement. Will the solution of those problems which have contributed to the growth of the movement deprive it of any reason for further existence, and thus require it to change or collapse? Does Communism, as it were, contain the seeds of its own destruction? Or will the strength of the totalitar-ian system enable it to outlive indefinitely the circumstances which called it into being, as so many despotic systems have in the past? Only the future can yield the answers to such questions.

Postscript: 1983

The nature of Communism in the Soviet Union has not changed fundamentally since the 1950's, and with some qualifications the same is true of Communism internationally. Although the history of the international movement has been replete with spectacular shifts and conflicts, by and large the roots of these developments can be traced in the events of the entire postwar period.

Soviet foreign policy since the fifties has continued to display the old pattern of tactical zig-zags between the confrontationist and accommodationist lines, depending on the calculation of practical Soviet interest as well as the occasional intrusion of domestic political struggles. The post-Stalin détente with the West, culminating in Khrushchev's visit to the United States in 1959, gave way the following year to a period of crisis and angry rhetoric, extending from the U-2 affair and the collapse of the Paris Summit Conference of 1960 through the Berlin Wall crisis of 1961 to the Cuban missile crisis in 1962. Then the political winds shifted to détente again with the Nuclear Test Ban Treaty of 1963, and held that direction, despite the Vietnam War and the Czechoslovakian crisis of 1968, on through the Strategic Arms Limitations Talks of the 1970's, the exchange of visits by President Nixon and General Secretary Brezhnev, and the Helsinki Accords of 1975 on European security. The late seventies witnessed a sharp Soviet turn back to confrontational rhetoric and more adventurist tactics, with intervention (sometimes by proxy) in Africa, the Middle East, and Afghanistan, accompanied by a stalemate in relations with the West and arms control matters.

In the meantime, the "socialist camp" of Communist governments and parties was suffering a progressive series of splits and deviations, traceable to the "polycentrism" espoused by Palmiro Togliatti at the time of the anti-Stalin campaign of 1956, and further back to the national communism of the early postwar years as well as to the special background of Communism in the Far East. De-Stalinization had broken the bonds of unquestioning ideological discipline within the Communist movement, and it became increasingly difficult for the Soviet leadership to maintain its international influence except by raw economic and military power. Most spectacular of the problems posed for Moscow was the Sino-Soviet schism and the Chinese Communists' pursuit of an ultra-radical line culminating in the "Great Proletarian Cultural Revolution" of the late sixties and early seventies. Meanwhile East European reformers repeatedly tried to move in the opposite direction and liberalize their regimes along the lines of the Yugoslav version of Communism. They were crushed in Czechoslovakia and Poland but made modest gains in Hungary. Some East European thinkers, exemplified by the Yugoslav philosopher Stojanović and the former East German functionary Bahro, advanced trenchant critiques of the Soviet and East European Communist system from the standpoint of a creative, unofficial Marxism analogous to the outlook of the Soviet dissident Roy Medvedev. In Western Europe most Communists responded to these manifestations of polycentrism by openly disavowing the Soviet Union as a political model and opting for democratic politics—i.e., the "Eurocommunism" exemplified by the Spanish Communist leader Santiago Carrillo. By the 1970's there were no significant, united non-ruling Communist parties legally operating anywhere in the world who were still controlled by Moscow, except in Portugal and perhaps in France.

Where distinctly new developments have occurred since the fifties is in the Third World, with the emergence of new Communist dictatorships or radical pro-Soviet regimes either through guerrilla warfare or military coups. Castro's Cuba is the prototype of an independent revolution drawn into the Communist camp. The

Communist-nationalist guerrilla revolution in Vietnam came to a long, drawn-out conclusion with the fall of Saigon and the creation of a united pro-Soviet state in 1975. Other movements, exemplified by the Popular Movement for the Liberation of Angola, have installed firmly pro-Soviet regimes led by "vanguard" parties that are organizationally Leninist and ideologically Marxist even if they lack any significant working-class base. They are distinct from the less doctrinaire Third-World nationalists—in the Arab world, for instance—with whom the Soviets have scored no better than an on-again, off-again relationship since the 1950's.

Apart from these forays at winning influence in the Third World the policy style of the Soviet Union has remained essentially stable, not to say rigid, in international as well as domestic affairs, with a basic reliance on military power to balance the influence of the United States and keep neighboring satellite states—Czechoslovakia, Poland, Afghanistan—under firm Soviet control. For the other Communist giant, the People's Republic of China, it has been quite a different matter in the tumultuous history of the past quarter-century. Searching for a future that would reconcile the claims of revolutionary emotion and national development, China moved from the latter-day Soviet model of bureaucratic industrialism to the repudiation of Soviet leadership and a new revolutionary upsurge reminiscent of Russia in the early days of War Communism. During the Cultural Revolution China reached a peak of puritanical and anti-intellectual fanaticism transcending anything in the history of the Russian Revolution. This was in no sense a class struggle but rather a battle of generations and attitudes legitimized by appeals to Marxism, Leninism and "Mao Tse-tung Thought." The ultimate extreme was reached by Mao's disciples of the Khmer Rouge in Cambodia who were well on their way to the annihilation of all marks of civilization in that unfortunate country before they were dislodged by the intervention of the more traditional Communists of Vietnam.

In China itself the left-wing tide was already receding when Mao Tse-tung died in 1976, and his death opened the way for a quick victory of the pragmatic wing of the Communist Party led by Deng Xiao-ping, against the infamous "Gang of Four" led by Mao's wife Chiang Ching. Conceding with Deng the impossibility of modernizing by exhortation and coercion alone, the Chinese Communists swung in the direction of the East European reformers and embraced the decentralized economic model of Russia of the 1920's, while keeping their distance both diplomatically and ideologically from the contemporary Soviet Union.

The proliferation of different interests and interpretations among Communist parties both in and out of power has accentuated the old tension between theory and practice and the habit of bending theory to fit the convenience of practice. It is ironic that many people in the West since the mid-seventies have reverted to the explanation of Communism as the pursuit of a binding ideological goal, at a time when Communist ideology has actually become a battlefield of conflicting political interests. Certainly the Soviet Union is not building the world's most powerful military force for the sake of realizing the utopian society: it is an imperial power synthesizing pre-capitalist motives of national expansion with the post-capitalist rhetoric of socialism, and striving by whatever means to hold its own in the balance of the two super-powers amidst a world that has become increasingly harder for either to control.

Postscript: 1993

The later 1980s and the first years of the 1990s saw a crisis in the international Communist movement as astounding as the attempted reform and ultimate collapse of the Communist system in the Soviet Union. The end of Communism internationally was all the more dramatic in view of the imperial power and ambition that the Soviet Union had manifested up to the early 1980s, although some of the weaknesses and vulnerability in the Communist position, particularly in Eastern Europe, had already become visible.

Facing the realities of its own internal crisis and the costs of sustaining its confrontation with the Western alliance, the Soviet Union under Gorbachev surrendered step by step both its superpower aspirations and its revolutionary appeal, giving up control over its former East European security zone, abandoning its traditional stance of ideological struggle against the capitalists, and pulling back from its efforts to extend its influence globally through Third World revolutionary movements. Thus the Cold War and Soviet imperialism peacefully faded away without any military catastrophe.

This relatively quiet demise of international Communism pointed up how empty was its shell of ideological conviction. Like the basic contradiction of Marxist theory and Soviet-style practice, revolutionary ambitions and superpower pretensions were undermined by the limitations in the real resources and achievements of the Communist system of politics and economics. 1989 was the watershed year, when cumulative signals of democratization and retrenchment on the part of the Soviet Union emboldened opposition forces in Eastern Europe and sapped the will of the local Communist regimes to resist change. Where Communism had been imposed by the Soviet Union it was most completely repudiated. Where it was only the rationale for Third-World nationalism it was easily dispensed with.

Both Soviet and East European Communists readily abandoned their ostensible beliefs when they could no longer rationalize ruling privilege or national status-seeking. Communists everywhere scrambled to turn themselves into nationalists or social-democrats or even fascists. The Communist revolutionary empire simply dissolved, with little regret and no resistance. This outcome suggested how much the old international polarization had been a matter only of attitudes and assumptions rather than real ideological conviction or material interests—and the extent to which Soviet competition with the West relied on one, unusable instrument, namely, nuclear weapons.

In much of the formerly Communist area, as in the former Soviet Union, the new freedom allowed old ethnic animosities to well up, worst of all in Yugoslavia as it broke apart in a vicious civil war. Outside Europe, hard-line Communists who had come to power on their own in China (plus the long-time Chinese satellite North Korea), in Vietnam, and in Cuba—clung to power while seeking a path of pragmatic reform. Nevertheless, Communism as a coherent and powerful international movement had ceased to exist, even before the breakup of the Soviet Union and the outright repudiation of Communist rule in the former Soviet republics. Russia remained a major power but only one of several, and a supplicant for aid from its former enemies.

A Documentary History of
Communism and the World

CHAPTER ONE

World Revolution, 1914–1920

Communism as an international revolutionary movement had its origin in the years of the First World War, when socialist parties not only in Russia but throughout Europe were split by the issues of the war and the Russian Revolution. Lenin, in exile in Switzerland, seized this split as an opportunity to mobilize the radical, anti-war factions of the various socialist parties in support of his conception of a world revolution against imperialism. This was the genesis of the Communist International, formally established in 1919, and its member Communist parties all over the world.

While the nascent Soviet government was able to survive the terms of peace with Germany and the efforts of the Allied powers to intervene in the Russian civil war, the Bolsheviks' expectations of imminent world revolution did not materialize. The legacy of the revolutionary war era was one revolutionary government confronting a hostile world with the aid of radical sympathizers whom it controlled as a unique arm of its foreign policy.

The "Imperialist War" and the Schism in Socialism

The outbreak of a general war in August, 1914, deeply shook the European socialist movement. The moderate wings dominant in most of the socialist parties put national defense ahead of social change, and voted to support their respective governments. The Bolsheviks and many other Russian socialists, together with leftwing splinter groups in the rest of Europe, appealed to the antinationalist tradition of Marxism and tried to make revolutionary capital out of the war. Lenin frankly hoped for the defeat of the tsarist government of Russia and urged revolutionaries everywhere to "turn the imperialist war into a civil war."

The European war, for which the governments and the bourgeois parties of all countries have been preparing for decades, has broken out. The growth of armaments, the extreme intensification of the struggle for markets in the epoch of the latest, the imperialist stage of capitalist development in the advanced countries, and the dynastic interests of the most backward East-European monarchies were inevitably bound to lead, and have led, to this war. Seizure of territory and subjugation of foreign nations, ruin of a competing nation and plunder of its wealth, diverting the attention of the working masses from the internal political crises in Russia, Germany, England and other countries, disuniting and nationalist doping of the workers and the extermination of their vanguard with the object of weakening the

FROM: Lenin, "The War and Russian Social-Democracy" (November, 1914; Selected Works, Vol. I, book 2, pp. 397, 404–6.

revolutionary movement of the proletariat—such is the only real meaning, substance and significance of the present war.

On Social-Democracy, primarily, rests the duty of disclosing the true meaning of the war and of ruthlessly exposing the falsehood, sophistry and "patriotic" phrasemongering spread by the ruling classes, the landlords and the bourgeoisie, in defence of the war. . . .

Under present conditions, it is impossible to determine, from the standpoint of the international proletariat, the defeat of which of the two groups of belligerent nations would be the lesser evil for Socialism. But for us, the Russian Social-Democrats, there cannot be the slightest doubt that from the standpoint of the working class and of the labouring masses of all the nations of Russia, the lesser evil would be the defeat of the tsarist monarchy, the most reactionary and barbarous of governments, which is oppressing the greatest number of nations and the largest mass of the population of Europe and Asia.

The immediate political slogan of the Social-Democrats of Europe must be the formation of a republican United States of Europe, but in contrast to the bourgeoisie, which is ready to "promise" anything in order to draw the proletariat into the general current of chauvinism, the Social-Democrats will explain that this slogan is utterly false and senseless without the revolutionary overthrow of the German, Austrian and Russian monarchies.

In Russia, in view of the fact that this country is the most backward and has not yet completed its bourgeois revolution, the task of the Social-Democrats is, as heretofore, to achieve the three fundamental conditions for consistent democratic reform, viz., a democratic republic (with complete equality and self-determination for all nations), confiscation of the landed estates, and an 8-hour day. But in all the advanced countries the war has placed on the order of the day the slogan of socialist revolution, and this slogan becomes the more urgent, the more the burdens of war press upon the shoulders of the proletariat, and the more active its role must become in the restoration of Europe after the horrors of the present "patriotic" barbarism amidst the gigantic technical progress of big capitalism. . . .

The transformation of the present imperialist war into a civil war is the only correct proletarian slogan; it was indicated by the experience of the [Paris] Commune and outlined by the Basle resolution [of the Socialist International] (1912), and it logically follows from all the conditions of an imperialist war among highly developed bourgeois countries. However difficult such a transformation may appear at any given moment, Socialists will never relinquish systematic, persistent and undeviating preparatory work in this direction once war has become a fact.

Only in this way can the proletariat shake off its dependence on the chauvinist bourgeoisie, and, in one form or another, more or less rapidly, take decisive steps towards the real freedom of nations and towards Socialism.

Long live the international fraternity of the workers against the chauvinism and patriotism of the bourgeoisie of all countries!

Long live a proletarian International, freed from opportunism!

The "Zimmerwald Left"

At a conference in the Swiss village of Zimmerwald in 1915 the antiwar socialists split over the revolutionary implications of the war. The left wing, which included Lenin and the Bolshevik representatives, vainly supported the uncompromising resolution written by Karl Radek, a Polish Jew who was high in the councils of the international Communist movement throughout the nineteen-twenties. Although the extremists were rebuffed at Zimmerwald, they had laid the organizational basis for the Third or Communist International which was formally launched in 1919.

The World War, which has been devastating Europe for the last year, is an imperialist war waged for the political and economic exploitation of the world, export markets, sources of raw material, spheres of capital investment, etc. It is a product of capitalist development which connects the entire world in a world economy but at the same time permits the existence of national state capitalist groups with opposing interests.

If the bourgeoisie and the governments seek to conceal this character of the World War by asserting that it is a question of a forced struggle for *national independence*, it is only to mislead the *proletariat*, since the war is being waged for the oppression of foreign peoples and countries. Equally untruthful are the legends concerning the defence of democracy in this war, since imperialism signifies the most unscrupulous domination of big capital and political reaction.

Imperialism can only be overcome by overcoming the contradictions which produced it, that is, by the *Socialist organisation* of the sphere of capitalist civilisation for which the objective conditions are already ripe.

At the outbreak of the war, the majority of the labour leaders had not raised the only possible slogan in opposition to imperialism. Prejudiced by nationalism, rotten with opportunism, *they surrendered the proletariat to imperialism, and gave up the principles of Socialism and thereby the real struggle for every-day interests of the proletariat.*

Social-patriotism and social-imperialism . . . is a more dangerous enemy to the proletariat than the bourgeois apostles of imperialism, since, misusing the banner of Socialism, it can mislead the unenlightened workers. *The ruthless struggle against social-imperialism constitutes the first condition for the revolutionary mobilisation of the proletariat and the reconstruction of the International.*

It is the task of the Socialist parties, as well as of the Socialist opposition in the now social-imperialist parties, to call and lead the labouring masses to the *revolutionary struggle* against the capitalist governments for the conquest of political power for the Socialist organisation of society.

Without giving up the struggle for every foot of ground within the framework of capitalism, for every reform strengthening the proletariat, without renouncing any means of organisation and agitation, the revolutionary Social-Democrats, on the contrary, must utilise all the struggles, all the reforms demanded by our minimum programme for the purpose of sharpening this war crisis as well as every social and political crisis of capitalism, of extending them to an attack upon its very foundations. By waging this struggle *under the slogan of Socialism* it will render the labouring masses immune to the slogans of the oppression of one people by another as expressed in the maintenance of the domination of one nation over

FROM: Proposed Resolution of the Zimmerwald Left at the Zimmerwald Conference in September, 1915—"The World War and the Tasks of Social-Democracy" (English translation in *Collected Works of V. I. Lenin*, Vol. XX, book 2, New York, International Publishers, 1929, pp. 386–87; reprinted by permission of the publisher).

another, in the cry for new annexations; it will render them deaf to the temptation of national solidarity which has led the proletarians to the battlefields.

The signal for this struggle is the struggle against the World War, for the speedy termination of the slaughter of nations. This struggle demands the refusal of war credits, quitting the cabinets, the denunciation of the capitalist, anti-Socialist character of the war from the tribunes of the parliaments, in the columns of the legal, and where necessary, illegal, press, the sharpest struggle caused by the results of the war (misery, great losses, etc.) for the organisation of street demonstrations against the governments, propaganda of international solidarity in the trenches, the encouragement of economic strikes, the effort to transform them into political strikes under favourable conditions. "Civil war, not civil peace"—that is the slogan!

As against all illusions that it is possible to bring about the basis of a lasting peace, the beginning of disarmament, by any decisions of diplomacy and the governments, the revolutionary Social-Democrats must repeatedly tell the masses of the people that only the social revolution can bring about a lasting peace as well as the emancipation of mankind.

Lenin on Imperialism

Like many of his Marxist colleagues, Lenin attempted to bring Marxism up to date to account for the World War and contemporary economic trends. His product was the book, *Imperialism, the Highest Stage of Capitalism*, for which he drew heavily from the work of the English economist J. A. Hobson. The essence of the argument was that the capitalist search for markets and profits made colony-grabbing and imperialist war between capitalist states inevitable. Lenin's presentation became the basis of the Communist view of the capitalist world.

. . . The principal feature of the latest stage of capitalism is the domination of monopolist combines of the big capitalists. These monopolies are most firmly established when *all* the sources of raw materials are captured by one group, and we have seen with what zeal the international capitalist combines exert every effort to make it impossible for their rivals to compete with them by buying up, for example, iron ore fields, oil fields, etc. Colonial possession alone gives the monopolies complete guarantee against all contingencies in the struggle with competitors, including the contingency that the latter will defend themselves by means of a law establishing a state monopoly. The more capitalism is developed, the more strongly the shortage of raw materials is felt, the more intense the competition and the hunt for sources of raw materials throughout the whole world, the more desperate is the struggle for the acquisition of colonies. . . .

Finance capital is interested not only in the already discovered sources of raw materials but also in potential sources, because present-day technical development is extremely rapid, and land which is useless today may be made fertile tomorrow if new methods are applied (to devise these new methods a big bank can equip a special expedition of engineers, agricultural experts, etc.), and if large amounts of capital are invested. This also applies to prospecting for minerals, to new methods of working up and utilizing raw materials, etc., etc. Hence, the inevitable striving of finance

FROM: Lenin, "Imperialism, the Highest Stage of Capitalism" (1916; *Selected Works*, Vol. I, book 2, pp. 517–20, 562–67).

capital to enlarge its economic territory and even its territory in general. In the same way that the trusts capitalize their property at two or three times its value, taking into account its "potential" (and not present) profits, and the further results of monopoly, so finance capital strives in general to seize the largest possible amount of land of all kinds in all places, and by every means, taking into account potential sources of raw materials and fearing to be left behind in the fierce struggle for the last scraps of undivided territory, or for the repartition of those that have been already divided. . . .

The interests pursued in exporting capital also give an impetus to the conquest of colonies, for in the colonial market it is easier to employ monopolist methods (and sometimes they are the only methods that can be employed) to eliminate competition, to make sure of contracts, to secure the necessary "connections," etc.

The non-economic superstructure which grows up on the basis of finance capital, its politics and its ideology, stimulates the striving for colonial conquest. . . .

We have seen that in its economic essence imperialism is monopoly capitalism. This in itself determines its place in history, for monopoly that grows out of the soil of free competition, and precisely out of free competition, is the transition from the capitalist system to a higher social-economic order. We must take special note of the four principal types of monopoly, or principal manifestations of monopoly capitalism, which are characteristic of the epoch we are examining.

Firstly, monopoly arose out of a very high stage of development of the concentration of production. This refers to the monopolist capitalist combines, cartels, syndicates and trusts. We have seen the important part these play in present-day economic life. At the beginning of the twentieth century, monopolies had acquired complete supremacy in the advanced countries, and although the first steps toward the formation of the cartels were first taken by countries enjoying the protection of high tariffs (Germany, America), Great Britain, with her system of free trade, revealed the same basic phenomenon, only a little later, namely, the birth of monopoly out of the concentration of production.

Secondly, monopolies have stimulated the seizure of the most important sources of raw materials, especially for the basic and most highly cartelized industries in capitalist society: the coal and iron industries. The monopoly of the most important sources of raw materials has enormously increased the power of big capital, and has sharpened the antagonism between cartelized and non-cartelized industry.

Thirdly, monopoly has sprung from the banks. The banks have developed from humble middlemen enterprises into the monopolists of finance capital. Some three to five of the biggest banks in each of the foremost capitalist countries have achieved the "personal union" of industrial and bank capital, and have concentrated in their hands the control of thousands upon thousands of millions which form the greater part of the capital and income of entire countries. A financial oligarchy, which throws a close network of dependence relationships over all the economic and political institutions of present-day bourgeois society without exception—such is the most striking manifestation of this monopoly.

Fourthly, monopoly has grown out of colonial policy. To the numerous "old" motives of colonial policy, finance capital has added the struggle for the sources of raw materials, for the export of capital, for "spheres of influence," i.e., for spheres for profitable deals, concessions, monopolist profits and so on, and finally, for economic territory in general. When the colonies of the European powers in

Africa, for instance, comprised only one-tenth of that territory (as was the case in 1876), colonial policy was able to develop by methods other than those of monopoly—by the "free grabbing" of territories, so to speak. But when nine-tenths of Africa had been seized (by 1900), when the whole world had been divided up, there was inevitably ushered in the era of monopoly ownership of colonies and, consequently, of particularly intense struggle for the division and the redivision of the world.

The extent to which monopolist capital has intensified all the contradictions of capitalism is generally known. It is sufficient to mention the high cost of living and the tyranny of the cartels. This intensification of contradictions constitutes the most powerful driving force of the transitional period of history, which began from the time of the final victory of world finance capital.

Monopolies, oligarchy, the striving for domination instead of striving for liberty, the exploitation of an increasing number of small or weak nations by a handful of the richest or most powerful nations—all these have given birth to those distinctive characteristics of imperialism which compel us to define it as parasitic or decaying capitalism. More and more prominently there emerges, as one of the tendencies of imperialism, the creation of the "rentier state," the usurer state, in which the bourgeoisie to an ever increasing degree lives on the proceeds of capital exports and by "clipping coupons." It would be a mistake to believe that this tendency to decay precludes the rapid growth of capitalism. It does not. In the epoch of imperialism, certain branches of industry, certain strata of the bourgeoisie and certain countries betray, to a greater or lesser degree, now one and now another of these tendencies. On the whole, capitalism is growing far more rapidly than before; but this growth is not only becoming more and more uneven in general, its unevenness also manifests itself, in particular, in the decay of the countries which are richest in capital (England). . . .

The receipt of high monopoly profits by the capitalists in one of the numerous branches of industry, in one of the numerous countries, etc., makes it economically possible for them to bribe certain sections of the workers, and for a time a fairly considerable minority of them, and win them to the side of the bourgeoisie of a given industry or given nation against all the others. The intensification of antagonisms between imperialist nations for the division of the world increases this striving. And so there is created that bond between imperialism and opportunism, which revealed itself first and most clearly in England, owing to the fact that certain features of imperialist development were observable there much earlier than in other countries. . . .

From all that has been said in this book on the economic essence of imperialism, it follows that we must define it as capitalism in transition, or, more precisely, as moribund capitalism. It is very instructive in this respect to note that the bourgeois economists, in describing modern capitalism, frequently employ catchwords and phrases like "interlocking," "absence of isolation," etc.; "in conformity with their functions and course of development," banks are "not purely private business enterprises; they are more and more outgrowing the sphere of purely private business regulation." And this very Riesser,* who uttered the words just quoted, declares with all seriousness that the "prophecy" of the Marxists concerning "socialization" has "not come true"!

*Riesser: author of a study of German banking, cited by Lenin—Ed.

What then does this catchword "interlocking" express? It merely expresses the most striking feature of the process going on before our eyes. It shows that the observer counts the separate trees, but cannot see the wood. It slavishly copies the superficial, the fortuitous, the chaotic. It reveals the observer as one who is overwhelmed by the mass of raw material and is utterly incapable of appreciating its meaning and importance. Ownership of shares, the relations between owners of private property "interlock in a haphazard way." But underlying the interlocking, its very base, is the changing social relations of production. When a big enterprise assumes gigantic proportions, and, on the basis of an exact computation of mass data, organizes according to plan the supply of primary raw materials to the extent of two-thirds, or three-fourths of all that is necessary for tens of millions of people; when the raw materials are transported in a systematic and organized manner to the most suitable place of production, sometimes hundreds or thousands of miles, when a single centre directs all the consecutive stages of work right up to the manufacture of numerous varieties of finished articles; when these products are distributed according to a single plan among tens and hundreds of millions of consumers (the distribution of oil in America and Germany by the American "oil trust")— then it becomes evident that we have socialization of production, and not mere "interlocking"; that private economic and private property relations constitute a shell which no longer fits its contents, a shell which must inevitably decay if its removal by artificial means be delayed; a shell which may continue in a state of decay for a fairly long period (if, at the worst, the cure of the opportunist abscess is protracted), but which will inevitably be removed. . . .

War, Peace and the Russian Provisional Government

Upon his return to Russia in 1917 after the fall of the Tsar, Lenin denounced the Provisional Government's war policy as a continuation of bourgeois imperialism, and called for a struggle to end the war through international proletarian revolution.

In the domain of foreign policy, which has now been brought to the forefront by objective circumstances, the new government is a government for the continuation of the imperialist war, a war being waged in alliance with the imperialist powers—Great Britain, France, and others—for the division of the capitalist spoils and for the strangling of small and weak nations.

Subordinated to the interests of Russian capital and of its powerful protector and master, Anglo-French imperialist capital, the wealthiest in the world, the new government, notwithstanding the wishes expressed in the most definite fashion on behalf of the undoubted majority of the peoples of Russia through the Soviet of Soldiers' and Workers' Deputies, has taken no real steps to put an end to the slaughter of peoples for the interests of the capitalists. It has not even published the secret treaties of an obviously predatory character (for the partition of Persia, the spoliation of China, the spoliation of Turkey, the partition of Austria, the annexation of Eastern Prussia, the annexation of the German colonies, etc.), which, as everybody knows, bind Russia to Anglo-French predatory imperialist capital. It

FROM: Lenin, "The Tasks of the Proletariat in Our Revolution: Draft of a Platform for the Proletarian Party," *Pravda*, May 13 (April 30), 1917 (English translation in *Selected Works*, Vol. II, book 1, pp. 26–27, 33–36, 45–49, 51, 55).

has *confirmed* these treaties concluded by tsarism, which for centuries robbed and oppressed more nations than other tyrants and despots, and which not only oppressed, but also disgraced and demoralized the Great-Russian nation by transforming it into an executioner of other nations.

The new government has confirmed these shameful cutthroat treaties and has not proposed an immediate armistice to all the belligerent nations, in spite of the clearly expressed demand of the majority of the people of Russia, voiced through the Soviets of Workers' and Soldiers' Deputies. It has evaded the issue with the help of solemn, sonorous, bombastic, but absolutely empty declarations and phrases, such as in the mouths of bourgeois diplomats have always served, and still serve, to deceive the trustful and naive masses of the oppressed people. . . .

Revolutionary defencism must be regarded as the most important and striking manifestation of the petty-bourgeois wave that has overwhelmed "nearly everything." It is precisely this that acts as the worst enemy of the further progress and success of the Russian revolution.

Those who have yielded on this point and have been unable· to extricate themselves are lost to the revolution. But the masses yield in a different way from the leaders; and they extricate themselves *differently*, by a different course of development, by different means.

Revolutionary defencism is, on the one hand, a result of the deception of the masses by the bourgeoisie, a result of the trustful lack of reasoning on the part of the peasants and a section of the workers; it is, on the other, an expression of the interests and standpoint of the small owner, who is to some extent interested in annexations and bank profits, and who "sacredly" guards the traditions of tsarism, which demoralized the Great Russians by making them do a hangman's work against the other peoples.

The bourgeoisie deceives the people by playing upon the noble pride of the revolution and by pretending that the *social and political* character of the war, as far as Russia is concerned, underwent a change beacuse of this stage of the revolution, because of the substitution of the bourgeois near-republic of Guchkov and Milyukov for the tsarist monarchy. . . .

What is required of us is the *ability* to explain to the masses that the social and political character of the war is determined not by the "good will" of individuals or groups, or even of nations, but by the position of the *class* which conducts the war, by the class *policy* of which the war is a continuation, by the *ties* of capital, which is the dominant economic force in modern society, by the *imperialist character* of international capital, by Russia's dependence in finance, banking and diplomacy upon Great Britain, France, etc. To explain this skillfully and in a way that would be comprehensible to the masses *is not easy*, none of us could do it at once without committing errors.

But such, and only such, must be the direction or, rather, the contents of our propaganda. The slightest concession to revolutionary defencism is *treason to Socialism* and a complete renunciation of *internationalism*, no matter by what fine phrases and "practical" considerations it may be justified. . . .

The war cannot be ended "at will." It cannot be ended by the decision of one of the warring parties. It cannot be ended by "sticking your bayonet in the ground," as one soldier, a defencist, expressed it.

The war cannot be ended by an "agreement" among the Socialists of the various countries, by the "action" of the proletarians of all countries, by the "will" of the peoples, and so forth. All the phrases of this kind, which fill the articles of the defencist and semidefencist, semi-internationalist papers as well as innumerable resolutions, appeals, manifestoes, and the resolutions of the Soviet of Soldiers' and Workers' Deputies—all such phrases are nothing but empty, innocent and pious wishes of the petty bourgeois. Nothing is more pernicious than such phrases as "ascertaining the will of the peoples for peace," as the *sequence* of revolutionary actions of the proletariat (after the Russian proletariat comes the "turn" of the German), etc. All this is in the spirit of Louis Blanc, sweet dreams, a game of "political campaigning," and in reality but a repetition of the fable of Vaska the cat.

The war is not a product of the evil will of rapacious capitalists although it is undoubtedly being fought *only* in their interests and they alone are being enriched by it. The war is a product of half a century of development of world capital and of its billions of threads and connections. It is *impossible* to escape from the imperialist war at a bound, it is *impossible* to achieve a democratic, noncoercive peace without overthrowing the power of capital and transferring state power to *another* class, the proletariat.

The Russian revolution of February-March 1917 was the beginning of the transformation of the imperialist war into a civil war. This revolution took the *first* step towards ending the war; but It requires a *second* step, namely, the transfer of the power of state to the proletariat, to make the end of the war a *certainty*. This will be the beginning of a "breach in the front" on a world-wide scale, a breach in the front of the interests of capital; and only after having broken through *this* front *can* the proletariat save mankind from the horrors of war and endow it with the blessings of a durable peace.

It is directly to such a "breach in the front" of capital that the Russian revolution has *already* brought the Russian proletariat by creating the Soviets of Workers' Deputies. . . .

Good people often forget the brutal and savage setting of the imperialist world war. This setting does not tolerate phrases, and mocks at innocent and pious wishes.

There is one, and only one kind of internationalism in deed: working wholeheartedly for the development of the revolutionary movement and the revolutionary struggle *in one's own* country, and supporting (by propaganda, sympathy and material aid) *such a struggle*, such, and only such a line in *every* country without exception.

Everything else is deception and Manilovism.*

In the period of over two years of the war the international socialist and working-class movement in *every* country has evolved three trends. Whoever ignores *reality* and refuses to recognize the existence of these three trends, to analyze them, to fight persistently for the trend that is really internationalist, dooms himself to impotence, helplessness and errors.

The three trends are:

The social-chauvinists, i.e., Socialists in words and chauvinists in deeds, people who recognize "defence of the fatherland" in an imperialist war (and above all in the present imperialist war).

*Manilovism: complacency and day-dreaming typified by a character in Gogol's *Dead Souls*—Ed.

These people are our *class* enemies. They have gone over to the bourgeoisie.

Such is the majority of the official leaders of the official Social-Democratic parties in *all* countries—Messrs. Plekhanov and Co. in Russia, the Scheidemanns in Germany, Renaudel, Guesde and Sembat in France, Bissolati and Co. in Italy, Hyndman, the Fabians and the Labourites (the leaders of the "Labour Party") in England, Branting and Co. in Sweden, Troelstra and his party in Holland, Stauning and his party in Denmark, Victor Berger and the other "defenders of the fatherland" in America, and so forth.

The second trend is that known as the "Centre," consisting of people who vacillate between the social-chauvinists and the true internationalists.

All those who belong to the "Centre" vow and swear that they are Marxists and internationalists, that they are for peace, for bringing every kind of "pressure" to bear upon the governments, for "demanding" in every way that their own government should "ascertain the will of the people for peace," that they are for all sorts of peace campaigns, for peace without annexations, etc., etc.,—*and for peace with the social-chauvinists*. The "Centre" is for "unity," the "Centre" is opposed to a split.

The "Centre" is a realm of honeyed petty-bourgeois phrases, of internationalism in words and cowardly opportunism and fawning on the social-chauvinists in deeds.

The fact of the matter is that the "Centre" is not convinced of the necessity for a revolution against one's own government; it does not preach revolution; it does not carry on a wholehearted revolutionary struggle; and in order to evade such a struggle it resorts to the tritest ultra-"Marxist" sounding *excuses*.

The social-chauvinists are our *class enemies, bourgeois* within the working-class movement. They represent a stratum, or groups, or sections of the working class which *objectively* have been bribed by the bourgeoisie (by better wages, positions of honour, etc.), and which help *their* bourgeoisie to plunder and oppress small and weak peoples and to fight *for* the division of the capitalist spoils. . . .

The third trend, the true internationalists, is most closely represented by the "Zimmerwald Left." (We reprint as a supplement its manifesto of September 1915, in order that the reader may become acquainted in the original with the inception of this trend.)

Its main characteristic feature is its complete rupture with both social-chauvinism and "Centrism," and its relentless revolutionary struggle against *its own* imperialist government and against *its own* imperialist bourgeoisie. Its principle is: "Our chief enemy is at home." It wages a ruthless struggle against honeyed social-pacifist phrases (a social-pacifist is a Socialist in words and a bourgeois pacifist in deeds; bourgeois pacifists dream of an everlasting peace *without* the overthrow of the yoke and domination of capital) and against all *subterfuges* employed to deny the possibility, or the appropriateness, or the timeliness of a proletarian revolutionary struggle and of a proletarian socialist revolution *in connection* with the present war.

The most outstanding representative of this trend in Germany is the Spartacus Group or the International Group, to which Karl Liebknecht belongs. Karl Liebknecht is a most celebrated representative of this trend and of the *new*, and genuine, proletarian International. . . .

The difference between the reformists and the revolutionaries among the Social-Democrats and Socialists generally was objectively bound to undergo a change under the conditions of an imperialist war. Those who confine themselves to "demanding" that the bourgeois governments should conclude peace or "ascertain the will of the peoples for peace," etc., are *actually* slipping into reforms. *For*, objectively, *the problem of the war* can be solved only in a *revolutionary way*.

There is no possibility of this war ending in a democratic, noncoercive peace and the liberation of the people from the burden of paying *billions* as interest to the capitalists, who have grown rich on "the war," except through a revolution of the proletariat.

The most varied reforms can be and must be demanded of the bourgeois governments, but without sinking to Manilovism and reformism one cannot demand that people and classes who are entangled by the thousands of threads of imperialist capital should *break* those threads. And unless they are broken, all talk of a war against war is idle and deceitful prattle.

The "Kautskyites," the "Centre," and revolutionaries in words and reformists in deeds, they are internationalists in words and accomplices of the social-chauvinists in deeds. . . .

To "wait" for international congresses or conferences is simply to *betray* internationalism, since it has been shown that even from Stockholm neither Socialists loyal to internationalism *nor even their letters* are allowed to enter here, although this is quite possible and although there exists a ferocious military censorship.

Our Party must not "wait," but must immediately *found* a Third International. Hundreds of Socialists imprisoned in Germany and England will thereupon heave a sigh of relief, thousands and thousands of German workers who are now organizing strikes and demonstrations, which are frightening that scoundrel and brigand, Wilhelm, will learn from *illegal* leaflets of our decision, of our fraternal confidence in Karl Liebknecht, and in him alone, of *our* decision to fight "revolutionary defencism" *even now*, they will read and be strengthened in their revolutionary internationalism.

To whom much has been given, of him much shall be demanded. There is no other land on earth as free as Russia is *now*. Let us make use of this freedom, not to advocate support of the bourgeoisie, or of bourgeois "revolutionary defencism," but in a bold, honest, proletarian, Liebknecht way, *to found the Third International*, an International uncompromisingly hostile both to the social-chauvinist traitors and to the vacillating "Centrists."

The October Revolution and the War: Decree on Peace

Among the decrees that Lenin immediately issued upon taking power in November, 1917, was a call for the immediate conclusion of peace by all the belligerent governments, on pain of being overthrown by the working class in each country.

The workers' and peasants' government created by the revolution of October 24–25 and relying on the Soviets of Workers', Soldiers' and Peasants' Deputies calls upon all the belligerent peoples and their governments to start immediate negotiations for a just, democratic peace.

By a just or democratic peace, for which the overwhelming majority of the

FROM: Decree on Peace, October 26 [November 8], 1917 (written by Lenin); *Selected Works*, Vol. II, book 1, pp. 328–30, 332–33.

working and toiling classes of all the belligerent countries, exhausted, tormented and racked by the war, are craving—a peace that has been most definitely and insistently demanded by the Russian workers and peasants ever since the overthrow of the tsarist monarchy—by such a peace the government means an immediate peace without annexations (i.e., without the seizure of foreign lands, without the forcible incorporation of foreign nations) and without indemnities.

This is the kind of peace the government of Russia proposes to all the belligerent nations to conclude immediately, and expresses its readiness to take all the resolute measures immediately, without the least delay, pending the final ratification of all the terms of such a peace by authoritative assemblies of the people's representatives of all countries and all nations.

In accordance with the sense of justice of the democracy in general, and of the toiling classes in particular, the government conceives the annexation or seizure of foreign lands to mean every incorporation into a large or powerful state of a small or weak nation without the precisely, clearly and voluntarily expressed consent and wish of that nation, irrespective of the time when such forcible incorporation took place, irrespective also of the degree of development or backwardness of the nation forcibly annexed to, or forcibly retained within, the borders of the given state, and irrespective, finally, of whether this nation resides in Europe or in distant, overseas countries.

If any nation whatsoever is forcibly retained within the borders of a given state, if, in spite of its expressed desire—no matter whether expressed in the press, at public meetings, in the decisions of parties, or in protests and uprisings against national oppression—it is not accorded the right to decide the forms of its state existence by a free vote, taken after the complete evacuation of the troops of the incorporating or, generally, of the stronger nation and without the least pressure being brought to bear, such, incorporation is annexation, i.e., seizure and violence.

The government considers it the greatest of crimes against humanity to continue this war over the issue of how to divide among the strong and rich nations the weak nationalities they have conquered, and solemnly announces its determination immediately to sign terms of peace to stop this war on the conditions indicated, which are equally just for all nationalities without exception.

At the same time the government declares that it does not regard the above-mentioned terms of peace as an ultimatum; in other words, it is prepared to consider any other terms of peace, but only insists that they be advanced by any of the belligerent nations as speedily as possible, and that in the proposals of peace there should be absolute clarity and the complete absence of all ambiguity and secrecy.

The government abolishes secret diplomacy, and, for its part, announces its firm intention to conduct all negotiations quite openly under the eyes of the whole people. It will immediately proceed to the full publication of the secret treaties endorsed or concluded by the government of landlords and capitalists from February to October 25, 1917. The government proclaims the absolute and immediate annulment of everything contained in these secret treaties in so far as it is aimed, as is mostly the case, at securing advantages and privileges for the Russian landlords and capitalists and at the retention, or extension, of the annexations made by the Great Russians. . . .

In proposing an immediate armistice, we appeal to the class-conscious workers of the countries that have done so much for the development of the proletarian movement. We appeal to the workers of England, where there was the Chartist movement, to the workers of France, who have in repeated uprisings displayed the strength of their class consciousness, and to the workers of Germany, who waged the fight against the Anti-Socialist Law and have created powerful organizations.

In the manifesto of March 14, we called for the overthrow of the bankers, but, far from overthrowing our own bankers, we entered into an alliance with them. Now we have overthrown the government of the bankers.

That government and the bourgeoisie will make every effort to unite their forces and drown the workers' and peasants' revolution in blood. But the three years of war have been a good lesson to the masses: the Soviet movement in other countries and the mutiny in the German navy, which was crushed by the junkers of Wilhelm the hangman. Finally, we must remember that we are not living in the wilds of Africa, but in Europe, where news can spread quickly.

The workers' movement will triumph and will pave the way to peace and Socialism.

Lenin Capitulates to Germany

The Eastern Front had been relatively quiet during 1917, and shortly after the Bolshevik Revolution a temporary armistice was agreed upon. Peace negotiations were then begun at the Polish town of Brest-Litovsk, behind the German lines. In conformity with their earlier anti-imperialist line, the Bolshevik negotiators, headed by Trotsky, used the talks as a forum for revolutionary propaganda, while most of the party expected the eventual resumption of war in the name of the revolution.

Lenin startled his followers in January, 1918, by bluntly demanding that the Soviet Republic meet the German conditions and conclude a formal peace in order to win what he regarded as an indispensable "breathing spell," instead of vainly risking the future of the revolution.

1. The position of the Russian revolution at the present moment is that nearly all the workers and the vast majority of the peasants undoubtedly side with the Soviet power and the socialist revolution which it has started. To that extent the socialist revolution in Russia is assured.

2. At the same time, the civil war, provoked by the frantic resistance of the wealthy classes, who perfectly realize that they stand before the last and decisive fight for the preservation of private ownership of the land and means of production, has not yet reached its climax. The victory of the Soviet power in this war is assured, but some time must inevitably elapse, no little exertion of effort will inevitably be required, a certain period of acute economic dislocation and chaos, such as attend all wars, and civil war in particular, is inevitable, before the resistance of the bourgeoisie is crushed.

3. Furthermore, this resistance, in its less active and nonmilitary forms—sabotage, hiring of the declassed elements and of agents of the bourgeoisie, who worm their way into the ranks of the Socialists in order to ruin their cause, and so on and so forth—has proved so stubborn and capable of assuming such diversified forms, that the fight against it will inevitably require some more time, and, in its main

FROM: Lenin, "Theses on the Question of Immediate Conclusion of a Separate and Annexationist Peace" (January 7 [20], 1918; *Selected Works*, Vol. II, book 1, pp. 385–87, 390–92).

forms, is scarcely likely to end before several months. And unless this passive and covert resistance of the bourgeoisie and its supporters is definitely crushed the socialist revolution cannot succeed.

4. Lastly, the organizational problems of the socialist transformation of Russia are so immense and difficult that their solution—in view of the abundance of petty-bourgeois fellow-travellers of the socialist proletariat, and of the latter's low cultural level—will also require a fairly long time.

5. All these circumstances taken together are such as to make it perfectly clear that for the success of Socialism in Russia a certain amount of time, several months at least, will be necessary, during which the hands of the socialist government must be absolutely free for achieving victory over the bourgeoisie in our own country first, and for launching on a wide scale far-reaching mass organizational work.

6. . . . That the socialist revolution in Europe must come, and will come, is beyond doubt. All our hopes for the *final* victory of Socialism are founded on this certainty and on this scientific prognosis. Our propagandist activities in general, and the organization of fraternization in particular, must be intensified and extended. But it would be a mistake to base the tactics of the Russian socialist government on attempts to determine whether the European, and especially the German, socialist revolution will take place in the next six months (or some such brief period), or not. Inasmuch as it is quite impossible to determine this, all such attempts, objectively speaking, would be nothing but a blind gamble.

7. The peace negotiations in Brest-Litovsk have by this date—January 7, 1918—made it perfectly clear that the upper hand in the German government . . . has undoubtedly been gained by the military party, which has virtually already presented Russia with an ultimatum . . . : either the continuation of the war, or an annexationist peace, i.e., peace on condition that we surrender all the territory we have occupied, while the Germans retain *all* the territory they have occupied and impose upon us an indemnity (outwardly disguised as payment for the maintenance of prisoners)—an indemnity of about three thousand million rubles, payable over a period of several years.

8. The socialist government of Russia is faced with the question—a question which brooks no postponement—of whether to accept this annexationist peace now, or at once to wage a revolutionary war. Actually speaking, no middle course is possible. No further postponement can now be achieved, for we have *already* done everything possible and impossible to protract the negotiations artificially. . . .

12. It is said that in a number of party statements we bluntly "promised" a revolutionary war, and that by concluding a separate peace we would be going back on our word.

That is not true. We said that in the era of imperialism it was *necessary* for a socialist government to "*prepare for and wage*" a revolutionary war; we said this in order to combat abstract pacifism and the theory that "defence of the fatherland" must be completely rejected in the era of imperialism, and, lastly, to combat the purely selfish instincts of a part of the soldiers, but we never gave any pledge to start a revolutionary war without considering how far it is possible to wage it at a given moment. . . .

13. Summing up the arguments in favour of an immediate revolutionary war, we have to conclude that such a policy might perhaps answer the human yearning for the beautiful, dramatic and striking, but that it would totally disregard the

objective relation of class forces and material factors at the present stage of the socialist revolution which has begun.

14. There can be no doubt that our army is absolutely in no condition at the present moment, and will not be for the next few weeks (and probably for the next few months), to beat back a German offensive successfully. . . .

17. Consequently, the situation at present in regard to a revolutionary war is as follows:

If the German revolution were to break out and triumph in the coming three or four months, the tactics of an immediate revolutionary war might perhaps not ruin our socialist revolution.

If, however, the German revolution does not eventuate in the next few months, the course of events, if the war is continued, will inevitably be such that grave defeats will compel Russia to conclude a still more disadvantageous separate peace, a peace, moreover, which would be concluded, not by a socialist government, but by some other (for example, a bloc of the bourgeois Rada* and the Chernovites,† or something similar). For the peasant army, which is unbearably exhausted by the war, will after the very first defeats—and very likely within a matter of weeks, and not of months—overthrow the socialist workers' government.

18. Such being the state of affairs, it would be absolutely impermissible tactics to stake the fate of the socialist revolution which has already begun in Russia merely on the chance that the German revolution may begin in the immediate future, within a period measurable in weeks. Such tactics would be a reckless gamble. We have no right to take such risks.

19. And the German revolution will by no means be made more difficult of accomplishment as far as its objective premises are concerned, if we conclude a separate peace. . . .

The Brest-Litovsk Treaty—Lenin's Defense

The issue of peace split the Bolshevik Party nearly in two, between the doctrinaire adherents of "revolutionary war," led by Bukharin and (somewhat less unequivocally) Trotsky, and the more cautious and practical-minded people like Zinoviev and Stalin who followed Lenin's lead. On February 23, 1918, the Central Committee finally voted to accept the German terms—loss of Poland, the Ukraine, and the Baltic region, and the cessation of all revolutionary propaganda abroad—by a scant five to four margin, with the middle group headed by Trotsky abstaining. The treaty was thereupon signed, on March 3. Ratification depended on approval by the Seventh Party Congress, to which Lenin appealed with the argument that peace was necessary so that the Soviet Republic could hold out until the onset of world revolution.

. . . International imperialism, with the entire might of its capital, with its highly organized military technique, which is a real force, a real fortress of international capital, could not under any circumstances, on any conditions, live side by

*Rada ["council"]: the Ukrainian nationalist regime in Kiev, 1917-1918—Ed.

†Chernovites: the Right SR's, led by V. M. Chernov—Ed.

FROM: Lenin, Report on War and Peace, delivered to the Seventh Congress of the Russian Communist Party (Bolsheviks), March 7, 1918 (*Selected Works*, Vol. II, book 1, pp. 422, 425, 429-30).

side with the Soviet Republic, both because of its objective position and because of the economic interests of the capitalist class which are embodied in it—it could not do so because of commercial connections, of international financial relations. In this sphere a conflict is inevitable. Therein lies the greatest difficulty of the Russian revolution, its greatest historical problem: the necessity of solving international problems, the necessity of calling forth an international revolution, of effecting this transition from our strictly national revolution to the world revolution. . . .

. . . History has now placed us in an extraordinarily difficult position; in the midst of organizational work of unparalleled difficulty we shall have to experience a number of painful defeats. If we consider the situation on a world-historical scale, there would doubtlessly be no hope of the ultimate victory of our revolution, if it were to remain alone, if there were no revolutionary movements in other countries. When the Bolshevik Party tackled the job alone, took it entirely into its own hands, we did so being convinced that the revolution was maturing in all countries and that in the end—but not at the very beginning—no matter what difficulties we experienced, no matter what defeats were in store for us, the international socialist revolution would come—because it is coming; would ripen—because it is ripening and will grow ripe. I repeat, our salvation from all these difficulties is an all-European revolution. . . . The German revolution is growing, but not in the way we would like it, not as fast as Russian intellectuals would have it, not at the rate our history developed in October—when we entered any town we liked, proclaimed the Soviet power, and within a few days nine-tenths of the workers came over to our side. The German revolution has the misfortune of not moving so fast. What do you think: must we reckon with the revolution, or must the revolution reckon with us? You wanted the revolution to reckon with you. But history has taught you a lesson. It is a lesson, because it is the absolute truth that without a German revolution we are doomed—perhaps not in Petrograd, not in Moscow, but in Vladivostok, in more remote places to which perhaps we shall have to retreat, and the distance to which is perhaps greater than the distance from Petrograd to Moscow. At all events, under all conceivable vicissitudes, if the German revolution does not come, we are doomed. Nevertheless, this does not in the least shake our conviction that we must be able to bear the most difficult position without blustering.

The revolution will not come as quickly as we expected. History has proved this, and we must be able to take this as a fact, to reckon with the fact that the world socialist revolution cannot begin so easily in the advanced countries as the revolution began in Russia—in the land of Nicholas and Rasputin, the land in which an enormous part of the population was absolutely indifferent as to what peoples were living in the outlying regions, or what was happening there. In such a country it was quite easy to start a revolution, as easy as lifting a feather.

But to start without preparation a revolution in a country in which capitalism is developed, in which it has produced a democratic culture and organization, provided it to everybody, down to the last man—to do so would be wrong, absurd. There we are only just approaching the painful period of the beginning of socialist revolutions. This is a fact. We do not know, no one knows; perhaps—it is quite possible—it will triumph within a few weeks, even within a few days, but we cannot stake everything on that. We must be prepared for extraordinary difficulties, for extraordinarily severe defeats, which are inevitable, because the revolution in Europe has not yet begun, although it may begin tomorrow, and when it does begin then, of course, we shall not be tortured by doubts, there will be no question about a revolutionary war, but just one continuous triumphal march. That will be, it will inevitably be so, but it is not so yet. This is the simple fact that history has taught us, with which she has hit us quite painfully—and a man who has been thrashed is worth two that haven't. That is why I think that after history has given us a very painful thrashing, because of our hope that the Germans cannot attack and that we can get everything by shouting "hurrah!", this lesson, with the help of our Soviet organizations, will be very quickly brought home to the masses all over Soviet Russia. . . .

The Brest-Litovsk Treaty—Bukharin's Attack

Bukharin pleaded at the Seventh Party Congress for the rejection of the Treaty of Brest-Litovsk on the ground that it tarnished the revolutionary appeal of the Soviet Republic at a time when, as he saw it, survival depended on evoking international revolutionary support.

The treaty was nevertheless approved by the party congress and officially ratified by the Congress of Soviets. The Left SR's then quit the cabinet in protest, after some inconsequential negotiations with Bukharin's Left Communists about the idea of forming a new coalition, removing Lenin as head of the government, and resuming the war. This became a count in the indictment of Bukharin when he was tried for treason in 1938.

Meanwhile, the Seventh Congress changed the official name of the party—from "Russian Social-Democratic Party (of Bolsheviks)" to "Russian Communist Party (of Bolsheviks)."

. . . Among the conditions of the peace are . . . points which reduce to nothing the international significance of the Russian revolution. And certainly we have said and say again that in the end the whole business depends on whether the international revolution is victorious or not. In the final reckoning the international revolution—and it alone—is our salvation. Even Comrade Lenin agrees with this. If we refrain from international propaganda, we also give up the sharpest weapon that we have at our disposal. International propaganda is a bell resounding throughout the world; if we refrain from using this bell, we are cutting our tongue off. . . . Up to now all the greatest force of the Russian revolution, all its greatest significance for the international proletarian movement consists in the fact that it has set forth an entirely clear, precise, definite program of action, which it has carried out not only in its newspaper, not only in its press, has carried out not just in words but in deeds. It is precisely the actions of the Soviet Republic, the clarity and definiteness of the program which it is carrying out, that have become its greatest attractive force. But now, when it will be declared to the whole world, when it will be known to all oppressed nations and all the proletariat that it [the Soviet Republic] is refraining from propaganda, that we have taken upon ourselves the holy mission of protecting German interests against English capital in colonial countries [Persia and Afghanistan] whose right to independence we had asserted as a slogan of struggle—excuse me, but I assert that this one point deals us such a blow, so undermines our Soviet power on all fronts, within and without—that we cannot buy at such a price, a two-day breathing spell which gives us nothing; it is inexpedient because here we not only make a compromise with capital, here we destroy our own socialist essence. . . .

FROM: Bukharin's Minority Report to the Seventh Party Congress, March 7, 1918 (*Seventh Congress of the RCP: Stenographic Report*, Moscow, State Press, 1923, pp. 40–44, 50; editor's translation).

. . . We do have a way out. The way out, which Lenin rejects but which from our point of view is the only one—this way out is revolutionary war against German imperialism. . . . Opportunists do not take account of the most important fact that the organization of a struggle grows in the very process of struggle. . . .

It is not necessary to point out that it is the greatest illusion to think that we could in the course of a few days utilize a breathing spell to create a formidable army, and fix the railroads, production and provisioning. There is no such prospect; we must reject it. Before us stands the prospect of steadily drawing broad circles of the population into the struggle during the process of this struggle. . . .

Before us we have a very real prospect which we must accept, because it is the only prospect, the only one in the sense of possibility and necessity—the prospect of war against international capital, which will bear the character of a civil war with this capital. . . .

. . . We say now that our task—in this we join you [i.e., Lenin and his supporters]—is for the workers really to dedicate themselves all the time to preparing for the coming inevitable moment, preparing for the terrible clash. On this depends the fate not only of the Russian revolution but of the international revolution as well. . . .

Therefore we propose breaking away from the policy which has been pursued up to now, annulling the peace treaty which gives us nothing and signifies our capitulation, and undertaking the proper preparations, the creation of a combat-ready Red Army. . . .

Intervention

At first with the aim of guarding Russian ports against the Germans, then, after the outbreak of the civil war, in the hope of overthrowing the Communists and getting Russia back into the war against Germany, the Allied powers sent in small contingents of troops and large amounts of money to support the anti-Communist or "White Russian" cause. The Soviet leaders responded in fury with charges of an imperialist conspiracy to snuff out the Revolution.

Workers! Like a vicious dog let off the leash, the entire capitalist press of your countries is howling for the 'intervention' of your Governments in Russian affairs, shrieking, 'now or never!' But even at this moment, when these hirelings of your exploiters have dropped their masks and are clamouring for an attack on the workers and peasants of Russia—even at this moment they lie unscrupulously, and shamelessly deceive you. For while threatening 'intervention' in Russian affairs, they are already conducting military operations against workers' and peasants' Russia.

On the Murmansk Railway which they have seized the Anglo-French bandits are already shooting Soviet workers. In the region of the Urals they are breaking up the workers' Soviets and shooting their representatives, using for this purpose the Czecho-Slovak troops, which are maintained at the expense of the French people and commanded by French officers.

FROM: Appeal of the Council of People's Commissars to the Toiling Masses of England, America, France, Italy and Japan on Allied Intervention in Russia, August 1, 1918 (English translation in Jane Degras, ed., *Soviet Documents on Foreign Policy*, London, Oxford, 1951, 1:88–92). Reprinted by permission of Oxford University Press.

Complying with the orders of your Governments, they are cutting off the Russian people from their food supplies, in order to force the workers and peasants to put their necks once more into the halter of the Paris and London Stock Exchanges. The present open attack of Franco-English capital on the workers of Russia is only the culmination of eight months' long underground struggle against Soviet Russia. From the first day of the October revolution, from the moment when the workers and peasants of Russia declared that they would no longer shed either their own or other people's blood for the sake of Russian or foreign capital, from the first day that they overthrew their exploiters and appealed to you to follow their example, to put an end to the universal slaughter, to put an end to exploitation—from that moment your exploiters vowed that they would destroy this country, in which the workers had dared for the first time in the history of humanity to throw off the yoke of capitalism, to get their necks out of the noose of war. Your Governments supported the Ukrainian Rada against the workers and peasants of Russia, that same Rada which sold itself to German imperialism and called in the help of German bayonets against the Ukrainian workers and peasants; they supported the Rumanian oligarchy, that same oligarchy which, by attacking on our south-western front, helped to destroy the defensive power of Russia. For hard cash their agents bought over that same General Krasnov who now, acting in concert with the German military authorities, is trying to cut Russia off from the coal of the Donetz and the grain of the Kuban, to render it a defenceless victim of German and Russian capital. They gave moral and financial support to the right wing of the Social-Revolutionary Party, that party of traitors to the revolution, who rose arms in hand against the workers' and peasants' Government.

But when they saw that all their attempts were unsuccessful, when it became clear that hired bandits were an insufficient force, they decided to sacrifice you too, and they are now openly attacking Russia, flinging the workers and peasants of France and England into the firing line.

You who, in the interests of capital, are shedding your blood, at the Marne and on the Aisne, in the Balkans, in Syria, and in Mesopotamia, you are to die also in the snows of north Finland and on the mountains of the Ural.

In the interests of capital you are to play the part of the executioner of the Russian workers' revolution.

To conceal the true nature of this crusade against the Russian workers' revolution your capitalists tell you that it is being undertaken not against the Russian revolution, but against German imperialism, to which they claim we have sold ourselves. . . .

Everything that the press of your capitalists and their agents say in justification of the savage assault upon Russia is nothing but hypocrisy, intended to conceal the facts of the case. It is for other purposes that they are preparing their campaign against Russia. They have three aims in view: their first aim is the seizure of as much Russian territory as possible so that its wealth and its railways can be used to secure payment to French and English capital of the interest on loans; their second aim is the suppression of the workers' revolution for fear that it may inspire you, and show you how to throw off the yoke of capitalism. Their third aim is to create a new eastern front so as to divert German forces from the western front to Russian territory.

The agents of your capitalists declare that this will weaken the pressure of the

German legions on you and hasten the moment of victory over German imperialism. They lie: they were unable to defeat Germany when a great Russian army was fighting, which gave the Allies numerical superiority; how much less are they able to secure victory on the field of battle now that the Russian army is only just being created. German imperialism can only be defeated when the imperialism of all States is defeated by the united onslaught of the world's proletariat. Not by carrying on the war, but by bringing it to an end, shall we achieve this object. Then both you and the German workers will be freed of the fear of the foreign bourgeoisie and its plans of conquest: the ending of the war of nations and the beginning of the international civil war—the war of the exploited against the exploiters—will finally put an end to all kinds of injustice, social as well as national.

The attempts to draw Russia into war will not save you from bloodshed; they can only endanger the Russian workers, the Russian workers' and peasants' revolution—and nobody wants this more than the leaders of the German military party, who, being close neighbours to the Russian revolution, are more afraid than anybody else of its inflammatory sparks. By acting as the docile tools of your Governments in their criminal conspiracy against Russia, you, the workers of France and England, America and Italy, become the executioners of the workers' revolution. . . .

We are convinced that should we retort to every blow of the rapacious 'Allies' by two blows, you would regard our action not only as legitimate defence, but also as the defence of your own interests, for the salvation of the Russian revolution is the common interest of the proletariat of all countries. We are certain that every measure taken against those who on Russian territory hatch plots against the Russian revolution will meet with your sincere sympathy, for these plots are directed against you as well as against us. Driven to fight Allied capitalism, which wishes to add new fetters to those fastened on us by German imperialism, we turn to you with the call:

Long live the solidarity of the workers of the world!

Long live the solidarity of the proletariat of France, England, America, and Italy, with the Russian proletariat!

Down with the bandits of international imperialism, long live the international revolution!

Long live peace between the nations!

The Prospect of International Revolution—Germany

The world revolution expected and relied on by the Bolsheviks seemed to be imminent in the months immediately after the end of World War I. Left-wing socialists in sympathy with Soviet Russia prepared for revolutionary struggle. In Germany Karl Liebknecht and Rosa Luxemburg organized the Spartacus League—the nucleus of the future German Communist Party—and in January, 1919, attempted to seize power. The revolt was put down by the moderate socialist government of the new German republic, and both Spartacus leaders were killed.

Proletarians! Men and Women of Labor! Comrades!
The revolution has made its entry into Germany. The masses of the soldiers, who for four years were driven to the slaughterhouse for the sake of capitalistic

FROM: "Manifesto of the Spartacus Group," December, 1918 (English translation in *The New York Times*, January 24, 1919).

profits, the masses of workers, who for four years were exploited, crushed, and starved, have revolted. That fearful tool of oppression—Prussian militarism, that scourge of humanity—lies broken on the ground. Its most noticeable representatives, and therewith the most noticeable of those guilty of this war, the Kaiser and the Crown Prince, have fled from the country. Workers' and Soldiers' Councils have been formed everywhere.

Proletarians of all countries, we do not say that in Germany all the power has really been lodged in the hands of the working people, that the complete triumph of the proletarian revolution has already been attained. There still sit in the government all those Socialists who in August, 1914, abandoned our most precious possession, the International, who for four years betrayed the German working class and at the same time the International.

But, proletarians of all countries, now the German proletarian himself is speaking to you. We believe we have the right to appear before your forum in his name. From the first day of this war we endeavored to do our international duty by fighting that criminal government with all our power and branding it as the one really guilty of the war. . . .

We know that also in your countries the proletariat made the most fearful sacrifices of flesh and blood, that it is weary of the dreadful butchery, that the proletarian is now returning to his home, and is finding want and misery there, while fortunes amounting to billions are heaped up in the hands of a few capitalists. He has recognized, and will continue to recognize, that your governments, too, have carried on the war for the sake of the big money bags. And he will further perceive that your governments, when they spoke of "justice and civilization" and the "protection of small nations," meant the profits of capital just as did ours when it talked about the "defense of the home"; and that the peace of "justice" and of the "League of Nations" amounts to the same base brigandage as the peace of Brest-Litovsk. Here, as well as there, the same shameless lust for booty, the same desire for oppression, the same determination to exploit to the limit the brutal preponderance of murderous steel.

The imperialism of all countries knows no "understanding," it knows only one right—capital's profits; it knows only one language—the sword; it knows only one method—violence. And if it is now talking in all countries, in yours as well as ours, about the "League of Nations," "disarmament," "rights of small nations," "self-determination of the peoples," it is merely using the customary lying phrases of the rulers for the purpose of lulling to sleep the watchfulness of the proletariat.

Proletarians of all countries! This must be the last war! We owe that to the 12,000,000 murdered victims, we owe that to our children, we owe that to humanity. . . .

Socialism alone is in a position to complete the great work of permanent peace, to heal the thousand wounds from which humanity is bleeding, to transform the plains of Europe, trampled down by the passage of the apocryphal horseman of war, into blooming gardens, to conjure up ten productive forces for every one destroyed, to awaken all the physical and moral energies of humanity, and to replace hatred and dissension with fraternal solidarity, harmony, and respect for every human being.

If representatives of the proletarians of all countries stretch out their hands to each other under the banner of socialism for the purpose of making peace, then peace will be concluded in a few hours. . . .

. . . The proletariat of Germany is looking toward you in this hour. Germany is pregnant with the social revolution, but socialism can only be realized by the proletariat of the world.

And therefore we call to you: "Arise for the struggle! Arise for action! The time for empty manifestos, platonic resolutions, and high-sounding words has gone by! The hour of action has struck for the International!" We ask you to elect Workers' and Soldiers' Councils everywhere that will seize political power and, together with us, will restore peace.

Not Lloyd George and Poincaré, not Sonnino, Wilson, and Erzberger or Scheidemann,* must be allowed to make peace. Peace is to be concluded under the waving banner of the socialist world revolution.

Proletarians of all countries! We call upon you to complete the work of socialist liberation, to give a human aspect to the disfigured world, and to make true those words with which we often greeted each other in the old days and which we sang as we parted: "And the International shall be the human race."

Klara Zetkin
Rosa Luxemburg
Karl Liebnecht
Franz Mehring

The Founding of the Communist International

In March, 1919, the Soviet Communist leaders assembled a casual group of foreign sympathizers in Moscow and proclaimed this to be the founding congress of the Third or Communist International (the "Comintern," following Marx's "International Workingmen's Association" and the Social-Democratic Second International). Designed as a sort of general staff of world revolution, the Comintern remained under firm Russian control (Zinoviev was its chairman from 1919 to 1926), though it attracted widespread foreign support in the years immediately after its establishment. The initial manifesto, written by Trotsky, summoned all the victims of "imperialism," proletarians and colonials, to rally to the Communist cause.

The moment of the last decisive battle came later than the apostles of social revolution had expected and hoped for. Yet it has come. We, the communists of today, representing the revolutionary proletariat of various countries in Europe, America and Asia, and assembled in "soviet-governed" Moscow, feel it incumbent upon us to continue and bring to completion the task outlined in the programme of seventy-two years ago. It is our object to summarize the revolutionary experience of the working classes, to purge the movement from the decomposing admixtures

---

*David Lloyd George, Prime Minister of Great Britain; Raymond Poincaré, President of the French Republic; Baron Sidney Sonnino, Italian Foreign Minister; Woodrow Wilson, President of the United States; Matthias Erzberger, leader of the German Catholic Center Party and signer of the 1918 armistice; Philip Scheidemann, Social-Democratic head of the provisional government in Germany—Ed.

FROM: "Manifesto of the Communist International to the Proletarians of the World," March 1919 (written by Trotsky; English translation in *The Communist International*, May 1, 1919; reprinted in U.S. House of Representatives, Committee on Un-American Activities, *The Communist Conspiracy*, May 29, 1956, Part I, sec. C, pp. 13, 16–21).

of opportunism and "social-patriotism," to unite the efforts of all truly revolutionary parties of the world's proletariat, thus facilitating and hastening the victory of the communistic revolution throughout the world. . . .

The state control over economic life, which elicited the strongest protest from capitalistic liberalism, has now become an accomplished fact. At present, there is no going back not only to free competition, but even to the oligarchy of trusts, syndicates and other economic octopuses. The issue lies between the imperialistic state and the state of the victorious proletariat, as to which of them shall henceforth be the steward of state-controlled production.

In other words: shall all labouring humanity become tributary slaves to the triumphant clique which, under the firm of "The League of Nations" and assisted by an "international" army and an "international" navy, will plunder and oppress some, throw tasty morsels to others and everywhere and on all occasions, forge fetters for the proletariat, with the sole aim of maintaining and perpetuating its own supremacy? Or shall the working classes of Europe and of other advanced countries take possession of the dilapidated, tottering structure of the world's economy and ensure its regeneration on socialist principles?

Nothing short of a dictatorship of the proletariat can reduce the duration of the present crisis. That dictatorship should not look back upon the past, nor take into account any hereditary privileges or rights of ownership, being solely guided by the necessity to succour the starving masses; it should, for that purpose, mobilize all forces and use all available means, introduce compulsory labour and labour discipline, thus to cure, within a few years, the gaping wounds inflicted by the war, and lift mankind to a new, hitherto unprecedented height. . . .

While they wrong and oppress small and weak nations in consigning them to hunger and humiliation, the allied imperialists talk a great deal (just as much, in fact, as the imperialists of the central empires did some time ago) of the nations' right of self-determination, a right which has now been trodden under foot in Europe and in all other parts of the world.

The proletarian revolution alone is capable of ensuring to the small peoples a free and independent existence. It will liberate the productive forces of all countries from the clutches of national states; it will unite the nations in the closest possible economic cooperation based on a common economic scheme, it will enable even the smallest and least numerous of nations to direct the affairs of its own national culture without the interference of any other state, and without any prejudice to the united and centralized economic body of Europe and of the world. . . .

No emancipation of the colonies is possible unless the working classes of the mother-country are emancipated. The workmen and peasants not only in Annam, Algiers, Bengal, but also in Persia and Armenia, will achieve their independence only in the hour when the working men of England and France throw over Lloyd-George and Clemenceau and take power into their own hands. In more advanced colonies, the struggle is not only being conducted under the banner of national emancipation, but it assumes, to a smaller or greater extent, the character of a purely social struggle. If capitalistic Europe forcibly involved the most backward parts of the world into the Maelstrom of capitalist interrelations, socialistic Europe is prepared to assist the emancipated colonies by its technics, by its organization, by its moral and intellectual influence, so as to facilitate their transition to properly-organized socialistic economy.

Colonial slaves of Africa and Asia! When the hour of the dictatorship of the proletariat in Europe strikes, the hour of your liberation shall have come.

The whole of the bourgeois world accuses the communists of having destroyed freedom and political democracy. This is not true. In acceding to power, the proletariat merely recognizes the utter impossibility of applying the methods of bourgeois democracy, and creates the conditions and forms of a new and a higher democracy, that of the working classes. The whole course of capitalistic development, particularly in its last imperialistic period, had been sapping at the roots of political democracy; not only did it divide the nations into two hostile classes, but it also doomed to economic vegetation and political impotency the numerous proletarian and petty-bourgeois strata, as well as the most hapless lower strata of the proletariat itself. . . .

In this realm of destruction, where not only the means of production and of transport, but the very institutions of political democracy are but a heap of blood-stained ruins, the proletariat is called upon to create its own apparatus for maintaining the cohesion of the working masses and ensuring the possibility of their revolutionary interference in the subsequent development of mankind. That apparatus is provided by workmen's councils (Soviets). The old parties, the old professional organizations (trade unions), as represented by their governing bodies, have proved utterly incapable not only of solving, but even of understanding, the problems set before them by the new era. The proletariat has created a new type of political organization, an apparatus wide enough to embrace the working masses irrespective of profession, and of their degree of political maturity, an apparatus pliant enough and capable of constant renovation and expansion to such an extent as to draw within its sphere new strata of the population and gather within its fold those of the urban and rural workers as are most akin to the proletariat. This unique organization of labour, having for its object the self-government, the social struggle and the ultimate accession to power of the working classes, has been tried in a number of countries and is the most essential achievement and the most powerful weapon of the proletariat in modern times. . . .

Civil war is being foisted upon the working classes by their deadly foes. The working classes cannot refrain from returning blow for blow, unless they forego their own interests and sacrifice their future—which is the future of mankind.

While they never artificially foster civil war, the communist parties strive to shorten its duration whenever it inexorably breaks out; they endeavour to reduce the number of its victims and, first of all, to ensure the victory of the proletariat. Hence the necessity of the timely disarmament of the middle classes, the arming of the working classes, the creation of a communistic army to defend the rule of the proletariat and the unhindered carrying out of the constructive programme of socialism. Thus the Red Army of Soviet Russia came into being. It is a bulwark for the conquests of the working classes against any assaults both from without and from within. The Soviet army is an integral part of the Soviet state. . . .

Bourgeois order has been sufficiently castigated by socialist critics. The object of the international communist party is to overthrow that organization and to replace it by the socialist state. We call upon all the working men and women of all countries to rally round the communist banner already floating over many a victorious battlefield.

Proletarians of all countries! In the struggle against imperialistic barbarism, against monarchy, against the privileged classes, against the bourgeois state and bourgeois property, against national oppression and the tyranny of classes in any shape or form—unite!

Proletarians of all countries, round the banner of workmen's councils, round the banner of the revolutionary struggle for power and the dictatorship of the proletariat, round the banner of the Third International—unite!

The Hungarian Soviet Republic

Aside from Russia, the only country in which Communists came to power during the era of the Comintern was Hungary, where the leftists under Bela Kun, in default of effective opposition, seized the opportunity in March, 1919, to establish a dictatorship on the Soviet model. The regime lasted only until August, 1919, when it was overthrown by Rumanian intervention with Anglo-French backing.

To All!

Today the proletariat of Hungary takes all authority into its hands. The collapse of the bourgeois world and the bankruptcy of the coalition compel the workers and peasants to take this step. Capitalistic production has collapsed. Communism alone can preserve the country from anarchy.

In foreign politics we are also faced by a complete catastrophe. The Paris Conference has decided to occupy nearly the whole of Hungary by arms, and regards the line of occupation as a definitive political frontier, thus making the supply of food and coal impossible. In the dictatorship of the proletariat lies our salvation. For this purpose the perfect unity of the proletariat is necessary. The Social Democratic Party and the Communist Party have therefore joined. The Hungarian Socialistic Party henceforth receives as members all the working men and women of the country.

This party empowers the Revolutionary Governing Council to assume the Government. It will develop the Workers', Peasants' and Soldiers' Councils throughout the country, which will exercise legislative, executive, and judicial powers. Hungary becomes a Soviet Republic, which will immediately proceed to carry into effect the principles of Socialism and Communism. The large estates, mines, large industrial concerns, banks and means of traffic will be socialized. Agrarian reform will be effected not by division into small lots, but by cooperative societies. Profiteers, and those who speculate on hunger and want, will be pitilessly dealt with.

The Governing Council demands iron discipline. The bandits of counter-revolution and the brigands of plunder will be punished with death. The Council organizes a powerful proletarian army to assert the dictatorship of workers and peasants against Hungarian capitalists and landlords as well as against Rumanian boiars [noblemen] and Czech bourgeois.

It declares its entire ideal and spiritual community with the Russian Soviet Government, to which it offers an armed alliance. It sends its fraternal greetings to the workers of England, France, Italy, and America, and calls upon them not to tolerate for one moment the wicked predatory campaign of their capitalistic gov-

FROM: Proclamation of the Revolutionary Governing Council of Hungary, March 22, 1919 (English translation in Enemy Press Supplement, London, April 10, 1919).

ernments against the Hungarian Soviet Republic. It invites to an armed alliance the workers of Czechoslovakia, Rumania, Serbia and Croatia against bourgeois, boiars, landlords, and dynasties. It calls on the workers of German-Austria and Germany to break with Paris and ally themselves with Moscow, to set up the Soviet Republic, and to face the conquering imperialists with arms in their hands.

We are conscious of the hardships and sacrifices before us. We must fight to free our food supplies and our mines, for the liberty of our brothers and our own existence. We trust in the heroism of the proletariat. We choose a course that will bring us hardships, misery and suffering, because only thus can we help to victory the cause of Socialism which will redeem the world. We call on all to work or to enter the proletarian army.

The Philosophy of Consciousness and Force: Lukács

The outstanding non-Soviet Communist theoretician in the early period of the International was the Hungarian literary critic György Lukács. While serving as Commissar of Education in the Bela Kun government Lukács announced a frankly revised conception of Marxism which put heavy stress on the factors of thought and power, in opposition to the strict economic determinism of the "vulgar Marxists." Theoretically speaking Lukács was a Stalinist before Stalin, though the straightforwardness of his innovations brought him Moscow's disfavor. Also distinguished by a humanitarian bent, Lukács once again gained note by participating in the short-lived Hungarian national Communist movement of 1956.

. . . *Paralleling the economic struggle a struggle is waged for society's consciousness. However, society's development of consciousness is synonymous with the possibility of leading society.* The proletariat achieves victory in its class struggle not only in the sphere of force, but equally in this struggle for the social consciousness, as during the last fifty or sixty years it has in an ascending line broken up bourgeois ideology and developed its own consciousness as henceforth the only standard social consciousness.

The most important weapon in this contest over consciousness, over social leadership, is historical materialism. Therefore historical materialism is just as much a function of the development and break-up of capitalist society as all other ideologies. . . .

. . . Historical materialism cannot at all be applied to the pre-capitalist social structure in the same way as to that of capitalistic development. Here we need much more developed, much more refined analyses, to indicate on the one hand what role among the forces which move society has been played by purely economic forces—insofar as such have ever existed in the strict sense of "purity"—and on the other hand to point out how these economic forces have influenced the rest of the structure of society. . . . Historical materialism has attained its greatest success in the analysis of the structure of society, of law, and of other structures on the same plane. . . . It becomes far less conclusive and creative when it is applied to literary, scientific, and religious creations.

Vulgar Marxism has completely neglected this distinction. . . .

FROM: Lukács, "The Change in the Function of Historical Materialism" (1919; in *Geschichte und Klassenbewusstsein* [History and Class Consciousness], Berlin, Malik Verlag, 1923, pp. 234, 244–47, 251–52; editor's translation).

This historical attitude of vulgar Marxism has by itself decisively influenced the conduct of the labor parties, their political theory and tactics. The question in which this divorce from vulgar Marxism is most clearly expressed is that of *force*: the role of force in the struggle to achieve and preserve victory in the proletarian revolution. . . .

Vulgar Marxist economism specifically disputes the significance of force in the transition from one economic system of production to another. It appeals to the "natural lawfulness" of economic development, which accomplishes this transition by its own supreme authority, without the assistance of crude, "non-economic" force. . . .

. . . For Marx the "ripeness" of the production relations for the transition from one form of production to another meant something entirely different from what it means for vulgar Marxism. The organization of the revolutionary elements as a class—not just "against capital," but "for itself," to change the simple forces of production into a lever for social transformation—is not only a problem of class consciousness, of the practical effectiveness of conscious action, but also the beginning of the suspension of the pure "natural lawfulness" of economism. It means that the "greatest productive force" [the workers] finds itself in rebellion against the system of production of which it is a part. A situation has arisen which can be resolved only by force. . . .

The qualitative distinction between the decisive, "last" crisis of capitalism . . . and the earlier ones is not just a simple change of its duration and depth, of quantity into quality. . . . This change is expressed in the fact that the proletariat ceases to be a simple object of the crisis; that the internal antagonism in capitalistic produc-tion . . . comes out into the open. The organization of the proletariat, whose aim has always been "to halt the ruinous consequences for its class of that natural law of capitalistic production" (Marx), moves from the stage of negativity . . . to activity. With this the structure of the crisis has decisively, qualitatively changed. . . . Force becomes the decisive economic factor in this situation.

This shows again that these "eternal natural laws" are valid only for a certain period of development. . . .

Vulgar Marxism . . . denies the significance of force "as an economic factor." For vulgar Marxism the theoretical underestimation of the significance of force in history and the denial of its role in the history of the past is a theoretical prepara-tion for opportunistic tactics. This elevation of the specific developmental laws of capitalist society to general laws is the theoretical foundation for the effort to make the existence of capitalist society practically eternal.

. . . The demand that socialism be realized without "non-economic" force, through the immanent laws of economic development, is actually synonymous with the eternal survival of capitalist society. . . .

· Communism in the U.S.A.

The American Socialist Party, after reaching the million-vote mark with Eugene Debs in the presidential election of 1912, split over the United States' entry into the war in 1917 just as

FROM: Manifesto of the Communist Party of America, September, 1919 (in U.S. House of Representatives, Committee on Un-American Activities, "Organized Communism in the United States," August 19, 1953, pp. 29–30, 34–35).

the Europeans had three years before. The radical anti-war wing, largely representing a European-born constituency, proclaimed itself the "Communist Party of America" in 1919, while a native American group led by the noted journalist John Reed formed a "Communist Labor Party." The two groups merged in 1920, but by that time the great Red Scare and repression by the Justice Department had reduced the Communist movement to a semi-underground sect. Thenceforth the American Communists had little significance in the world of American domestic politics, but they are of interest as an exemplification of all the subsequent developments in the international Communist movement.

The world is on the verge of a new era. Europe is in revolt. The masses of Asia are stirring uneasily. Capitalism is in collapse. The workers of the world are seeing a new life and securing new courage. Out of the night of war is coming a new day.

The spectre of Communism haunts the world of capitalism. Communism, the hope of the workers to end misery and oppression.

The workers of Russia smashed the front of international Capitalism and Imperialism. They broke the chains of the terrible war; and in the midst of agony, starvation and the attacks of the capitalists of the world, they are creating a new social order.

The class war rages fiercely in all nations. Everywhere the workers are in a desperate struggle against their capitalist masters. The call to action has come. The workers must answer the call.

The Communist Party of America is the party of the working class. The Communist Party proposes to end capitalism and organize a workers' industrial republic. The workers must control industry and dispose of the products of industry. The Communist Party is a party realizing the limitations of all existing workers' organizations and proposes to develop the revolutionary movement necessary to free the workers from the oppression of Capitalism. The Communist Party insists that the problems of the American worker are identical with the problems of the workers of the world.

A giant struggle is convulsing the world. The war is at an end, but peace is not here. The struggle is between the capitalist nations of the world and the international proletariat, inspired by Soviet Russia. The Imperialisms of the world are desperately arraying themselves against the onsweeping proletarian revolution. . . .

The war made a shambles of civilization. It proved the utter incapacity of capitalism to direct and promote the progress of humanity. Capitalism has broken down.

But the Socialist movement itself broke down under the test of war. The old dominant moderate Socialism accepted and justified the war. It acted against the proletarian revolution and united with the capitalists against the workers. Out of this circumstance developed the forces of revolutionary Socialism now expressed in the Communist International. . . .

The proletarian revolution comes at the moment of crisis in Capitalism, of a collapse of the old order. Under the impulse of the crisis, the proletariat acts for the conquest of power, by means of mass action. Mass action concentrates and mobilizes the forces of the proletariat, organized and unorganized; it acts equally against the bourgeois state and the conservative organizations of the working class. Strikes of protest develop into general political strikes and then into revolutionary mass action for the conquest of the power of the state. Mass action becomes political in purpose while extraparliamentary in form; it is equally a process of revolution and the revolution itself in operation.

The state is an organ of coercion. The bourgeois parliamentary state is the organ of the bourgeoisie for the coercion of the proletariat. Parliamentary government is the expression of bourgeois supremacy, the form of authority of the capitalist over the worker. Bourgeois democracy promotes the dictatorship of capital, assisted by the press, the pulpit, the army and the police. Bourgeois democracy is historically necessary, on the one hand, to break the power of feudalism, and, on the other, to maintain the proletarian in subjection. It is precisely this democracy that is now the instrument of Imperialism, since the middle class, the traditional carrier of democracy, accepts Imperialism. The proletarian revolution disrupts bourgeois democracy. It disrupts this democracy in order to end class divisions and class rule, to realize industrial self-government of the workers. Therefore it is necessary that the proletariat organize its own state *for the coercion and suppression of the bourgeoisie.* Proletarian dictatorship is a recognition of the fact; it is equally a recognition of the fact that in the Communist reconstruction of society the proletariat alone counts as a class.

While the dictatorship of the proletariat performs the negative task of crushing the old order, it performs the positive task of constructing the new. Together with the government of the proletarian dictatorship, there is developed a new "government," which is no longer government in the old sense, since it concerns itself with the management of the production and not with the government of persons. Out of workers' control of industry, introduced by the proletarian dictatorship, there develops the complete structure of Communist Socialism—industrial self-government of the communistically organized producers. When this structure is completed, which implies the complete expropriation of the bourgeoisie, economically and politically, the dictatorship of the proletariat ends, in its place coming the full, free social and individual autonomy of the Communist order.

The Communist International, issuing directly out of the proletarian revolution in action, is the organ of the International revolutionary proletariat; just as the League of Nations is the organ of the joint aggression and resistance of the dominant Imperialism.

The Communist International represents a Socialism in complete accord with the revolutionary character of the class struggle. It unites all the conscious revolutionary forces. It wages war equally against Imperialism and moderate Socialism—each of which has demonstrated its complete inability to solve the problems that now press down upon the workers. The Communist International issues its call to the conscious proletariat for the final struggle against Capitalism.

It is not a problem of immediate revolution. The revolutionary epoch may last for years, and tens of years. The Communist International offers a program both immediate and ultimate in scope.

The old order is in decay. Civilization is in collapse. The workers must prepare for the proletarian revolution and the Communist reconstruction of society.

The Communist International calls!

Workers of the world, unite!

Leninist Discipline in the Comintern

The early years of the Communist International were a period of turmoil from the organizational point of view, as the Russian Communists strove to split the European socialist parties and bring their left-wing elements under firm international discipline. The Second Comintern Congress, in August, 1920, laid down "twenty-one conditions"—largely drafted by Lenin— to which member Communist parties would have to subscribe. They were required to commit themselves to the political pattern which had emerged in Russia—violent revolution under the exclusive leadership of a strictly disciplined Communist party—as well as to unquestioning acceptance of the decisions of the International and the interests of the Soviet Republic.

The Second Congress of the Communist International rules that the conditions for joining the Communist International shall be as follows:

1. The general propaganda and agitation should bear a really Communist character, and should correspond to the programme and decisions of the Third International. The entire party press should be edited by reliable Communists who have proved their loyalty to the cause of the Proletarian revolution. The dictatorship of the proletariat should not be spoken of simply as a current hackneyed formula, it should be advocated in such a way that its necessity should be apparent to every rank-and-file working man and woman, to each soldier and peasant, and should emanate from everyday facts systematically recorded by our press day by day. . . .

2. Every organization desiring to join the Communist International shall be bound systematically and regularly to remove from all the responsible posts in the labor movement (Party organizations, editors, labor unions, parliamentary factions, co-operatives, municipalities, etc.), all reformists and followers of the "centre," and to have them replaced by Communists, even at the cost of replacing at the beginning "experienced" men by rank-and-file working men.

3. The class struggle in almost every country of Europe and America is entering the phase of civil war. Under such conditions the Communists can have no confidence in bourgeois laws. They should create everywhere a parallel illegal apparatus, which at the decisive moment should do its duty by the party, and in every way possible assist the resolution. In every country where in consequence of martial law or of other exceptional laws, the Communists are unable to carry on their work lawfully, a combination of lawful and unlawful work is absolutely necessary.

4. A persistent and systematic propaganda and agitation is necessary in the army, where Communist groups should be formed in every military organization. Wherever, owing to repressive legislation, agitation becomes impossible, it is necessary to carry on such agitation illegally. But refusal to carry on or participate in such work should be considered equal to treason to the revolutionary cause, and incompatible with affiliation with the Third International.

5. A systematic regular propaganda is necessary in the rural districts. The working class can gain no victory unless it possesses the sympathy and support of at least part of the rural workers and of the poor peasants. . . .

6. Every party desirous of affiliating with the Third International should renounce not only avowed social patriotism, but also the falsehood and the hypocrisy of social pacifism; it should systematically demonstrate to the workers that

FROM: Conditions of Admission to the Communist International, approved by the Second Comintern Congress, August, 1920 (English translation in *The Communist Conspiracy*, Part I, sec. C, pp. 40–44).

without a revolutionary overthrow of capitalism no international arbitration, no talk of disarmament, no democratic reorganization of the League of Nations will be capable of saving mankind from new Imperialist wars.

7. Parties desirous of joining the Communist International must recognize the necessity of a complete and absolute rupture with reformism and the policy of the "centrists," and must advocate this rupture amongst the widest circles of the party membership, without which condition a consistent Communist policy is impossible. . . .

8. In the Colonial question and that of the oppressed nationalities there is necessary an especially distinct and clear line of conduct of the parties of countries where the bourgeoisie possesses such colonies or oppresses other nationalities. Every party desirous of belonging to the Third International should be bound to denounce without any reserve all the methods of "its own" imperialists in the colonies, supporting not only in words but practically a movement of liberation in the colonies. It should demand the expulsion of its own Imperialists from such colonies, and cultivate among the workingmen of its own country a truly fraternal attitude towards the working population of the colonies and oppressed nationalities, and carry on a systematic agitation in its own army against every kind of oppression of the colonial population.

9. Every party desirous of belonging to the Communist International should be bound to carry on systematic and persistent Communist work in the labor unions, co-operatives and other labor organizations of the masses. It is necessary to form Communist groups within the organizations, which by persistent and lasting work should win over labor unions to Communism. These groups should constantly denounce the treachery of the social patriots and of the fluctuations of the "centre." These Communist groups should be completely subordinated to the party in general.

10. Any party belonging to the Communist International is bound to carry on a stubborn struggle against the Amsterdam "International" of the yellow labor unions.*

11. Parties desirous of joining the Third International shall be bound to inspect the personnel of their parliamentary factions, to remove all unreliable elements therefrom, to control such factions, not only verbally but in reality, to subordinate them to the Central Committee of the party, and to demand from each proletarian Communist that he devote his entire activity to the interests of real revolutionary propaganda.

12. All parties belonging to the Communist International should be formed on the basis of the principle of democratic centralism. At the present time of acute civil war the Communist Party will be able fully to do its duty only when it is organized in a sufficiently thorough way, when it possesses an iron discipline, and when its party centre enjoys the confidence of the members of the party, who are to endow this centre with complete power, authority and ample rights.

13. The Communist parties of those countries where the Communist activity is legal, should make a clearance of their members from time to time, as well as those of the party organizations, in order systematically to free the party from the petty bourgeois elements which penetrate into it.

*I.e., the socialist International Federation of Trade Unions, with headquarters in Amsterdam— Ed.

14. Each party desirous of affiliating with the Communist International should be obliged to render every possible assistance to the Soviet Republics in their struggle against all counter-revolutionary forces. The Communist parties should carry on a precise and definite propaganda to induce the workers to refuse to transport any kind of military equipment intended for fighting against the Soviet Republics, and should also by legal or illegal means carry on a propaganda amongst the troops sent against the workers' republics, etc.

15. All those parties which up to the present moment have stood upon the old social and democratic programmes should, within the shortest time possible, draw up a new Communist programme in conformity with the special conditions of their country, and in accordance with the resolutions of the Communist International. . . .

16. All the resolutions of the congresses of the Communist International, as well as the resolutions of the Executive Committee, are binding for all parties joining the Communist International. The Communist International, operating under the conditions of most acute civil warfare, should be centralized in a better manner than the Second International. At the same time, the Communist International and the Executive Committee are naturally bound in every form of their activity to consider the variety of conditions under which the different parties have to work and struggle, and generally binding resolutions should be passed only on such questions upon which such resolutions are possible.

17. In connection with the above, all parties desiring to join the Communist International should alter their name. Each party desirous of joining the Communist International should bear the following name: Communist Party of such and such a country, section of the Third Communist International. The question of the renaming of a party is not only a formal one, but is a political question of great importance. The Communist International has declared a decisive war against the entire bourgeois world, and all the yellow Social Democratic parties. It is indispensable that every rank-and-file worker should be able clearly to distinguish between the Communist parties and the old official "Social Democratic" or "Socialist" parties, which have betrayed the cause of the working class. . . .

21. Those members of the party who reject the conditions and the theses of the Third International, are liable to be excluded from the party.

CHAPTER TWO

One Communist Country, 1921–1939

Throughout the interwar period Russia—or the Soviet Union, as it officially became known in 1922—stood alone as the land of the Marxist workers' revolution. Recognizing in 1921 that the international revolutionary tide was ebbing in the face of the "stabilization of capitalism," the Soviet leadership put a priority on national survival and security through normalization of relations with the outside world and the pursuit of power politics including cultivation of non-Communist allies. The parties of the Communist International were brought under increasing Russian control—the "Bolshevization of the Comintern"—to make them support Russia's foreign policy and to eliminate sympathizers with the succession of ill-fated opposition factions within Russia. A particularly sensitive case was China, where the alliance tactics demanded by the Russians failed, and the nascent Communist movement was nearly obliterated by Chiang Kaishek's Nationalist government before the new Communist leader Mao Tse-tung evolved his novel strategy of guerrilla revolution.

From 1928 to 1934—the "Third Period" after revolution and normalization—Soviet policy and the line enjoined upon the Comintern were bolder in rhetoric, even in America, while Stalin was consummating his revolution from above within Russia and disposing of his Communist enemies both at home and abroad. Thanks in part to Stalin's refusal during these years to cooperate with democratic governments and parties, the Soviet Union found itself confronted by deadly enemies both to the east and to the west in the form of militarist Japan and Nazi Germany. Stalin responded with the new line of Collective Security (preached at the League of Nations by Foreign Commissar Litvinov) and the doctrine of the Popular Front to guide foreign Communist parties into alliance with democrats and Socialists. Believing that the Western democracies had left him holding the bag after the failure to stop Franco in the Spanish Civil War and the appeasement of Hitler at Munich, Stalin resolved to come to terms with his most threatening neighbor. In Soviet Russia's deepest descent into diplomatic expediency, he concluded the Non-Aggression Pact with Germany that launched the Second World War and set the stage for his country's emergence as the hegemonic power in Eastern Europe.

The Stabilization of Capitalism and the Revolutionary Mission

At the Third Congress of the Comintern in 1921 the leaders of the movement were compelled to recognize that the old order had withstood the challenge of proletarian revolution

FROM: "Theses on the World Situation and the Tasks of the Comintern," Third Comintern Congress, July 4, 1921 (English translation in Degras, *The Communist International, 1919-1943: Documents*, London, Oxford University Press, 1956, Vol. I, pp. 230–31, 234, 236, 238–39). Reprinted by permission of Oxford University Press.

everywhere outside Russia. Nevertheless they urged upon the Communist parties the duty of vigilance, discipline and struggle in preparation for the next upsurge of revolutionary sentiment.

The revolutionary movement at the end of the imperialist war and after it was marked by an amplitude unprecedented in history. . . . It did not, however, end with the overthrow of world capitalism, or even of European capitalism.

During the year which has passed between the second and third congresses of the Communist International, a series of working class risings and struggles have ended in partial defeat (the advance of the Red Army on Warsaw in August 1920, the movement of the Italian proletariat in September 1920, the rising of the German workers in March 1921).

The first period of the post-war revolutionary movement, distinguished by the spontaneous character of its assault, by the marked imprecision of its aims and methods, and by the extreme panic which it aroused among the ruling classes, seems in essentials to be over. The self-confidence of the bourgeoisie as a class, and the outward stability of their State organs, have undeniably been strengthened. The panic fear of communism has abated, even if it has not altogether disappeared. The leaders of the bourgeoisie are even boasting of the power of their State machine and have gone over to an offensive against the workers in all countries both on the economic and the political front.

Consequently the Communist International puts to itself and to the entire working class the following questions: To what extent do the new relations between the bourgeoisie and the proletariat correspond with the real relation of forces? Are the bourgeoisie really about to re-establish the social equilibrium destroyed by the war? Are there reasons for thinking that after the political upheavals and class struggles a new and prolonged epoch of the restoration and expansion of capitalism is about to open? Does it not follow from this that the programme and tactics of the Communist International should be revised? . . .

The period of demobilization, when the massacre that had been prolonged for four years had ceased, the period of transition from a state of war to a state of peace, inevitably accompanied by an economic crisis arising from the exhaustion and chaos of war, rightly appeared most dangerous in the eyes of the bourgeoisie. In fact in the two years following its end the countries which had been ravaged by war became the scene of powerful proletarian movements.

The fact that a few months after the war it was not the apparently inevitable crisis but economic recovery which set in was one of the chief reasons why the bourgeoisie retained their dominant position. This period lasted about a year and a half. Industry absorbed practically all the demobilized workers. Although as a rule wages did not catch up with food prices, they rose enough to create a mirage of economic gain. It was precisely the favourable economic circumstances of 1919–1920 which, by ameliorating the most acute phase of liquidation of the war, encouraged the self-confidence of the bourgeoisie, and raised the question of the opening of a new epoch of organic capitalist development. At bottom, however, the recovery of 1919–1920 did not mark the beginning of the restoration of capitalist economy after the war; it only continued the artificial prosperity created by the war. . . .

The general world economic situation, and above all the decline of Europe, will give rise to a long period of grave economic difficulties, of shocks, of partial and general crises. The international relations established as a result of the war and the treaty of Versailles make the situation even more difficult. Imperialism was born of the pressure of the productive forces to abolish national frontiers and to create a single economic territory in Europe and in the world. The result of the conflict of hostile imperialisms has been to create in central and eastern Europe new frontiers, new tariffs, and new armies. In the economic and political sense Europe has relapsed into the Middle Ages. Its exhausted and devastated territory has now to support armies one and a half times as large as in 1914, that is, at the height of the 'armed peace'. . . .

The conclusion by some capitalist countries of treaties of peace and commercial agreements with Soviet Russia does not mean that the world bourgeoisie have abandoned the idea of destroying the Soviet Republic. It is probably no more than a temporary change in the forms and methods of struggle. . . .

The differences between the Communist International and the social-democrats of both groups do not consist in our having fixed a date for the revolution, while they reject utopianism and putschism. The difference is that the social-democrats obstruct real revolutionary development by doing all they can, whether in the government or in opposition, to help reestablish the stability of the bourgeois State, while the communists take advantage of every opportunity and of every means to overthrow or to destroy the bourgeois State.

In the two and a half years which have passed since the end of the war, the proletariat of many countries has shown more energy, militancy, and devotion, than would have been required for a victorious revolution if at the head of the working class there had been a strong international communist party centralized and ready for action. But for a number of historical reasons it was the Second International which stood at the head of the proletariat during and immediately after the war, and that organization was and still is an invaluable political instrument in the hands of the bourgeoisie. . . .

It cannot be denied that the open revolutionary struggle of the proletariat for power is at the present moment slackening and slowing down in many countries. But after all it could not be expected that the post-war revolutionary offensive, once it failed to win an immediate victory, would follow an unbroken upward curve of development. Political movements also have their cycles, their ups and downs. The enemy does not remain passive; he fights. If the proletarian attack is now crowned with success, the bourgeoisie pass at the first chance to the counter-attack. The loss of some positions, won without difficulty, is followed by a temporary depression among the proletariat. But it is equally undeniable that the curve of capitalist development is downwards, with a few passing upward movements, while the curve of revolution is rising although it shows a few falls. . . .

Capitalism can be restored only by infinitely greater exploitation, by the loss of millions of lives, by the reduction of the standard of living of other millions below the minimum by perpetual uncertainty, and this makes for constant strikes and revolts. It is under this pressure and in these struggles that the mass will to overthrow capitalist society grows.

The chief task of the communist party in the present crisis is to direct the defensive struggles of the proletariat, to broaden and deepen them, to link them together and, in harmony with the march of events, to transform them into decisive political struggles for the final goal. But if events develop more slowly and a period of recovery follows in a greater or lesser number of countries the present economic crisis, that would not in any way mean the beginning of an 'organic' epoch. So long as capitalism exists, recurrent fluctuations are inevitable. They will characterize capitalism in its death agony as they did in its youth and its maturity. . . .

Whether the revolutionary movement in the forthcoming period advances more rapidly or slows down, in either case the communist party must remain the party of action. It stands at the head of the fighting masses, formulating clearly and vigorously the watchwords of the battle, exposing the evasive slogans of social-democracy, designed for compromise. Throughout the changing course of the struggle, the communist party strives to consolidate its organizational footholds, to train the masses in active manœuvring, to arm them with new methods aimed at open conflict with the forces of the enemy. Utilizing every respite to assimilate the lessons of the preceding phase, the communist party strives to deepen and extend class conflicts, to co-ordinate them nationally and internationally by unity of aim and action, and in this way, as spearhead of the proletariat, to sweep aside every obstacle on the road to its dictatorship and to the social revolution.

Mongolia—The First Satellite

In the course of consolidating their rule in Siberia in the wake of the Russian Civil War, the Soviet authorities intervened in 1921 in Outer Mongolia, a former Tsarist sphere of influence, to install in power the Communist-oriented Mongolian People's Party led by Sukhe Bator. Communications exchanged between the Mongolian revolutionaries and the Soviet authorities made clear the dependence of the former on Soviet backing.

The death of Sukhe Bator was followed by purges of moderate elements and formalization of the Mongolian People's Republic, after which the country conformed to the successive phases of Soviet policy under Khorloin Choibalsan, an avowed imitator of Stalin. Mongolia remained largely pastoral, however, until the industrialization and collectivization drive of the 1950's under Choibalsan's successor Yumjagin Tsedenbal. It then lined up firmly with the Soviets in their dispute with Communist China.

Mongolia is significant as a prototype, both theoretical and tactical, of Soviet moves to establish satellite Communist regimes and later to co-opt national liberation movements.

a) Sukhe Bator's Appeal to Russia

We, members of the People's Party, in the name of our Party turn to great Russia with a request for aid. We, together with service-elements (Mongolian army troops) of our country, on whose military strength we rely, aspire to restore the Autonomy of Mongolia and to proclaim the Khutukhtu Bogdo [Jebtsun Damba Khutukhtu] as a limited monarch. Then we wish to take necessary measures to limit the hereditary rights of the princes. Having attained the independence of our country, we, profiting by the experience of other countries, will struggle for the rights and interests of our people. The development of national self-awareness of the arats [commoners] will permit us in coming years to carry the revolution further, to the point of finally liquidating the privileges of the hereditary princes. Therefore we ask:

1. To extend necessary aid to the People's Party of Mongolia, and to assist in restoring Mongolian Autonomy.

FROM: Sukhe Bator, letter to Boris Shumiatsky (head of the Soviet administration in Irkutsk known at the time as the Far Eastern Republic), August 28, 1920, in Khorloin Choibalsan, *Short History of the Mongolian People's Revolution*, Russian edition, Moscow, 1952, pp. 25–26 (English translation in Robert A. Rupen, *Mongols of the Twentieth Century*, Bloomington, Ind., Indiana University Publications, 1964, I:139). Reprinted by permission of Robert A. Rupen.

2. To designate a Soviet representative at Kyakhta who will serve as a connecting link between the Soviet Government and the People's Party.

On our side, we consider it necessary. . . . to organize at Urga a Central Committee of the Party, to elect leaders of the Committee. The elected Central Committee must, first, establish relations with the population; second, to form an army capable of defending the purposes of the Party; third, to send Party members to Irkutsk for military training and political education. Besides this, the Central Committee should also lead the work of Party organizations throughout the country. Simultaneously with the election of the Central Committee, it is necessary to assign people who will control the Central Committee, to assure the correctness and purity of its work.

[Also] to organize a Mongolian people's cooperative and establish ties with cooperatives founded in Russia, so that the cattle and raw materials of Mongolia can be sent to Russia in exchange for industrial goods. Besides, it is desirable that Russian cooperatives organize on Mongolian territory industrial enterprises for processing local raw materials. For this it is necessary to send authorized representatives of the Mongolian People's Party to Wang Küre, Kyakhta, and the border-post, Khabtagai.

b) The People's Party Platform

1. The "power and culture" of the Mongols is to be raised to a level comparable to that of other people.

2. There must be an independent Mongolian State, with no foreign domination. To attain this, the Party ". . . aims at the ultimate goal of the union of all Mongolian tribes into a single self-governing State." The immediate purpose is, ". . . liberation from the power of the Chinese despots, the restoration and resumption of the recently-suppressed Autonomous State of Outer Mongolia."

3. The Mongolian tribes do not on principle oppose the idea of forming part of an all-China federation; indeed, this would be desirable. But such a federation would have to provide and guarantee "broad autonomous rights." Such a federal organization, eliminating the subjection of any one of the constituent units to any of the others, would be desirable, ". . . to assist in defense against danger from foreign imperialists." . . .

4. Mongolian State-existence should be established immediately and popular control should be strengthened.

5. The Mongolian People's Party should cooperate with other Mongolian parties which are "of such a trend"; but parties which ". . . sold out to the Chinese are declared enemies of the people."

6. Questions of external and internal policy, and also of religious life, questions of change of long-observed customs, traditions, and economy way-of-life, our Party will resolve according to the spirit of our times, the experience of the peoples of the world, and in conformity with the character of future changes in world events, in the interests of the welfare and progress of the Mongolian people. Thus, branches which are useless or inimical, not conforming to the spirit of the times,

FROM: Proclamation of the Mongolian People's Party, Constituting the Political Platform of the Mongolian Revolution, adopted at the First Congress of the Mongolian People's Party, March 1–6, 1921 (English translation in Rupen, *Mongols of the Twentieth Century*, I:142–43). Reprinted by permission of Robert A. Rupen.

or which are dying out, will be removed through sheer necessity, as obsolete and unhealthy, as far as possible by mild, and in border-cases by firm, measures.

7. The Party desires friendly contact with revolutionary organizations in other countries, including those in China and Russia.

8. Mongolia feels a common bond especially with other small countries oppressed by more powerful States, and the Mongolian People's Party therefore desires to cooperate with organizations aiming to end such oppression in those countries.

9. The Party recognizes the "right of freedom" for the people, and hopes to eliminate ". . . obstacles to the realization of this right, forbidding only those actions which are contrary to the interests of the people and the policies of the State."

c) Mongolia's Appeal for Soviet Troops

The People's Revolutionary Government of Mongolia addresses to the Government of the Russian Socialist Federated Soviet Republic a request not to withdraw the Soviet troops from the territory of Mongolia until the complete removal of the menace from the common enemy, who is now seeking reinforcements in the Eastern Steppes. The People's Revolutionary Government finds it necessary to address this request to the Government of the R.S.F.S.R., because the Mongolian Government has not as yet completed the organization of the apparatus of the new authority. The presence of the Soviet troops is dictated by circumstances, its purpose being to preserve the security of the territory of Mongolia and of the frontiers of the R.S.F.S.R. The People's Provisional Revolutionary Government of Mongolia is confident that the Government of the R.S.F.S.R. will realize the seriousness of the situation and the common interest in the defeat of the common enemy, and will accede to this request.

d) Chicherin's Reply

The Russian Soviet Government, in alliance with the Government of the Far Eastern Republic,* ordered its troops, side by side with the revolutionary army of the Provisional Government of Mongolia, to deal a crushing blow to their common enemy the Tsarist General, Ungern, who has subjected the Mongolian people to unprecedented enslavement and oppression, violated the rights of autonomous Mongolia, at the same time threatening the security of Soviet Russia and the inviolability of the territory of the fraternal Far Eastern Republic. The appearance of the Soviet troops on the territory of autonomous Mongolia has for its sole aim the destruction of the common enemy, thus removing the danger which threatens the Soviet territory, and safeguarding the free development and self-determination of autonomous Mongolia.

FROM: Appeal of the Provisional Revolutionary Government of Mongolia, *Izvestiya*, August 10, 1921 (English translation in Leo Pasvolsky, *Russia in the Far East*, New York, Macmillan, 1922, pp. 176–77).

FROM: Reply of Foreign Commissar Chicherin to the Appeal of the People's Revolutionary Government of Mongolia, *Izvestiya*, August 12, 1921 (English translation in Pasvolsky, *Russia in the Far East*, pp. 177–79).

*Far Eastern Republic: the temporary Soviet-sponsored administration of eastern Siberia—Ed.

Welcoming the first steps of the People's Revolutionary Government of Mongolia on the road toward creating a new order in its country, now freed from the enemy by common effort, the Russian Government notes with great satisfaction the Appeal addressed to it by the People's Revolutionary Government of Mongolia, which appeal expresses the wish that the Soviet troops should not be removed from the territory of Mongolia until the complete destruction of the common enemy shall have been encompassed. Considering this proposal a manifestation of the steadfast, close and friendly bonds which unite the liberated people of Mongolia with the workmen and peasants of Russia who have thrown off the yoke of the exploiters, the Russian Government declares that it recognizes fully the seriousness of the situation and the common interest of Russia and Mongolia in the destruction of the common enemy. Having firmly decided to withdraw its troops from the territory of autonomous Mongolia, which is bound to Soviet Russia only by the ties of mutual friendship and common interests, just as soon as the menace to the free development of the Mongolian people and to the security of the Russian Republic and of the Far Eastern Republic shall have been removed, the Russian Government, in complete harmony with the People's Revolutionary Government of Mongolia, notes that this moment has not yet arrived. In response to the request addressed to it by the People's Revolutionary Government of Mongolia, the Russian Government announces its decision to give this request complete satisfaction.

The Russian Government is convinced that, in the near future, by the united efforts of the two peoples who are struggling against the violence of the Tsarist generals and against foreign oppression and exploitation, the free development of the Mongolian people will be secured on the basis of its autonomy, and that, as a result of the organization of the apparatus of popular revolutionary authority in Mongolia, such authority will be definitely established and firmly secured there.

The Return to Power Politics

Along with their revolutionary rhetoric the Soviet leaders seized every opportunity to form cooperative relations with amenable governments in order to stabilize their own uncertain circumstances. In 1920-21 they concluded treaties of diplomatic recognition and non-aggression with most of their neighbors in the Middle East and Eastern Europe, including a peace treaty and boundary settlement ending their short war with Poland. Then, in 1922, simultaneously with their first participation in an international diplomatic meeting (the Genoa Conference on world monetary problems), the Soviets astounded the international community by concluding a treaty of mutual support with the German Weimar Republic which they had just been trying to overthrow.

The German Government, represented by Foreign Minister Dr. Walter Rathenau, and the Government of the Russian Socialist Federated Soviet Republic, represented by People's Commissar Chicherin, have agreed on the following stipulations:

Article 1. The two Governments are agreed that the issues between the German Reich and the RSFSR over questions stemming from the state of war between Germany and Russia shall be handled on the following basis:

a) The German Reich and the RSFSR mutually renounce compensation for their

FROM: Treaty of Rapallo, in *Deutsche-sowjetische Beziehungen von den Verhandlungen in Brest-Litovsk bis zum Abschluss des Rapallovertrages*, Berlin, Staatsverlag der D.D.R., 1971, Vol. II, pp. 585-87 (editor's translation).

war expenses as well as war damage, i.e., the damage to them and their citizens in the war zone that has arisen from military measures including all requisitions effected in enemy territory. Likewise both parties renounce compensation for civil damages that the citizens of one party have been caused by so-called exceptional war laws or by forcible measures of state organs of the other party.

b) Public and private legal relations affected by the state of war, including the question of the treatment of merchant ships that have fallen into the hands of the other party, will be settled on the basis of reciprocity.

c) Germany and Russia mutually renounce repayment of expenditures on both sides for war prisoners. Likewise the German Government renounces repayment of the expenditures made by it for the members of the Red Army interned in Germany. The Russian Government renounces for its part repayment for the proceeds of the sale made by Germany of the military material brought into Germany by these internees.

Article 2. Germany renounces all claims resulting from the application of laws and measures of the RSFSR to German citizens or their personal rights or to claims of the German Reich and its states against Russia, or resulting from measures otherwise taken by the RSFSR or its organs against citizens of the Reich or their personal rights, provided that the Government of the RSFSR does not satisfy similar claims of a third state.

Article 3. Diplomatic and consular relations between the German Reich and the RSFSR shall be resumed immediately. The admission of consuls on both sides shall be regulated by a special agreement.

Article 4. Both governments are further agreed that as regards the general rights of citizens of one party in the territory of the other party, and the general regulation of mutual trade and economic relations, the most favored nation principle shall govern. The most favored nation principle does not extend to the preferential rights and accommodations that the RSFSR grants to a Soviet Republic or other such state that was previously a part of the former Russian Empire.

Article 5. Both governments will mutually deal with the economic difficulties of both countries in a benevolent spirit. In the spirit of a fundamental settlement of this question on an international basis they will enter into a preliminary exchange of views. The German government declares itself ready, as it has recently indicated, to support agreements contemplated by private firms as far as possible and to facilitate their execution.

Article 6. Articles 1(b) and 4 of this treaty shall go into force upon ratification; the other provisions of this treaty shall do so immediately. Prepared in parallel versions at Rapallo, 16 April 1922.

The End of the German Revolution

Early Communist hopes for international revolution had rested on Germany, which they regarded as the country with the most powerful working class. The German Communists attempted a series of uprisings, and in 1923, at the time of the great inflation, it appeared to

FROM: Zinoviev, *Problems of the German Revolution* (1923; excerpts translated in Xenia J. Eudin and Harold H. Fisher, *Soviet Russia and the West*, pp. 214-15; reprinted by permission of the publisher, Stanford University Press. Copyright, 1957, by the Board of Trustees of Leland Stanford Junior University).

the Russians that the proletariat was about to take power in Germany. As it happened, the main attempt was called off, isolated Communist risings were put down, and the German Communist Party remained more or less on the defensive until it was suppressed by Hitler.

The 1923 setback to their revolutionary hopes induced the Soviet leaders to adopt the "united front" policy of alliance with whatever reformist or nationalist groups would agree to cooperate with the USSR.

. . . German events are developing with the certainty of fate. . . .

. . . Soon everyone will see that the autumn months of 1923 mark a turning point not only for Germany, but also for the world in general. . . .

The social basis of the coming revolution is absolutely clear. In the cities the workers are definitely numerically superior (to the rest of the population). These workers have followed the counterrevolutionary German Social Democratic Party in one way or another . . . (but) this worker-giant is now convinced that the country and the working class can be saved only by revolution.

From the moment the German working class turns its back upon the German Social Democrats and follows the Communist Party, the fate of Germany is sealed. . . .

The forthcoming German revolution will be a proletarian class revolution. The twenty-two million German workers who make up its army represent the cornerstone of the international proletariat. They will meet the capitalists with an international revolution. According to the highest estimates, in 1917 Russia had eight to ten million workers among a population of 160 million. Germany, with a population of sixty million, has more than twenty million workers. With us, the working class was only a small minority; in Germany it is the principal element, the majority of the population.

Most important of all, the German revolution will operate from a powerful industrial base. It is true that German industries are in a very difficult position. . . . But even so, German industries represent a formidable power. In that sense, Lenin was correct when he said: "In Western Europe, and especially in a country such as Germany, it will be much more difficult to start a proletarian revolution than in Russia. But it will be much easier to continue and to finish it." The German proletariat has preponderance both in industry and in agriculture. . . .

. . . One can say that the role of the peasants in Russia, war-weary, exhausted by continued ravages and devastation, and pushed to the abyss by the actions of capitalists, will be played in Germany by the middle class in the towns. The middle class will naturally vacillate between the proletariat and the bourgeoisie. It may even support the enemies of the revolution more often than not. But in the end it will provide (us with) auxiliary forces. The urban and rural proletariat will under no circumstances abandon revolutionary ideas. Today it has succeeded, and in a truly short time, in neutralizing the petty bourgeois elements and in gaining the sympathy of some of them. . . .

The attitude of the German petty bourgeoisie in the cities is due partly to the brutal policies of the Entente . . . and partly to the egotism of the German capitalist bourgeoisie, which has been ruinous to the middle classes. We, the Marxists, know that industrial capital destroys the petty bourgeoisie, and consequently proletarianizes most of them. But it is in Germany that we see for the first time that process being accomplished on a considerable scale. . . .

All the difficulties (of the German proletarian revolution) in achieving a domestic correlation of forces are secondary to the difficulties from the outside that will come into being the day after victory is won. The threat of an immediate war on the part of the French, Czech, and Polish bourgeoisie, the possibility of an English blockade—these are the main international political difficulties that will confront the German revolution. . . .

Imperialism will undoubtedly attempt to organize an international front against the German proletarian revolution. But its success is doubtful. Six years of struggle against the Russian revolution have shown that to erect a united front is no easy matter. There is bound to be a struggle in the camp of the imperialist policy of conquest, and a social-class policy in the broad sense. . . .

It goes without saying that the German proletariat must prepare for the worst, that is, it must expect international imperialism to interpret its revolution not as an isolated episode but as affecting the face of all European bourgeoisie. It must make its plans accordingly. . . .

Recognition

The great breakthrough in Soviet Russia's pursuit of diplomatic normalization was *de jure* recognition of the Soviet regime by the first Labour government of Ramsay MacDonald in Britain early in 1924. The act was hailed by the Soviet government as a monument of people-to-people cooperation. Recognition and normalization of commercial relations by most of the major powers quickly followed, only the United States holding out until the Roosevelt administration took office in 1933.

Having heard the communication concerning the full *de jure* recognition of the Union of Soviet Socialist Republics by Great Britain and the establishment of full normal diplomatic relations between the two States, the Second Congress of Soviets of the Union of Soviet Socialist Republics notes with satisfaction that this historic step was one of the first acts of the first Government of Great Britain chosen by the working class.

The workers' and peasants' government of the Union of Soviet Socialist Republics which originated in the great Revolution made the struggle for peace its foremost object, and has throughout its existence persistently striven for the re-establishment of international relations between all peoples. Unfortunately no previous British Government went to meet the Government of the Union of Soviet Socialist Republics and, on the contrary, as late as last May, the Union of Soviet Socialist Republics was confronted by British diplomacy with the fact of an ultimatum which threatened to interrupt trade relations which were commencing and was pregnant with direct peril to European peace.

The working class of Great Britain has been throughout this period the true ally of the working masses of the Union of Soviet Socialist Republics in their struggle for peace. The people of the Union of Soviet Socialist Republics remember the efforts of the working masses of Great Britain and the advanced section of British public opinion for the ending of the boycott, the blockade, and armed intervention. They realized that the recognition which has resulted is the consequence of the

FROM: Resolution of the Second Congress of Soviets on *De Jure* Recognition by Britain, February 2, 1924 (English translation in *The Times* of London, February 4, 1924).

unfaltering will of the British people which unanimously demanded the political recognition of the Soviet Government as a necessary condition for the establishment of universal peace, the economic reconstruction of the world after the ruin caused by the Imperialistic war, and, in particular, for the successful fight against industrial stagnation and unemployment in Great Britain itself.

As a result of these united efforts of the pacific policy of the Soviet Government under the guidance of V. I. Lenin and of the loudly expressed determination of the British people, there has resulted at last the establishment of normal relations between the two countries in a form worthy of both great peoples, and laying the foundations for their friendly cooperation.

In the tense atmosphere of international relations to-day fraught with the dangers of a new world conflict and justly constituting a subject for anxiety amongst the working people of all countries, this step of the British Labour Government acquires special and striking importance.

This second Congress of Soviets of the Union of Soviet Socialist Republics declares that cooperation between the peoples of Great Britain and the Union of Soviet Socialist Republics remains as before one of the first cares of the Soviet Union Government which, in keeping with all its preceding policy of peace, will make every effort to settle all disputed questions and misunderstandings and to develop and consolidate economic relations which are so necessary for the economic and political progress of the people of both countries and of the whole world.

This Second Congress of Soviets of the Union of Soviet Socialist Republics stretches out its hand with friendly fraternal greeting to the British people and empowers the Union Government to undertake the necessary proceedings with the British Government arising out of the fact of the recognition of the Soviet Government.

Bolshevizing the Comintern

The disappointment of revolutionary hopes and the complexities of Soviet Russia's conventional diplomacy put a premium on Moscow-centered orthodoxy if the Communist International were to be preserved as a reliable instrument of Soviet policy. To this end the Russian-controlled Comintern leadership intensified its demand for the foreign Communists to commit themselves to the Leninist principles of conspiratorial discipline, and proceeded to expel most of the original leaders of the foreign parties when they resisted these terms.

The Slowing Down of World Revolution and the Slogan of Bolshevization

Already at the time of the third world congress of the Comintern it was becoming clear that we were approaching a slowing-down phase in the development of the world revolution. . . . This gives the slogan of bolshevization not less, but more importance.

A bolshevik is not one who joins the party at the height of the revolutionary flood, but one who knows how to go on for years, if necessary for decades, building up the party even when the tide is ebbing and revolutionary development slows

FROM: Executive Committee of the Communist International, Theses on the Bolshevization of Communist Parties, April, 1925 (English translation [abridged] in Degras, *The Communist International: Documents*, II:189-92, 197-200). Reprinted by permission of Oxford University Press.

down. . . . A bolshevik party does not come into existence by itself when the revolutionary wave reaches its climax. It takes part in every struggle and builds itself up over the years in the course of these struggles. . . .

The communist party must be elastic enough to be able to make the transition to illegality in good order, should circumstances require it, without getting into a panic; legality should not be lightly surrendered, however, and legal must be combined with illegal work, and every legal foothold utilized by the party to break through the constraints of illegality and place itself at the head of open mass movements to prepare the revolution. . . .

Right-Wing Dangers and Ultra-Left Deviations

The slogan of bolshevization arose in the struggle against the right danger. . . . The correct slogan of the third world congress, 'To the masses,' was so wrongly applied in a number of countries over the past two years that there was a real danger of independent communist tactics being replaced by a policy of communist 'coalition' with the counterrevolutionary social-democracy. . . .

But bolshevization is impossible without a simultaneous struggle against ultra-left tendencies, which are frequently only the obverse of opportunism. . . . The mistakes of the ultra-left, for example in regard to communist participation in reformist and reactionary unions, could destroy communist parties for years to come. . . .

Communist Parties and Bolshevik Parties

In themselves communism, Marxism, and bolshevism are one and the same. 'Communist party' and 'bolshevik party' are, in themselves, identical concepts. In practice, however, they are not always one and the same. Some important sections of the Comintern still have to complete the development from left social-democracy (and in some cases from anarchosyndicalist ideology) to genuine communism. . . .

Bolshevization and the Conditions of Struggle

It should not be thought that there is one panacea which can be applied uniformly in the bolshevization of all Comintern parties. True bolshevization requires careful consideration of the concrete circumstances of time and place. . . . It would be the greatest mistake to transfer Russia's experience mechanically to other countries, a mistake against which Lenin uttered a warning. There is much in the experience of the Russian revolution which Lenin considered of general significance for other countries. . . .

Bolshevization and Some Theoretical Mistakes in the Communist Camp
(particularly the Mistakes of Luxemburgians)

Mastery of Leninism and its practical application in building communist parties is impossible unless attention is paid to the errors of some prominent Marxists who tried, but not quite successfully, to apply Marxism to the conditions of the new epoch.

These include the errors of the 'left' communists in Russia, the group of Dutch Marxists (Gorter and Pannekoek), and also the errors of Rosa Luxemburg. The closer these political leaders stand to Leninism, the more dangerous are their views in those respects in which they do not coincide with Leninism. . . .

Trotskyism is a particularly dangerous deviation from Leninism; it is a variety of menshevism combining 'European' opportunism with 'left-radical' phrases which frequently conceal its politically passive character. Trotskyism is not an isolated deviation towards menshevism, but a year-long system of struggle against Lenin-ism. Nor is Trotskyism a purely Russian phenomenon; it is international in charac-ter. To achieve Leninism in the Comintern means to expose Trotskyism in all parties and to liquidate it as a tendency. . . .

Bolshevization and Questions of Organization

. . . The basic form of organization of every bolshevik party is the party cell in the factory. . . .

Besides the factory cell, and work in such organizations as trade unions, factory committees, consumers' co-operatives, etc., steps should be taken to establish a whole series of non-party subsidiary organizations—tenants' leagues, unemployed committees, ex-service men's associations, etc. (with communist cells working in them). Bolshevization requires our parties to use every opportunity to make this organizational network as dense and closely woven as possible. . . .

The initiative in creating such organizations must be taken by the party leader-ship through the party members, who must then take the management of these organizations into their own hands. Communists must form factions in these organizations, receiving instructions from the party leadership. . . .

Bolshevization and the Problem of Party Cadres

To create a bolshevik party it is necessary over the years to forge strong party cadres. Such cadres are not formed by means of formal elections, but rather by selection in the course of practical work. The process of selection is necessarily slow; from the party cell up to the party centre it occurs in the course of the strug-gle which tests the members. . . .

The communist cadres of organizers must be trained in the sense that their work in preparing the revolution should not be a spare-time job; all their time must be given to the revolutionary struggle; they must be wholly and completely at the disposal of the party. The communist organizer and cadre worker . . . must live and work among the masses in the factory, the shop or mine, always ready to be sent elsewhere by the party in the interests of the cause. . . .

Bolshevization, Party Democracy, and Discipline

. . . The forms of internal party organization are subordinate to the overriding interests of the struggle for the proletarian dictatorship. But in all circumstances the communist party must preserve a certain freedom of criticism within the party, a spirit of equality among the party members. . . . This is in accordance with the interests of stimulating the entire party mass, securing the co-operation of all the lower party bodies and the cells in the political and organizational life of the party, and arousing the initiative of the workers in the party.

Iron proletarian discipline is one of the most important pre-conditions of bolshevization.

Bolshevization and the International Leadership

. . . Bolshevization is incompatible with separatist and federalist tendencies. The world party of Leninism must be strongly fused, not by mechanical discipline, but by unity of will and action. . . . Every party must give its best forces to the international leadership. It must be brought home to the broadest masses that in the present epoch serious economic and political battles of the working class can be won only if they are led from one centre and on an international scale.

No Communist Party should recoil from illegal work. Illegality is a condition in which many Communist Parties must now work and which in the epoch of the increased intensification of the social struggles might extend to many Parties of the Comintern which to-day are still legal.

Every Communist Party must reckon with illegality as a possible and probable condition, and must be prepared to transfer to illegal work. Whenever the political situation becomes seriously acute, it must take the proper measures which will enable it to continue its work illegally after its organization has been prohibited; it must keep its whole technical apparatus for illegality in readiness. But all unnecessary playing with illegality must be avoided and the Party must defend its legality to the bitter end.

On the other hand the Parties which are compelled to work illegally must take advantage of every passing opportunity of conducting legal activity and for the extension of such opportunities.

The Party should not allow any form of legal activity to be taken from it (election campaigns, parliamentary activity, the legal press, factory councils, trade unions, educational societies, co-operatives, sick benefit societies, etc.). The masses of workers and peasants must become accustomed to protect the legal opportunities of their Party, and to meet every attack of the bourgeoisie and the social traitors against these opportunities with mass demonstrations (strikes, demonstrations, etc.).

European Marxism—Gramsci

A number of attempts were made by Western Communist theoreticians in the 1920's to refine Marxist theory in the voluntaristic direction pointed to by Lukács, and thereby take account of the complexities of modern society. Ultimately most influential of these creative Marxists was Antonio Gramsci, leader of the semi-underground Italian Communist Party under Mussolini until his imprisonment in 1926. In custody until just before his death in 1937, Gramsci was nevertheless able to compose voluminous theoretical commentaries stressing the historical role of intellectual and political factors and the power of ideological "hegemony" of the ruling class. This reflected the staying power of capitalism in the West as well as the necessity for an activist and educational role on the part of the Communist Party.

Are intellectuals an autonomous and independent social group, or does every social group have its own particular specialised category of intellectuals? The problem is a complex one, because of the variety of forms assumed to date by the real historical process of formation of the different categories of intellectuals. . . .

The relationship between the intellectuals and the world of production is not as direct as it is with the fundamental social groups but is, in varying degrees, "medi-

FROM: Antonio Gramsci, *Selections from the Prison Notebooks* (London, Lawrence & Wishart, 1971), pp. 5, 12, 180–85, 365–66, 407–09). Reprinted by permission of the publisher.

ated" by the whole fabric of society and by the complex of superstructures, of which the intellectuals are, precisely, the "functionaries." It should be possible both to measure the "organic quality" [*organicità*] of the various intellectual strata and their degree of connection with a fundamental social group, and to establish a gradation of their functions and of the superstructures from the bottom to the top (from the structural base upwards). What we can do, for the moment, is to fix two major superstructural "levels": the one that can be called "civil society," that is the ensemble of organisms commonly called "private," and that of "political society" or "the State." These two levels correspond on the one hand to the function of "hegemony" which the dominant group exercises throughout society and on the other hand to that of "direct domination" or command exercised through the State and "juridical" government. The functions in question are precisely organisational and connective. The intellectuals are the dominant group's "deputies" exercising the subaltern functions of social hegemony and political government. These comprise:

1. The "spontaneous" consent given by the great masses of the population to the general direction imposed on social life by the dominant fundamental group; this consent is "historically" caused by the prestige (and consequent confidence) which the dominant group enjoys because of its position and function in the world of production.

2. The apparatus of state coercive power which "legally" enforces discipline on those groups who do not "consent" either actively or passively. This apparatus is, however, constituted for the whole of society in anticipation of moments of crisis of command and direction when spontaneous consent has failed. . . .

. . . In the "relation of forces" various moments or levels must be distinguished, and they are fundamentally the following:

1. A relation of social forces which is closely linked to the structure, objective, independent of human will, and which can be measured with the systems of the exact or physical sciences. The level of development of the material forces of production provides a basis for the emergence of the various social classes, each one of which represents a function and has a specific position within production itself. This relation is what it is, refractory reality: nobody can alter the number of firms or their employees, the number of cities or the given urban population, etc. By studying these fundamental data it is possible to discover whether in a particular society there exist the necessary and sufficient conditions for its transformation—in other words, to check the degree of realism and practicability of the various ideologies which have been born on its own terrain, on the terrain of the contradictions which it has engendered during the course of its development.

2. A subsequent moment is the relation of political forces; in other words, an evaluation of the degree of homogeneity, self-awareness, and organisation attained by the various social classes. This moment can in its turn be analysed and differentiated into various levels, corresponding to the various moments of collective political consciousness, as they have manifested themselves in history up till now. The first and most elementary of these is the economic-corporate level: a tradesman feels *obliged* to stand by another tradesman, a manufacturer by another manufacturer, etc., but the tradesman does not yet feel solidarity with the manufacturer; in other words, the members of the professional group are conscious of its unity and homogeneity, and of the need to organise it, but in the case of the wider social

group this is not yet so. A second moment is that in which consciousness is reached of the solidarity of interests among all the members of a social class—but still in the purely economic field. Already at this juncture the problem of the State is posed—but only in terms of winning politico-juridical equality with the ruling groups: the right is claimed to participate in legislation and administration, even to reform these—but within the existing fundamental structures. A third moment is that in which one becomes aware that one's own corporate interests, in their present and future development, transcend the corporate limits of the purely economic class, and can and must become the interests of other subordinate groups too. This is the most purely political phase, and marks the decisive passage from the structure to the sphere of the complex superstructures; it is the phase in which previously germinated ideologies become "party," come into confrontation and conflict, until only one of them, or at least a single combination of them, tends to prevail, to gain the upper hand, to propagate itself throughout society—bringing about not only a unison of economic and political aims, but also intellectual and moral unity, posing all the questions around which the struggle rages not on a corporate but on a "universal" plane, and thus creating the hegemony of a fundamental social group over a series of subordinate groups. It is true that the State is seen as the organ of one particular group, destined to create favourable conditions for the latter's maximum expansion. But the development and expansion of the particular group are conceived of, and presented, as being the motor force of a universal expansion, of a development of all the "national" energies. In other words, the dominant group is coordinated concretely with the general interests of the subordinate groups, and the life of the State is conceived of as a continuous process of formation and superseding of unstable equilibria (on the juridical plane) between the interests of the fundamental group and those of the subordinate groups—equilibria in which the interests of the dominant group prevail, but only up to a certain point, i.e. stopping short of narrowly corporate economic interest. . . .

3. The third moment is that of the relation of military forces, which from time to time is directly decisive. . . .

A further question connected with the foregoing is whether the fundamental historical crises are directly determined by economic crises. . . . The specific question of economic hardship or well-being as a cause of new historical realities is a partial aspect of the question of the relations of force, at the various levels. Changes can come about either because a situation of well-being is threatened by the narrow self-interest of a rival class, or because hardship has become intolerable and no force is visible in the old society capable of mitigating it and of re-establishing normality by legal means. Hence it may be said that all these elements are the concrete manifestation of the conjunctural fluctuations of the totality of social relations of force, on whose terrain the passage takes place from the latter to political relations of force, and finally to the military relation which is decisive. . . .

Structures and superstructures form an "historical bloc." That is to say the complex, contradictory and discordant *ensemble* of the superstructures is the reflection of the *ensemble* of the social relations of production. From this, one can conclude: that only a totalitarian system of ideologies gives a rational reflection of the contradiction of the structure and represents the existence of the objective conditions for the revolutionising of praxis. If a social group is formed which is one hundred percent homogeneous on the level of ideology, this means that the premisses exist one hundred percent for this revolutionising: that is that the "rational" is actively and actually real. This reasoning is based on the necessary reciprocity between structure and superstructure, a reciprocity which is nothing other than the real dialectical process. . . .

The claim, presented as an essential postulate of historical materialism, that every fluctuation of politics and ideology can be presented and expounded as an immediate expression of the structure, must be contested in theory as primitive infantilism, and combated in practice with the authentic testimony of Marx. . . . Among [Marx's] precautions the following examples can be enumerated:

1. The difficulty of identifying at any given time, statically (like an instantaneous photographic image), the structure. Politics in fact is at any given time the reflection of the tendencies of development in the structure, but it is not necessarily the case that these tendencies must be realised. A structural phase can be concretely studied and analysed only after it has gone through its whole process of development, and not during the process itself, except hypothetically and with the explicit proviso that one is dealing with hypotheses.

2. From this it can be deduced that a particular political act may have been an error of calculation on the part of the leaders [*dirigenti*] of the dominant classes, an error which historical development, through the parliamentary and governmental "crises" of the directive [*dirigenti*] classes, then corrects and goes beyond. Mechanical historical materialism does not allow for the possibility of error, but assumes that every political act is determined, immediately, by the structure, and therefore as a real and permanent (in the sense of achieved) modification of the structure. The principle of "error" is a complex one: one may be dealing with an individual impulse based on mistaken calculations or equally it may be a manifestation of the attempts of specific groups or sects to take over hegemony within the directive groupings, attempts which may well be unsuccessful.

3. It is not sufficiently borne in mind that many political acts are due to internal necessities of an organisational character, that is they are tied to the need to give coherence to a party, a group, a society. This is made clear for example in the history of the Catholic Church. . . .

The Rise of Communism in China

In response to the anti-imperialist appeal of the Russian Revolution, a small Chinese Communist Party, composed primarily of intellectuals, was organized in 1921 by Ch'en Tu-hsiu and Li Ta-chao, dean and librarian, respectively, at Peking University. Guided by the Comintern, the Chinese Communists pursued an alliance with the Nationalist Party (Kuomintang) of Sun Yat-sen and Chiang Kai-shek, who were waging a successful struggle in the midtwenties to make themselves rulers of all China. However, at the moment of victory in 1927 Chiang broke with the Communists and decimated the party with arrests and executions. The Russians blamed the Chinese Communist leadership for "opportunism" and belatedly ordered revolutionary uprisings, to no avail except where Mao Tse-tung, former assistant to Li Ta-chao, organized peasant guerrilla activity in the south-central mountains.

FROM: Manifesto of the Chinese Communist Party, "On the Current Situation ," June 10, 1922 (English translation in Conrad Brandt, Benjamin Schwartz, and John K. Fairbank, *A Documentary History of Chinese Communism*, Cambridge, Mass., Harvard University Press, 1952, pp. 55-58, 62; this and subsequent selections reprinted by permission of the publisher).

a) The Founding of the Chinese Communist Party

. . . The revolution of 1911 had two historical tasks: first, the overthrow of the Manchu dynasty and, second, the liberation of China from foreign oppression and the transformation of China into an independent state. In this second objective the 1911 revolution aimed to create, within a framework of racial and national independence, favourable conditions for the industrial development of China. The 1911 revolution expressed the transition from the political system of feudalism to a democratic regime, from manual labour and an artisan economy to capitalist production. . . .

The result of the revolution's defeat has been a strengthening of the world imperialist yoke in China and of the reactionary regime of her own militarists. The so-called republican rule is in the hands of militarists who, under conditions of a semi-feudal economy, use it to join their own actions with those of the world imperialists, who are concluding an agreement with the Chinese military clique regarding loans for their military needs and for the state's self-preservation. The foreign states are making use of the opportunity to invest their capital in China, thus acquiring, by means of a system of financial enslavement, "spheres of influence" in China and special rights and privileges. . . .

The socio-economic conditions in China affect the middle, intermediary classes with particular force. The owners of small enterprises are being deprived of property; artisans fill the ranks of the army of the unemployed; peasants sell their land to landlords for absurd sums of money because they are unable to conduct their own economy, owing to the continuously rising cost of living.

These conditions will remain unchanged so long as power remains in the hands of the feudal-lord government, in the hands of militarists; so long as power is not seized from their hands; and so long as a democratic government is not established.

Democratic government means a democratic party government. We have in mind the creation of power on the basis of a total reorganization of the entire political system of administration. Basically, this demand entails the overthrow of the authority of the reactionary, counterrevolutionary elements and groups by revolutionary methods, by a democratic party, or by a bloc of democratic groupings which will organize power to conform to the historical requirements of their own country and with consideration for the realities of the new international environment. . . .

The postulate must be clear to everyone that the political struggle is not a struggle between individuals for power, but a manifestation and expression of class struggle—the social struggle of the proletariat against the bourgeoisie in the period of revolution and, in the period of bourgeois revolution, the struggle of the bourgeoisie against the feudal lords and the system of feudal economy. The postulate must also be clear that only such freedom is precious as is achieved in the process of hard struggle and at the price of human blood, in distinction from those methods of struggle which are used by our class enemies.

The struggle for democracy is a struggle of one class, a struggle which aims to overthrow the dominance of another class; it is the replacement of one system by another, and in no event can it be regarded as a struggle of one individual or one group for the overthrow of another individual or group.

A real democratic party must possess two characteristic elements: (1) its principles must be correlated with the concepts of democracy; and (2) its actions must consist in an active struggle against feudalism in the form of the military. Of all the political parties existing in China, only the Kuomintang can be characterized as a revolutionary party, yet it possesses only a relative amount of democratic and revolutionary spirit. The programme of this party has not yet been fully elaborated. But its three principles, "of the people, for the people, and by the people" . . . in conjunction with plans for the industrial development of China . . . reflect the democratic spirit of the Kuomintang. . . .

For all of us, the only way by which we can liberate ourselves from the hard yoke of the military is to join the democratic struggle against the relics of the past—a struggle for freedom and peace. The government opposition game, played by the bourgeoisie, the intelligentsia, and the politicians, cannot be trusted. We all want peace, but real peace rather than false peace. We welcome a war to achieve the triumph of democracy, to overthrow the military and the militarists and to liberate the Chinese people.

The Chinese Communist Party, as the vanguard of the proletariat, struggles for working-class liberation and for the proletarian revolution. Until such time as the Chinese proletariat is able to seize power in its own hands, considering the present political and economic conditions of China's development and all the historical processes now going on in China, the proletariat's urgent task is to act jointly with the democratic party to establish a united front of democratic revolution to struggle for the overthrow of the military and for the organization of a real democratic government. . . .

b) The Comintern and China

. . . During the last two years, imperialism has suffered a heavy defeat in China, the effects of which will contribute considerably to the aggravation of the crisis of world capitalism. . . .

The further victories of the revolutionary armies of Canton, supported by the broad masses of the Chinese people, will lead to victory over the imperialists, to the achievement of the independence of China, and to its revolutionary unification, which will consequently increase in numerous ways its power of resistance to imperialism. . . .

To overthrow the militarists completely, the economic and political struggle of the peasantry, which constitutes the overwhelming majority of the population, must be developed as a part of the anti-imperialist struggle. The fear that the aggravation of the class struggle in the countryside will weaken the anti-imperialist front is baseless. . . . The refusal to assign the agrarian revolution a prominent place in the national-liberation movement, for fear of alienating the dubious and indecisive co-operation of a section of the capitalist class, is wrong. This is not the revolutionary policy of the proletariat. The Communist Party must be free from such mistakes. . . .

FROM: "Theses on the Chinese Situation and Plan of Action for the Chinese Communists," adopted at the Seventh Plenum of the Executive Committee of the Communist International, November–December, 1926 (English translation in Xenia J. Eudin and Robert C. North, *Soviet Russia and the East, 1920–1927: A Documentary Survey*, Stanford, Calif., Stanford University Press, 1957, pp. 356, 359–62; reprinted by permission of the publisher; copyright 1957 by the Board of Trustees of Leland Stanford Junior University).

The supreme necessity of winning influence over the peasantry determines the relation of the Communist Party to the Kuomintang and to the Canton government likewise. The machinery of the national-revolutionary government provides a very effective way to reach the peasantry. The Communist Party must use this machinery.

In the newly liberated provinces (local) governments of the type of the Canton government will be set up. The Communists and their revolutionary allies must penetrate the new governments, so as to give practical expression to their agrarian programs by using the governmental machinery to confiscate land, reduce taxes, invest real power in the peasant committees. . . .

For this reason and many other equally important reasons, the point of view that the Communist Party must leave the Kuomintang is incorrect. The whole process of development of the Chinese revolution, its character and its prospects, demand that the Communists stay in the Kuomintang and intensify their work in it. . . .

The Communist Party of China must strive to develop the Kuomintang into a real people's party—a solid revolutionary bloc of the proletariat, the peasantry, the urban petty bourgeoisie and the other oppressed and exploited strata—a party dedicated to a decisive struggle against imperialism and its agents. . . .

. . . The Canton government, in spite of its bourgeois-democratic character, essentially and objectively contains the germs of a revolutionary petty bourgeois state—a democratic dictatorship of the revolutionary bloc of the proletariat, peasantry, and the urban petty bourgeoisie. The petty-bourgeois democratic movement becomes revolutionary in China because it is an anti-imperialist movement. The Canton government is revolutionary primarily because it is anti-imperialist. Being primarily anti-imperialist, the Chinese revolution and the government created by it must strike at the root of imperialist power in China. Repudiation of unequal treaties and abolition of territorial concessions will not be sufficient to weaken the position of imperialism. The blow must be dealt at the economic basis of imperalist power; the revolutionary government must gradually confiscate the railways, concessions, factories, mines, banks, and other business enterprises owned by foreign capital. By so doing it will immediately outstrip the narrow boundary of bourgeois democracy and enter into the state of transition to revolutionary dictatorship. . . .

c) The 1927 Debacle

. . . In the recent resolution of the Executive Committee of the Communist International it was pointed out that the leadership of our Party had committed grave errors of opportunism. The Executive Committee of the Communist International called on the entire Party to criticize itself thoroughly and correct such mistakes. The mistakes mentioned here are neither individual nor incidental but rather result from the grievously erroneous opportunist line carried out by the leadership of our Party. . . .

The Chinese Communist Party should spread and encourage the class struggle of the proletariat and help every workers' struggle against the bourgeoisie. The Communist International has repeatedly instructed the Chinese Communist Party to fight for the improvement of the material conditions of the working masses, and for the betterment of living conditions in the factories and in society, for the

FROM: Circular Letter of the Central Committee of the Chinese Communist Party, to All Party Members, August 7, 1927 (Brandt, Schwartz, Fairbank, pp. 102–3, 106–7, 109–10, 116–17).

immediate abolition of the laws which oppress the workers, and for the realization of such rights as the eight-hour working day, increase of wages, and recognition of workers' rights to organize unions and to strike. At the same time, the Communist International points out that it is necessary to arm the workers speedily, boldly, and resolutely, especially those elements which are most class-conscious and best organized. This course is considered absolutely essential by the Communist International. Such directives of the Communist International are in keeping with the struggle of the workers themselves in the industrial areas and the actions of the rank and file Party members. But the leading organ of our Party has developed a different course. It has simply hindered and minimized the class struggle and the revolutionary actions of the workers. Instead of spreading and promoting strike movements, the Central Committee, together with the leaders of the Kuomintang, decided on an arbitrary method of mediation and ruled that the final authority belonged to the government. Under the government of a coalition of classes, led at this first stage by the bourgeoisie, this kind of policy actually served merely to protect the interests of the bourgeoisie and greatly obstructed the workers' movement. . . .

The question of agrarian revolution is the crux of the bourgeois-democratic revolution in China. The Communist International has repeatedly explained itself concerning this question. . . . Agrarian revolution consists of confiscation and nationalization of land—this is the major content of the internal social economy in the new stage of the Chinese revolution. The main thing at present is to employ the "mass-type" revolutionary methods to solve the land problem [and allow] the tens of millions of peasants to solve this problem by rising from below. The Central Committee should be the vanguard of this movement and direct it. In the government, the Communist Party should carry out such a policy so that the government itself will act to support the agrarian revolution. Only thus can the present government be turned into the centre of political organization of the workers' and peasants' movement, and the organ of the dictatorship of the workers and peasants. . . .

The relation between the Party and the Communist International was also not in accordance with accepted organizational procedure. There has never been a case in the history of the Communist International where the instructions and resolutions were actually rejected in such a critical situation. This was no longer merely a simple breach of discipline, but a criminal act against the Chinese and international Communist movement. The Chinese revolution does not merely have a national significance, but also forms a major sector in the world revolution. The fate of the world revolution will be decided by the fate of the Chinese revolution. The Chinese Communist Party not only carried out an erroneous policy, a policy that brought the revolution to defeat, that voluntarily liquidated the revolution and capitulated to the enemy, but also would not admit its errors or obey the instructions of the Communist International. . . .

The Communist International has severely criticized the opportunist line of the Central Committee, which has in reality betrayed the [Chinese] revolution. We agree that this criticism is entirely just and that the policy of the Executive Committee of the Communist International regarding the Chinese problem is entirely correct. We welcome the recent instructions of the Communist International which have made possible the unmasking of the past mistakes of the [Party] leadership and have saved our Party [from destruction]. We positively agree that, in the past,

the leadership of the Central Committee carried out an opportunist, unrevolution-
ary policy and that it is necessary to carry out a thorough revision of our policy on
the basis of the lessons of the past. . . .

d) Mao Tse-tung on the Peasant Revolution

China is the only country in the world today where one or more small areas
under Red political power have emerged in the midst of a White regime which
encircles them. We find on analysis that one reason for this phenomenon lies in the
incessant splits and wars within China's comprador and landlord classes. So long as
these splits and wars continue, it is possible for an armed independent regime of
workers and peasants to survive and grow. In addition, its survival and growth
require the following conditions: (1) a sound mass base, (2) a sound Party organization, (3) a fairly strong Red Army, (4) terrain favourable to military operations,
and (5) economic resources sufficient for sustenance. . . .

Since the struggle in the border area is exclusively military, both the Party and
the masses have to be placed on a war footing. How to deal with the enemy, how to
fight, has become the central problem in our daily life. An independent regime
must be an armed one. Wherever such an area is located, it will be immediately
occupied by the enemy if armed forces are lacking or inadequate, or if wrong tactics are used in dealing with the enemy. As the struggle is getting fiercer every day,
our problems have become extremely complex and serious. . . .

After receiving political education, the Red Army soldiers have become class-
conscious, learned the essentials of distributing land, setting up political power,
arming the workers and peasants, etc., and they know they are fighting for themselves, for the working class and the peasantry. Hence they can endure the hardships of the bitter struggle without complaint. Each company, battalion or regiment
has its soldiers' committee which represents the interests of the soldiers and carries
on political and mass work. . . .

Apart from the role played by the Party, the reason why the Red Army has been
able to carry on in spite of such poor material conditions and such frequent
engagement is its practice of democracy. The officers do not beat the men; officers
and men receive equal treatment; soldiers are free to hold meetings and to speak
out; trivial formalities have been done away with; and the accounts are open for all
to inspect. The soldiers handle the mess arrangements and, out of the daily five
cents for cooking oil, salt, firewood and vegetables, they can even save a little for
pocket money, amounting to roughly six or seven coppers per person per day,
which is called "mess savings." All this gives great satisfaction to the soldiers. The
newly captured soldiers in particular feel that our army and the Kuomintang army
are worlds apart. They feel spiritually liberated, even though material conditions in
the Red Army are not equal to those in the White army. The very soldiers who had
no courage in the White army yesterday are very brave in the Red Army today; such
is the effect of democracy. The Red Army is like a furnace in which all captured
soldiers are transmuted the moment they come over. In China the army needs
democracy as much as the people do. Democracy in our army is an important
weapon for understanding the feudal mercenary army. . . .

FROM: Mao, "The Struggle in the Chingkang Mountains" (Report to the Central Committee
of the Chinese Communist Party, November, 1928; English translation in *Selected Works of Mao
Tse-tung*, Peking Foreign Languages Press, 1965, Vol. I, pp. 73, 80–81, 83, 97–98).

We fully agree with the Communist International's resolution on China. There is no doubt that China is still at the stage of the bourgeois-democratic revolution. The programme for a thorough democratic revolution in China comprises, externally, the overthrow of imperialism so as to achieve complete national liberation, and, internally, the elimination of the power and influence of the comprador class in the cities, the completion of the agrarian revolution in order to abolish feudal relations in the villages, and the overthrow of the government of the warlords. We must go through such a democratic revolution before we can lay a real foundation for the transition to socialism. In the past year we have fought in many places and are keenly aware that the revolutionary tide is on the ebb in the country as a whole. While Red political power has been established in a few small areas, in the country as a whole the people lack the ordinary democratic rights, the workers, the peasants and even the bourgeois democrats do not have freedom of speech or assembly, and the worst crime is to join the Communist Party. Wherever the Red Army goes, the masses are cold and aloof, and only after our propaganda do they slowly move into action. Whatever enemy units we face, there are hardly any cases of mutiny or desertion to our side and we have to fight it out. This holds even for the enemy's Sixth Army which recruited the greatest number of "rebels" after the May 21st Incident.* We have an acute sense of our isolation which we keep hoping will end. Only by launching a political and economic struggle for democracy, which will also involve the urban petty bourgeoisie, can we turn the revolution into a seething tide that will surge through the country.

The Russian Opposition and Communism Abroad

At the time of their last stand in 1927 the Trotsky Opposition made a burning issue out of the mistakes which they alleged the Soviet leadership to have committed in pursuance of the "united front" policy. The purge of the Chinese Communists by Chiang Kai-shek was the occasion for a bitter Trotskyist attack on the "petty-bourgeois" compromises made by the leadership and on the effort to cover up failure by muzzling the Opposition. This international issue contributed to Stalin's determination to destroy the Opposition. Trotsky's expulsion from the Communist Party then evoked serious disagreements in the foreign Communist parties, but this only gave Stalin the opportunity to tighten Russian control over the Comintern in the course of disciplining the Trotskyist dissidents.

Comrades,
    The serious mistakes which have been permitted in the work of leading the Chinese revolution have contributed to a severe defeat, from which it is possible to escape only by returning to Lenin's path. The extremely abnormal circumstances under which the discussion of questions connected with the Chinese revolution is going on create an extraordinarily tense situation in the party. The one-sided "discussion" being conducted in the pages of *Pravda* and *Bolshevik*, and the intentional distortion of the views of the Opposition (for example, attributing to it the demand to quit the Kuomintang), testify to the desire of the leading group in the Central

*May 21, 1927: occasion of military repression of the labor and peasant movement in the province of Hunan—Ed.

FROM: The Declaration of the Eighty-Four, May, 1927 (editor's translation from copy in the Trotsky Archive, Houghton Library, Harvard University).

Committee to cover its mistakes by hunting down the Opposition. All this directs the party's attention on a false path. . . .

All the prerequisites were present for arming the Chinese workers (primarily in Shanghai and Hankow). And nevertheless the heroic proletariat of Shanghai was revealed to be unarmed, and the mass of the Hankow workers are not armed even now, in spite of the fact that the "Left" Kuomintang men are ruling in Hankow.

The "leadership" in China *in fact* concluded that it could not arm the workers, could not organize revolutionary strikes, could not finally support the peasants against the landlords, could not issue a daily Communist newspaper, could not criticize the domination of the bourgeois of the Right Kuomintang and the petty-bourgeois of the "Left" Kuomintang, could not organize Communist cells in Chiang Kai-shek's army, could not proclaim the slogan of soviets—in order "not to drive away" the bourgeoisie, in order "not to frighten" the petty-bourgeoisie, in order not to shake the government of the "bloc of four classes." In answer to this, thanks to this, one ought to expect, the Chinese "national" bourgeoisie, after waiting for a convenient moment, mercilessly shoots down the Chinese workers, and appeals for the help of the imperialists, today the Japanese, tomorrow the Americans, and the day after tomorrow the English. . . .

The Chinese defeat can be reflected in the most direct manner in the fate of the USSR in the immediate future. If the imperialists succeed for an extended period in pacifying China, they will then move against us, against the USSR. The defeat of the Chinese revolution can bring war against the USSR vastly nearer. Meanwhile, the party is deprived of the opportunity of judging the Chinese question, which is now for it, the first party of the Comintern, the most important question. Principled consideration of the questions of the Chinese revolution is suppressed. And at this very time in fact only a furious one-sided discussion is being conducted, i.e., in the sense of hunting down the Opposition, with the objective of concealing the incorrect line of the leading core of the Central Committee. . . .

Between the incorrect line in the Chinese question and the incorrect line in the question of the Anglo-Russian Committee* there is a close internal connection. That same line is proceeding now in the whole policy of the Comintern. In Germany hundreds of skilled Left proletarians are being expelled from the party merely because they have shown solidarity with the Russian Opposition. The Right elements in all the parties are getting more and more preponderance. The crudest Right mistakes (in Germany, Poland, France, etc.) go unpunished. The slightest voice of criticism on the Left leads to lopping off. The authority of the All-Union Communist Party and the October Revolution are thus utilized for the turn of the Communist parties to the right, away from the Leninist line. All this taken together deprives the Comintern of the possibility of preparing and conducting the struggle against war in a Leninist manner.

For any Marxist it is indisputable that the incorrect line in China and in the question of the Anglo-Russian Committee is not accidental. It continues and completes the incorrect line in internal policy.

The economy of the Soviet Union has completed, in general and as a whole, its restoration period. In the course of this period substantial success was achieved in

---

*The Anglo-Russian Committee of Trade-Union Unity, an organ of tenuous cooperation which the Russian oppositionists wanted to abandon after the failure of the British general strike in 1926—Ed.

economic construction. In industry, agriculture, and the other branches of the economy of the Union of Soviet Socialist Republics we are either approaching or have overtaken the pre-war level. . . .

But . . . instead of a Marxist analysis of the real situation of the proletarian dictatorship in the USSR, the party offers up the false, petty-bourgeois "theory of socialism in one country," which has nothing in common with Marxism, with Leninism. This crude retreat from Marxism makes it more difficult for the party to see the *class content* of the economic processes which are going on. Meanwhile it is precisely in the terms unfavorable for the workers and in the burdensome position of the broad popular masses that the *negative manifestations* of the period of the revolution through which we are living are comprised. . . .

The *international situation* is becoming more and more tense. The danger of war is increasing. The central task of the All-Union Communist Party and of the whole vanguard of the international proletariat now consists of *preventing war (or perhaps just postponing it for as long a time as possible), in order to support and defend in whatever way the policy of peace, which only our party and soviet rule are able to carry out in the end.*

The cause of the USSR is the cause of the international proletariat. The most important task of the international proletariat is to avert the danger of a new war which hangs over the head of the USSR. But this cannot be done through the path of a bloc with the traitors of the General Council [of the British Trades Union Congress]. Any serious struggle for the prevention of war is impossible in alliance with Purcell and Citrine. It is possible to get closer to the Social-Democratic and nonparty *workers*, to draw them into the struggle against war, only by going *over the heads* of these treacherous leaders, and in struggle with them. . . .

Recriminations in China

Ch'en Tu-hsiu, co-founder of the Chinese Communist Party, was made a scapegoat for the 1927 debacle and ousted from the leadership. In turn he denounced Stalin's "opportunistic" interference and vainly tried to organize a Trotskyist opposition group. The issues Ch'en raised were opened again by the Chinese Communist leadership after the death of Mao, although Ch'en himself is still regarded as a "Right capitulationist."

. . . Since the time when I followed the appeal to organize a Chinese Communist Party in 1920, I have sincerely carried out to the utmost the opportunistic policy of the leaders of the International, Stalin, Zinoviev, Bukharin, and the others, who led the Chinese Revolution to a shameful and terrible defeat. Although I worked hard day and night, my mistakes nevertheless outweighed my merits. . . .

I categorically hold that the objective causes of the defeat of the late Chinese revolution have secondary significance, and that the chief cause of the defeat was the error of opportunism, i.e., the falseness of our whole policy in relation to the bourgeois Kuomintang. . . .

Under the direction of such a consistently opportunistic policy how could the Chinese proletariat and the Communist Party clearly see their own future? How

FROM: Ch'en, "Open letter to All Members of the Chinese Communist Party," December 10, 1929 (editor's translation from excerpts of Russian version in *Biuleten' Oppozitsii* [The Bulletin of the Opposition], Paris, no. 15-16, September-October, 1930, pp. 20-23).

could they have their own independent policy? They just capitulated step by step before the bourgeoisie and submitted to it. And then when it suddenly began to exterminate us, we definitely did not know what to do. . . .

If we had the forces to rearrange the old committee and reorganize the Kuomintang, why could we not organize soviets? Why did we have to send our workers and peasant leaders into the bourgeois Kuomintang, which at that time was exterminating workers and peasants? Or why did we have to embellish this Kuomintang with our leaders? . . .

Once the party had consistently made such radical mistakes, other subordinate mistakes, large and small, inevitably had to issue from them. I, whose understanding was not sufficiently clear, whose opinion was not sufficiently resolute, deeply mired in the atmosphere of opportunism [*sic*], sincerely supported the opportunistic policy of the Third International. I unconsciously became an instrument of the narrow Stalin faction; I did not have an opportunity to develop; I could not save the party; I could not save the revolution. . . .

We must openly and objectively admit that the whole past and present opportunistic policy came and now comes from the Third International. The Comintern must bear the responsibility. The Chinese party, which had scarcely emerged from infancy, did not have the capacity to create a theory for itself and then establish a policy. But the leading organ of the Chinese party must bear responsibility for the fact that it blindly carried out the opportunistic policy of the Third International. . . .

Dear comrades! The party's present errors do not refer to particular problems; they reveal, as in the past, the whole opportunistic policy which Stalin has conducted in China. Responsible functionaries of the Central Committee of the Chinese Communist Party who have agreed to become Stalin's mouthpieces have since lost whatever political conscience they had, they have gotten worse and worse and can no longer be saved. . . .

Every member of our party is responsible for the salvation of the party. We must turn back to the spirit and policy of Bolshevism, unite with strength and a united spirit, and work undeviatingly on the side of the international opposition led by Comrade Trotsky, i.e., to struggle under the banner of real Marxism and Leninism, resolutely, firmly, and to the end, against the opportunism of the Comintern and the Central Committee of the Chinese Communist Party. . . .

The "Third Period"

In August, 1928, simultaneously with his attack on Bukharin and the Right Opposition inside Russia, Stalin initiated a "left turn" for the Comintern at its Sixth Congress, justifying the shift as a response to the "third period" of post-war capitalism. He then proceeded to weed Bukharin's sympathizers out of the leadership of the foreign Communist parties, just as he had done with the Trotskyists earlier. By this time most of the original founders of the Communist parties were eliminated from the movement, which henceforth until the 1950's was completely subservient to Moscow.

FROM: "Communism and the International Situation," Theses of the Sixth Congress of the Comintern, August 19, 1928 (English translation in U.S. House of Representatives, Committee on Un-American Activities, *The Communist Conspiracy*, May 29, 1956, Part I, sec. C, pp. 233-34, 268-69).

After the first world imperialist war the international Labour movement passed through a series of historical phases of development, expressing various phases of the general crisis of the capitalist system.

The *first* period was the period of extremely acute crisis of the capitalist system, and of direct revolutionary action on the part of the proletariat. This period reached its apex of development in 1921, and culminated, on the one hand, with the victory of the U.S.S.R. over the forces of foreign intervention and internal counter-revolution and with the consolidation of the Communist International. On the other hand, it ended with a series of severe defeats for the Western European proletariat and the beginning of the general capitalist offensive. The final link in the chain of events in this period was the defeat of the German proletariat in 1923. This defeat marked the starting point of the *second* period, a period of gradual and partial stabilisation of the capitalist system, of the restoration of capitalist economy, of the development and expansion of the capitalist offensive and of the continuation of the defensive battles fought by the proletarian army weakened by severe defeats. On the other hand, this was a period of rapid restoration in the U.S.S.R., of extremely important successes in the work of building up socialism, and also of the growth of the political influence of the Communist Parties over the broad masses of the proletariat. Finally came the *third* period, which, in the main, is the period in which capitalist economy is exceeding the pre-war level, and in which the economy of the U.S.S.R. is also almost simultaneously exceeding the pre-war level (the beginning of the so-called "reconstruction period," the further growth of the socialist form of economy on the basis of a new technique). For the capitalist system this is the period of rapid development of technique and accelerated growth of cartels and trusts, and in which tendencies of development towards State capitalism are observed. At the same time, it is a period of intense development of the contradictions of world capitalism, operating in forms determined by the whole of the preceding process of the crisis of capitalism (contraction of markets, the U.S.S.R., colonial movements, growth of the inherent contradictions of imperialism). This third period, in which the contradiction between the growth of the productive forces and the contraction of markets become particularly accentuated, is inevitably giving rise to a fresh series of imperialist wars; among the imperialist States themselves, wars of the imperialist States against the U.S.S.R., wars of national liberation against imperialism and imperialist intervention, and to gigantic class battles. The intensification of all *international* antagonisms (antagonisms between the capitalist States and the U.S.S.R., the military occupation of Northern China—which is the beginning of the partition of China—the mutual struggles between the imperialists, etc.), the intensification of the *internal* antagonisms in capitalist countries (the swing to the left of the masses of the working class, growing acuteness of the class struggle), and the wide development of *colonial movements* (China, India and Syria), which are taking place in this period, will inevitably lead—through the further development of the contradictions of capitalist stabilisation—to capitalist stabilisation becoming still more precarious and to the severe intensification of the general crisis of capitalism. . . .

The international working class, and the toilers generally, look to the Soviet Union as their champion, and their attitude towards the Soviet Union is one of growing sympathy. Bearing this in mind, and also that the broad masses of the workers will understand much better than in 1917 that the next imperialist war against the Soviet Union will be open class war; that the masses of the toilers are now wiser from the experience that they had of the first imperialist war and that the vanguard of the proletariat now has a strong revolutionary organization in the shape of the Communist International, it may be safely asserted that the opportunities for fighting against war are far greater now than they were in previous times, and consequently that there is every reason for adopting bolder tactics.

(a) The possibilities of preventing war against the Soviet Union by intensifying class struggles to the point of revolutionary, mass action against the bourgeois governments are much greater at the present time than the possibilities for such action were in 1914. An example of revolutionary action was given by the British workers in 1920, when, by forming Councils of Action, they forced their government to abandon their intention of declaring war against the Soviet Union.

(b) The conditions favorable for transforming a war against the Soviet Union into civil war against the bourgeoisie will be much more speedily created for the proletariat than in an ordinary imperialist war.

(c) Therefore, although the Communists in capitalist countries must reject the phrase "Reply to war by general strike," and have no illusions whatever about the efficacy of such phrases, nevertheless in the event of war against the Soviet Union becoming imminent, they must take into consideration the increased opportunities for employing the weapon of mass strikes and the general strike, prior to the outbreak of war and during the mobilization.

(d) In the event of an attack upon the Soviet Union the Communists in oppressed nations, as well as those in imperialist countries, must exert all their efforts to rouse rebellion or wars of national liberation among the national minorities in Europe and in the colonial and semi-colonial countries against the imperialist enemies of the Soviet State.

In view of the fact that the "enemy" in such a war is the Soviet Union, *i.e.*, the fatherland of the international proletariat, the following changes must be made in tactics as compared with the tactics employed in "purely" imperialist war:

(a) The proletariat in the imperialist countries must not only fight for the defeat of their own governments in this war, but must actively strive to secure victory for the Soviet Union.

(b) Therefore, the tactics and the choice of means of fighting will not only be dictated by the interests of the class struggle at home in each country, but also by considerations for the outcome of the war at the front, which is a bourgeois class war against the proletarian State.

(c) The Red Army is not an "enemy" army, but the army of the international proletariat. In the event of a war against the Soviet Union, the workers in capitalist countries must not allow themselves to be scared from supporting the Red Army and from expressing this support by fighting against their own bourgeoisie, by the charges of treason that the bourgeoisie may hurl against them.

Although the proletariat in imperialist countries is not bound by the duty of "national defense," in the land of the proletarian dictatorship, however, national defense is an unfailing revolutionary duty. Here, the defenders are the armed proletariat supported by the poor peasantry. The victory of the October Revolution gave a Socialist fatherland to the workers of the world, *viz*, the Soviet Union.

Defense of the Soviet Union is a matter of class interest for the international proletariat as well as a debt of honor. In 1919–1921, the Soviet Government was able to defeat the interventionist forces of fourteen States, among which were the most powerful imperialist States, because the international proletariat intervened on behalf of the proletarian dictatorship in the U.S.S.R. by revolutionary mass action. A renewed imperialist attack on the Soviet Union will prove that, in spite of all the preparations made for this attack and in spite of the counter-revolutionary efforts of the Social Democrats, this international proletarian solidarity still exists.

The proletariat's allies in the defense of the U.S.S.R. are: (1) The rural poor and the mass of the middle peasants; and (2) the national revolution and liberation movements of the colonies and semi-colonies.

The international policy of the U.S.S.R. is a *peace policy*, which conforms to the interests of the ruling class in Soviet Russia, *viz.*, the proletariat, and to the interests of the international proletariat. This policy rallies all the allies of the proletarian dictatorship around its banner and provides the best basis for taking advantage of the antagonisms among the imperialist States. The aim of this policy is to guard the international revolution and to protect the work of building up Socialism—the progress of which is revolutionizing the world. It strives to put off the conflict with imperialism as long as possible. In regard to the capitalist States, to their mutual relationships and to their relationships with their colonies, this policy implies: opposition to imperialist war, to predatory colonial campaigns, and to pacifism, which camouflages these campaigns. . . .

China in the "Third Period"

Pursuant to Stalin's "left turn," the Chinese Communist Party was placed under the leadership of Li Li-san, a doctrinaire advocate of immediate proletarian revolution and an enemy of Mao's peasant strategy. After the failure of Li's urban insurrectionism Moscow replaced him with Wang Ming, a slavish follower of Soviet orthodoxy who nevertheless spoke with some prescience about war with Japan as an opportunity for revolution.

Meanwhile the center of gravity of Chinese Communism had shifted to Mao's peasant guerrilla army. Under heavy pressure from the Nationalist government Mao's troops executed the famous "Long March" in 1934–35 and relocated their Communist government at Yenan in northwest China. At the Tsunyi Party Conference in 1935 Mao asserted control of the party and censured Wang Ming for a "left" deviation, following which, in 1936, he promulgated his strategy of revolutionary guerrilla warfare.

Both Li Li-san and Wang Ming reappeared in the Chinese Communist Central Committee in 1945 and Li became Minister of Labor in 1949, but neither achieved real influence. Wang eventually returned to Moscow and contributed to Soviet polemics against China in the 1960's.

a) Li Li-san and the Proletarian Line

. . . The major signs of the revolutionary rising tide are the heightened political struggle of the revolutionary vanguard and of the general and even the backward masses, and the outbreak of great political strikes in the major cities. But serious

FROM: Li-san, Resolution, "The New Revolutionary Rising Tide and Preliminary Successes in One or More Provinces," adopted by the Politbureau of the Chinese Communist Party, June 11, 1930 (Brandt, Schwartz, Fairbank, pp. 188, 190–91, 193–94).

rightist or even liquidationist concepts will inevitably result if [one] considers only the superficial unevenness in the development [of the revolution] in the cities and countryside, and neglects [to consider] the workers' struggle, the sharpening of class antagonisms, the rapid growth of revolutionary spirit and determination on the part of the broad masses, and the bankruptcy of the ruling power of the ruling class; that is, the conditions under which every incident may lead to the outbreak of a great revolutionary struggle. The major reason why the workers' strike movement has not yet turned into a revolutionary rising tide decidedly does not lie in a lag of revolutionary consciousness on the part of the workers, nor in their lack of desire for revolution; rather it lies in the fact that the ruling class, about to collapse, is waging a last-ditch battle in the cities, using all possible methods—white terror and trickery—to suppress the workers' struggle. Thus the urban struggle is more intense and cruel than that in the countryside; this is why we must redouble our efforts in city work for the ultimate victory in the revolution. But the major handicaps in our present work are rightist ideas of doubt and pessimism regarding the workers' struggle. The elimination of such waverings is the major prerequisite for speeding the arrival of the rising tide in the workers' struggles. . . .

The great struggle of the proletariat is the decisive force in the winning of preliminary successes in one or more provinces. Without an upsurge of strikes of the working class, without armed insurrection in key cities, there can be no successes in one or more provinces. It is a highly erroneous concept to pay no special attention to urban work, and to plan "to use village [forces] to besiege the cities" and "to rely on the Red Army alone to occupy the cities." Henceforth, the organization of political strikes and their expansion into a general strike, as well as the strengthening of the organization and training of the workers' militia to set up a central force for armed insurrections, are the major tactics in preparing for preliminary successes in one or more provinces. Particular attention should be directed to [the fact that] the ruling class will [stage] a final struggle in the cities. This cruel struggle will be even fiercer than that in the rural areas; therefore, [we] must redouble our efforts in urban work, set up strong bases in the key cities—especially among workers of important industries—awaken the will of the broad masses to struggle to the death. These are the most grave tasks for the present and the tactical problems that must be solved first.

In view of the present objective economic and political conditions of China, a rising tide of proletarian struggles unaccompanied by peasant uprising, soldiers' mutinies, powerful assaults by the Red Army, and a [whole] combination of various revolutionary forces, also will not lead the revolution to victory. Also it will be unattainable if one of the above four revolutionary forces is lacking. The liquidationists who look down on the peasantry and [want to] liquidate the Red Army, are undoubtedly [spreading] reactionary ideas, attempting to weaken the ally of the proletariat and to destroy the fighting power of the revolution. The great revolutionary role of the peasantry has even a higher significance in China; the birth of the Red Army in the agrarian revolution is a special feature of China, which can never be understood by the Trotskyite liquidationists. . . .

Another factor decisive for the victory and transformation of the revolution is the mighty support from the already successful proletariat of the Soviet Union, and especially the outbreak of proletarian revolutions in capitalist countries. Because of China's semi-colonial nature, the victory of socialism in the Chinese revolution will be inseparable from the world revolution. The unprecedentedly fierce struggle of the Chinese revolution against the imperialists will inevitably heighten the world revolutionary upsurge; on the other hand, without a revolutionary rising tide of the world proletariat, it would be difficult to assure the continued success of the Chinese revolution. Therefore, it is at present our grave duty—and one of the main factors in the preparation for the victory and transformation of the revolution—that [we should] intensify propaganda for the Chinese revolution among the world proletariat, and, in particular, strengthen the alliance [with the latter] in the struggle. . . .

b) Wang Ming and the Moscow Orientation

. . . After the Manchurian events, in September, 1931,* and the creation of the central soviet government,† our general line was concretized to form the following three-fold slogan:

1. National revolutionary war of the armed nation against Japanese and other imperialisms to defend the integrity, independence and unity of China;

2. Overthrow of the Kuomintang as the government of national betrayal and national disgrace, as a condition of the successful carrying out of the national-revolutionary war;

3. Only the Soviet government and the Red Army of China can consistently carry out and lead the national-revolutionary war against Japanese and other imperialisms and achieve full national liberation. . . . The [Central Committee] placed before the party a clear and precise theoretical line. It stated that the starting point of the economic policy of the Chinese Soviet Republic at the present moment ought to be determined by the following considerations:

a. The character of the revolution at the given stage, that is, the fact that it is a bourgeois-democratic revolution;

b. The present stage of the Soviet Republic, that is, a state of prolonged and continuous civil war, of economic backwardness and scattered disposition of the present territories, and

c. The prospects of the revolution, that is, the struggle for the noncapitalist path of further development. . . .

One of the principal reasons which go to explain the successes of our Red Army and of the Soviet government in the struggle against the fifth Kuomintang expedition was the victorious completion in four years of the first Five-Year Plan in the U.S.S.R. and the recital of its results in the report of Comrade Stalin. Our party has popularized far and wide Comrade Stalin's report delivered at the January Plenum of the [Central Committee] and the [Central Control Commission] of the C.P.S.U., especially the part which directly deals with China. For instance the place where Comrade Stalin, in speaking of the harm caused by relegating the tasks of industrialization to the rear, directly declared:

FROM: Wang, "Revolution, War, and Intervention in China, and the Tasks of the Communist Party" (Speech to the Thirteenth Plenum of the Executive Committee of the Communist International, December, 1933; English translation in *Revolutionary China Today*, New York, Workers Library Publishers, 1934, pp. 33, 35–36, 40–41, 52, 54).

*The Japanese seizure of Manchuria—Ed.

†I.e., in Mao's guerrilla territory—Ed.

"Our position would then have been more or less analogous to the present position of China, which has no heavy industry, has no war industry of its own and is pecked at by everybody who cares to do so."

Our party, availing itself of these words of Comrade Stalin and of the triumph of the first Five-Year Plan, declares resolutely and firmly before all China, before the whole world, that only the Chinese Bolsheviks and the Chinese Soviet Republic which they head can change China from a country without a war industry, incapable of defending itself, an object of military operations by foreign enemies, into a country having its own heavy and war industries, capable of defending itself and powerful enough to repulse all attacks from without. Only the Chinese Bolsheviks and the Chinese Soviet Republic they head can change China from a country economically backward, politically dependent and colonial into a country economically developed and politically independent. . . .

The present-day international and internal situation of China is doubtless still more favorable than before for the further development and the victory of the soviet revolution in China. We have shown above that in the near future two perspectives are possible: either the decisive victory of the soviet revolution in China will prevent the outbreak of a world imperialist war for the Pacific and a war of the imperialists against the U.S.S.R.; or an imperialist war, primarily *a war of the Japanese and other imperialists against the Soviet Union will precede the decisive victory of the Soviet revolution in China. The endless and open acts of provocation, intrigues and even military feelers of the Japanese militarists in Manchuria on the Chinese Eastern Railway, at the borders of the Mongolian People's Republic and at the Soviet Far Eastern borders speak with sufficient eloquence of the nearness of the anti-Soviet war and of the possibility of its outbreak at any moment. In either event we, the [Communist Party of China] consider the following to be our basic task: A struggle for the decisive victory of the soviet revolution in all China,* or in other words, in the words of Comrade Molotov, "the complete defeat of the enemy and the victory of the Red Army." In our opinion these words suit not only the tasks of the C.P.S.U. in case of an attack by the Japanese or other imperialists upon the U.S.S.R. but they also fit the basic tasks of the C.P.C. in the very near future. . . .

c) Guerrilla Warfare and the Ascendancy of Mao

China's revolutionary war, which began in 1924, has passed through two stages, i.e., the stage of 1924–27 and the stage of 1927–36; from now on it will enter the stage of the national anti-Japanese revolutionary war. The revolutionary war in all the three stages has been and will be led by the Chinese proletariat and its party, the Chinese Communist Party. The chief enemies in China's revolutionary war are imperialism and the feudal forces. Although the Chinese bourgeoisie may take part in the revolutionary war on certain historical occasions, yet owing to its selfish character and its lack of political and economic independence, it is neither willing nor able to lead China's revolutionary war to complete victory. The masses of the Chinese peasantry and of the urban petty bourgeoisie are willing to take part actively in the revolutionary war and to bring about its complete victory. They are the main forces in the revolutionary war, yet small-scale production, which is their

FROM: Mao Tse-tung, *Strategic Problems of China's Revolutionary War* (Peking, Foreign Language Press, 1954), pp. 22–23, 34–39, 56–59.

characteristic and limits their political outlook (a section among the unemployed being imbued with anarchist ideology), renders them unable to give correct leadership in the war. Thus, in an era when the proletariat has already appeared on the political stage, the responsibility of leadership in China's revolutionary war inevitably falls on the shoulders of the Chinese Communist Party. At such a time any revolutionary war will certainly end in defeat if the leadership of the proletariat and the Communist Party is lacking or is forsaken. For of all the social strata and political groups in semicolonial China only the proletariat and the Communist Party are the most openminded and unselfish, possess the most farsighted political outlook and the highest organizational quality, and are also the readiest to learn with an open mind from the experiences of the advanced proletariat of the world and its parties as well as to apply what they have learned in their own undertakings. Hence only the proletariat and the Communist Party can lead the peasantry, the urban petty bourgeoisie, and the bourgeoisie, overcome the narrowmindedness of the peasantry and the petty bourgeoisie, the destructiveness of the unemployed masses, and the vacillation and lack of thoroughness of the bourgeoisie (provided no mistake is made in the Communist Party's policy), and thereby lead the revolution and the war to the path of victory. . . .

What then are the characteristics of China's revolutionary war?

I think there are four.

The first is that China is a vast semicolonial country which is unevenly developed both politically and economically, and which has gone through the revolution of 1924-27. . . .

Let us now analyze this characteristic.

The unevenness of political and economic development in China—the coexistence of a frail capitalist economy and a preponderant semifeudal economy; the coexistence of a few modern industrial and commercial cities and the boundless expanses of stagnant rural districts; the coexistence of several millions of industrial workers on the one hand and, on the other, hundreds of millions of peasants and handicraftsmen under the old regime; the coexistence of big warlords controlling the central government and small warlords controlling the provinces; the coexistence of two kinds of reactionary armies, *i.e.*, the so-called central army under Chaing Kai-shek and the troops of miscellaneous bands under the warlords in the provinces; and the coexistence of a few railway and steamship lines and motor roads on the one hand and, on the other, the vast number of wheelbarrow paths and trails for pedestrians only, many of which are even difficult for them to negotiate.

China is a semicolonial country—the disunity among the imperialist countries has caused the disunity among the various ruling blocs in China. A semicolonial state controlled by several countries is different from a colony controlled by a single country.

China is a vast country—"When the east is still dark, the west is lit up; when night falls in the south, the day breaks in the north"; hence one need not worry about whether there is room enough to move around.

China has gone through a great revolution which has provided us with the seeds of the Red Army, the Chinese Communist Party which leads the Red Army, and the masses who have participated in a revolution.

We have said, therefore, that the first characteristic of China's revolutionary war is that China is a vast semicolonial country which has gone through a revolution and is unevenly developed politically and economically. This characteristic basically determines not only our political strategy and tactics, but also our military strategy and tactics.

The second characteristic is the great strength of the enemy.

What is the situation of the Kuomintang, the enemy of the Red Army? It is a party that has seized political power and has relatively stabilized it. It has gained the support of the principal counterrevolutionary countries in the world. It has remodeled its army which has thus become different from any other army in Chinese history and, on the whole, similar to the armies of the modern states in the world; its army is supplied much more abundantly with arms and other equipment than the Red Army, and is greater in numerical strength than any army in Chinese history, even than the standing army of any country in the world. . . .

The third characteristic is that the Red Army is weak and small.

The Chinese Red Army was born after the failure of the first great revolution, starting as guerrilla units. It finds itself existing not only in a period of reaction in China but in a period of relative political and economic stability in the reactionary capitalist countries in the world.

Our political power is dispersed and isolated in mountainous or remote regions, and is deprived of any outside help. In economic and cultural conditions the revolutionary base areas are more backward than the Kuomintang areas. The revolutionary bases embrace only rural districts and small towns. They were extremely small in the beginning and have not grown much larger since. Moreover, they are often shifted and the Red Army possesses no really consolidated bases.

The Red Army is small in number, its arms are poor, and its access to food, bedding, clothing and other supplies is extremely difficult.

This characteristic presents a sharp contrast to the preceding one. The strategy and tactics of the Red Army are based on this sharp contrast.

The fourth characteristic is the Communist Party's leadership and the agrarian revolution.

This characteristic is the inevitable result of the first one. It gives rise to the following two features. On the one hand, China's revolutionary war, though taking place in a period of reaction in China and throughout the capitalist world, can yet be victorious because it is led by the Communist Party and supported by the peasantry. Because we have secured the support of the peasantry, our base areas, though small, possess great political power and stand firmly opposed to the political power of the Kuomintang, which encompasses a vast area; in a military sense, this creates colossal difficulties for the attacking Kuomintang troops. The Red Army, though small, has great fighting capacity, because its men under the leadership of the Communist Party have sprung from the agrarian revolution and are fighting for their own interests, and because officers and men are politically united.

On the other hand, our situation contrasts sharply with that of the Kuomintang. Opposed to the agrarian revolution, the Kuomintang is deprived of the support of the peasantry. Despite the great size of its army it cannot arouse the bulk of the soldiers or many of the lower-rank officers, who used to be small producers, to risk their lives voluntarily for its sake. Officers and men are politically disunited and this reduces its fighting capacity. . . .

. . . Under the slogan of safeguarding the revolutionary base areas and safeguarding China, we can rally the greatest majority of the people to fight single-mindedly because we are the victims of oppression and aggression. The Red Army of the Soviet Union defeated its enemies also by defensive warfare during the civil war. It not only carried on the war under the slogan of defending the Soviets when the imperialist powers organized the Whites for an onslaught, but also carried out military mobilization under the slogan of defending the capital when the October Uprising was being prepared. All defensive battles in a just war cannot only exercise a lulling influence on the politically alien elements but mobilize the backward sections of the masses to join in the war.

When Marx said that once an armed uprising is started there must not be a moment's pause in the attack, he meant that the masses, having taken the enemy by surprise in an uprising, must not allow the reactionary ruling classes any chance to retain or recover their political power, but must seize this moment to spring a surprise attack on the nation's reactionary ruling forces, and that they must never feel satisfied with the victories they have won, underrate the enemy, relent in their attacks, or hesitate to go forward, lest they should miss the chance of annihilating the enemy and court failure for the revolution. This is correct. This does not mean, however, that we revolutionaries should not adopt defensive measures even when we are already locked in a battle with an enemy stronger than ourselves and are hard pressed by him. Any one who thinks so would be a first-class idiot.

Our past war was on the whole an offensive against the Kuomintang, though militarily it assumed the form of smashing the enemy's campaigns of "encirclement and annihilation."

In military terms, our warfare consists in the alternate adoption of the defensive and the offensive. It makes no difference to us whether our offensive is regarded as following the defensive or preceding it, because the turning point comes when we smash the campaigns of "encirclement and annihilation." It remains a defensive until a campaign of "encirclement and annihilation" is smashed, and then it immediately begins as an offensive. . . .

In the civil war, when the Red Army surpasses the enemy in strength, there will no longer be any use for strategic defensive in general. Then our only directive will be strategic offensive. Such a change depends on an overall change in the relative strength of the enemy and ours. The only defensive measures that remain will be of a partial character.

American Communism in the "Third Period"

The line enjoined by Stalin on the foreign Communists until 1934 was one of uncompromising hostility to democratic and reformist movements. Hitler's seizure of power in Germany was thereby facilitated, while Earl Browder of the Communist Party of the USA denounced Roosevelt's New Deal as fascist.

The situation of the United States confirms most strikingly the correctness of the draft thesis before us, when it speaks of "the tremendous strain of the internal antagonism . . . as well as of the international antagonisms." The policies of the Roosevelt administration, known as the "New Deal," called into being by the crisis

FROM: Earl Browder, Speech at the Thirteenth Plenum of the Executive Committee of the Communist International, January 1934 (in *The Communist International*, January 15, 1934, pp. 75–77).

and by these "tremendous strains," have by no means softened these strains and antagonisms, but on the contrary have intensified them. Precisely the period of the Roosevelt regime has marked not alone the sharpening of the international relations of the U.S., but also the internal class relations.

Roosevelt's policy called for "national concentration" and "class peace." But in spite of the apparent surface successes of his regime, even the "honeymoon period" of the New Deal has been marked by rising mass struggles, by great class battles, by a radicalization of large sections of all the toiling masses of the population. . . . Never before in modern times has the "strain of internal class antagonisms" in the U.S. been so sharp and so general.

Characteristic for the whole system of policies known as the New Deal is their nature as preparations for war. The economic contents of these measures are those of war economy. . . . Simultaneously, U.S. oppression of the colonies and semicolonies takes on sharper forms, as the resistance of the colonial masses grows. . . .

If we witness all these developments during what may be called the "honeymoon" period of the Roosevelt regime, when the illusions created by an unprecedented demagogy were bolstered up for a time by a rapid rise in production stimulated by an enormous speculative market (the flight from the dollar)—then we have every reason to expect the growth and intensification of class conflicts, and of all the contradictions of capitalism, now when the Roosevelt program has already exposed its inability to improve the condition of the masses, when production again declines precipitately, when rising prices and inflation cut further sharply into the living standards of the masses, and when demagogy is rapidly being reinforced with a sharp development of fascist ideology and terror directed against the struggling masses.

International social-fascism* has hailed the Roosevelt policies as "steps in the direction of socialism." The British Labor Party and Trade Union Congress have adopted the Roosevelt program as their own, demanding that it can be imitated in Britain. In this way they are but continuing, in the period of crisis, that complete ideological subordination to the bourgeoisie which, during the period of American prosperity, created out of the figure of Henry Ford the reformist "saviour." The American Socialist Party has not lagged behind in this respect; Norman Thomas and Morris Hillquit hastened to pay a public visit to Roosevelt, upon his assumption of office, to congratulate him upon his policies, which they hailed as nothing less than a "revolution" in the interests of the masses.

But the fascist direction in which the Roosevelt policies are carrying the U.S. is becoming clear to the whole world. Nowhere is this more manifest than in the efforts to merge the reformist American Federation of Labor into the machinery of government, under the avowed banner of the fascist conception of the "corporate state," prohibition of strikes, compulsory arbitration, governmental fixing of wages, and even control of the inner life of the trade unions. For the edification of the masses this was spoken of as a "partnership of capital and labor, together with the government." Under this program the A.F. of L. is given governmental support and even financial assistance, and a determined effort is made to control and eventually choke off the strike movement, by driving the workers into the A.F. of L. where it is hoped the official leadership will be able to bring the masses under control. . . .

*I.e., democratic Socialists—Ed.

International Trotskyism

Trotsky's sympathizers in the Communist parties outside Russia, after vainly trying to hold on as left opposition groups within their respective organizations, began to build an independent movement. In 1934 they proclaimed the establishment of a "Fourth International" to challenge the Third, which, they contended, had betrayed the world revolution because of its identification with Stalin's bureaucratic nationalism. Apart from a considerable response in South-East Asia the Fourth International never advanced beyond the status of a splinter group; it ceased to be a significant force after Trotsky's assassination in 1940.

. . . The two parties of the proletariat, into whose hands history successively gave the imposing task of overthrowing the bourgeoisie and opening the road to socialism, have failed abysmally. Social democracy and Stalinism both collapsed at the first blow, like eggshells sucked dry, in Germany, then in Austria, then in Latvia, then in Bulgaria. (The social democracy, be it noted, died politically twenty years ago; it proved no less despicable in its second incarnation.) . . .

Neither of the two parties came to their miserable end because of some aberration, springing out of conditions peculiar to Germany, or Austria. Their demolition is rather to be traced to the fundamental theories and practices common to their respective Internationals. The generic name of these theories is nationalistic opportunism.

The modern social democratic parties were nurtured on the skimmed milk of the imperialist expansion of their respective national fatherlands. . . .

What distinguishes the Stalinist parties from the social democratic is not so much the outcome of their policy—the effects have been equally calamitous in both cases—as it is the different origin of their nationalism. The Stalinist parties were not poisoned at the well of imperialist nationalism, but at the well once fed exclusively by the springs of a proletarian revolution. The theory of "socialism in one country" is an expression of the nationalist degeneration of the Soviet Union. There is not, nor can there be, an inherent conflict between the interests of the Soviet Union and the interests of the world revolution. The interests of a parasitic Soviet bureaucracy, however, can and do conflict with the interests of the world revolution. The generalized formulation of this conflict is implicit in the theory of "socialism in one country."

The Soviet bureaucracy, myopically attributing longevity to phenomena of a temporary character, does not believe in the possibilities of a world revolution for several decades to come. With this conviction pervading all their thoughts, the bureaucrats want above all else the safeguarding of Russia's territorial integrity in order to construct a nationally walled-off utopia. This course had led inexorably to the transformation of the Third International from the general staff of the world revolution into a Soviet border patrol. Internationalism requires the subordination of each country to the interests of the world revolution. Nationalism means the subordination of the world movement to the interests of the Stalinist bureaucracy in the Soviet Union. . . .

The revolutionary vanguard needs a new Communist International. The masses are confused, it is true. They are being confused by the social democrats of all

FROM: "For the Fourth International," lead article in *The New International*, Vol. I, No. 1, July, 1934 (pp. 1–3).

shades and disguises, who tell them that the Second International is good enough, that it can be reformed, if not today then tomorrow, if not tomorrow then . . . after Fascism triumphs in a few more countries. They are being confused by the Stalinists who tell them that the Third International was right yesterday, today, tomorrow and forever. They are being confused by the vacillators and opportunists who deceive them with stories about uniting the Second and the Third, or about forming some other International—not a "sectarian" one, God forbid! but one in which all "good revolutionary parties outside the Second and the Third" will find shelter for the night. The Fourth International will not bring confusion into the ranks of the working class. It will bring a flaming sword whose edge cuts through the web of lies and deceit and hypocrisy, and whose light brings clarity. . . .

The Fourth International? This is no meaningless phrase. *It is a fighting program!* It means a fight to the death against Fascism, imperialism, war. It means an intransigent struggle against treacherous social reformism, bureaucratic Stalinism, cowardly compromising centrism of all species. It means the unconditional struggle to defend the Soviet Union which social democrats and Stalinists left in the lurch in Germany when they permitted the arch-anti-Sovietist Hitler to come to power without a battle. It means the militant struggle for revolutionary Marxism, for the final victory of the working class. . . .

. . . As yesterday, so today, we shall continue to work with all our strength for all the fundamental theories of Marx, Engels, Lenin and Trotsky, which have been tested through and through and confirmed a thousand times over and from every angle. With its modest resources, *The New International* will defend the revolutionary teachings of Marxism in every domain, taking up every challenge and refuting all over again those "new" anti-Marxists who have merely refurbished the well-riddled views of old revisionists. Our banner is hoisted and unfurled. The class-conscious militants will rally to it and plant it on the citadels of capitalism.

For the Fourth International! For revolutionary Marxism!

Collective Security

The stunning about-face in Soviet foreign policy in the face of the new German and Japanese threat was personified by Foreign Commissar Maxim Litvinov, an Old Bolshevik who had spent many years of exile in England. Litvinov led the Soviet Union into membership in the League of Nations and military alliances with France and Czechoslovakia. On the first anniversary of Soviet membership he spoke to the League Assembly on his conception of disarmament and Collective Security to maintain peace.

I am afraid that also, on future occasions, when settling disputes between its Members, the League of Nations will inevitably come up against the obstacle created by the absence of a universally adopted definition of aggression, and I am wondering whether the time has not come for considering this question anew and disconnecting it from the little wheels in the mechanism of the League with which it has been linked up. I do hope that the Council will take up this problem, even if it requires some preliminary preparation by way of diplomacy. . . .

While speaking on disarmament, I cannot help recalling another proposal of the

FROM: Litvinov, Speech at the Assembly of the League of Nations on its Annual Report, September 14, 1935 (League of Nations Official Journal, Supplement 138, pp. 71ff.)

Soviet government which is probably covered with the thickest layer of dust in the archives of the League. To many it may seem paradoxical that I am again raising the question of total disarmament when the most modest attempts at a partial reduction of armaments have failed. My answer to this is that I always contested the thesis that total disarmament is Utopian and partial disarmament easily realisable. I maintained, and am still maintaining, on the contrary, that the utmost difficulty is presented by partial and the least difficulty by total disarmament, given the will to do it. If what had seemed feasible has proved Utopian, let us try whether what seems Utopian will not prove feasible. The overwhelming majority of States which declare their fidelity to the idea of peace and their readiness to defend this idea with all means could not give more convincing proof of their peaceable disposition than by consenting to a new thorough investigation of the total disarmament problem. The Soviet delegation, at any rate, will take care that this problem does not sink into complete oblivion.

Of course, I am interested not solely in proposals submitted by the Soviet Government. I have learned, for instance, with regret that the question of bringing the Covenant into harmony with the Pact of Paris with a view to the complete outlawing of war has again been adjourned for an indefinite period. The solution of this problem would have put an end once for all to the discreditable disputes one hears here as to whether the League should avert armed conflicts or legalise them. . . .

The anxiety which has been tormenting the world for the last three years is far from decreasing, but, on the contrary, is growing. It is not only the Ethiopian question that matters or that matters so much, there are other ominous dangers facing Europe and the whole world. We owe it, fortunately, to this anxiety that all peaceable countries, all sincere friends of peace, have convinced themselves on the indivisibility of peace and of the necessity of collective security. . . .

The Soviet Union, too, has made its contribution to the system of regionally strengthening the peace of Europe. It spared no effort jointly with the Governments of France and of Czechoslovakia in order to put into practice a regional pact in the eastern part of Europe. Unfortunately, for reasons over which we had no control, we did not succeed in associating in this work of peace all the States belonging to that region, and we therefore could only conclude pacts of mutual assistance with France and Czechoslovakia, having the same aim and the same character as a regional pact. There can be no doubt that these pacts have in a large degree contributed to the strengthening of the feeling of security, thus performing in the east of Europe the same functions as does the Locarno Treaty in the western part of Europe. Such pacts cannot be regarded as a threat to anyone but would-be violators of peace; they do not affect anybody's interests and are exclusively serving the cause of peace and, consequently, the cause of humanity.

We know of another political conception that is fighting the idea of collective security and advocating bilateral pacts, and this not even between all States, but only between States arbitrarily chosen for this purpose. This conception can have nothing in common with peaceful intentions. Not every pact of non-aggression is concluded with a view to strengthening general peace. While non-aggression pacts concluded by the Soviet Union with its neighbours include a special clause for suspending the pact in cases of aggression committed by one of the parties against any third State, we know of other pacts of non-aggression which have no such clause. This means that a State which has secured by such a pact of nonaggression its rear or its flank obtains the facility of attacking with impunity third States. No wonder that the advocates of such pacts stand also for the localisation of war. But he who says localisation of war means freedom of war, its legalisation. A bilateral non-aggression pact may become in this way a means of security of aggression. We have thus two clearly defined political conceptions—security of peaceable nations on one hand, and security of aggression on the other. Fortunately, the latter theory is common to a few countries and stigmatises them before the whole world as probable disturbers of the peace. . . .

The Popular Front and Anti-Fascism

Paralleling the new Soviet policy of collective security, the Communist International received instructions at its Seventh (and last) Congress in August, 1935, to promote cooperation with liberal and socialist groups wherever such "Popular Front" alliances could be arranged. By thus playing revolution down, the Communists experienced a considerable heightening of their appeal, and Popular Front governments came to power temporarily in France and Spain.

In face of the towering menace of fascism to the working class and all the gains it has made, to all toilers and their elementary rights, to the peace and liberty of the peoples, the Seventh Congress of the Communist International declares that *at the present historical stage it is the main and immediate task of the international labor movement to establish the united fighting front of the working class.* For a successful struggle against the offensive of capital, against the reactionary measures of the bourgeoisie, against fascism, the bitterest enemy of all the toilers, who, without distinction of political views, have been deprived of all rights and liberties, it is imperative that unity of action be established between all sections of the working class, irrespective of what organization they belong to, even before the majority of the working class unites on a common fighting platform for the overthrow of capitalism and the victory of the proletarian revolution. But it is precisely for this very reason that this task makes it the duty of the Communist Parties to take into consideration the changed circumstances and to apply the united front tactics *in a new manner,* by seeking to reach agreements with the organizations of the toilers of various political trends for joint action on a factory, local, district, national and international scale.

With this as its point of departure, the Seventh Congress of the Communist International enjoins the Communist Parties to be guided by the following instructions when carrying out the united front tactics.

1. *The defense of the immediate economic and political interests of the working class, the defense of the latter against fascism,* must be the starting point and form the main content of the workers' united front in all capitalist countries. In order to set the broad masses in motion, such slogans and forms of struggle must be put forward as arise from the vital needs of the masses and from the level of their fighting capacity at the given stage of development. Communists must not limit themselves to merely issuing appeals to struggle for proletarian dictatorship, but must show the masses *what they are to do today* to defend themselves against capitalist plunder and fascist

FROM: Resolution of the Seventh World Congress of the Communist International, August, 1935, "The Offensive of Fascism and the Tasks of the Communist International in the Fight for the Unity of the Working Class against Fascism" (English translation in *Seventh World Congress of the Communist International,* New York, Workers' Library Publishers, 1935).

barbarity. They must strive, through the joint action of the labor organizations, to mobilize the masses around *a program of demands that are calculated to really shift the burden of the consequences of the crisis on to the shoulders of the ruling classes; demands, the fight to realize which, disorganizes fascism, hampers the preparations for imperialist war, weakens the bourgeoisie and strengthens the positions of the proletariat.* . . .

2. Without for a moment giving up their independent work in the sphere of Communist education, organization and mobilization of masses, the Communists, in order to render the road to unity of action easier for the workers, *must strive to secure joint action with the Social Democratic Parties,* reforming trade unions and other organizations of the toilers against the class enemies of the proletariat, on the basis of short or long-term agreements. . . .

5. Joint action with the Social-Democratic Parties and organizations not only does not preclude, but on the contrary, *renders still more necessary the serious and well-founded criticism of* reformism, of Social-Democracy as the ideology and practice of class collaboration with the bourgeoisie, and the patient exposition of the principles and program of Communists to the Social-Democratic workers. . . .

6. *Election campaigns* must be utilized for the further development and strengthening of the united fighting front of the proletariat. While coming forward independently in the elections and unfolding the program of the Communist Party before the masses, the Communists must seek to establish a united front with the Social-Democratic Parties and the trade unions (also with the organizations of the toiling peasants, handicraftsmen, etc.), and exert every effort to prevent the election of reactionary and fascist candidates. In face of fascist danger, the Communists may, *while reserving for themselves freedom of political agitation and criticism,* participate in election campaigns on *a common platform and with a common ticket of the anti-fascist front,* depending on the growth and success of the united front movement, also depending on the electoral system in operation. . . .

Emphasizing the special importance of forming a united front in the sphere of the economic struggle of the workers and the establishment of the unity of the trade union movement as a most important step in consolidating the united front of the proletariat, the Congress makes it a duty of the Communists to adopt all practical measures for the realization of the unity of the trade unions by industries and on a national scale. . . .

Communism and the Spanish Civil War

In accordance with the Popular Front policy, the Spanish Communists gave their full support to the republican government of Spain during the civil war which followed General Franco's rebellion of July, 1936. Thanks to this line and the importance of Soviet aid, the Communists exercised strong (but neither exclusive nor revolutionary) influence in the government of the republic until it was overwhelmed by Franco in March, 1939.

José Diaz, General Secretary of the Communist Party of Spain, made it clear in a speech to the Central Committee in March, 1937, that revolutionary policies would be postponed until after the defeat of the fascists. The Communists denounced the revolutionary extremism of the Trotskyist POUM ("Workers' Party of Marxist Unit"), and supported the government's suppression of the Anarchist uprising in Barcelona in May, 1937.

FROM: Diaz, "For Unity, until Victory" (Report to the Central Committee of the Communist Party of Spain, March 5, 1937, pp. 10, 12-14, 17-18, 38, 46-48; editor's translation).

The Communist position in Spain is significant as a link between their old avowedly revolutionary line and their post-World-War-II appeal on an ostensibly reformist or nationalist basis—*vide* Diaz's stress on the role of the "new" type of "democratic" republic.

. . . Realizing the new character which our struggle acquired when the war began, our party announced the slogan of broadening the Popular Front, of turning toward the union of all Spaniards. For this it took account of the fact that the civil war was now transformed into a war of independence, a war of national liberation. . . .

Our struggle, which in its basic content is a national one, also has a marked international character. This international character of our struggle has been defined, in a few words but in the manner of a genius, by our great comrade Stalin. . . . Stalin, in his historic telegram to the Central Committee of our party, says the following:

"In helping the revolutionary masses of Spain as much as possible, the workers of the Soviet Union are only doing their duty. They realize that to liberate Spain from the oppression of the fascist reactionaries is not the private affair of the Spaniards, but the common cause of all advanced and progressive humanity." . . .

We are fighting for the Democratic Republic, for a Democratic and Parliamentary Republic of a new type, with deep social content. The struggle which is going on in Spain does not have as its object the establishment of a democratic republic such as can be seen in France or in any other capitalist country. No; the Democratic Republic for which we are fighting is different. We are fighting to destroy the material bases on which reaction and fascism rest, for without the destruction of these bases a true political democracy cannot exist.

In our struggle we are pursuing *the annihilation of the material bases of semifeudal Spain*, tearing out the roots of fascism. . . .

We must annihilate the big landholders. . . .

We must also *destroy the economic and political power of the Church*, which was a center of conspiracy against the popular masses and one of the firmest supports of semifeudal Spain, and for this we must proceed with the confiscation and nationalization of its property. Let it be well understood that *fighting the Church* in its semifeudal economic and political structure is not the same thing as *fighting religion*, but the contrary, for only a republican and democratic Spain, liberal and progressive, will be able to guarantee freedom of religion in our country.

We must also proceed with the *liquidation of militarism*. . . .

We must likewise *break up the great financial oligarchies*. . . .

In addition to these fundamental points, whose solution will mean the disappearance of the semifeudal castes which have been dominant in Spain, and the transformation of the material and social base of our new Democratic and Parliamentary Republic, it is necessary to proceed, as the complement of what this should be, to the establishment of *true* universal suffrage, to the direct participation of all the people in elections and in the posts of political and economic leadership of the country. Thus we will move directly to the inauguration of a true democracy, which will permit wide channels to be opened for the economic, political, and cultural progress of our people. . . .

. . . The fact of not having clearly understood the character of our struggle leads organizations and parties associated with ours to adopt extremist attitudes which in no way benefit the cause of the people, but far from carrying us rapidly to victory, seriously obstruct the attainment of it. To these equivocal positions correspond those premature attempts at "socialization" and "collectivization." . . . Today, when there is a Popular Front government in which all the forces who are fighting against fascism are represented, this is not advisable, but is self-defeating. Now it is necessary to move rapidly to coordinate production and intensify it under a single administration to provide everything necessary for the front and the rear. To persist now in these attempts is to go against the interests which are supposedly being defended. To announce those premature attempts at "socialization" and "collectivization" while the war has still not been decided, at moments when the enemy within, aided by fascism without, is violently attacking our positions and endangering the fate of our country, is absurd and equivalent to becoming accomplices of the enemy. Such attempts reveal the failure to understand the character of our struggle, which is the struggle for the defense of the Democratic Republic, in which all the popular forces needed to win the war can and must combine.

It is said that the Communists have renounced their revolutionary program. No; what has happened is that we conform to the realities of the struggle and the necessities of the war. . . .

We have not abandoned our revolutionary program just because we did not carry forward these unfortunate attempts. What is happening is that today it is impossible to have a more revolutionary program than the one which the Communist Party has placed before the people. We plan our tactics and our strategy in accordance with the given situation. That is, we Marxist-Leninists apply to each concrete situation the tactics and strategy which correspond to that situation; and he who pretends to jump stages, with resounding names, wishing to do the impossible, will smash against the difficulties of the situation. But the harm is not that they smash themselves; the harm is that with their lack of understanding they compromise everyone's cause and endanger the freedom of Spain. . . .

In spite of everything, at all cost, we must maintain the Popular Front. Whatever the difficulties which are found in our path, the Communist Party will continue to be the most vigorous defender of the Popular Front and of its expression in power: the legitimate government. Our party will permit no one to attack the union of the anti-fascist forces with impunity. Our slogan is, "United now to win the war, and united afterward to reap the fruits of victory"; he who tries to break the union of the Popular Front, he who tries to break the union of the Spanish people struggling for the independence of Spain and staking everything on this struggle, is working consciously or unconsciously in favor of our enemies. . . .

Who are the enemies of the people? The enemies of the people are the fascists, the Trotskyists, and the "uncontrollables." . . . Our principal enemy is fascism. Against it we are concentrating all of the people's vigor and hatred. Against it we are setting all the forces ready to annihilate it; but our hatred is also directed, with the same concentrated force, against the agents of fascism who hide themselves behind pretended revolutionary slogans as POUM'ists, disguised Trotskyists, the better to accomplish their mission as agents of our enemies waiting in ambush in our own territory. We cannot annihilate the Fifth Column without also annihilating those who also defend politically the enemy's slogans directed at disrupting and disuniting the anti-fascist forces. The slogans of the enemy are: Against the Democratic Republic, against the anti-Fascist Popular Front, against the Popular Front government, against the regular army, etc., and above all against the Soviet Union on account of its magnificent solidarity with the Spanish people in this struggle. Although the Trotskyists try to conceal themselves with other apparently more revolutionary slogans, such as the social republic, workers' government, red militia, they cannot avoid revealing their fascist ears. . . .

It is a serious error to consider the Trotskyists as a fraction of the workers' movement. This is an unprincipled group of counterrevolutionaries classified as agents of international fascism. The recent Moscow trial has shown in the light of day that the chief of the band, Trotsky, is a direct agent of the Gestapo. In his hatred of the Soviet Union, of the great Bolshevik Party and of the Communist International, he joined hands with the fascists. . . .

Chinese Communism Under Mao

When the Japanese invaded China in 1937, Mao offered to form a "united front" with the Nationalist government and moderated his program accordingly. In 1940 in his celebrated pamphlet, "On the New Democracy," he spelled out his new approach to revolution by easy steps, led by the Communist Party as a surrogate for the proletariat. Meanwhile, at their new headquarters in Yenan Mao and Party Secretary Liu Shao-ch'i launched an indoctrination program to instill Stalin-style discipline in the party, culminating in the "Thought Reform" movement of 1942–44.

a) The Anti-Japanese "United Front"

. . . To resist Japan we need a strengthened united front which means the mobilization of the people of the whole country to participate in the united front. To resist Japan we need a solid united front, which means the necessity of common policies. Common policies should be the guiding principle of the united front. They will also serve as a binding force of the united front, binding tightly, as with a cord, all the organizations and individuals from all the parties, groups, classes and armies that participate in it. Only thus can solidarity be achieved. We are opposed to the old form of control because it is unsuitable to the national revolutionary war. We welcome the establishment of a new system of control to replace the old, that is, by promulgating common policies to set up a revolutionary order. For only thus can the needs of the war of resistance be met.

What should our common policies be? They are the Three People's Principles of Dr. Sun Yat-sen and the Ten Great Policies for Anti-Japanese Resistance and National Salvation announced by the Chinese Communist Party. . . .

Communism is to be implemented in a future stage of the revolutionary development. Communists do not wishfully envisage the realization of the historically determined revolution. This is the basic reason why the Chinese Communist Party has raised the slogans of an anti-Japanese national united front and a united democratic republic. As to the implementation of the Three People's Principles, the Chinese Communist Party agreed to it during the first united front formed ten years ago at the First National Congress of the Kuomintang, and they were indeed carried out on a national scale between 1925 and 1927 by every faithful Commu-

FROM: Mao, "Urgent Tasks of the Chinese Revolution since the Formation of the Kuomintang-Chinese Communist Party United Front" (September, 1937; Brandt, Schwartz, Fairbank, pp. 252–54, 257).

nist and every faithful Kuomintang member. Unfortunately in 1927 the united front was shattered, resulting in the suspension of the Three People's Principles during the past decade. However, as far as the Chinese Communist Party is concerned, all the policies carried out by it during the last ten years have been in harmony with the revolutionary spirit of Dr. Sun Yat-sen's Three People's Principles and the three great policies. The Chinese Communist Party has never ceased its firm resistance to imperialism; this is the principle of nationalism. The soviet system of people's representative councils is nothing else than the principle of democracy, and the agrarian revolution is without a doubt the principle of people's livelihood. Why, then, has the Chinese Communist Party announced the abolition of soviets and the cessation of land confiscation? This we have explained before. It is not that these measures are undesirable, but that armed invasion by Japanese imperialists has brought about changes in class relations in China, thus making imperative and making possible the alliance of all classes in the fight against Japanese imperialism. Furthermore, a democratic united front is being formed internationally, to fight against the danger of fascism. Therefore, the formation of a national, democratic united front in China is today a necessity in China. . . .

Our race and nation now stand at a critical hour of survival. May the Kuomintang and the Chinese Communist Party work in close harmony! May all our fellow countrymen who do not want to be slaves rally together on the foundation of Kuomintang-Chinese Communist Party solidarity! The realization of all necessary reforms in order to overcome numerous difficulties—such is the urgent task now facing us in the Chinese revolution. The accomplishment of this task will certainly bring about the defeat of Japanese imperialism. If we devote our efforts [to this task] our future is indeed bright. . . .

b) Liu Shao-ch'i on the Training of a Party Member

A Communist Party member must not only clearly determine his Communist philosophy of life and his world view, but must also explicitly determine the correct relationship between his individual interests and the interests of the party. The Marxist principle is that the interests of the individual are subordinate to the interests of the party, the interest of the part is subordinate to the interest of the whole, the short-range interest is subordinate to the long-range, and the national interest is subordinate to the international.

The Communist Party is a political party representing the proletariat. The Communist Party has no interest or aim aside from the interest of the liberation of the proletariat. However, the final liberation of the proletariat must also be the final liberation of all mankind. . . .

. . . Therefore, the individual interests of the party member are subordinate to the interests of the party, which means subordinate to the interests of class and national liberation, of Communism and of social progress. . . .

. . . Fundamentally, it is in the struggle against various dark forces within and without the party that we reform the world and mankind, and at the same time reform our party and ourselves. The intra-party struggle is a reflection of the class struggle outside the party. In the class struggle outside the party—in the revolu-

FROM: Liu, "On the Training of a Communist Party Member" (August, 1939; Brandt, Schwartz, Fairbank, pp. 336, 343–44).

tionary struggle of the broad masses—the party is tempered, developed, and strengthened; at the same time, the party achieves consolidation and unity in the intra-party struggle and gives planned, correct, powerful leadership to the revolutionary struggle of the broad masses. It is therefore fundamentally incorrect and of benefit to the enemy to adopt the attitude of liberalism towards various errors, defects, and undesirable phenomena in the party, to attempt to blot out divergencies in principle in the party, to evade the intra-party struggle, to conceal the party's internal contradictions or to exhibit negligence; because they are in contradiction to the rules of development of the class struggle and to our basic viewpoint of reforming the world and mankind through struggle. It is therefore also incorrect to separate the intra-party struggle from the class struggle outside the party—from the revolutionary movement of the broad masses—and transform it into empty talk; because the party cannot be tempered, developed, or strengthened if it is separated from the revolutionary struggle of the broad masses. Yet it is also incorrect to carry things to the other extreme and adopt a categorical attitude towards all comrades who have errors or defects [which are] not incurable, to carry on the intra-party struggle mechanically, or to subjectively manufacture intra-party struggles within the party. Because this is also injurious to the party, it gives the enemy an opportunity to mount an attack on our party. This also runs completely counter to the rules of the party's development. Loyal comrades in the party who have committed errors should not be utterly denounced from the start; instead they should be persuaded, educated, and tempered with a friendly, sympathetic attitude, and only when absolutely necessary should they be publicly attacked and expelled. Of course, we cannot allow anyone to harm the party's interests, and we must take precautions lest opportunists, spies, Trotskyites, and two-faced elements take advantage of every opportunity to harm the party's interests. . . .

c) Mao on the "New Democracy"

. . . The historical characteristic of the Chinese revolution is that it is divided into two steps, that of democracy and that of socialist. The first step is not democracy in the general sense, but a new and specific kind, of a Chinese type—i.e., new democracy. . . .

Evidently, if the nature of the present Chinese society is colonial, semicolonial, and semi-feudal, then the progress of the Chinese revolution must be in two steps. The first step is to turn the colonial, semi-colonial, and semi-feudal society into an independent democratic society; the second step is to push the revolution forward to build up a socialist society. The present phase of the Chinese revolution carried out by us is the first step.

The beginning of the first step of the Chinese revolution can be traced back to the Opium War when the Chinese society began to change from a feudal society to a semi-colonial, semi-feudal society. . . .

But a change took place in the Chinese bourgeois-democratic revolution after the outbreak of the first imperialist World War and the establishment of a socialist state on one-sixth of the land surface of the globe, i.e., after the Russian revolution

FROM: Mao, "On the New Democracy" (January 1940; Brandt, Schwartz, Fairbank, pp. 264–68, 270–73, 275).

of 1917. Before that time, the Chinese bourgeois-democratic revolution was within the orbit of the old bourgeois-democratic world revolution and was a part of it.

From then on, the Chinese bourgeois-democratic revolution changed and came within the orbit of the new bourgeois-democratic revolution. From the standpoint of the revolutionary front, it is a part of the world proletarian-socialist revolution. . . .

As to the first stage or the first step in this colonial and semi-colonial revolution—according to its social nature, it is fundamentally still a bourgeois-democratic revolution in which the objective requirement is still basically to clear away the obstacles in the way of capitalist development; nevertheless, this revolution is no longer the old type led solely by the bourgeoisie for the building of capitalist society and a state of the bourgeois dictatorship, but a new type of revolution wholly or partly led by the proletariat, the first stage of which aims at the setting up of a new democratic society, a new state of the joint dictatorship, of all revolutionary classes. The fundamental character of this revolution will not change until the [arrival of the stage of] socialist revolution, even though, during its progress, it may pass through a number of stages in accordance with the possible changes in the conditions of enemies and allies.

This kind of revolution, because it is a great blow to the imperialists, is bound to be opposed and not tolerated by the imperialists; on the other hand, it is permitted by the socialist country and socialistic international proletariat.

Therefore, it is inevitable that this revolution will become a part of the proletarian-socialist world revolution. . . .

Today those who are capable of leading the people to defeat Japanese imperialism and put democracy into practice are the saviours of the people. If the Chinese bourgeoisie is capable of fulfilling this duty, it certainly deserves every praise. Otherwise, the responsibility on the whole cannot but fall on the shoulders of the proletariat.

Therefore, no matter what the circumstances, the Chinese proletariat, peasantry, intelligentsia, and other petty-bourgeois elements are the main force upon which the fate of China depends. These classes either have awakened or are awakening, and are bound to be the basic parts of the state and government framework in the democratic Republic of China. The democratic Republic of China which we are aiming to construct now can only take the form of dictatorship of all anti-imperialist and anti-feudal people, i.e., a new democratic republic. In other words, a republic of the Three People's Principles in the true revolutionary sense as put forward by Dr. Sun Yat-sen including the Three Great Policies. . . .

In such a republic as that mentioned above, our economy must be the economy of the new democracy, just as the politics is the politics of the new democracy.

Big banks, big industries, and big business shall be owned by this republic. "In order that private capital may not manipulate the livelihood of the people, all native-owned or foreign-owned enterprises, either monopolist or of a dimension too large for private efforts to manage such as banks, railroads, airlines, etc., will be managed and controlled by the state. This is the essence of restriction of capital." This was a slogan statement made by the Kuomintang in the declaration of its First National Congress. This is the correct course for the economic constitution of the new democratic republic; at the same time, however, the state will not confiscate other capitalist private property and will not forbid the development of capitalist production that "cannot manipulate the people's livelihood." This is because the Chinese economy is still in a very backward state.

It will adopt certain necessary measures to confiscate the land of big landlords and distribute it among peasants without any, or with very little, land, in order to realize Dr. Sun's slogan, "The tiller should own his land," and to liquidate the feudal relations in rural areas. This is not to build up socialist agriculture, but to turn the land into the private property of the peasants. The rich peasant economy will also be allowed to exist in the rural areas. This is the policy of "the equalization of landownership," the correct slogan of which is, "The tiller should own his land." . . .

. . . The Chinese revolution is in essence a revolution of the peasantry; the present war of resistance is in essence a war of resistance of the peasantry. The politics of new democracy is in essence [the politics of] the transfer of power to the peasantry. The new, genuine Three People's Principles are in their essence the principles of a peasant revolution. The content of popular culture is in essence [the question of] the elevation of the cultural [level] among the peasantry. The anti-Japanese war is in essence a peasant war. . . . Therefore, the peasant question becomes the fundamental question of the Chinese revolution, and the force of the peasantry is the main force of the Chinese revolution. Besides the peasantry, the second [largest] section of the Chinese population consists of workers. China has several millions of industrial workers. Without them, China would not be able to live on, for it is they who are the producers in the industrial economy. Without the workers, the [Chinese] revolution would not be able to succeed, for it is they who are the leaders of the revolution and have the highest revolutionary spirit. Under these conditions the revolutionary, new or genuine Three People's Principles must adopt the policy of [aiding] the workers and peasants. If there is such a Three People's Principles which does not adopt this policy, does not truly protect and assist them, does not endeavour to "awaken the people," then it is bound to decay. . . .

The culture of the new democracy is the anti-imperialist and anti-feudal culture of the masses, or, in terms of present-day China, the culture of the anti-Japanese united front. It can only be led by the cultural thought of the proletariat, i.e., Communist thought; it cannot be led by the thought of any other class. The culture of the new democracy, in short, is "the proletarian-led anti-imperialist and anti-feudal culture of the masses." . . .

China should absorb on a great scale the progressive culture of foreign countries as a raw material for her own cultural food. Such absorption was not sufficient in the past. This refers not only to the socialist and new democratic culture, but also to the ancient cultures of foreign countries, which are useful to us; for instance, the cultural heritage of the capitalist countries in their earlier period of growth. These foreign materials we must not treat as we treat our food. We submit our food to the mouth for chewing and to the stomach and intestines for digestion, add to it saliva, pepsin, and other secretions of the intestines to separate it into the essence and the residue, and then absorb the essence of our nourishment and pass off the residue. It should never be indiscriminately and uncritically absorbed. The thesis of "wholesome Westernization" is a mistaken viewpoint. To absorb blindly foreign materials has done China much harm. The same attitude is necessary for the Chinese Communists in the application of Marxism to China. We must unify appropriately the general truth of Marxism and the concrete actuality of the Chinese revolution, i.e., we must adopt the national form before we can make Marxism useful and not apply it subjectively and dogmatically. Subjective and formal Marxists are only playing with Marxism and the Chinese revolution, and there is no place for them in the revolutionary ranks of China. Chinese culture must have its own form, i.e., a national form. A national form and a new democratic content—this is our new culture of today. . . .

The combination of new democratic politics, new democratic economics, and new democratic culture is the Republic of New Democracy. It is truly a republic in name and in reality. And that is the New China we aim to build.

The New China stands before every one of us. We should be ready to receive it.

The mast of the ship New China is appearing on the horizon. We should clap our hands to welcome it.

Raise both your hands! The New China is ours! . . .

d) The "Thought Reform" Movement

Mao on Literature and Art

. . . The various fronts of our struggle for the liberation of the Chinese people may be grouped into two: the civil and the martial; they are the cultural front and the military front. We must rely on armed troops to conquer the enemy, but this in itself is not enough. A cultural army is also indispensable for uniting ourselves and conquering the enemy. This cultural army has materialized in China since May Fourth,* it has helped the Chinese revolution, and has caused a gradual decrease in the territory dominated by a feudalistic and slavish culture which has yielded to imperialistic encroachments. . . .

The purpose of our meeting today is to make literature and art become a constructive part of the whole revolutionary machine; to use it as a powerful weapon for uniting and educating the people and for crushing and destroying the enemy, as well as to help the people wage the struggle against the enemy with one heart and one mind. . . .

. . . In the world of today, all culture or literature and art belong to some one definite class, some one definite party, i.e., some one definite political line. Art for art's sake, art which transcends class or party, art which stands as a bystander to, or independent of, politics, does not in actual fact exist. Since art is subordinate to class and party in a society which has classes and parties, it must undoubtedly follow the political demands of those classes and parties. . . . If it deviates from these, it will deviate from the basic needs of the masses. Proletarian literature and art are one part of the entire proletarian revolutionary cause: as Lenin says, "a screw in the whole machine." Therefore, the literary and artistic work of the Party has a definite and set position in the Party's entire revolutionary work. . . .

Under the great principle of unity in the war of resistance we must allow the

FROM: Mao, Speeches at the Forum on Literature and Art, Yenan, May 2 and 23, 1942 (Brandt, Schwartz, Fairbank, pp. 408, 414-15, 417-18).

*May 4, 1919: occasion of student demonstrations against Japan and the Far-Eastern provisions of the Treaty of Versailles, which launched the "May Fourth Movement" of nationalistic intellectual revival.—Ed.

inclusion of literary and artistic works representing every kind and sort of political attitude. However, our criticism will be firm upon our principle and standpoint. We must give severe judgment to all works of literature and art that are anti-national, anti-scientific, anti-masses, and anti-Communistic in viewpoint, because these so-called works of literature and art, their motivation and effect, all harm the unity of the war effort. . . .

There is a political standard, there is an artistic standard; what is the relationship between the two? Politics is not synonymous with art, nor is a general view of the world synonymous with the methodological theories of artistic creation. We not only do not recognize abstract and eternal political standards, but also do not recognize such standards for art. Every class society and every separate class within that society has different political and artistic standards. But no matter what kind of class society or what kind of separate class within that class society it may be, it always puts the political standard first and artistic standard second. The bourgeois class always rejects the proletarian works of literature and art, no matter how high their standards may be. The proletarian classes must . . . reject the reactionary political nature of the bourgeois works of literature and art, and assimilate their art only in a critical manner. It is possible for some things [which are] politically, basically reactionary to have a certain artistry, for example the fascist literature and art. However, the more artistic a work which is reactionary in content, the more harmful does it become to the people and the more it ought to be rejected. The common characteristics in the literature and art of the exploiting classes in their period of decline are the inconsistencies between their reactionary political content and their artistic form. Our demand, then, is a unity of politics and art, a unity of content and form, and a unity of revolutionary political content and an artistic form of as high a standard as possible. Works of art which are deficient in artistry, no matter how advanced they are politically, will not have any force. For this reason, we oppose works of art whose content is harmful and also oppose the so-called "slogan type" tendency which only considers the content and not the form. We must carry on this twofold struggle in the problem of literature and art. . . .

The Central Committee on Leadership

If any work or mission lacks a general, universal slogan, the broad masses cannot be moved to action, but if there is nothing more than a general slogan and the leaders do not make a concrete, direct and thorough application of it with those from a particular unit who have been rallied around the slogan, [if the leaders] fail to break through at some point and gain experience, or fail to use acquired experience in later guiding other units, there is then no way for the leaders to test the correctness of the general slogan and there is no way for them to carry out its contents; there is then the danger that the general slogan will have no effect. . . .

The experience of the reform movement of 1941 has also proved that in the process of reform, the reforms of each concrete unit must produce a leading nucleus of minority activists who are the core of the administrative leadership of that unit and it must also bring this leading nucleus into close union with the broad masses engaged in study; in this way only can reform fulfill its mission. If

FROM: Resolution of the Central Committee of the Chinese Communist Party "On Methods of Leadership," June 1, 1943 (English translation in Boyd Compton, *Mao's China: Party Reform Documents, 1942–44*, Seattle, University of Washington Press, 1952, pp. 176–79, 183; reprinted by permission of the publisher).

there is only a positive spirit on the part of the leading nuclei, it (the reform) becomes an empty flurry of activity on the part of a minority; yet if there is only a positive spirit on the part of the broad masses, with no powerful leading nucleus to organize the positive spirit of the masses properly, the masses' spirit then cannot endure, nor can it move in a correct direction or be elevated to a high standard.

In all our Party's actual work, correct leadership must come from the masses and go to the masses. This means taking the views of the masses (unintegrated, unrelated views) and subjecting them to concentration (they are transformed through research into concentrated systematized views), then going to the masses with propaganda and explanation in order to transform the views of the masses, and seeing that these [views] are maintained by the masses and carried over into their activities. It also means an examination of mass activities to ascertain the correctness of these views. Then again, there is concentration from the masses and maintenance among the masses. Thus the process is repeated indefinitely, each time more correctly, vitally, and fruitfully. This is the epistemology and methodology of Marxism-Leninism. . . .

. . . Comrades in all areas should reflect carefully and develop their own creative abilities. The more bitter the struggle becomes, the more necessary is the demand for close union between men of the Communist Party and the broad masses, the more necessary to Communist Party members is the close union between general slogans and particular guidance, and [the more necessary] is the thorough disruption of subjectivistic and bureaucratic methods of leadership. All leading comrades of our Party must forthwith adopt scientific methods of leadership and oppose them to subjective and bureaucratic methods of leadership, overcoming the latter with the former. Subjectivists and bureaucratists who do not understand the principles of uniting leadership with the masses and combining the general and the particular, greatly hamper the development of Party work. We must therefore oppose subjectivistic and bureaucratic methods of leadership, and universally and profoundly promote methods of leadership which are scientific

The Nazi-Soviet Pact

In 1939, after the Munich Agreement strained Russia's ties with Britain and France, the Soviet government commenced negotiations with Germany and threw the world (and especially the international Communist movement) into consternation by concluding the nonaggression treaty of August, 1939. Molotov, at the time both premier (1930-1941) and foreign commissar (1939-1949 and 1953-1956), defended the deal strictly in terms of national interest and "peaceful coexistence." Nevertheless the loyalties of many foreign Communists were rudely shaken by the maneuver, which registered the clear ascendency of Soviet national security over the fortunes of the international revolutionary movement.

. . . The conclusion of a pact of non-aggression between the U.S.S.R. and Germany is of tremendous positive value, eliminating the danger of war between Germany and the Soviet Union. . . .

FROM: Molotov, "The Meaning of the Soviet-German Non-Aggression Pact" (Speech to the Supreme Soviet, August 31, 1939; English translation in *The Strategy and Tactics of World Communism: Supplement I*, "One Hundred Years of Communism, 1848-1948" (U.S. House of Representatives Document No. 619, 80th Congress, 2nd Session), Washington, Government Printing Office, 1948, p. 158, 160-63).

The decision to conclude a non-aggression pact between the U.S.S.R. and Germany was adopted after military negotiations with France and Great Britain had reached an impasse owing to the insuperable differences I have mentioned. As the negotiations had shown that the conclusion of a pact of mutual assistance could not be expected, we could not but explore other possibilities of ensuring peace and eliminating the danger of war between Germany and the U.S.S.R. If the British and French governments refused to reckon with this, that is their affair. It is our duty to think of the interests of the Soviet people, the interests of the Union of Soviet Socialist Republics. (*Prolonged applause*) All the more since we are firmly convinced that the interests of the U.S.S.R. coincide with the fundamental interests of the people of other countries. (*Applause*) But that is only one side of the matter.

Another circumstance was required before the Soviet-German Non-Aggression Pact could come into existence. It was necessary that in her foreign policy Germany should make a turn towards good-neighborly relations with the Soviet Union.

Only when this second condition was fulfilled, only when it became clear to us that the German Government desired to change its foreign policy so as to secure an improvement of relations with the U.S.S.R., was the basis found for the conclusion of a Soviet-German Non-Aggression Pact. Everybody knows that during the last six years, ever since the National-Socialists (Nazis) came into power, political relations between Germany and the U.S.S.R. have been strained. Everybody also knows that despite the differences of outlook and political systems, the Soviet government endeavored to maintain normal business and political relations with Germany. . . .

. . . Stalin declared . . . that the Soviet Union stands for strengthening business relations with all countries. But at the same time Stalin warned us against warmongers who are anxious in their own interests to involve our country in conflicts with other countries.

Exposing the hullabaloo raised in the British, French, and American press about Germany's "plans" for the seizure of the Soviet Ukraine, Stalin said:

"It looks as if the object of this suspicious hullabaloo was to incense the Soviet Union against Germany, to poison the atmosphere and to provoke a conflict with Germany without any visible grounds."

As you see, Stalin hit the nail on the head when he exposed the machinations of the Western European politicians who were trying to set Germany and the Soviet Union at loggerheads.

It must be confessed that there were some short-sighted people even in our own country who, carried away by oversimplified anti-fascist propaganda, forgot about this provocative work of our enemies. Mindful of this, Stalin even then suggested the possibility of other, unhostile, good-neighborly relations between Germany and the U.S.S.R. It can now be seen that on the whole Germany correctly understood these statements of Stalin and drew practical conclusions from them. . . . The conclusion of the Soviet-German Non-Aggression Pact shows that Stalin's historic pre-vision has been brilliantly confirmed. (*Loud applause*).

Voices are now heard testifying to the lack of understanding of the most simple reasons for the improvement of political relations between the Soviet Union and Germany which has begun. For example, people ask with an air of innocence how the Soviet Union could consent to improve political relations with a state of a fascist type. "Is that possible?" they ask. But they forget that this is not a question of our attitude towards the internal regime of another country but of the foreign relations between the two states. They forget that we hold the position of not interfering in the internal affairs of other countries and, correspondingly, of not tolerating interference in our own internal affairs. . . .

. . . In our foreign policy towards non-Soviet countries, we have always been guided by Lenin's well-known principle of the peaceful coexistence of the Soviet state and of capitalist countries. . . .

August 23, 1939, the day the Soviet-German Non-Aggression Pact was signed, is to be regarded as a date of great historical importance. The Non-Aggression Pact between the U.S.S.R. and Germany marks a turning point in the history of Europe, and not only of Europe. Only yesterday the German fascists were pursuing a foreign policy hostile to us. Yes, only yesterday we were enemies in the sphere of foreign relations. Today, however, the situation has changed and we are enemies no longer.

The art of politics in the sphere of foreign relations does not consist in increasing the number of enemies for one's country. On the contrary, the art of politics in this sphere is to reduce the number of such enemies and to make the enemies of yesterday good neighbors, maintaining peaceable relations with one another. . . .

CHAPTER THREE

The Expansion of Communism—Westward

In the critical years of World War II and its aftermath, Communist power moved beyond the boundaries of the USSR and became really international. In most instances, the essential characteristics of the movement remained as they had been fixed during the first decade of Stalinism in Russia, with unrelenting emphasis on industrialization and totalitarian controls. Soviet Russia went through this period with no structural change apart from further tightening of the control system, and Soviet norms were imposed on or accepted by foreign Communists as they came to power in Eastern Europe or the Far East.

In the expansion of Communism after World War II the nature of its appeal and the methods of acquiring power had become quite different from what the movement originally envisaged. Instead of leading a mass revolutionary upsurge the Communists won their new footholds either through wartime national resistance movements or in consequence of Soviet occupation and secret intrigue. Prior to the 1960's Communists came to power nowhere except in countries where the authority of the old rulers was actually dissolved in the course of the war. It was no longer the "proletarian revolution" but a military and police usurpation.

Russia in the Second World War

After the German invasion of the USSR in June, 1941, the Communist view of the world was once again revised. Stalin stressed that Russia was fighting a "patriotic war" to defend the sovereign rights of nations, and hailed the positive aspects of his American and British allies. Revolution was to all intents and purposes ignored.

a) Stalin on the Patriotic War

. . . In our country the German invaders, i.e., the Hitlerites, are usually called fascists. The Hitlerites, it appears, consider this wrong and obstinately persist in calling themselves "National-Socialists." Hence, the Germans are trying to assure us that the Hitler party, the party of German invaders, which is plundering Europe and has engineered this dastardly attack on our socialist country, is a socialist party. Is this possible? What can there be in common between socialism and the bestial Hitler invaders who are plundering and oppressing the peoples of Europe?

Can the Hitlerites be regarded as *nationalists*? No, they cannot. Actually, the Hitlerites are now not nationalists but *imperialists*. As long as the Hitlerites were

FROM: Stalin, Speech on the Twenty-Fourth Anniversary of the October Revolution, to the Moscow Soviet and Representatives of Moscow Party and Public Organizations, November 6, 1941 (English translation in Stalin, *On the Great Patriotic War of the Soviet Union*, Moscow, Foreign Languages Publishing House, 1954, pp. 35–37, 44–45).

engaged in assembling the German lands and reuniting the Rhine district, Austria, etc., there might have been some ground for calling them nationalists. But after they seized foreign territories and enslaved European nations—the Czechs, Slovaks, Poles, Norwegians, Danes, Netherlanders, Belgians, the French, Serbs, Greeks, Ukrainians, Byelorussians, the inhabitants of the Baltic countries, etc.—and began to reach out for world domination, the Hitler party ceased to be a nationalist party, for from that moment it became an imperialist, predatory, oppressor party.

The Hitler party is a party of imperialists, and of the most rapacious and predatory imperialists in the world at that.

Can the Hitlerites be regarded as *socialists*? No, they cannot. Actually, the Hitlerites are the sworn enemies of socialism, arrant reactionaries and Black-Hundreds,* who have robbed the working class and the peoples of Europe of the most elementary democratic liberties. In order to cover up their reactionary, Black-Hundred nature, the Hitlerites denounce the internal regime of Britain and America as a plutocratic regime. But in Britain and the United States there are elementary democratic liberties, there are trade unions of workers and other employees, there are workers' parties, there are parliaments; whereas in Germany, under the Hitler regime, all these institutions have been destroyed. One need but compare these two sets of facts to perceive the reactionary nature of the Hitler regime and the utter hypocrisy of the German fascist buncombe about a plutocratic regime in Britain and in America. In point of fact the Hitler regime is a copy of the reactionary regime which existed in Russia under tsarism. As we know, the Hitlerites suppress the rights of the workers, the rights of the intellectuals and the rights of nations as readily as the tsarist regime suppressed them; they organize medieval pogroms against the Jews as readily as the tsarist regime did.

The Hitler party is a party of enemies of democratic liberties, a party of medieval reaction and Black-Hundred pogroms. . . .

Lenin distinguished between two kinds of war—predatory, and therefore unjust wars, and wars of liberation, just wars.

The Germans are now waging a predatory war, an unjust war, aimed at seizing foreign territory and subjugating foreign peoples. That is why all honest people must rise against the German invaders, as against an enemy.

Unlike Hitler Germany, the Soviet Union and its Allies are waging a war of liberation, a just war, aimed at liberating the enslaved peoples of Europe and the U.S.S.R. from Hitler's tyranny. That is why all honest people must support the armies of the U.S.S.R., Great Britain, and the other Allies, as armies of liberation.

We have not, and cannot have, any such war aims as the seizure of foreign territories and the subjugation of foreign peoples—whether it be the peoples and territories of Europe or the peoples and territories of Asia, including Iran. Our first aim is to liberate our territories and our peoples from the German fascist yoke.

We have not, and cannot have, any such war aims as that of imposing our will and our regime upon the Slavonic or other enslaved nations of Europe, who are expecting our help. Our aim is to help these nations in the struggle for liberation they are waging against Hitler's tyranny and then to leave it to them quite freely to arrange their lives on their lands as they think fit. There must be no interference whatever in the internal affairs of other nations! . . .

---

*Black-Hundreds: term for violent right-wing groups in pre-revolutionary Russia—Ed.

b) Stalin on the Two Camps

. . . It may now be regarded as beyond dispute that in the course of the war imposed upon the nations by Hitlerite Germany, a radical demarcation of forces and the formation of two opposite camps have taken place: the camp of the Italo-German coalition, and the camp of the Anglo-Soviet-American coalition.

It is equally beyond dispute that these two opposite coalitions are guided by two different and opposite programmes of action.

The programme of action of the Italo-German coalition may be characterized by the following points: race hatred; domination of the "chosen" nations; subjugation of other nations and seizure of their territories; economic enslavement of the subjugated nations and spoliation of their national wealth; destruction of democratic liberties; universal institution of the Hitler regime.

The programme of action of the Anglo-Soviet-American coalition is: abolition of racial exclusiveness; equality of nations and inviolability of their territories; liberation of the enslaved nations and restoration of their sovereign rights; the right of every nation to manage its affairs in its own way; economic aid to war-ravaged nations and assistance in establishing their material welfare; restoration of democratic liberties; destruction of the Hitler regime. . . .

It is said that the Anglo-Soviet-American coalition has every chance of winning, and would certainly win if it did not suffer from an organic defect which might weaken and disintegrate it. This defect, in the opinion of these people, is that this coalition consists of heterogeneous elements having different ideologies, and that this circumstance will prevent them from organizing joint action against the common enemy.

I think that this assertion is wrong.

It would be ridiculous to deny the difference in the ideologies and social systems of the countries that constitute the Anglo-Soviet-American coalition. But does this preclude the possibility, and the expediency, of joint action on the part of the members of this coalition against the common enemy who threatens to enslave them? Certainly not. Moreover, the very existence of this threat imperatively dictates the necessity of joint action among the members of the coalition in order to save mankind from reversion to savagery and medieval brutality. Is not the programme of action of the Anglo-Soviet-American coalition a sufficient basis upon which to organize a joint struggle against Hitler tyranny and to vanquish it? I think it is quite sufficient. . . .

Dissolution of the Comintern

A specifically antirevolutionary gesture was the dissolution of the Communist International in May, 1943, ostensibly on the grounds that it no longer served the interests of the working-

FROM: Stalin, Speech on the Twenty-Fifth Anniversary of the October Revolution, to the Moscow Soviet and Representatives of Moscow Party and Public Organizations, November 6, 1942 (*On the Great Patriotic War of the Soviet Union*, pp. 87–88, 90–91).

FROM: Resolution of the Presidium of the Executive Committee of the Communist International, May 22, 1943, proposing the dissolution of the International (English translation in *The Strategy and Tactics of World Communism*, pp. 165–68).

class movement in different countries. Victory over Germany was made the supreme goal of the Communist movement. Nevertheless, postwar events were to show that Soviet authority over the Communist movement continued unabated, and that this authority could again turn the movement in the aggressive direction.

The historic rule of the Communist International, which was founded in 1919 as a result of a political union of the great majority of the old pre-war working-class parties, consisted in upholding the principles of the working-class movement, in helping to promote consolidation in a number of countries of the vanguard of the foremost workers in the real working-class parties, and in helping them mobilize workers for the defense of their economic and political interests, and for the struggle against Fascism and the war which the latter was preparing and for the support of the Soviet Union as the chief bulwark against Fascism.

The Communist International from the first exposed the real meaning of the Anti-Comintern Pact* as a weapon for the preparation of war by the Hitlerites. Long before the war it ceaselessly and tirelessly exposed the vicious, subversive work of the Hitlerites, who masked it by their screams about so-called interference of the Communist International in the internal affairs of these states.

But long before the war it became more and more clear that, with increasing complications in internal and international relations of various countries, any sort of international center would encounter insuperable obstacles in solving the problems facing the movement in each separate country.

Deep differences of the historic paths of development of various countries, differences in their character and even contradictions in their social orders, differences in the level and the tempo of their economic and political development, differences finally in the degree of consciousness and organization of workers, conditioned different problems affecting the working class of the various countries.

The whole development of events in the last quarter of a century and the experience accumulated by the Communist International convincingly showed that the organizational form of uniting workers chosen by the First Congress of the Communist International, answered conditions of the first stages of the working-class movement, but it has been outgrown by the growth of this movement and by the complications of its problems in separate countries and has even become a drag on the further strengthening of the national working class parties.

The World War that the Hitlerites have let loose has still further sharpened the differences in the situation of the separate countries and has placed a deep dividing line between those countries that fell under the Hitlerite tyranny and those freedom-loving peoples who have united in a powerful anti-Hitlerite coalition.

In countries of the Hitlerite bloc the fundamental task of the working class, toilers and all honest people consists in giving all help for the defeat of this bloc by sabotage of the Hitlerite military machine from within and by helping to overthrow the governments guilty of war.

In countries of the anti-Hitlerite coalition the sacred duty of the widest masses of the people, and in the first place of foremost workers, consists in aiding by every means the military efforts of the governments of these countries aimed at the

---

*Anti-Comintern Pact: treaty of alliance between Germany and Japan, 1936, later extended to include Italy and Germany's lesser allies; ostensibly directed against Communism—Ed.

speediest defeat of [the] Hitlerite bloc and the assurance of the friendship of nations based on their equality. . . .

. . . Taking into account the growth and the political maturity of Communist parties and their leading cadres in separate countries and also having in view the fact that during the present war some sections have raised the question of the dissolution of the Communist International as the directing center of the international working-class movement, the Presidium of the Executive Committee of the Communist International, in the circumstances of the World War, not being able to convene a Congress of the Communist International, puts forth the following proposal for ratification by the sections of the Communist International:

The Communist International, as the directing center of the international working-class movement, is to be dissolved, thus freeing the sections of the Communist International from their obligations arising from the statutes and resolutions of the Congresses of the Communist International.

The Presidium of the Executive Committee of the Communist International calls on all supporters of the Communist International to concentrate their energies on the whole-hearted support of and active participation in the war of liberation of the peoples and the states of the anti-Hitlerite coalition for the speediest defeat of the deadly enemy of the working class and toilers—German Fascism and its associates and vassals.

Guerrilla Revolution in Yugoslavia

In German-occupied Yugoslavia the Communist Party under Josip Broz Tito won a dominant place in the guerrilla resistance movement. These "Partisans" denounced the monarchy and fought its supporters, though for the time being they denied plans of Communist revolution. When Germany collapsed Yugoslavia was effectively under one-party Communist control, and the reorganization of the country's political and economic life rapidly followed.

a) The Jajce Assembly of the Anti-Fascist Council of National Liberation

(a) The so-called Yugoslav Government abroad is deprived of all the rights of a legal Government, as also of the rights of representing the peoples of Yugoslavia in foreign countries.

(b) King Peter II Karadjordjević is forbidden to return to the country until after the liberation of the entire country, when the problem of the king as well as the question of monarchy can be decided.

(c) It is recommended that the Anti-Fascist National Council should reexamine all international treaties or obligations undertaken by the so-called Yugoslav Government abroad.

(d) International treaties or obligations which may in future be contracted by the fugitive Yugoslav Government in the name of Yugoslavia and of her peoples will not be recognized.

FROM: Statement issued by the Second Assembly of the Anti-Fascist Council of National Liberation, Jajce (Bosnia), November 29, 1943 (English translation in *Free Europe*, December 31, 1943, p. 222; reprinted in *Documents on International Affairs, 1939–1946* (London, Royal Institute of International Affairs and Oxford University Press), Vol. II: "Hitler's Europe," p. 334).

b) Declaration by the National Liberation Committee of Yugoslavia

The National Liberation Movement, since the very beginning of our struggle against the occupier, endeavoured to unite all the national forces. The leaders of this movement always placed the cause of the liberation of the country from the barbarous Fascist invaders above all other interests of particular political and social groups and classes. For this reason, while the most sanguinary battles with the occupiers and their henchmen were raging, all efforts were made to enable those who love their people and freedom to assemble in one united front of national liberation. These efforts were crowned with success. A United Front of National Liberation, embracing a great majority of the population of Yugoslavia, became the basis of the armed resistance of the entire nation against the occupier, the basis on which the partisan detachments developed and the regular units of the Army of National Liberation of Yugoslavia were formed.

For over two and a half years the true forces of resistance in Yugoslavia witnessed with great bitterness how all the emigrant governments, one after the other, instead of helping the superhuman struggle of the peoples of Yugoslavia for the freedom of their country, stubbornly continued in their hostile attitude towards the National Liberation Movement, and through their Minister Draza Mihajlović waged an armed struggle against their own people at the side of the occupier. The peoples' representatives at the second session of the Anti-Fascist Council of November 29, 1943, in their resolutions condemned the treacherous work of the émigré governments and, expressing the strivings of all the peoples of Yugoslavia, issued historical resolutions on the creation of a federative democratic Yugoslavia.

The National Liberation Movement of Yugoslavia is in its essence a movement which has been endorsed by the entire people, and is both national and democratic. Therefore, we must emphasise once more that the leaders of the Movement of National Liberation of Yugoslavia have before them one single important aim: to fight against the occupiers and their lackeys and build up a federative democratic Yugoslavia, and not—as our enemies accuse us—the aim of introducing Communism.

Stalin's War Aims

Until the end of World War II Stalin expressed hope for permanent postwar cooperation with the United States and Britain. The menace of Germany still loomed far greater in his thinking than the prospects of Communist expansion. But when Soviet troops moved into the countries of Eastern Europe in 1944, the Soviet government began to maneuver local Communists into positions of power, ostensibly in the name of creating "friendly" and "democratic" regimes. With respect to Poland, Stalin made it clear to his allies at the time of the Yalta Conference that he intended to back the Communist-dominated "Committee of National Liberation" in opposition to the authority of the London government-in-exile, though he did promise free elections in the future.

FROM: Declaration by the National Liberation Committee of Yugoslavia, August, 1944 (English translation in *Free Europe*, September 8, 1944, p. 75; reprinted in *Documents on International Affairs, 1939–1946*, Vol. II: "Hitler's Europe," pp. 337–38).

FROM: Stalin, Speech on the Twenty-Seventh Anniversary of the October Revolution, to the Moscow Soviet and Representatives of Moscow Party and Public Organizations, November 6, 1944 (*On the Great Patriotic War of the Soviet Union*, pp. 200–205, 207–8).

a) On Germany and the World Order

. . . The past year has witnessed the triumph of the common cause of the anti-German coalition, for the sake of which the peoples of the Soviet Union, Great Britain, and the United States of America have united in a fighting alliance. . . .

. . . There is talk of disagreements among the three powers on certain questions concerning security. Of course there are disagreements, and there will be on a number of other questions too. Disagreements even exist among people who belong to the same party. How much more so must this be the case among representatives of different countries and different parties. The surprising thing is not that differences exist, but that there are so few, and that these are, as a rule, settled almost every time in a spirit of unity and coordination of action of the three Great Powers. It is not the disagreements that count, but the fact that they do not go beyond the limits dictated by the interests of unity among the three Great Powers, and that, in the final analysis, they are settled in conformity with the interests of this unity. It is common knowledge that more serious disagreements existed among us on the question of opening the second front. It is known, however, that, in the final analysis, these disagreements were settled in the spirit of complete harmony. . . .

Since the fighting alliance of the democratic countries has stood the test of over three years of war, and since this alliance is sealed with the blood of the people who have risen to defend their freedom and honour, there can be no doubt that it will stand the test of the concluding stage of the war. (Prolonged applause) . . .

To win the war against Germany means consummating a great historical cause. But winning the war does not yet mean ensuring the peoples a durable peace and reliable security in the future. The task is not only to win the war, but also to prevent the outbreak of fresh aggression and another war, if not for ever, then at least for a long time to come.

After her defeat Germany will, of course, be disarmed economically, as well as militarily and politically. It would be naive to think, however, that she will make no attempt to recuperate her strength and embark on new aggression. It is common knowledge that the German rulers are already making preparations for another war. History shows that quite a short period, a matter of twenty or thirty years, is sufficient to enable Germany to recover from defeat and recuperate her strength. What means are available to prevent fresh aggression on Germany's part and, if war breaks out nevertheless, to strangle it at the very outset and prevent it from developing into a big war? . . .

Apart from the complete disarming of aggressor nations there is only one means of achieving this: to set up a special organization consisting of representatives of the peaceful nations, for the protection of peace and for ensuring security; to place at the disposal of the leading body of this organization the minimum of armed forces necessary to prevent aggression; and to make it the duty of this organization to utilize these armed forces without delay, in the event of necessity, to prevent or liquidate aggression and punish those responsible for it.

This must not be a replica of the League of Nations of sad memory, which possessed neither the powers nor the means with which to prevent aggression. It will be a new, special, fully-empowered international organization, which will have at its

FROM: Stalin to President Roosevelt, December 27, 1944 (in *Foreign Relations of the United States: The Conferences at Malta and Yalta 1945* [U.S. House of Representatives Document No. 154, 84th Congress, 1st Session], Washington, Government Printing Office, 1955, pp. 221–22).

disposal all that is necessary for protecting peace and preventing fresh aggression.

Can we count on the activities of this international organization being sufficiently effective? They will be effective if the Great Powers who have borne the brunt of the burden of the war against Hitler Germany continue to act in a spirit of unanimity and harmony. They will not be effective if this essential condition is violated. . . .

b) On Poland

The Polish National Committee has made serious achievements in the strengthening of the Polish state and the apparatus of governmental power in the territory of Poland, in the expansion and strengthening of the Polish army, in carrying into practice of a number of important governmental measures and, in the first place, of the agrarian reform in favor of the peasants. All this has led to consolidation of democratic powers of Poland and to powerful strengthening of authority of the National Committee among the wide masses in Poland and among wide social Polish circles abroad.

It seems to me that now we should be interested in the support of the Polish National Committee and all those who want and are capable to work together with it and that is especially important for the Allies and for the solution of our common task—the speeding of the defeat of Hitlerite Germany. For the Soviet Union, which is bearing the whole burden for the liberation of Poland from German occupationists, the question of relations with Poland under present conditions is the task of daily close and friendly relations with a power which has been established by the Polish people on its own soil and which has already grown strong and has its own army which together with the Red Army is fighting against the Germans.

I have to say frankly that if the Polish Committee of National Liberation will transform itself into a Provisional Polish Government then, in view of the above-said, the Soviet Government will not have any serious ground for postponement of the question of its recognition. It is necessary to bear in mind that in the strengthening of a pro-Allied and democratic Poland the Soviet Union is interested more than any other power not only because the Soviet Union is bearing the main brunt of the battle for liberation of Poland but also because Poland is a border state with the Soviet Union and the problem of Poland is inseparable from the problem of security of the Soviet Union. To this we have to add that the successes of the Red Army in Poland in the fight against the Germans are to a great degree dependent on the presence of a peaceful and trustworthy rear in Poland, and the Polish National Committee fully takes into account this circumstance while the *émigré* government and its underground agents by their terroristic actions are creating a threat of civil war in the rear of the Red Army and counteract the success of the latter. . . .

The Yalta Conference

The meeting of Roosevelt, Churchill and Stalin at Yalta in the Crimea in February, 1945, is rightly considered the watershed between wartime collaboration and post-war confrontation

FROM: Protocol of the Proceedings of the Crimea Conference, February 11, 1945 (in *Foreign Relations of the United States: The Conferences at Malta and Yalta, 1945,* pp. 975, 977–80, 984).

between the Soviet Union and the Western powers. Roosevelt and Churchill made important concessions to Stalin regarding the Polish border, German reparations and Soviet influence in post-war Europe, while Stalin promised to support the creation of the United Nations and assist in the defeat of Japan—for a price.

The Crimea Conference of the Heads of the Governments of the United States of America, the United Kingdom, and the Union of Soviet Socialist Republics which took place from February 4th to 11th came to the following conclusions.

I. *World Organisation*

It was decided:
that a United Nations Conference on the proposed world organisation should be summoned for Wednesday, 25th April, 1945, and should be held in the United States of America. . . .

II. *Declaration on Liberated Europe*

The following declaration has been approved:
"The Premier of the Union of Soviet Socialist Republics, the Prime Minister of the United Kingdom and the President of the United States of America have consulted with each other in the common interests of the peoples of their countries and those of liberated Europe. They jointly declare their mutual agreement to concert during the temporary period of instability in liberated Europe the policies of their three governments in assisting the peoples liberated from the domination of Nazi Germany and the peoples of the former Axis satellite states of Europe to solve by democratic means their pressing political and economic problems.

"The establishment of order in Europe and the re-building of national economic life must be achieved by processes which will enable the liberated peoples to destroy the last vestiges of Nazism and Fascism and to create democratic institutions of their own choice. This is a principle of the Atlantic Charter—the right of all peoples to choose the form of government under which they will live—the restoration of sovereign rights and self-government to those peoples who have been forcibly deprived of them by the aggressor nations.

"To foster the conditions in which the liberated peoples may exercise these rights, the three governments will jointly assist the people in any European liberated state or former Axis satellite state in Europe where in their judgment conditions require (*a*) to establish conditions of internal peace; (*b*) to carry out emergency measures for the relief of distressed peoples; (*c*) to form interim governmental authorities broadly representative of all democratic elements in the population and pledged to the earliest possible establishment through free elections of governments responsive to the will of the people; and (*d*) to facilitate where necessary the holding of such elections. . . .

III. *Dismemberment of Germany*

It was agreed that Article 12(*a*) of the Surrender Terms for Germany should be amended to read as follows:
"The United Kingdom, the United States of America and the Union of Soviet Socialist Republics shall possess supreme authority with respect to Germany. In the

exercise of such authority they will take such steps, including the complete disarmament, demilitarisation and the dismemberment of Germany as they deem requisite for future peace and security."

The study of the procedure for the dismemberment of Germany was referred to a Committee, consisting of Mr. Eden (Chairman), Mr. Winant and Mr. Gousev. This body would consider the desirability of associating with it a French representative.

IV. *Zone of Occupation for the French and Control Council for Germany*

It was agreed that a zone in Germany, to be occupied by the French Forces, should be allocated to France. This zone would be formed out of the British and American zones and its extent would be settled by the British and Americans in consultation with the French Provisional Government.

It was also agreed that the French Provisional Government should be invited to become a member of the Allied Control Council for Germany.

V. *Reparation*

The following protocol has been approved:

1. Germany must pay in kind for the losses caused by her to the Allied nations in the course of the war. Reparations are to be received in the first instance by those countries which have borne the main burden of the war, have suffered the heaviest losses and have organised victory over the enemy.

2. Reparation in kind is to be exacted from Germany in three following forms:

a) Removals within 2 years from the surrender of Germany or the cessation of organised resistance from the national wealth of Germany located on the territory of Germany herself as well as outside her territory (equipment, machine-tools, ships, rolling stock, German investments abroad, shares of industrial, transport and other enterprises in Germany etc.), these removals to be carried out chiefly for purpose of destroying the war potential of Germany.

b) Annual deliveries of goods from current production for a period to be fixed.

c) Use of German labour.

3. For the working out on the above principles of a detailed plan for exaction of reparation from Germany an Allied Reparation Commission will be set up in Moscow. It will consist of three representatives—one from tke Union of Soviet Socialist Republics, one from the United Kingdom and one from the United States of America.

4. With regard to the fixing of the total sum of the reparation as well as the distribution of it among the countries which suffered from the German aggression the Soviet and American delegations agreed as follows:

"The Moscow Reparation Commission should take in its initial studies as a basis for discussion the suggestion of the Soviet Government that the total sum of the reparation in accordance with the points (*a*) and (*b*) of the paragraph 2 should be 20 billion dollars and that 50% of it should go to the Union of Soviet Socialist Republics."

The British delegation was of the opinion that pending consideration of the reparation question by the Moscow Reparation Commission no figures of reparation should be mentioned.

The above Soviet-American proposal has been passed to the Moscow Reparation Commission as one of the proposals to be considered by the Commission.

VI. *Major War Criminals*

The Conference agreed that the question of the major war criminals should be the subject of enquiry by the three Foreign Secretaries for report in due course after the close of the Conference.

VII. *Poland*

The following Declaration on Poland was agreed by the Conference:

"A new situation has been created in Poland as a result of her complete liberation by the Red Army. This calls for the establishment of a Polish Provisional Government which can be more broadly based than was possible before the recent liberation of the Western part of Poland. The Provisional Government which is now functioning in Poland should therefore be reorganised on a broader democratic basis with the inclusion of democratic leaders from Poland itself and from Poles abroad. This new Government should then be called the Polish Provisional Government of National Unity.

"M. Molotov, Mr. Harriman and Sir A. Clark Kerr are authorised as a commission to consult in the first instance in Moscow with members of the present Provisional Government and with other Polish democratic leaders from within Poland and from abroad, with a view to the reorganisation of the present Government along the above lines. This Polish Provisional Government of National Unity shall be pledged to the holding of free and unfettered elections as soon as possible on the basis of universal suffrage and secret ballot. In these elections all democratic and anti-Nazi parties shall have the right to take part and to put forward candidates.

"When a Polish Provisional Government of National Unity has been properly formed in conformity with the above, the Government of the U.S.S.R., which now maintains diplomatic relations with the present Provisional Government of Poland, and the Government of the United Kingdom and the Government of the U.S.A. will establish diplomatic relations with the new Polish Provisional Government of National Unity, and will exchange Ambassadors by whose reports the respective Governments will be kept informed about the situation in Poland.

"The three Heads of Government consider that the Eastern frontier of Poland should follow the Curzon Line with digressions from it in some regions of five to eight kilometres in favour of Poland. They recognise that Poland must receive substantial accessions of territory in the North and West. They feel that the opinion of the new Polish Provisional Government of National Unity should be sought in due course on the extent of these accessions and that the final delimitation of the Western frontier of Poland should thereafter await the Peace Conference." . . .

Agreement Regarding Entry of the Soviet Union Into the War Against Japan
TOP SECRET
AGREEMENT
The leaders of the three Great Powers—the Soviet Union, the United States of America and Great Britain—have agreed that in two or three months after Ger-

many has surrendered and the war in Europe has terminated the Soviet Union shall enter into the war against Japan on the side of the Allies on condition that:

1. The *status quo* in Outer-Mongolia (The Mongolian People's Republic) shall be preserved;

2. The former rights of Russia violated by the treacherous attack of Japan in 1904 shall be restored, viz:

(*a*) the southern part of Sakhalin as well as all the islands adjacent to it shall be returned to the Soviet Union,

(*b*) the commercial port of Dairen shall be internationalized, the preeminent interests of the Soviet Union in this port being safeguarded and the lease of Port Arthur as a naval base of the USSR restored,

(*c*) the Chinese-Eastern Railroad and the South-Manchurian Railroad which provides an outlet to Dairen shall be jointly operated by the establishment of a joint Soviet-Chinese Company it being understood that the preeminent interests of the Soviet Union shall be safeguarded and that China shall retain full sovereignty in Manchuria;

3. The Kuril islands shall be handed over to the Soviet Union.

It is understood, that the agreement concerning Outer-Mongolia and the ports and railroads referred to above will require concurrence of Generalissimo Chiang Kai-Shek. The President will take measures in order to obtain this concurrence on advice from Marshal Stalin.

The Heads of the three Great Powers have agreed that these claims of the Soviet Union shall be unquestionably fulfilled after Japan has been defeated.

For its part the Soviet Union expresses its readiness to conclude with the National Government of China a pact of friendship and alliance between the USSR and China in order to render assistance to China with its armed forces for the purpose of liberating China from the Japanese yoke.

I. STALIN
FRANKLIN D. ROOSEVELT
WINSTON S. CHURCHILL

FEBRUARY 11, 1945.

The Revival of International Communism

The Communist Party of the United States was an extreme example of the subordination of revolution to considerations of winning the war and assuring the peace. In May, 1945, Jacques Duclos, second-in-command of the French Communist Party, published an attack on Earl Browder's reformist perspective which led to Browder's replacement by William Z. Foster as the American Communist leader. This signaled the revival of militance throughout the international Communist movement.

The Teheran Conference [of Roosevelt, Churchill, and Stalin, December, 1943] served as Browder's point of departure from which to develop his conceptions favorable to a change of course in the American Communist Party. However, while justly stressing the importance of the Teheran Conference for victory in the war

FROM: Duclos, "On the Dissolution of the Communist Party of the United States," *Daily Worker*, May 24, 1945.

against fascist Germany, Earl Browder drew from the Conference decisions erroneous conclusions in no wise flowing from a Marxist analysis of the situation. Earl
Browder made himself the protagonist of a false concept of the ways of social evolution in general, and in the first place, the social evolution of the U.S.

Earl Browder declared, in effect, that at Teheran capitalism and socialism had
begun to find the means of peaceful co-existence and collaboration in the framework of one and the same world; he added that the Teheran accords regarding
common policy similarly pre-supposed common efforts with a view of reducing to
a minimum or completely suppressing methods of struggle and opposition of force
to force in the solution of internal problems of each country. . . .

The Teheran agreements mean to Earl Browder that the greatest part of Europe,
west of the Soviet Union, will probably be reconstituted on a bourgeois democratic
basis and not on a fascist-capitalist or Soviet basis.

"But it will be a capitalist basis which is conditioned by the principle of complete democratic self-determination for each nation, allowing full expression within
each nation of all progressive and constructive forces and setting up no obstacles to
the development of democracy and social progress in accordance with the varying
desires of the peoples. It means a perspective for Europe minimizing, and to a
great extent eliminating altogether, the threat of civil war after the international
war." . . .

And Earl Browder adds: "Whatever may be the situation in other lands, in the
United States this means a perspective in the immediate postwar period of
expanded production and employment and the strengthening of democracy within
the framework of the present system—and not a perspective of the transition to
socialism.

"We can set our goal as the realization of the Teheran policy, or we can set ourselves the task of pushing the United States immediately into socialism. Clearly,
however, we cannot choose both.

"The first policy, with all its difficulties, is definitely within the realm of possible
achievement. The second would be dubious, indeed, especially when we remember
that even the most progressive section of the labor movement is committed to capitalism, is not even as vaguely socialistic as the British Labor Party.

"Therefore, the policy for Marxists in the United States is to face with all its
consequences the perspective of a capitalist postwar reconstruction in the United
States, to evaluate all plans on that basis, and to collaborate actively with the most
democratic and progressive majority in the country, in a national unity sufficiently
broad and effective to realize the policies of Teheran." . . .

1. The course applied under Browder's leadership ended in practice in liquidation of the independent political party of the working class in the U.S.

2. Despite declarations regarding recognition of the principles of Marxism, one
is witnessing a notorious revision of Marxism on the part of Browder and his supporters, a revision which is expressed in the concept of a long-term class peace in
the United States, of the possibility of the suppression of the class struggle in the
postwar period and of establishment of harmony between labor and capital. . . .

Nationalization of monopolies actually in no sense constitutes a socialist
achievement, contrary to what certain people would be inclined to believe. No, in
nationalization it is simply a matter of reforms of a democratic character, achievement of socialism being impossible to imagine without preliminary conquest of
power.

Everyone understands that the Communists of the United States want to work to achieve unity in their country. But it is less understandable that they envisage the solution of the problems of national unity with the good will of the men of the trusts, and under quasi-idyllic conditions, as if the capitalist regime had been able to change its nature by some unknown miracle.

In truth, nothing justifies the dissolution of the American Communist Party, in our opinion. Browder's analysis of capitalism in the United States is not distinguished by a judicious application of Marxism-Leninism. The predictions regarding a sort of disappearance of class contradictions in the United States correspond in no wise to a Marxist-Leninist understanding of the situation. . . .

It is scarcely necessary to recall that the material bases for fascism reside in the trusts, and the great objective of this war, the annihilation of fascism, can only be obtained to the extent in which the forces of democracy and progress do not shut their eyes to the economic and political circumstances which engendered fascism.

The American Communists have an especially important role to play in the struggle taking place between the progressive forces of the earth and the fascist barbarism.

Without any doubt they would have been in a better position to play this role in the interests of their country and human progress if, instead of proceeding to dissolve their Party, they had done everything to strengthen it and make of it one of the elements of the assembling of the broad democratic masses of the United States for the final crushing of fascism, that shame of the 20th Century. It would be useless to hide the fact that fascism has more or less concealed sympathizers in the United States, as it has in France and other countries.

The Cold War

Stalin's pre-election speech of Feb. 9, 1946, has long been considered by Western policy makers and historians as a declaration of renewed revolutionary hostility against the capitalist West. His actual text, apart from a brief reminder of the Marxist theory of imperialist war, was mainly a self-congratulatory appraisal of Soviet success in World War II (see volume 1, p. 232). But following Winston Churchill's famous "Iron Curtain" speech at Fulton, Missouri, on March 5, Stalin flatly accused the West of plotting war on the Soviet Union.

a) Stalin's Pre-election Speech

Comrades!

Eight years have elapsed since the last election to the Supreme Soviet. This was a period abounding in events of decisive moment. The first four years passed in intensive effort on the part of Soviet men and women to fulfill the Third Five-Year Plan. The second four years embrace the events of the war against the German and Japanese aggressors, the events of the Second World War. Undoubtedly, the war was the principal event in the past period.

It would be wrong to think that the Second World War was a casual occurrence or the result of mistakes of any particular statesmen, though mistakes undoubtedly were made. Actually, the war was the inevitable result of the development of world economic and political forces on the basis of modern monopoly capitalism. Marx-

FROM: Stalin, Pre-election Speech of February 9, 1946 (English translation in *The Strategy and Tactics of World Communism*, pp. 168–70).

ists have declared more than once that the capitalist system of world economy har-
bors elements of general crises and armed conflicts and that, hence, the development
of world capitalism in our time proceeds not in the form of smooth and even progress but through crises and military catastrophes.

The fact is, that the unevenness of development of the capitalist countries usually leads in time to violent disturbance of equilibrium in the world system of capitalism, that group of capitalist countries which considers itself worse provided than
others with raw materials and markets usually making attempts to alter the situation and repartition the "spheres of influence" in its favor by armed force. The
result is a splitting of the capitalist world into two hostile camps and war between
them.

Perhaps military catastrophes might be avoided if it were possible for raw materials and markets to be periodically redistributed among the various countries in
accordance with their economic importance, by agreement and peaceable settlement. But that is impossible to do under present capitalist conditions of the development of world economy.

Thus the First World War was the result of the first crisis of the capitalist system
of world economy, and the Second World War was the result of a second crisis.

That does not mean of course that the Second World War is a copy of the first.
On the contrary, the Second World War differs materially from the first in nature.
It must be borne in mind that before attacking the Allied countries the principal
fascist states—Germany, Japan and Italy—destroyed the last vestiges of bourgeois
democratic liberties at home, established a brutal terrorist regime in their own
countries, rode roughshod over the principles of sovereignty and free development
of small countries, proclaimed a policy of seizure of alien territories as their own
policy and declared for all to hear that they were out for world domination and the
establishment of a fascist regime throughout the world.

Moreover, by the seizure of Czechoslovakia and of the central areas of China,
the Axis states showed that they were prepared to carry out their threat of enslaving all freedom-loving nations. In view of this, unlike the First World War, the
Second World War against the Axis states from the very outset assumed the character of an anti-fascist war, a war of liberation, one the aim of which was also the restoration of democratic liberties. The entry of the Soviet Union into the war against
the Axis states could only enhance, and indeed did enhance, the anti-fascist and liberation character of the Second World War.

It was on this basis that the anti-fascist coalition of the Soviet Union, the United
States of America, Great Britain and other freedom-loving states came into being—
a coalition which subsequently played a decisive part in defeating the armed forces
of the Axis states.

That is how matters stand as regards the origin and character of the Second
World War.

By now I should think everyone admits that the war really was not and could
not have been an accident in the life of nations, that actually this war became the
war of nations for their existence, and that for this reason it could not be a quick
lightning affair.

As regards our country, for it this war was the most bitter and arduous of all
wars in the history of our Motherland.

But the war was not only a curse. It was at the same time a great school in which all the forces of the people were tried and tested. The war laid bare all facts and events in the rear and at the front, it tore off relentlessly all veils and coverings which had concealed the true faces of the states, governments and parties and exposed them to view without a mask or embellishment, with all their shortcomings and merits.

The war was something like an examination for our Soviet system, for our State, for our Government, for our Communist Party, and it summed up the results of their work, saying to us as it were: "Here they are, your people and organizations, their deeds and their lives. Look at them well and reward them according to their deeds."

This was one of the positive aspects of war. . . .

b) Stalin's Reply to Churchill

A few days ago a *Pravda* correspondent approached Stalin with a request to clarify a series of questions connected with the speech of Mr. Churchill. Comrade Stalin gave clarifications, which are set out below in the form of answers to the correspondent's questions.

Q. How do you assess the last speech of Mr. Churchill which was made in the United States?

A. I assess it as a dangerous act calculated to sow the seed of discord among the Allied governments and hamper their cooperation.

Q. Can one consider that the speech of Mr. Churchill is damaging to the cause of peace and security?

A. Undoubtedly, yes. In substance, Mr. Churchill now stands in the position of a fire-brand of war. And Mr. Churchill is not alone here. He has friends not only in England but also in the United States of America.

In this respect, one is reminded remarkably of Hitler and his friends. Hitler began to set war loose by announcing his racial theory, declaring that only people speaking the German language represent a fully valuable nation. Mr. Churchill begins to set war loose also by a racial theory, maintaining that only nations speaking the English language are fully valuable nations, called upon to decide the destinies of the entire world.

In substance, Mr. Churchill and his friends in England and the United States present nations not speaking the English language with something like an ultimatum: "Recognize our lordship voluntarily and then all will be well. In the contrary case, war is inevitable."

But the nations have shed their blood during five years of cruel war for the sake of liberty and the independence of their countries, and not for the sake of exchanging the lordship of Hitler for the lordship of Churchill.

It is, therefore, highly probable that the nations not speaking English and which, however, make up an enormous majority of the world's population, will not consent to go into a new slavery. The tragedy of Mr. Churchill lies in the fact that he, as a deep-rooted Tory, cannot understand this simple and obvious truth.

There is no doubt that the set-up of Mr. Churchill is a set-up for war, a call to war with the Soviet Union. It is also clear that such a set-up as that of Mr. Chur-

FROM: Stalin, "Answer to *Pravda* Correspondent," *Pravda*, March 14, 1946 (English translation in *The New York Times*, March 14, 1946).

chill is incompatible with the existing treaty of alliance between England and the U.S.S.R. . . .

Q. How do you assess that part of Mr. Churchill's speech in which he attacks the democratic regime of the European countries which are our neighbors and in which he criticizes the good neighborly relations established between these countries and the Soviet Union?

A. This part of Mr. Churchill's speech is a mixture of the elements of libel with the elements of rudeness and lack of tact. Mr. Churchill maintains that Warsaw, Berlin, Prague, Vienna, Budapest, Belgrade, Bucharest and Sofia, all these famous cities and the populations of those areas, are within the Soviet sphere and are all subjected to Soviet influence and to the increasing control of Moscow.

Mr. Churchill qualifies this as the "boundless expansionist tendencies of the Soviet Union." It requires no special effort to show that Mr. Churchill rudely and shamelessly libels not only Moscow but also the above-mentioned states neighborly to the U.S.S.R.

To begin with, it is quite absurd to speak of the exclusive control of the U.S.S.R. in Vienna and Berlin, where there are Allied control councils with representatives of four States, where the U.S.S.R. has only one-fourth of the voices.

It happens sometimes that some people are unable to refrain from libel, but still they should know a limit.

Secondly, one cannot forget the following fact: the Germans carried out an invasion of the U.S.S.R. through Finland, Poland, Rumania, Bulgaria* and Hungary. The Germans were able to carry out the invasion through these countries by reason of the fact that these countries had governments inimical to the Soviet Union.

As a result of the German invasion, the Soviet Union has irrevocably lost in battle with the Germans, and also during the German occupation and through the expulsion of Soviet citizens to German slave labor camps, about 7,000,000 people. In other words, the Soviet Union has lost in men several times more than Britain and the United States together.

It may be that some quarters are trying to push into oblivion these sacrifices of the Soviet people which insured the liberation of Europe from the Hitlerite yoke.

But the Soviet Union cannot forget them. One can ask, therefore, what can be surprising in the fact that the Soviet Union, in a desire to ensure its security for the future, tries to achieve that these countries should have governments whose relations to the Soviet Union are loyal? How can one, without having lost one's reason, qualify these peaceful aspirations of the Soviet Union as "expansionist tendencies" of our Government? . . .

Mr. Churchill further maintains that the Communist parties were very insignificant in all these Eastern European countries but reached exceptional strength, exceeding their numbers by far, and are attempting to establish totalitarian countries everywhere; that police-government prevailed in almost all these countries, even up to now, with the exception of Czechoslovakia, and that there exists in them no real democracy. . . .

The growth of the influence of communism cannot be considered accidental. It is a normal function. The influence of the Communists grew because during the

---

*Stalin misspoke here: Bulgaria and the Soviet Union have no common border and were never officially at war until the Red Army occupied Bulgaria in 1944—Ed.

hard years of the mastery of fascism in Europe, Communists showed themselves to be reliable, daring and self-sacrificing fighters against fascist regimes for the liberty of peoples. . . .

It is they, millions of these common people, having tried the Communists in the fire of struggle and resistance to fascism, who decided that the Communists deserve completely the confidence of the people. Thus grew the Communists' influence in Europe. Such is the law of historical development.

Of course, Mr. Churchill does not like such a development of events. And he raised the alarm, appealing to force. But he also did not like the appearance of the Soviet regime in Russia after the First World War. Then, too, he raised the alarm and organized an armed expedition of fourteen states against Russia with the aim of turning back the wheel of history.

But history turned out to be stronger than Churchill's intervention and the quixotic antics of Churchill resulted in his complete defeat. I do not know whether Mr. Churchill and his friends will succeed in organizing after the Second World War a new military expedition against eastern Europe. But if they succeed in this, which is not very probable, since millions of common people stand on guard over the peace, then one man confidently says that they will be beaten, just as they were beaten twenty-six years ago.

The "People's Democracies"

Between 1945 and 1947 the local Communist parties were given positions of decisive political influence throughout Soviet-occupied Eastern Europe, although there were no mass upheavals and usually no overt overthrow of governments. The Hungarian-born Soviet economist Eugene Varga expounded the official explanation of these satellite states as transitional societies whose socialist direction was assured by the new quality of their governments.

One of the most important political results of the Second World War is the emergence of democratic states of a new type: Yugoslavia, Bulgaria, Poland, Czechoslovakia and, also, Albania.* We understand by a "democracy of a new type" a state of affairs in a country where feudal remnants—large-scale landowner-ship—have been eliminated, where the system of private ownership of the means of production still exists but large enterprises in the spheres of industry, transport and credit are in state hands, while the state itself and its apparatus of coercion serve not the interests of a monopolistic bourgeoisie but the interests of the working people in town and countryside.

The social structure of these states differs from all those hitherto known to us; it is something totally new in the history of mankind. It is neither a bourgeois dicta-torship nor a proletarian dictatorship. The old state apparatus has not been smashed, as in the Soviet Union, but re-organized by means of a continuous inclu-sion in it of the supporters of the new regime. They are not capitalist states in the ordinary sense of the word. Neither, however, are they Socialist states. The basis

FROM: Varga, "Democracy of a New Type" (English translation in *The Labour Monthly*, August–September, 1947; reprinted by permission).

*Varga fails to list Hungary and Rumania, and later on asserts erroneously that the new democracies were all Slavic.

for their transition to Socialism is given by the nationalization of the most important means of production and by the essential character of the state. They may, with the maintenance of the present state apparatus, gradually pass over to Socialism, developing to an ever-increasing extent the socialist sector which already exists side by side with the simple commodity sector (peasant and artisan) and the capitalist sector, which has lost its dominant position. . . .

The change in the character of the state—its transformation from a weapon of domination in the hands of the propertied classes into the state of the working people—this is what determines the real significance of the transfer of a decisive part of the means of production into the hands of the state in the countries of a democracy of a new type.

The change in the character of the state explains also why the influence of nationalization on the distribution of the national revenue is totally different in the democratic states of a new type from that in the bourgeois-democratic countries such as Great Britain.

Nationalization in the new democratic states signifies a special sort of economic revolution. The property of traitors to the country, of fascist capitalists, was confiscated without compensation. Other big capitalists received compensation, but their income after compensation was only a small part of the surplus value which they previously appropriated. . . .

The second important feature of the economies of the countries of democracy of a new type is the complete and final elimination of large-scale landlordism, of this feudal survival inside the capitalist system of economy. The social and political power of the big landowners, dating back a thousand years, has been destroyed. The big landed properties were confiscated by the state and distributed among peasants having little land and landless agricultural laborers. The number of peasant households (i.e., private owners of land) increased very considerably in these countries.

The division of the lands among many hundreds of thousands of peasants who had little or no land has converted the overwhelming majority of these peasants into loyal supporters of the new regime. The mistake made by the Hungarian Communists in 1919, when they wanted to leap over an essential historical stage by converting the confiscated large landed properties into state farms, instead of dividing them up among the peasants and so satisfying the land hunger, has nowhere been repeated.

The cultivation of land by the peasants using their own resources and giving them the opportunity of selling their produce on the market (in some countries only after fulfilling tax payments and deliveries to the state) make possible the preservation or re-emergence of commodity capitalist relations in the economy of the country. As Lenin pointed out, "Small-scale production engenders capitalism and the bourgeoisie continuously, daily, hourly, spontaneously and on a mass scale."

Thus, the social order in the states of democracy of a new type is not a socialist order, but a peculiar, new, transitional form. The contradiction between the productive forces and relations of production becomes mitigated in proportion as the relative weight of the socialist sector increases. . . .

As regards the class struggle, however, there exists a difference in principle between the states of democracy of a new type and the old bourgeois countries. In the old bourgeois countries the state is a weapon of domination in the hands of the propertied classes. The entire state apparatus—officials, judges, police and as a last resort, the standing army—is on the side of the propertied classes.

The opposite is to be seen in the countries of new democracy. Here the state protects the interests of the working people against those who live by appropriating surplus value. When conflicts arise the armed forces of the State are to be found, not on the side of the capitalists, but on the side of the workers. . . .

In this connection an important theoretical question arises: the idea was widely held in the Communist parties that the political domination of the working people, as is the case in the Soviet Union, could only be realized in the form of soviet power. This is not correct, nor is it an expression of Lenin's opinion. . . .

The rise of the states of new democracy shows clearly that it is possible to have political rule by the working people even while the outward forms of parliamentary democracy are still maintained. . . .

It is equally understandable that these countries maintain close, friendly relations with the Soviet Union. This is so not only because it was precisely the victorious troops of the Soviet Union that liberated their countries (Yugoslavia being, in part, an exception) from German occupation, and not only because they are all Slav states, but primarily because the present social order brings them close to the Soviet Union, because of all the great powers the Soviet Union alone is interested in the maintenance and further progressive development of the social order and political regime existing in these countries and can afford them diplomatic support against the reactionary offensive from outside.

The Soviet Union is at the same time interested in the maintenance by these countries of the existing regime and their further development in a progressive direction. The present regime in these countries provides the guarantee that they will not, in the future, again voluntarily serve as a *place d'armes* for any power which tries to attack the Soviet Union. . . .

The Cominform

By 1947 the Communist international line had become aggressively anti-Western. A new international Communist center, the so-called "Communist Information Bureau," was organized to link the Communist parties of the Soviet Union and the East European states together with the two powerful Western Communist parties, the French and Italian. Speaking at the founding conference of the Cominform, Zhdanov recast the Communist view of World War II and represented the current world situation as a bitter contest between the "socialist camp" and "American imperialism."

The end of the Second World War brought with it big changes in the world situation. The military defeat of the bloc of fascist states, the character of the war as a war of liberation from fascism, and the decisive role played by the Soviet Union in the vanquishing of the fascist aggressors sharply altered the alignment of forces between the two systems—the Socialist and the Capitalist—in favour of Socialism.

What is the essential nature of these changes?

FROM: Zhdanov, Report on the International Situation, at the Founding Conference of the Communist Information Bureau in Poland, September, 1947 (English translation in *The Strategy and Tactics of World Communism*, pp. 212–216, 219, 222–24, 228–29).

The principal outcome of World War II was the military defeat of Germany and Japan—the two most militaristic and aggressive of the capitalist countries. The reactionary imperialist elements all over the world, notably in Britain, America and France, had reposed great hopes in Germany and Japan, and chiefly in Hitler Germany: firstly as in a force most capable of inflicting a blow on the Soviet Union in order to, if not having it destroyed altogether, weaken it at least and undermine its influence; secondly, as in a force capable of smashing the revolutionary labour and democratic movement in Germany herself and in all countries singled out for Nazi aggression, and thereby strengthening capitalism generally. This was the chief reason for the pre-war policy of "appeasement" and encouragement of fascist aggression, the so-called Munich policy consistently pursued by the imperialist ruling circles of Britain, France, and the United States.

But the hopes reposed by the British, French, and American imperialists in the Hitlerites were not realized. The Hitlerites proved to be weaker, and the Soviet Union and the freedom-loving nations stronger than the Munichists had anticipated. As a result of World War II the major forces of bellicose international fascist reaction had been smashed and put out of commission for a long time to come.

This was accompanied by another serious loss to the world capitalist system generally. Whereas the principal result of World War I had been that the united imperialist front was breached and that Russia dropped out of the world capitalist system, and whereas, as a consequence of the triumph of the Socialist system in the U.S.S.R., capitalism ceased to be an integral, world wide economic system, World War II and the defeat of fascism, the weakening of the world position of capitalism and the enhanced strength of the anti-fascist movement resulted in a number of countries in Central and Southeastern Europe dropping out of the imperialist system. In these countries new, popular, democratic regimes arose. . . .

The war immensely enhanced the international significance and prestige of the U.S.S.R. The U.S.S.R. was the leading force and the guiding spirit in the military defeat of Germany and Japan. The progressive democratic forces of the whole world rallied around the Soviet Union. The socialist state successfully stood the strenuous test of the war and emerged victorious from the mortal struggle with a most powerful enemy. Instead of being enfeebled, the U.S.S.R. became stronger. . . .

. . . America's aspirations to world supremacy encounter an obstacle in the U.S.S.R., the stronghold of anti-imperialist and anti-fascist policy, and its growing international influence, in the new democracies, which have escaped from the control of Britain and American imperialism, and in the workers of all countries, including America itself, who do not want a new war for the supremacy of their oppressors. Accordingly, the new expansionist and reactionary policy of the United States envisages a struggle against the U.S.S,R., against the labour movement in all countries, including the United States, and against the emancipationist, anti-imperialist forces in all countries.

Alarmed by the achievements of Socialism in the U.S.S.R., by the achievements of the new democracies, and by the post-war growth of the labour and democratic movement in all countries, the American reactionaries are disposed to take upon themselves the mission of "saviours" of the capitalist system from Communism.

The frank expansionist program of the United States is therefore highly reminiscent of the reckless program, which failed so ignominiously, of the fascist aggressors, who, as we know, also made a bid for world supremacy.

Just as the Hitlerites, when they were making their preparations for piratical aggression, adopted the camouflage of anti-Communism in order to make it possible to oppress and enslave all peoples and primarily and chiefly their own people, America's present-day ruling circles mask their expansionist policy, and even their offensive against the vital interests of their weaker imperialist rival, Great Britain, by fictitious considerations of defense against Communism. The feverish piling up of armaments, the construction of new military bases and the creation of bridge-heads for the American armed forces in all parts of the world is justified on the false and pharisaical grounds of "defence" against an imaginary threat of war on the part of the U.S.S.R. . . .

Soviet foreign policy proceeds from the fact of the co-existence for a long period of the two systems—capitalism and socialism. From this it follows that co-operation between the U.S.S.R. and countries with other systems is possible, provided that the principle of reciprocity is observed and that obligations once assumed are honoured. Everyone knows that the U.S.S.R. has always honoured the obligations it has assumed. The Soviet Union has demonstrated its will and desire for co-operation. . . .

In their ideological struggle against the USSR, the American imperialists, who have no great insight into political questions, demonstrate their ignorance by laying primary stress on the allegation that the Soviet Union is undemocratic and totalitarian, while the United States and Great Britain and the whole capitalist world are democratic. On this platform of ideological struggle—on this defence of bourgeois pseudo-democracy and condemnation of Communism as totalitarian—are united all the enemies of the working class without exception, from the capitalist magnates to the Right Socialist leaders, who seize with the greatest eagerness on any slanderous imputations against the USSR suggested to them by their imperialist masters. The pith and substance of this fraudulent propaganda is the claim that the earmark of true democracy is the existence of a plurality of parties and of an organized opposition minority. On these grounds the British Labourites, who spare no effort in their fight against Communism, would like to discover antagonistic classes and a corresponding struggle of parties in the USSR. Political ignoramuses that they are, they cannot understand that capitalists and landlords, antagonistic classes, and hence a plurality of parties, have long ceased to exist in the USSR. They would like to have in the USSR the bourgeois parties which are so dear to their hearts, including pseudo-socialistic parties, as an agency of imperialism. But to their bitter regret these parties of the exploiting bourgeoisie have been doomed by history to disappear from the scene. . . .

One of the lines taken by the ideological campaign that goes hand in hand with the plans for the enslavement of Europe is an attack on the principle of national sovereignty, an appeal for the renouncement of the sovereign rights of nations, to which is opposed the idea of a world government. The purpose of this campaign is to mask the unbridled expansion of American imperialism which is ruthlessly violating the sovereign rights of nations, to represent the United States as a champion of universal laws, and those who resist American penetration as believers in obsolete and selfish nationalism. The idea of a world government has been taken up by bourgeois intellectual cranks and pacifists, and is being exploited not only as a means of pressure, with the purpose of ideologically disarming the nations that defend their independence against the encroachments of American imperialism, but also as a slogan specially directed against the Soviet Union, which indefatigably and consistently upholds the principle of real equality and protection of the sovereign rights of all nations, big and small. Under present conditions imperialist countries like the USA, Great Britain and the states closely associated with them become dangerous enemies of national independence and the self-determination of nations, while the Soviet Union and the new democracies are a reliable bulwark against encroachments on the equality and self-determination of nations. . . .

The Truman doctrine, which provides for the rendering of American assistance to all reactionary regimes which actively oppose the democratic peoples, bears a frankly aggressive character. . . .

The vague and deliberately guarded formulations of the Marshall Plan amount in essence to a scheme to create a bloc of states bound by obligations to the United States, and to grant American credits to European countries as a recompense for their renunciation of economic, and then of political, independence. Moreover, the cornerstone of the Marshall Plan is the restoration of the industrial areas of Western Germany controlled by the American monopolies. . . .

The dissolution of the Comintern, which conformed to the demands of the development of the labour movement in the new historical situation, played a positive role. The dissolution of the Comintern once and for all disposed of the slanderous allegation of the enemies of Communism and the labour movement that Moscow was interfering in the internal affairs of other states, and that the Communist Parties in the various countries were acting not in the interests of their nations, but on orders from outside. . . .

But the present position of the Communist Parties has its shortcomings. Some comrades understood the dissolution of the Comintern to imply the elimination of all ties, of all contact, between the fraternal Communist Parties. But experience has shown that such mutual isolation of the Communist Parties is wrong, harmful and, in point of fact, unnatural. . . .

The Communist Coup in Czechoslovakia

Increasing East-West tension was reflected in the breakdown of the last case of Communist—non-Communist cooperation, when the Communists took over full power in Czechoslovakia in February, 1948. Communist moves to cement their control over the police provoked the protest resignations of the anti-Communist cabinet ministers, and the Communists took advantage of this to form a new government which, with the support of Social-Democrats manipulated by crypto-Communists in their leadership, was able to command a parliamentary majority. The new regime immediately began to destroy all organized opposition and complete the nationalization of the economy. When the Communist premier Gottwald spoke in justification of the coup shortly afterwards, he illustrated the new Communist appeal to all the "people" against the "reactionaries," whom he identified with the enemies of the nation. At the same time he made it clear that all political organizations in the country would be "regenerated"—i.e., converted into auxiliaries of the Communist dictatorship. Gottwald's report was approved unanimously by the now rubber-stamp National Assembly.

Honourable Members of the Constituent National Assembly! On February 20th, 1948, the members of the government representing the National Socialist,

FROM: Gottwald, "Program of Action of the New Czechoslovak Government" (Speech to the Constituent National Assembly, March 10, 1948; English translation in Gottwald, *Selected Speeches and Articles, 1929–53*, Prague, Orbis, 1954, pp. 158, 160, 162–66, 171–73).

the Catholic People's and the Slovak Democratic Parties handed in their resignations. Thereby an open government *crisis was provoked.* On the 25th of February, 1948, the President of the Republic accepted the resignations of these members of the government and sanctioned our proposals for the reconstruction of the government. Thus the government crisis was overcome. Today the newly formed government comes before the Constituent National Assembly with a declaration of its programme. By approving of this government declaration, the Constituent National Assembly will have confirmed the solution of the government crisis also in *a parliamentary manner.* . . .

During the occupation . . . it became more and more clear that, after the Germans, their Czech and Slovak helpmates had also to be chased from power, and that their power must be gripped at the roots, which were their great possessions, amassed through long years of exploitation of the people. In short, it had become clear that *in the liberated Republic it was the people that must wield the decisive power. Not on paper, but in fact.*

And so, after the liberation of Czechoslovakia by the glorious Soviet Army, we nationalized banking and the heavy and big industries; we transferred the Germans from our country and delivered the soil, the banks and the factories, which had formerly belonged to them, not into the hands of Czech and Slovak capitalists, but into the hands of Czech and Slovak peasants, workers and tradesmen, into the hands of the nation; we did away with the bureaucratic police-state system, and by the setting up of National Committees we placed our public administration in the hands of the people; we did not allow the revival of the pre-Munich reactionary political parties, which were simply the tools of the Czech and Slovak bourgeoisie; and the Government of the National Front was formed, as the executive of the union of workers, peasants, tradesmen, and the intelligentsia. By these various means the former ruling class was ousted from political power, and was hit in its weakest spot, its property. *And in the new people's democracy the principle that the people is the source of all power began to be put into practice.* . . .

Reactionaries who had misused their economic position to enrich themselves once again and who had gained complete control in several parties of the former National Front so that by their help they directly entered the government—these reactionaries decided on a frontal attack upon the people's democratic regime. The *immediate* aim of reaction was to bring about a realignment of forces in the government and in the whole state before the elections, because they feared defeat in the elections. The *ultimate* aim of reaction was, however, completely to overthrow the people's democratic order, to take from the people all that the liberation and national revolution had brought them, to return to former owners what had been nationalized, and to reinstate the absolute power of the big and powerful masters. As regards *foreign policy,* reaction wanted to separate us from the Soviet Union and our other allies and link up the Republic once more with those who have Munich on their conscience. . . .

On the surface, it was just a case of eight officials of the National Security Corps in Prague being removed from their jobs. In reality, the attack of reaction was being concentrated against the whole of the state security service. These gentlemen reckoned on getting the national Security Corps again into reactionary hands, again under reactionary leadership and, as a result, on being able to use the Security Corps against the people as it was used in the unhappy time before Munich. . . .

The overwhelming majority of the people understood clearly that here it was a question of a dangerous attempt to overthrow the people's democratic regime and to bring to nothing all that the people had gained from the liberation. That is why such a storm of anger and resistance was raised by the people, which swept through the Republic from the Bohemian Forest to the Tatras between February 20th and 25th, and which tumbled down the sinister plans of reaction like a house of cards. . . .

I should like to emphasize that the following measures will have to be taken before the elections:

A state organization set up for all *domestic wholesale trade*, and a state organization for *export and import trade*.

The *nationalization* of all capitalist enterprises employing more than 50 persons, and the complete nationalization of certain branches in which the public interest demands this change.

These measures are necessary first and foremost on *economic* grounds. They will ensure that tens of milliards of crowns' worth of values which were previously drained away from the national income and misused partly for purposes harmful to the nation are preserved for the nation, for the community. These measures are also necessary for reasons of *state policy*. The sector in which further nationalization is to be introduced was and is a hot-bed of subversive intrigues, and it is here that the roots of the government crisis of last February are to be found. These roots of anti-state and anti-popular plotting must be torn out. And they *will* be torn out!

Finally, we must also draw the political conclusions from the February crisis. I have already said that certain parties in the former National Front fell completely into the hands of reaction and were its tools. I have said that the reconstructed government is an expression of the *regenerated* National Front. To this I must expressly add that the component parts of the regenerated National Front can only be *regenerated* political parties and non-party organizations. The agents of reaction must be *unconditionally* removed from these parties and organizations! We are under an obligation to our people in town and country to put this into effect. We are under an obligation to the nation and to the Republic to put this into effect. We are in duty bound to do so if we want to guarantee a peaceful and free development, as well as the independence of our Republic.

This purge of our public life is now going on. It is being carried out by the Action Committees of the National Front which have spontaneously arisen. This purge must not take the form of political revenge; still less must it be a series of campaigns to settle personal accounts. The Central Committee of the National Front has given clear directions to this effect, and the government will co-operate with it in seeing that they are carried out. In a task of this kind it is not possible to prevent a certain amount of encroachments and misunderstandings. I therefore solemnly declare that where such have occurred, they will be put right again. But I declare equally solemnly: We shall not stop half-way! The infiltration of agents of reaction into leading positions in our public life must be stopped and any repetition of their penetration prevented. Our common people do not want February 1948 to be repeated some months later.

The February storm has also cleared the horizon as far as our *foreign policy* is concerned. The lengths to which our reactionaries went in this direction, misusing as they did freedom of speech and of the printed word, exceeded all bounds. By systematic indictment against our allies, they undermined our international position and so threatened the security, indeed the very foundations of the existence of our Republic. This state of affairs has now been ended. It can no longer appear that the foreign policy of the Republic is falling between two chairs. Let it be said to all sides that Czechoslovakia is and will remain a true and dependable member of the Slav family, and that she also feels herself to be an ally of the other People's Democracies. . . .

The Berlin Blockade and the Division of Germany

The Cold War reached its most acute point in 1948 when four-power administration of Germany broke down and the Soviets tried to force the Western powers to abandon their occupation sectors in West Berlin by cutting off all ground communication across the Soviet zone of East Germany. The memorable Berlin Airlift kept the city supplied until the Soviets lifted the blockade in the spring of 1949. By that time plans were well under way on both sides to set up separate German governments in the West and the East—the German Federal Republic and the Soviet-dominated German Democratic Republic, respectively.

The decisions adopted at the Yalta and Potsdam conferences, as well as the agreement of the four powers on the control machinery in Germany, set as their aim the demilitarization and democratization of Germany, undermining the very basis of German militarism, and prevention of the revival of Germany as an aggressive power, and hence, the conversion of Germany into a peace-loving and democratic state. These agreements stipulate Germany's obligation to pay reparations and thus, even if only partially, to compensate for the damage done to countries that suffered from German aggression.

In accordance with these agreements, the governments of the four powers accepted the responsibility for administering Germany and undertook to determine jointly the status of Germany or of any areas, including Berlin, that are part of the German territory, and conclude a peace treaty with Germany which should be signed by a democratic government of Germany adequate for the purpose.

The highly important agreements by the four powers in relation to Germany have been violated by the Governments of the United States of America, Great Britain, and France. Measures for the demilitarization of Germany have not been completed and such an important center of German war industry as the Ruhr region has been removed from the control of the four powers. Fulfillment of the decision on reparations from the Western zones of occupation of Germany has been disrupted by the Governments of the United States of America, Great Britain, and France. The quadripartite council has ceased to function.

Since the London conference of the three powers with the participation of the Benelux countries, measures are being carried out by the Governments of the United States of America, Great Britain, and France aimed at splitting and dismembering Germany, including the preparation now taking place for the appointment of a separate government for the Western zones of Germany and the separate currency reform carried out June 18 of this year for the Western zones of occupation. . . .

The Soviet Government must reject as altogether unfounded the declaration of

FROM: Soviet note to the U.S. Government, July 14, 1948 (*The New York Times*, July 15, 1948).

the Government of the United States of America to the effect that measures for restricting transport and communications between Berlin and the Western zones of occupation of Germany, introduced by the Soviet command to protect the economy of the Soviet zone from disorganization, allegedly constitute a violation of existing agreements relating to the administration of Berlin. . . .

The Government of the United States declares that temporary measures introduced by the Soviet command for restricting transport and communications between Berlin and the Western zones created difficulties in the supply of the Berlin population in the Western sectors.

It cannot, however, be denied that these difficulties were caused by the actions of the Governments of the United States, Great Britain, and France and, above all, by their separate actions in introducing a new currency in the Western zones of Germany and a special currency in the Western sectors of Berlin.

Berlin is in the center of the Soviet zone and is part of that zone.

The interests of the Berlin population do not admit to a situation where there has been introduced into Berlin, or even only into the Western sectors of Berlin, a currency that is not in circulation in the Soviet zone. Moreover, the introduction of a separate currency reform in the Western zones of Germany placed Berlin, and with it the entire Soviet zone of occupation, in a position where the entire mass of currency notes invalidated by the Western zones threatened to pour into Berlin and into the Soviet occupation zone of Germany.

The Soviet command was compelled, therefore, to adopt urgent measures to safeguard the interest of the population as well as the economy of the Soviet zone of occupation and the area of "Greater Berlin." . . .

The Soviet-Yugoslav Break

In June, 1948, the solid front of Communist states was broken by the expulsion of Yugoslavia from the Cominform. By resisting Soviet control the Yugoslav Communists incurred charges of un-Marxist deviation, and despite their professions of orthodoxy were read out of the movement. Tito's position, however, was geographically and politically strong enough for him to hold out against Soviet pressure.

a) The Cominform Resolution

. . . The leaders of the Communist Party of Yugoslavia have taken a stand unworthy of Communists, and have begun to identify the foreign policy of the Soviet Union with the foreign policy of the imperialist powers, behaving toward the Soviet Union in the same manner as they behave to the bourgeois states. Precisely because of this anti-Soviet stand, slanderous propaganda about the "degeneration" of the CPSU (B), about the "degeneration" of the USSR, and so on, borrowed from the arsenal of counterrevolutionary Trotskyism, is current within the Central Committee of the Communist Party of Yugoslavia.

The Information Bureau denounces this anti-Soviet attitude of the leaders of the Communist Party of Yugoslavia, as being incompatible with Marxism-Leninism and only appropriate to nationalists.

FROM: Resolution of the Communist Information Bureau, June 28, 1948, "Concerning the Situation in the Communist Party of Yugoslavia" (English translation in *The Soviet-Yugoslav Dispute*, London, Royal Institute of International Affairs, 1948, pp. 62–63, 68–70).

In home policy, the leaders of the Communist Party of Yugoslavia are departing from the positions of the working class and are breaking with the Marxist theory of classes and class struggle. They deny that there is a growth of capitalist elements in their country, and consequently, a sharpening of the class struggle in the countryside. This denial is the direct result of the opportunist tenet that the class struggle does not become sharper during the period of transition from capitalism to socialism, as Marxism-Leninism teaches, but dies down, as was affirmed by opportunists of the Bukharin type, who propagated the theory of the peaceful growing over of capitalism into socialism.

The Yugoslav leaders are pursuing an incorrect policy in the countryside by ignoring the class differentiation in the countryside and by regarding the individual peasantry as a single entity, contrary to the Marxist-Leninist doctrine of classes and class struggle, contrary to the well-known Lenin thesis that small individual farming gives birth to capitalism and the bourgeoisie continually, daily, hourly, spontaneously and on a mass scale. Moreover, the political situation in the Yugoslav countryside gives no grounds for smugness and complacency. In the conditions obtaining in Yugoslavia, where individual peasant farming predominates, where the land is not nationalized, where there is private property in land, and where land can be bought and sold, where much of the land is concentrated in the hands of kulaks, and where hired labour is employed—in such conditions there can be no question of educating the Party in the spirit of glossing over the class struggle and of reconciling class contradictions without by so doing disarming the Party itself in face of the difficulties connected with the construction of socialism. . . .

. . . The Information Bureau unanimously concludes that by their anti-Party and anti-Soviet views, incompatible with Marxism-Leninism, by their whole attitude and their refusal to attend the meeting of the Information Bureau, the leaders of the Communist Party of Yugoslavia have placed themselves in opposition to the Communist Parties affiliated to the Information Bureau, have taken the path of seceding from the united Socialist front against imperialism, have taken the path of betraying the cause of international solidarity of the working people, and have taken up a position of nationalism.

The Information Bureau condemns this anti-Party policy and attitude of the Central Committee of the Communist Party of Yugoslavia.

The Information Bureau considers that, in view of all this, the Central Committee of the Communist Party of Yugoslavia has placed itself and the Yugoslav Party outside the family of the fraternal Communist Parties, outside the united Communist front and consequently outside the ranks of the Information Bureau.

The Information Bureau considers that the basis of these mistakes made by the leadership of the Communist Party of Yugoslavia lies in the undoubted fact that nationalist elements, which previously existed in a disguised form, managed in the course of the past five or six months to reach a dominant position in the leadership of the Communist Party of Yugoslavia, and that consequently the leadership of the Yugoslav Communist Party has broken with the international traditions of the Communist Party of Yugoslavia and has taken the road of nationalism.

Considerably overestimating the internal, national forces of Yugoslavia and their influence, the Yugoslav leaders think that they can maintain Yugoslavia's independence and build socialism without the support of the Communist Parties of other countries, without the support of the people's democracies, without the support of the Soviet Union. They think that the new Yugoslavia can do without the help of these revolutionary forces.

Showing their poor understanding of the international situation and their intimidation by the blackmailing threats of the imperialists, the Yugoslav leaders think that by making concessions they can curry favor with the Imperialist states. They think they will be able to bargain with them for Yugoslavia's independence and, gradually, get the people of Yugoslavia oriented on these states, that is, on capitalism. In this they proceed tacitly from the well-known bourgeois-nationalist thesis that "capitalist states are a lesser danger to the independence of Yugoslavia than the Soviet Union."

The Yugoslav leaders evidently do not understand or, probably, pretend they do not understand, that such a nationalist line can only lead to Yugoslavia's degeneration into an ordinary bourgeois republic, to the loss of its independence and to its transformation into a colony of the imperialist countries.

The Information Bureau does not doubt that inside the Communist Party of Yugoslavia there are sufficient healthy elements, loyal to Marxism-Leninism, to the international traditions of the Yugoslav Communist Party and to the united socialist front.

Their task is to compel their present leaders to recognize their mistakes openly and honestly and to rectify them; to break with nationalism, return to internationalism; and in every way to consolidate the united socialist front against imperialism.

Should the present leaders of the Yugoslav Communist Party prove incapable of doing this, their job is to replace them and to advance a new internationalist leadership of the Party.

The Information Bureau does not doubt that the Communist Party of Yugoslavia will be able to fulfill this honourable task.

b) The Yugoslav Reply

In connection with the publication of the Resolution of the Information Bureau, the Central Committee of the Communist Party of Yugoslavia makes the following statement:

1. The criticism contained in the Resolution is based on inaccurate and unfounded assertions and represents an attempt to destroy the prestige of the CPY both abroad and in the country, to arouse confusion amongst the masses in the country and in the international workers' movement, to weaken the unity within the CPY and its leading role. . . .

2. The Resolution maintains, without citing any proof, that the leadership of the CPY carried out a hostile policy towards the USSR. The statement that Soviet military specialists in Yugoslavia have been treated with scant respect, and that Soviet civilian citizens have been under the surveillance of state security agents, does not in the least correspond to the truth. . . .

On the contrary, it is correct, as stated in the letter to the CC of the CPSU of 13 April, and based on numerous reports of members of the CPY to their Party organizations as well as on statements of other citizens of our country, that from

FROM: Statement of the Central Committee of the Communist Party of Yugoslavia on the Resolution of the Communist Information Bureau on the Situation in the Communist Party of Yugoslavia, June 29, 1948 (*The Soviet-Yugoslav Dispute*, pp. 73-75, 78-79).

the liberation up to date the Soviet intelligence service sought to enroll them. The CC of the CPY considered and considers that such an attitude towards a country where the Communists are the ruling party and which is advancing toward socialism is impermissible. . . .

4. The CC of the CPY cannot but reject with deep indignation the assertions that the leading ranks in the CPY are deviating to the course of a kulak party, to the path of the liquidation of the Communist Party of Yugoslavia, that there is no democracy in the Party, that methods of military leadership are fostered within the Party, that the most basic rights of Party members are trampled upon by the Party and that the mildest criticism of irregularities in the Party is answered by sharp reprisals, etc. Could the members of the Party who dauntlessly faced death in thousands of battles, tolerate in the Party a state of affairs unworthy of both men and Communists? The assertion that criticism is not allowed in the Party and similar statements are a terrible insult to every member of our Party, a degradation of the heroic and glorious past of the Party and its present heroic struggle for the reconstruction and development of the country. . . .

8. . . . The Information Bureau has committed a breach of the principles on which it was based and which provide for the voluntary adoption of conclusions by every Party. The Information Bureau, however, not only forces the leaders of the CPY to admit errors which they did not commit but also calls members of the CPY to rebellion within the Party, to shatter the unity of the Party. The CC of the CPY can never agree to a discussion about its policy on the basis of inventions and uncomradely behaviour without mutual confidence. Such a basis is not one of principle and in this and only in this sense the CC of the CPY considered that it was not on an equal footing in the discussion and that it could not accept discussion on that basis. Further, in connection with the above, the CC of the CPY resolutely rejects the accusation that the CPY has passed on to positions of nationalism. By its entire internal and foreign policy, and especially by its struggle during the national liberation war and the proper solution of the national question in Yugoslavia, the CPY has given proof of the exact opposite.

By the above-mentioned unjust charges, the greatest historical injustice has been done to our Party, our working class and working masses, the peoples in Yugoslavia in general and their unselfish and heroic struggle. . . .

The CC of the CPY calls upon the Party membership to close their ranks in the struggle for the realization of the Party line and for even greater strengthening of Party unity, while it calls upon the working class and other working masses, gathered in the People's Front, to continue to work even more persistently on the building of our socialist homeland. This is the only way, the only method to prove in full and by deeds the unjustness of the above-mentioned charges.

National Communism

The Soviet-Yugoslav break was quickly followed by political crises in the other East European satellite states, as the Russians moved to crush potential independent-mindedness among the local Communist leaders. In Poland, Wladyslaw Gomulka, General Secretary of the Polish United Workers (i.e., Communist) Party was ousted after being forced to admit a "right-nationalist deviation," and spent the years from 1951 to 1956 in jail or under house arrest. In Hungary and Bulgaria in 1949 and in Czechoslovakia in 1952 show trials of former Communist leaders were staged on the model of the Moscow Trials of 1936–38.

The indictment of László Rajk, formerly Minister of the Interior and Minister of Foreign Affairs in Hungary, illustrates the charges of plotting and espionage leading to the execution of the national Communists. In most cases (including Rajk) the victims were posthumously "rehabilitated" in 1956 during Khrushchev's de-Stalinization campaign.

a) Poland—Gomulka's Confession

Today's plenum is being held under the banner of struggle with the right-nationalist deviation in the leadership of the party, and under the banner of self-criticism by those comrades who in their political consciousness acknowledge the commission of the mistakes which contributed to the occurrence of this deviation. I wish to speak, comrades, about my own mistakes which I made in the period just past, mistakes which must be assessed not only as to their content, but also in the light of the fact that I committed them at a time when I held the position of General Secretary of the Party. . . .

I realize, comrades, that my position was an expression of disbelief in the revolutionary forces of the working class, that its sources went deep, that it is one further expression of the right deviation, that it is an expression of the Social-Democratic, opportunistic tendencies which developed in me to the greatest degree just at that time of crisis, at that turning point in history.

My actual attitude regarding the issue of group, collective work on the farms expressed what the resolution of the Political Bureau defines as an orientation toward automatism,* since I had no other conception. To that conception of the road to socialism I could not counterpose any other conception. I recoiled and shielded myself from the conception of the reconstruction of the village on the basis of collective farms, by rejecting it as premature for our conditions. Therefore automatism was actually manifested in my attitude, leaving agriculture to develop by itself—let it develop spontaneously in any way it will. Now I realize that such automatism would lead to the steady growth of the capitalist sector in our economy. I realize now that such automatism would quickly lead to the growth of the class of rich farmers and capitalism in the village, that leaving the village on the path of automatic development would lead to ideological distortions in our Party, would simply lead to our Party failing to promote or even have any other conception—it would actually rest on the basis of the conception of capitalist enterprise in the agricultural, peasant sector. I realize that this automatism would consequently lead in practice to the restoration of capitalistic relationships not only in the agricultural sector but equally in the sector of industry, in the urban sector. Therefore I also understand now that it was right and necessary to put forth the perspective of collective farming, without waiting for the maturation of the base of production, the technical cadres or the cadres of specialists, either here or anywhere else. This had to be affirmed, comrades, in order to realize just what is our Polish road to socialism of which we have spoken so often. I am not quite prepared today—these matters do not seem clear enough to me—to indicate the elements of the Polish road to socialism. It seems to me that it would be incorrect to assert that

FROM: Gomulka, Speeches at the Plenum of the Central Committee of the Polish United Workers' Party, September, 1948 (*Nowe Drogi* [New Roads], September-October, 1948, pp. 40–42, 50, 141–44; editor's translation with the assistance of Yvonne Starcheska).

*I.e., letting nature take its course—Ed.

in general there is no Polish road, that there is only one mold, one such method. After all, conditions are different; at present we are living in another period of history; collectivization was carried out in the Soviet Union in another period of history, under other conditions, in another situation with another pattern of class forces—and we will carry out the reconstruction of the village under other conditions. So therefore there must be some elements of a Polish road to socialism. . . .

I understand that the tendencies toward separating our Polish road from the Soviet experience and practice are completely false. Without studying this practice, without an intimate connection between our road and the Soviet road there is no question that we would fall into new error in this sector.

Nowhere in the world outside the Soviet Union has socialism been built, and nowhere in the world has any party had, nor can it have, such practice and such experience as the CPSU. Therefore it would also be entirely false even to think that there is some wholly different conception, some other means of solving the problem of agricultural production, the problems of building socialism. I also understand that the distinctiveness of our road does not mean its absolute differentiation from the Soviet road. I have been helped to understand this problem by my comrades' severe criticism and their indication of the necessity of the class struggle which we must carry through, for which we must mobilize the Party, mobilize the working class and the masses of the poor peasantry. In reaching the correct position on this question I was aided by my comrades' criticism.

Please, comrades, it is clear that the core of the right-nationalist complex of which I speak was of necessity my attitude toward the Soviet Union, toward the CPSU. I have examined myself more than once from this point of view, and I admit that in actual practice my attitude reduced not so much to the party relationship between the CPSU and the PPR [Polish Worker's Party], but rather to the governmental relationship between Poland and the USSR, a good, friendly relationship of allies, but only the governmental and not the party relationship. I never conceived that Poland could step forward on the road to socialism, that it could assure the development of its people and its government, its independence, its sovereignty, without the support of the Soviet Union. I understood these things, although it was difficult for me—as I often appreciated intellectually—to demonstrate my attitude toward the Soviet Union in practice, particularly on the ideological and party plane.

I will do everything possible to root out my underestimation of the actual role of the USSR, an underestimation which was an expression of tendencies of nationalistic provincialism. I want to demonstrate this in practice, and not only in words, so that in this way I will contribute to the realization of the goals and intentions which have inspired me. . . .

b) Hungary—The Rajk Trial

At the end of May, 1945, László Rajk returned to Hungary. He succeeded in concealing his past and playing the part of a much-persecuted Communist, steeled in the Spanish struggle. He rose to be the secretary of the Greater Budapest district

FROM: Indictment of László Rajk, September, 1949 (English translation in *Hungary: László Rajk and his Accomplices before the People's Court, Budapest*, 1949; extracts reprinted in *Documents on International Affairs*, 1949–50, pp. 390–91, 395).

of the Hungarian Communist Party, a member of the National Assembly, Minister of Home Affairs and finally Minister of Foreign Affairs. Naturally he continued his old activities. About this he admitted in his statement: "I regularly and constantly informed the American intelligence agents of every question that cropped up in the Ministry of Home Affairs and later in the Ministry of Foreign Affairs."

American intelligence in Hungary gave increasing prominence to the Yugoslav spies of the foreign espionage services, the envoys of Tito. Foully abusing the fraternal sympathy of Hungarian democracy with the working people of Yugoslavia, Tito's diplomatic representatives and other official envoys built up their net of espionage with the greatest effrontery from the moment they first set foot on Hungarian soil at the beginning of 1945. First of all they recruited László Rajk for their service, as they were acquainted with his past as police informer and spy. . . .

László Rajk, as cabinet minister and member of the National Assembly, that is, as a public servant, grossly abusing his official position, gave secrets to foreign powers which seriously endangered the interests of the Hungarian state; by so doing he committed the crimes of espionage and sedition.

The coming into prominence of the Yugoslav spies was connected with the fact that American spies, *agents provocateurs*, and Trotskyists like Rajk himself had come into power in liberated Yugoslavia. The Gestapo had sent, from French internment camps alone, 150 of these people to Yugoslavia for espionage work at the same time as Rajk himself had been sent home. These spies formed the bulk of the circle around Tito and they systematically forced back the honest elements among the Yugoslav partisans, those who were true to their people. Encouraged by this success, the American imperialists set themselves no smaller target than, with the assistance of Tito and company, to attempt to bring the countries of the people's democracies over to their side. Rajk said of this: "Rankovich, Yugoslav Minister of Home Affairs, told me squarely that the people's democracies must unite under the leadership of Yugoslavia and Tito.". . .

About Hungary Rajk said in his statement, "Very soon after this Tito was to begin an intensive campaign against the leaders of the Hungarian government and state. They were to accuse Rakosi* of revisionism† to say that under his leadership the Hungarian government attempted to annex territories peopled by Hungarians. Having thus created differences between the Hungarian and Yugoslav people they were at the appropriate moment to raise the issue in the Yugoslav Parliament. This action was to be followed by frontier incidents for which Yugoslav would make Hungary responsible."

According to the plan proposed by Rankovich, these frontier incidents would serve the purpose of giving a formal pretext to Yugoslavia for violent military intervention against Hungary, for the armed occupation of part of Hungarian territory. This intervention was to take place at a time when the Soviet Union would be occupied by being involved in some sort of international complication. Part of the armed military action would be for sections of the Yugoslav Army to be sent across the frontier wearing Hungarian uniforms. The plan also provided for the invasion of Hungary by gendarmes, arrow-cross men and Horthyists** in Hungarian uni-

*Mátyás Rákosi: deputy premier and actual dictator of Hungary, 1947–53 and 1955–56—Ed.

†Evidently in the sense of "revising" the country's boundaries—Ed.

**Arrow Cross: pre-1945 Hungarian fascist organization; Admiral Nicholas Horthy: Regent of Hungary, 1920–1945—Ed.

form—all collected in the British and American occupation zones and passing through Yugoslav territory.

The plan involved the physical liquidation of some of the ministers of the Hungarian government, first of all, of Mátyás Rákosi, [Minister of Defense] Mihaly Farkas and Ernö Gerö [president of the economic council].

Yugoslav Communism

To defend themselves against Cominform denunciations after their expulsion in 1948, the Yugoslav Communists looked for Marxist arguments against the USSR, and began to remodel their own system to distinguish it from Stalinism. A leading role in stating their theoretical case against the "bureaucratic" and "imperialist" distortions of socialism in the Soviet Union was taken by Vice-President Milovan Djilas. Particular reforms that followed aligned Yugoslavia with the Soviet model of the NEP, including a decentralized economy, private farming and a measure of intellectual freedom. Touted above all was the principle of "workers' self-management" through nominally elected councils (reminiscent of the Workers' Opposition in Russia in 1920–21), which Tito made the cornerstone of his independent Communist ideology.

a) The Critique of Stalinsim

. . . Taking as a point of departure the economic laws of development toward communism, Marx and Lenin foresaw two dangers threatening the triumphant working class in socialism: from the overthrown bourgeoisie on the one hand and its own bureaucracy on the other. It was not accidental that Marx asked that civil service employees be elected and that only for a certain period of time, after which they were to go into production. Engels and Lenin emphasized often that with the change in economic relations, that is, with the liquidation of private capitalist ownership over the means of production, changes in political relationships do not come about immediately, easily and automatically. The development of dictatorship of the proletariat, socialist democracy, can therefore go in two directions: in the direction of its own disappearance to the extent that socialism itself strengthens, or in the direction of strengthening and transformation of bureaucracy into a privileged caste which lives at the expense of society as a whole. . . .

The development of production forces in the Soviet Union has reached a point where social relations no longer correspond to it. Neither does the method of management of the process of production itself or the method of distribution of the goods produced. The classic antagonism between productive forces and relationships in production has arisen. But this antagonism in the Soviet Union is not the same as that in earlier class social formations, for the relationships of property are different than they were then. Although we have there the existence of capitalist, and even precapitalist remnants, they do not play an essential role in social development, for property relationships have been destroyed and it is on these that remnants could base their further development. This is therefore a new historical phenomenon in which new, socialist relationships of ownership and new development of production forces no longer suit the method of management of that property itself and the production forces themselves.

Let us see the forms in which this process appears: introduction of unequal rela-

FROM: Djilas, *On New Roads of Socialism* (Speech at a pre-election rally of Belgrade students, March, 1950; English edition, Belgrade, Jugoslovenska Knjiga, 1950, pp. 8–12, 17–18).

tions and exploitation of other socialist countries; un-Marxist treatment of the role of the leaders which often takes the shape of even vulgar historical falsifications and idolatries similar to those in absolute monarchies; differences in pay which are greater than in bourgeois bureaucracies themselves, ranging from 400 to 15,000 rubles; ideological promotion of Great-Russian nationalism and underestimation and subordination of the role, culture and history of other peoples; a policy of division of spheres of influence with the capitalist states; monopolization of the interpretation of Marxist ideology and the tactics of the international working class movement; introduction of lying and slandering methods into the working-class movement; neglect of study of Marx, Engels and Lenin, and especially their premises about the laws of the transition period and communist society; underestimation of the role of consciousness—especially the consciousness of the masses—in the struggle for a new society; tendencies toward actual liquidation of socialist democracy and transforming it into a mere form; rendering impossible a struggle of opinions and putting brakes on the initiative of the masses, that is, the basic productive forces, and by that very fact productive forces in general; revision of the philosophical foundations of Marxism, etc., etc. Seeing all this, drawing conclusions from the conflict between the Central Committee of the Communist Party of the Soviet Union and the Soviet Government and the Central Committee of the Yugoslav Communist Party and the Yugoslav Government and seeking theoretical explanations both of the phenomenon and practice, many comrades pose the question whence such phenomena, in every way characteristic of class formations; what do they mean and why must they exist in socialism? Further, where, actually, are the roots of these phenomena? Is what is taking place in the Soviet Union some new kind of class society, is it state capitalism, or "deviations" within socialism itself?

. . . The basis which is the point of departure (socialist revolution and dictatorship of the proletariat, nationalization of capitalist property and struggle for socialist construction) is the same here and in the USSR. Both here and there, these bases are progressive as beginnings. But the tendencies of development, which came about as the result of different general historic conditions and dissimilar conditions in both countries, are unlike. There we see the creation of a privileged bureaucratic stratum, bureaucratic centralism, temporary transformation of the state into "a force above society." (Some of the reasons for this are the fact that the USSR was for a long time the only socialist country, that it was backward, surrounded by capitalism, that the masses had a relatively weak conscious role in the struggle for socialist building and that there were relatively weak foreign and internal revolutionary forces.) Here, in our country, there is also a tendency toward domination by bureaucracy for, as we see in Marx, it is a law that this becomes a danger, a necessarily conditioned phenomenon, a necessary remnant of the old class society in the struggle for the creation of a new classless society. But here, these tendencies will not and cannot win, because historical conditions are different, because the relationship of forces, which changes in struggle every day, is different, because the tendencies of development are different—toward accelerating the decrease of the role of bureaucracy, toward giving greater initiative to the masses and actual power (to put it that way) to the direct producers in the process of production. . . .

. . . Bureaucratic elements in the USSR, who have frozen their privileged position, are attempting to find the solution to the internal crisis in the outside world, that is, to hush it temporarily by foreign successes, by exploitation and subordination of other socialist countries. And since methods of exploitation and subordination of peoples in the contemporary world, which is divided and in which the world market is still dominated by capitalism, can only be capitalistic, they inevitably appear as a struggle for spheres of influence and as a brake to the further development of socialism, as a struggle for the victory of socialism, only there, to that extent and in that form that suits the narrow, hegemonistic interests of that privileged stratum. That is why what is directly advantageous to that stratum becomes, for it, theoretically true and justified. Thence the ever broader and more ruthless orientation toward Great-Russian nationalism, the backwardness of the masses and their obscure instincts, inherited from the past, which were always stimulated and appealed to by the bourgeoisie. But this has a new, different character here—the character of bureaucratic, imperialistic expansion and domination by the bureaucracy of one nation over other nations. Reliance on historic nationalistic backwardness, in the given conditions, is possible only for the biggest nations where these remnants are the strongest precisely because it has long been the ruling nation. Thence subjective idealism—despite its materialistic and dialectic phraseology—in the philosophy and science of the USSR, which is unfolding on the basis of untrue and undialectic proclamations to the effect that there are no more internal contradictions there. It is on this erroneous basis that their scientific methodology and practice is founded and it must substitute apologetics for scientific work, and routine for revolutionary practice. . . .

b) Workers' Self-Management

The Federal Assembly is today considering the draft of one of the most important bills in socialist Yugoslavia—the bill on management of state economic enterprises and higher economic associations by the workers. The adoption of this bill will be the most significant historic act of the Federal Assembly next to the Law of Nationalization of the Means of Production. When the state took over the means of production, that still did not mean fulfillment of the action slogan of the working-class movement—"the factories for the workers." The mottoes "the factories for the workers" and "the land for the peasants" are not abstract propaganda slogans, but mottoes which have deep meaning. They contain the entire program of socialist relations in production, in regard to social ownership, in regard to the rights and duties of working people. Therefore, they can be and they must be realized in practice if we are really to build socialism. . . .

Today, the Soviet leaders and all the servile leaders of other communist parties are disputing our revolution, our hard struggle. They are not only trying to deny that we are Marxists and that we are building socialism, but they also say that we are fascists. There is no length to which they have not gone in blackening our name. This is simply the most ordinary kind of unethical propaganda worthy of fascist mouthpieces of the type of Goebbels and others. . . .

. . . The essence of our road to socialism . . . can be defined in a few words:

FROM: Tito, *Workers Manage Factories in Yugosavia* (Speech to the Yugoslav Federal Assembly, April, 1950; English edition, Belgrade, Yugostampa, 1950, pp. 9, 13, 22, 24–25, 29–30, 36, 41–42).

our road to socialism consists in the application of Marxist science to the given stage, in the closest possible harmony with the specific conditions existing in our country. For us, that science is not a dogma but a means of leadership, a means for orientation in every concrete situation, regardless of how complicated it may be. We are endeavoring to introduce the spirit of that science into everything we do, for we are deeply convinced that this is correct. It has turned out in practice that the principles of this science are correct, thanks to the brilliant scientific forecasts of our great teachers. And in the present stage of international development, they are fully valid. Any departure from these principles under any excuse whatsoever would mean revision and betrayal of not only the working class but all progressive mankind. . . .

How do things look in the Soviet Union thirty-one years after the October Revolution? The October Revolution made it possible for the state to take the means of production into its hands. But these means are still, after 31 years, in the hands of the state. Has the slogan "the factories for the workers" been put into practice? Of course not. The workers still do not have any say in the management of the factories. They are managed by directors who are appointed by the state, that is, by civil service employees. The workers only have the possibility and the right to work but this is not very different from the role of the workers in capitalist countries. The only difference for workers is that there is no unemployment in the Soviet Union, and that is all. Therefore, the leaders of the Soviet Union have not, so far, put through one of the most characteristic measures of a socialist state, that of turning over the factories and other economic enterprises to the workers so that they may manage them. . . .

. . . After the Second World War, when a whole series of new socialist states emerged in the proximity of the Soviet Union, there could no longer be any question of the capitalist encirclement of the Soviet Union. To say that the functions of the state as an armed force, not only of the army but also the so-called punitive organs, are directed only outwards means talking with no connection with reality, just as it has no connection with the present situation in the Soviet Union. What is the tremendous bureaucratic, centralistic apparatus doing? Are its functions directed outwards? Who deports millions of citizens of various nationalities to Siberia and the Far North? Can anyone claim that these are measures against the class enemy, can anyone say that whole nations are a class to be destroyed? Who is obstructing the struggle of opinions in the Soviet Union? Is not all this being done by one of the most centralized, most bureaucratic state apparatuses, which bears no resemblance whatsoever to a state machine that is withering away? Stalin is right in one thing here if it is applied to the present period and that is that this state machine really has functions regarding the outside world. But this must be added, too—that these functions are aimed where they are necessary and where they are not. They are directed at interfering in the internal affairs of other countries and against the will of people of those countries. Therefore, these are least of all the functions of a socialist state that is withering away but rather resemble the functions of an imperialist state machine which is fighting for spheres of influence and the subjugation of other peoples. . . .

By turning over the factories, mines, etc., to the workers to manage, we will make it impossible for an infectious disease to take hold there, a disease bearing the name of bureaucracy. This disease is unbelievably easily and rapidly carried over from bourgeois society and it is dangerous in the transition period. Like a polyp with thousands of tentacles it obstructs and impedes the correct and rapid process of development. Bureaucracy is among the biggest enemies of socialism precisely because it insinuates itself unnoticed into all the pores of social activity and people are not conscious of it in the beginning. It would be erroneous to think that bureaucracy has not taken root in our country, too. It has begun worming its way into various institutions, into the state apparatus and into the economy, but we are conscious of that and have already undertaken a whole series of measures to render it impossible. It is not enough simply to undertake periodical drives against it but to wage incessant struggle and to educate people. . . .

From now on, the state ownership of the means of production—factories, mines, railways—is passing gradually on to a higher form of socialist ownership. State ownership is the lowest form of social ownership and not the highest, as the leaders of the USSR consider it to be. Therein lies our road to socialism and that is the only right road as regards the withering away of state functions in the economy. Let the Cominformists remember that their slanderous hue and cry cannot obscure the correctness of our building of socialism.

On the other hand, this bill on the participation of working collectives, of our working people, in the management of the economy of our country is the best answer to the question of where there is true democracy—here in our country, or in the much praised and lauded western democracy. In our country, democracy is based on a material basis for the broadest masses of working people. It is felt by the masses, they are making use of it to build a better and happier future for all the working people of our country. . . .

Stalin on the Inevitability of War

In his last theoretical pronouncement Stalin argued that while war might still break out among capitalist countries, the Soviet Union could avoid involvement.

It is said that the contradictions between capitalism and socialism are stronger than the contradictions among the capitalist countries. Theoretically, of course, that is true. It is not only true now, today; it was true before the Second World War. And it was more or less realized by the leaders of the capitalist countries. Yet the Second World War began not as a war with the U.S.S.R., but as a war between capitalist countries. Why? First, because war with the U.S.S.R., as a socialist land, is more dangerous to capitalism than war between capitalist countries; for whereas war between capitalist countries puts in question only the supremacy of certain capitalist countries over others, war with the U.S.S.R. must certainly put in question the existence of capitalism itself. Secondly, because the capitalists, although they clamour, for "propaganda" purposes, about the aggressiveness of the Soviet Union, do not themselves believe that it is aggressive, because they are aware of the Soviet Union's peaceful policy and know that it will not itself attack capitalist countries. . . .

. . . When the United States and Britain assisted Germany's economic recovery, they did so with a view to setting a recovered Germany against the Soviet Union, to

FROM: Stalin, *Economic Problems of Socialism in the USSR* (English edition, Moscow, Foreign Languages Publishing House, 1952, pp. 39–41).

utilizing her against the land of socialism. But Germany directed her forces in the first place against the Anglo-French-American bloc. And when Hitler Germany declared war on the Soviet Union, the Anglo-French-American bloc, far from joining with Hitler Germany, was compelled to enter into a coalition with the U.S.S.R. against Hitler Germany.

Consequently, the struggle of the capitalist countries for markets and their desire to crush their competitors proved in practice to be stronger than the contradictions between the capitalist camp and the socialist camp.

What guarantee is there, then, that Germany and Japan will not rise to their feet again, will not attempt to break out of American bondage and live their own independent lives? I think there is no such guarantee.

But it follows from this that the inevitability of wars between capitalist countries remains in force.

It is said that Lenin's thesis that imperialism inevitably generates war must now be regarded as obsolete, since powerful popular forces have come forward today in defence of peace and against another world war. That is not true.

The object of the present-day peace movement is to rouse the masses of the people to fight for the preservation of peace and for the prevention of another world war. Consequently, the aim of this movement is not to overthrow capitalism and establish socialism—it confines itself to the democratic aim of preserving peace. In this respect, the present-day peace movement differs from the movement of the time of the First World War for the conversion of the imperialist war into civil war, since the latter movement went farther and pursued socialist aims.

It is possible that in a definite conjuncture of circumstances the fight for peace will develop here or there into a fight for socialism. But then it will no longer be the present-day peace movement; it will be a movement for the overthrow of capitalism. . . .

CHAPTER FOUR

The Expansion of Communism—Eastward

The rise and triumph in the 1940's of Communism in China together with its counterparts elsewhere in Asia initially appeared to be an even more decisive gain for Moscow's influence than the expansion of Soviet control into Eastern Europe. Mao Tse-tung's victory seemed to bear out the theory of imperialism as a revolt of the backward and exploited East against the capitalist West. Nevertheless the success of Communism in China, in a large country with a different culture and very different conditions, and under the leadership of the one Communist Party which Moscow had not succeeded in controlling, entailed a new challenge to the unity of the Russia-centered movement.

The Chinese Communist path to power, as a peasant guerrilla movement waging a war of national resistance against the Japanese from 1937 to 1945 and a civil war against Chiang Kai-shek's Nationalist government from 1946 to 1949, was anomalous from the Marxist standpoint because it was not based on the working class and lacked a definite class struggle except that of peasants against landlords. The pattern, copied by other Far Eastern Communist movements, was to mobilize any available social groups under the discipline of the Communist Party by appealing to nationalistic and anti-imperialist emotions, and to develop a substitute "proletariat" not by social selection but by ideological "remolding." Here Communism approached most closely to the qualities of a militant religious faith, culminating in the bizarre episode of the Cultural Revolution of the late 1960's.

Mao's War Aims

By the end of World War II the Communist position in China was greatly strengthened, thanks to the widespread peasant guerrilla movement which the Communist Party had built behind the Japanese lines in North China. This made the party a major contender for power. In April, 1945, Mao outlined the coalition regime which he expected for China after the defeat of Japan, but he made it clear that it would be led by the Communists and exclude the Kuomintang. It was, in effect, to be the application of his "New Democracy."

. . . A decisive victory has been scored in the sacred and just war against fascist aggressors throughout the world; the time is near for the Chinese people to defeat the Japanese invaders in collaboration with our Allies; but China, still hard pressed by the Japanese invaders, is not yet united and a grave crisis still exists in China. In such circumstances, what should we do? Indubitably, what China urgently needs is the establishment, through uniting all political parties and groups and non-partisan leaders, of a democratic, provisional coalition government, so that democratic

FROM: Mao, "On Coalition Government" (April, 1945; Brandt, Schwartz, Fairbank, pp. 295–96, 299–302, 305–06, 311–14).

reforms may be instituted, the present crisis overcome, all anti-Japanese forces mobilized and united for the defeat of the Japanese invaders in effective collaboration with our Allies, and the Chinese people liberated from the hands of the Japanese. . . .

The leading ruling clique in the Kuomintang has persisted in maintaining a dictatorial rule and carried out a passive policy against Japan while it has upheld a policy of opposing the people within the country. In this way, the Kuomintang armies have shrunk to half their former size and the major part of them has almost lost its combat ability; in this way, a deep chasm exists between the Kuomintang government and the people, and a serious crisis of poverty, discontent, and revolts among the people is engendered; thus the ruling clique of the Kuomintang has not only greatly reduced its role in the war against Japan, but, moreover, has become an obstacle to the mobilization and unification of all the anti-Japanese forces in the country.

Why did this serious situation come into existence under the leadership of the major ruling clique of the Kuomintang? Because this ruling clique represents the interests of China's big landlords, big bankers, and the big compradore class. This reactionary and extremely small stratum monopolizes all the important organs of military, political, economic, and cultural bodies under the Kuomintang government. They place the preservation of their own vested interests in the first place and interests of the war against Japan in the second place. . . .

Under the over-all premise of annihilating the Japanese aggressors and of building a new China, the fundamental views of us Chinese Communist Party members are, at the present stage, identical with those held by the overwhelming majority of the Chinese populace. These are, firstly, that China should not have a feudalistic, fascist, anti-popular system of government exclusively controlled by big landowners and big bourgeoisie, because such a system has been proved to be entirely bankrupt by the chief ruling cliques of the Kuomintang in their eighteen years' rule. Secondly, China cannot, and therefore should not, attempt to build a state along the old-type democratic lines entirely ruled by the liberal bourgeois dictatorship. For in China, the liberal bourgeoisie has so far proved itself to be weak economically and politically, while on the other hand there has been born in China a politically powerful new factor that leads the broad masses of the peasant class, the petty bourgeoisie, the intellectuals, and other democratic elements—the awakened Chinese proletariat and its leader, the Chinese Communist Party. Thirdly, in the present stage, while the task of the Chinese people is still to oppose imperialistic and feudal oppression, while the requisite social and economic conditions are still lacking in China, the Chinese people cannot, and therefore should not, attempt to build a socialist state system.

Then, what is our proposal? We want to build, after annihilating the Japanese aggressors, a system of government based on the support of the overwhelming majority of the people, on the united front and the coalition of democratic alliance. We call this the New Democratic system of government.

Some people wonder if the Communists, once in power, will establish a dictatorship by the proletariat and a one-party system, as they have done in Russia. Our answer is that a New Democratic state of a union of several democratic classes is different in principle from a socialist state of a proletarian dictatorship. China, throughout the period of her New Democratic system, cannot and should not have a system of government of the character of a one-class dictatorship or a one-party autocracy. We have no reason not to co-operate with political parties, social groups, or individuals outside the Communist Party, who adopt a co-operative, but not a hostile, attitude. Russian history has created the Russian system . . . . Chinese history will create the Chinese system. A special type, a New Democratic type of state with a union of several democratic classes will be produced, which will be entirely necessary and rational to us and different from the Russian system. . . .

Under the New Democratic system of government, a policy of readjusting the relations between capital and labour will be adopted. On the one hand, the interests of workers will be protected. An eight to ten-hour-day system, according to varying circumstances, will be adopted, as well as suitable relief for the unemployed, social security, and the rights of labour unions. On the other hand, reasonable profits of state, private, and co-operative enterprises will be guaranteed. In general, this will enable both labour and capital to work jointly for the development of industrial production.

Large amounts of capital will be needed for the development of industries. Where will it come from? It can only come from two sources: mainly from dependence on the accumulated capital of the Chinese people, and at the same time from borrowing foreign aid. We welcome foreign investments if such are beneficial to China's economy and are made in observance of China's laws. . . .

The basic principles in the Chinese Communist Party's foreign policy are the establishment and consolidation of friendly relations with all nations on the basis of the thorough annihilation of the Japanese aggressors, the maintenance of world peace, mutual respect for national independence and equality, and the mutual promotion of national and popular interests and friendship, as well as the solution of all war-time and post-war problems such as the co-ordination of action in the war, peace conferences, trade, foreign investments, etc. . . .

We maintain that the Kuomintang government must end its hostile attitude towards the Soviet Union and immediately improve the Sino-Soviet relationship. The Soviet Union was the first nation to abrogate the unequal treaties and to sign equal new treaties with China. During the First Kuomintang National Congress, summoned by Dr. Sun Yat-sen himself in 1924, and the subsequent Northern Expedition, the Soviet Union was the only nation that assisted the Chinese war of liberation. After the war of resistance broke out on July 7, 1937, the Soviet Union was again the first to come to the aid of China in her fight against the Japanese aggressors. The Chinese people express their thankfulness to the Soviet government and its people for this help. We believe that the final, thorough solution of Pacific problems is impossible without participation of the Soviet Union.

We believe that the great efforts, sympathy, and help to China by both the governments and peoples of the two great nations, Great Britain and the United States, especially the latter, in the common cause of fighting the Japanese aggressors, deserve our thanks.

But we request the governments of all Allies, especially the British and the United States governments, to pay serious attention to the voice of the overwhelming majority of the Chinese people, so that their foreign policy may not go against the will of the Chinese people, and so as to avoid impairing our friendship or losing the friendship of the Chinese people. We believe that any foreign government that helps the Chinese reactionaries to stop the Chinese people's pursuit of democracy will be committing a grave error. . . .

The Chinese Civil War

Civil war between the Communists and the Kuomintang broke out again in 1946 despite American mediation, and continued until the Kuomintang forces collapsed in the first half of 1949. Late in 1947 Mao put forth an analysis of Communist strength and expressed confidence of victory despite American support of Chiang. However, Mao indicated that success involved new problems of tightening and purifying the Communist movement.

The revolutionary war of the Chinese people has now reached a turning point. That is, the Chinese People's Liberation Army (PLA) has repelled the attacks of the millions of reactionary troops of Chiang Kai-shek, the running dog of America; and has enabled itself to go over to the offensive. . . .

. . . Our enemy's superiority in military strength was only a temporary phenomenon, a factor playing only a temporary role; the aid of American imperialism was likewise a factor playing only a temporary role; while the anti-popular nature of Chiang Kai-shek's war and the support or opposition of the people are factors playing a constant role; and in these respects the PLA held superiority. The war of the PLA is a patriotic, just and revolutionary war which must of necessity obtain the support of the people throughout the country. This is the political basis for the victory over Chiang Kai-shek. The experience of eighteen months of war fully bears out our judgment . . . .

At present, the rear areas of the PLA are much more consolidated than they were eighteen months ago. That is the outcome of our Party's firmly siding with the peasants in reforming the agrarian system. During the anti-Japanese war, for the sake of establishing an anti-Japanese united front with the KMT and uniting all people who at the time were still capable of resisting Japan, our party on its own initiative changed from the policy before the anti-Japanese war of confiscating landlords' lands and distributing them to the peasants to that of reducing rents and interests—this was entirely necessary.

After the Japanese surrender, the peasants urgently demanded land and we therefore made a timely decision to change the agrarian policy of reducing rents and interest to one of confiscating the lands of the landlord class and distributing them to the peasants. . . .

The Basic Program on Chinese Agrarian Law stipulates that under the principle of eliminating the agrarian system of feudal and semi-feudal exploitation and carrying out the agrarian system of land to the tillers, the land shall be equally distributed according to population. . . . Poor peasants' leagues and their elected committees, comprising the masses of poor peasants and farm laborers, must be organized in the villages. These shall be the legal organs for carrying out agrarian reform, and the poor peasants' leagues should become the backbone leading all

FROM: Mao, "The Present Situation and Our Tasks" (December, 1947; English translation by the New China News Agency, reprinted in H. Arthur Steiner, ed., *Maoism: A Sourcebook—Selections from the Writings of Mao Tse-tung*, Los Angeles, editor's mimeographed edition, 1952, pp. 85, 87, 89–92, 95–96).

rural struggles. Our line is to rely on poor peasants and solidly unite with middle peasants to destroy the feudal and semi-feudal exploitation system of the landlord class and old-type rich peasants. . . .

For the sake of resolutely and thoroughly carrying out agrarian reform and consolidating the rear areas of the PLA, it is necessary to reorganize and purify the ranks of the party. The movement for the reformation of ideology and style of work within our party during the period of the anti-Japanese war in general attained success. This success lay, in the main, in the fact that our party's leading organs as well as many cadres have gone a step further in their grasp of such a basic orientation as the integration of the universal truth of Marxism-Leninism with the concrete practice of the Chinese revolution.

In this respect, our party has taken a great stride forward in comparison with the several historical periods prior to the anti-Japanese war. However, the question of impure composition and working style of the party's local organizations, and especially of the party's primary rural organizations, was not solved. During the eleven years from 1937 to 1947, our party organization developed from several tens of thousands of party members to 2,700,000 party members. This is a huge leap forward. It has made our party an unprecedentedly powerful party. It provided us with the possibilities of defeating Japanese imperialism and repelling the offensives of Chiang Kai-shek, and leading the Liberated Areas of more than 100,000,000 population and a PLA 2,000,000 strong. But along with this came defects. That is, many landlord, rich peasant and *lumpen*-proletarian* elements took this opportunity to slip into our party. They dominate many party, government and mass organizations in the rural areas; lord it over, bully and oppress the people, and distort the Party's policies, causing these organizations to become alienated from the masses of the people and preventing agrarian reform from being thorough.

Such serious conditions place before us the task of reorganizing and purifying the ranks of the party. If this task is not solved we cannot make progress in the rural areas. . . .

Without the broadest united front, comprising the overwhelming majority of the entire national population, the victory of the Chinese New Democratic Revolution is impossible. But this is not all. This united front must also be under the firm leadership of the Chinese Communist Party. Without the firm leadership of the Chinese Communist Party, no revolutionary united front can be victorious. . . .

. . . Crisis, like a volcano, is daily menacing American imperialism: American imperialism is sitting right on this volcano. This situation forced American imperialist elements to establish a plan for enslaving the world: to plunge like wild beasts into Europe, Asia and other places, muster the reactionary forces of various countries—these dregs spat out by the people—to organize the imperialist, anti-democratic front against all democratic forces headed by the Soviet Union, and prepare war—scheming at some remote time in the future to unleash World War III and defeat the democratic forces. This is a wild plan. The democratic forces of the whole world must, and entirely can, defeat this plan. The strength of the world anti-imperialist camp exceeds that of the imperialist camp. The superiority is with us, not with the enemy. The anti-imperialist camp headed by the Soviet Union has already been formed. . . .

---

*"*Lumpen*-proletarian": from the German, "ragged proletarian"—Ed.

We are clearly aware of the fact that there will be all kinds of obstruction and difficulties in our path of advance. We should prepare to cope with the greatest degree of resistance and struggle on the part of all foreign and domestic enemies. Only if we are able to grasp the science of Marxism-Leninism, have faith in the masses, stand closely together with the masses and lead them forward will we be entirely capable of surmounting any obstacle and conquering any difficulty and will our strength be matchless. This is the historic era in which capitalism and imperialism of the whole world are moving toward their doom, in which Socialism and Democracy of the whole world are moving toward victory. The light of dawn is just before us. We should put forth our efforts.

Communist Victory in China

By the middle of 1949 Communist control was extended to the whole of mainland China, as Chiang Kai-shek took refuge in Taiwan. Mao announced the main policies which he intended to pursue—dictatorship and "re-education," to mobilize the whole population in building up the country and fighting the enemies of Communism.

. . . The experience of several decades, amassed by the Chinese people, tells us to carry out the people's democratic dictatorship. That is, the right of reactionaries to voice their opinions must be abolished and only the people are allowed to have the right of voicing their opinions.

Who are the "people"? At the present stage in China, they are the working class, the peasant class, the petty bourgeoisie, and national bourgeoisie. Under the leadership of the working class and the Communist Party, these classes unite together to form their own state and elect their own government [so as to] carry out a dictatorship over the lackeys of imperialism—the landlord class, the bureaucratic capitalist class, and the Kuomintang reactionaries and their henchmen representing these classes—to suppress them, allowing them only to behave properly and not to talk and act wildly. If they talk and act wildly their [action] will be prohibited and punished immediately. The democratic system is to be carried out within the ranks of the people, giving them freedom of speech, assembly, and association. The right to vote is given only to the people and not to the reactionaries. These two aspects, namely, democracy among the people and dictatorship over the reactionaries, combine to form the people's democratic dictatorship.

Why should it be done this way? Everybody clearly knows that otherwise the revolution would fail, and the people would meet with woe and the State would perish.

"Don't you want to eliminate state authority?" Yes, but we do not want it at present, we cannot want it at present. Why? Because imperialism still exists, the domestic reactionaries still exist, and classes in the country still exist. Our present task is to strengthen the apparatus of the people's state, which refers mainly to the people's army, people's police, and people's courts, for the defence of the country, and the protection of the people's interests; and with this as a condition, to enable China to advance steadily, under the leadership of the working class and the Communist Party, from an agricultural to an industrial country, and from a New Democratic to a Socialist and Communist society, to eliminate classes and to

FROM: Mao, "On the People's Democratic Dictatorship" (July, 1949; Brandt, Schwartz, Fairbank, pp. 456–61).

realize the state of universal fraternity. The army, police, and courts of the state are instruments by which classes oppress classes. To the hostile classes the state apparatus is the instrument of oppression. It is violent, and not "benevolent." "You are not benevolent." Just so. We decidedly will not exercise benevolence towards the reactionary acts of the reactionaries and reactionary classes. Our benevolence applies only to the people, and not to the reactionary acts of the reactionaries and reactionary classes outside the people. . . .

. . . Re-education of the reactionary classes can only be carried out in the state of the people's democratic dictatorship. If this work is well done the main exploiting classes of China—the landlord and bureaucratic capitalist classes—will be finally eliminated. [Of the exploiting classes] there remain the national bourgeoisie, among many of whom appropriate educational work can be carried out at the present stage. When socialism is realized, that is, when the nationalization of private enterprises has been carried out, they can be further educated and reformed. The people have in their hands a powerful state apparatus and are not afraid of the rebellion of the national bourgeois class.

The grave problem is that of educating the peasants. The peasants' economy is scattered. Judging by the experience of the Soviet Union, it requires a very long time and careful work to attain the socialization of agriculture. Without the socialization of agriculture, there will be no complete and consolidated socialism. And to carry out the socialization of agriculture a powerful industry with state-owned enterprises as the main component must be developed. The state of the people's democratic dictatorship must step by step solve this problem. . . .

The national bourgeoisie is of great importance at the present stage. Imperialism is still standing near us and this enemy is very fierce. A long time is required for China to realize true economic independence and become free from reliance on imperialist nations. Only when China's industries are developed, and she no longer depends economically on powerful nations, can there be real independence. The proportion of China's modern industry in the entire national economy is still very small. There are still no reliable figures at present, but according to certain data it is estimated that modern industry only occupies about ten per cent of the total productive output in the national economy of the whole country. To cope with imperialist oppression, and to raise our backward economic status one step higher, China must utilize all urban and rural factors of capitalism which are beneficial and not detrimental to the national economy and the people's livelihood, and unite with the national bourgeoisie in a common struggle. Our present policy is to restrict capitalism and not to eliminate it. . . .

We must overcome difficulties, and must master what we do not know. We must learn economic work from all who know the ropes (no matter who they are). We must acknowledge them as our teachers, and learn from them respectfully and earnestly. We must acknowledge our ignorance, and not pretend to know what we do not know, nor put on bureaucratic airs. Stick to it, and eventually it will be mastered in a few months, one or two years, or three or five years. At first some of the Communists in the U.S.S.R. also did not know how to do economic work, and the imperialists also waited for their failure. But the Communist Party of the Soviet Union won. Under the leadership of Lenin and Stalin they not only could do revolutionary work but also reconstruction work. They have already built up a great and brilliant socialist state. The Communist Party of the U.S.S.R. is our best teacher from whom we must learn. We can rely wholly on the weapon of the people's democratic dictatorship to unite all people throughout the country, except the reactionaries, and advance steadily towards the goal. . . .

The Sino-Soviet Alliance

While Soviet aid to the Chinese Communists during the civil war was not conspicuous and probably not decisive, the Chinese Communists never faltered in their professions of solidarity with the USSR. The USSR maintained relations with the nationalist government of China until 1949, but then quickly recognized the new Communist republic. A formal treaty of alliance was concluded in Moscow early in 1950.

The new Treaty of Friendship, Alliance and Mutual Assistance, the Agreement on the Chinese Changchun [South-Manchurian] Railway, Port Arthur and Dairen, the Agreement on granting credit to China have been signed today between the People's Republic of China and the Union of Soviet Socialist Republics and notes have been exchanged. The conclusion of the above treaty and agreements is based on the vital interests of the great peoples of China and the Soviet Union and indicates fraternal friendship and eternal co-operation between China and the Soviet Union. The conclusion of the treaty and agreements is a special expression of fervent assistance to the revolutionary cause of the Chinese people on the part of the Soviet Union directed by the policy of Generalissimo Stalin. There is no doubt that this close and sincere co-operation between China and the Soviet Union is of extremely profound historical importance and will inevitably have immense influence upon and consequences for the cause of peace and justice for the peoples of the East and the whole world.

The great friendship between our two powers has been built up since the October Socialist Revolution. However imperialism and the counter-revolutionary government of China hampered further co-operation between us. The victory of the Chinese people has brought about radical changes in the situation. The Chinese people, under the leadership of Chairman Mao Tse-tung, have set up the People's Republic of China and have formed a state having unprecedented unity and this has made sincere co-operation possible between our two great states. Thanks to the meetings and the exchange of opinions between Generalissimo Stalin and Chairman Mao Tse-tung, this possibility became a reality and the friendship, alliance and mutual assistance between China and the Soviet Union are sealed now with the signed treaty. The imperialist bloc headed by American imperialism has resorted to all kinds of provocative methods attempting to frustrate the friendship between our two nations but these ignominious attempts have utterly failed.

The significance of the treaty and agreements between China and the Soviet Union is of particular importance for the new-born People's Republic of China. This treaty and these agreements will help the Chinese people to realize that they are not alone, and will help in the restoration and development of Chinese economy. . . .

Permit me on behalf of the Chinese people to express gratitude to Generalissimo Stalin and the Soviet Government for this great friendship. . . .

FROM: Chou En-lai, Speech on the Signing of the Sino-Soviet Agreements of Feb. 14, 1950 (English translation in *People's China*, March 1, 1950, pp. 28–29).

Long live permanent friendship and eternal co-operation between China and the Soviet Union! . . .

National Minorities in China—Tibet

In 1951, Chinese Communist forces entered Tibet, which in the past had usually been under Chinese suzerainty. An agreement was concluded by which Tibet was promised internal autonomy. The agreement broke down in 1959, as Communist moves toward socialism and tighter control precipitated an abortive Tibetan uprising.

1. The Tibetan people shall unite and drive out imperialist aggressive forces from Tibet so that the Tibetan people shall return to the big family of the motherland—the People's Republic of China.

2. The local government of Tibet shall actively assist the People's Liberation Army to enter Tibet and consolidate the national defences.

3. In accordance with the policy towards nationalities laid down in the Common Programme of the Chinese People's Political Consultative Conference, the Tibetan people have the right of exercising regional autonomy under the unified leadership of the Central People's Government.

4. The central authorities will not alter the existing political system in Tibet. The central authorities also will not alter the established status, functions and powers of the Dalai Lama. Officials of various ranks shall hold office as usual.

5. The established status, functions and powers of the Panchen Ngoerhtehni* shall be maintained.

6. By the established status, functions and powers of the Dalai Lama and of the Panchen Ngoerhtehni are meant the status, functions and powers of the Thirteenth Dalai Lama and of the Ninth Panchen Ngoerhtehni when they were in friendly and amicable relations with each other.

7. The policy of freedom of religious belief laid down in the Common Programme of the Chinese People's Political Consultative Conference shall be carried out.

The religious beliefs, customs and habits of the Tibetan people shall be respected, and lama monasteries shall be protected. The central authorities will not effect a change in the income of the monasteries.

8. Tibetan troops shall be reorganised step by step into the People's Liberation Army and become a part of the national defence forces of the People's Republic of China.

9. The spoken and written language and school education, etc., of the Tibetan nationality shall be developed step by step in accordance with the actual conditions in Tibet.

10. Tibetan agriculture, livestock raising, industry and commerce shall be developed step by step, and the people's livelihood shall be improved step by step in accordance with the actual conditions in Tibet.

FROM: Agreement between the Chinese Central People's Government and the Tibetan Government on the Administration of Tibet, May 23, 1951 (English translation by New China News Agency; reprinted in *Documents on International Affairs*, 1951, pp. 577–78).

*The Panchen Lama, Tibetan spiritual leader, who had been at odds with the Dalai Lama, the theocratic head of the Tibetan government—Ed.

11. In matters related to various reforms in Tibet, there will be no compulsion on the part of the central authorities. The local government of Tibet should carry out reforms of its own accord, and when the people raise demands for reform, they shall be solved by means of consultation with the leading personnel of Tibet.

12. Insofar as former pro-imperialist and pro-Kuomintang officials resolutely sever relations with imperialism and with the Kuomintang and do not engage in sabotage or resistance, they may continue to hold office irrespective of their past.

13. The People's Liberation Army entering Tibet shall abide by all the above mentioned policies and shall also be fair in all buying and selling and shall not arbitrarily take a needle or thread from the people.

14. The Central People's Government shall have the centralised handling of all external affairs of the area of Tibet; and there will be peaceful co-existence with neighbouring countries and the establishment and development of fair commercial and trading relations with them on the basis of equality, mutual benefit and mutual respect for territory and sovereignty.

15. In order to ensure the implementation of this agreement, the Central People's Government shall set up a military and administrative committee and a military area headquarters in Tibet, and apart from the personnel sent there by the Central People's Government shall absorb as many local Tibetan personnel as possible to take part in the work. . . .

The Korean War and Industrialization in China

The anti-imperialist sentiments of the Chinese Communists were charged with new intensity with Chinese involvement in the Korean War. In February, 1953, Chou En-lai spoke to the People's Political Consultative Council (the provisional legislative body) to report on the government's political and military strength, and to call for a major industrialization effort in the Five-Year Plan which was just beginning.

Under the leadership of the Communist Party of China, the Chinese people have become further organized, on a nationwide scale, through the trade unions, peasant associations, the New Democratic Youth League, the women's federations, the students' federation, the industrialists and merchants' associations, the Sino-Soviet Friendship Association, and the people's organizations in the spheres of literature, arts and sciences. By relying on the strength of the broad masses of the people, we have, during the past 3 years, carried out such great struggles as land reform, the suppression of counter-revolutionaries, the movement to resist American aggression and aid Korea, the "3-anti" movement (against corruption, waste and bureaucratism) and the "5-anti" movement (against bribery, tax evasion, fraud, theft of state property, and theft of state economic secrets) and the ideological remoulding of intellectuals.

Educated by these struggles, the Chinese people have raised their political consciousness to a level never known before. In this respect, the most striking achievements are: the drawing of a sharp distinction between ourselves and the

FROM: Chou, Political Report to the Fourth Session of the First National Committee of the PPCC, February, 1953 (*Current Background*, No. 228, February 8, 1953, pp. 3-4, 9-10).

enemy by the masses of the people in our country; the destruction of the remaining influence of the domestic counter-revolutionaries and the imperialists; the repudiation of decadent capitalist ideology and the further consolidation of the leading role of the working class and of socialist ideology. All this has strengthened our people's democratic united front more than ever, welding hundreds of millions of people into an organized and conscious force. Throughout the past year, all groups of the people in our country have taken up the study of the "Selected Works of Mao Tse-tung" and the Common Program. More recently, they have embarked on the study of Comrade Stalin's "Economic Problems of Socialism in the USSR" and Comrade Malenkov's report to the 19th Congress of the CPSU. These studies will arm us and enable us to work and remould ourselves better and more consciously.

Since the return of the Tibetan people to the great family of the motherland, solidarity between the Han [Chinese] and Tibetan people has made immense progress. National autonomous areas are being built up step by step in the areas inhabited by the minority nationalities. Patriotism and political consciousness are growing daily among the peoples of all nationalities. Fraternal relations of equality, cooperation, friendliness and solidarity among all these nationalities are being increasingly consolidated. United within one big family in our great motherland, these nationalities have embarked on developments of historic importance in their political, economic and cultural life.

All these achievements show that the leading position of the working class of our country has been strengthened economically, politically and ideologically; that our economy, which was disrupted by prolonged wars, has been rehabilitated and that a solid foundation has been built for the people's democratic dictatorship. This has created favorable conditions for our long-term, planned, large-scale national construction.

It must be pointed out that these successes were attained mainly in the process of the great struggle to resist American aggression and aid Korea. Two and a half years ago, the American imperialists launched their heinous war of aggression against our neighbor, Korea, crossed the 38th Parallel and pushed to the bank of the Yalu and Tumen Rivers along the borders of our country. At the same time, they occupied our territory of Taiwan. In order to preserve peace in the Far East and the World, to safeguard the security of our country and to support the just struggle of the Korean people against aggression, the Chinese people resolutely started their great campaign to resist American aggression and aid Korea. Hundreds of thousands of the finest sons and daughters of the Chinese people joined the Chinese People's Volunteers and have fought shoulder to shoulder with the Korean People's Army, repelling the U.S. imperialist aggression and forcing the enemy back to the 38th Parallel, thereby upsetting the timetable of the American imperialists for a war of worldwide aggression, increasing the internal contradictions within the camp of imperialism and placing increasingly serious difficulties in the way of the frantic scheme of the American imperialists to attack the camp of peace and democracy and extend aggression. This armed struggle against aggression by the Chinese people has not, as the imperialists imagined, caused any halt or interruption in the social transformation and economic rehabilitation of China. On the contrary, it has greatly stimulated the Chinese people's great spirit of patriotism and internationalism, infinitely strengthened their moral and political unity, conspicuously elevated the international status of our country, powerfully expanded the world movement against war and in defence of peace and reinforced the strength and influence of the world camp of peace and democracy headed by the Soviet Union. This great struggle to resist American aggression and aid Korea has been a tremendous driving force in every aspect of our work of national transformation and rehabilitation. The people of our country have everywhere ardently joined in the struggle by signing patriotic pacts increasing production and practising economy. In the course of this struggle, they have resolutely rooted out any pro-America, worship-America or fear-America ideology which had been left among a section of the people as the residue of reactionary Kuomintang indoctrination. The people of our country have answered the American imperialist war schemes by enthusiastic participation in the campaign for signatures for world peace. They have defeated American germ warfare by their patriotic mass sanitation movement. The campaign to resist American aggression and aid Korea has, in fact, guaranteed and accelerated the early and successful completion of our work of social transformation and economic rehabilitation. . . .

. . . In 1953, the first year of the first five-year plan, our industry and agriculture will register a marked rise in output compared with 1952. . . .

Our planned national construction is on a grand scale from the very beginning; the tasks before us are both immense and glorious and fraught with many difficulties. Our weightiest and central task throughout this year is therefore to mobilize the working class and all the other people of the whole country to concentrate their efforts in overcoming difficulties and to exert themselves to fulfill and overfulfill the plan of construction for 1953. To complete this complex and arduous task, we must develop intensive, precise work at every link in the process. We must guarantee the income of the state and ensure that our plans of economic construction, national defence and social and cultural development are not affected by any shortage of funds. . . .

We must rally all industrialists and merchants whose enterprises are beneficial to the national interests and the people's livelihood, and enable them to develop their initiative under the leadership of the state economy and the unified national plan. We must make a serious study of advanced Soviet experience, propagate the application of advanced experience, organize patriotic emulation and economy campaigns on the broadest mass base and gradually lift the living standards of the workers and peasants by raising the level of industrial and agricultural production.

We must make all working comrades understand that we are facing new things and new tasks, that we can overcome difficulties, fulfill our tasks, master our work and make fewer errors only by setting ourselves firmly against arrogance and complacency, by making every effort to learn humbly and by correcting our mistakes and shortcomings. We must strengthen our state discipline, oppose bureaucratism and commandism, mete out punishment to law-breakers and keep a strict watch against sabotage and destruction by vicious elements. It is our belief that under the correct leadership of Chairman Mao Tse-tung and the Chinese Communist Party and with the assistance of advanced Soviet technique and the Soviet experts, the intelligent, industrious workers, peasants and intellectuals of China will certainly be able to bring their great initiative and creativeness into play and to carry out every concrete task and plan. . . .

The Collectivization of the Chinese Peasants

Late in 1953 the Chinese Communist leadership ordered the general collectivization of the nation's agriculture. With an eye to Russian experience, the decision cautioned against the use of violence, but the organization of "cooperatives" was rapidly pushed. By 1957 it was substantially complete.

The general line of the party during the transition period is to gradually bring into realization socialist industrialization of the state and to effect, step by step, socialist reform of agriculture, handicraft industry and capitalist industry and commerce. According to the general line of the party, the national economic construction would not only bring our industrial economy to a high point but our agricultural economy to a relatively high level. However, the isolated, scattered, conservative and backward individual economy limits the development of the productive forces of agriculture and an ever greater contradiction between individual economy and socialist industrialization is making itself increasingly felt. It has become more and more evident that the small-scale agricultural production cannot satisfy the demand of the broad peasantry to improve their living conditions, nor can it meet the increasing need of the entire national economy. To further raise the productive forces of agriculture, the most fundamental task of the party in its rural work would be to educate the peasants through measures most acceptable and understandable to them and stimulate them to gradually get organized and carry out the socialist reform of agriculture. This will make it possible for our agriculture to change from a state of backward individual economy into one of advanced cooperative economy aiming at large-scale production, for the contradiction between the two types of economy, industrial and agricultural, to be gradually overcome, and for the peasants to gradually but completely free themselves from the state of poverty and, instead, enjoy a happy and prosperous life.

According to the nation's experiences, the concrete way for the gradual organization of China's peasants is to organize them through temporary mutual-aid teams which operate a simple form of collective labor, and year-round mutual-aid teams which have certain division of labor among their members on the basis of collective labor and with a small amount of property owned in common; then through agricultural cooperatives in which the members pool their land as shares and there is unified management and more property owned in common; and finally to agricultural cooperatives of a higher form (or collective farms) with collective peasant ownership which is entirely socialist in character. This is the path laid down by the party for the gradual, step-by-step socialist transformation of agriculture. . . .

There inevitably will grow in rural villages a conflict between socialism and capitalism as the two develop. The conflict will become more and more evident as the agricultural economy restores and gradually improves. The party's policy is to actively and carefully channel the peasants' activeness in individual economy to mutual aid and cooperation through numerous, concrete, appropriate and varied forms, so as to overcome the spontaneous tendency toward capitalism and gradually lead them to socialism. . . .

FROM: Decision of the Central Committee of the Chinese Communist Party on the Development of Agricultural Producer Cooperatives, December 16, 1953 (*Current Background*, No. 278, February 15, 1954, pp. 1-2, 4, 13).

Cooperative farming must in all cases be developed along the basic principle of voluntariness. To carry out socialist reform in small peasant economy, we must not resort to the simple method of calling upon the masses to start it, nor should we command the poor peasants and middle peasants to join the cooperatives, nor could we use the means of depriving the peasants of their production materials by turning them into common property. If we should resort to such means, it would be a criminal act of sabotaging the workers' and peasants' alliance and also the poor peasants' and middle peasants' alliance, hence a criminal act against agricultural cooperation. . . .

North Korea and the Korean War

After occupying northern Korea in 1945, the Russians created a "People's Democratic Republic of Korea" in their zone in 1948, with the Communist Kim Il Sung as premier. North Korean troops attacked the American-sponsored Republic of Korea in the South in June, 1950, and thus began the Korean War, which, after involving the United States and Communist China, dragged on until 1953. At the time of Chinese intervention in December, 1950, Premier Kim Il Sung expressed high hopes of victory and unification of all of Korea under his rule.

During the two past months of the sacred war for the liberation of our glorious motherland, the People's Army—the off-spring of our motherland and of our people—was forced to make a temporary, strategic retreat under the weight of the offensive by superior forces of aggressors' troops of several imperialist states headed by the American imperialist interventionists. However, our retreat was a temporary one and was carried out with the aim of delivering a crushing blow to the enemy, with the aim of routing, annihilating and expelling the enemy from our native soil, in order to obtain complete victory in the great liberation war.

The entire Korean people, who rose in the just struggle for the freedom, honor and independence of their motherland, never bowed before the enemy at the hardest moment of the retreat; on the contrary, they rallied even closer around the republic's government and by their practical efforts for the good of their country and people demonstrated their firm determination to attain conclusive victory over the enemy at any cost. This firm determination of the Korean people was manifested in the awesome partisan movement of the entire people, which spread all over the territory of South and North Korea under the enemy's temporary occupation, in the widespread activity of the underground agencies of the government and of the Workers' [Communist] Party, and in the patriotic, self-sacrificing work of helping the People's Army and the Chinese people's volunteer detachments.

The people's strength is inexhaustible. This inexhaustible strength is invincible. From the support of the great Soviet and Chinese peoples, from that of the people of the people's democracies and of the freedom-loving people of the entire world, the Korean people draw firm trust in victory and inexhaustible strength in their just struggle for the freedom, honor and independence of their motherland.

FROM: Kim Il Sung, Address to the Korean People on the Occasion of the Liberation of Pyongyang, December, 1950 (English translation in *The Current Digest of The Soviet Press*, II:48, January 6, 1951, p. 3). This and subsequent selections copyright by *The Current Digest of the Soviet Press*, published weekly at The Ohio State University; reprinted by permission.

Dear warriors of the People's Army! Chinese people's volunteers and partisans! Dear fellow countrymen, brothers and sisters! The enemy is retreating in disorder, but he has not yet been completely routed. With mad fury, the enemy is striving to regroup and to achieve his perfidious aim at any cost. The road to conclusive victory lies before us. But we must remember that we shall still encounter all sorts of difficulties and obstacles along it. We can win the final victory only after a grim struggle, overcoming difficulties and accepting sacrifices. . . .

All the Korean people must rally still closer around the government of the Korean People's Democratic Republic and march boldly toward victory in the patriotic war of liberation.

Vengeance and death to the accursed enemies—the American interventionists and [South Korean President] Syngman Rhee's band of traitors—who have caused great sufferings to our motherland and our people!

Glory to the valorous People's Army and to the heroic units of the Chinese people's volunteers, conducting the offensive and destroying the enemy!

Glory to the men and women partisans daringly operating in the enemy's rear!

Long live the united Korean people!

Long live the Korean People's Democratic Republic! . . .

Communism in Vietnam

Next to China the most significant manifestation of Communism in Asia emerged in the former French possessions of Indo-China. The Communist Party of Indo-China was founded by Ho Chi Minh (born Nguyen Tat Thanh), who became a Communist as a young man in France in 1920. Given the chance to build a mass movement by the Japanese occupation in Vietnam in World War II, Ho identified his cause with anti-French nationalism and successfully applied Mao Tse-tung's peasant guerrilla tactics. When Japan surrendered, Ho temporarily occupied Hanoi and proclaimed Vietnam's independence from the French.

In 1946 fighting broke out between French colonial forces and Ho Chi Minh's Communist-led Viet Minh movement, who were compelled to resume their guerrilla war. After the Communist victory in China Ho adopted a more openly Communist program and in 1951 reorganized his movement as the Vietnam Labor Party with an all-class nationalist appeal similar to the line that had prevailed in China.

By his victory at Dien Bien Phu in 1953 Ho Chi Minh forced the French to the bargaining table, and at the Geneva Conference in 1954 it was agreed to divide Vietnam temporarily between the Communists in the North and the French in the South. Power in the South then passed to a conservative native government underwritten by the United States. In 1961 the Communists resumed guerrilla warfare against the Saigon regime, ostensibly as a movement of Southerners but actually controlled and supported from the North.

a) The Independence Movement

"All men are created equal. They are endowed by their Creator with certain inalienable Rights; among these are Life, Liberty and the pursuit of Happiness."

This immortal statement was made in the Declaration of Independence of the

FROM: Declaration of Independence of the Democratic Republic of Vietnam, Septemher 2, 1945 (English translation in *Vietnamese Studies*, no. 24, Hanoi, Foreign Languages Publishing House, 1970, pp. 195–99; reprinted in Robert F. Turner, *Vietnamese Communism: Its Origins and Development*, Stanford, Calif., Hoover Institution, 1975, pp. 334–36).

United States of America in 1776. In a broader sense, this means: All the peoples on the earth are equal from birth, all the peoples have a right to live and to be happy and free.

The Declaration, made in 1791 [actually 1789] at the time of the French Revolution, on the Rights of Man and the Citizen, also states: "All men are born free and with equal rights, and must always remain free and have equal rights."

Those are undeniable truths.

Nevertheless, for more than eighty years, the French imperialists, abusing the standard of Liberty, Equality and Fraternity, have violated our Fatherland and oppressed our fellow-citizens. They have acted contrary to the ideals of humanity and justice.

In the field of politics, they have deprived our people of every democratic liberty.

They have enforced inhuman laws; they have set up three distinct political regimes in the North, the Centre and the South of Viet Nam in order to wreck our national unity and prevent our people from being united.

They have built more prisons than schools. They have mercilessly slain our patriots; they have drowned our uprisings in rivers of blood. They have fettered public opinion; they have practised obscurantism against our people. To weaken our race they have forced us to use opium and alcohol.

In the field of economics, they have fleeced us to the bone, impoverished our people and devastated our land.

They have robbed us of our ricefields, our mines, our forests, our raw materials. They have monopolized the issue of bank-notes and the export trade.

They have invented numerous unjustifiable taxes, and reduced our people, especially our peasantry, to a state of extreme poverty.

They have hampered our national bourgeoisie from prospering; they have mercilessly exploited our workers.

In the autumn of 1940, when the Japanese fascists violated Indochina's territory to establish new bases against the Allies, the French imperialists went down on their bended knees and handed over our country to them.

Thus, from that date, our people were subjected to the double yoke of the French and the Japanese. Their sufferings and miseries increased. The result was that from the end of last year to the beginning of this year, from Quang Tri province to the North of Viet Nam, more than two million of our fellow-citizens died from starvation. On the 9th of March, French troops were disarmed by the Japanese. The French colonialists either fled or surrendered, showing that not only were they incapable of "protecting" us, but that, in the span of five years, they had twice sold our country to the Japanese.

On several occasions before the 9th of March, the Viet Minh league had urged the French to join forces with it against the Japanese. Instead of agreeing to this proposal, the French colonialists so intensified their terrorist activities against the Viet Minh members that before fleeing they massacred a great number of political prisoners detained at Yen Bay and Cao Bang.

Notwithstanding all this, our fellow-citizens have always manifested a tolerant and humane attitude towards the French. Even after the Japanese coup de force of March 1943, the Viet Minh League helped many Frenchmen to cross the frontier, rescued some of them from Japanese jails and protected French lives and property.

From the autumn of 1940, our country had in fact ceased to be a French colony and had become a Japanese possession.

After the Japanese had surrendered to the Allies, our whole people rose up to regain our national sovereignty and to found the Democratic Republic of Viet Nam.

The truth is that we have wrested our independence from the Japanese and not from the French.

The French have fled, the Japanese have capitulated. Emperor Bao Dai has abdicated. Our people have broken the chains which for nearly a century have fettered us, and have won independence for the Fatherland. Our people at the same time have overthrown the monarchic regime that has reigned supreme for tens of centuries. In its place has been established the present Democratic Republic.

For these reasons, we, members of the Provisional Government, representing the whole Vietnamese people, declare that from now on we break off all relations of a colonial character with France; we repeal all the international obligations that France has so far subscribed to on behalf of Viet Nam and we abolish all the special rights the French have unlawfully acquired in our Fatherland.

The whole Vietnamese people, animated by a common purpose, are determined to fight to the bitter end against any attempt by the French colonialists to reconquer our country.

We are convinced that the Allied nations, which at Teheran and San Francisco have acknowledged the principles of self-determination and equality of nations, will not refuse to recognize the independence of Viet Nam.

A people that has courageously opposed French domination for more than eighty years, a people that has fought side by side with the Allies against the fascists during these last years, such a people must be free and independent.

For those reasons, we, members of the Provisional Government of the Democratic Republic of Viet Nam, solemnly declare to the world that Viet Nam has the right to be free and independent, and in fact it is so already. The entire Vietnamese people are determined to mobilize all their physical and mental strength, to sacrifice their lives and property in order to safeguard their freedom and independence. [Signed by Ho Chi Minh, President, and fourteen other leaders.]

b) From Nationalism to Communism

Dear fellow countrymen and women!
The world of today is clearly divided into two camps:
There is the anti-democratic imperialist camp led by the American imperialists and composed of imperialist states and reactionary governments, lackeys of imperialism. They plan to seize the lands of other peoples in order to dominate the world; to suppress the national liberation movements of the peoples; to destroy world peace and democracy and to provoke a third world war which would plunge mankind into darkness and misery.

There is the anti-imperialist democratic camp headed by the Soviet Union and composed of the countries of socialism and People's Democracy, of the oppressed peoples, and of the working people and progressives in capitalist countries. This

FROM: "Manifesto of the Viet-Nam Lao Dong Party," February, 1951 (English translation in *People's China*, May 1, 1951, Supplement, pp. 2–3).

camp is striving to carry on the work of national liberation, for the defence of national independence and the maintenance of world peace and democracy, and it seeks to enhance the unity, progress and happiness of mankind.

That the democratic camp has become stronger than the imperialist camp is clearly shown by the fact that the Soviet Union is daily growing more prosperous and powerful; that the work of national construction is swiftly moving ahead in the People's Democracies; that the Chinese People's Revolution has been victorious; and that the Korean people are waging a successful struggle.

Our country and our people stand in the democratic camp.

The French colonialists stand in the imperialist camp. They want to plunder our land. In this they have the all-out assistance of the American imperialists. Our people, who definitely do not want to be enslaved, are determined to fight in defence of their land and homes. They are now preparing for an early general counter-offensive.

The forces of our resistance spring from the people. Over 90 per cent of our people are working people, that is, the workers, peasants and intellectual workers. Thus, the working people are the main driving force of our armed resistance and of our national construction.

The central task of the working class and the working people of Viet-Nam now is to unite the entire people, to carry the War of Resistance to complete victory, to build an independent, united, democratic, strong and prosperous Viet-Nam, and to fully realise People's Democracy so as to gradually advance towards socialism. In order to fulfill this task, the working class and the working people of Viet-Nam must have a vanguard army, a general staff, a powerful, clear-sighted, determined, pure and thoroughly revolutionary political party: the Viet-Nam Lao Dong Party.

The Viet-Nam Lao Dong Party will be composed of the most patriotic, the most enthusiastic, the most revolutionary workers, peasants and intellectual workers. It will be comprised of those who are determined to serve the Motherland, to serve the people, to serve labor, who place the overall interests of the country and the people above their own personal interests and who set the example in the War of Resistance and in national construction.

The theoretical foundation of the party is Marxism-Leninism.

The principle of organization of the party is democratic centralism.

The discipline of the party is a strict, voluntary discipline.

The policy of the party aims to serve the interests of the country and the people.

The law governing the development of the party is criticism and self-criticism.

The present main tasks of the Viet-Nam Lao Dong Party are: to unite and lead the working class, the working people and the whole Viet-Nam nation in their liberation struggle; to wipe out the aggressive French colonialists and defeat the American interventionists; and to lead the War of Resistance of the people of Viet-Nam to complete victory, thereby making Viet-Nam a genuinely independent and united country. . . .

The workers who are production fighters in enterprises shall have their living conditions improved and take part in the running of enterprises.

The peasants who are production fighters in the rural areas shall benefit from the reduction of land rent and interest rates, and from appropriate agrarian reforms.

The intellectual workers shall be encouraged and assisted to develop their abilities.

Small-scale traders and small workshop owners shall be assisted to develop their trade and handicrafts.

The national bourgeoisie shall be encouraged, assisted and guided in their undertakings in order to contribute to the development of the national economy.

The right of patriotic landlords to collect land rent in accordance with law shall be guaranteed.

National minorities shall be given every assistance and shall enjoy perfect equality of all rights and duties.

Effective help shall be extended to women so as to achieve equality between men and women.

Followers of all religions shall enjoy freedom of belief and worship.

Overseas citizens of Viet-Nam in foreign countries shall be given protection.

The lives and properties of foreign residents in Viet-Nam shall be protected. In particular, Chinese nationals, if they so desire, shall be allowed to enjoy the same rights and perform the same duties as citizens of Viet-Nam.

In the sphere of external affairs, the Viet-Nam Lao Dong Party recommends that the people of Viet-Nam closely unite with and help the peoples of Cambodia and Laos in their struggle for independence, and, jointly with them, liberate the whole of Indo-China; actively support the national liberation movements of oppressed peoples; closely unite with the Soviet Union, China and other People's Democracies; and closely ally themselves with the peoples of France and of the French colonies so as to contribute to the anti-imperialist struggle for the defence of world peace and democracy. . . .

All compatriots at home and abroad! Unite closely around the People's Government of the Viet-Nam Democratic Republic, the Viet-Nam Lao Dong Party and the leader of the people, of the working class and working people of Viet-Nam— President Ho Chi Minh!

The Viet-Nam Lao Dong Party earnestly requests other organisations sincerely to criticize Party cadres and rank and file members and the policy of the Party, so that it can make constant progress and act in accordance with the wishes of the people.

Confident in the efforts of all Party members, in the support of the workers and the response from the entire people, the Viet-Nam Lao Dong Party will certainly fulfill its tasks:

To lead the resistance to complete victory;
To develop the People's Democratic regime;
To contribute to the defense of world peace and democracy;
To march towards socialism.

c) The Viet Cong

Compatriots in the country and abroad!

Over the past hundred years the Vietnamese people repeatedly rose up to fight against foreign aggression for the independence and freedom of their fatherland. In 1945, the people throughout the country surged up in an armed uprising, over-

FROM: Manifesto of the South Viet Nam National Liberation Front (1961; English translation in *South Viet-Nam National Front for Liberation: Documents*, South Viet-Nam, Giai Phong Publishing House, 1968, pp. 11–15; reprinted in Turner, *Vietnamese Communism*, pp. 416–20).

threw the Japanese and French domination and seized power. When the French colonialists invaded our country for the second time our compatriots, determined not to be enslaved again, shed much blood and laid down many lives to defend their national sovereignty and independence. Their solidarity and heroic struggle during nine years led the resistance war to victory. The 1954 Geneva Agreements restored peace in our country and recognized "the sovereignty, independence, unity and territorial integrity of Viet Nam."

Our compatriots in South Viet Nam would have been able to live in peace, to earn their livelihood in security and to build a decent and happy life.

However, the American imperialists, who had in the past helped the French colonialists to massacre our people, have now replaced the French in enslaving the southern part of our country through a disguised colonial regime. They have been using their stooge—the Ngo Dinh Diem administration—in their downright repression and exploitation of our compatriots, in their manoeuvres to permanently divide our country and to turn its southern part into a military base in preparation for war in Southeast Asia.

The aggressors and traitors, working hand in glove with each other, have set up an extremely cruel dictatorial rule. They persecute and massacre democratic and patriotic people, and abolish all human liberties. They ruthlessly exploit the workers, peasants and other labouring people, strangle the local industry and trade, poison the minds of our people with a depraved foreign culture, thus degrading our national culture, traditions and ethics. They feverishly increase their military forces, build military bases, use the army as an instrument for repressing the people and serving the U.S. imperialists' scheme to prepare an aggressive war.

Never, over the past six years, have gun shots massacring our compatriots ceased to resound throughout South Viet Nam. Tens of thousands of patriots here have been murdered and hundreds of thousands thrown into jail. All sections of the people have been living in a stifling atmosphere under the iron heel of the U.S.-Diem clique. Countless families have been torn away and scenes of mourning are seen everywhere as a result of unemployment, poverty, exacting taxes, terror, massacre, drafting of manpower and pressganging, usurpation of land, forcible house removal, and herding of the people into "prosperity zones," "resettlement centres" and other forms of concentration camps.

High anger with the present tyrannical regime is boiling among all strata of the people. Undaunted in the face of barbarous persecution, our compatriots are determined to unite and struggle unflaggingly against the U.S. imperialists' policy of aggression and the dictatorial and nepotic regime of the Ngo Dinh Diem clique. Among workers, peasants and other toiling people, among intellectuals, students and pupils, industrialists and traders, religious sects and national minorities, patriotic activities are gaining in scope and strength, seriously shaking the U.S.-Diem dictatorial regime.

The attempted coup d'état of November II, 1960, in Saigon in some respects reflected the seething anger among the people and armymen, and the rottenness and decline of the U.S.-Diem regime. However, there were among the leaders of this coup political speculators who, misusing the patriotism of the armymen, preferred negotiation and compromise rather than to overthrow Ngo Dinh Diem. Like Ngo Dinh Diem, they persisted in following the pro-American and traitorous path, and also used the anti-Communist signboard to oppose the people. That is why the coup was not supported by the people and large numbers of armymen and, consequently, ended in failure.

At present, our people are urgently demanding an end to the cruel dictatorial rule; they are demanding independence and democracy, enough food and clothing, and peaceful reunification of the country.

To meet the aspirations of our compatriots, the *South Viet Nam National Front for Liberation* came into being, pledging itself to shoulder the historic task of liberating our people from the present yoke of slavery.

The *South Viet Nam National Front for Liberation* undertakes to unite all sections of the people, all social classes, nationalities, political parties, organizations, religious communities and patriotic personalities, without distinction of their political tendencies, in order to struggle for the overthrow of the rule of the U.S. imperialists and their stooges—the Ngo Dinh Diem clique—and for the realization of independence, democracy, peace and neutrality pending the peaceful reunification of the fatherland.

The *South Viet Nam National Front for Liberation* calls on the entire people to unite and heroically rise up as one man to fight along the line of a program of action summarized as follows:

1. To overthrow the disguised colonial regime of the U.S. imperialists and the dictatorial Ngo Dinh Diem administration—lackey of the United States—and to form a national democratic coalition administration.

2. To bring into being a broad and progressive democracy, promulgate freedom of expression, of the press, of belief, of assembly, of association, of movement and other democratic freedoms. To grant general amnesty to all political detainees, dissolve all concentration camps dubbed "prosperity zones" and "resettlement centres," abolish the fascist 10–59 law and other anti-democratic laws.

3. To abolish the economic monopoly of the United States and its henchmen, to protect home-made products, encourage home industry and trade, expand agriculture and build an independent and sovereign economy. To provide jobs for the unemployed, increase wages for workers, armymen and office employees. To abolish arbitrary fines and apply an equitable and rational tax system. To help those who have gone South to return to their native places if they so desire, and to provide jobs for those among them who want to remain in the South.

4. To carry out land rent reduction, guarantee the peasants' rights to till their present plots of land, redistribute communal land and advance toward land reform.

5. To do away with enslaving and depraved U.S.-style culture, build a national and progressive culture and education. To wipe out illiteracy, open more schools, carry out reforms in the educational and examination system.

6. To abolish the system of American military advisers, eliminate foreign military bases in Viet Nam and build a national army for the defence of the fatherland and the people.

7. To guarantee equality between men and women and among different nationalties and the right to autonomy of the national minorities; to protect the legitimate interests of foreign residents in Viet Nam; to protect and take care of the interests of Vietnamese living abroad.

8. To carry out a foreign policy of peace and neutrality, to establish diplomatic relations with all countries which respect the independence and sovereignty of Viet Nam.

9. To re-establish normal relations between the two zones, pending the peaceful reunification of the fatherland.

10. To oppose aggressive war; to actively defend world peace.

Compatriots!

Ours are a heroic people with a tradition of unity and indomitable struggle. We cannot let our country be plunged into darkness and mourning. We are determined to shatter the fetters of slavery and wrest back independence and freedom.

Let us all rise up and unite!

Let us close our ranks and fight under the banner of the *South Viet Nam National Front for Liberation* to overthrow the rule of the U.S. imperialists and Ngo Dinh Diem—their henchman.

Workers, peasants and other toiling people! The oppression and misery which are now heavily weighing on you must be ended. You have the strength of tens of millions of people. Stand up enthusiastically to save your families and our fatherland.

Intellectuals! The dictatorial rulers have stripped us of the most elementary human rights. You are living in humiliation and misery. For our great cause, stand up resolutely!

Industrialists and traders! A country under the sway of foreign sharks cannot have an independent and sovereign economy. You should join in the people's struggle.

Compatriots of all national minorities! Compatriots of all religious communities! Unity is life, disunity is death. Smash all U.S.-Diem schemes of division. Side with the entire people in the struggle for independence, freedom and equality among all nationalities.

Notables! The interests of the nation are above all else. Support actively the struggle for the overthrow of the cruel aggressors and traitors.

Patriotic officers and soldiers! You have arms in your hands. Listen to the sacred call of the fatherland. Be definitely on the side of the people. Your compatriots have faith in your patriotism.

Young men and women! You are the future of the nation. You should devote your youthful ardour to serving the fatherland.

Compatriots living abroad! Turn your thoughts toward the beloved fatherland, contribute actively to the sacred struggle for national liberation

At present the movement for peace, democracy and national independence is surging up throughout the world. Colonialism is irretrievably disintegrating. The time when the imperialists could plunder and subjugate the people at will is over. This situation is extremely favourable for the struggle to free South Viet Nam from the yoke of the U.S. imperialists and their stooges. Peace-loving and progressive people in the world are supporting us. Justice is on our side, and we have the prodigious strength of the unity of our struggle to free South Viet Nam from the yoke of the U.S. imperialists and their stooges. Peace-loving and progressive people in the world are supporting us. Justice is on our side, and we have the prodigious strength of the unity of our entire people. We will certainly win! The U.S. imperialist aggressors and the Ngo Dinh Diem traitorous clique will certainly be defeated. The cause of liberation of South Viet Nam will certainly triumph.

Compatriots around the country!

Let us unite and march forward confidently and valiantly to score brilliant victories for our people and our fatherland!

Communism in India

The Communist Party of India responded to independence in 1947 with vain efforts to enhance its power by violence. Repeated changes of leadership ended in 1951 with the ascendancy of Ajoy Ghosh and a policy of peaceful preparation of revolution in accordance with specifically Indian conditions. This line was expressed in a new party program and statement of policy, which included some frank comments about the peculiarities of Asian Communism. Later, in the 1960's, the Indian Communists split three ways, into pro-Moscow, pro-Peking and neutralist parties.

India Will Strike Its Own Path to Freedom & People's Rule.

The experience of the last four years has taught the people of our country that the present government, and the present system, cannot solve their main problems of life. It cannot give them land and bread, work wages, peace and freedom. They are coming to realise the necessity of changing the present government, which mainly serves the interests of feudal landlords and big monopoly financiers and the hidden power behind them all, the vested interests of British imperialism.

The Communist Party has, therefore, adopted a programme, in which it says that it "regards as quite mature the task of replacing the present anti-democratic and anti-popular Government by a new Government of People's Democracy." . . .

Past Policies

There are a large number of people who think that [the present] government can be replaced by a People's Democratic Government by utilizing the Parliament ushered in by the new Constitution. Such feelings are encouraged and fed not only by this government and the vested interests but even by the Right-wing Socialists, who preach that the very fact of a strong opposition party on the parliamentary floor will shake the government and make it topple down.

But hardly had the people started to believe in the efficacy of the new Constitution which they thought was the outcome of their anti-imperialist struggles of the past, when even the fiction of the fundamental rights and guarantees is thrown out of that very Constitution and the freedom of person, the press, speech and assembly, which the masses wanted to use to shake up this anti-democratic Government, are subjected to the rule of the police baton and the bureaucrat.

Even the most hardened liberal would now feel ashamed to maintain, let alone the Communist Party and other democrats and revolutionaries, that this government and the classes that keep it in power will ever allow us to carry out a fundamental democratic transformation in the country by parliamentary methods alone.

Hence, the road that will lead us to freedom and peace, land and bread, as outlined in the programme of the party, has to be found elsewhere.

History, enlightened for us by Marx, Engels, Lenin and Stalin, places before us its vast experience, arising out of struggles which have led nearly half of humanity to socialism, freedom and real democracy, at the head of which stands the Soviet Union and in which the great Chinese and People's Democracies join hands.

Thus, our main road is already charted out for us. Even then, each country has to seek its own path also. What is the path for us? . . .

FROM: Policy Statement of the Communist Party of India (in *Cross Roads*, Bombay, June 8, 1951, pp. 3, 6).

Controversies inside the C.P.I. . . .

For a time, it was advocated that the main weapon in our struggle would be the weapon of general strike of industrial workers followed by countrywide insurrection as in Russia.

Later, on the basis of a wrong understanding of the lessons of the Chinese Revolution, the thesis was put forward that since ours is a semicolonial country like China, our revolution would develop in the same way as in China, with the partisan war of the peasantry as its main weapon.

Among comrades, who at different periods accepted the correctness of the one or the other of these views, there were differences of the estimate of the situation in the country, on the degree of isolation of the present government from the people, and on many other vital issues. It was clear that these differences had to be resolved in order that the party could lead the people to victory.

After long discussion, running for several months, the party has now arrived at a new understanding of the correct path for attaining the freedom of the country and the happiness of the people, a path which we do not and cannot name as either Russian or Chinese.

It should be, and is, one that conforms to the teachings of Marx, Engels, Lenin and Stalin, and that utilizes the lessons given by all the struggles of history, especially the Russian and Chinese, the Russian because it was the first Socialist Revolution in the world carried out by the working class, under the leadership of the Communist Party of Lenin and Stalin in a capitalist and imperialist country; and the Chinese because it was the first People's Democratic Revolution in a semicolonial, dependent country, under the leadership of the Communist Party, in which even the national bourgeoisie took part.

AT THE SAME TIME, ONE HAS TO REMEMBER THAT EVERY COUNTRY HAS ITS OWN PECULIARITIES, NATURAL AND SOCIAL, WHICH CANNOT FAIL TO GOVERN ITS PATH TO LIBERATION.

In what way then shall our path be different from the Chinese path?

China & India

First, let us see where we are the same as the Chinese. It is in the character of our revolution. The thing of primary importance for the life of our country, same as it was in China, is agriculture and the peasant problem. We are essentially a colonial country, with a vast majority of our people living on agriculture. Most of our workers also are directly connected with the peasantry and interested in the problem of land.

OUR REAL FREEDOM TODAY MEANS TAKING THE LAND FROM THE FEUDAL LANDLORDS AND HANDING IT OVER WITHOUT PAYMENT TO THE PEASANT. THIS ANTI-FEUDAL TASK, WHEN FULFILLED, ALONE WILL MEAN THE REAL LIBERATION FOR OUR COUNTRY BECAUSE THE MAIN PROPS OF IMPERIALIST INTERESTS IN OUR COUNTRY, AS THEY WERE IN CHINA, ARE THE FEUDALS, SO, LIKE THE CHINESE, WE HAVE TO FIGHT FEUDALISM AND IMPERIALISM. OUR REVOLUTION IS ANTI-FEUDAL, ANTI-IMPERIALIST.

That makes the struggles of the peasantry of prime importance. Drawing upon the fact that in China the liberation war was fought mainly on the basis of the partisan struggles of the peasantry, during which the peasants took land from the feudal landlords, and, in the process, created the Liberation Army, it was asserted that in India too, the path would be the same, that is, the path of partisan struggle of the peasantry would almost alone lead us to liberation.

The Central Committee finds that drawing upon the Chinese experience in this way and to come to such a conclusion would mean neglecting to look to other factors of the Chinese Revolution and also neglecting to look into our own specific conditions. For example:

We CANNOT fail to take note of the fact that when the Chinese Party began to lead the peasantry in the liberation struggle, it had already an army which it inherited from the split in the Revolution of 1925.

We CANNOT fail to note the fact that China had no unified and good communication system, which prevented the enemy from carrying out concentrated and swift attacks on the liberation forces. India is different in this respect from China, in that it has a comparatively more unified, well organized and far-flung system of communications.

India has a far bigger working class than China had during her march to freedom.

Further, we cannot fail to note the fact that the Chinese Red Army was surrounded and threatened with annihilation again and again until it reached Manchuria. There, with the industrial base in hand, and the great friendly Soviet Union in the rear, the Chinese Liberation Army, free from the possibility of any attack in the rear, rebuilt itself and launched the final offensive which led it to victory.

The geographical situation in India in this respect is altogether different.

Points of Similarity

This does not mean that there is nothing in common between us and China excepting the stage of our revolution and its main task. On the contrary? Like China, India is of vast expanses. Like China, India has a vast peasant population. Our Revolution, therefore will have many features in common with the Chinese Revolution. But, peasant struggles along the Chinese path alone cannot lead to victory in India.

Moreover, we must bear in mind that the Chinese party stuck to the peasant partisan war alone, not out of a principle, but out of sheer necessity. In their long-drawn struggles, the party and the peasant bases got more and more separated from the working class and its organisations, which prevented the party and the Liberation Army from calling into action the working class in factories, shipping and transport to help it against the enemy.

Because it happened so with the Chinese, why make their necessity into a binding principle for us and fail to bring the working class into practical leadership and action in our liberation struggle?

SUCH AN OUTLOOK IGNORES THE FACT THAT WE HAVE A BIG WORKING CLASS AND THAT IT HAS A ROLE TO PLAY, WHICH CAN BE DECISIVE IN OUR STRUGGLE FOR FREEDOM. THE GRAND ALLIANCE OF THE WORKING CLASS AND THE PEASANTRY, ACTING IN UNISON, THE COMBINATION OF WORKERS' AND PEASANTS' STRUGGLES, UNDER THE LEADERSHIP OF THE COMMUNIST PARTY, AND

UTILISING ALL LESSONS OF HISTORY FOR THE CONDUCT OF THE STRUGGLES IS TO BE THE PATH FOR US.

It can thus be seen that while the previous line of reliance on the general strike in the cities neglected the role of the peasantry, the subsequent one of partisan struggle minimised the role of the working class, which in practice meant depriving the peasantry of its greatest friend and leader. The working class remained leader only "in theory," only through the party, because the party is defined as the party of the working class.

Both the lines in practice meant ignoring the task of building the alliance of the working class and the peasantry, as the basis of the United National Front, ignoring the task of building the United National Front, ignoring the task of putting the working class at the head of this Front in the liberation struggle. . . .

The main question is not, whether there is to be armed struggle or not, the main question is not whether to be nonviolent or violent. It is our opponents who pose for us the question whether our creed is violence or non-violence. Such a poser is a poser of Gandhian ideology, which in practice, misleads the masses and is a poser of which we must steer clear.

MARXISM AND HISTORY HAVE ONCE AND FOR ALL DECIDED THE QUESTION FOR THE PARTY AND THE PEOPLE OF EVERY COUNTRY IN THE WORLD LONG AGO. ALL ACTION OF THE MASSES IN DEFENCE OF THEIR INTERESTS TO ACHIEVE THEIR LIBERATION IS SACROSANCT. HISTORY SANCTIONS ALL THAT THE PEOPLE DECIDE TO DO TO CLEAR THE LUMBERLOAD OF DECADENCE AND REACTION IN THEIR PATH TO PROGRESS AND FREEDOM. . . .

We have to realise that although the masses are getting fast radicalised and moving into action in many parts of the country, the growth of the mass movement has not kept pace with the growth of discontent against the present government and its policies and methods. To ascribe this to repression alone would be wrong. This weakness of the mass movement is due, above all, to the weakness of our party and the division in the camp of progressive forces.

The party, therefore, must strive to overcome this division and must stress the supreme need for unity of all progressive forces, build this unity in action and itself grow into a mass party by drawing into its fold the best elements from the fighting masses. . . .

CHAPTER FIVE

Coexistence and Polycentrism, 1953–1964

Thanks to its great expansion during Stalin's time Communism became a multi-national movement, though it still appeared—with the exception of Yugoslavia—to be firmly united around its center in Moscow. After Stalin's death in 1953 the centrifugal potential of a movement implanted in many diverse countries broke out into the open. Titoism was the prototype for this emergence of polycentrism, and de-Stalinization was the occasion.

Stalin's heirs in Russia tried to salvage their control over the international movement by acknowledging national differences and apologizing for Stalin's transgressions. Khrushchev's mission of penance to Belgrade in 1955 symbolized the new stance, which he elaborated both in his secret speech against Stalin at the Twentieth Party Congress and by his public speech at the same gathering on "peaceful coexistence" and "separate roads to socialism." Taking him at his word, Communists in Poland and Hungary defied Soviet control, and the Hungarians rose in armed revolt. Khrushchev was compelled to put the Hungarian uprising down by force, which did not prevent reform later on; the Poles secured reforms, which did not preclude periodic repression by their own leadership later on. But the signal effect of the events of 1956, as became clear in retrospect, was to cut the bonds of unquestioning Muscovite discipline that had held the Communist movement together ever since the 1920's.

The most consequential outcome of this rupture was the schism—at first ideological, then a profound divergence and antagonism in national policy—between Soviet Russia and Communist China. Repudiating Khrushchev's leadership as "revisionist," Mao Tse-tung and his lieutenants launched into an escalating series of radical policy innovations that ultimately brought China into the realm of a new kind of social revolution, one which disgusted the Soviets but found a curious echo among the New Left in the West. Meanwhile the divergence of Moscow and Peking had created a state of bipolarity and a zone of latitude in the movement within which Communist parties and even governments could stake out positions of national individuality. Albania became a mouthpiece for China; Rumania claimed neutrality despite its Stalinist internal regime; many Third World Communist parties, notably the Indian, split into pro-Moscow and pro-Peking factions; and the major Communist parties of Europe began to reconcile themselves to the democratic way in politics.

Simultaneously with the ferment he had uncorked in the Communist movement, Khrushchev pressed for an end to the Cold War with the West. Following the truces that ended the Korean and (temporarily) Vietnam wars in 1953 and 1954, Khrushchev went to the first and only post-war four-power summit meeting of heads of state at Geneva in 1955, overcame the ill will of the Hungarian and Suez crises in 1956, and went on to press the themes of détente and disarmament culminating in his 1959 visit to the United States. The following year, perhaps under pressure from the neo-Stalinist faction at home, Khrushchev reverted abruptly to Cold War politics. Embarrassed by the American U-2 reconnaissance planes that had been traversing Soviet airspace until one was downed on May Day of 1960, he broke up the scheduled Paris Summit Conference, turned up his anti-imperialist rhetoric, ostentatiously resumed nuclear weapons testing, brought the situation in divided Berlin almost to the point of armed conflict, and embraced the new revolution of Fidel Castro in Cuba. In 1963, perhaps as the domestic political scene became momentarily relaxed after his adversary Frol Kozlov had a heart attack, Khrushchev reversed himself again to resume the strategy of détente and conclude the Nuclear Test Ban Treaty. But his brief resumption of hard-line diplomacy left permanent consequences: the division of Germany, cemented by the Berlin Wall; the parting of the ways with China; and the Communist bridgehead in Cuba, setting a precedent for a new form of Communist expansion through the cooptation of Third World nationalist revolutionaries.

Malenkov on Peaceful Cooperation

No sooner had Stalin breathed his last than the Soviet government took steps to alleviate international tensions, presumably including advice to the Chinese to accept a cease-fire ending the Korean War. Prime Minister Malenkov expounded the moderate line in a speech to the Supreme Soviet in August, 1953.

. . . Desirous of promoting peaceful cooperation with all countries, the Soviet Government attaches particular importance to strengthening the Soviet Union's relations with its neighbours. To elevate these relations to the level of genuine good-neighbourliness is the aim for which we are striving and will continue to strive.

The Soviet Union has no territorial claims on any country, and none, in particular, on any of its neighbours. Respect for the national liberty and sovereignty of all countries, big and small, is an inviolable principle of our foreign policy. It goes without saying that the fact that our social and economic system differs from that of some of our neighbours cannot be an obstacle to the furtherance of friendly relations with them. The Soviet Government has, on its part, taken measures to promote neighbourly friendship with such countries, and everything now depends on the readiness of their governments actively to co-operate in establishing the friendship in fact, and not only in word, friendship which presumes mutual concern for safeguarding the peace and security of our countries. . . .

The active and persistant efforts for peace of the Soviet Union and the entire democratic peace camp have yielded definite results. A change in the international atmosphere is to be observed. After a long period of mounting tension, one feels for the first time since the war a certain easing of the international situation. Hundreds of millions of people are becoming increasingly hopeful that a way can be found of settling disputes and outstanding issues. This is a reflection of the deep desire of the peoples for stable and prolonged peace.

We cannot, however, close our eyes to the fact that there are forces which are

FROM: Malenkov, Speech to the Supreme Soviet of the USSR, August 8, 1953 (English translation in *Soviet News*, August 15, 1953; reprinted in *Documents on International Affairs*, 1953, pp. 22–25, 30).

working against the policy of relaxing international tension and trying to frustrate it at any cost. That is why the Korean armistice negotiations were so protracted, why strategic bridgeheads are being built in West Germany and Japan, why provocations are instigated against the countries of the democratic camp, and why the policy of atomic blackmail is persisted in.

The aggressive elements are stubbornly working against relaxation of international tension because they fear that if developments take this course they will have to curtail armaments programmes, which are a source of huge profits to the munitions manufacturers and which create artificial employment for industry. They fear for their fabulous profits. These elements are afraid that if international tension is lessened, more millions upon millions of people will realize that the North Atlantic bloc, which was ostensibly established for defence, actually constitutes the principal danger to peace. The aggressive elements are also aware that if now, at the time of international tension, the North Atlantic bloc is torn by internal conflicts and contradictions, it may fall to pieces altogether if that tension is relaxed. . . .

Soviet foreign policy is clear.

The Soviet Union will consistently and firmly pursue a policy of preserving and consolidating peace, will promote co-operation and business relations with all states which have a like desire, and strengthen the ties of brotherly friendship and solidarity with the great Chinese people, with all the People's Democracies.

We firmly stand by the belief that there are no disputed or outstanding issues today which cannot be settled peacefully by mutual agreement between the parties concerned.

This also relates to disputed issues between the United States of America and the Soviet Union. We stand, as we have always stood, for the peaceful co-existence of the two systems. We hold that there are no objective reasons for clashes between the United States of America and the Soviet Union. The security of the two states and of the world, and the development of trade between the United States of America and the Soviet Union, can be ensured on the basis of normal relations between the two countries. . . .

China and Coexistence

Following the armistice that concluded the Korean War in 1953, Chinese Communist foreign policy began to emphasize accommodations with non-Communist Asian states. An agreement with India in 1954 stated "five principles" of coexistence, which the Chinese proclaimed as the basis of their policy. In 1955 China participated in the Bandung Conference of Asian and African states, at which Chou En-lai proclaimed the community of interest of these countries against the Western colonial powers and sought to allay fears about Chinese expansion.

a) The "Five Principles" of Coexistence

. . . Recently India and China have come to an agreement in which they have laid down certain principles which should guide relations between the two countries. These principles are: (1) mutual respect for each other's territorial integrity and sovereignty, (2) non-aggression, (3) non-interference in each other's internal

---

FROM: Communiqué on Talks between Jawaharlal Nehru and Chou En-lai, June 28, 1954 (*India News*, July 3, 1954; reprinted in *Documents on International Affairs*, 1954, pp. 313-314).

affairs, (4) equality and mutual benefit and (5) peaceful co-existence. The Prime Ministers reaffirmed their principles and felt that they should be applied in their relations with other countries in Asia as well as in other parts of the world. If these principles are applied not only between various countries, but also in international relations generally, they would form a solid foundation for peace and security, and the fears and apprehensions that exist today would give place to a feeling of confidence.

The Prime Ministers recognized that different social and political systems exist in various parts of Asia and the world. If, however, the above-mentioned principles are accepted and acted upon and there is no interference by any one country with another, this difference should not come in the way of peace or create conflicts. With assurance of the territorial integrity and sovereignty of each country and of non-aggression, there would be peaceful co-existence and friendly relations between the countries concerned. This would lessen the tensions that exist in the world today and help in creating a climate of peace. . . .

b) The Bandung Conference

The Chinese Delegation has come here to seek unity and not to quarrel. We Communists do not hide the fact that we believe in communism and that we consider the socialist system a good system. There is no need at this Conference to publicize one's ideology and the political system of one's country, although differences do exist among us.

The Chinese Delegation has come here to seek common ground, and not to create divergence. Is there any basis for seeking common ground among us? Yes, there is. The overwhelming majority of the Asian and African countries and peoples have suffered and are still suffering from the calamities of colonialism. This is acknowledged by all of us. If we seek common ground in doing away with the sufferings and calamities under colonialism, it will be very easy for us to have mutual understanding and respect, mutual sympathy and support, instead of mutual suspicion and fear, mutual exclusion and antagonism. . . .

Now first of all I would like to talk about the question of different ideologies and social systems. We have to admit that among our Asian and African countries, we do have different ideologies and different social systems. But this does not prevent us from seeking common ground and being united. Many independent countries have appeared since the Second World War. One group of them are countries led by the Communist parties; another group of them are countries led by nationalists. There are not many countries in the first group. But what some people dislike is the fact that the 600 million Chinese people have chosen a political system which is socialist in nature and led by the Chinese Communist Party and that the Chinese people are no longer under the rule of imperialism. The countries in the second group are greater in number, such as India, Burma, Indonesia and many other countries in Asia and Africa. Out of the colonial rule both of these groups of countries have become independent and are still continuing their struggle for complete independence. Is there any reason why we cannot understand and respect each other and give support and sympathy to each other? There is every reason to make the five principles the basis for establishIng friendly co-operation and good

FROM: Chou En-lai, Speech to the Bandung Conference, April 19, 1955 (in *Asia-Africa Speaks from Bandung*, Jakarta, 1955; reprinted in *Documents on International Affairs*, 1955, pp. 409–11).

neighbourly relations among us. We Asian and African countries, with China included, are all backward economically and culturally. If our Asian-African Conference does not exclude anybody, why couldn't we understand each other and enter into friendly cooperation?

Secondly, I would like to talk about the question as to whether there is freedom of religious belief. Freedom of religious belief is a principle recognized by all modern nations. We Communists are atheists, but we respect all those who have religious belief. We hope that those who have religious belief will also respect those without. China is a country where there is freedom of religious belief. There are in China, not only seven million Communists, but also tens of millions of Islamists and Buddhists and millions of Christians and Catholics. Here in the Chinese Delegation, there is a pious Imam of the Islamic faith. Such a situation is no obstacle to the internal unity of China. Why should it be impossible in the community of Asian and African countries to unite those with religious belief and those without? The days of instigating religious strife should have passed, because those who profit from instigating such strife are not those among us.

Thirdly, I would like to talk about the question of the so-called subversive activities. The struggle of the Chinese people against colonialism lasted for more than a hundred years. The national and democratic revolutionary struggles led by the Chinese Communist Party finally achieved success only after a strenuous and difficult course of thirty years. It is impossible to relate all the sufferings of the Chinese people under the rule of imperialism, feudalism and Chiang Kai-shek. At last, the Chinese people have chosen their state system and the present government. It is by the efforts of the Chinese people that the Chinese revolution has won its victory. It is certainly not imported from without. The point cannot be denied even by those who do not like the victory of the Chinese Revolution. As a Chinese proverb says: "Do not do unto others what you yourself do not desire." We are against outside interference; how could we want to interfere in the internal affairs of others? . . .

The Warsaw Pact

The early post-Stalin overtures to the West met with little response; on the contrary, the North Atlantic Treaty Organization was stiffened in 1955 with the inclusion of West Germany. The Soviets responded by formalizing their military coordination wirh the satellite countries in the Warsaw Pact. This reinforced the political and economic integration of the Soviet bloc initiated with the Council of Economic Mutual Assistance (Comecon) in 1949.

The contracting parties:

Confirm once again their striving for the creation of a system of collective security in Europe based on the participation of all European states, irrespective of their social or state structure, which would make it possible to unite their efforts in the interest of insuring peace in Europe.

Taking into consideration at the same time the situation which has arisen in Europe as the result of the ratification of the Paris agreements envisaging the for-

FROM: Treaty of Friendship, Cooperation and Mutual Assistance between the People's Republic of Albania, the People's Republic of Bulgaria, the Hungarian People's Republic, the German Democratic Republic, the Polish People's Republic, the Rumanian People's Republic, the Union of Soviet Socialist Republics, and the Czechoslovak Republic, May 14, 1955 (English translation in *The New York Times*, May 15, 1955).

mation of a new military alignment in the form of the West European Union with the participation of Western Germany, which is being remilitarized, and her inclusion in the North Atlantic bloc, which increases the danger of a new war and creates a threat to the national security of peace-loving states;

Being convinced of the fact that in these circumstances peace-loving states in Europe must take measures necessary to safeguard their security and in the interests of preserving peace in Europe;

Guided by the aims and principles of the United Nations Charter, in the interests of the further strengthening and developing of friendship, collaboration and mutual assistance in accordance with the principles of respecting the independence and sovereignty of the states and non-interference in their internal affairs;

Have decided to conclude the present treaty of friendship, collaboration and mutual assistance. . . .

Article I

The high contracting parties undertake, in accordance with the United Nations Charter, to abstain in their international relations from threats of violence or its use and to settle international disputes by peaceful means, so as not to put each other or international peace in danger.

Article II

The contracting parties declare their readiness to cooperate in all international actions with the purpose of insuring international peace and security.

With that, the contracting parties will strive to reach agreement with states desiring to cooperate in that cause and take measures to reduce armaments and ban atomic, hydrogen, and other kinds of weapons of mass destruction.

Article III

The contracting parties will consult mutually on all important international problems affecting their common interests, taking as their guide the interests of strengthening international peace and security. They will immediately consult each time in the event of a threat of armed attack against one or several states, signatories to the pact, in the interest of insuring their mutual defense and of maintaining peace and security.

Article IV

In case of armed aggression in Europe against one or several states party to the pact by a state or group of states, each state member of the pact, in order to put into practice the right to individual or collective self-defense, in accordance with Article 51 of the U.N. Charter, will afford to the state or states which are the objects of such an aggression immediate assistance, individually and in agreement with other states party to the pact, with all means which appear necessary, including the use of armed force.

The parties to the pact will immediately take joint measures necessary to establish and preserve international peace and security.

Article V

The contracting powers agree to set up a joint command of their armed forces to be allotted by agreement between the powers, at the disposal of this command and used on the basis of jointly established principles.

They will also take other agreed measures necessary to strengthen their defenses in order to protect the peaceful toil of their peoples, guarantee the integrity of their frontiers and territories and insure their defense against possible aggression.

Article VI

With the object of carrying out consultations prescribed by the present treaty between the states participating in the treaty and for the examination of questions arising in connection with the fulfillment of this treaty, a political consultative committee is being set up in which each state participating in the treaty will be represented by a member of its Government or another specially appointed representative.

The committee may set up any auxiliary organs it considers necessary.

Article VII

The contracting parties undertake not to enter into any coalitions or unions and not to enter into any agreements whose aims are contrary to the aims of this treaty.

The contracting parties declare that their obligations under existing international agreements are not contrary to the terms of the present treaty.

Article VIII

The contracting parties declare that they will act in a spirit of friendship and cooperation in order further to develop the economic and cultural ties between them, and will be guided by principles of mutual respect and will not interfere in the internal affairs of each other. . . .

Article XI

The present treaty will remain in force for twenty years. Those states which do not give notice of abrogation one year before the treaty expires will remain bound by it for a further ten years.

In the event of a system of collective security being set up in Europe and a pact to this effect being signed—to which each party to this treaty will direct its efforts—the present treaty will lapse from the day such a collective security treaty comes into force.

Drawn up in Warsaw May 14, 1955, in one copy each in Russian, Polish, Czech and German, each text being equally valid.

Khrushchev and Tito

In May, 1955, Khrushchev went to Belgrade to apologize for Yugoslavia's expulsion from the Soviet bloc and restore close relations. The Cominform was dissolved, but Tito was careful to avoid Soviet control, and after he took an independent position on the Hungarian uprising of 1956, he was once again repudiated by the Russians.

FROM: Khrushchev, Speech on Arrival at Belgrade, May 26, 1955 (English translation in *Soviet News*, May 27, 1955; reprinted in *Documents on International Affairs*, 1955, pp. 265–66).

Dear Comrade Tito, dear comrades, members of the government and leaders of the Union of Communists of Yugoslavia, dear comrades and citizens.

In the name of the Presidium of the Supreme Soviet of the U.S.S.R., of the government of the Soviet Union and of the Central Committee of the Communist Party of the Soviet Union, on behalf of the Soviet people I extend cordial greetings to you and to the working people of the glorious capital of Yugoslavia, Belgrade, to all the fraternal peoples of Yugoslavia. . . .

The peoples of our countries are bound by ties of an age-old fraternal friendship and joint struggle against common enemies. This friendship and militant co-operation had been especially strengthened in the hard trials of the struggle against the fascist invaders, in the years of the Second World War. . . .

It will be remembered that those years witnessed the development of the best relations between the peoples of the Soviet Union and Yugoslavia, between our states and our Parties. But those good relations were disturbed in the years that followed.

We sincerely regret that, and we resolutely sweep aside all the bitterness of that period.

On our part, we have no doubt about the part played in provoking that bitterness in the relations between Yugoslavia and the U.S.S.R. by Beria, Abakumov* and other exposed enemies of the people. We have thoroughly investigated the materials upon which the grave accusations against and insults to the leaders of Yugoslavia were based at that time. Facts indicate that those materials were fabricated by the enemies of the people, the contemptible agents of imperialism who had fraudulently wormed their way into the ranks of our Party. . . .

True to the teachings of the founder of the Soviet state, Vladimir Ilich Lenin, the government of the Soviet Union bases its relations with other countries, big and small, on the principles of the peaceful co-existence of states, on the principles of equality, non-interference, respect for sovereignty and national independence, on the principles of non-aggression and recognition that any encroachments by states upon the territorial integrity of other states are impermissible.

We hope that the relations between our countries will in the future too develop on the basis of these principles, for the good of our peoples. And that will be another major contribution to the efforts to ease international tension, to sustain and strengthen general peace.

We fully appreciate Yugoslavia's desire to promote relations with all states, in the West and in the East. We believe that greater friendship and contact between our countries will help to improve relations between all countries, irrespective of social system, and to advance the cause of general peace.

Khrushchev On Peaceful Coexistence

Simultaneously with his spectacular though unofficial repudiation of Stalin in February, 1956, Khrushchev publicly enunciated a position with even more far-reaching implications

---

*V. S. Abakumov: Beria's deputy for state security; tried and shot in December, 1954—Ed.

FROM: Khrushchev, Report of the Central Committee to the Twentieth Party Congress, February, 1956 (English translation in *Current Soviet Policies*, II:36–38). Copyright by *The Current Digest of the Soviet Press*; reprinted by permission.

for Communism as an international revolutionary movement. This was his doctrine of peaceful coexistence with capitalism and separate roads to socialism, including a possible nonviolent path, reflecting the conditions and traditions of different countries.

Comrades! I should like to dwell on some fundamental questions concerning present-day international development which determine not only the present course of events but also future prospects.

These are the questions of peaceful coexistence of the two systems, the possibility of preventing wars in the present era, and the forms of transition to socialism in different countries.

Let us examine these questions briefly.

The peaceful coexistence of the two systems. The Leninist principle of peaceful coexistence of states with different social systems has always been and remains the general line of our country's foreign policy.

It has been alleged that the Soviet Union advances the principle of peaceful coexistence merely out of tactical considerations, considerations of expediency. Yet it is common knowledge that we have always, from the very first years of Soviet power, stood with equal firmness for peaceful coexistence. Hence it is not a tactical move, but a fundamental principle of Soviet foreign policy.

This means that, if there is indeed a threat to the peaceful coexistence of countries with differing social-political systems, it by no means comes from the Soviet Union or the socialist camp. Is there a single reason why a socialist state should want to unleash aggressive war? Do we have classes and groups that are interested in war as a means of enrichment? We do not; we liquidated them long ago. Or perhaps do we not have enough territory or natural resources, do we lack sources of raw materials or markets for our goods? No, we have enough of all those, and to spare. Why then should we want war? We do not want it. As a matter of principle we renounce any policy that might lead to millions of people being plunged into war for the sake of the selfish interests of a handful of billionaires. Do those who shout about the "aggressive intentions" of the U.S.S.R. know all this? Of course they do. Why then do they keep up the monotonous, old refrain about an imaginary "Communist aggression"? Only to muddy the waters, to conceal their own plans for world domination, for a "crusade" against peace, democracy and socialism.

To this day, the enemies of peace allege that the Soviet Union is out to overthrow capitalism in other countries by "exporting" revolution. It goes without saying that among us Communists there are no supporters of capitalism. But this does not at all mean that we have interfered or plan to interfere in the internal affairs of countries where the capitalist order exists. Romain Rolland was right when he said: "Freedom is not brought in from abroad in baggage trains, like Bourbons." (*Stir in the hall.*) It is ridiculous to think that revolutions are made to order. One often hears representatives of bourgeois countries reasoning thus: "The Soviet leaders claim that they are for peaceful coexistence between the two systems. At the same time, they declare that they are fighting for communism and say that communism is bound to win in all countries. How can there be any peaceful coexistence with the Soviet Union if it is fighting for communism?" This interpretation is formed under the influence of bourgeois propaganda. The ideologists of the bourgeoisie, distorting the facts, deliberately confuse questions of ideological struggle with questions of relations between states in order to make the Communists of the Soviet Union seem aggressive people.

When we say that the socialist system will win in the competition between the two systems—the capitalist and the socialist—this by no means signifies that its victory will be achieved through armed interference by the socialist countries in the internal affairs of capitalist countries. Our certainty of the victory of communism is based on the fact that the socialist mode of production possesses decisive superiority over the capitalist mode of production. Precisely because of this, the ideas of Marxism-Leninism are more and more capturing the minds of the broad masses of the working people in the capitalist countries, just as they have captured the minds of millions of men and women in our country and the people's democracies. (*Prolonged applause.*) We believe that all the working people on earth, once they have become convinced of the advantages communism brings, will sooner or later take the road of struggle for the construction of a socialist society. (*Prolonged applause.*) Building communism in our country, we are resolutely against war. We have always held and continue to hold that the establishment of a new social system in one or another country is the internal affair of the peoples of the countries concerned. This is our position, based on the great Marxist-Leninist teaching. The principle of peaceful coexistence is gaining ever wider international recognition. This principle has become one of the cornerstones of the foreign policy of the Chinese People's Republic and the other people's democracies. It is being actively implemented by the Republic of India, the Union of Burma, and a number of other countries. And this is natural, for there is no other way in present-day conditions. Indeed there are only two ways: either peaceful coexistence or the most destructive war in history. There is no third way. . . .

As long as imperialism exists, the economic base giving rise to wars will also remain. That is why we must display the greatest vigilance. As long as capitalism survives in the world, reactionary forces, representing the interests of the capitalist monopolies, will continue their drive toward military gambles and aggression and may try to unleash war. But war is not a fatalistic inevitability. Today there are mighty social and political forces possessing formidable means to prevent the imperialists from unleashing war and, if they try to start it, to give a smashing rebuff to the aggressors and frustrate their adventurist plans. For this it is necessary for all anti-war forces to be vigilant and mobilized; they must act as a united front and not relax their efforts in the struggle for peace. The more actively the peoples defend peace, the greater the guarantee that there will be no new war. (*Stormy, prolonged applause.*)

Forms of transition to socialism in different countries. In connection with the radical changes in the world arena, new prospects are also opening up in regard to the transition of countries and nations to socialism.

As far back as on the eve of the great October socialist revolution, V. I. Lenin wrote: "All nations will arrive at socialism—this is inevitable—but not all will do so in exactly the same way. Each will contribute something of its own in one or another form of democracy, one or another variety of the dictatorship of the proletariat, one or another rate at which socialist transformations will be effected in the various aspects of social life. There is nothing more primitive from the viewpoint of theory or more ridiculous from that of practice than to paint *this* aspect of the future in a monotonous gray 'in the name of historical materialism.' The result would be nothing more than Suzdal daubing" (V. I. Lenin, "Works" [in Russian], Vol. XXIII, p. 58).

Historical experience has fully confirmed this brilliant precept of Lenin's. Now, alongside the Soviet form of reorganizing society on socialist foundations, we have the form of people's democracy.

This form sprang up in Poland, Bulgaria, Czechoslovakia, Albania, and the other European people's democracies and is being employed in conformity with the specific historical social and economic conditions and peculiarities of each of these countries. It has been thoroughly tried and tested for ten years and has fully proved its worth.

Much that is unique in socialist construction is being contributed by the Chinese People's Republic, possessing an economy which was exceedingly backward and bore a semifeudal and semicolonial character until the triumph of the revolution. Having taken over the decisive commanding positions, the people's democratic state is pursuing a policy of peaceful reorganization of private industry and trade and their gradual transformation into components of the socialist economy in the course of the socialist revolution.

Leadership of the great cause of socialist reconstruction by the Communist Party of China and the Communist and Workers' Parties of the other people's democracies in keeping with the peculiarities and specific features of each country is creative Marxism in action. In the Federal People's Republic of Yugoslavia, where power belongs to the working people and society is founded on public ownership of the means of production, unique specific forms of economic management and organization of the state apparatus are arising in the process of socialist construction.

It is quite probable that the forms of transition to socialism will become more and more varied; moreover, achieving these forms need not be associated with civil war under all circumstances. Our enemies like to depict us Leninists as advocates of violence always and everywhere. True, we recognize the need for the revolutionary transformation of capitalist society into socialist society. It is this that distinguishes the revolutionary Marxists from the reformists, the opportunists. There is no doubt that in a number of capitalist countries violent overthrow of the dictatorship of the bourgeoisie and the sharp aggravation of class struggle connected with this are inevitable. But the forms of social revolution vary. And it is not true that we regard violence and civil war as the only way to remake society. . . .

In present-day conditions the working class in many capitalist countries has a genuine opportunity to unite the overwhelming majority of the people under its leadership and to ensure that the basic means of production are placed in the hands of the people. Rightist bourgeois parties and the governments which they form are suffering failure more and more often. In these conditions, the working class, uniting around itself the working peasantry, the intellectuals and all patriotic forces, and firmly rebuffing opportunist elements incapable of renouncing a policy of collaboration with the capitalists and landlords, has an opportunity to defeat the reactionary, antipopular forces, to win a firm majority in parliament and to turn the parliament from an agency of bourgeois democracy into an instrument of genuinely popular will. (*Applause.*) In such a case this institution, traditional in many highly developed capitalist countries, may become an agency of genuine democracy for the working people.

De-Stalinization and Polycentrism

The publication of Khrushchev's criticism of Stalin produced a major crisis in the Communist parties outside Russia. The East European satellites were in ferment, while many Western Communist leaders expressed grave misgivings or actually quit the movement. Palmiro Togliatti, head of the Communist Party of Italy, raised broad questions of the defects which permitted Stalinism, and considered the possibility of decentralizing the Communist movement.

. . . We must admit openly and without hesitation that while the XXth Congress greatly aided the proper understanding and solution of many serious and new problems confronting the democratic and socialist movement, and while it marks a most important milestone in the evolution of Soviet society, it is not possible, however, to consider satisfactory the position which was taken at the Congress and which today is being fully developed in the Soviet press regarding the errors of Stalin and the causes and conditions which made them possible.

The basic cause of everything allegedly lies in the "personality cult," and in the cult of one person with specific and serious faults who lacked modesty, leaned toward personal power, who at times erred because of incompetence, was not loyal in his relations with the other leaders, who had a megalomania for self-aggrandizement and excessive self-love, was suspicious in the extreme, and at the end through the exercise of personal power reached the point where he detached himself from the people, neglected his work, and even submitted to an obvious form of persecution mania. . . .

. . . As long as we confine ourselves, in substance, to denouncing the personal faults of Stalin as the cause of everything we remain within the realm of the "personality cult." First, all that was good was attributed to the superhuman, positive qualities of one man: now all that is evil is attributed to his equally exceptional and even astonishing faults. In the one case, as well as in the other, we are outside the criterion of judgment intrinsic in Marxism. The true problems are evaded, which are why and how Soviet society could reach and did reach certain forms alien to the democratic way and to the legality which it had set for itself, even to the point of degeneration. . . .

We are reminded, first of all, that Lenin, in his last speeches and writings, stressed the danger of bureaucracy which threatened the new society. It seems to us that undoubtedly Stalin's errors were tied in with an excessive increase in the bureaucràtic apparatus in Soviet economic and political life, and perhaps, above all in party life. And here it is extremely difficult to distinguish between cause and effect. The one gradually became the expression of the other. Is this excessive bureaucratic burden also a traditional outgrowth of political and organizational forms and customs of Old Russia? . . .

The first years after the revolution were hard and terrible years marked by superhuman difficulties, foreign intervention, war, and civil war. A maximum of power centralization was required along with severe repressive measures to crush the counter-revolution. . . . At this time the fight erupted between groups who

FROM: Togliatti Interview, "Nine Questions on Stalinism," *Nuovi Argomenti*, June 16, 1956 (English translation in *The Anti-Stalin Campaign*, New York, Columbia Universiry Press, 1956, pp. 119–25, 138–39; reprinted by permission of the publisher).

were at odds over the possibilities of socialist economic development, and this naturally had a widespread influence on all of Soviet life. This struggle also had all the elements of a real battle, which was decisive in determining who would assume power, and which had to be won at any price.

And it was in this period that Stalin assumed a positive role, and the sound forces of the party rallied and united around him. Now it can be observed that these forces rallied around Stalin and, guided by him, accepted such modifications in the function of the party and of its directing organisms, i.e., the new functioning of the apparatus controlled from above, as a result of which either they could not offer opposition when the evils began to appear, or else at the outset they did not fully understand that they were evils.

Perhaps we are not in error in asserting that the damaging restrictions placed on the democratic regime and the gradual emergence of bureaucratic organizational forms stemmed from the party.

More important it seems to me should be a close examination of that which followed, when the first Five-Year Plan was carried out, and agricultural collectivization was realized. Here we are dealing with fundamental questions. The successes attained were great, in fact, superlative. . . .

In the exaltation of the achievements there prevailed, particularly in the then current propaganda but also in the general political line, a tendency to exaggerate, to consider all problems already solved and objective contradictions, difficulties, and differences, which are always inherent in the development of a society, as having been overcome. . . .

When reality came into play and difficulties came to light as the result of the imbalance and contrasts which still existed everywhere, there occurred little by little, until at last it was the main force, the tendency to consider that, always and in every case, every evil, every obstacle in the application of the plan, every difficulty in supplying provisions, in delivering raw materials, in the development of the various sectors of industry or agriculture, etc.—all was due to sabotage, to the work of class enemies, counterrevolutionary groups operating clandestinely, etc. It is not that these things did not exist; they did indeed exist. The Soviet Union was surrounded by merciless enemies who were ready to resort to any means to damage and to check its rise. But this erroneous trend in judging the objective situation caused a loss of the sense of limits, made them lose the idea of the borderline between good and evil, friend and enemy, incapacity or weakness and conscious hostility and betrayal, contrasts and difficulties which come from things and from the hostile action of one who has sworn to ruin you. Stalin gave a pseudo-scientific formulation to this fearful confusion through his erroneous thesis of the inherent increase in enemies and in the sharpening of the class struggle with the progress of building socialism. This made permanent and aggravated the confusion itself and was the origin of the unheard-of violations of socialist legality which have been denounced publicly today. . . .

What the CPSU has done remains, as I said, as the first great model of building a socialist society for which the way was opened by a deep, decisive revolutionary breach. Today, the front of socialist construction in countries where the Communists are the leading party has been so broadened (amounting to a third of the human race) that even for this part the Soviet model cannot and must not any longer be obligatory. In every country governed by the Communists, the objective and subjective conditions, traditions, the organizational forms of the movement can and must assert their influence in different ways. In the rest of the world there are countries where we wish to start socialism although the Communists are not the leading party. In still other countries, the march toward socialism is an objective for which there is a concentration of efforts coming from various movements, which, however, have not yet reached either an agreement or a reciprocal understanding. The whole system becomes polycentric, and even in the Communist movement itself we cannot speak of a single guide but rather of a progress which is achieved by following paths which are often different. One general problem, common to the entire movement, has arisen from the criticisms of Stalin—the problem of the perils of bureaucratic degeneration, of stifling democratic life, of the confusion between the constructive revolutionary force and the destruction of revolutionary legality, of separation of the economic and political leadership from the life, criticism, and creative activity of the masses. We shall welcome a contest among the Communist parties in power to find the best way to avoid this peril once and for all. It will be up to us to work out our own method and life in order that we, too, may be protected against the evils of stagnation and bureaucratization, in order that we may learn to solve together the problems of freedom for the working masses and of social justice, and hence gain for ourselves ever increasing prestige and membership among the masses.

The "October Revolution" in Poland

In June, 1956, while hopes for reform were sweeping Eastern Europe, Poland was shaken by a workers' uprising in the city of Poznan. The Stalinists lost their hold on the Polish Communist Party, and in October Gomulka was reinstated as Secretary General in defiance of the Russians. Gomulka then addressed his Central Committee on the nation's economic straits and the need for a more gradual, humane, and national road to socialism

When I addressed the November Plenum of the Central Committee of the Polish United Workers' Party seven years ago, I thought that it was my last speech to the members of the Central Committee. Although only seven years have elapsed since that time, or eight years since the August Plenum, where an abrupt change occurred in the party's policy, these years constitute a closed historic period. I am deeply convinced that that period has gone into the irrevocable past. There has been much evil in those years. The legacy that this period left the party, the working class, and the nation is more than alarming in certain spheres of life. . . .

The working class recently gave a painful lesson to the party leadership and the Government. When seizing the weapon of strike and going out to demonstrate in the streets on the black Thursday last June, the Poznan workers shouted in a powerful voice: Enough! This cannot go on any longer! Turn back from the false road. . . .

The Poznan workers did not protest against People's Poland, against socialism

FROM: Gomulka, Speech to the Central Committee of the Polish United Workers' [Communist] Party, October 20, 1956 (English translation in Paul Zinner, ed., *National Communism and Popular Revolt in Eastern Europe*, New York, Columbia University Press, 1956, pp. 197, 206–7, 209–10, 212, 222, 226–28, 230–33, 235–36, 238; this and following selections reprinted by permission of the publisher).

when they went out into the streets of the city. They protested against the evil which was widespread in our social system and which was painfully felt also by them, against the distortions of the fundamental principles of socialism, which is their idea. . . .

The clumsy attempt to present the painful Poznan tragedy as the work of imperialist agents and provocateurs was very naive politically. Agents and provocateurs can be and act anywhere, but never and nowhere can they determine the attitude of the working class. . . .

Among the charges which were raised against me in the past was that my attitude in different matters stemmed from an alleged lack of faith in the working class. This is not true. I have never lost faith in the wisdom, common sense, self-lessness, and revolutionary attitude of the working class. In these values of the working class I believe also today. I am convinced that the Poznan workers would not have gone on strike, that they would not have demonstrated in the streets, that no men would have been found among them who even resorted to arms, that our fraternal, workers' blood would not have been shed there had the party, that is the leadership of the party, presented the whole truth to them. It was necessary to recognize without any delays the just claims of the workers; it was necessary to say what can be done today and what cannot be done; it was necessary to tell them the truth about the past and the present. There is no escaping from truth. If you cover it up, it will rise as an awful specter, frightening, alarming, and madly raging. . . .

The loss of the credit of confidence of the working class means the loss of the moral basis of power.

It is possible to govern the country even in such conditions. But then this will be bad government, for it must be based on bureaucracy, on infringing the rule of law, on violence. The essence of the dictatorship of the proletariat, as the broadest democracy for the working class and the working masses, becomes in such conditions deprived of its meaning. . . .

. . . We must tell the working class the painful truth. We cannot afford at the present moment any considerable increase of wages, for the string has already been stretched so tight that it can break. . . .

The road to setting up a vast network of cooperative farms in Poland's countryside is a long one. A quantitative development of producer cooperation cannot be planned because, on the basis of voluntary entry in a cooperative, this would amount to planning the growth in human consciousness, and that cannot be planned. The consciousness of the masses is shaped by their experience in life. It is shaped by facts. There are not a few facts in our present state of cooperative farming which repel the peasant masses from the cooperative farms. Such facts must be liquidated. . . .

What is immutable in socialism can be reduced to the abolition of the exploitation of man by man. The roads of achieving the goal can be and are different. They are determined by various considerations of time and place. The model of socialism can also vary. It can be such as that created in the Soviet Union; it can be shaped in a manner as we see it in Yugoslavia; it can be different still.

Only by way of the experience and achievements of various countries building socialism can the best model of socialism under given conditions arise. . . .

. . . The mapping out of the Russian road to socialism passed gradually from the hands of the Central Committee into the hands of an even smaller group of people, and finally became the monopoly of Stalin. This monopoly also encompassed the theory of scientific socialism.

The cult of personality is a specific system of exercising power, a specific road of advancing in the direction of socialism, while applying methods contrary to socialist humanism, to the socialist conception of the freedom of man, to the socialist conception of legality. . . .

The cult of personality cannot be confined solely to the person of Stalin. The cult of personality is a certain system which prevailed in the Soviet Union and which was grafted to probably all Communist Parties, as well as to a number of countries of the socialist camp, including Poland.

The essence of this system consisted in the fact that an individual, hierarchic ladder of cults was created. Each such cult comprised a given area in which it functioned. In the bloc of socialist states it was Stalin who stood at the top of this hierarchic ladder of cults. All those who stood on lower rungs of the ladder bowed their heads before him. Those who bowed their heads were not only the other leaders of the Communist Party of the Soviet Union and the leaders of the Soviet Union, but also the leaders of Communist and Workers Parties of the countries of the socialist camp. The latter, that is the First Secretaries of the Central Committees of the Parties of the various countries who sat on the second rung of the ladder of the cult of personality, in turn donned the robes of infallibility and wisdom. . . .

That system violated the democratic principles and the rule of law. Under that system, the characters and consciences of men were broken, people were trampled underfoot and their honor was besmirched. Slandering, falsehood and lies, even provocations, served as instruments in the exercise of authority.

In Poland, too, tragic events occurred when innocent people were sent to their death. Many others were imprisoned, often for many years, although innocent, including Communists. Many people were submitted to bestial tortures. Terror and demoralization were spread. On the soil of the cult of personality, phenomena arose which violated and even nullified the most profound meaning of the people's power.

We have put an end to this system, or we are putting an end to it once and for all. Great appreciation should be expressed to the 20th Congress of the CPSU which so greatly helped us in the liquidation of this system. . . .

The road of democratization is the only road leading to the construction of the best model of socialism in our conditions. We shall not deviate from this road and we shall defend ourselves with all our might not to be pushed off this road. And we shall not allow anyone to use the process of democratization to undermine socialism. Our party is taking its place at the head of the process of democratization and only the party, acting in conjunction with the other parties of the National Front, can guide this process in a way that will truly lead to the democratization of relations in all the spheres of our life, to the strengthening of the foundation of our system, and not to their weakening.

The party and all the people who saw the evil that existed in the past and who sincerely desire to remove all that is left of the past evil in our life today in order to strengthen the foundations of our system should give a determined rebuff to all persuasions and all voices which strive to weaken our friendship with the Soviet Union.

If in the past not everything in the relations between our party and the CPSU and between Poland and the Soviet Union shaped up in the manner it should have in our view, then today this belongs to the irrevocable past. . . .

Among the main ailments of the past period was also the fact that the Sejm [Parliament] did not fulfill its constitutional task in state life. We are now facing elections to the new Sejm which ought to occupy in our political and state life the place assigned to it by the Constitution. The elevation of the role of the Sejm to that of the supreme organ of state power will probably be of the greatest importance in our democratization program. . . .

Postulating the principle of the freedom of criticism in all its forms, including criticism in the press, we have the right to demand that each criticism should be creative and just, that it should help to overcome the difficulties of the present period instead of increasing them or sometimes even treating demagogically certain phenomena and problems.

We have the right to demand from our youth, especially from university students, that they should keep their ardor in the search for roads leading to the improvement of our present reality, within the framework of the decisions which will be adopted by the present Plenum. . . .

. . . Our party should say clearly to the young people: march in the vanguard of this great and momentous process of democratization but always look up to your leadership, to the leadership of all People's Poland—to the party of the working class, to the Polish United Workers Party.

The Hungarian Revolution

Firing on demonstrators in Budapest by the political police on October 22, 1956, served as the signal for a nation-wide popular uprising against the Soviet-sponsored regime in Hungary. While revolutionary workers' councils took power in some localities, the government was turned over to the reformer, Imre Nagy, in the hope of appeasing the populace. Nagy promised reform, ended one-party Communist rule by forming a coalition government, and took the fatal step of repudiating Hungary's treaty ties with the USSR. The new party secretary János Kádár meanwhile announced formation of a new Communist party frankly espousing national communism. On November 4 the experiment in liberal Communist rule was rudely terminated by Soviet military intervention, aided by Kádár and others who betrayed the revolutionary regime. Resistance, in some cases even in the name of Communism, went vainly on for some days after the Russians overthrew Nagy, but effective force was lacking to prevent the restoration of the Communist dictatorship under Kádár. Nagy was captured by trickery and executed; twenty-six years later, in June 1989, the reform Communists conducted a ceremonial funeral for him, shortly before they too were swept away.

The Hungarian revolution is notable as the event where the forces and circumstances—armed uprising by intellectuals and workers—most nearly approximated the Bolshevik Revolution in Russia. It is appropriately ironic that this movement was directed against the power of the imperialism which that revolution in Russia had brought into being.

a) Demands of a Workers' Council

End the massacre of Hungarians in Budapest! Do not believe deceptions! Let them withdraw Soviet troops from Hungary! Strike! . . .

FROM: Resolution of the Workers' Council of Miskolc and Borsod County, Hungary, October 25, 1956 (Broadcast by Radio Free Miskolc; English translation in M. J. Lasky, ed., *The Hungarian Revolution: A White Book*, New York, Praeger, 1957, p. 80; this and following selections reprinted by permission of the editor).

We have had enough—enough of the autocracy of certain leaders. We too want socialism but according to our own special Hungarian conditions, which reflect the interests of the Hungarian working class and the Hungarian nation, and our most sacred national sentiments.

We demand that all persons who compromised themselves by the cult of personality be eliminated immediately. . . .

We demand that those Communists and non-Communists be given the most important positions in government and party life who, in following the principles of proletarian internationalism, honor above all else our Hungarian national traditions and our thousand-year history.

We demand the revision of the institutions of the state security authority and the elimination immediately of all leaders and functionaries who are compromised. . . .

We demand a public trial of Mihaly Farkas* before an independent court, regardless whether this trial may reflect on individuals currently holding important office.

With regard to the grave errors committed in the field of planned economy we demand the immediate dismissal of the responsible leaders of the planning offices.

We demand an increase of real wages.

We believe our demands will be realized when our parliament ceases to be an electoral machine, and the members of parliament cease being yes-men.

We demand that March 15th be proclaimed a national holiday, and we also demand that October 6th be a national memorial day.* . . .

b) Recommendation of the National Trade Union Council on Workers' Councils

The Trade Union Council Presidium recommends that workers and employees embark on the introduction of worker-management in factories, workshops, mines and everywhere else. They should elect Workers' Councils. . . .

The tasks of the Workers' Councils: A Workers' Council shall decide all questions connected with production, administration and management of the plant. Therefore: (a) it should elect from among its own members a council of 5-15 members, which in accordance with direct instructions of the Workers' Council, shall decide questions connected with the management of the factory—it will hire and fire workers, economic and technical leaders; (b) it will draw up the factory's production plan and define tasks connected with technical development; (c) the Workers' Council will choose the wage-system best suited to conditions peculiar to the factory, decide on the introduction of that system as well as on the development of social and cultural amenities in the factory; (d) the Workers' Council will decide on investments and the utilisation of profits; (e) the Workers' Council will determine the working conditions of the mine, factory, etc.; (f) the Workers' Council will be responsible to all the workers and to the State for correct management.

*Because of his responsibility for the purge of Rajk—Ed.

*March 15: the pre-Communist national holiday, anniversary of the Revolution of 1848; October 6: date of the reinterment of Rajk after his posthumous rehabilitation, 1956—Ed.

FROM: Recommendation of the Presidium of the National Trade Union Council of Hungary, on the establishment of Workers' Councils, October 27, 1956 (Broadcast by Radio Kossuth; English translation in Lasky, *The Hungarian Revolution*, pp. 100–101).

At present the principal task of the Workers' Councils is to effect and ensure order, discipline and production. With the help of all the workers, their electors, the Workers' Council should defend the factory, the source of their livelihood.

On this basis of the aforesaid, the Presidium of the Trade Union Council recommends the setting up of Workers' Councils.

c) Nagy on the Formation of a New Government

During the course of the past week bloody events took place with tragic rapidity. The fatal consequences of the terrible mistakes and crimes of these past 10 years unfold before us in these painful events which we are witnessing and in which we are participating. During the course of 1,000 years of history, destiny was not sparing in scourging our people and nation. But such a thing has never before afflicted our country.

The government condemns the viewpoints according to which the present formidable movement is a counterrevolution. Without doubt, as always happens at times of great popular movements, this movement too was used by criminal elements to compromise it and commit common criminal acts. It is also a fact that reactionary and counterrevolutionary elements had penetrated into the movement with the aim of overthrowing the popular democratic regime.

But it is also indisputable that in these stirrings a great national and democratic movement, embracing and unifying all our people, developed with elemental force. This movement aims at guaranteeing our national freedom, independence, and sovereignty, of advancing our society, our economic and political system on the way of democracy—for this is the only foundation for socialism in our country. This great movement exploded because of the grave crimes committed during the past historic period.

The situation was further aggravated by the fact that up to the very last, the [party] leadership had not decided to break finally with the old and criminal policy. It is this above all which led to the tragic fraticidal fight in which so many patriots died on both sides. In the course of these battles was born the government of democratic national unity, independence, and socialism which will become the true expression of the will of the people. This is the firm resolution of the government. . . .

The government wishes to rest in the first place on the support of the fighting Hungarian working class, but also, of course, on the support of the entire Hungarian working population. We have decided to work out a broad program, in the framework of which we wish to settle old and justified demands and rectify damages to the satisfaction of the working class, among other things on the question of wages and work norms, the raising of minimum pay in the lowest wage brackets and of the smallest pensions, taking into account the number of years worked, and the raising of family allowances. . . .

The Hungarian Government has come to an agreement with the Soviet Government that the Soviet forces shall withdraw immediately from Budapest and that simultaneously with the formation of our new Army they shall evacuate the city's territory. The Hungarian Government will initiate negotiations in order to settle

FROM: Imre Nagy, Radio Address Announcing the Formation and the Program of a New Government, October 28, 1956 (Zinner, *National Communism*, pp. 428–32).

relations between the Hungarian People's Republic and the Soviet Union, among other things with regard to the withdrawal of Soviet forces stationed in Hungary, in the spirit of Soviet-Hungarian friendship and the principle of the mutual equality and the national independence of socialist countries.

After the reestablishment of order we shall organize a new and unified state police force and we shall dissolve the organs of state security. No one who took part in the armed fighting need fear further reprisals. The government will put proposals before the National Assembly for the restoration of the emblem of Kossuth as the national emblem and the observance of March 15 once again as a national holiday.

People of Hungary!

In these hours of bitterness and strife one is prone to see only the dark side of the past twelve years. We must not let our views become clouded. These twelve years contain lasting, ineradicable, historic achievements which you, Hungarian workers, peasants, and intellectuals, under the leadership of the Hungarian Workers Party brought into being by virtue of hard labor and sacrifice. Our renascent popular democracy relies on the strength and self-sacrifice which you have displayed in our founding labors and which constitute the best guarantee of our country's happier future.

d) Kádár on a National-Communist Party

Hungarian workers, peasants, and intellectuals! In a fateful hour we appeal to those who, inspired by loyalty to the people and the country and the pure ideals of socialism, were led to a party which later degenerated to a medium of despotism and national slavery through the blind and criminal policy of the Hungarian representatives of Stalinism—Rakosi and his clique. This adventurous policy unscrupulously frittered away the moral and ideological heritage which you acquired in the old days through honest struggle and blood sacrifice in the fight for our national independence and our democratic progress. Rakosi and his gang gravely violated our national decency and pride when they disregarded the sovereignty and freedom of our nation and wasted our national wealth in a lighthearted manner. In a glorious uprising, our people have shaken off the Rakosi regime. They have achieved freedom for the people and independence for the country, without which there can be no socialism.

We can safely say that the ideological and organizational leaders who prepared this uprising were recruited from among your ranks. Hungarian Communist workers, journalists, university students, the youth of the Petöfi Circle,* thousands and thousands of workers and peasants, and veteran fighters who had been imprisoned on false charges fought in the front line against the Rakosiite despotism and political hooliganism. We are proud that you, permeated by true patriotism and loyalty to socialism, honestly stood your ground in the armed uprising and led it.

We are talking to you frankly. The uprising of the people has come to a crossroads. The Hungarian democratic parties will either have enough strength to stabilize our achievements or we must face an open counterrevolution. The blood of

FROM: Kádár, Radio Address, November 1, 1956 (Zinner, *National Communism*, pp. 464–66).

*Petöfi Circle: a national-Communist intellectual group, named after the nineteenth-century Hungarian poet Alexander Petöfi, active in pressing demands for reform—Ed.

Hungarian youth, soldiers, workers, and peasants was not shed in order that Rakosiite despotism might be replaced by the reign of the counterrevolution. . . .

In these momentous hours the Communists who fought against the despotism of Rakosi have decided, in accordance with the wish of many true patriots and socialists, to form a new party. The new party will break away from the crimes of the past once and for all. It will defend the honor and independence of our country against anyone. On this basis, the basis of national independence, it will build fraternal relations with any progressive socialist movement and party in the world.

On this basis, the basis of national independence, does it desire friendly relations with every country, far and near, and in the first place with the neighboring socialist countries. It defends and will defend the achievements of the Hungarian Republic—the land reform, the nationalization of factories, mines, and banks, and the indisputable social and cultural gains of our people.

It defends and will defend the cause of democracy and socialism, whose realization it seeks not through servile copying of foreign examples, but on a road suitable to the historic and economic characteristics of our country, relying on the teachings of Marxism-Leninism, on scientific socialism free of Stalinism and any kind of dogmatism, and on the revolutionary and progressive traditions of Hungarian history and culture. . . .

e) Nagy on Soviet Intervention

This is Imre Nagy, Premier, speaking. In the early hours of this morning, the Soviet troops launched an attack against our capital city with the obvious intention of overthrowing the lawful, democratic, Hungarian Government. Our troops are fighting. The government is in its place. I inform the people of the country and world public opinion of this.

f) Kádár on a Pro-Soviet Regime

The Hungarian Revolutionary Worker-Peasant Government has been formed. The mass movement which started on October 23 in our country had the noble aims of remedying anti-party and anti-democratic crimes committed by Rakosi and his associates and defending national independence and sovereignty. Through the weakness of the Imre Nagy government and through the increased influence of counterrevolutionary elements who edged their way into the movement, socialist achievements, our people's state, our worker-peasant power, and the existence of our country have become endangered.

This has prompted us, Hungarian patriots, to form the Hungarian Revolutionary Worker-Peasant Government. . . .

With growing impudence the counterrevolutionaries are ruthlessly persecuting the followers of democracy. Arrow Cross members and other beasts are murdering the honest patriots, our best comrades. We know that many questions are still awaiting solution in our country and that we have to cope with many difficulties.

FROM: Imre Nagy, Radio Announcement of November 4, 1956 (Zinner, *National Communism*, p. 472).

FROM: Kádár, "Appeal to the Hungarian People," November 4, 1956 (Zinner, *National Communism*, pp. 474–76, 478).

The life of the workers is still far from what it should be in a country building socialism. Simultaneously, with the progress attained during the past twelve years, the clique of Rakosi and Gerö has committed many grave mistakes and gravely violated legality. . . .

Making use of the mistakes committed during the building of our people's democratic system, the reactionary elements have misled many honest workers and particularly the major part of the youth, who joined the movement with honest and patriotic intentions. . . .

. . . By utilizing the weakness of Imre Nagy's government, counterrevolutionary forces are indulging in excesses, murdering and looting in the country, and it is to be feared that they will gain the upper hand. We see with deep sadness and a heavy heart into what a terrible situation our beloved Fatherland has been driven by those counterrevolutionary elements, and often even by well-meaning progressive people, who willy-nilly abused the slogans of freedom and democracy and thus opened the way to reaction.

Hungarians, brethren, patriots, soldiers, citizens! We must put an end to the excesses of the counterrevolutionary elements. The hour of action has struck. We will defend the power of the workers and peasants and the achievements of the people's democracy. We will create order, security, and calm in our country. The interest of the people and the country is that they should have a strong government, a government capable of leading the country out of its grave situation. It is for this reason that we formed the Hungarian Revolutionary Worker-Peasant Government. . . .

The Hungarian Revolutionary Worker-Peasant Government, in the interest of our people, working class, and country, requested the command of the Soviet Army to help our nation in smashing the sinister forces of reaction and restoring order and calm to the country. . . .

g) Broadcast by "Free Radio Rajk"

We have very little to say to the Soviet masters. They have convinced not only the whole world, but also all Communists, that they do not care for Communism, that they simply prostituted Communism . . . to Russian imperialism.

We also want to speak of the traitors . . . the János Kádárs, who play the dirty role of colonial governors. . . . We send them the message that we consider them all traitors to Communism. . . . [Kádár's] crime and that of his accomplices is clear and the sentence has already been pronounced. We Hungarian Communists will see to it that the sentence is carried out. . . .

The Disintegration of the American Communist Party

The events of 1956, beginning with the repudiation of the Stalin cult in the USSR and ending with the Soviet intervention in Hungary, dealt a crushing blow to what was left of the Communist movement in North-West Europe and the United States. Bitter dissension broke out among the American Communist leadership over the issue of independence from Mos-

FROM: Broadcast by Free Radio Rajk, Hungary, November 5, 1956 (English translation in Lasky, *The Hungarian Revolution*, p. 250).

FROM: Joseph Clark's Letter of Resignation, *The Daily Worker*, September 9, 1957.

cow, and in the fall of 1957 the anti-Moscow leaders followed the majority of the rank and file in breaking with the party. Most prominent among the dissenters were John Gates and Joseph Clark, respectively editor-in-chief and foreign editor of the *Daily Worker*. Clark's statement of resignation was a soul-searching analysis of the failure of American communism.

Editor, *Daily Worker*:

Regretfully, this will be the last time I speak my piece as an editor of the *Daily Worker* and member of the Communist Party. After 28 years of association I am resigning from both because I find it is no longer possible to serve the cause of American socialism through them.

I continue to adhere as strongly as ever to the ideal which brought me into the Communist movement—a world free from poverty, racism, injustice and war. This has become a categorical imperative in the atomic age. Unless the exploitation of man by man is ended it is impossible to conceive of humanity living in both peace and freedom.

It is a grievous comment on the situation in our country, as well as in the Communist Party, that I am the first to resign from the party by making it known through the *Daily Worker*. The most recent meeting of the party's National Committee was told that at least 7,000 of the 17,000 reported members last year, have left the organization. About 60,000 quit in the previous decade. However, the great majority could not resign publicly because they were never able to declare their affiliation in the first place. This is because freedom of thought and association in our country has been infringed by legislation such as the Smith and McCarran acts.

Furthermore, many who resigned were concerned, as I am, lest opponents of democracy and socialism utilize their resignations to defame the high ideals for which they joined the Communist Party and to which we have devoted some of the best years of our lives.

. . . Fundamentally, the demise of the party is related to that of every other socialist movement in our country since the days of the first Marxists here. Not content with growing directly out of the struggles of the American people, and basing themselves on the specific conditions of American life, these movements have unwittingly tried to impose their dogmas on the struggles.

The party became a sect primarily because history rode roughshod over dogma. Since the trend is toward aggravation of this process the party has become a hindrance rather than a means for advancing socialism. . . .

. . . My view is that socialism can be served only by a complete break with Stalinism. The latter perverted socialism by substituting autocracy for democracy. But Marxists have always advocated socialist democracy, which they uphold as more libertarian than any yet attained.

It is my view that to advance the all-important goal of American-Soviet friendship one must win the people for strong opposition to the cold war diplomacy of John Foster Dulles. But to do this one must also take a critical view of what is wrong in the Soviet Union. . . .

The only effective posture from which American Marxists can work for American-Soviet friendship—necessary if mankind is to survive in a time of hydrogenheaded ICBM weapons—is that of independence. The issue was posed directly at the last convention of the party by the letter of Jacques Duclos, who, for a second time, meddled in the affairs of the American Communist movement. The essence of the Duclos letter was rejected by the convention. But, unfortunately, it was not argued or specifically refuted in a way which would establish beyond a shadow of a doubt the independence of the American Communist Party and demolish the slanders of J. Edgar Hoover. I refer particularly to Duclos' declaration that proletarian internationalism "implies solidarity with the foreign policy of the Soviet Union."

History is replete with instances where the opposite is true. In 1939 internationalism required support for the anti-Hitler war, not the shameful neutrality of both the French and American Communist parties. And in 1956 proletarian internationalism required solidarity with the Hungarian workers opposing Soviet intervention. It demanded support for the Hungarian workers who formed a solid phalanx of workers councils and for their 100 percent solid general strike. It meant solidarity with the views expressed by Janos Kadar in his Nov. 1 radio address, when he was still with the Hungarian masses, and said: "Our people have proved with their blood their intention to support unflinchingly the Government's (Nagy's) efforts for the complete withdrawal of Soviet forces."

There is no prospect that party leaders will rebuff the Duclos argument quoted above, not in generalities, but with specific reference to the Duclos letter. All efforts that I made to get a specific refutation of the Duclos statement were rebuffed. Therefore to remain in the party tends to lend support to the disastrously un-Marxist policy which has time and again isolated us from the American workers, as in 1939.

Communism on a world scale has been the major current in our time through which socialist transformations have taken place. The successful revolutions in Russia, China and Yugoslavia, and the socialist transformation in Poland last October, have advanced socialism as an issue for our time. But these revolutions have created no guides or patterns for socialism in most Western countries, and certainly not for ours. Marxism realized its greatest triumph in the Russian and Chinese revolutions. It also reached its most serious crisis as a result of Stalinist perversion of the Communist movement. Within the Communist countries there is great hope for socialism in the complete elimination of Stalinism which deprives socialism of its humanism and high moral principles and which replaced scientific method with a religious-type dogma.

Within our own country communism has made an important contribution to the welfare of the people. A high-point was reached in the decade of 1935–1945. We were to some degree in the mainstream of American labor and of the country. Social security, the industrial organization of labor, the development of a popular folk culture, integration of the Negro people, were important achievements of American democracy to which we contributed. But that is past and no movement can live in the past. Even during the period of our greatest success we were never a mass party and we were never able to bring socialism into the arena of American political thought and action.

It therefore seems to me that we are entering a period when all questions relating to socialism and America are up for reconsideration. Certainly no organization exists today as a proper vehicle for socialism. No fixed dogma can guide our study. Our starting point must be American reality, as it is today, not as it was a century ago when Marx studied it. We must begin from facts. This is a virtue of Marxism we have often forgotten. And we must above all maintain the moral and humanist essence of socialism. . . .

Marxist Revisionism in Poland

Following the "October Revolution" of 1956, Poland temporarily enjoyed considerable freedom of expression, and a notable intellectual ferment commenced. Many Polish Communists, particularly the intellectuals, reacted against the decade of Stalinist controls with sharp criticism of Communist dogmatism and demands for further freedom. Outstanding among these "revisionists" was the young philosopher Leszek Kolakowski, who managed to publish some of the most penetrating criticisms of Marxist doctrine, before Gomulka pressed the lid of orthodoxy on again. Kolakowski has since pursued an academic career in the West as a noted critic of Marxism.

. . . It is enough to believe in the inevitability of progress to believe simultaneously in the progressiveness of inevitability. It is enough to believe in Providence in order to bless the brick which hits one on the head. When the spirit of history assumes the difficult role of Divine Providence, it must accordingly demand humble gratitude for every blow it inflicts on its chosen. The demiurge of progress which guards the world demands the worship of his every creation and image. What could be easier than to prove that this or that national leader, this or that system of government, or of social relations, is the demiurge's anointed, even if its external appearance terrifies people with its simian hide? . . . How . . . is it possible to reconcile the conviction of the existence of historical necessity with the conviction that this necessity must be realized by brutal and terroristic means? How can this be reconciled with acceptance of any universal values, that is, with the conviction that certain actions are called for and others prohibited in all circumstances? Moral duty is the belief, perpetuated in a given social environment, that certain human actions are ends in themselves and not merely means to an end, and that other actions are counter-ends in themselves; that is, they are prohibited. If historical necessity is considered either as an unlimited process without a final end, or if an ultimate end is ascribed to it, though still unrealized and subject only to a promise of the future, and if, simultaneously, moral judgments are subject to the realization of that necessity, then there is nothing in contemporary life which can be considered an end in itself. In other words, moral values in the strict sense of the term cease to exist altogether. Can the view of the world of reality be reconciled with the view of the world of values? . . .

. . . Marx's predictions referred to a change in economic structure and were formulated in those terms. Ordinary scientific criticism did not permit going into further details so happily indulged in by Fourier and the majority of the utopians. The details of Lenin's programs, formulated before the October Revolution, went considerably further. Yet, to this very day, we cannot positively decide which part of those programs was based on peculiarly Russian conditions, and which retained, or was intended to retain, universal validity for the period of transition from capitalism to Socialism. We can almost certainly take for granted Marx's fundamental assumption that the development of capitalist technology creates the tendency to

FROM: Kolakowski, "Responsibility and History" (September, 1957; English translation in *East Europe*, February, 1958, pp. 18–21; March, 1958, pp. 26–28).

endow the means of production with a collective ownership; and this assumption is confirmed, in general outline, by historical experience. However, in the course of how many revolutions won and lost, how many wars and crises, how many years and decades, according to what geographical and chronological circumstances, in the course of what progress and regress, and in what diverse forms, a Socialist way of life will be realized cannot be deduced authoritatively from a superficial knowledge of the "laws of history." These questions are answered by the experiences of everyday life, daily shocking us with new surprises like a virtuoso magician.

. . . How can we free the morality of daily life from the nightmare of the philosophy of history and from those pseudo-dialectics which, by transforming morality into an instrument of history, in fact make history the pretext for disgraceful behavior? . . .

The danger is based on a complete substitution of criteria of usefulness, which the demiurge of history derives from our actions, for moral criteria. The greater the degree of certainty we have concerning the demiurge's intentions, the greater the threat. The sectarian spirit is the natural enemy of the skeptical spirit, and skepticism is the best possible antidote, however difficult to apply generally, against the insane fanaticism of visionaries. This centuries-old truth should be refurbished from time to time whenever historical experiences which demonstrate this truth with particular clarity recur. When one achieves an absolute and unshakeable certainty that the kingdom of heaven is around the corner, that the "Third Order," of which Joachim of Floris* wrote, is nearing its triumph and simultaneously approaching the final establishment of a new historical era, the ultimate one which "really" gives happiness and is "really" different from all the others, the only one to scotch the serpent's head and put an end to human suffering, when therefore we are hypnotized by boundless conviction that we are on the threshold of some kind of second coming, it is no wonder that this single messianic hope will become the sole law of life, the only source of moral precept, and the only measure of virtue. A consistent messianist must be convinced that he cannot hesitate to do anything that might help to bring about the new era. Morality, then, speaks in the language of the Apocalypse. It sees "a new heaven and a new earth" and knows simultaneously that before the far side is reached the four angels will destroy a third of mankind, burning stars will fall, the abyss will open, the seven vessels of God's wrath will be poured over the world, and glory will illuminate the victor who crushes the heathen with an iron rod. The historiosophy of the Apocalypse, of Joachim of Floris and of Thomas Munzer,† has been revived to some extent in the Communist movement. Although in this latter case it was supported by an honest and prolific effort of scientific analysis, it acted like a messianic vision in the operations of the mass movement. Probably it could not have been different, but awareness of this cannot provide us with a sense of security precisely because we want to prove that out of more or less reliable knowledge of historical necessities, we still cannot deduce the rules of our conduct.

In any case we take note of one of many practical lessons, which states that one

---

*Joachim of Floris: Heretical Italian monk of the twelfth century, who prophesied the coming of a new "age of the Holy Spirit," to succeed those of the "Father" and the "Son"—Ed.

†Thomas Munzer: Anabaptist leader of the German peasants' revolt of 1524–25—Ed.

needs a certain skepticism in the face of excessive certainty. Experience shows that, as Marx wrote, it is still easy to enslave people by an independent historical process. . . .

Nobody is free from positive or negative responsibility because his individual actions constitute only a fragment of a specific historical process. . . . If a social system exists which needs criminals for some of its tasks, one may be sure that these criminals will be found, but it does not follow that as a result of this certainty every individual criminal is freed from responsibility. In order to take upon oneself the role of such an instrument of the system, one must intrinsically be a criminal, one must voluntarily commit a specific act subject to moral judgement. We therefore support the doctrine of the total responsibility of the individual for his own deeds, and the amorality of the historical process. . . .

It is not true that the philosophy of history determines our main choices in life. Our moral sensibility does this. We are not Communists because we have recognized Communism as historical necessity; we are Communists because we have joined the side of the oppressed against their masters, the side of the persecuted against their persecutors. Although we know that the correct theoretical division of society is not into "rich" and "poor," not into "persecuted" and "persecutors," when we must make a *practical* choice apart from the theory, that is, a fundamental option, we are then morally motivated, and not motivated by theoretical considerations. It cannot be otherwise because even the most convincing theory is not by itself capable of making us lift a finger. A practical choice is a choice of values; that is, a moral act which is something for which everyone bears his own personal responsibility.

The Reaffirmation of International Communist Solidarity

In November, 1957, a world-wide conference of Communist parties (excepting only Yugoslavia) was held in Moscow to repair the damage done to Communist discipline by de-Stalinization and the Polish and Hungarian revolutions. The conference demanded conformity against "revisionism" (i.e., Yugoslavia) and "dogmatism" (i.e., diehard Stalinists) but echoed Khrushchev's line on different roads to socialism, Popular Front tactics, and the possibility of non-violent revolution.

The Communist and Workers' Parties taking part in this conference declare that the Leninist principle of peaceful coexistence of the two systems, which has been further developed in contemporary circumstances in the decisions of the 20th Party Congress, is the firm foundation of the foreign policy of the socialist countries and the reliable foundation of peace and friendship among the peoples. The five principles advanced jointly by the Chinese People's Republic and the Republic of India and the program adopted by the Bandung conference of African and Asian countries correspond to the interests of peaceful coexistence. The struggle for peace and peaceful coexistence have now become the demands of the broadest masses in all countries of the world.

FROM: Declaration of the Conference of Representatives of Communist and Workers' Parties of Socialist Countries, Moscow, November, 1957 (English translation in *The Current Digest of the Soviet Press* [hereafter cited as CDSP], IX: 47, January 1, 1958, pp. 4–7). This and following sections reprinted by permission of *The Current Digest of the Post-Soviet Press*.

The Communist Parties regard the struggle for peace as their foremost task. Together with all peace-loving forces, they will do all in their power to prevent war.

The conference considers that strengthening of the unity and fraternal cooperation of the socialist states and of the Communist and Workers' Parties of all countries and closing of the ranks of the international working class, national-liberation and democratic movements take on special importance in the present situation. . . .

Intensification of the struggle against opportunist trends in the workers' and Communist movement is of great importance at the present stage. The conference stresses the necessity of resolutely overcoming revisionism and dogmatism in the ranks of the Communist and Workers' Parties. Revisionism and dogmatism in the workers' and Communist movement are today, as they have been in the past, of an international nature. Dogmatism and sectarianism hinder the development of Marxist-Leninist theory and its creative application in specific changing conditions, replace study of the specific situation with quotations and pedantry, and lead to the Party's isolation from the masses. A party that has locked itself up in sectarianism and that has lost contact with the broad masses can by no means bring victory to the cause of the working class. . . .

The forms of the transition of different countries from capitalism to socialism may vary. The working class and its vanguard—the Marxist-Leninist party—seek to bring about socialist revolution by peaceful means. Realization of this possibility would accord with the interests of the working class and of all the people and with the over-all national interests of the country.

In present-day conditions in a number of capitalist countries the working class, headed by the vanguard, has the possibility—on the basis of a worker's and people's front or of other possible forms of agreement and political cooperation among the different parties and public organizations—to unite the majority of the people, win state power without civil war, and ensure the transfer of the basic means of production to the hands of the people. . . .

In conditions in which the exploiting classes resort to violence against the people, it is necessary to bear in mind another possibility—nonpeaceful transition to socialism. Leninism teaches and history confirms that the ruling classes never relinquish power voluntarily. In these conditions the severity and forms of the class struggle will depend not so much on the proletariat as on the resistance of the reactionary circles to the will of the overwhelming majority of the people, on the use of force by these circles at one or another stage of the struggle for socialism.

In each country the real possibility of one or another means of transition to socialism depends on the specific historical conditions.

The Communist Parties stand for the establishment of cooperation with socialist parties both in the struggle for improving the working people's living conditions, for extending and preserving their democratic rights, for winning and defending national independence and for peace among peoples and in the struggle for winning power and building socialism. . . . The participants in the conference unanimously express their firm confidence that, by rallying their ranks and thereby rallying the working class and the peoples of all countries, the Communist and Workers' Parties will undoubtedly surmount all obstacles on the path of progress and hasten great new victories for the cause of peace, democracy and socialism on a world scale.

The Yugoslav Alternative

Disabused of renewed Soviet friendship by the intervention in Hungary in 1956, Tito's Yugoslavia proceeded to formalize its independent line in 1958 in a new Program of the League of Communists of Yugoslavia (as the Communist Party had been renamed). Meanwhile the leading Titoist theoretician, Vice-President Djilas, went too far in his argument for democratization; in 1954 he was ousted from all his party and government positions for a "reactionary deviation." Nevertheless, he completed a book, *The New Class*, analyzing the bureaucratic degeneration of Communism along the lines sketched by Trotsky and Rakovsky in Russia in the 1930's. For allowing the manuscript to be smuggled out and published in the West, Djilas was tried and jailed, and he has continued to suffer periodic repression for his stubborn opposition to the one-party regime in Yugoslavia.

a) Official—The Program of the League of Communists of Yugoslavia

. . . The entire social development in the Soviet Union had to begin with the concentration of all forces on the construction of the material basis of the new society. This was the only way to prevent a restoration of capitalism in the Soviet Union. This general situation, however, required extraordinary efforts and great self-denial of the whole working class and the working people of the Soviet Union. . . .

. . . In this general situation, social development called for an emphasis on the organizing role of the leading forces of society—the Communist Party and the Soviet State—first in the fields of economic life, then in all life of society. This is what led to the great concentration of power in the hands of the state apparatus.

However, this concentration of power in the state apparatus began to be accompanied by bureaucratic-state tendencies, mistakes and deformities in the development of the political system of the state. This, in turn, caused a sharper and more convulsive manifestation of the numerous contradictions typical of the transition period from capitalism to socialism.

In the end, this practice gradually led not only to the ever stronger power of the state but to the rule by one man. This is the practice which produced the "cult of personality" and attempts at its theoretical and ideological justification. . . .

Along these lines a pragmatist revision of certain fundamental scientific propositions of Marxism-Leninism was carried out, first in the theory of the state and the Party, then in philosophy, political economy and the social sciences generally.

The Marxist-Leninist theory of the dictatorship of the proletariat as a political system of government in a state which is withering away and as an instrument of the struggle of the working class in the process of destroying the economic foundations of capitalism and creating the political and material conditions for a free development of new, socialist relations—this Marxist-Leninist theory was transformed into Stalin's theory of the state which is not withering away, which has to grow ever stronger in all areas of social life. To the apparatus of this state is assigned too big a part in the construction of socialism and in the solution of the

FROM: *Yugoslavia's Way: The Program of the League of the Communists of Yugoslavia* (translated by Stoyan Pribichevich, New York: All-Nations Press, 1958), pp. 42–45, 64–65, 120–122, 129–130, 132–133, 152, 173. Reprinted by permission of the publisher.

inner contradictions of the transition period, a part which sooner or later must begin to obstruct the development of the socialist factors in society and economy.

On the international scene, that is, in certain aspects of the Soviet foreign policy and in relations among the socialist countries, phenomena of this kind also appeared after the Second World War. These showed most strikingly in Stalin's action against socialist Yugoslavia, action unanimously condemned at the Twentieth Congress of the Communist Party of the Soviet Union as obviously contrary to the real interests of socialism.

In resisting this pressure and in fighting for the independence of their country, the Yugoslav Communists and the peoples of Yugoslavia not only fought for their right to free socialist development but contributed to the indispensable fight against state-bureaucratic and other anti-socialist deformities in the development of socialism and in the relations among nations which have chosen the socialist path. This resistance, therefore, was socialist and progressive by definition, and precisely for this reason it contributed to the strengthening and advancing of socialism throughout the world. . . .

. . . Every aspect of ideological monopoly that hampers free socialist development in socialist countries is a brake on international socialism in general. For this reason, the League of the Communists of Yugoslavia regards as particularly useful today the creation of such forms of international cooperation as would on the broadest possible basis unite efforts toward solution of the common practical problems of peace and of the struggle for, and the building of, socialism. . . .

To proclaim the path and form of the socialist development of any country as the only correct ones is nothing but dogma, obstructing the process of the socialist transformation of the world. The general aims of socialism are common, but the tempo and forms of the movement of society toward these aims are and must be different, depending on the concrete conditions in individual countries or parts of the world. Consequently, freedom of internal socialist development and absence of any imposition of various forms, noninterference in the internal life and progress of various movements, and a free and equal exchange of experience and socialist theoretical thought should be the basic principle of mutual relations among socialist countries and socialist movements. . . .

Assigning an indispensable and important role to the state in the first stages of socialist construction, and also aware of statist deformation which this role may cause in the development of socialist relations, the Yugoslav Communists believe that the state, that is, its administrative apparatus and measures, are not at all the main instrument of socialist construction and solution of the inner contradictions of socialist development. The state apparatus cannot be the decisive, permanent and all-embracing factor in the development of new social relations. The Yugoslav Communists must not, nor do they wish to, become a power through the use of the state apparatus instead of through the working class and working people. Only the social and economic interest of the working class, of the working people who produce with the social means of production, and socialist consciousness based on that interest, can be the basic, permanent motive power of social progress.

The Communists do not renounce their leading social role. Social consciousness plays the decisive part in the solution of the contradictions of socialist development. But the leading socialist forces can be victorious only if they act in accordance with the objective laws of development and with the needs of society in general; and in particular, if they act in accordance with the social and economic interests of the working class, that is, the working people who produce with the social means of production. . . .

Simultaneously, the Communists will continue the struggle for keeping key positions of state authority in firm revolutionary hands—positions on which depend further development of socialist society and defense of that society against the various internal and foreign anti-socialist forces. The great socialist, democratic, humane and peaceful goals that the Yugoslav socialist society has set itself can be achieved most quickly and least painfully if the enemies of socialism are allowed no opportunity to bring obstacles and disturbances into our internal social life. . . .

Social ownership of the means of production was put into practice in Yugoslavia through a revolutionary transformation. It covers all means of production except those used in personal labor of peasants and craftsmen. Social ownership of the means of production in Yugoslavia has not only completely liquidated private capitalist ownership; it has become a firm foundation and guarantee of such social relations in production where conditions of any ownership monopoly are gradually eliminated. This means elimination, also, of any economic and political monopoly— of any monopoly by individuals and of any monopoly by the socialist state.

The actual social substance of this process consists in the development of self-management of producers in production, in self-government of the working people in the Commune, District, Republic and Federation, and in a clear delimitation of the rights and duties of all these organs. . . .

Yugoslavia has carried out a radical agrarian reform finally limiting individual holdings to 24.71 acres of arable land. This substantially restricts the possibility of capitalist tendencies to assert themselves in private agricultural production.

Considering that land holdings in Yugoslavia are almost exclusively small or medium-sized, the League of the Communists believes that the process of socialization of land will not consist in a forced general nationalization or other similar means but primarily in socialization of agricultural production based on the increasingly stronger forces of production in the economy, and especially in agriculture; in a gradual socialist transformation of the village; in uniting the peasants through cooperatives or in cooperation of the peasants with the social sector of agricultural production. This cooperation is in the first place based on the use of the means of modern large-scale agricultural production, which can be exclusive social property. . . .

The League of the Communists of Yugoslavia believes that the right of individual ownership by citizens of various objects of consumption and use, on which a more varied and more comfortable life of citizens depends, is also an essential personal right and incentive to creative personal initiative.

The prerequisite of the socialist character and scope of the right to individual ownership is that it does not become a source of personal enrichment by exploiting others, that it does not stem from any special social privilege, that it does not restrict others in enjoying the same right—that, in a word, it returns the individual to society, no longer confining him within the bounds of selfishness and isolation.

The source of individual ownership must be work. Such individual ownership is not abolished in socialism. It must be protected and continuously expanded, because socialism as a whole aims not only at general social progress but also at personal happiness of man. In this sense, a constant inner striving to satisfy as much as possible human needs, activities, tastes, desires, is peculiar to socialism. . . .

The experience of Yugoslavia and of a number of other countries shows that over-all economic plans, no matter how "perfect," cannot exhaust innumerable possibilities, forms or incentives afforded by the spontaneous development of economic forces. Therefore the economic system and plan must not abolish that indispensable degree of independence of the working man, enterprise or other social-economic units without which no conscious initiative is possible and without which man ceases to be creator. They must not suppress either the individual or the collective material interest of the producers in production and work, that is, their constant striving for a higher degree of material welfare, which is one of the essential motive powers of their activity. . . .

The Communists will pay particular attention to the development of Workers' Councils. Workers' Councils are democratic economic-political organs of social self-management through which direct producers independently manage enterprises and take a decisive part in the development of the forces of production—within a single coordinated social economic plan and in accordance with the general interests of the community, expressed in a single coordinated economic system. The motive power of the activity of the direct producers in Workers' Councils, aimed at more productive labor and faster development of the forces of production, is their desire continuously to improve their living conditions and the general material standard of the social community through better individual work, better operation of the enterprise and faster general economic progress of the social community; and to develop freely their individual creative abilities and inclinations, in harmony with the general interests of the working people.

Workers' Councils are neither representatives of the owner nor the collective owner of the means of production. They manage the means of production on behalf of the social community and in their work are stimulated by their own material and moral-political aspirations. Just for this reason, they are the most suitable social-economic instrument of struggle against both bureaucratism and selfish individualism.

b) Unofficial—Djilas, *The New Class*

All so-called *bourgeois* revolutions, whether achieved from below, i.e., with participation of the masses as in France, or from above, i.e., by *coup d'état* as in Germany under Bismarck, had to end up in political democracy. That is understandable. Their task was chiefly to destroy the old despotic political system, and to permit the establishment of political relationships which would be adequate for already existing economic and other needs, particularly those concerning the free production of goods.

The case is entirely different with contemporary Communist revolutions. These revolutions did not occur because new, let us say socialist, relationships were already existing in the economy, or because capitalism was "overdeveloped." On the

FROM: Djilas, *The New Class: An Analysis of the Communist System* (pp. 19–23, 27–28, 38–39, 101–2, 153, 155, 162–63; reprinted by permission of the publisher).

contrary. They did occur because capitalism was not fully developed and because it was not able to carry out the industrial transformation of the country.

In France, capitalism had already prevailed in the economy, in social relationships, and even in the public conscience prior to inception of the revolution. The case is hardly comparable with socialism in Russia, China, or Yugoslavia. . . .

This leads to an apparent contradiction. If the conditions for a new society were not sufficiently prevalent, then who needed the revolution? Moreover, how was the revolution possible? How could it survive in view of the fact that the new social relationships were not yet in the formative process in the old society?

No revolution or party had ever before set itself to the task of building social relationships or a new society. But this was the primary objective of the Communist revolution.

Communist leaders, though no better acquainted than others with the laws which govern society, discovered that in the country in which their revolution was possible, industrialization was also possible, particularly when it involved a transformation of society in keeping with their ideological hypothesis. Experience—the success of revolution under "unfavorable" conditions—confirmed this for them; the "building of socialism" did likewise. This strengthened their illusion that they knew the laws of social development. In fact, they were in the position of making a blueprint for a new society, and then of starting to build it, making corrections here and leaving out something there, all the while adhering closely to their plans.

Industrialization, as an inevitable, legitimate necessity of society, and the Communist way of accomplishing it, joined forces in the countries of Communist revolutions. . . .

. . . In Communist revolutions, force and violence are a condition for further development and even progress. In the words of earlier revolutionaries, force and violence were only a necessary evil and a means to an end. In the words of Communists, force and violence are elevated to the lofty position of a cult and an ultimate goal. In the past, the classes and forces which made up a new society already existed before the revolution erupted. The Communist revolutions are the first which have had to create a new society and new social forces. . . .

War, or more precisely, national collapse of the state organization, was unnecessary for past revolutions, at least for the larger ones. Until now, however, this has been a basic condition for the victory of Communist revolutions. This is even valid for China; true, there the revolution began prior to the Japanese invasion, but it continued for an entire decade to spread and finally to emerge victorious with the end of the war. The Spanish revolution of 1936, which could have been an exception, did not have time to transform itself into a purely Communist revolution, and, therefore, never emerged victorious.

The reason war was necessary for the Communist revolution, or the downfall of the state machinery, must be sought in the immaturity of the economy and society. In a serious collapse of a system, and particularly in a war which has been unsuccessful for the existing ruling circles and state system, a small but well-organized and disciplined group is inevitably able to take authority in its hands. . . .

. . . The masses of a nation also participated in a Communist revolution; however, the fruits of revolution do not fall to them, but to the bureaucracy. For the bureaucracy is nothing else but the party which carried out the revolution. . . .

. . . Revolutionaries who accepted the ideas and slogans of the revolution literally, naively believing in their materialization, are usually liquidated. The group
which understood that revolution would secure authority, on a social-political-
Communist basis, as an instrument of future industrial transformation, emerges
victorious. . . .

This new class, the bureaucracy, or more accurately the political bureaucracy,
has all the characteristics of earlier ones as well as some new characteristics of its
own. . . .

. . . In spite of its illusions, it represented an objective tendency toward industrialization. Its practical bent emanated from this tendency. The promise of an ideal
world increased the faith in the ranks of the new class and sowed illusions among
the masses. At the same time it inspired gigantic physical undertakings.

Because this new class had not been formed as a part of the economic and social
life before it came to power, it could only be created in an organization of a special
type, distinguished by a special discipline based on identical philosophic and ideological views of its members. A unity of belief and iron discipline was necessary to
overcome its weaknesses.

The roots of the new class were implanted in a special party, of the Bolshevik
type. Lenin was right in his view that his party was an exception in the history of
human society, although he did not suspect that it would be the beginning of a
new class.

To be more precise, the initiators of the new class are not found in the party of
the Bolshevik type as a whole but in that stratum of professional revolutionaries
who made up its core even before it attained power. It was not by accident that
Lenin asserted after the failure of the 1905 revolution that only professional
revolutionaries—men whose sole profession was revolutionary work—could build a
new party of the Bolshevik type. It was still less accidental that even Stalin, the
future creator of a new class, was the most outstanding example of such a professional revolutionary. The new ruling class has been gradually developing from this
very narrow stratum of revolutionaries. . . .

. . . The new class may be said to be made up of those who have special privileges and economic preference because of the administrative monopoly they
hold. . . .

Just as personality, various social classes, and ideas still live, so do the nations
still live; they function; they struggle against despotism; and they preserve their distinctive features undestroyed. If their consciences and souls are smothered, they are
not broken. Though they are under subjugation, they have not yielded. The force
activating them today is more than the old or bourgeois nationalism; it is an imper-
ishable desire to be their own masters, and, by their own free development, to
attain an increasingly fuller fellowship with the rest of the human race in its eternal
existence. . . .

History does not have many movements that, like Communism, began their
climb with such high moral principles and with such devoted, enthusiastic, and
clever fighters, attached to each other not only by ideas and suffering, but also by
selfless love, comradeship, solidarity, and that warm and direct sincerity that can be
produced only by battles in which men are doomed either to win or die. . . .

. . . During the climb to power, intolerance, servility, incomplete thinking,
control of personal life—which once was comradely aid but is now a form of oli-

garchic management—hierarchical rigidity and introversion, the nominal and neglected role of women, opportunism, self-centeredness, and outrage repress the
once-existent high principles. The wonderful human characteristics of an isolated
movement are slowly transformed into the intolerant and Pharisaical morals of a
privileged caste. Thus, politicking and servility replace the former straightforwardness of the revolution. Where the former heroes who were ready to sacrifice everything, including life, for others and for an idea, for the good of the people, have
not been killed or pushed aside, they become self-centered cowards without ideas
or comrades, willing to renounce everything—honor, name, truth, and morals—in
order to keep their place in the ruling class and the hierarchical circle. The world
has seen few heroes as ready to sacrifice and suffer as the Communists were on the
eve of and during the revolution. It has probably never seen such characterless
wretches and stupid defenders of arid formulas as they become after attaining
power. . . .

Throughout history there have been no ideal ends which were attained with
non-ideal, inhumane means, just as there has been no free society which was built
by slaves. Nothing so well reveals the reality and greatness of ends as the methods
used to attain them. . . .

No regime in history which was democratic—or relatively democratic while it
lasted—was predominantly established on the aspiration for ideal ends, but rather
on the small everyday means in sight. Along with this, each such regime achieved,
more or less spontaneously, great ends. On the other hand, every despotism tried
to justify itself by its ideal aims. Not a single one achieved great ends.

Absolute brutality, or the use of any means, is in accord with the grandiosity,
even with the unreality, of Communist aims.

By revolutionary means, contemporary Communism has succeeded in demolish-
ing one form of society and despotically setting up another. At first it was guided
by the most beautiful, primordial human ideas of equality and brotherhood; only
later did it conceal behind these ideas the establishment of its domination by whatever means. . . .

China From Reform to Radicalization

After closely following the Soviet lead since 1949 in political organization, economic planning, foreign policy, ideology and even architecture, Communist China began in the later
1950's to set its own policy guidelines and even to challenge the Soviets' ideological leadership. The Chinese first reacted to de-Stalinization by proposing even freer criticism—the "let
all the flowers bloom" line enunciated by Lu Ting-yi, head of the Communist Party propaganda department. Mao spoke on the positive force of "non-antagonistic contradictions"
and warned against using force in matters of belief, while maintaining vigilance against
"revisionism."

In the latter part of 1957 China's general line was abruptly reversed, as Mao undertook
to outflank the Soviets on the left. General Secretary Teng Hsiao-p'ing announced a new rectification campaign to root out "bourgeois" thinking, and so-called "rightists" in the government and intellectual life were denounced in large numbers. As the Second Five-Year Plan
took effect in 1958, Liu Shao-ch'i proclaimed the program of the "Great Leap Forward" to
accelerate industrialization and the achievement of socialism by mobilizing popular effort
and enthusiasm. This was followed in the fall of 1958 by orders to reorganize the countryside into "people's communes," larger and more fully collectivist than the Soviet collective
farms, and implicitly bringing China further toward the Marxist ideal than the Soviet Union

had yet come. Both the Great Leap and the communes in fact disrupted production and soon had to be compromised, but the Chinese were now committed to solving their problems—including tension with the United States over Taiwan and the Nationalist-held off-shore islands—by militancy and force. These were the circumstances—focused by China's condemnation of the new Yugoslav party program as revisionist heresy—that set the stage for the open political rupture between China and the Soviet Union in 1960.

a) Lu Ting-yi, "Let All Flowers Bloom Together"

If China is to become wealthy and powerful, apart from the need of consolidating the people's regime, developing the economic and educational enterprises and fortifying the national defense, it is also necessary to bring prosperous development to literature, the arts and scientific work. We cannot afford to go without any of these things.

To bring prosperous development to literature, the arts and scientific work, it is necessary to adopt the policy of "letting all the flowers bloom together and all schools contend in airing their views." In literary and art work, if there is "only one flower in bloom," no matter how good the flower may be, it would not lead to prosperity. . . .

We must be able to see also that although literature and arts and scientific research are closely related with class struggle, nonetheless they cannot be identified with politics in an absolute sense. Political struggle is an instrument for manifesting class struggle directly. In the case of literature and arts and social science, while they can also manifest class struggle directly, they can also manifest the latter in a more devious way. It is fallacious to entertain the rightist unilateral view of "literature and arts for the sake of literature and arts" and "science for the sake of science" on the ground that literature and arts and science bear no relations with politics. On the other hand, to identify literature and arts and science with politics would also lead to another one-sided view. This is the mistake of "leftist" simplicity.

The party's policy advocates freedom of independent thinking in the work of literature and art and in the work of scientific research, freedom of debate, freedom of creative work and freedom to criticize, freedom to express one's opinion, and freedom to maintain one's opinion and to reserve one's opinion. . . .

The CCP Central Committee has pointed out that it is necessary to support this principle: In academic criticism and discussion, nobody is in a privileged position. It is wrong for anybody to look upon himself as the "authority," to suppress criticism, to neglect the mistaken thoughts of the bourgeoisie or to adopt the attitude of liberalism or even surrenderism. . . .

(1) Natural sciences including medicine have no class character. They have their own laws of development. Their relation with social systems is only that under bad social systems, these sciences develop slowly and under better social systems they can develop quickly. These are questions which have already been solved theoretically. Therefore, it is erroneous to put on class labels such as "feudal," "capitalist," "socialist," "proletarian," or "bourgeois," to certain medical theories, or theories of biology or other natural sciences; for instance, to say that "Chinese traditional medicine is feudal," "Western medicine is capitalist," "Pavlov's theory is socialist,"

FROM: Lu Ting-yi, "Let All Flowers Bloom Together, Let Diverse Schools of Thought Contend" (Speech of May 26, 1956; *Current Background*, No. 406, August 15, 1956, pp. 3–4, 6–8, 11, 15).

"Michurin's theory is socialist," or the "theory of heredity of Mendel-Morgan is capitalist." We must never believe in this fallacy. Some people fall victim to this fallacy because of their sectarian sentiment. Some fall victim to this fallacy unconsciously because they want to give undue stress to the need of learning advanced Soviet sciences. We must treat the different things according to their circumstances and cannot indulge in generality.

Simultaneously with pointing out the above mentioned error, we must also point out another kind of mistake. This is the negation of the Pavlov and Michurin theories as important theories. People also fall victim to this fallacy on different grounds. Some want to negate the Soviet scientific achievement because of their political anti-Soviet sentiment. Some are just unable to yield to the theories because they belong to another school of thought. The former involves the question of political viewpoint, while the latter involves the question of academic thought. We must treat them in a different way and cannot indulge in generality.

(2) The party makes only one demand of works of literature and art, that is, "to serve the workers, peasants and soldiers." Today, this means that they should serve all working people, including the intelligentsia. We regard socialist realism as the best method of creation. But it is by no means the only one. While serving the workers, peasants and soldiers, any author can use whatever method he thinks best to create and vie with the others. . . .

b) Mao, on the Correct Handling of Contradictions Among the People

Unification of the country, unity of the people and unity among our various nationalities—these are the basic guarantees for the sure triumph of our cause. However, this does not mean that there are no longer any contradictions in our society. It would be naive to imagine that there are no more contradictions. To do so would be to fly in the face of objective reality. We are confronted by two types of social contradictions—contradictions between ourselves and the enemy and contradictions among the people. . . .

The contradictions between ourselves and our enemies are antagonistic ones. Within the ranks of the people, contradictions among the working people are non-antagonistic, while those between the exploiters and the exploited classes have, apart from their antagonistic aspect, a non-antagonistic aspect. . . . Our people's government is a government that truly represents the interests of the people and serves the people, yet certain contradictions do exist between the government and the masses. These include contradictions between the interests of the state, collective interests and individual interests; between democracy and centralism; between those in positions of leadership and the led, and contradictions arising from the bureaucratic practices of certain state functionaries in their relations with the masses. . . .

In our country, the contradiction between the working class and the national bourgeoisie is a contradiction among the people. The class struggle waged between the two is, by and large, a class struggle within the ranks of the people. . . . The

FROM: Mao, "On the Correct Handling of Contradictions Among the People" (Revised text of speech to the Eleventh Session of the Supreme State Conference, February 27, 1957; in *People's China*, July 1, 1957, supplement, pp. 3–7, 9, 11–12, 14–16, 18–19, 21).

contradiction between exploiter and exploited, which exists between the national bourgeoisie and the working class, is an antagonistic one. But, in the concrete conditions existing in China, such an antagonistic contradiction, if properly handled, can be transformed into a non-antagonistic one and resolved in a peaceful way. . . .

Our dictatorship is known as the people's democratic dictatorship, led by the working class and based on the worker-peasant alliance. That is to say, democracy operates within the ranks of the people, while the working class, uniting with all those enjoying civil rights, the peasantry in the first place, enforces dictatorship over the reactionary classes and elements and all those who resist socialist transformation and oppose socialist construction. By civil rights, we mean, politically, freedom and democratic rights.

But this freedom is freedom with leadership and this democracy is democracy under centralized guidance, not anarchy. Anarchy does not conform to the interests or wishes of the people.

Certain people in our country were delighted when the Hungarian events took place. They hoped that something similar would happen in China, that thousands upon thousands of people would demonstrate in the streets against the people's government. Such hopes ran counter to the interests of the masses and therefore could not possibly get their support. In Hungary, a section of the people, deceived by domestic and foreign counter-revolutionaries, made the mistake of resorting to acts of violence against the people's government, with the result that both the state and the people suffered for it. . . .

The year 1956 saw the transformation of privately owned industrial and commercial enterprises into joint state-private enterprises as well as the organization of co-operatives in agriculture and handicrafts as part of the transformation of our social system. The speed and smoothness with which this was carried out are closely related to the fact that we treated the contradiction between the working class and the national bourgeoisie as a contradiction among the people. . . .

In building a socialist society, all need remoulding, the exploiters as well as the working people. Who says the working class doesn't need it? Of course, remoulding of the exploiters and that of the working people are two differing types of remoulding. The two must not be confused. In the class struggle and the struggle against nature, the working class remoulds the whole of society, and at the same time remoulds itself. . . .

Our industrialists and business men can be thoroughly remoulded only in the course of work; they should work together with the staff and workers in the enterprises, and make the enterprises the chief centres for remoulding themselves. It is also important for them to change certain of their old views through study. Study for them should be optional. After they have attended study groups for some weeks, many industrialists and business men on returning to their enterprises find they speak more of a common language with the workers and the representatives of state shareholding, and so work better together. They know from personal experience that it is good for them to keep on studying and remoulding themselves. . . .

Our intellectuals have made some progress, but they should not be complacent. They must continue to remould themselves, gradually shed their bourgeois world outlook and acquire a proletarian, Communist world outlook so that they can fully meet the needs of the new society and closely unite with the workers and peasants.

This change in world outlook is a fundamental one, and up till now it cannot yet be said that most of our intellectuals have accomplished it. . . .

"Let a hundred flowers blossom," and "let a hundred schools of thought contend," "long-term co-existence and mutual supervision"—how did these slogans come to be put forward?

They were put forward in the light of the specific conditions existing in China, on the basis of the recognition that various kinds of contradictions still exist in a socialist society, and in response to the country's urgent need to speed up its economic and cultural development.

The policy of letting a hundred flowers blossom and a hundred schools of thought contend is designed to promote the flourishing of the arts and the progress of science; it is designed to enable a socialist culture to thrive in our land. Different forms and styles in art can develop freely and different schools in science can contend freely. We think that it is harmful to the growth of art and science if administrative measures are used to impose one particular style of art or school of thought and to ban another. . . . While criticizing doctrinairism, we should at the same time direct our attention to criticizing revisionism. Revisionism, or rightist opportunism, is a bourgeois trend of thought which is even more dangerous than doctrinairism. The revisionists, or right opportunists, pay lip-service to Marxism and also attack "doctrinairism." But the real target of their attack is actually the most fundamental elements of Marxism. They oppose or distort materialism and dialectics, oppose or try to weaken the people's democratic dictatorship and the leading role of the Communist Party, oppose or try to weaken socialist transformation and socialist construction. Even after the basic victory of the socialist revolution in our country, there are still a number of people who vainly hope for a restoration of the capitalist system. They wage a struggle against the working class on every front, including the ideological front. In this struggle, their right-hand men are the revisionists. . . .

c) Teng Hsiao-p'ing, on the Movement to Rectify Work Style

. . . The movement for rectifying the work style within the ranks of the people involves questions in two different social categories. For the bourgeoisie and the bourgeois intelligentsia it involves the acceptance of the socialist transformation. For the petty bourgeoisie (peasants and independent workers in urban and rural areas) and particularly for the well-to-do middle peasant, it is also a matter of accepting the socialist transformation. For the working class and the general ranks of the Communist Party it is a question of rectifying the work style. . . .

It is necessary to wage a resolute struggle against the enemy, to adopt methods of exposure, isolation and dispersal and, against certain persons, the methods of punishment and suppression. Within the ranks of the people the basic method to be applied is the method of education, the method of "rally—criticize—rally." It is also necessary to resort to legal punishment of violators of laws among the people. This punishment also has educational value. . . .

FROM: Teng, "On the Movement to Rectify Work Style," Report to the Chinese Communist Party Central Committee, September 23, 1957 (*The Current Digest of the Soviet Press*, IX: 43, December 4, 1957, pp. 20–22).

The party will pursue a consistent policy toward bourgeois elements. Toward the bourgeois industrialists and merchants the party follows a policy of redemption and will strive to see that they continue to serve socialism. A course of prolonged coexistence and mutual control will be practiced in regard to democratic parties and groups. In the realm of science and culture the party will stand by the policy of "let a hundred flowers bloom, a hundred schools of thought contend." The premise for such courses and political aims is socialism. The party is resolutely insisting that the bourgeois elements and the bourgeois intelligentsia should in the end be re-educated and gradually become one with the working class. Under no circumstances is it possible to allow the leading role of the party, the dictatorship of the proletariat and democratic centralism to be shaken. It is impossible to permit the basic political aims of the party to be shaken, i.e., the policy of liquidating counterrevolutionaries, the policy of collectivization, centralized purchasing and selling of farm products, etc. It is important to intensify Marxist-Leninist propaganda and political education. It is essential to criticize false ideologies. Poisonous weeds must be uprooted. We allow poisonous weeds to grow in order to educate the masses by negative examples, to root out poisonous weeds and use them for fertilizers, to steel the proletariat and the broad popular masses in battle. . . .

The bourgeois intelligentsia, in addition to the fact that a small segment of it adheres to right-wing views, also suffers from other seriously mistaken views, specifically individualism, liberalism, anarchism, leveling and nationalism. At this stage of ideological education, criticism and self-analysis is essential to eliminate these mistaken views through systematic criticism.

The ideological re-education of the intelligentsia will take a long time, possibly more than ten years. . . .

. . . As a result of collectivization the question of the ownership of the means of production has been essentially settled, but this does not mean that there are no problems in the countryside. Some of the peasants still lack a clear understanding of the relationship between the state, the cooperative and the family, and individualism and provincialism are still in existence among them and are expressed in the form of scorn for the state and the collective interests.

The overwhelming majority of the well-to-do middle peasants joined the cooperatives under the pressure of the general circumstances, but most of them vacillate in their ideological outlook. A small portion of those elements which resolutely supported capitalism, after being compelled to enter cooperatives, headed the movement for withdrawal from the cooperatives or engaged in activity outside the cooperatives designed to undermine the cooperatives. Counterrevolutionary elements, hostile elements and a segment of the landlords and kulaks also engaged in subversive activity at every opportunity.

Serious right-deviationist ideas were also found within the party recently, ideas that the struggle between the two paths in the countryside was over and that the class line could not be further emphasized, that attention could be concentrated on production and that socialist education of the peasantry could be relaxed. Less attention was paid to the subversive activity of reactionary elements and these elements were not resolutely rebuffed in time. . . .

. . . The movement has shown that the old workers are a basic arm of the party and socialism. Among the new workers—nearly 65% of the workers at present— more than half are persons who come from the peasantry, students and the poor of the cities. They are largely contaminated by the ideology and work style of the petty bourgeoisie. Three percent of the new workers (5% in some organizations) are former landlords, kulaks, capitalists, police, soldiers of the reactionary army and declassed elements among whom the ideology and depraved customs of the exploiting class have not been completely eradicated.

The situation in the party derives from the following social and ideological factors: 1) The majority of party members are from nonproletarian classes; 2) party organizations have developed relatively rapidly, insufficient attention has been devoted to the quality of party membership, and ideological and political work has lagged behind the growth of the party; 3) An even more important factor is that most persons joined the party after the victory of the revolution without having a true socialist world view and, after joining the party, they found themselves for a long time in a situation in which collaboration with the bourgeoisie existed in the country; thus they have not participated directly in a sharp class struggle with the bourgeoisie. Among the 1,880,000 Communist intelligentsia the majority have not been steeled in the work of production and have not had effective training in the class struggle. . . .

d) Liu Shao-ch'i on the "Great Leap Forward"

. . . The spring of 1958 witnessed the beginning of a leap forward on every front in our socialist construction. Industry, agriculture and all other fields of activity are registering greater and more rapid growth. . . .

The upsurge in agriculture last winter and this spring gave a vigorous push to the new industrial upsurge of this year. The rapid development of industry in turn has prompted an even swifter growth of agriculture. . . .

The current mighty leap forward in socialist construction is the product not only of the successful development of the anti-rightist struggle and the rectification campaign but also of a correct implementation of the Party's general line—to build socialism by exerting our utmost efforts, and pressing ahead consistently to achieve greater, faster, better and more economical results.

Comrade Mao Tse-tung has often said that there are two ways of carrying on socialist transformation and construction: one will result in doing the work faster and better; the other slowly and not so well. Which way shall we take? This has been an issue. . . . The Central Committee of the Party and Comrade Mao Tse-tung have always taken a clear-cut stand, insisting that the way of working faster and better be adopted and the other way, of working slowly and not so well, be rejected. However on this question some comrades still clung to such outmoded ideas as "keeping to the right is better than keeping to the left," "it is better to go slower than faster" or "it is better to take small steps than to go striding forward." The struggle between the two ways of dealing with this question was not fully decided until the launching of the rectification campaign and the anti-rightist struggle. . . .

. . . The following are the basic points of our general line, which is to build socialism by exerting our utmost efforts, and pressing ahead consistently to achieve greater, faster, better and more economical results:

FROM: Liu, Report on the Work of the CCP Central Committee delivered to the Second Session of the Eighth National Congress of the Chinese Communist Party, May 5, 1958 (official translation reprinted in *Current Background*, no. 507, June 2, 1958, pp. 7–13, 19–21, 23–25).

To mobilize all positive factors and correctly handle contradictions among the people;

To consolidate and develop socialist ownership, i.e., ownership by the whole people and collective ownership, and consolidate the proletarian dictatorship and proletarian international solidarity;

To carry out a technological revolution and a cultural revolution step by step, while completing the socialist revolution on the economic, political and ideological fronts;

To develop industry and agriculture simultaneously while giving priority to heavy industry; and

With centralized leadership, overall planning, proper division of labor and coordination, to develop national and local industries, and large, small and medium-sized enterprises simultaneously.

Through all this we will build our country, in the shortest possible time, into a great socialist country with a modern industry, modern agriculture and modern science and culture. . . .

The central task of the rectification campaign is to handle correctly the contradictions among the people and improve human relations in socialist labor and all other group activities. We have in the main accomplished the socialist transformation of the means of production, which is the prerequisite for changing the relationships between men. . . . However, many of the administrative personnel and brain workers have not yet learnt to treat the masses on a footing of complete equality; they have not yet done away with some survivals of the working style of the Kuomintang and still have certain bureaucratic airs. This makes it difficult for them to gain the full confidence of the masses. . . .

. . . We have a population of more than 600 million and our Party has ties of flesh and blood with this vast population. By relying on this great force we can, or soon can, do anything within the realms of human possibility. It is true that for the time being this population of 600 million and more is economically poor and culturally is like a clean sheet of white paper. But what does this matter to Marxist-Leninist revolutionaries? Comrade Mao Tse-tung has put it well: "In addition to other characteristics, our more than 600 million people are characterized by poverty and 'whiteness.' This appears to be a bad thing, but in fact it is a good thing. Poor people want to change, to work hard and make a revolution. A clean sheet of white paper has nothing written on it and is therefore well suited for writing the newest and most beautiful words on and for drawing the newest and most beautiful pictures." Isn't this a fact? Our 600 million and more people have already far surpassed the most advanced capitalist countries in the West in the speed of the upsurge of their revolutionary consciousness and of the victories of their revolutionary struggles and will definitely far surpass them too in the speed of economic and cultural growth. In history, it is always the newcomers who outstrip the old, always the new-born things, which for a time appear weak and small but represent what is progressive, that defeat the moribund things, which appear powerful but represent what is conservative. Within a very short historical period we shall certainly leave every capitalist country in the world far behind us. And so, shouldn't we have confidence in ourselves and discard everything that smacks of superstition, fear and feelings of inferiority?

The inevitable victory of our cause is also grounded in the fraternal aid of the countries in the socialist camp headed by the great Soviet Union—which is internationally the most important factor in our favor. We shall continue to draw on the advanced experience of the Soviet Union and other countries, continue to strengthen mutual assistance and cooperation with the other countries in the socialist camp and shoulder to shoulder with our fraternal parties in all countries, raise still higher the banner of Marxism-Leninism and reinforce the militant solidarity of the international Communist movement. We resolutely support the peace proposals of the Soviet Union, the efforts of the peoples of all lands to safeguard peace, and all national movements which oppose aggression, defend their sovereign rights and seek independence. The struggles of the people of all countries support our cause and through our work we in turn support the people of all countries.

Comrades! Let us, on the basis of the Party's general line for socialist construction, strengthen ceaselessly the unity of the entire Party and unity between the Party and all the people. Let us strengthen ceaselessly our solidarity with the Soviet Union and other countries in the socialist camp and with all the peoples of the world in the common cause of peace, democracy and socialism. Victory will surely be ours!

e) Resolution of the Central Committee on the Establishment of Communes

. . . The main basis for the development of people's communes is the overall and continuous leap forward in agricultural production in the whole country and the growing elevation of the political consciousness of the 500 million peasants. After the basic victory over the road of capitalism on the economic, political and ideological fronts, agricultural capital construction has been developed on an unprecedented scale, and we have basically built the new foundation for agricultural production to be developed under comparatively stable conditions, free from the menaces of flood and drought. With the overcoming of rightist conservatism, and the breaking down of conventions in agricultural technical measures, agricultural production is leaping forward at high speed, and the output of agricultural products is increasing by one hundred percent, several hundred percent, over one thousand percent, and several thousand percent. This has further promoted the ideological liberation of the people. Large-scale agricultural capital construction and advanced agricultural technical measures demand the employment of more manpower. The development of industry in the rural areas also demands the transfer of a portion of manpower from the agricultural front. Thus the demand is more and more urgent for the mechanization and electrification of our countryside. In the struggle for agricultural capital construction and the quest for bumper harvests, the breaking down of boundaries between cooperatives, between *hsiang* [townships], and between *hsien* [counties] in order to carry out extensive cooperation, the "militarization" of organization, the placing of activities on a "combatant" basis, and the collectivization of daily living have become mass actions, and they

FROM: Resolution of the Central Committee of the Chinese Communist Party, "On the Establishment of People's Communes in the Rural Areas," August 29, 1958 (English translation in *Survey of China Mainland Press*, U.S. Consulate-General, Hong Kong, No. 1853, September 15, 1958, pp. 1–2, 4).

have further raised the Communist consciousness of the 500 million peasants. Common mess halls, kindergartens, nurseries, tailoring teams, barbershops, public baths, "happiness homes" [old people's homes], agricultural middle schools, and schools for turning out red and expert personnel are leading the peasants to a collective life of greater happiness, and are further fostering and steeling the collectivism of the masses of the peasants. . . .

According to present conditions, the scale of the organization of the people's commune should in general be fixed at one commune to a *hsiang* with about 2,000 households. . . .

The steps taken in the establishment of people's communes consist of the merger of small cooperatives into large cooperatives, and their change into communes. This is the common demand of the broad masses of the people today. The poor peasants and the lower middle peasants resolutely support such a course. The majority of the upper middle peasants also support it. . . .

When the stage of the system of ownership by the whole people is reached, it is still socialist in nature, such as is the case with the state-owned industry, i.e., "from each according to his ability, to each according to his labor." After another period of many years, when social products have been greatly increased, the Communist ideological awakening and ethical standards of all the people have been greatly raised, universal education is practiced and elevated, the differences between workers and peasants, between urban and rural areas, and between mental and physical labor (all these differences having been left over from the old society had to be preserved during the period of socialism) are gradually wiped out, the remnants of the bourgeois state power which reflect these different cases of inequality have been gradually eliminated, and the function of the state is only to deal with aggression from enemies outside and plays no longer a role in domestic affairs, then and only then will our society enter the age of communism, "from each according to his ability, to each according to his need" will be practiced.

After the establishment of the people's communes, there is also no need to hastily change the original system of distribution, to avoid unfavorable effects on production. We must start from concrete conditions. Where conditions are ripe, the wage systems may be taken up. Where conditions are not yet ripe, for the time being we may continue to adopt such systems as originally practiced, that of "the three contracts and one bonus award," or else we may adopt the system of fixing production quotas and paying wages on the basis of labor days. When the conditions are ripe, changes may then be instituted.

Though the people's communes still practice the system of collective ownership, and the distribution system, whether it be the wage system or remuneration according to labor days, is still "to each according to his labor" and not "to each according to his need"; nevertheless the people's commune will be the best organizational form for the building of socialism and the gradual transition to communism. It will develop into the basic social unit of the future communist society.

Our task at the present stage is the building of socialism. The establishment of people's communes is undertaken first of all for the acceleration of socialist construction, and the building of socialism is to actively make preparations for transition to communism. It appears now that the realization of communism in our country is no longer a thing of the distant future. We should actively employ the form of the people's commune to produce a concrete path for transition to communism.

Revolt and Repression in Tibet

The radicalism of the Great Leap Forward entailed tighter central control over China's extensive national minority regions. In Tibet, local forces loyal to the Buddhist theocracy of the Dalai Lama rose in revolt. Central troops crushed the uprising and effectively put an end to Tibet's autonomy, while the Dalai Lama fled into exile in India.

The following order is herewith proclaimed:

Most of the officials of the Tibet Local Government and the upper strata reactionary clique colluded with imperialism, assembled rebellious bandits, carried out rebellion, ravaged the people, put the Dalai Lama under duress, tore up the seventeen-article agreement on measures for the peaceful liberation of Tibet* and, on the night of March 19, directed the Tibetan Local Army and rebellious elements to launch a general offensive against the People's Liberation Army garrison in Lhasa.

Such acts, which betray the motherland and disrupt unification, are not allowed by law. In order to safeguard the unification of the country and national units, in addition to enjoining the Tibet military area command of the Chinese People's Liberation Army to put down the rebellion thoroughly, the decision is that from this day the Tibet Local Government is dissolved and the preparatory committee for the Tibet Autonomous Region shall exercise the functions and powers of the Tibet Local Government.

During the time when the Dalai Lama Dantzen-Jaltso, chairman of the Preparatory Committee for the Tibet Autonomous Region, is under duress by the rebels, Panchen Erdeni Ghuji-geltseng, vice chairman of the Preparatory Committee, will act as the chairman. . . . Eighteen traitorous elements . . . are relieved of their posts as members of the Preparatory Committee for the Tibet Autonomous Region and of all their other posts and are to be punished individually under law.

Sixteen persons . . . are appointed members of the Preparatory Committee for the Tibet Autonomous Region.

It is to be hoped that the Preparatory Committee for the Tibet Autonomous Region will lead all the people of Tibet, ecclesiastical and secular, to unite as one and make common efforts to assist the People's Liberation Army to put down the rebellion quickly, consolidate national defense, protect the interests of the people of all nationalities, secure social order and strive for the building of a new democratic and socialist Tibet.

Khrushchev in America

Khrushchev's pursuit of better relations with the West led to an exchange of visits by high Soviet and American officials (including Vice-President Nixon), culminating in Khrushchev's own tour of the United States in September, 1959. On his return to Moscow he reported on his perception of America's interest in peace, and incidentally tried to explain away his remark about "burying the capitalists."

FROM: Order of Premier Chou En-lai dissolving the Local Government of Tibet, March 28, 1959 (English text in *The New York Times*, March 29, 1959).

*See pp. 135–36.

FROM: Khrushchev, Speech upon his return to Moscow, September 28, 1959 (English translation in *New Times*, #40, October, 1959, Supplement, pp. 35, 37, 39–40)

Dear Comrades:

We have just stepped off the plane which made a nonstop flight from Washington to Moscow. (*Applause.*) We have come straight here to this meeting, dear Muscovites, in order to share our impressions with you and to tell you about the results of our stay in the United States of America, which we visited at the invitation of President Dwight D. Eisenhower.

In accepting that invitation, we were prompted by the consideration that the international situation and the relations between our states—our two Great Powers, the Soviet Union and the United States—have for a long time been strained. To preserve such a state of affairs would mean to preserve a situation in which there may be all kinds of surprises fraught with grave consequences for our peoples and for the peoples of the whole world. That is why the more farsighted statesmen in a number of countries have come to realize the need to make some effort to put an end to the cold war, to remove the tension in international relations, clear the atmosphere and create more or less normal relations between states. The peoples could then live and look to the future without fear. . . .

. . . In our age of tremendous technological progress, in circumstances where there exist states with different social systems, international problems can be successfully solved only on the basis of the principle of peaceful coexistence. There is no other way. Those who say that they do not understand what peaceful coexistence is, and are afraid of it, are wittingly or unwittingly helping to further the cold war which is bound to spread unless we intervene and stop it. It will reach a point of such intensity that a spark may at any moment set off a world conflagration. In that war much will perish. It will be too late to discuss what peaceful coexistence means when such terrible means of destruction as atomic and hydrogen bombs, and ballistic missiles, which practically cannot be intercepted and can carry nuclear weapons to any point on the globe, go into action. Not to reckon with this, means to close one's eyes and stop one's ears, to hide one's head in the sand as the ostrich does at the approach of danger. If we humans imitate the ostrich and hide our heads in the sand, then, I ask you, what is the use of having a head if it is incapable of averting the danger to life? (*Prolonged applause.*)

No, we must show human reason, we must have faith in the human intellect, faith in the possibility of achieving agreement with statesmen of different countries and in combining efforts to mobilize people for the task of averting the threat of war. We must have the courage and determination to act in defiance of those who persist in continuing the cold war. We must stop it from spreading, melt the ice and normalize international relations. From this lofty rostrum, before you Muscovites, before my whole people, my government and Party, I must say that President Eisenhower displayed wise statesmanship in appraising the present world situation, displayed courage and determination. (*Stormy applause.*) Notwithstanding the complex situation prevailing in the United States, the President, a man who enjoys the absolute confidence of his people, proposed an exchange of visits between the heads of government of our two countries. We give him due credit for this important initiative aimed at strengthening the cause of peace. (*Prolonged applause.*) In taking this step, he was confident that we would accept the hand he proffered us, inasmuch as we have repeatedly addressed both President Eisenhower and other heads of government to that effect. And the President was not mistaken. (*Applause.*) . . .

During the first half of our tour, we could not help noticing that one and the same story was repeated each time. Speakers claimed that I had once said that we would "bury the capitalists." At first I patiently explained what I had actually said, that we would "bury capitalism"* in the sense that socialism would inevitably replace that moribund social system, just as in its time capitalism had replaced feudalism. But as time went on, I saw that the people who persisted in repeating this sort of question did not really need any explanations. They were pursuing a definite purpose, namely, to use the Communist bogey to frighten people who have only the vaguest notion of what Communism is. . . .

But I can tell you in all frankness, dear comrades, that as a result of my talks and discussions of concrete questions with the U.S. President, I have gained the impression that he sincerely wishes to see the end of the cold war, to create normal relations between our countries and to help improve relations among all countries. (*Stormy applause.*) Peace today is indivisible, it cannot be secured by the efforts of two or three countries alone. Hence it is necessary that all nations, all states participate in the fight for peace.

The President and I exchanged views on the question of disarmament. He stated that the Government of the United States was studying our proposal and that the United States, like ourselves, wants total, controlled disarmament.

It would seem that there are, at present, no reasons for delaying settlement of this question. But, on the other hand, disarmament is too serious a question for one to expect one's partners to settle it hastily, right off the bat. It must, of course, be studied with a view to finding a solution that would really create confidence and ensure disarmament and the peaceful coexistence of states. . . .

I would like to tell you, dear comrades, that I have no doubt that the President is prepared to exert his efforts and his will to bring about agreement between our two countries, to create friendly relations between our two peoples and to settle pressing problems in the interest of a durable peace. (*Applause.*)

At the same time, it is my impression that there are forces in America which are not operating in the same direction as the President. These forces stand for continuing the cold war and the arms race. Whether these forces are great or small, influential or uninfluential, whether the forces backing the President—and he has the support of the absolute majority of the American people—can win, are questions I would not be too hasty to answer. . . .

In our actions we base ourselves on reason, on truth, on the support of the whole people. Moreover, we rely on our mighty potential. And those who wish to preserve the cold war with a view sooner or later to turning it into a hot war had best know that in our time only a madman can start war, who himself will perish in its flames. (*Applause.*)

The peoples must strait-jacket such madmen. We believe that statesmanship, that human reason will triumph. (*Applause.*) In the splendid words of Pushkin, "Let reason triumph! May darkness be banished!" (*Prolonged applause.*)

Dear comrade Muscovites! We are boundlessly happy to be home again, to see the dear faces of Soviet people. (*Applause.*)

Long live the great Soviet people who are successfully building communism under the leadership of the glorious Party of Lenin! (*Prolonged applause.*)

---

*Khrushchev actually made this boast at a reception at the Polish Embassy in Moscow in November, 1956—Ed.

Long live Soviet-American friendship! (*Prolonged applause.*)

Long live friendship among all the peoples of the world! (*Stormy, prolonged applause. All rise.*)

Khrushchev's Rupture with America and China

Following the U-2 Affair in May 1960 and the abortive Paris Summit Conference, Khrushchev reverted to vitriolic anti-American and anti-imperialistic rhetoric, and appeared in this confrontationist mood at the U.N. General Assembly session in New York in September of the same year (the occasion of the unforgettable shoe-banging incident). A meeting of representatives of eighty-one Communist parties was held in Moscow in November, 1960, to reaffirm the militant solidarity of the movement and to reinforce Moscow's ideological defenses against the "dogmatism and sectarianism" represented by the Chinese and the Albanians.

Our time, whose main content is the transition from capitalism to socialism initiated by the Great October Socialist Revolution, is a time of struggle between the two opposing social systems, a time of socialist revolutions and national-liberation revolutions, a time of the breakdown of imperialism, of the abolition of the colonial system, a time of transition of more peoples to the socialist path, of the triumph of socialism and communism on a world-wide scale.

It is the principal characteristic of our time that the world socialist system is becoming the decisive factor in the development of society. . . .

The world capitalist system is going through an intense process of disintegration and decay. Its contradictions have accelerated the development of monopoly capitalism into state-monopoly capitalism. By tightening the monopolies' grip on the life of the nation, state-monopoly capitalism closely combines the power of the monopolies with that of the state with the aim of saving the capitalist system and increasing the profits of the imperialist bourgeoisie to the utmost by exploiting the working class and plundering large sections of the population. . . .

The decay of capitalism is particularly marked in the United States of America, the chief imperialist country of today. U.S. monopoly capital is clearly unable to use all the productive forces at its command. The richest of the developed capitalist countries of the world—the United States of America—has become a land of especially big chronic unemployment. Increasing under-capacity operation in industry has become permanent in that country. Despite the enormous increase in military appropriations, which is achieved at the expense of the standard of life of the working people, the rate of growth of production has been declining in the post-war years and has been barely above the growth of population. Over-production crises have become more frequent. The most developed capitalist country has become a country of the most distorted, militarised economy. More than any other capitalist country, the United States drains Asia, and especially Latin America, of their riches, holding up their progress. U.S. capitalist penetration into Africa is increasing. U.S. imperialism has become the biggest international exploiter.

The U.S. imperialists seek to bring many states under their control, by resorting

FROM: Statement of the Meeting of Representatives of the Communist and Workers' Parties, November, 1960 (English translation in *New Times*, #50, 1960, Supplement, pp. 1–3, 5–8, 10–16).

chiefly to the policy of military blocs and economic "aid." They violate the sovereignty of developed capitalist countries as well. The dominant monopoly bourgeoisie in the more developed capitalist countries, which has allied itself with U.S. imperialism, sacrifices the sovereignty of their countries, hoping with support from the U.S. imperialists to crush the revolutionary liberation forces, deprive the working people of democratic freedoms and impede the struggle of the masses for social progress. U.S. imperialism involves those countries in the arms race, in a policy of preparing a new war of aggression and carrying on subversive activities against socialist and neutral countries. . . .

The common interests of the peoples of the socialist countries and the interests of peace and socialism demand the proper combination of the principles of socialist internationalism and socialist patriotism in politics. Every Communist Party which has become the ruling party in the state, bears historical responsibility for the destinies of both its country and the entire socialist camp. . . .

The imperialist reactionaries, who try to arouse distrust for the Communist movement and its ideology, continue to intimidate the people by alleging that the Communists need wars between states to overthrow the capitalist system and establish a socialist system. The Communist Parties emphatically reject this slander. The fact that both world wars, which were started by the imperialists, ended in socialist revolution by no means implies that the way to social revolution is necessarily through world war, especially now that there exists a powerful world system of socialism. Marxist-Leninists have never considered that the way to social revolution lies through wars between states.

The choice of social system is the inalienable right of the people of each country. Socialist revolution cannot be imported, nor imposed from without. It is a result of the internal development of the country concerned, of the utmost sharpening of social contradictions in it. The Communist Parties, which guide themselves by the Marxist-Leninist doctrine, have always been against the export of revolution. At the same time they fight resolutely against imperialist export of counter-revolution. They consider it their internationalist duty to call on the peoples of all countries to unite, to rally all their internal forces, to act vigorously and, relying on the might of the world socialist system, to prevent or firmly resist imperialist interference in the affairs of any people who have risen in revolution. . . .

The Communist Parties have unanimously condemned the Yugoslav variety of international opportunism, a variety of modern revisionist "theories" in concentrated form. After betraying Marxism-Leninism, which they termed obsolete, the leaders of the League of Communists of Yugoslavia opposed their anti-Leninist revisionist programme to the Declaration of 1957; they set the L.C.Y. against the international Communist movement as a whole, severed their country from the socialist camp, made it dependent on so-called "aid" from U.S. and other imperialists, and thereby exposed the Yugoslav people to the danger of losing the revolutionary gains achieved through a heroic struggle. . . .

The further development of the Communist and working-class movement calls, as stated in the Moscow Declaration of 1957, for continuing a determined struggle on two fronts—against revisionism, which remains the main danger, and against dogmatism and sectarianism.

Revisionism, Right-wing opportunism, which mirrors bourgeois ideology in theory and practice, distorts Marxism-Leninism, robs it of its revolutionary essence, and thereby paralyses the revolutionary will of the working class. It disarms and demobilises the workers and all working people, in their struggle against oppression by imperialists and exploiters, for peace, democracy and national liberation, for the triumph of socialism.

Dogmatism and sectarianism in theory and practice can also become the main danger at some stage of development of individual parties, unless combated unrelentingly. They rob revolutionary parties of the ability to develop Marxism-Leninism through scientific analysis and apply it creatively according to the specific conditions. They isolate Communists from the broad masses of the working people, doom them to passive expectation or Leftist, adventurist actions in the revolutionary struggle. . . .

Marxism-Leninism is a great integral revolutionary doctrine, the guiding light of the working class and working people of the whole world at all stages of their great battle for peace, freedom and a better life, for the establishment of the most just society, communism. Its great creative, revolutionising power lies in its unbreakable link with life, in its continuous enrichment through a comprehensive analysis of reality. On the basis of Marxism-Leninism, the community of socialist countries and the international Communist working-class and liberation movements have achieved great historic successes, and it is only on its basis that all the tasks facing the Communist and Workers' Parties can be effectively accomplished.

The Meeting sees the further consolidation of the Communist Parties on the basis of Marxism-Leninism, of proletarian internationalism, as a primary condition for the unification of all working-class, democratic and progressive forces, as a guarantee of new victories in the great struggle waged by the world Communist and working-class movement for a happy future for the whole of mankind, for the triumph of the cause of peace and socialism.

The Berlin Crisis and the Wall

Defied by the Western powers in his efforts to force them out of Berlin, and faced with a growing drain of working-age people out of East Germany, Khrushchev invoked the Warsaw Pact to support the surprise action by the East German government in August, 1961, to seal off West Berlin from the East with the construction of the infamous wall.

a) Warsaw Pact Communiqué

The Governments of the Warsaw Treaty member states have been striving for a peaceful settlement with Germany for a number of years. In so doing, they are guided by the fact that this question has long since been ripe and brooks no further delays.

It is generally known that the Government of the U.S.S.R., with the full agreement and support of all member states of the Warsaw Treaty organization, approached the Governments of the countries which had participated in the war against Hitler Germany with a proposal to conclude a peace treaty with two German states and to settle on this basis the question of West Berlin by granting it the status of a demilitarized, free city.

FROM: Communiqué of the Warsaw Pact Powers, August 13, 1961 (English text in *The New York Times*, August 14, 1961).

This proposal took into account the situation obtaining practically in Germany and Europe in the post-war period. This proposal is not directed against anybody's interests, and its only aim is to do away with the leftovers of World War II and to consolidate world peace.

The governments of the Western Powers have not so far shown willingness to achieve an agreed solution of this question through negotiations between all sides concerned. Moreover, to the peaceful proposals of the Socialist countries, the Western powers reply by stepping up their military preparations, fanning up war hysteria and by threatening to use armed forces. . . .

The Governments of the Western powers, in every way encouraging the arming of Western Germany, grossly violate the most important international agreements envisaging eradication of German militarism and prevention of its revival in any form.

The Western powers, far from having made any efforts to normalize the situation in West Berlin, on the contrary continue using it intensively as a center of subversive activities against the G.D.R. [East Germany] and all other countries of the Socialist commonwealth.

In no other point of the world are so many espionage and subversive centers of foreign states to be found as in West Berlin, where they can act with some impunity. These numerous subversive centers are smuggling their agents to the G.D.R. for all sorts of subversion, recruiting spies and inciting hostile elements to organize sabotage and to provoke disturbances in the G.D.R.

The present situation regarding the traffic on the borders of West Berlin is being used by the F.R.G. [West German] ruling quarters and intelligence agencies of the NATO countries for undermining the G.D.R.'s economy.

The government bodies and military concerns of the F.R.G., through deceit, bribery, and blackmail, make some unstable elements in the G.D.R. leave for Western Germany. These deceived people are compelled to serve with the Bundeswehr, or recruited to the intelligence agencies of different countries to be sent back to the G.D.R. as spies and saboteurs.

A special fund has even been formed for such subversive activities against the G.D.R. and other Socialist countries. Recently West German Chancellor Adenauer asked the NATO Governments to increase this fund.

It is highly indicative that the subversive activities directed from West Berlin have greatly increased of late, right after the Soviet Union, the G.D.R. and other Socialist countries have advanced proposals for immediate peaceful settlement with Germany. This subversive activity inflicts damage not only on the German Democratic Republic but also affects the interests of other countries of the Socialist camp.

In the face of the aggressive aspirations of the reactionary forces of the F.R.G. and its NATO allies, the Warsaw Treaty member states cannot but take necessary measures for insuring their security, and primarily the security of the German Democratic Republic in the interests of the German peoples themselves.

The Governments of the Warsaw Treaty member states address the People's Chamber and the Government of the G.D.R., and all working people of the German Democratic Republic, with a proposal to establish such an order on the borders of West Berlin which would securely block the way for the subversive activity against the Socialist camp countries, so that reliable safeguards and effective control can be established around the whole territory of West Berlin including its border with Democratic Berlin.

It goes without saying that these measures must not affect the existing order of traffic and control on the ways of communication between West Berlin and Western Germany.

The Governments of the Warsaw Treaty member states understand, of course, that protective measures along the borders of West Berlin will somewhat inconvenience the population. But the entire responsibility for the obtaining situation rests exclusively with the Western powers, and with the F.R.G. in the first place.

If so far the borders of West Berlin have remained opened, this was done in the hope that the Western powers would not abuse the goodwill of the Government of the German Democratic Republic. But they, disregarding the interests of the German people and Berlin population, used the order now operating on the border of West Berlin for their own perfidious, subversive aims.

Stronger protection and control on the border with West Berlin must put an end to the present abnormal situation.

At the same time, the Governments of the Warsaw Treaty member states find it necessary to emphasize that this necessity will disappear when a peaceful settlement with Germany is achieved, and the questions awaiting their solution will be settled on this basis.

b) East German Decree

On the basis of the statement by the Warsaw Treaty member countries and the decision of the People's Chamber, the Council of Ministers of the German Democratic Republic adopted the following decree:

The interests of preserving peace demand that an end be put to the machinations of the West German revanchists and militarists and that the way be opened, through conclusion of a German peace treaty, to the preservation of peace and the revival of Germany as a peaceful, anti-imperialist, neutral state.

The viewpoint of the Bonn Government that World War II is not yet formally ended is tantamount to demanding freedom for militarist provocations and civil war measures.

This imperialist policy, which is being carried out under the signboard of anti-communism, constitutes continuation of the aggressive aims of the Fascist German imperialism of the time of the Third Reich.

From the defeat of Hitler Germany in World War II, the Bonn Government has drawn the conclusion that the piratical policy of the German monopoly capital and its Hitler generals must be tried once more through rejection of a German national state policy and conversion of Western Germany into a NATO member state, into a satellite country of the United States.

This fresh threat to the German and other European peoples on the part of German militarism could become a grave danger, because the provisions of the Potsdam agreement on eradication of militarism and Nazism were constantly violated in the West German Federal Republic and the front-line city of West Berlin.

FROM: Decree of the Council of Ministers of the German Democratic Republic, August 13, 1961 (English text in *The New York Times*, August 14, 1961).

The revanchist policy, with its increasing territorial claims to the German Democratic Republic and Germany's neighbor states, has been intensified in Western Germany, which is closely connected with speedy armament and atomic arming of the West German Bundeswehr.

The Adenauer Government is systematically carrying out, with regard to the German Democratic Republic, preparations for a civil war.

The citizens of the German Democratic Republic visiting Western Germany are being increasingly subjected to terroristic persecutions. West Germany and West Berlin espionage organizations are systematically luring citizens of the German Democratic Republic and organizing regular slave traffic.

As follows from official [West German] Government documents and principled statement by the Christian Democratic Union-Christian Socialist Union, C.D.U.-C.S.U. party leadership, the aim of this aggressive policy and sabotage is to include the whole of Germany into the NATO Western military bloc and to extend the militarists' domination from the Federal Republic of Germany to the German Democratic Republic as well. The West German militarists want, with the help of all sorts of fraudulent maneuvers, as, for instance, free elections, at first to extend their military base to the Oder [River] and then start another big war.

The West German revanchists and militarists are abusing the peaceful policy of the U.S.S.R. and the Warsaw Treaty states on the German question, in order to damage not only the German Democratic Republic but also other states of the Socialist camp by means of rampant, hostile propaganda, by enticing people and by sabotage.

For all these reasons, the Council of Ministers of the German Democratic Republic, in accordance with the decision of the Political Consultative Committee of the Warsaw Treaty member states, and with a view of insuring peace in Europe, protecting the German Democratic Republic and in the interests of the security of the Socialist camp states, decided to take the following measures:

To put an end to the hostile activities of the revanchist and militarist forces of Western Germany and West Berlin, such control is to be introduced on the borders of the German Democratic Republic, including the border with the Western sectors of Greater Berlin, which is usually introduced along the borders of every sovereign state.

Reliable safeguards and effective control must be insured on the West Berlin borders in order to block the way to the subversive activities.

The citizens of the German Democratic Republic may cross these borders only with special permission.

Until West Berlin is turned into a demilitarized neutral free city, the citizens of the capital of the German Democratic Republic will have to have a special permit for crossing the border to West Berlin.

The West Berlin civilians may visit the capital of the German Democratic Republic (Democratic Berlin) on presenting West Berlin identity cards.

Revanchist politicians and agents of West German militarism are not permitted to enter the territory of the G.D.R. capital (Democratic Berlin).

As regards visits to Democratic Berlin by the citizens of the West German Federal Republic, former decisions on control remain valid.

These decisions do not affect the visits of the citizens of other states to the capital of the German Democratic Republic.

As regards the traveling of West Berlin citizens abroad along the communications lines in the German Democratic Republic, former decisions remain valid.

This decree in no way revises former decisions on transit between West Berlin and West Germany via the German Democratic Republic.

The Minister of Home Affairs, Minister of Transport and Mayor of Greater Berlin are instructed to issue appropriate instructions on the enactment of this decree.

This decree on the measures for insuring peace, protecting the German Democratic Republic and its capital of Berlin in particular, and for insuring the security of other Socialist states, remains valid till the conclusion of a German peace treaty.

Cuba—From Nationalism to Communism

A major strategic advance for the Soviet Union was the capture of the Cuban Revolution for the Communist cause in the early 1960's. Fidel Castro had taken power in January, 1959, after waging Mao-style guerrilla warfare against the Batista dictatorship, without any previous indication of Communist affiliation. Backed at the last minute by the Cuban Communist Party, Castro rapidly radicalized his regime, fell out with the United States over the nationalization of American plantations and businesses, and welcomed the aid that the Soviet Union offered in 1960 when Khrushchev shifted to his confrontationist line. Gravely threatened when the U.S. launched an abortive attempt at counter-revolutionary intervention at the Bay of Pigs in the spring of 1961, Castro boldly announced that he had always been an instinctive Marxist-Leninist. Then Khrushchev attempted to convert his Cuban political foothold into a military one by installing Soviet missiles, precipitating the crisis that brought him to the verge of war with the U.S.A. Khrushchev was compelled to withdraw the missiles but won American acquiescence in the continuation of the Castro regime.

a) Castro's Conversion to Communism

I consider myself more revolutionary today than I was even on the first of January [1959]. Was I a revolutionary on the first of January? Yes, I believe I was a revolutionary on the first of January. That is, all of the ideas I have today I had on the first of January.

Now then, am I at this moment a man who has studied thoroughly all of the political philosophy of the Revolution, the entire history? No, I have not studied it thoroughly. Of course, I am absolutely convinced and have the intention—an intention we all ought to have—to study. Recently, while looking through some books up there in the capital, I found that when I was a student I had read up to page 370 of *Capital*. That's as far as I got. When I have the time, I plan to continue studying Karl Marx's *Capital*.

In my student years I had studied the Communist Manifesto and selected works of Marx, Engels, and Lenin. Of course, it is very interesting to reread now the things I read at that time. Well, now, do I believe in Marxism? I believe absolutely in Marxism! Did I believe on the first of January? I believed on the first of January. Did I believe on the 26th of July?* I believed on the 26th of July! Did I understand it as I do today, after almost ten years of struggle? No, I did not understand it as I do today. Comparing what I understood then with what I understand today,

FROM: *Fidel Castro Speaks on Marxism-Leninism*, television address, December 1, 1961 (English edition, New York, Fair Play for Cuba Committee, 1962, pp. 46-47, 63-65).

*1953, date of Castro's first abortive coup—Ed.

there is a great difference. Did I have prejudices? Yes, I had prejudices on the 26th of July, yes. Could I have been called a thoroughgoing revolutionary on the 26th of July? No, I could not have been called a thoroughgoing revolutionary. Could I be called a thoroughgoing revolutionary today? That would mean that I feel satisfied with what I know and, of course, I am not satisfied. Do I have any doubt about Marxism and do I feel that certain interpretations were wrong and have to be revised? No, I do not have the slightest doubt!

What occurs to me is precisely the opposite: the more experience we gain from life, the more we learn what imperialism is—and not by word, but in the flesh and blood of our people—the more we have to face up to that imperialism; the more we learn about imperialist policies throughout the world, in South Vietnam, in the Congo, in Algeria, in Korea, everywhere in the world; the more we dig deeper and uncover the bloody claws of imperialism, the miserable exploitation, the abuse they commit in the world, the crimes they commit against humanity, the more, in the first place, we feel sentimentally Marxist, emotionally Marxist, and the more we see and discover all the truths contained in the doctrine of Marxism. The more we have to face the reality of a revolution and the class struggle, and we see what the class struggle really is, in the setting of a revolution, the more convinced we become of all of the truths Marx and Engels wrote and the truly ingenious interpretations of scientific socialism Lenin made.

The more we read today, with the experience, the load of experience we have, in those books, the more convinced we become of their inspired vision, of the foresight they had. . . .

. . . We had to choose between remaining under the domination, under the exploitation and, furthermore, the insolence of imperialism, to go on putting up with Yankee ambassadors giving the orders here, keeping our country in the state of poverty it was in, or making an anti-imperialist revolution, making a socialist revolution.

There was no alternative. We chose the only honorable road, the only loyal road that we could follow for our country, and in keeping with the tradition of our revolutionary forefathers, in keeping with the tradition of all those who fought for the good of our country. That is the path we have followed: the path of anti-imperialist struggle, the path of the socialist Revolution. Moreover, there was no room for any other position. Any other position would have been a false position, an absurd position. We will never adopt such a position, nor will we ever waver. Never!

Imperialism should know well that, for all time, we will never have anything to do with it. And imperialism must know that however great our difficulties, however hard our struggle to build our country, to build the future of our country, to write a history worthy of our country, imperialism must not harbor the slightest hope so far as we are concerned.

Many who did not understand these things before understand them today. And they will understand them more and more. For all of us, these things become ever clearer, more evident, and more indisputable.

This is the path that the Revolution had to follow: the path of anti-imperialism and the path of socialism, that is, the path of nationalization of all the big industries, nationalization of big business, nationalization and social ownership of the basic means of production; a path of planned development of our economy at a pace that our resources permit, and that the aid we are receiving from abroad permits. Another truly favorable thing for our Revolution has been the fact that we have been able to count on the aid and solidarity which have enabled us to carry our Revolution forward without the enormous sacrifices that other peoples have had to make.

The Revolution had to be anti-imperialist and socialist. Good. There could have been only one anti-imperialist and socialist Revolution, because there is but one revolution. And that is the great dialectical truth of mankind: imperialism, and imperialism versus socialism. The result of this: the victory of socialism, the triumph of the epoch of socialism, the overcoming of the state of capitalism and imperialism, the establishment of the era of socialism, and later on the era of communism. . . .

What is the socialism we have to apply here? Utopian socialism? We simply have to apply scientific socialism. That is why I began by saying with complete frankness that we believe in Marxism, that we believe it is the most correct, the most scientific theory, the only truly revolutionary theory. I say that here with complete satisfaction (*applause*) and with complete confidence: I am a Marxist-Leninist, and I shall be a Marxist-Leninist to the end of my life (*prolonged applause*).

And what kind of Marxist-Leninist am I? Am I a half-way one? We revolutionaries don't know how to be anything halfway. We only know how to be 100 percent something. And to that we shall dedicate our efforts, our energies, our entire selves. Moreover, it is a great satisfaction to have been illiterate at the age of eighteen and to feel revolutionary as I do now at thirty odd years—I think the "odd years" run to thirty-six (*laughter and applause*). I've learned a thing or two in eighteen years, and still have a lot to learn! And that is what we are telling the people, with complete candor, with complete loyalty, with all clarity, as I have always spoken to the people, always with complete frankness.

Did I have prejudices? I believe it is good to talk about that. Did I have prejudices about the Communists? Yes. Was I ever influenced by imperialist and reactionary propaganda against the Communists? Yes. What did I think about the Communists? Did I think they were thieves? No, never; I always regarded the Communists—at the university and elsewhere—as honorable and honest people and all that. . . . But, well, that is no special merit, because almost everyone recognizes these qualities in them. Did I have the idea they were sectarian? Yes. Why did I have such opinions about the Communists? Simply, I am absolutely convinced that the ideas I had about the Communists—not about Marxism, nor about the Communist Party—like the ideas many people have, were the product of the propaganda and prejudices instilled in us since childhood, practically from school age, in the university, in the movies and everywhere else. I should say so. Do I believe they could make mistakes? Yes, I believe they can make mistakes. Marx, Engels and Lenin could make mistakes, and they themselves were the first to admit that they could be wrong, that they could err, because they did not think themselves infallible. . . .

b) Khrushchev on the Missile Crisis

To complete the liquidation of the conflict dangerous for the cause of peace, in order to give confidence to the peoples striving for peace, to reassure the people of

FROM: Khrushchev, Note of October 28, 1962, to President Kennedy (*Department of State Bulletin*, XLVII:1220, November 12, 1962, pp. 743–45).

America who, I am sure, want peace, as much as the people of the Soviet Union, the Soviet Government, in addition to the previous order about the cessation of further works pertaining to the disposition of military equipment, has given a new order about dismantling this equipment, which you call "offensive," its packing and withdrawing back to the Soviet Union.

Mr. President, I would like to repeat once more what I have already stated in my previous letters to you—that the Soviet Government rendered its economic assistance, as well as its aid with arms to the Government of the Republic of Cuba, since Cuba, the Cuban people were living under a constant danger of an invasion of Cuba. . . .

The Cuban people desire to build up their life in their own interests, without interfering from outside. This is its right and the Cuban people must not be blamed for the desire to be the masters of their country, to dispose of the fruits of their labour.

The danger of invading Cuba and all the other ventures which result in creating tension as regards Cuba, are designed to engender uncertainty in the Cuban people, to intimidate them, to prevent them from building a new life undisturbed.

Mr. President, I want once more to state clearly that we could not be indifferent to that and the Soviet Government decided to help Cuba with means of defence against aggression. These were only the means for defensive purposes. We have sent there defence means which you call "means of offence," have supplied them there to prevent the aggression against Cuba, to prevent reckless action.

With respect and confidence I regard your statement set forth in your message of 27th October, 1962, that Cuba will not be attacked, will not be invaded, not only by the United States, but also by other countries of the western hemisphere, as pointed in your message. So the motives which prompted us to render Cuba our assistance of this nature, are no longer applicable. Therefore, we have given the order to our officers (and the said means, as I have informed you, are in the hands of Soviet officers) to carry out the necessary measures as regards discontinuing the construction of the mentioned installations, their dismantling and withdrawing to the Soviet Union.

As I have already informed you in the letter of 27th October, we are both ready to come to an agreement that representatives of the U.N.O. may verify the dismantling of these means. Thus, if taking for a basis your assurances you have made, and our orders on dismantling, all the necessary conditions for the elimination of the conflict arisen, are on hand.

I note with satisfaction that you have responded to my call as to eliminate the dangerous situation mentioned, as well as to create conditions for more thoughtful assessment of the international situation fraught with great dangers in our age of thermo-nuclear weapons, rocket technology, space ships, global rockets and other lethal weapons.

All people are concerned with maintaining peace. Therefore, we who are invested with trust and great responsibility, should not allow the situation to be aggravated and should remove those hotbeds where there has been created the dangerous situation fraught with grave consequences for the cause of peace. And if we succeed, along with the aid of other people of good will, in liquidating this tense situation, we should also take care that there should not arise other dangerous conflicts which might lead to a world thermo-nuclear catastrophe. . . .

Our concern is that there be no war in the world at all, that the Cuban people live in peace. But, besides, Mr. President, it is an open secret that we have our people in Cuba. According to the agreement with the Cuban government we have there our officers, instructors who train the Cubans, mainly ordinary people, specialists, agronomists, animal husbandry experts, irrigation and soil improvement experts, ordinary workers, tractor drivers and others. We are concerned about them. I would like to ask, Mr. President, to take into account that the violation of air space of Cuba may also bring dangerous consequences. If you do not wish that, it would be advisable not to give cause for the creation of a dangerous situation. At present we must be very cautious and avoid taking such steps which will be of no use for the defence of the States involved in the conflict, but will cause irritation and even provoke a fatal step. Therefore, we must display sobriety and wisdom and refrain from such steps.

We value peace, perhaps even more than other peoples, because we went through a terrible war against Hitler. But our people will not waver in the face of any ordeal. Our people trust their own government, and we assure our people and the world public that the Soviet Government will not allow [itself] to be provoked. But if provocators unleash a war, they will not escape the responsibility for the grave consequences of the war. But we are confident that reason will triumph, war will not be unleashed and there will be ensured peace and the security of peoples.

The Sino-Soviet Schism

The first cracks in the ostensibly firm alliance of the Soviet and Chinese Communists appeared in 1958 with Soviet rejection of Mao's new radical line and Chinese disappointment over Khrushchev's rapprochement with the United States. By 1960 the Soviets had terminated all military and economic aid for China and in 1962 they backed India against China in their border clash. Negotiations between the Chinese and Soviets came to an impasse in 1963, when each side denounced the other for abandoning Marxism-Leninism.

a) The Chinese View

It is the common and sacred duty of the Communist and Workers' parties of all countries to uphold and strengthen the unity of the international Communist movement. The Chinese and Soviet parties bear a heavier responsibility for the unity of the entire Socialist [i.e., Communist] camp and international Communist movement and should of course make commensurately greater efforts.

A number of major differences of principle now exit in the international Communist movement. But however serious these differences, we should exercise patience and find ways to eliminate them so that we can unite our forces and strengthen the struggle against our common enemy. . . .

If Communists isolate themselves from the revolutionary demands of the masses, they are bound to lose the confidence of the masses and will be tossed to the rear by the revolutionary current.

FROM: Letter of the Central Committee of the Communist Party of China to the Central Committee of the Communist Party of the Soviet Union, June 14, 1963 (English translation in *Peking Review*, June 21, 1963; reprinted in William E. Griffith, *The Sino-Soviet Rift*, Cambridge, Mass., MIT Press, 1964, pp. 259-60, 269-72, 281, 288).

If the leading group in any party adopts a nonrevolutionary line and converts it into a reformist party, then Marxist-Leninists inside and outside the party will replace them and lead the people in making revolution. In another kind of situation, the bourgeois revolutionaries will come forward to lead the revolution and the party of the proletariat will forfeit its leadership of the revolution. When the reactionary bourgeoisie betray the revolution and suppress the people, an opportunist line will cause tragic and unnecessary losses to the Communists and the revolutionary masses.

If Communists slide down the path of opportunism, they will degenerate into bourgeois nationalists and become appendages of the imperialists and the reactionary bourgeoisie.

There are certain persons* who assert that they have made the greatest creative contributions to revolutionary theory since Lenin and that they alone are correct. But it is very dubious whether they have ever really given consideration to the extensive experience of the entire world Communist movement, whether they have ever really considered the interests, the goal and tasks of the international proletarian movement as a whole, and whether they really have a general line for the international Communist movement which conforms with Marxism-Leninism. . . .

The national-liberation movements of Asia, Africa and Latin America and the revolutionary movements of the people in the capitalist countries are a strong support to the Socialist countries. It is completely wrong to deny this.

The only attitude for the Socialist countries to adopt towards the revolutionary struggles of the oppressed peoples and nations is one of warm sympathy and active support; they must not adopt a perfunctory attitude, or one of national selfishness or of great-power chauvinism.

Lenin said, "Alliance with the revolutionaries of the advanced countries and with all the oppressed peoples against any and all [of] the imperialists—such is the external policy of the proletariat." Whoever fails to understand this point and considers that the support and aid given by the Socialist countries to the oppressed peoples and nations are a burden or charity is going counter to Marxism-Leninism and proletarian internationalism.

The superiority of the Socialist system and the achievements of the Socialist countries in construction play an exemplary role and are an inspiration to the oppressed peoples and the oppressed nations.

But this exemplary role and inspiration can never replace the revolutionary struggles of the oppressed peoples and nations. No oppressed people or nation can win liberation except through its own staunch revolutionary struggle.

Certain persons have onesidedly exaggerated the role of peaceful competition between Socialist and imperialist countries in their attempt to substitute peaceful competition for the revolutionary struggles of the oppressed peoples and nations. According to their preaching, it would seem that imperialism will automatically collapse in the course of this peaceful competition and that the only thing the oppressed peoples and nations have to do is to wait quietly for the advent of this day.

What does this have in common with Marxist-Leninist views?

Moreover, certain persons have concocted the strange tale that China and some

*I.e., Khrushchev and his supporters—Ed.

other Socialist countries want "to unleash wars" and to spread Socialism by "wars between states." As the Statement of 1960 points out, such tales are nothing but imperialist and reactionary slanders. To put it bluntly, the purpose of those who repeat these slanders is to hide the fact they are opposed to revolutions by the oppressed peoples and nations of the world and opposed to others supporting such revolutions. . . .

Every Socialist country must rely mainly on itself for its construction.

In accordance with its own concrete conditions, every Socialist country must rely first of all on the diligent labor and talents of its own people, utilize all its available resources fully and in a planned way, and bring all its potential into play in Socialist construction. Only thus can it build Socialism effectively and develop its economy speedily.

This is the only way for each socialist country to strengthen the might of the entire Socialist camp and enhance its capacity to assist the revolutionary cause of the international proletariat. Therefore, to observe the principle of mainly relying on oneself in construction is to apply proletarian internationalism concretely. . . .

b) The Soviet View

What is the gist of the differences between the CPC on the one hand and the CPSU and the international Communist movement on the other? This question is no doubt asked by everyone who studies the letter from the CPC central committee of June 14.

At a first glance many theses in the letter may seem puzzling: whom are the Chinese comrades actually arguing with? Are there Communists who, for instance, object to socialist revolution or who do not regard it as their duty to fight against imperialism and to support the national-liberation movement? Why does the CPC leadership set out these theses with such obsession?

The question may also arise why it is impossible to agree with the positions of the Chinese comrades set forth in their letter on many important problems? Take, for instance, such cardinal problems as war and peace. In its letter the CPC central committee speaks of peace and peaceful co-existence.

The essence of the matter is that having started an offensive against the positions of the Marxist-Leninist parties on cardinal problems of today, the Chinese comrades first ascribe to the CPSU and other Marxist-Leninist parties views which they have never expressed and which are alien to them; secondly, by paying lip service to formulae and positions borrowed from the documents of the Communist movement, they try to camouflage their erroneous views and incorrect positions. To come out openly against the people's struggle for peace and for peaceful co-existence between states with different social systems, against disarmament, etc., would mean to expose their positions in the eyes of the Communists of the whole world and all peaceloving peoples and to repulse them. Therefore the further the polemics develop and the clearer the weakness of the positions of the CPC leadership becomes, the more zealously it resorts to such camouflage.

If this method of the Chinese comrades is not taken into consideration, it may

FROM: Open Letter from the CPSU Central Committee to Party Organizations and All Communists of the Soviet Union, *Pravda*, July 14, 1963 (English translation in *Soviet News*, July 17, 1963; reprinted in Griffith, *The Sino-Soviet Rift*, pp. 296–300, 322, 324–25).

even seem from outside that the dispute has acquired a scholastic nature, that separate formulae far removed from vital problems are the points at issue.

In point of fact, however, the questions which bear on vital interests of the peoples are in the centre of the dispute.

These are the questions of war and peace, the question of the role and development of the world-socialist system, these are the questions of the struggle against the ideology and practice of the "cult of the individual," these are the questions of the strategy and tactics of the world labour movement and the national liberation struggle. . . .

The CPSU central committee believes it to be its duty to tell the party and the people with all frankness that in questions of war and peace the CPC leadership has cardinal differences, based on principle, with us and with the world Communist movement. The essence of these differences lies in a diametrically opposite approach to such vital problems as the possibility of averting thermonuclear world war, peaceful co-existence between states with different social systems and the interconnection between the struggle for peace and the development of the world revolutionary movement. . . .

And what is the position of the CPC leadership? What do the theses that they propagate mean: an end cannot be put to wars so long as imperialism exists; peaceful co-existence is an illusion; it is not the general principle of the foreign policy of socialist countries; the peace struggle hinders the revolutionary struggle?

These theses mean that the Chinese comrades are acting contrary to the general course of the world Communist movement in questions of war and peace. They do not believe in the possibility of preventing a new world war; they underestimate the forces of peace and socialism and overestimate the forces of imperialism; in fact they ignore the mobilisation of the masses for the struggle with the war danger.

It emerges that the Chinese comrades do not believe in the ability of the peoples of the socialist countries, of the international working class, and of all democratic and peace-loving forces to frustrate the plans of the war-mongers and to achieve peace for our and future generations. What stands behind the loud revolutionary phrases of the Chinese comrades? Lack of faith in the forces of the working class and its revolutionary capabilities, lack of faith both in the possibility of peaceful co-existence and in the victory of the proletariat in class struggle. All peaceloving forces unite in the struggle to avert war. They differ as to their class composition and their class interests. But they can be united by the stuggle for peace and to avert war, because the nuclear bomb does not adhere to the class principles—it destroys everybody within the range of its devastating force.

To adopt the course proposed by the Chinese comrades means to alienate the masses of the people from the Communist Parties which have won the sympathies of the peoples by their insistent and courageous struggle for peace.

Socialism and peace are now inseparable in the minds of the broad masses!

The Chinese comrades obviously underestimate the whole danger of thermonuclear war. "The atomic bomb is a paper tiger"; "it is not terrible at all," they contend. . . .

Is it permissible to ask the Chinese comrades if they realise what sort of "ruins" a nuclear rocket world war would leave behind?

The CPSU central committee, and we are convinced that all our party and the whole Soviet people unanimously support us in this, cannot share the views of the Chinese leadership about the creation "of a thousand times higher civilisation" on the corpses of hundreds of millions of people. Such views are in crying contradiction with the ideas of Marxism-Leninism. . . .

It is generally known that under present conditions a world war would be a thermonuclear war. The imperialists will never agree to withdraw from the scene voluntarily, to lie in the coffin of their own free will, without having used the extreme means they have at their disposal.

Apparently the people who refer to the thermonuclear weapon as a "paper tiger" are not fully aware of the destructive force of this weapon.

We soberly consider this. We ourselves produce the thermonuclear weapon and have manufactured it in sufficient quantity. We know its destructive force full well. And if imperialism starts a war against us we shall not hesitate to use this formidable weapon against the aggressor; but if we are not attacked, we shall not be the first to use this weapon. . . .

One of the clear examples of the special line of the leadership of the CPC in the socialist camp and the international Communist movement is its position on the Albanian question. As is well known, in the second half of 1960 the Albanian leaders openly came out with a left opportunist platform on the main questions of our day and began to promote a hostile policy in relation to the CPSU and other fraternal parties. The Albanian leadership started an anti-Soviet campaign in the country, which led to a rupture of political, economic and cultural ties with the Soviet Union.

The overwhelming majority of Communist and Workers' Parties resolutely condemned this anti-Leninist activity of the Albanian leaders. The leaders of the CPC took an absolutely different position and did everything in their power to use the Albanian leaders as their mouthpiece. It is now known that the Chinese comrades openly pushed them on to the road of open struggle against the Soviet Union and the other socialist countries and fraternal parties. . . .

The Communist Party of the Soviet Union has stood, and continues to stand, for close friendship with the Communist Party of China. There are serious differences between us and the leaders of the CPC, but we consider that the relations between the two parties, between our two peoples, should be built, proceeding from the fact that we have the same aim—the building of a new communist society, from the fact that we have the same enemy—imperialism. United, the two great powers, the Soviet Union and the People's Republic of China, can do much for the triumph of communism. Our friends and enemies are well aware of that.

The Nuclear Test Ban

Simultaneously with the final Sino-Soviet rupture Khrushchev reverted to the line of accommodation with the West, and concluded the treaty with the U.S. and Britain banning nuclear tests in the atmosphere. France and China refused to accept the ban, and Khrushchev took the occasion to denounce the Chinese threat to peace.

The initialling in Moscow of the treaty banning nuclear weapon tests in the atmosphere, in outer space and under water has been eagerly welcomed by the people everywhere. . . .

FROM: Statement of the Soviet Government, *Pravda*, August 4, 1963 (English translation in *New Times*, #32, 1963, Supplement, pp. 35–37, 40).

On July 31, the government of the Chinese People's Republic issued a statement on the results of the Moscow test-stoppage negotiations. In it, the C.P.R. government declares that it is opposed to the treaty and will not accede to it. The C.P.R. government even describes the treaty as a "fraud," alleging that it "dupes the peoples of the whole world" and "contradicts the aspirations of the peace-loving peoples of all countries."

The Soviet government considers it necessary, in this connection, to state the following.

The test-ban treaty is of fundamental importance for further exploration of ways and means of resolving the controversial questions that may divide the world. The fact that states with differing social systems—and moreover Great Powers, whose contradictions have on more than one occasion threatened to plunge mankind into the abyss of world war—were able to work out a mutually acceptable solution for one of the most pressing international problems, is proof that the policy of peaceful coexistence is both correct and effective. The peoples can see that there is a real possibility of easing international tension and halting the arms race, which imposes such a heavy burden upon them.

The results of the Moscow talks provide hope that outstanding international issues, upon which the strengthening of world peace depends, can be resolved. That is exactly what the Soviet government has been working for. During the Moscow three-power negotiations it again presented a comprehensive programme of action for promoting peace. It envisages a series of immediate steps to eliminate the menace of thermonuclear conflict, notably conclusion of a non-aggression pact between the NATO and Warsaw Treaty countries. Once again the Soviet government appealed for elimination of the survivals of World War II, conclusion of a German peace treaty and normalization, on that basis, of the position in West Berlin.

The Soviet programme of strengthening peace accords with the vital interests of the peoples. It is warmly supported by the governments and peoples of the socialist states, by public opinion in Asia, Africa and Latin America, by millions of working people in the capitalist countries, by progressives the world over. . . .

Everywhere, on every continent, the fraternal Marxist-Leninist parties have signified their complete approval of the treaty. They see in it a major result of the consistently pursued foreign policy of the Communist movement, aimed at strengthening the forces of peace and progress. Everyone concerned for peace approves the outcome of the Moscow talks. Against this background of unanimous approval, those who have ventured openly to oppose the treaty can be counted on the fingers of one hand. Nor is that surprising, for he who today opposes prohibition of nuclear testing, no matter what verbal subtleties he resorts to, stands exposed as an enemy of the policy of peaceful co-existence, relaxation of international tension and of the undermining of the forces of aggression and war.

The few days since the conclusion of the Moscow three-power talks have clearly shown who resents this new and important success of the peace forces. They are, primarily, the so-called "wild men" in the United States, who hold up the "Communist menace" bogey and clamorously complain that the treaty makes it impossible for the United States to devise weapons of still greater destructive power. They are the extremists among the West-German militarists and revanchists, who continue to plot fresh military gambles. They are the extremists among the French ruling element who, for some unknown reason, have decided that French grandeur lies not in assisting international détente or in friendship with other nations, but in friendship with the H-bomb and in building up a nuclear arsenal at any cost.

When such views are expressed by spokesmen of the most bellicose imperialist forces, no one is surprised. But when the test-ban treaty is opposed by Communists, and moreover Communists in the leadership of a socialist country, that is bound to rouse legitimate surprise. How can the leaders of a socialist country reject out of hand an international agreement that helps strengthen peace and accords with the peoples' aspirations and vital interests? Only disregard of the fundamental interests of the peoples, who have long been demanding an end to nuclear explosions, could suggest the interpretation of the purpose and meaning of the treaty the Chinese government has sought to give in its statement. . . .

The C.P.R. government tries to cancel out facts known to the whole world. That its attempts to cast aspersions on the Soviet attitude on nuclear weapons are unfounded, is evident from the fact alone that, way back in 1946, the Soviet Union was the first to propose permanent prohibitions of nuclear weapons and destruction of their stockpiles. Though it has the most advanced nuclear weapons and the most efficient means of delivery, the Soviet Union has for many years worked perseveringly and consistently to secure prohibition of nuclear and thermonuclear weapons, discontinuance of their production, destruction of all stockpiles, cessation of all testing and the break-up of national war machines.

At the U.N. General Assembly in 1959, the head of the Soviet government, N. S. Khrushchev, proposed general and complete disarmament, and that proposal became the peoples' banner in the fight for lasting peace. Prohibition and complete destruction of all nuclear weapons and of all means of delivery forms the basis, the backbone, of the Soviet disarmament programme. It is generally known that the Soviet government is also urging such immediate measures to restrict the nuclear arms race as denuclearized zones in various parts of the world and closure of military bases on foreign territory. . . .

Expressing the will of the entire Soviet people, the Soviet government rejects the fabrications about its foreign policy contained in the C.P.R. government's statement. No inventions and no attacks can change Soviet foreign policy, given us by the great Lenin, further developed in the decisions of our Party's Twentieth and Twenty-second Congresses and in the CPSU Programme, and unanimously endorsed by the Soviet people and the international Communist movement. Guided by that policy, the Soviet Union will continue unswervingly to follow its course of peace and friendship among the nations, to work for general and complete disarmament, peaceful settlement of international issues, including European security, and for the triumph of the Leninist principles of peaceful co-existence. . . .

Rumania's Independent Path

The Sino-Soviet schism confronted other Communist governments and parties with the challenge to take sides and the opportunity to assert their independence by professing neutrality between Moscow and Peking. This was the stance of Rumania, already resentful of Soviet plans to keep it as a raw-material-producing country instead of industrializing. Rumania con-

FROM: Statement of the Rumanian Workers' Party, "On the Problems of the World Communist and Workers' Movement," April 26, 1964 (English translation [abridged] in *East Europe*, June, 1964, pp. 25–30).

tinues to maintain an independent foreign policy though it adheres to the Stalinist model internally.

The world Communist movement and the socialist camp are now faced with the danger of a split. Since the public polemic began, the Rumanian Workers' Party has given its full support to the proposals aimed at putting an end to it, has repeatedly appealed and insisted that it cease without delay, and has spoken out for settling controversial issues in conformity with the norms jointly established at the 1957 and 1960 conferences concerning relations among the Communist parties. . . .

The Central Committee of the Rumanian Workers' Party informed the other fraternal parties of the approach it had made and stated that it was necessary for all Communist and Workers parties to discontinue the public polemic in the interest of finding ways and means to insure unity. At the same time, we voiced our hope that our party's proposals and position would meet with understanding and support. . . .

The public polemic, joined by numerous fraternal parties, is proceeding with growing intensity: a particularly serious situation has been created in the world Communist movement. The question arises as to what the prospects of this situation are should the public polemic not be terminated and should it continue to aggravate relations among the Communist and Workers parties, among the socialist states and their peoples, thus aggravating the danger of splitting the world Communist movement and the camp of the socialist countries. . . .

The victories of the Rumanian People's Republic and the other socialist countries show that the successful solution of the tasks of developing the economy depends first and foremost on the utilization of each country's internal possibilities through an intense mustering of its own forces and the maximum use of natural resources. Decisive for the development of the countries which inherited economic backwardness from capitalism is socialist industrialization—the only road which insures the harmonious, balanced and ever-ascending as well as rapid growth of the entire national economy. . . .

At the same time, the economic and technical-scientific progress of the socialist countries relies on the relations of cooperation and mutual assistance established between them. . . .

In regard to the method of economic cooperation, the socialist countries—which are members of COMECON—have established that the main means of achieving the international socialist division of labor, the main form of cooperation between their national economies, is to coordinate plans on the basis of bilateral and multilateral agreements.

During the development of the relations of cooperation among the socialist countries which are COMECON members, ways and means have been suggested, such as a joint plan and a single planning body for all member countries, interstate technical-productive branch unions, enterprises jointly owned by several countries, interstate economic complexes, and so forth.

Our party has very clearly expressed its point of view, declaring that since the essence of the suggested measures lies in shifting some functions of economic management from the competence of the respective state to the competence of superstate bodies or organisms, these measures are not in keeping with the principles which underlie relations among the socialist countries.

The idea of a single planning body for all COMECON countries has the most serious economic and political implications. The planned management of the national economy is one of the fundamental, essential and inalienable attributes of the sovereignty of the socialist state. . . . The sovereignty of the socialist state requires that it effectively and fully avail itself of the means to practically implement these attributes, holding in its hands all the levers of managing economic and social life. Transmitting such levers to the competence of superstate or extrastate bodies would make of sovereignty an idea without any content. . . .

Bearing in mind the diversity of the conditions of socialist construction, there are not and there can be no unique patterns and recipes; no one can decide what is and what is not correct for other countries or parties. It is up to every Marxist-Leninist party, it is a sovereign right of each socialist state, to elaborate, choose, or change the forms and methods of socialist construction. . . .

As far back as the last stage in the Comintern's existence it became obvious that the solution of the problems of the workers movement, in one country or another, by an international center no longer suited the stage of development of the world Communist parties, went as far as the removal and replacement of leading cadres and even of entire central committees, as far as imposing leaders from without, the suppression of distinguished leading cadres of various parties, as far as censuring and even dissolving Communist parties. . . .

In 1948 the Communist Party of Yugoslavia was condemned and excluded from the Cominform, and Yugoslavia—a country which builds socialism—was expelled from the community of socialist states. In some socialist countries there were numerous cases of expulsion from the party, arrests, trials, and suppressions of many leading party and state cadres. Their rehabilitation was only possible after the 20th CPSU Congress had exposed and criticized the personality cult and the practices the latter had engendered.

Our party regarded as correct and highly appreciated the critical analysis made by the 20th CPSU Congress of the personality cult, as well as the fact that the necessity was underlined of most consistently applying Leninist standards in party life and throughout the world Communist movement. . . .

There is not and cannot be a "parent" party and a "son" party, parties that are "superior" and parties that are "subordinate"; rather there is the great family of Communist and Workers parties which have equal rights.

No party has or can have a privileged place, or can impose its line or opinions on other parties. Each party makes its own contribution to the development of the common treasure store of Marxist-Leninist teaching, to enriching the forms and practical methods of revolutionary struggle for winning power and building socialist society.

In discussing and confronting different points of view on problems concerning the revolutionary struggle or socialist construction, no party must label as anti-Marxist or anti-Leninist the fraternal party whose opinions it does not share. . . .

Taking advantage of the present state of affairs in the Communist movement, all kinds of dissatisfied, anti-party and dissolving elements of a series of parties are rising against the party leaderships, setting up splinter groups, calling themselves "true Marxist-Leninist parties," and struggling to split the working class movement of the respective country. It is regrettable that these groups met with favorable appraisals and support on the part of the Chinese comrades. . . .

Owing to their prestige, the CPSU and the CCP have a particular responsibility and role in reestablishing the unity of the Communist movement. We address and appeal to all fraternal parties and above all to the two big parties, the CPSU and the CCP. Let all of us unite to bar the road to a split, to safeguard the unity and cohesion of the countries of the socialist camp, the world Communist and working class movement. . . .

CHAPTER SIX

Schism and Détente, 1964–1976

During the major part of the Brezhnev era Soviet relations with the outside world were, like the internal policies of the regime, extraordinarily steady as compared with the crises and conflicts that had marked earlier periods. Soviet policy toward the West remained in the accommodationist mode initiated under Khrushchev and confirmed in 1963; toward China it remained unremittingly hostile. Most Soviet initiatives, such as ventures in the Middle East and the 1968 intervention in Czechoslovakia, were essentially reactive.

For Communism outside the Soviet Union the period of the sixties and seventies was a different story, marked by division and disarray hitherto unimaginable. China escalated its independent radicalism in the Cultural Revolution of 1966–69 and renounced the Soviet model as a "capitalist road." Youthful radicals all over the world, disillusioned with Soviet totalitarianism and the pragmatism of the official Communist parties, broke off into Maoist splinter groups (represented by the tiny Progressive Labor Party in America) or joined the anti-authoritarian causes of the New Left, much to the disgust of Moscow. East Europeans, in contrast, sought paths of moderation and relaxation, expressed in theory by various dissenters and in practice by certain governments (successful in Hungary, unsuccessful in Czechoslovakia). Among Communists in most parts of Western Europe, similar currents of democratization and independence prevailed in the movement of Eurocommunism, which thereby ceased to conform to traditional definitions of Marxism-Leninism.

As a result of these deviations to the left or to the right, Moscow found itself with no reliable Communist allies other than those kept in line by a Soviet military presence or economic coercion. Under these circumstances it was in Moscow's obvious interest to pursue détente with the Western powers, while it concentrated on closing the gap with the United States in heavy industry and nuclear arms. Marked by major treaties and reciprocal visits of governmental chiefs, détente reached a climax in the years 1972 to 1975, the sunniest period in East-West relations since the Grand Alliance of World War II.

The Cultural Revolution in China

After a period of retrenchment following his ill-conceived "Great Leap Forward," Mao Tse-tung returned to the task of renewing his revolution from within and averting the menace of the Soviet-style "capitalist road," i.e., self-serving bureaucracy. The upshot was the extraordinary episode of the Cultural Revolution, when youthful Red Guards with Mao's blessings

FROM: Decision of the Central Committee of the Chinese Communist Party concerning the Great Proletarian Cultural Revolution (the "sixteen points"), August 8, 1966 (English translation in *Peking Review*, August 12, 1966, pp. 6–11).

disrupted much of the normal functioning of government, industry and education in the name of a new puritan egalitarianism.

1. *A New Stage in the Socialist Revolution*

The great proletarian cultural revolution now unfolding is a great revolution that touches people to their very souls and constitutes a new stage in the development of the socialist revolution in our country, a deeper and more extensive stage.

At the Tenth Plenary Session of the Eighth Central Committee of the Party, Comrade Mao Tse-tung said: To overthrow a political power, it is always necessary, first of all, to create public opinion, to do work in the ideological sphere. This is true for the revolutionary class as well as for the counter-revolutionary class. This thesis of Comrade Mao Tse-tung's has been proved entirely correct in practice.

Although the bourgeoisie has been overthrown, it is still trying to use the old ideas, culture, customs and habits of the exploiting classes to corrupt the masses, capture their minds and endeavour to stage a come-back. The proletariat must do just the opposite: it must meet head-on every challenge of the bourgeoisie in the ideological field and use the new ideas, culture, customs and habits of the proletariat to change the mental outlook of the whole of society. At present, our objective is to struggle against and crush those persons in authority who are taking the capitalist road, to criticize and repudiate the reactionary bourgeois academic "authorities" and the ideology of the bourgeoisie and all other exploiting classes and to transform education, literature and art and all other parts of the superstructure that do not correspond to the socialist economic base, so as to facilitate the consolidation and development of the socialist system.

2. *The Main Current and the Zigzags*

The masses of the workers, peasants, soldiers, revolutionary intellectuals and revolutionary cadres form the main force in this great cultural revolution. Large numbers of revolutionary young people, previously unknown, have become courageous and daring pathbreakers. They are vigorous in action and intelligent. Through the media of big-character posters and great debates, they argue things out, expose and criticize thoroughly, and launch resolute attacks on the open and hidden representatives of the bourgeoisie. In such a great revolutionary movement, it is hardly avoidable that they should show shortcomings of one kind or another, but their main revolutionary orientation has been correct from the beginning. This is the main current in the great proletarian cultural revolution. It is the main direction along which the great proletarian cultural revolution continues to advance.

Since the cultural revolution is a revolution, it inevitably meets with resistance. This resistance comes chiefly from those in authority who have wormed their way into the Party and are taking the capitalist road. It also comes from the old force of habit in society. At present, this resistance is still fairly strong and stubborn. . . .

3. *Put Daring Above Everything Else And Boldly Arouse the Masses*

The outcome of this great cultural revolution will be determined by whether the Party leadership does or does not dare boldly to arouse the masses. . . .

Some units are controlled by those who have wormed their way into the Party and are taking the capitalist road. Such persons in authority are extremely afraid of being exposed by the masses and therefore seek every possible pretext to suppress the mass movement. They resort to such tactics as shifting the targets for attack and turning black into white in an attempt to lead the movement astray. When they find themselves very isolated and no longer able to carry on as before, they resort still more to intrigues, stabbing people in the back, spreading rumours, and blurring the distinction between revolution and counter-revolution as much as they can, all for the purpose of attacking the revolutionaries.

What the Central Committee of the Party demands of the Party committees at all levels is that they persevere in giving correct leadership, put daring above everything else, boldly arouse the masses, change the state of weakness and incompetence where it exists, encourage those comrades who have made mistakes but are willing to correct them to cast off their mental burdens and join in the struggle, and dismiss from their leading posts all those in authority who are taking the capitalist road and so make possible the recapture of the leadership for the proletarian revolutionaries.

4. Let the Masses Educate Themselves in the Movement

In the great proletarian cultural revolution, the only method is for the masses to liberate themselves, and any method of doing things on their behalf must not be used.

Trust the masses, rely on them and respect their initiative. Cast out fear. Don't be afraid of disorder. Chairman Mao has often told us that revolution cannot be so very refined, so gentle, so temperate, kind, courteous, restrained and magnanimous. Let the masses educate themselves in this great revolutionary movement and learn to distinguish between right and wrong and between correct and incorrect ways of doing things. . . .

5. Firmly Apply the Class Line Of the Party

Who are our enemies? Who are our friends? This is a question of the first importance for the revolution and it is likewise a question of the first importance for the great cultural revolution.

Party leadership should be good at discovering the Left and developing and strengthening the ranks of the Left, and should firmly rely on the revolutionary Left. During the movement this is the only way to isolate thoroughly the most reactionary Rightists, win over the middle and unite with the great majority so that by the end of the movement we shall achieve the unity of more than 95 per cent of the cadres and more than 95 per cent of the masses.

Concentrate all forces to strike at the handful of ultra-reactionary bourgeois Rightists and counter-revolutionary revisionists, and expose and criticize to the full their crimes against the Party, against socialism and against Mao Tse-tung's thought so as to isolate them to the maximum.

The main target of the present movement is those within the Party who are in authority and are taking the capitalist road.

Care should be taken to distinguish strictly between the anti-Party, anti-socialist Rightists and those who support the Party and socialism but have said or done something wrong or have written some bad articles or other works.

Care should be taken to distinguish strictly between the reactionary bourgeois scholar despots and "authorities" on the one hand and people who have the ordinary bourgeois academic ideas on the other.

6. *Correct Handling of Contradictions Among the People*

A strict distinction must be made between the two different types of contradictions: those among the people and those between ourselves and the enemy. Contradictions among the people must not be made into contradictions between ourselves and the enemy; nor must contradictions between ourselves and the enemy be regarded as those among the people. . . .

7. *Be on Guard Against Those Who Brand the Revolutionary Masses As "Counter-Revolutionaries."* . . .

8. *The Question of Cadres*

The cadres fall roughly into the following four categories:
(1) good;
(2) comparatively good;
(3) those who have made serious mistakes but have not become anti-Party, anti-socialist Rightists;
(4) the small number of anti-Party, anti-socialist Rightists.

In ordinary situations, the first two categories (good and comparatively good) are the great majority.

The anti-Party, anti-socialist Rightists must be fully exposed, hit hard, pulled down and completely discredited and their influence eliminated. At the same time, they should be given a way out so that they can turn over a new leaf.

9. *Cultural Revolutionary Groups, Committees and Congresses*

Many new things have begun to emerge in the great proletarian cultural revolution. The cultural revolutionary groups, committees and other organizational forms created by the masses in many schools and units are something new and of great historic importance.

These cultural revolutionary groups, committees and congresses are excellent new forms of organization whereby under the leadership of the Communist Party the masses are educating themselves. They are an excellent bridge to keep our Party in close contact with the masses. They are organs of power of the proletarian cultural revolution.

The struggle of the proletariat against the old ideas, culture, customs and habits left over from all the exploiting classes over thousands of years will necessarily take a very, very long time. Therefore, the cultural revolutionary groups, committees and congresses should not be temporary organizations but permanent, standing mass organizations. They are suitable not only for colleges, schools and government and other organizations, but generally also for factories, mines, other enterprises, urban districts and villages.

It is necessary to institute a system of general elections, like that of the Paris Commune, for electing members to the cultural revolutionary groups and committees and delegates to the cultural revolutionary congresses. The lists of candidates should be put forward by the revolutionary masses after full discussion, and the elections should be held after the masses have discussed the lists over and over again.

The masses are entitled at any time to criticize members of the cultural revolutionary groups and committees and delegates elected to the cultural revolutionary congresses. If these members or delegates prove incompetent, they can be replaced through election or recalled by the masses after discussion.

The cultural revolutionary groups, committees and congresses in colleges and schools should consist mainly of representatives of the revolutionary students. At the same time, they should have a certain number of representatives of the revolutionary teaching staff and workers.

10. *Educational Reform*

In the great proletarian cultural revolution a most important task is to transform the old educational system and the old principles and methods of teaching.

In this great cultural revolution, the phenomenon of our schools being dominated by bourgeois intellectuals must be completely changed.

In every kind of school we must apply thoroughly the policy advanced by Comrade Mao Tse-tung, of education serving proletarian politics and education being combined with productive labour, so as to enable those receiving an education to develop morally, intellectually and physically and to become labourers with socialist consciousness and culture.

The period of schooling should be shortened. Courses should be fewer and better. The teaching material should be thoroughly transformed, in some cases beginning with simplifying complicated material. While their main task is to study, students should also learn other things. That is to say, in addition to their studies they should also learn industrial work, farming and military affairs, and take part in the struggles of the cultural revolution as they occur to criticize the bourgeoisie.

11. *The Question of Criticizing By Name in the Press*

In the course of the mass movement of the cultural revolution, the criticism of bourgeois and feudal ideology should be well combined with the dissemination of the proletarian world outlook and of Marxism-Leninism, Mao Tse-tung's thought. . . .

12. *Policy Towards Scientists, Technicians and Ordinary Members Of Working Staffs*

As regards scientists, technicians and ordinary members of working staffs, as long as they are patriotic, work energetically, are not against the Party and socialism, and maintain no illicit relations with any foreign country, we should in the present movement continue to apply the policy of "unity, criticism, unity." Special care should be taken of those scientists and scientific and technical personnel who have made contributions. Efforts should be made to help them gradually transform their world outlook and their style of work.

13. *The Question of Arrangements For Integration With the Socialist Education Movement in City And Countryside*

The cultural and educational units and leading organs of the Party and government in the large and medium cities are the points of concentration of the present proletarian cultural revolution.

The great cultural revolution has enriched the socialist education movement in both city and countryside and raised it to a higher level. . . .

14. *Take Firm Hold of the Revolution And Stimulate Production*

The aim of the great proletarian cultural revolution is to revolutionize people's ideology and as a consequence to achieve greater, faster, better and more economical results in all fields of work. If the masses are fully aroused and proper arrangements are made, it is possible to carry on both the cultural revolution and production without one hampering the other, while guaranteeing high quality in all our work.

The great proletarian cultural revolution is a powerful motive force for the development of the social productive forces in our country. Any idea of counterposing the great cultural revolution against the development of production is incorrect.

15. *The Armed Forces*

In the armed forces, the cultural revolution and the socialist education movement should be carried out in accordance with the instructions of the Military Commission of the Central Committee and the General Political Department of the People's Liberation Army.

16. *Mao Tse-tung's Thought Is the Guide for Action in the Great Proletarian Cultural Revolution*

In the great proletarian cultural revolution, it is imperative to hold aloft the great red banner of Mao Tse-tung's thought and put proletarian politics in command. The movement for the creative study and application of Chairman Mao Tse-tung's works should be carried forward among the masses of the workers, peasants and soldiers, the cadres and the intellectuals, and Mao Tse-tung's thought should be taken as the guide for action in the cultural revolution.

In this complex great cultural revolution, Party committees at all levels must study and apply Chairman Mao's works all the more conscientiously and in a creative way. In particular, they must study over and over again Chairman Mao's writings on the cultural revolution and on the Party's methods of leadership, such as *On New Democracy, Talks at the Yenan Forum on Literature and Art, On the Correct Handling of Contradictions Among the People, Speech at the Chinese Communist Party's National Conference on Propaganda Work, Some Questions Concerning Methods of Leadership* and *Methods of Work of Party Committees.*

Party committees at all levels must abide by the directions given by Chairman Mao over the years, namely that they should thoroughly apply the mass line of "from the masses and to the masses" and that they should be pupils before they become teachers. They should try to avoid being one-sided or narrow. They should foster materialist dialectics and oppose metaphysics and scholasticism.

The great proletarian cultural revolution is bound to achieve brilliant victory under the leadership of the Central Committee of the Party headed by Comrade Mao Tse-tung.

Hungary—Kádár and "Goulash Communism"

Half a decade after the suppression of the Hungarian uprising of 1956, the Soviet-installed leader János Kádár began to show signs of a flexibility and pragmatism similar to Yugoslavia. Proclaiming that "whoever is not against us is with us," he relaxed controls over intellectual life, made consumer well-being an economic priority, and in 1966 espoused a major shift from central planning to market socialism under the label of the "New Economic Mechanism." Officially put into operation in 1968, the NEM quickly gave the Hungarians the highest consumer living standards in the Soviet orbit.

a) Whoever Is Not Against Us Is With Us

At the time of the cult of personality, tens and hundreds of thousands of persons in society felt relieved of the obligation to think and be responsible. For if there is a situation when it is said that there are five men or one man in the country who know everything, see everything, and think of everything, then this means that we really don't have to rack our brains. At the time of the cult of personality this way of thinking was no accident, since if there is no broad discussion of the decisions, if people have nothing to say about what has to be done, then they don't feel any kind of responsibility about it, either. Now that the cult of personality is over, the situation has changed: people really have to think to form their opinions, they have to make decisions in their own areas of work, and they have to take the responsibility for these. . . .

A process of great significance has taken place in this country during the past three years, and it has affected the entire society: the socialist reorganization of the villages. One characteristic of this process is worth recalling. After the conditions were ripe, our Central Committee decided that the organization of the masses had to be begun. At this time, however, the Central Committee did not specify in one single case the percentage to be fulfilled in the individual counties and in the country. . . .

Believe me, we can be a hundred times more assured about the fate of the country if we know that hundreds of thousands or, I may safely say, millions of conscientious people are concerned with the fate of the country than if only fifteen, five, or even perhaps one single man were concerned with it. The socialist upheaval which is able to generate the energy of the entire liberated population frees a tremendous amount of power if it is not hamstrung by the cult of personality.

People are still heard saying about our policy: "If what the Central Committee, Parliament, and the government says happened everywhere, we would be for it heart and soul, but it does not happen everywhere." In other words, there are still people who do not exactly implement the policy proclaimed by the Party, which the government wants to enforce, and which the Patriotic People's Front considers its own in agreement with the Party. We are also fighting people like these. And we are going to fight those who nurture concepts which hinder progress, who are too lazy to think, and who do not want to accept responsibility. . . .

Naturally we also continue to fight rightist ideas. . . .

We must strengthen cooperation between Party members and those outside the Party. We have to strengthen the idea of the popular front and its influence on the masses. We have to strengthen the different committees and their work. Basically this means that we have to keep deepening the trust of the masses, because this is the foundation of our policy. Without this, without a trust in the masses, we cannot exist. And we must also strengthen our trust in the individual. . . .

FROM: János Kádár, Speech to the National Council of the Patriotic People's Front, December 9, 1961 (English translation in William Juhasz, ed., *Hungarian Social Science Reader, 1945–1963*, New York and Munich, Aurora, 1965, pp. 276–79).

Western political commentators say—because they also keep needling us, and that is really not so bad, since we consider them unpaid fellow workers, paid by imperialism (laughter) to keep searching for the faults of Communists—well, they say now the following: this Kádár group is very cunning, they want to fool everybody. Because Rákosi used to say a long time ago: "Whoever is not with us is against us." Kádár now says: "Whoever is not against us is with us." (laughter) The western political commentators are bringing up "faults" like these nowadays. We can safely acknowledge this. Indeed, we do believe that whoever is not against the Hungarian People is with us; whoever is not against the Popular Front is with it, whoever is not against the Hungarian Communist Party is with it. Of course, some of those who share our opinions are more conscientious and also share our long-range aims, another group is with us in the simple everyday things. For example, there are many hundreds of thousands who are not Marxists but who respect our Party and our government for having created a legal order and a normal atmosphere in the country. They are with us, and we must further develop our policy in this spirit. . . .

At the Seventh Congress of the Hungarian Socialist Workers' Party, important statements of principle were made on this point, and we said that we must guard the purity of Marxism-Leninism, because that is our compass. We have to guard our Party, the revolutionary Party of the working class, which is the leading power in the social life of the Hungarian people and one of the chief guarantees of a socialist future. We also said the Patriotic People's Front is an important part of our social life and of the realization of our goals. . . .

We can interpret this correctly only by saying that Marxist-Leninist theory, the Party, and the Patriotic Peoples Front are individually and jointly only tools in our struggle. The main task of the Party and, in a certain sense of the word, the people's front, is leadership, activation and organization. The Seventh Congress of the Hungarian Socialist Workers' Party itself took great pains to make this clear: these are not ends in themselves, but they are subordinate to the great aim, to the assurance of a better life for our people and our socialist future. We do not build a socialist society because there is a Marxism-Leninism which prescribes it, or because there is a Patriotic People's Front which helps to lead the popular masses in some direction, but just the reverse: we need good theory, a good Party and a good people's front, we have to build up a socialist society because this assures a better life for the people, the welfare of the country, and the nation. If this view is strengthened in hundreds of thousands of people who work and who represent the people's front to others, then this part of our work will be strengthened, its mass power increased, and the solidarity of the people and the national unity which we are trying to build up will be strengthened. Leading is not reigning, and the work we are doing is serving a cause than which there is nothing holier: the service of our socialist country, of the Hungarian People's Republic, and our people. We must always bear in mind that we are not the new chosen group for reigning but people called to the service of the masses. . . .

The meaning of all kinds of deliberations, just like the meaning of life, is not nice words but whatever we can achieve by them. Deliberations of this kind must be permeated by the feeling that through them a bit more wheat, perhaps more corn, more meat, more milk, or a few good books, or—God forgive—a few understandable poems of correct interpretation will be made available. In these conditions, deliberations have a meaning.

b) The New Economic Mechanism

Esteemed congress, dear comrades, economic work constitutes the most important aspect of our party's activities in the completion period of a socialist society. The formulation of an appropriate economic policy is the task of leading party organs, while the party as a whole mobilizes and organizes the working masses to accomplish the economic tasks.

Our activities in economic work have been guided by the objectives of economic policy defined by the eighth congress. Proceeding from the demands of an intensive development of the people's economy, the congress has specified an intensification of economic considerations, the improvement of productivity, the reduction of prime costs, and the improvement of quality as the building principles of economic activities. The Central Committee's December 1964 and December 1965 economic resolutions, resolutions of fundamental significance, were aligned to these objectives and put them into concrete form. In conformity with our party's resolutions, we have increased our efforts to accelerate the improvement of work productivity and enforce economic considerations in all spheres of work. . . .

Last May the Central Committee passed a decision on a comprehensive reform of our economic mechanism. The reform's purpose is to allow better utilization of our resources and to speed up the rate of development and improve living conditions. The reform makes it possible for a sizable amount of the decision-making to be transferred from the government and ministries to the competence of the enterprises and councils. Transferring the power of decision of a great mass of economic questions to the enterprises and councils makes it possible for the organs of government to turn their attention to exercising supervision, to work out the main proportions (foe arranyok) of the national economy, and to draw up long-term plans.

Central planning will continue to have a first class role. The central plan is to decide: ratios of production and accumulation; main proportions of investments; technical development of the branches of the national economy; influences on the structure of consumption; questions of the development of our participation in the international division of labor; changes in the allocation of the production forces; and the most important factors of social-cultural affairs and the living standard. On the other hand, we expect the mechanism of goods manufacture and the market to achieve the more resilient adaptation of supply to demand with respect to the production of certain goods, and enterprises striving to make the most efficient use of their own economic resources.

The point at issue is not to have a separate functioning of central planning and the laws of the market from now on, but to have a union between the two, in which the paramount role is played by central planning because its task will be to regulate the main processes of the national economy and the market mechanism itself.

When transforming the planning system we are aware that this demands changes in the contents of planning and in the system of working out a plan.

FROM: János Kádár, Report to the Ninth Congress of the Hungarian Socialist Workers' [Communist] Party, November 28, 1966, *Nepszabadsag*, November 29, 1966 (English translation in Foreign Broadcast Information Service *Daily Report*, Washington, #241 (37S), December 14, 1966, pp. 19, 23–25).

Owing to the reform of the mechanism, the planning organs can pay more attention to the study of basic economic trends and to the comprehensive analysis of their mutual influence.

In this connection, the importance of the role of long-term planning and the need for regulations affecting long-term perspectives will necessarily grow. The approved plan prescribes an obligatory line of action for the government and all central organs. The place and role of enterprises will undergo a change in principle under the further developed, new system of socialist planned economy. Up to now socialist enterprises have essentially been mechanical implementors, organizers of the tasks posed to them in the national economy plan. Under the new system of direction, enterprises have at their disposal financial means, investment funds and funds for incentives. They themselves engage in market research, directly negotiate with their suppliers, and develop contacts with their clients. Direct relations between enterprises with regard to the acquisition and sale of the means of production by way of trading must become more and more the general rule.

Under the new economic mechanism the state will not generally prescribe compulsory plan indexes for the enterprises. The enterprises will draw up their own plans on the basis of information received from the central organs and their own knowledge of the market. The state, in its role as proprietor, regulates the operation of the enterprises, but the method and form of this regulation will change.

Generally speaking, the state will insure the realization of the plan's objectives not by direct instructions but by economic means and economic policy, such as a suitable credit policy, or by regulating the use of the net income of the enterprises, as well as other means. The aim of the socialist planned economy is to meet requirements. The husbandry of enterprises serves the interests of society when their activity is directed in the most profitable way to meeting financially sound demands, when they produce goods needed by society.

Enterprise profits are tools. After the introduction of the new economic system, the trend shown by profits will not be the only but the principal indication of the efficiency of production, of the quality of economic activity in the enterprises. The reform of the economic mechanism calls for producer's prices that are in harmony with the actual values, with the social work that goes into the production process.

A general review of prices must take place by 1 January 1968, and the method of determining prices must be changed. In the next few years the producer's prices of some goods will have to be raised, while the price of others will be lowered. The alteration of producer's prices may affect consumer prices in some cases and to some extent.

The changes in consumer prices must not entail a lowering of the population's living standard, which must rise in accordance with provisions of the plan. The effort to keep price levels stable—while achieving a certain flexibility—will remain an important feature of our price policy. The reform also embraces other important questions of socialist construction, such as material incentives and a more direct application of the socialist principle of distribution according to work. In the future we must strive to raise, first of all, workers' wages, while everybody should pay for what he consumes. Wages should reflect the workers' actual performance more exactly. This is what a more direct application of the socialist principle of distribution according to work means.

Therefore, we must proceed more boldly in respect to differentiating between wages and earnings, too. In the course of the reform of the economic mechanism, opportunities must be created for a successful enterprise to provide for its efficient workers and employees certain limited extra earnings in addition to the profit sharing in force up to now. Incentives for good work should be stepped up in this way, too. A more consistent assertion of the principle of distribution according to work and adaptation to the actual performance of individuals and enterprises increases the prestige of labor.

With our socialist planned economy we shall continue to insure an adequate level and an even growth of social employment, an increase in real incomes, and an improvement in living conditions. But we intend to achieve these aims with different economic means—in a way in which the consequences of good and poor work, the presence or absence of expertise, and the presence or absence of industriousness will be more clearly distinguishable both in the individual and the enterprise.

In socialist production relations enormous possibilities have opened up for initiative and creative effort on the part of experts and workers alike. Initiative, dynamic work, and the rejection of that which is conservative and obsolete have become some of the main features of socialist work. These characteristics of our socialist building work must be further strengthened; the implementation and dissemination of good initiatives must be furthered.

Looking in depth at our current methods of husbandry and leadership, we can say that in spite of every success of our work up to now there are restrictions, over-centralized licensing, regulations, which impede the introduction of new processes. We are justified in expecting that the new economic mechanism will augment the prestige of the directing organs of state. State discipline will be given new content. It will not be possible to pass responsibility for something on to others and the petty bickering over minutia will cease, but the weight of real direction will grow. We must now do all we can to insure that the detailed measures in connection with the reform of the economic mechanism are in harmony with the basic principles that have been approved and that it is possible to introduce the reform in full by January 1968.

The Vietnam War and The Tet Offensive

In 1965 the United States initiated direct military intervention to rescue the government of South Vietnam from the Viet Cong guerrillas supported by North Vietnam. Late in 1967 the Communists resolved on a decisive offensive and advised their forces accordingly. The actual attack began on January 31, 1968, the day after "Tet," the Vietnamese New Year's Day, with urban uprisings and frontal attacks all over South Vietnam. The offensive was a tactical failure, exhausting the fighting ability of the Viet Cong, but politically it marked the beginning of the end of the Americans' will to continue their intervention.

Upon receipt of this letter, you are required to formulate a plan to prepare the minds of the Party, Group, agencies and the people by convening a Party Branch meeting (one night) to:

FROM: Directive from Province Party Standing Committee to District and Local Party Organs on Forthcoming Offensive and Uprisings, November 1, 1967 (English translation in *Vietnam Documents and Research Notes*, Saigon, U.S. Mission, 1971; reprinted in Gareth Porter, ed., *Vietnam: the Definitive Documentation of Human Decisions*, Stanfordville, N.Y., Earl M. Coleman Enterprises, 1979, II: 477–480).

—Report the new situation in towns and rural areas. The time is now more favorable [for an offensive] than ever before. This is to notify you that an offensive and uprising will take place in the very near future and we will mount stronger attacks on towns and cities, in coordination with the widespread [uprising] movement in the rural areas. The enemy will be thrown into utmost confusion. No matter how violently the enemy may react, he cannot avoid collapse. This is not only a golden opportunity to liberate hamlets and villages but also an opportunity to liberate district seats, province capitals and South Viet-Nam as a whole.

Our victory is close at hand. The conditions are ripe. Our Party has carefully judged the situation. We must act and act fast. This is an opportunity to fulfill the aspirations of the entire people, of cadre, of each comrade and of our families. We have long suffered hardships, death and pain. We are looking for an opportunity to avenge evil done to our families, to pay our debt to the Fatherland, to display our loyalty to the country, affection for the people and love for our families. We cannot afford to miss this rare opportunity. All Party members and cadre must be willing to sacrifice their lives for the survival of the Fatherland.

This opportunity is like an attack on an enemy post in which we have reached the last fence and the enemy puts up a fierce resistance. We only need to make a swift assault to secure the target and gain total victory.

If we are hesitant and fearful of hardships and misery, we will suffer heavy losses, fail to accomplish the mission and feel guilty for failing our nation, our people, our families and our comrades who have already sacrificed themselves. It is time for us to take the initiative in penetrating into enemy bases in provinces, districts and villages, attacking him five or ten times more violently to score brilliant achievements.

Make all comrades realize that the purpose of the revolutionary activities conducted for many years is mainly to support this phase, in this decisive hour. Even though we make sacrifices, we will gain glorious victory, not only for the people, but also for our Fatherland and families. If we adopt a hesitant attitude, we will not only belittle the value of human beings but also lower the prestige of revolutionary party members. This means we will lose self-respect and we will not be worthy of enjoying the rights of man. . . .

How Will The Uprising Be Conducted?

There are two fundamental steps:

First, annihilate the enemy's political power. It is fundamental that we capture all tyrants from the village and hamlet administrative machinery and a number of spies. If we are not successful in this area the uprising will not be able to take place.

Second, organize our political power, specifically our [own] district, village and hamlet administrative machinery.

To conduct an uprising, you must have a roster of all the tyrants and spies and be familiar with the way they live and where they live. Then use suicide cells to annihilate them by any means. The following tasks should also be achieved on the same night:

Conduct meetings and give information on the current situation (about 10 to 15 minutes). *Make use of the populace immediately* in sabotage and support activities and in raid operations against the spies. The masses should be encouraged to go on strike. Dig trenches and make spikes all night long, and contribute to the transformation of the terrain. All people in each family, regardless of their ages, should be encouraged to take part [in the uprising]. This is the best way of motivating the populace and of elevating their pride. . . . Make appeals to enemy personnel from the Popular, Regional and Special Forces to surrender. Once the task is achieved, make use of a number of agents under legal cover to organize insurrection committees in white [South Vietnamese-controlled] hamlets and villages. At the same time, transfer the determined-to-die cells to the next hamlet or village to push the revolutionary movement forward quickly. . . .

In those areas where the local or main force units are garrisoned, the District Party Committee will coordinate with the commanders of these units to activate a local Joint Uprising Committee. In addition to the activation of the determined-to-die teams and the task force charged with the missions of attacking the district headquarters and destroying lines of communication, a certain number of cells will be organized in support of the efforts to destroy the tyrants and pacification workers operating in the weak or white villages. However, the bulk of our forces will be assigned to carry out plans designed to destroy the enemy [armed forces]. Meanwhile, special emphasis must be placed on building the guerrilla warfare movement. . . .

While the uprising is at its apex in the countryside and the masses are seething with fervor, we must make the most of circumstances to lead the masses to realize that, more than ever before, we must commit all manpower and resources to the speedy liberation of our homeland. We must knock on every inhabitant's door to borrow the maximum possible amount of money and food, which will then be taken immediately without resorting to the normal procedures followed previously. In this connection we must act strongly and get high goals. Concurrently we must motivate the populace to store up food, salt, fuel and other staples.

It behooves all comrades to review their past experiences pertaining to uprising as well as consolidation so they will perform their tasks well. . . .

The Soviet Union, Israel, and Zionism

Beginning with vigorous support of Egypt in the Suez crisis of 1956, the Soviet Union steadily pursued a strategy of wooing anti-Western Arab governments and simultaneously condemning Israel and Zionism. This attitude was sharpened after Israel's preemptive attack in 1967 on Egypt and Syria and the annexation of the West Bank of the Jordan. In the early seventies the Soviet Union overtly allied itself with the Palestine Liberation Organization.

It is becoming more and more apparent that Israel is a predatory imperialist state. Those who until June, 1967, believed that the existence of the state of Israel was threatened by its Arab neighbours have had their eyes opened by recent events.

This last year has also dispelled various illusions about the Israeli state as a haven for Jews flocking to Mount Zion to realise the principles of the Old Testament.

The fall of Israel and its betrayal of social progress stem from the vices of imperialism, and it is becoming clearer and clearer that imperialism is the course on which Israel is set. The architects of the domestic and foreign policy of this small

FROM: K. Ivanov, "Israel, Zionism, and International Imperialism," *International Affairs*, June, 1968 (reprinted in Walter Laqueur, *The Struggle for the Middle East*, New York, Macmillan, 1969, pp. 277, 279-80, 284-289).

state have been trampling more and more often the rules of the comity of nations, and this disgraceful defiance of the rest of the world is the root of the calamities that have befallen Israel's neighbours and bodes ill for the Israelis themselves. . . .

Israel's actions are openly aimed against the interests of the Arab people and of all the other peoples of the world. In January, for instance, the Israeli military authorities demonstratively prevented the release of foreign ships stranded in the Suez Canal. By hampering the creation of conditions for a resumption of shipping through the Suez Canal, Israel has inflicted substantial material damage on the countries of Europe, Asia and East Africa who normally make great use of the canal. Incidentally, this is doing the United States a good turn, for, in contrast to Britain, France, Italy or India, the United States stands to gain from keeping the canal closed, as this gives American shipping companies vast super-profits. . . .

An absolute majority of countries have resolutely condemned in one form or other any territorial changes in the Middle East and the establishment of an intolerable precedent there in the seizure of foreign territories by armed force. The Security Council resolution of November 22, 1967, likewise said that annexations were inadmissible. The fearless militarists at Mount Zion pretend that they do not care and that Israel can ignore with more or less complete impunity the mandatory decisions of the Security Council and flout world opinion. This brazen extremist policy is capable of dealing a blow at the very foundations of the United Nations, and its authority and prestige. At present, Israel, the Portuguese colonialists and the South African racialists constitute a little group of states in the United Nations who ignore the rules of international law, the comity of nations and the decisions of high and authoritative international organisations.

With the support of the U.S.A., Israel has in fact made a bid at becoming an outright colonialist power. Prominent politicians in Tel Aviv have been making wild statements to the effect that they refuse to give up the territories they have won and that it would be absurd and dangerous to withdraw their troops from their present positions. There are some kinds of people in Western Europe who applaud these wild speeches. But the strange thing is that Israel has been clearly setting its mind on open campaigns of aggrandisement at a time when even the major imperialist powers—the U.S.A., Britain and West Germany—have not dared advertise their neocolonialist policy or risk any head-on collisions with the world of emergent nations in the former colonies and dependent countries. . . .

The ideological exposure and defeat of Zionism as a political trend acquires considerable importance today for the international working-class movement and for all progressive and peaceloving forces in the world. Back in 1903, Lenin emphasised that 'the Zionist idea is absolutely false and essentially reactionary' (V.I. Lenin, *Collected Works*, Vol. 7, Moscow, 1961, p. 99). It took organisational and ideological shape at the end of the 19th century among bourgeois Jewish leaders in Germany, Austria and Russia, and later in France and the U.S.A.

From the outset, Zionism operated as an avowed and implacable enemy of Marxism and the international working-class movement. Zionism is based on principles contradictory to Marxism. Its aim is incredibly narrow. It is to 'gather' the Jews in the 'promised land,' namely, Israel, which, according to the canons of the ancient Judaic religion, will have neither social nor political inequality. Instead of irreconcilable class struggle against the bourgeoisie and the landowners, the Zionists preach the unity of all classes inside a sort of class-free and supraclass Jewish community; instead of overthrowing the power of the bourgeoisie and establishing the dictatorship of the working class, they establish ties and collaborate with the most reactionary groups of exploiters, who for various reasons support the immigration of Jews to Palestine. . . .

Zionist leaders are trying to instil into the minds of Jews in various countries, including the Socialist countries, that they have a 'dual citizenship'—one, a secondary one, in the country of actual domicile, and the other, the basic, spiritual and religious one, in Israel. Those were the very tricks used by the leaders of the Third Reich in the interests of German imperialism. In this way the Nazis set up their 'fifth column' in other countries, and in the same way modern Zionism tries to secure international support for Israel and its aggressive expansionist policy.

Only people who are politically blind can fail to see the danger lurking in this concept of 'dual citizenship.' The imperialist intelligence services and psychological warfare agencies have been spending hundreds of millions of dollars to subvert and corrupt the international working class and anti-imperialist movement as a whole, and especially the fraternal militant community of the Socialist countries. In this context, the 'dual citizenship' concept and the 'bridge-building' policy are two sides of ideological and political subversion and indirect aggression designed for the ultimate restoration of capitalism. . . .

The Soviet people are also well aware of the lying methods used by the Zionist imperialist agents who are trying to depict the exposure and prosecution of Zionism as a sign of anti-Semitism. From year to year, centres of psychological warfare against Socialism in New York and Tel Aviv have been spreading slander about an imaginary persecution of Jews in the Soviet Union. They call their malicious and shameless lies 'freedom of speech'. . . .

Like many European nations, the Jews suffered terribly from this imperialist barbarity. But imperialism has a stranglehold on men regardless of nationality. Hitlerism was not only an expression of the qualities of a German nation stupefied. It was an example of aggressive imperialism as such. In Israel the once persecuted have themselves become avid persecutors and villains. They applaud the current crimes of imperialism. There is a good reason for this: Zionism has made a close alliance with the most reactionary and aggressive force in the world today—U.S. imperialism.

The crisis in Israel's imperialist policy, the crisis in modern Zionism is closely bound up with that period of world history when the movement for the liberation of the oppressed nations and nationalities in Europe and for their equality went beyond Europe and became a world-wide movement. The colonial oppression of the countries of Asia, Africa and Latin America is essentially the same thing as Hitlerism, but organised on a world-wide scale by international imperialism. And when the question arose of liberating all nations oppressed by imperialism from every form of colonialism and neocolonialism, the Zionists and the rulers of imperialist Israel found themselves on the other side of the barricade, in the ranks of the enemies of Socialism and progress. The old ties of Jewish financiers and Zionist leaders with big monopoly capital, with the Rothschilds and Kuhn-Loebs, completed the vicious circle. . . .

The Soviet people take a consistently Leninist and internationalist stand against aggressive imperialist policy and bellicose Zionism and make a clear-cut distinction between the struggle against all types of nationalism, Zionism and great-power

chauvinism, and the struggle for complete national equality and fraternal cooperation of all nations and nationalities in the Soviet Union, including, of course, the
Jews. The struggle against Zionism in the ideology and policy of Leninism is
organically and indissolubly bound up with the struggle against anti-Semitism, a
product of the self-same bourgeois society. . . .

In the 50 years since the October Revolution, not only nations, but nationalities
as well, have undergone profound and all-round Socialist transformation. Honest
Soviet people of Jewish nationality have become men and women of Socialist
nationality; they are as profoundly instilled with the spirit of Socialism and internationalism in foreign relations as are people of all other fraternal nations and
nationalities inhabiting the great, victorious and powerful Socialist Soviet Union.
For the exploiting classes (and this applies to *all* nations and nationalities in this
country) have been eliminated in the U.S.S.R. once and for all, the bourgeois mode
of production has been supplanted by its opposite, the Socialist mode of production and social ideals, which are quite different from those in the U.S.A., Israel or
in tsarist Russia, have triumphed in every sphere of life. That is *the essence* of the
Socialist transformation of all nations and nationalities which has taken place in
this country in the 50 years of Soviet power. And that is also a source of the Soviet
people's sense of legitimate pride and moral superiority.

The Prague Spring

Of all the satellite countries of Eastern Europe Czechoslovakia had evidenced the least spirit
of reform until the fall of Khrushchev weakened the political grip of party chief and President Antonin Novotný. In January, 1968, the Czechoslovak Communist Central Committee
removed Novotný and installed Alexander Dubček, who proceeded to abolish censorship and
initiate a real democratization of the country's political life. This aspiration was formalized in
the "Action Program" adopted by the party in April.

The challenge of Czechoslovak revisionism and probable fears for the solidity of the Warsaw Pact prompted the Soviet leadership to decide on forcible intervention, and on August
20, 1968, Soviet forces together with other Warsaw Pact contingents (East German, Polish,
Hungarian, and Bulgarian) bloodlessly occupied Czechoslovakia. Dubček's reforms were
suspended, and Dubček himself was ousted the following year and replaced by the collabora-
tionist Gustav Husak. Meanwhile, in justification of the occupation, Moscow enunciated
what the West termed the "Brezhnev Doctrine," that the preservation of socialism set limits
to a satellite country's sovereignty.

a) The Action Program

In the past, the leading role of the Party was often conceived as a monopolistic
concentration of power in the hands of Party bodies. This corresponded to the
false thesis that the Party is the instrument of the dictatorship of the proletariat.
This harmful conception weakened the initiative and responsibility of the State,
economic and social institutions and damaged the Party's authority, and prevented
it from carrying out its real functions. The Party's goal is not to become a universal
"caretaker" of the society, to bind all organizations and every step taken in life by

FROM: The Action Program of the Communist Party of Czechoslovakia, in Paul Ello, ed.,
Czechoslovakia's Blueprint for Freedom, Washington, Acropolis, 1968, pp. 110, 116, 118–22,
131–32, 138–39, 146–49, 151, 168, 173, 178. Reprinted by permission of the publisher.

its directives. Its mission lies primarily in arousing socialist initiative, in showing the ways and actual possibilities of Communist perspectives, and in winning over all workers for them through systematic persuasion, as well as by the personal examples of Communists. . . .

The main thing is to reform the whole political system so that it will permit the dynamic development of socialist social relations, combine broad democracy with a scientific, highly qualified management, strengthen the social order, stabilize socialist relations and maintain social discipline. The basic structure of the political system must, at the same time, *provide firm guarantees against a return to the old methods of subjectivism and highhandedness from a position of power.* Party activity has, so far, not been turned systematically to that end, in fact, obstacles have frequently been put in the way of such efforts. All these changes necessarily call for . . . a new Czechoslovak constitution. . . .

The whole *National Front,* the political parties which form it, and the social organizations, will take part in the creation of state policy. *The political parties* of the National Front are partners whose political work is based on the joint political programme of the National Front and is naturally bound by the Constitution of the Czechoslovak Socialist Republic, is fully based on the socialist character of social relations in our country. The Communist Party of Czechoslovakia considers the National Front to be a political platform which does not separate the political parties into the government and the opposition in the sense that opposition would be created to the state policy as the policy of the whole National Front and a struggle for political power in the state were to exist. Possible differences in the viewpoints of individual component parts of the National Front, or divergency of views as to the policy of the state, are all to be settled on the basis of the common socialist conception of the National Front policy by way of political agreement and unification of all component parts of the National Front. Formation of political forces striving to negate this conception of the National Front, to remove the National Front as a whole from political power, was ruled out as long ago as 1945 after the tragic experience of both our nations with the prewar political development of the then Czechoslovak Republic; it is naturally unacceptable for our present republic.

The Communist Party of Czechoslovakia considers the *political management* of the Marxist-Leninist concept of the development of socialism as a precondition for the right development of our socialist society. It will assert the Marxist-Leninist concept as the leading political principle in the National Front and in all our political system by seeking, through the means of political work, such support in all the component parts of our system and *directly among the masses of workers and all working people* that will ensure its leading role in a democratic way.

Voluntary social organizations of the working people cannot replace political parties, *but the contrary is also true: political parties in our country cannot exclude common-interest organizations of workers and other working people from directly influencing state policy,* its creation and application. Socialist state power cannot be monopolized either by a single party, or by a coalition of parties. It must be open to all political organizations of the people. *The Communist Party of Czechoslovakia will use every means to develop such forms of political life that will ensure the expression of the direct say and will of the working class and all working people in political decision-taking in our country.* . . .

Voluntary social organizations must be based on really voluntary membership and

activity. People join these organizations because they express their interests, therefore they have the right to choose their own officials and representatives who cannot be appointed from outside. These principles should be the foundation of our
unified mass organizations the activities of which are still indispensable but which
should meet, by their structure, their working methods, and their ties with their
members, the new social conditions.

The implementation of *constitutional freedoms of assembly and association* must be
ensured this year so that the possibility of setting up voluntary organizations,
special-interest associations, societies, etc. is guaranteed by law to meet the actual
interests and needs of various strata and categories of our citizens, without bureaucratic interference and without monopoly of any individual organization. Any restrictions in this respect can be imposed only by law and only the law can stipulate
what is anti-social, forbidden, or punishable. Freedoms guaranteed by law are
applicable in this sense, in compliance with the constitution, also to citizens of
individual creeds and religious denominations.

The effective influence of views and opinions of the working people on all our
policy, opposition to all tendencies to suppress the criticism and initiative of the
people, cannot be guaranteed if we do not ensure constitution-based freedom of
speech and all political and personal rights of all citizens, systematically and consistently, by all legal means available. *Socialism cannot mean only liberation of the
working people from the domination of exploiting class relations, but must make more provisions for a fuller life of the personality than any bourgeois democracy.* The working
people, who are no longer ordered about by any class of exploiters, can no longer
be prescribed by any arbitrary interpretation from a position of power, what
information they may or may not be given, which of their opinions can or cannot
be expressed publicly, where public opinion may play a role and where not. Public
opinion polls must be systematically used in preparing important decisions and the
main results of the research are to be published. Any restriction may be imposed
only on the basis of a law stipulating what is anti-social—which in our country is
mainly the criminal law. The Central Committee of the Communist Party of
Czechoslovakia considers it necessary to define more exactly than hitherto in the
shortest possible time by a press law, when a state body can forbid the propagation
of certain information (in the press, radio, television, etc.) and exclude the possibility of preliminary factual censorship. It is necessary to overcome the holding up,
distortion, and incompleteness of information, to remove any unwarranted secrecy
of political and economic facts, to publish the annual balance sheets of enterprises,
to publish even alternatives to various suggestions and measures, to extend the
import and sale of foreign press. . . .

Legal norms must guarantee more exactly *the freedom of speech of minority interests
and opinions* also (again within the framework of socialist laws and in harmony with
the principle that decisions are taken in accordance with the will of the majority).
The *constitutional freedom of movement*, particularly the travelling of our citizens
abroad, *must be precisely guaranteed by law*; in particular, this means that a citizen
should have the legal right to long-term or permanent sojourn abroad and that
people should not be groundlessly placed in the position of emigrants; at the same
time it is necessary to protect by law the interests of the state, for example, as
regards the drain of some categories of specialists, etc.

We must gradually solve in the whole legal code the task of how *to protect in a*

better and more consistent way the personal rights and property of citizens, we must especially remove those stipulations that virtually put individual citizens at a disadvantage against the state and other institutions. . . .

*The Party policy is based on the principle that no undue concentration of power must
occur, throughout the state machinery, in one sector, one body, or in a single individual.* It
is necessary to provide for such a division of power and such a system of mutual
supervision that any faults, or encroachments of any of its links are rectified in
time, by the activities of another link. This principle must be applied not only to
relations between the elected and executive bodies, but also to the inner relations
of the state administration machinery and to the standing and activities of courts of
law. . . .

The Central Committee of the Communist Party of Czechoslovakia deems it
necessary *to change the organization of the security force* and to split the joint organization into two mutually independent parts—State Security and Public Security.
The State Security service must have such a status, organizational structure, numerical state, equipment, methods of work, and qualifications which are in keeping
with its work of defending the state from the activities of enemy centres abroad.
Every citizen who has not been culpable in this respect must know with certainty
that his political convictions and opinions, his personal beliefs and activities, cannot be the object of attention of the bodies of the State Security service. The Party
declares clearly that this apparatus *should not be directed and used to solve internal political questions* and controversies in socialist society. . . .

. . . *The programme of democratization of the economy includes particularly the provision of ensuring the independence of enterprises and enterprise groupings and their relative
independence from state bodies, a full and real implementation of the right of the consumer to determine his consumption and his style of life, the right of a free choice of working
activity, the right and real possibility of different groups of the working people and different social groups to formulate and defend their economic interests in shaping the economic
policy.*

In developing democratic relations in the economy we at present consider as the
most important task the final formulation of the economic position of enterprises,
their authority and responsibility.

The economic reform will increasingly push whole working teams of socialist
enterprises into positions in which they will feel directly the consequences of both
the good and bad management of enterprises. The Party therefore deems it necessary that the whole working team which bears the consequences should also be able
to influence the management of the enterprise. There arises the need of democratic
bodies in enterprises with determined rights towards the management of the enterprise. Managers and head executives of the enterprises, which would also appoint
them to their functions would be accountable to these bodies for the overall results
of their work. These bodies must become a direct part of the managing mechanism
of enterprises, and not a social organization. (They cannot therefore be identified
with trade unions.) These bodies would be formed by elected representatives of the
working team and by representatives of certain components outside the enterprise
ensuring the influence of the interests of the entire society and an expert and qualified level of decision-making; the representation of these components must also be
subordinated to democratic forms of control. . . .

We are putting great hope into reviving the positive functions of the market as a necessary mechanism of the functioning of socialist economy and for checking whether the work in enterprises has been expended in a socially useful way. However, we have in mind not the capitalist, but the socialist market, and not its uncontrolled but its regulated utilization. The plan and the national economic policy must appear as a positive force contributing to the normalization of the market and directed against tendencies of economic imbalance and against monopolistic control of the market. The society must do the planning with due insight and perspective, it must scientifically discover the possibilities of its future development and choose its most reasonable orientation. This, however, cannot be achieved by suppressing the independence of other subjects of the market (enterprises and the population), since this would on the one hand undermine the interest ensuring economic rationality, on the other hand it would deform information and decision-making processes which are indispensably necessary for the functioning of the economy. . . .

The development of international economic relations will continue to be based on economic cooperation with the Soviet Union and the other socialist countries, particularly those aligned in the Council of Mutual Economic Assistance. At the same time, however, it should be seen that the success of this cooperation will increasingly depend on the competitiveness of our products. The position of our country in the development of international division of labour will strengthen with the more general convertibility of our products. In our relations with the CMEA countries we shall strive for the fuller application of criteria of economic calculations and mutual advantage of exchange.

We shall also actively support the development of economic relations with all other countries in the world, which show interest in them on the basis of equality, mutual advantages and without discrimination. . . .

The basic aim of the Party in developing the economic policy is the steady growth of the standard of living. However, the development of the economy was in the past one-sidedly focussed on the growth of heavy industry with long-term returnability of investments. This was done to a considerable extent at the expense of the development of agriculture and the consumer goods industry, the development of the production of building materials, trade, services and non-productive basic assets, particularly in housing construction. This one-sided character of the former economic development cannot be changed overnight. If, however, we take advantage of the great reserve existing in the organization of production and work, as well as in the technical and economic standard of production and products, if we consider the possibilities offered by a skillful utilization of the new system of management, we can substantially speed up the creation of resources and on this basis raise the growth of nominal wages and the general standard of living. . . .

We reject administrative and bureaucratic methods of implementing cultural policy, we dissociate ourselves from them and we shall oppose them. Artistic work must not be subjected to censorship. We have full confidence in men of culture and we expect their responsibility, understanding and support. We appreciate how the workers in culture helped force through and create the humanistic and democratic character of socialism and how actively they participated in eliminating the retarding factors of its development. . . .

The basic orientation of Czechoslovak foreign policy was born and verified at the time of the struggle for national liberation and in the process of the socialist reconstruction of this country—*it is in alliance and cooperation with the Soviet Union and the other socialist states. We shall strive for friendly relations with our allies—the countries of the world socialist community—to continue, on the basis of mutual respect, to intensify sovereignty and equality, and international solidarity.* In this sense we shall contribute more actively and with a more elaborated concept to the joint activities of the Council of Mutual Economic Aid and the Warsaw Treaty.

In the relationship to the developing countries, socialist Czechoslovakia will be contributing to the strengthening of the anti-imperialist front and supporting within its power and possibilities all the nations opposing imperialism, colonialism, neo-colonialism and striving for the strengthening of their sovereignty and national independence and for economic development. Therefore we shall continue supporting the courageous struggle of the Vietnamese people against American aggression. We shall also be enforcing a political settlement of the Middle East crisis.

We shall actively pursue the policy of peaceful coexistence towards advanced capitalist countries. Our geographical position, as well as the needs and capacities of an industrial country, require that we should carry out a more active European policy aimed at the promotion of mutually advantageous relations with all states and international organisations and at safeguarding collective security of the European continent. . . .

We are not concealing the fact that difficult moments and extraordinarily exacting and responsible work face us in the coming months and years. For the fulfilment of the forthcoming progressive tasks it will be necessary to unite as many citizens of our Republic as possible, all who are concerned with the welfare of this country, with its peace efforts, with a flourishing socialism. . . . Let the Action Programme become a programme of the revival of socialist efforts in this country. There is no force which could resist the people who know what they want and how to pursue their aim.

b) The Brezhnev Doctrine

In connection with the events in Czechoslovakia, the question of the correlation and interdependence of the national interests of the socialist countries and their international duties acquires particular topical and acute importance.

The measures taken by the Soviet Union, jointly with other socialist countries, in defending the socialist gains of the Czechoslovak people are of great significance for strengthening the socialist community, which is the main achievement of the international working class.

We cannot ignore the assertions, made in some places, that the actions of the five socialist countries run counter to the Marxist-Leninist principle of sovereignty and the rights of nations to self-determination.

The groundlessness of such reasoning consists primarily in that it is based on an abstract, nonclass approach to the question of sovereignty and the rights of nations to self-determination.

The peoples of the socialist countries and Communist parties certainly do have and should have freedom for determining the ways of advance of their respective countries.

However, none of their decisions should damage either socialism in their coun-

FROM: S. Kovalev, "Sovereignty and International Duties of Socialist Countries," *Pravda*, September 25, 1968 (English translation in *The New York Times*, September 26, 1968).

try or the fundamental interests of other socialist countries, and the whole working class movement, which is working for socialism.

This means that each Communist party is responsible not only to its own people, but also to all the socialist countries, to the entire Communist movement. Whoever forgets this, in stressing only the independence of the Communist party, becomes one-sided. He deviates from his international duty.

Marxist dialectics are opposed to one-sidedness. They demand that each phenomenon be examined concretely, in general connection with other phenomena, with other processes.

Just as, in Lenin's words, a man living in a society cannot be free from the society, a particular socialist state, staying in a system of other states composing the socialist community, cannot be free from the common interests of that community.

The sovereignty of each socialist country cannot be opposed to the interests of the world of socialism, of the world revolutionary movement. Lenin demanded that all Communists fight against small-nation narrow-mindedness, seclusion and isolation, consider the whole and the general, subordinate the particular to the general interest.

The socialist states respect the democratic norms of international law. They have proved this more than once in practice, by coming out resolutely against the attempts of imperialism to violate the sovereignty and independence of nations.

It is from these same positions that they reject the leftist, adventurist conception of "exporting revolution," of "bringing happiness" to other peoples.

However, from a Marxist point of view, the norms of law, including the norms of mutual relations of the socialist countries, cannot be interpreted narrowly, formally, and in isolation from the general context of class struggle in the modern world. The socialist countries resolutely come out against the exporting and importing of counterrevolution.

Each Communist party is free to apply the basic principles of Marxism-Leninism and of socialism in its country, but it cannot depart from these principles (assuming, naturally, that it remains a Communist party).

Concretely, this means, first of all, that, in its activity, each Communist party cannot but take into account such a decisive fact of our time as the struggle between two opposing social systems—capitalism and socialism. . . .

The antisocialist elements in Czechoslovakia actually covered up the demand for so-called neutrality and Czechoslovakia's withdrawal from the socialist community with talk about the right of nations to self-determination.

However, the implementation of such "self-determination," in other words, Czechoslovakia's detachment from the socialist community, would have come into conflict with its own vital interests and would have been detrimental to the other socialist states.

Such "self-determination," as a result of which NATO troops would have been able to come up to the Soviet border, while the community of European socialist countries would have been split, in effect encroaches upon the vital interests of the peoples of these countries and conflicts, at the very root of it, with the right of these people to socialist self-determination.

Discharging their internationalist duty toward the fraternal peoples of Czechoslovakia and defending their own socialist gains, the U.S.S.R. and the other socialist states had to act decisively and they did act against the antisocialist forces in Czechoslovakia. . . .

Naturally the Communists of the fraternal countries could not allow the social-ist states to be inactive in the name of an abstractly understood sovereignty, when they saw that the country stood in peril of antisocialist degeneration. . . .

Formal observance of the freedom of self-determination of a nation in the con-crete situation that arose in Czechoslovakia would mean freedom of "self-deter-mination" not of the popular masses, the working people, but of their enemies.

The antisocialist path, "neutrality," to which the Czechoslovak people were pushed would bring it to the loss of its national independence.

World imperialism, on its part, supported the antisocialist forces in Czechoslo-vakia, tried to export counterrevolution to that country in this way. . . .

Those who speak about the "illegal actions" of the allied socialist countries in Czechoslovakia forget that in a class society there are not and there cannot be non-class laws.

Laws and legal norms are subjected to the laws of the class struggle, the laws of social development. These laws are clearly formulated in Marxist-Leninist teaching, in the documents jointly adopted by the Communist and Workers' parties.

Formally juridical reasoning must not overshadow a class approach to the matter. . . .

The interests of the socialist community and of the whole revolutionary move-ment, the interests of socialism in Czechoslovakia demand complete exposure and political isolation of the reactionary forces in that country, consolidation of the working people and consistent implementation of the Moscow agreement between the Soviet and Czechoslovak leaders.

There is no doubt that the actions of the five allied socialist countries in Czecho-slovakia directed to the defense of the vital interests of the socialist community, and the sovereignty of socialist Czechoslovakia first and foremost, will be increasingly supported by all those who have the interest of the present revolutionary move-ment, of peace and security of peoples, of democracy and socialism at heart.

The New Left and Maoism

In the late 1960's new currents of youthful radicalism, often sympathetic to the Cultural Revolution in China, swept the Western world. Soviet spokesmen took a dim view of the movement, including its most sensational manifestation in the May, 1968, student uprising in Paris, and its most famous mentor, the German-American philosopher Herbert Marcuse. Student and racial disturbances in the United States were generally less ideological, but the Progressive Labor Party, a small left-wing offshoot of the CP-USA organized in 1965, tried to give a revolutionary stamp to their agitation. Disillusioned with China over its "revision-ist" tendency in international affairs, the PLP disappeared from view in the seventies.

a) Moscow on Marcuse and the May Uprising

Marcuse, Marcuse, Marcuse. The name of this seventy-year-old German-Ameri-can philosopher, who has stepped out of the darkness of unrecognition, is repeated endlessly by the Western press. . . .

FROM: Yuri Zhukov, "Werewolves," *Pravda*, May 30, 1968 (English translation in Klaus Meh-nert, *Moscow and the New Left*, (Berkeley, University of California Press, 1975, pp. 145–50). Reprinted by permission of the publisher.

Recently this gentleman visited Paris. There he spoke at a UNESCO colloquium dedicated to the 150th anniversary of the birth of Marx. His report was entitled "The Revision of the Marxist Concept of Revolution." However, it was really not even a revision of Marxism but an attempt to refute it. Pitiful and inconsistent, but nevertheless an attempt. As the newspapers reported, Marcuse stated that at the present time the "working class, having integrated itself (?!) into the capitalist system, can no longer play the revolutionary role which Marx had intended for it. The power of capital can, consequently, be overthrown only by forces located outside the system: people of the colonies, Negroes or young people, still not integrated in the system."

As one would expect, the philosophers-Marxists participating in the colloquium gave this false prophet the refutation he deserved. Some were amazed: Why did Marcuse say that the working class "could no longer play a revolutionary role" at the very moment when in the capitalist world, and in particular in France where he spoke, the wave of an acute class struggle was breaking so highly? However, the more far-sighted people understood: Marcuse was catapulted from far-off San Diego to Paris just for this reason. It was necessary to put into use all means in order to attempt to interfere and bring chaos into the ranks of those struggling against the old order, and—mainly!—to attempt to put young people, especially students, in opposition to the basic force of the working class.

There was thus a good reason why, at this time, the *New York Times* invented a new term, "THE DE-COMMUNIZATION (!) OF MARXISM." There was also a reason why, with clear sympathy for the Paris students of Marcuse, it wrote that their flag "IS THE BLACK FLAG OF ANARCHY, AND NOT THE RED FLAG OF COMMUNISM." . . .

The bourgeois ideologists understand that during the serious sharpening of the class struggle their old theories of "people's capitalism," "convergence" (the gradual converging of the two opposed systems) do not have the power to influence the fighting proletariat. Consequently, the "ultra-left," anarchist slogans are released, very frequently, saturated with the ideas of Mao Tse-tung. With their help it is attempted to spread confusion, to lead astray the impetuous but politically uneducated young people, split them up, and to convert those with whom this succeeds into blind tools of the provocateurs.

Marcuse is not alone. In the FRG [Federal Republic of Germany] there are people who speak along his lines, saying that the West German working class cannot be revolutionary as long as, together with the bourgeois, it "participates in the exploitation of the Third World." In Italy the socialist delegate Codignola supports the thesis of Marcuse on the necessity of an "uprising" against the "industrial society in general" since, and he explained this to a correspondent of *L'Express*, "the present society, whether it is capitalist or socialist, is becoming more and more like an industrial enterprise."

However, quite similar to the demonstrations which are now being called by the Peking leaders to support, apparently, the struggle of the French workers for their rights, but in which the main blow is being directed against the French Communist Party and the USSR, the noisy followers of Marcuse in West Europe use their little fists to threaten the working class and the Communists.

This same goal is served by the turbid arguments of Marcuse and his students on the struggle *against "industrial civilization" in general*, without any distinction as to whether this refers to capitalist or socialist order. At the Sorbonne followers of Marcuse announced this "programmatic declaration":

"The beginning revolution questions not only capitalist society but industrial civilization in general. The consumer society should die a violent death. The society of alienation (!) also should die a violent death. We want a new and original society. We reject a society in which the certainty that you will not starve to death is exchanged for the risk of dying of boredom." . . .

The bourgeois press is now using bright colors to depict the "tricks" of a certain 23-year-old from the FRG: Cohn-Bendit, who until recently studied at the University in Paris and there engaged in divisive activities among the student body.

When . . . the French working class on May 13 organized a million-person demonstration in support of the legitimate demands of the students for a democratic reform of the university, this very same Cohn-Bendit with a handful of his followers—Trotskyites, anarchists, and "Maoists"—vainly attempted to confuse and divide the ranks of the demonstrators, hurling out the provocative slogans, "Let's storm the Elysée Palace!" . . .

Blasphemously using the name of Marx, the werewolves are attempting to undertake a "de-communization of Marxism" to divide and bring internal quarreling to progressive forces, and thus carry out the quite explicit social imperatives of the enemies of the working movement, who are seriously concerned about the intensification of the class struggle in their nations. This struggle is led by the working class, which, as *L'Humanité* stresses, is "powerful and organized and knows where it is going. It is the decisive force and is, in the final account, the sole revolutionary class since it has nothing to lose but its chains."

The leading force has been, is, and always will be the Communists, drawing their force from the great teachings of Marx and Lenin. And no matter how much unrequested "advisors" from the *New York Times* now prophesy the "de-communization of Marxism," no matter how much the bourgeois press advertises the reflections of Marcuse and the activities of his students, the plans of the enemies of the working class will fail.

b) Maoism in America—The Progressive Labor Party

The Progressive Labor Party is a revolutionary, Communist party. We believe that under capitalism the big bosses like GM control everything, including the government, and maintain a dictatorship of boss rule. We believe that in struggles like the present one, auto workers can learn the scientific lessons about the way society moves—based on a study of Communist ideas, Marxism-Leninism. Using this understanding, under the leadership of a worker-led Communist party, we can abolish the capitalist dictatorship, abolish profiteering off human labor and set up a government that puts power in the hands of the working people. . . .

Progressive Labor Party is a Communist party made up of workers and their allies . . . But we are not the phoney Communist Party USA which long ago gave

FROM: Leaflets and position statements of the Progressive Labor Party, 1969–70, excerpts in U.S. House of Representatives, 92nd Congress, 1st Sessions, Hearings before the Committee on Internal Security, April 13, 14 and November 18, 1971, *The Progressive Labor Party*, pp. 4140, 4313, 4320–22.

up on workers' revolution. PLP fights to strengthen workers' struggles against the bosses and politicians. This way we can build the power to destroy the system of exploitation—Capitalism. . . .

ONLY AN ARMED REVOLUTION LED BY the working class can destroy this U.S. ruling class and its state. The movement for reform must build a mass revolutionary movement in order to end poverty, racism, war, and exploitation forever.

This revolutionary movement must smash the bosses' bourgeois dictatorship and set up a dictatorship of the proletariat. . . .

The victory of the revolutionary forces in China serves as another lesson that negotiations with the revisionists or the imperialists are bound to lead to defeat. Comrade Mao Tse-tung and the hundreds of millions of Chinese people show that the best defense against ideological and military encroachment is to fight back; and to fight to the end. They have shown that the path to winning is unrelenting efforts against imperialism, nationalism, and revisionism. . . .

The U.S. War in Vietnam is an imperialist war which is aimed at preserving an important area of the world for exploitation by U.S. big business bosses. It is an attempt by the U.S. ruling class (that is, the class of corporation owners and bankers who hold power in the U.S. and live off the labor of working people here and abroad) to put down the rebellion of Vietnamese workers and peasants against the oppression they suffer at the hands of U.S. imperialism. . . .

Here in the U.S., workers are fighting back harder each year against the system that is driving down their real wages, causing inflation, higher taxes, speed-up on the job. This year, many workers will follow the example of the GE workers who held out for over three months trying to get a decent living.

And the workers that are fighting back the hardest, from work slowdowns, wildcat strikes to armed rebellion are black workers, who are the hardest hit by the bosses' profit drive. A cornerstone of the whole imperialist system is racism, which pushes black workers into the worst, lowest paying jobs, the most unemployment, worst and most dangerous living conditions, in order to create superprofits. Just as black workers are leading the fight against racism and oppression, black students are also in many cases leading this fight on the campuses. The ruling class is more afraid of this fight than any other, and has responded with vicious attacks against black workers and students, such as the bloody repression of ghetto rebellions (using in many cases the same military used against Vietnamese workers and peas-ants), the attacks on the Black Panthers, shooting of students involved in campus fights (such as Orangeburg, Texas State and others), the jailing of students at San Fernando Valley State College for fighting racism last year.

Racism is one of the key tools which the ruling class uses to divide workers (and students) to keep them fighting each other instead of uniting to fight their com-mon enemy—the bosses. Without fighting racism, no movement will be built which can defeat the imperialist bosses.

It is also the same system which is responsible for the countless other ways in which people's lives are made miserable. For example, the extra oppression of women, who it is estimated work an average of 99 hours a week, most of it unpaid housework. Or, for example, pollution of the air and water by the same bosses who provide dangerous working conditions in their factories because safety isn't profitable.

Why can all of these things happen, no matter who gets elected to what post in government? Because essentially a handful of exploiters exercise a *class dictatorship* over workers and other oppressed people. They run the government, the courts, the cops, the armies, the press and the schools and hold all the power.

The only thing that will end all of this oppression once and for all is completely wiping out imperialist rule. This means overthrowing the government which presently serves only the bosses, and setting up in its place a government run by the working people. Under this system only the bosses would be repressed, and instead of being stolen by profit-hungry corporation owners, what workers produce will go to them and their allies. We call this the DICTATORSHIP OF THE PROLETARIAT.

The establishment of worker's power is a long range fight. . . . Progressive Labor Party (PLP) is involved in and helping to build the programs of Students for a Democratic Society (SDS) aimed at fighting racism and imperialism, and allying with workers on campuses across the country.

Even though these short-range struggles are necessary, we have to be able to see beyond them, and make them part of a strategy to win which will keep the gains we make from being taken back again. Marxism-Leninism is the science which will enable us to analyze the whole situation and figure out—how can we win? Revolutionary experience shows that a party, such as PLP is striving to build, which bases its outlook on Marxism-Leninism and has the goal of working class revolution, is necessary. This party can unite all workers and oppressed people, black and white, men and women, workers and students, to finally win. . . .

Dissent in Yugoslavia—*Praxis*

Even Yugoslavia, the most reformed Communist state, was stirred by the ferment of the sixties. The "Praxis" group, so-called from their journal of that name, aimed a Marxist critique at the authoritarian survivals of Stalinism in the Soviet sphere. Svetozar Stojanović, Professor of Philosophy at the University of Belgrade, was able to expound this view in book form before the nervous Yugoslav authorities suppressed the publication of *Praxis* and ousted most of its members from their academic positions.

Our century abounds in ideological-political myths. The most prominent of them—the myth above myths of our age—is the statist myth of socialism. With the degeneration of the October Revolution a new exploitative class system was created, a system which stubbornly tries to pass itself off as socialism. Unfortunately, almost everyone believes in the socialist identity of Stalinist society.

The ideologues of "socialist" statism announced long ago that their society had completed the construction of socialism and had begun the construction of communism. They operate on the assumption that the construction of communism can be based upon an omnipotent state. Thus, in addition to the statist myth of social-

FROM: Svetozar Stojanović, *Between Ideals and Reality: A Critique of Socialism and its Future*, 1969 (English translation by Gerson S. Sher, New York, Oxford University Press, 1973, pp. 37, 40–42, 49–52, 59–60, 63–65). Copyright 1973 by Oxford University Press. Reprinted by permission.

ism, there is also the statist myth of communism. Marxists may argue over adequate interpretations of Marx's conception of the socialist state, but *statist communism*, even at first glance, is completely absurd to anyone who knows anything about the authentic Marx. . . .

Marx expected the socialist revolution to occur in the wealthiest capitalist countries. But Lenin rejected this assumption in both the theoretical and practical-political senses; indeed, historical practice has proved him right insofar as socialist revolutions have actually taken place in the undeveloped rather than the developed countries. On the other hand, those who found in Marx's assumption a more hidden, indirect sense of foreboding and caution were not far from the truth, either.

The absence of a large, developed industrial proletariat was one of the decisive causes of the statist perversion of the socialist revolution. Moreover, the small proletariat which did exist was decimated in the revolutionary struggle. We shall cite only some of the other extremely unfavorable factors in this respect: the feudal-capitalistic economic and social legacy of Russia, the atmosphere bred by a tradition of political absolutism and a low standard of education and culture, the world war, the obstinate counterrevolution and foreign intervention which devastated the land, the absence of effective support from the workers' movements of the developed countries, and the prolonged hostile encirclement. In such conditions the tendency toward statism was all the stronger and its victory all the more certain. Nevertheless, it cannot be said that the struggle for socialism was doomed in advance to failure. There is no "iron law" of revolutionary degeneration.* The triumph of the statist tendency, which as a rule has a great deal of vigor and endurance, can be prevented by persistent struggle on the part of the revolutionary forces.

But let us go half a century into the past. In Russia the revolutionary party had to take it largely upon itself to accomplish the mission of a yet undeveloped industrial proletariat. After the seizure and consolidation of power, it found itself confronted with a choice: either to develop the social self-government of the soviets of workers', soldiers', and peasants' deputies, or to base the entire system permanently and exclusively upon the state-party apparatus. It must be kept in mind that the idea of socialist self-government—based upon workers' self-management—was only theoretically sketched out in Marx's analysis of the Paris Commune and in Lenin's *State and Revolution.* Exactly how a socialist economy was going to look in practice was left quite vague. And to a certain extent this difficulty as well contributed to the victory of the statist tendency. . . .

In Stalinist society, where there are concentrations of political and economic power, wealth, and social prestige on the one hand, and of subjugation and exploitation on the other, the real relations between the ruling group and the proletariat can only be seen in terms of the following categorical symmetry: statist class—working class.

The statist class "adheres" firmly to Marxism (adapted, of course, to meet the circumstances) as its ideology. It uses the Marxist interpretation of socialism as the stage of preparation for classless society in order to lower an ideological veil over

---

*Robert Michels explicitly applied his "iron law of oligarchy" to the socialist movement: "The socialists may conquer, but not socialism, which would perish in the moment of its adherents' triumph." *Political Parties: A Sociological Study of the Oligarchic Tendencies of Modern Democracy* (Glencoe, Ill., 1915, 1949), p. 391.

class reality. When the Constitution of the U.S.S.R. was proclaimed in 1937, Stalin declared that the exploiting class had disappeared forever—and this at the very time that the new ruling class was passing through an intensive formative period. This is hardly unusual:

For each new class which puts itself in the place of one ruling class before it, is compelled, merely in order to carry through its aim, to represent its interest as the common interest of all the members of society . . . ; it will give its ideas the form of universality, and represent them as the only rational, universally valid ones.*

The statist class modestly legitimizes itself as the representative of the class which it actually exploits. . . .

In order to avoid any misunderstanding and at the same time to neutralize another possible objection to my thesis, I wish to emphasize that we may appreciate the progressiveness of statism over the capitalism of tsarist Russia without any sense of discomfort. The October Revolution did indeed run out of steam after a while. Nevertheless, statism did produce a great deal of progress in Russia. Our concern here is with a completely ascendant ruling class.

The U.S.S.R. has been transformed from backward Russia into one of two economic, political, cultural, and military superpowers of the world. Its share in world industry has grown from three per cent to twenty per cent, and its gross product is more than half that of the United States. While Russia's population was among the most illiterate and uneducated in the world, the U.S.S.R. today ranks among the highest both in its level of literacy and in the number of personnel working in the cultural, artistic, technical, and medical fields. Its free child care, and medical and social care, as well as schooling, are among the best in the world. In no other country has the emancipation of women proceeded with such speed. The above evidence is usually justly supplemented by citing the fact that the U.S.S.R. played the greatest role in defeating nazism in World War II.

However, even given the great progress made by the U.S.S.R., it does not at all follow that Stalinism was justified. The correct question does not involve how much progress there was, but whether there was an optimum degree of progress. Would there have been less progress or more had the Stalinist path not been chosen? Obviously any answer to this question can only be hypothetical.

How does this progress look as viewed from the other side? The final balance also includes: the millions of victims of Stalinism; the annihilation of the commanding cadres of the Red Army and the real unpreparedness of the U.S.S.R. to defend itself, for which it had to pay with an inordinate amount of human death and material destruction; the disarray of the Communist parties unable to organize resistance to nazism and thus help Russia; an agriculture ruined by a bloody period of collectivization from which it did not recover for a long time; the excessively low level of social science and philosophy; the stagnation of individual arts, also due to their vulgar politicization; and finally, the subordination of the international Communist movement to the Stalinist party with serious consequences, especially for the internal development of the Eastern European countries. The conclusion to be drawn from all this is that the U.S.S.R. would have been stronger in a political, cultural, and moral sense had the forces of Stalinism not triumphed. . . .

Beginning with the bloody collectivization of the peasantry in the U.S.S.R. at

---

*Marx, *The German Ideology*, pp. 40–41.

the end of the 1920's, through the mass extermination of Communists in the 1930's, the Stalinist offensive against Yugoslavia from 1943 on, the military intervention in Hungary in 1956, and concluding with the occupation of Czechoslovakia—and we only cite a few examples—Marxists have despairingly asked themselves the same question time and again: How is all this possible in *socialism*? But as the question is incorrectly formulated, no satisfactory answer can be given. We must liberate ourselves from the theoretical framework surrounding this question and simply ask: How is all this possible?

"Socialism" in which debureaucratization and democratization, economic decentralization, the elimination of political terror and censorship, the introduction of workers' self-management, the attainment of national sovereignty, and so on—in which all this represents counterrevolution, can hardly be called socialism in Marx's sense of the term. Nevertheless, many people are still trying to convince the *Stalinist oligarchy* that its aggression against Czechoslovakia dealt a serious blow to the cause of *socialism*, and are naïvely awaiting some positive results.

The case of Czechoslovakia has put all Marxists up against the wall. They must either unmask the statist myth of socialism or whirl helplessly within the circle of questions of how this is possible in socialism. If they opt for the second alternative, they still concede implicitly that socialism is at fault for the Czech case as well. With the aggression against Czechoslovakia the last socialist veil fell from the face of the oligarchic-statist system. Palliative explanations will no longer suffice. . . .

Under the pretense of preventing a bourgeois counterrevolution, the Stalinist oligarchy carried out a statist *counterrevolutionary* intervention in Czechoslovakia. On this occasion the internal system of the U.S.S.R. was manifested as well in its relations with the other countries of Eastern Europe. A small degree of relaxation in discipline within the Warsaw bloc was not essentially disturbing the U.S.S.R.'s dominant position in defining the external policy and internal arrangement of the countries of the bloc. The Stalinist oligarchy does not even permit different paths to statism, much less to socialism. . . .

Hope of socialist changes in the U.S.S.R. in the *long* run can be based upon the following factors: Statism, having carried out rapid industrialization, has thereby created a mass industrial proletariat to serve as its own "gravedigger." As we have seen, history already knows of attempts of the Eastern European working class to create its own organs of self-management. In this connection we should also count on the boomerang effect of the Marxist self-rationalization of statism. True Marxism, with its revolutionary-humanist program, the core of which is a plea for free association of the producers, will exert strong pressure in the direction of socialist change.

The Stalinist party has not seen fit to strike self-management totally from its program, but "merely" to postpone it to the communist future. But this postponement cannot go on indefinitely without irrevocably forfeiting the Marxist and Communist ideological legitimacy which the statist party has gone to such lengths to establish. Fifty years after the revolution the working class has still not won the right to participate in the management of the enterprise, although it has already won this right in some capitalist countries. Statism has provided the opportunity for mass education and has created an extremely large intelligentsia. It can be assumed that one part of it will help the masses to penetrate the ideological veil of statism and to shatter the information vacuum into which that system has cast them.

Détente

Notwithstanding the fall of Khrushchev, the Vietnam War, and the various changes of administration in the United States, Soviet-American relations steadily improved from the mid-sixties to the early seventies, culminating in President Nixon's visit to Moscow in 1972 to sign the treaties limiting intercontinental and anti-ballistic missiles. The visit was reciprocated when Brezhnev travelled to the U.S. the following year, and the mood of détente peaked in 1975 with the signing of the Helsinki Agreement on European security and human rights.

a) Nixon in Russia

Esteemed Mr. President, esteemed Mrs. Nixon, ladies and gentlemen, comrades: Let me, on behalf of the Presidium of the Supreme Soviet of the U.S.S.R. and the Soviet Government, greet you, Mr. President, your wife, and all those who accompany you on your visit to the Soviet Union. This is the first official visit by a President of the United States of America in the history of relations between our countries. This alone makes your visit and meetings between you and the Soviet leaders a momentous event. The results of the talks will predetermine in many ways prospects of relations between the Soviet Union and the United States. Their results will, apparently, have an effect on the further development of the international situation either toward a lasting peace and stronger universal security or toward greater tension.

We proceed from the fact that personal contacts and frank exchange of opinions between the leaders of states help search for mutually acceptable decisions in line with the interests of the peoples and of preserving peace, and overcome difficulties caused by factors of different origin and character.

Therefore great importance is attached in the Soviet Union to Soviet-American talks which should cover a wide range of questions. We approach these talks from realistic positions and will make every effort in accordance with the principles of our policy to achieve positive results and try to justify the hopes placed in our countries and beyond them in the Soviet-American summit meeting in Moscow.

We expect a similar approach from the American side.

Mr. President, you already had today a meeting with L. I. Brezhnev, General Secretary of the CPSU Central Committee, during which an exchange of opinions was started on the problems of Soviet-American relations and the present international situation.

The principles of our policy in international affairs and in relations with other states, the United States of America included, are well known. They were recently set forth again most definitely and clearly in the decisions of the 24th Congress of our party and the just-closed plenary meeting of the CPSU Central Committee. We have been guided and intend to be guided unswervingly by these principles in our practical activities. The Soviet Union, together with the countries of the Socialist community and all other peace forces, comes out consistently in defense of peace, for the deliverance of the present and future generations from the threat of war, from the disasters of a nuclear conflict, and for the elimination of hotbeds of war.

We stand for a radical turn toward relaxation of the existing tensions in all continents of the world, for freeing the peoples from the heavy arms burden, for a

FROM: Toast by President Nikolai V. Podgorny at Dinner Honoring President Nixon, Moscow, May 22, 1972 (*Department of State Bulletin*, LXVI:1722, June 26, 1972, pp. 863–64).

peaceful political settlement of problems through negotiation and with due account taken of the aspirations and will of the peoples and their inalienable right to decide their destinies themselves without interference and pressure from outside.

As far back as in the early years of the young Soviet state, its founder V. I. Lenin substantiated the objective need for and possibility of peaceful coexistence of countries with different social systems. Today, as before, the Soviet Union is prepared to develop and deepen relations of business cooperation and mutually beneficial ties with states of a different social system.

This fully applies to the relations with the United States also in the sense that peaceful coexistence must not be limited to absence of war. When we say that there is no exception for the United States in our policy of peaceful coexistence, these words are backed by our actual striving for the improvement and development of Soviet-American relations. The Soviet Union deems it possible and desirable to establish not merely good but friendly relations between the U.S.S.R. and the United States, certainly, not at the expense of any third countries or peoples. . . .

I would like to propose a toast to the success of the talks, to their serving the interests of the peoples of our countries, the interests of peace and international security.

To the health of Mr. President and Mrs. Nixon.

b) The SALT I Treaty

The United States of America and the Union of Soviet Socialist Republics, hereinafter referred to as the Parties,

Convinced that the Treaty on the Limitation of Anti-Ballistic Missile Systems and this Interim Agreement on Certain Measures with Respect to the Limitation of Strategic Offensive Arms will contribute to the creation of more favorable conditions for active negotiations on limiting strategic arms as well as to the relaxation of international tension and the strengthening of trust between States,

Taking into account the relationship between strategic offensive and defensive arms,

Mindful of their obligations under Article VI of the Treaty on the Non Proliferation of Nuclear Weapons,

Have agreed as follows:

Article I

The Parties undertake not to start construction of additional fixed land-based intercontinental ballistic missile (ICBM) launchers after July 1, 1972.

Article II

The Parties undertake not to convert land-based launchers for light ICBMs, or for ICBMs of older types deployed prior to 1964, into land-based launchers for heavy ICBMs of types deployed after that time.

Article III

The Parties undertake to limit submarine-launched ballistic missile (SLBM) launchers and modern ballistic missile submarines to the numbers operational and

FROM: Interim Agreement on Limitation of Strategic Offensive Arms, May 26, 1972 (*Department of State Bulletin*, LXVI:1722, June 26, 1972, pp. 920-21).

under construction on the date of signature of this Interim Agreement, and in addition to launchers and submarines constructed under procedures established by the Parties as replacements for an equal number of ICBM launchers of older types deployed prior to 1964 or for launchers on older submarines.

Article IV

Subject to the provisions of this Interim Agreement, modernization and replacement of strategic offensive ballistic missiles and launchers covered by this Interim Agreement may be undertaken.

Article V

1. For the purpose of providing assurance of compliance with the provisions of this Interim Agreement, each Party shall use national technical means of verification at its disposal in a manner consistent with generally recognized principles of international law.

2. Each Party undertakes not to interfere with the national technical means of verification of the other Party operating in accordance with paragraph 1 of this Article.

3. Each Party undertakes not to use deliberate concealment measures which impede verification by national technical means of compliance with the provisions of this Interim Agreement. This obligation shall not require changes in current construction, assembly, conversion, or overhaul practices.

Article VI

To promote the objectives and implementation of the provisions of this Interim Agreement, the Parties shall use the Standing Consultative Commission established under Article XIII of the Treaty on the Limitation of Anti-Ballistic Missile Systems in accordance with the provisions of that Article.

Article VII

The Parties undertake to continue active negotiations for limitations on strategic offensive arms. The obligations provided for in this Interim Agreement shall not prejudice the scope of terms of the limitations on strategic offensive arms which may be worked out in the course of further negotiations. . . .

For the United States of America:
RICHARD NIXON, President of the United States of America
For the Union of Soviet Socialist Republics:
LEONID I. BREZHNEV, General Secretary of the Central Committee of the CPSU

c) Brezhnev in America

Esteemed Mr. President, esteemed Mrs. Nixon, ladies and gentlemen, comrades: Tonight it is my very pleasant duty to welcome you, Mr. President, and your wife and members of the U.S. Government and other distinguished American guests here at the Soviet Embassy in Washington.

FROM: Brezhnev, Toast at Soviet Embassy dinner, June 21, 1973 (*Department of State Bulletin*, LXLX:1778, July 23, 1973, pp. 117-19).

On behalf of my comrades and myself, I would like first of all to cordially thank you personally, Mr. President and Mrs. Nixon, and other members of your family, for the warmth and consideration with which you have been surrounding us from the very start of our visit to your country.

At the same time I would like to say that we are grateful to all Americans who have shown their friendly feelings toward us and taken a lively interest in our visit and our negotiations. In all this we see a confirmation of the respect harbored by the people of the United States toward Soviet people and evidence of the mutual desire of our two peoples to live together in peace and friendship.

An awareness of our high duty and responsibility is permeating the entire course of our meetings. Our talks bear the hallmark of a vigorous pace, a broad scope, and a businesslike and constructive spirit. Each day, all this is yielding tangible results, bringing us closer to the jointly set objectives of securing a further major advance in the development of Soviet-American relations, of lessening the threat of war, and of strengthening peace and security on our planet.

The contribution made by our two nations to the attainment of this paramount goal will undoubtedly raise Soviet-American relations to a new level. In May of last year we agreed that in the nuclear age there is no alternative to conducting relations between our countries on the basis of peaceful coexistence. We can now confidently say that this fundamental principle is being increasingly imbued with concrete substance.

We are convinced that the results of our talks will strengthen still more the relations of peace and mutual trust between the Soviet Union and the United States. At the same time, new vistas will be opened for the constructive development of those relations.

The new step forward which it has proved possible to take through joint efforts in so vitally important and at once so complex a problem as the limitation of Soviet and American strategic arms is also something that cannot fail to cause satisfaction.

The agreement achieved on the basic principles for further negotiations on this problem contains everything to give a new impetus and a clear direction to joint work on important agreements designed not only to curb but also to reverse the race of the most formidable and costly types of rocket nuclear arms and thus to permit our countries to switch more resources to constructive purposes and use them to better man's life.

Atomic energy, too, must ever increasingly serve the aims of peace. The readiness of our two nations to promote that objective through joint efforts has been reflected in the agreement on cooperation in the field of the peaceful uses of atomic energy which President Nixon and I also signed today.

In pursuance of the line jointly initiated during last year's meeting in Moscow, a new series of agreements on cooperation between the U.S.S.R. and the United States in several other fields of science, technology, and culture was signed in the course of this visit. This we also value highly. It will give Soviet-American relations still greater diversity and stability. At the same time, we are sure the development of such cooperation will benefit other peoples, too, since it is aimed at solving problems that are important for all mankind.

Of course, in the relations between our two countries there are still quite a few outstanding problems and, I would say, some unfinished business. In particular this relates to the sphere of strategic arms limitation and also to commercial and economic matters. . . .

. . . The Soviet Union's line at improving relations with the United States is not some temporary phenomenon. It is a firm and consistent line reflecting the permanent principles of Soviet foreign policy formulated by the great founder of the Soviet state, V. I. Lenin. It is a line that rests on the full support of our people.

Soviet people believe that most Americans, too, approve of the jointly initiated line aimed at strengthening peace and cooperation between the peoples of the Soviet Union and of the United States.

Unfortunately the tight schedule of our talks has not left me much of a chance to learn more about your great country and to get a closer look at the life of Americans. But the little I have managed to see seemed to me to be very interesting indeed. To some extent I hope to be able to fill in that gap when, at your invitation, Mr. President, we go to the west coast of the United States, to California, long famous for the beauty of its nature and more recently for its surging industrial development.

I would like to use this very pleasant opportunity when we are all together here at the Soviet Embassy to confirm the invitation conveyed to you, Mr. President, on behalf of the Presidium of the U.S.S.R. Supreme Soviet and the Soviet Government to make an official visit to the Soviet Union in 1974. . . .

The cause of developing Soviet-American relations is indeed moving forward. In two years Soviet and American astronauts will fly into outer space to carry out the first major joint experiment in man's history. Now they know that from up there in space our planet looks even more beautiful, though small. It is big enough for us to live in peace, but too small to be subjected to the threat of nuclear war.

I shall be making no mistake if I say that the spirit of our talks and the main direction of our joint efforts were determined by an awareness of one major factor: Everything must be done for the peoples of the world to live free from war, to live in security, cooperation, and communication with one another. That is the imperative command of the times, and to that aim we must dedicate our joint efforts. . . .

d) The Helsinki Accords

Declaration on Principles Guiding Relations between Participating States

The participating States,

Reaffirming their commitment to peace, security and justice and the continuing development of friendly relations and co-operation;

Recognizing that this commitment, which reflects the interest and aspirations of peoples, constitutes for each participating State a present and future responsibility, heightened by experience of the past;

Reaffirming, in conformity with their membership in the United Nations and in accordance with the purposes and principles of the United Nations, their full and active support for the United Nations and for the enhancement of its role and effectiveness in strengthening international peace, security and justice, and in prompting the solution of international problems, as well as the development of friendly relations and co-operation among States;

Expressing their common adherence to the principles which are set forth below

FROM: Conference on Security and Cooperation in Europe: Final Act, Helsinki, August 1, 1975 (*Department of State Bulletin*, LXXIII:1888, September 1, 1975, pp. 324–26).

and are in conformity with the Charter of the United Nations, as well as their common will to act, in the application of these principles, in conformity with the purposes and principles of the Charter of the United Nations;

Declare their determination to respect and put into practice, each of them in its relations with all other participating States, irrespective of their political, economic or social systems as well as of their size, geographical location or level of economic development, the following principles, which all are of primary significance, guiding their mutual relations:

I. *Sovereign equality, respect for the rights inherent in sovereignty*

The participating States will respect each other's sovereign equality and individuality as well as all the rights inherent in and encompassed by its sovereignty, including in particular the right of every State to juridical equality, to territorial integrity and to freedom and political independence. They will also respect each other's right freely to choose and develop its political, social, economic and cultural systems as well as its right to determine its laws and regulations.

Within the framework of international law, all the participating States have equal rights and duties. They will respect each other's right to define and conduct as it wishes its relations with other States in accordance with international law and in the spirit of the present Declaration. They consider that their frontiers can be changed, in accordance with international law, by peaceful means and by agreement. They also have the right to belong or not to belong to international organizations, to be or not to be a party to bilateral or multilateral treaties including the right to be or not to be a party to treaties of alliance; they also have the right to neutrality.

II. *Refraining from the threat or use of force*

The participating States will refrain in their mutual relations, as well as in their international relations in general, from the threat or use of force against the territorial integrity or political independence of any State, or in any other manner inconsistent with the purposes of the United Nations and with the present Declaration. No consideration may be invoked to serve to warrant resort to the threat or use of force in contravention of this principle.

Accordingly, the participating States will refrain from any acts constituting a threat of force or direct or indirect use of force against another participating State. Likewise they will refrain from any manifestation of force for the purpose of inducing another participating State to renounce the full exercise of its sovereign rights. Likewise they will also refrain in their mutual relations from any act of reprisal by force.

No such threat or use of force will be employed as a means of settling disputes, or questions likely to give rise to disputes, between them.

III. *Inviolability of frontiers*

The participating States regard as inviolable all one another's frontiers as well as the frontiers of all States in Europe and therefore they will refrain now and in the future from assaulting these frontiers.

Accordingly, they will also refrain from any demand for, or act of, seizure and usurpation of part or all of the territory of any participating State.

IV. *Territorial integrity of States*

The participating States will respect the territorial integrity of each of the participating States.

Accordingly, they will refrain from any action inconsistent with the purposes and principles of the Charter of the United Nations against the territorial integrity, political independence or the unity of any participating State, and in particular from any such action constituting a threat or use of force.

The participating States will likewise refrain from making each other's territory the object of military occupation or other direct or indirect measures of force in contravention of international law, or the threat of them. No such occupation or acquisition will be recognized as legal.

V. *Peaceful settlement of disputes*

The participating States will settle disputes among them by peaceful means in such a manner as not to endanger international peace and security, and justice. . . .

Participating States, parties to a dispute among them, as well as other participating States, will refrain from any action which might aggravate the situation to such a degree as to endanger the maintenance of international peace and security and thereby make a peaceful settlement of the dispute more difficult.

VI. *Non-intervention in internal affairs*

The participating States will refrain from any intervention, direct or indirect, individual or collective, in the internal or external affairs falling within the domestic jurisdiction of another participating State, regardless of their mutual relations.

They will accordingly refrain from any form of armed intervention or threat of such intervention against another participating State.

They will likewise in all circumstances refrain from any other act of military, or of political, economic or other coercion designed to subordinate to their own interest the exercise by another participating State of the rights inherent in its sovereignty and thus to secure advantages of any kind.

Accordingly, they will, inter alia, refrain from direct or indirect assistance to terrorist activities, or to subversive or other activities directed towards the violent overthrow of the regime of another participating State.

VII. *Respect for human rights and fundamental freedoms, including the freedom of thought, conscience, religion or belief*

The participating States will respect human rights and fundamental freedoms, including the freedom of thought, conscience, religion or belief, for all without distinction as to race, sex, language or religion.

They will promote and encourage the effective exercise of civil, political, economic, social, cultural and other rights and freedoms all of which derive from the inherent dignity of the human person and are essential for his free and full development.

Within this framework the participating States will recognize and respect the freedom of the individual to profess and practise, alone or in community with others, religion or belief acting in accordance with the dictates of his own conscience.

The participating States on whose territory national minorities exist will respect the right of persons belonging to such minorities to equality before the law, will afford them the full opportunity for the actual enjoyment of human rights and fundamental freedoms and will, in this manner, protect their legitimate interests in this sphere. . . .

VIII. *Equal rights and self-determination of peoples*

The participating States will respect the equal rights of peoples and their right to self-determination, acting at all times in conformity with the purposes and principles of the Charter of the United Nations and with the relevant norms of international law, including those relating to territorial integrity of States.

By virtue of the principle of equal rights and self-determination of peoples, all peoples always have the right, in full freedom, to determine, when and as they wish, their internal and external political status, without external interference, and to pursue as they wish their political, economic, social and cultural development. . . .

IX. *Co-operation among States*

The participating States will develop their co-operation with one another and with all States in all fields in accordance with the purposes and principles of the Charter of the United Nations. . . .

X. *Fulfilment in good faith of obligations under international law*

The participating States will fulfil in good faith their obligations under international law, both those obligations arising from the generally recognized principles and rules of international law and those obligations arising from treaties or other agreements, in conformity with international law, to which they are parties. . . .

Eurocommunism

The swing of Western Communists away from Soviet-style orthodoxy and toward the democratic reformism long defended by Social Democrats was articulated most dramatically by the longtime Spanish Communist leader Santiago Carrillo, who espoused the new line upon his emergence from underground politics following the death of Franco and the dismantling of his dictatorship in 1975-76. Most European Communist parties, above all the Italian, subscribed to this criticism of the internal and external conduct of the Soviet regime. Of major Communist parties functioning in democratic countries, only the Portuguese and the French continued to support Soviet positions.

. . . Our policy in the Popular Front period already contained in embryo the conception of an advance to socialism with democracy, with a multiparty system, parliament, and liberty for the opposition. As for the excesses that took place in one direction or another, and they did take place, excesses that would have been unthinkable in a normal democratic situation, the cause of these might be sought in the passions of a civil war unleashed by the right, which opened up the deep wounds inflicted by age-old oppression and exploitation. As a result, it is not only from a Marxist analysis of present-day reality, but also from our own complex experience, that we derive the arguments in favour of the democratic socialism we advocate for our country.

Whilst there are in our past political positions features on which our present political line is based—I am referring here to the case of Spain—anyone who examines the experience of the Western European Communist parties after the Second World War will see that they have adjusted their activity to democratic practices, without overstepping them at any time. In 1945 Communists were taking part as ministers in all the governments of Western Europe except in Britain and the Federal Republic of Germany, and not just because the anti-Hitler coalition existed between the USSR and the western powers, although this helped, but because during the resistance to Hitlerism in Europe, the Communists were in the forefront— as on every occasion when liberty had to be fought for—and thus won an outstanding position among the forces which in each country played the leading part in opening the way to victory.

The years from 1945 to 1947 were the years of the greatest democratic expansion on our continent. In 1947 the beginning of the Cold War created a new correlation of forces; there was the union between the social-democratic forces and the bourgeoisie under the aegis of the United States, against the Communists. Following this, the Communists left the governments and went into opposition without attempting, in any western country, to hold on by force to the positions they were losing in the governments.

It will be said that this attitude corresponded to the division of zones of influence established at Yalta by the great powers. What is certain, however, is that in Greece, at that time, civil war was raging and the Communists were fighting with arms in their hands against the existing authorities, who were backed by the Americans, and it seems clear that at Yalta Greece remained on the western side. In countries like Italy and France the Communists were very strong and if the party had called on them to recover the arms that had been buried in the resistance, they would have done so and would have fought. Perhaps they would have been defeated, but they would have put up a considerable fight. Nevertheless they preferred to follow the democratic rules. They continued to develop a strategy directed towards unity and democracy—one which at that time might have seemed utopian— and in the course of long experience they worked out their own road to socialism based on democracy. It seems more convenient to many persons to judge the Western Communists by this or that phrase, or by the acts of other brother parties, than by the entire road which they have travelled—a road which has been long enough and consistent enough to provide the best of proofs.

In the course of charting the new roads, what was hardest to accomplish was the winning of autonomy in relation to the Soviet Union. The traditional links which united the Communists with the USSR had been maintained after the war, in spite of the dissolution of the Communist International, among other things because of the immense growth of Soviet prestige throughout the world, following the outstanding and decisive part played by the USSR in defeating Nazism.

The Cold War seemed, not only to Communists, but also to many people who were simply progressive, to be yet another repetition of the imperialist attempts to destroy the socialist gains with fire and sword. The theories of Foster Dulles and his like bore this out. At a time when, in addition, the United States had an overwhelming nuclear superiority, the idea would not readily have occurred to any Communist of breaking the bonds of deep feeling uniting him with the country of the first socialist revolution. . . .

It is true that we Communists have revised theses and formulas which we once regarded as articles of faith. It is true that long years of struggle against fascism have helped us see more clearly the true value of democracy—its true and, I would add, its permanent value. It is true that we have overcome a certain underestimation, already left far behind us, of so-called *formal liberties*. The monstrous crimes of imperialism, its obvious degeneration in all fields, have made freedom and democracy more precious to us. At the same time we have looked, without blinkers, at the weaknesses of democracy in the socialist societies in process of being born, and we have become more severely critical of deformations and breaches of democracy which we used to attribute earlier to reasons that made them seem less intolerable and led us even arrogantly to justify them in face of the class enemy.

We shall not, however, abandon the revolutionary ideas of Marxism; the ideas of the class struggle, historical materialism and dialectical materialism; the conception of a world-wide revolutionary process which is putting an end to imperialism—a process understood not as the defeat of this or that country, but as the defeat of a social system increasingly harmful to all countries, including those enabled by history to use that instrument to obtain a higher standard of living and lord it over the rest. Such a victory over an unjust system has to be supported by all countries, with their own struggle.

I am insisting on this, because some of those who see changes in our positions ask us whether we are not going back to the traditional positions of social democracy. Within our own movement, too, there is no lack of such more or less veiled accusations.

We are not returning to social democracy! In the first place because we are not in any way discarding the idea of coming to power in a revolutionary way, if the ruling classes were to close the democratic paths and a set of circumstances were to develop in which the revolutionary road would be possible. When we look at the present situation in Spain, with its specific features, we Communists, aware of its complexity, declare with a full sense of responsibility that today it is possible to pass from dictatorship to democracy without the use of force. It is one of those historical situations which are not easily repeated. And we are convinced, for the reasons given, that with democracy the road can be opened up to a new model of socialism which will maintain and increase liberties, without refusing them to an opposition prepared to wage the struggle at the ballot box and in the representative institutions. . . .

Socialism triumphed first in countries predominantly agricultural, because the revolutionary vanguard was able to combine the class contradictions with all kinds of contradictions peculiar to imperialism. There will be some who regard this as an historical anomaly. It is certainly the case that if socialism had triumphed first of all in the advanced countries, its results would have been more tangible and attractive, and would have come more quickly, for all mankind. Probably we would not have experienced the inadequacies, the distortions and even the degeneration that have occurred. . . .

As I see it, there is no doubt that the *dictatorship of the proletariat* was an unavoidable historical necessity, just as has been the case with revolutionary violence. I would add that such an instrument might still be necessary in some underdeveloped countries where revolution may occur as a result of the response to armed aggression by imperialism or to regimes of terror and violence which at some time or other may be plunged into crisis, come into collision with the majority of society and be unwilling to give way.

On the other hand, I am convinced that the dictatorship of the proletariat is not the way to succeed in establishing and consolidating the hegemony of the forces of the working people in the democratic countries of developed capitalism. In the first part of this essay I have already tried to explain why. I am convinced that in these latter countries socialism is not only the decisive broadening and development of democracy, the negation of any totalitarian conception of society, but that the way to reach it is along the democratic road, with all the consequences which this entails.

In this sphere, and at the risk of being accused of heresy, I am convinced that Lenin was no more than half right when he said:

The transition from capitalism to communism, naturally, cannot fail to provide an immense abundance and diversity of political forms, but the essence of all of them will necessarily be a single one: *the dictatorship of the proletariat* (*Collected Works*, vol. 25, p. 413).

He was no more than half right because the essence of all the various political forms of transition to socialism is, as we can judge today, *the hegemony of the working people*, while *the diversity and abundance of political forms* likewise entails the possibility of *the dictatorship of the proletariat not being necessary*. . . .

In actual fact the lack of democratic 'credibility' of us Communists among certain sections of the population in our countries is associated—rather than with our own activity and policy—with the fact that in countries where capitalist ownership has disappeared, the dictatorship of the proletariat has been implanted, with a one-party system, as a general rule, and has undergone serious bureaucratic distortions and even very grave processes of degeneration.

The contradictory aspect of this is that for many years, while we ourselves were pursuing a democratic policy, we took to ourselves and defended that model as if it had been our own, without any critical attitude. This, which was justified when the USSR was the only socialist country, ceased to be so after the Second World War, when the correlation of forces on the world scene had undergone a radical change.

Because of this, the struggle for socialism is demanding with increasing urgency that there should be internal criticism in the working-class and Communist movement, helping to find the correct roads for overcoming the shortcomings and errors and for arriving at an explanation of historical phenomena which still remain in a shadowy half-light.

The schema of a proletarian state outlined by Lenin in *The State and Revolution* has not been realised anywhere, and least of all in the country which has been presented to us and still is being presented to us today as the ideal model. Commenting on and developing the ideas of Marx and Engels in this work, Lenin says that all previous revolutions improved the State machine, and that what is needed is to smash it, to destroy it, and that this is the main and fundamental conclusion of the Marxist theory of the State.

With the October Revolution in the USSR, one type of State was destroyed; but in its place there has arisen a State much *improved*, that is to say, much more powerful, more organised, with mighty instruments of control—a State which, while speaking in the name of society, also finds itself situated above society. . . .

If all States are instruments for the domination of one class over another and if in the USSR there are no antagonistic classes and objectively there is no need to suppress other classes, then over whom does that State exercise domination?

The October Revolution has produced a State which is evidently not a bourgeois State, but neither is it as yet the proletariat organised as the ruling class, or a genuine workers' democracy.

Within that State there grew up and operated the Stalin phenomenon, with a series of formal characteristics similar to those of the fascist dictatorships. . . .

For a long time, with the formula of the 'cult of the individual', we attributed those phenomena to the personal characteristics of Stalin, and it is certainly true that they played a big part in this. We Marxists do not deny the role of individuals in history. But why was it that an individual with Stalin's characteristics, even though they had been condemned by Lenin, succeeded in imposing himself? It is true that Stalin knew how to exploit, with consummate skill, the contradictions that existed between the different groups that took shape within the leadership of the Communist Party of the Soviet Union, how to set himself up as the unifier and proceed to get rid of anyone able to obstruct his rise. Yet we must ask ourselves whether the practical significance of Stalin was not more in keeping with *the type of State* which was actually taking shape, with the objective realities that surrounded him, than was the case with his opponents, especially from the moment when illness reduced Lenin's possibilities of action and then caused his premature death.

It is clear that the Stalin phenomenon, which has been a form of totalitarianism extensively exploited by capitalist propaganda, has weakened the democratic credibility of the Communist parties among a section of the population in our countries.

The condemnation of the Stalinist horrors, pronounced by Khrushchev, temporarily broke up the entire system erected by Stalin, both in the USSR and in the socialist countries of the East. Events followed in Hungary and Poland, where there was formed, spontaneously and tacitly, a heterogeneous 'national front' against the Stalin system of rule. Whereas in Poland there was a Communist opposition to that system, capable of rectifying the situation, this did not happen in Hungary. It was Soviet troops who restored 'order': a fresh blow against the international prestige of Communism and one which also had repercussions as far as our own parties were concerned.

There were a number of years during which Khrushchev personified a new spirit of receptiveness towards the outside world and of greater freedom inside the country. This coincided with successes such as the launching of the first Sputnik, Gagarin's journey into space, new currents in Soviet literature and cinema, a cleaning up of the special repressive bodies and greater supervision over them. This was a period which resulted in a rise in the international prestige of the Soviet Union; however, it came to a speedy end.

Khrushchev was deposed by a sort of palace coup. His mistakes were 'exposed', when we had all come to believe that at last there was a collective leadership jointly responsible for good and ill. It is true that under Khrushchev's leadership there had arisen the conflicts with China—conflicts which he treated, in the light of what has since been emerging, with unquestionable levity and lack of awareness and with methods somewhat redolent of Stalin.

In actual fact, one of the causes of Khrushchev's downfall may have been his inability to transform the State apparatus created under Stalin, the *system* of political power to which Togliatti had referred and which eventually crushed Khrushchev. That system has not been transformed; it has not been made more democratic and it has even retained many of its aspects of coercion in relations with the socialist states of the East, as was brought out with brutal clarity by the occupation of Czechoslovakia.

The massive and annihilating repression of Stalin's day has ended. Khrushchev, deposed, died at home in his bed. There has been progress, tarnished by forms of oppression and repression in certain fields—and naturally in that of culture. Yet we still do not find ourselves looking at a State that can be regarded as a workers' democracy.

CHAPTER SEVEN

New Confrontations, 1975–1985

Toward the middle of the decade of the seventies, without any corresponding shift in internal politics, the pattern of Soviet international behavior rather abruptly changed. The signal at least coincidentally was the collapse of South Vietnam in 1975 after the removal of American troops from the war. A wide array of Soviet moves followed, to co-opt nationalistic revolutionary movements on the Cuban model and help them take power all over the Third World.

The installation of the MPLA in Angola was the prototype of this new strategy, then extended to Mozambique, Ethiopia, South Yemen, Afghanistan and Nicaragua. Soviet tactics in these areas were adroit and effective, especially the utilization of Cuban proxy forces and sentiments of anti-Zionism. On the other hand, in attempting to shore up the new Communist regime in Afghanistan the Soviets found themselves embroiled with a native resistance movement similar to what the United States had confronted in Vietnam.

While the Soviets nominally continued the line of détente, the success of their forward strategy and their progress toward nuclear and naval parity with the United States, coupled with heightened concern over Soviet human rights violations, proved fatal to the atmosphere of détente. Intervention in Afghanistan in 1979 and the crisis over the Solidarity movement in Poland in 1980–81, coinciding with the pronounced shift to the right in American politics, brought East-West relations virtually to a new state of Cold War. The American boycott in 1980 of the first Olympic Games ever to be held in Moscow, followed by the American-Soviet polemics over the downing of a South Korean airliner by a Soviet fighter plane, symbolized the confrontationist mood of the early 1980's, which the passage of leadership in Washington from Carter to Reagan and in Moscow from Brezhnev to Andropov did nothing to alleviate.

The trend toward moderation among Communists outside the area of direct Soviet influence nevertheless continued and even extended to China. After the death of Mao in 1976 China went through a virtual counterrevolution under the new leadership of Deng Xiao-ping [Teng Hsiao-p'ing],* repudiating not only the radicalism of the Cultural Revolution but also the earlier Soviet model of forced industrialization. In 1978–79 China's contest with the Soviet Union for influence in Southeast Asia produced the first cases [apart from border incidents] of military action between Communist governments, when the Soviet-backed government of united Vietnam intervened in Cambodia to suppress the Chinese-backed ultra-radicals and was in turn attacked by the Chinese in retaliation. Meanwhile the long history of hostility between China and the United States had been ended by the establishment of first *de facto* and then *de jure* diplomatic relations, thereby confront-

*The new "pin-yin" transliteration of Chinese names went into effect in 1979—Ed.

ing the Soviets with the two-front threat that they most feared. With the balance of power swinging against the Soviets, nuclear weapons and Third World anti-imperialism remained their high cards in the unpredictable game of global power status.

The Unification of Vietnam

American intervention in the Vietnam war came to a close with the Paris Accords of 1973. Two years later the forces of North Vietnam overwhelmed the Saigon government and finally unified the country. Shortly afterward the National Liberation Front and the People's Revolutionary Government of South Vietnam were dissolved, and the united "Socialist Republic of Vietnam" was proclaimed with a rigorous line of absorbing the South into a Soviet-style modernization drive.

A new page in our national history has begun. The first session of the Sixth Unified-Vietnam National Assembly, in accordance with the wishes of the people, recently decided to rename our country the Socialist Republic of Vietnam. The ever-victorious red banner with gold star of our people which first appeared during the Cochin China Uprising is the national flag. Two ripe rice stalks and half a bicycle gear on a red background with a gold star form the national emblem. The song "Tien Quan Ca" [Send Troops Forward Singing], which has been closely associated with the revolutionary struggle of our people since the days of preparing for the 1945 August General Uprising, is the national anthem. Heroic Hanoi, continuing the tradition of Dong Do and Thang Long, is the Capital of the Socialist Republic of Vietnam and the political, cultural, and economic center of the country. The National Assembly has selected the posts and organizations to lead our socialist State.

The Socialist Republic of Vietnam has come into being. A country of 50 million people is firmly progressing toward socialism. A country with a long civilization, after gaining complete independence and unification, is quickly turning to building the most advanced social system.

This important incident marks the historical turn of the revolution and social life of our country. The stage of the people's democratic national revolution under the democratic republican government has come to a glorious conclusion and the stage of socialist revolution throughout the country under the socialist republican government has begun. Our entire country is carrying out the strategic task of socialist revolution under the leadership of the party and the management of an undivided State, a socialist State. Regarding our people, this is the inheritance of the essence and wonderful traditions of our elders for holding up the high points of development with abundant and great vitality. . . .

Our country has walked a path full of thorns but one filled with victorious and brilliant heroic character also. Coming to the age of Ho Chi Minh and the present age of socialist revolution, our Fatherland is entering a period of the most all-round and brilliant development in history.

FROM: Editorial, "Long Live the Socialist Republic of Vietnam," *Nhan Dan* [Hanoi], July 3, 1976 (English translation in Joint Publications Research Service, Washington, #67787, pp. 26–28).

The birth of the Socialist Republic of Vietnam is the fruit of our people's long struggle. During 31 unforgettable years filled with heroic stories, counting from after the August Revolution, our country has had the "great honor of being a small country which has bravely fought and defeated two large imperialists, France and America, and made worthy contributions to the national liberation movement." During these 31 years full of trials and feats of war, our people, through their blood, sweat, and intelligence, have done great honor to our Fatherland.

In this sacred historical moment, enthusiastically celebrating the birth of the Socialist Republic of Vietnam, the entire party and army and all the people are above all expressing their deep gratitude to our beloved President Ho, our great class and national leader and the person who contributed his whole life to liberating the people, unifying the Fatherland, and building socialism in our country and who declared the birth of the Democratic Republic of Vietnam and led our people to today's glorious victory.

We respectfully bow and thank the heroes and war dead and all the people who bravely fought and made sacrifices for the independence and unification of the Fatherland and for socialism.

The Vietnamese revolution has moved to the stage of carrying on a socialist revolution throughout the country. With the establishment of the Socialist Republic of Vietnam, our people have clearly affirmed their firm resolve to build a wonderful society in their Vietnamese Fatherland and carry out completely President Ho's Testament of "building a peaceful, reunified, independent, democratic, and prosperous Vietnam and making a worthy contribution to the world revolution."

Successfully building a prosperous socialist country is the ideal, spiritual motive force, and daily target of action of each Vietnamese. Our party is resolved to continue and complete its historical mission of leading the socialist State and manifesting the ownership rights of the people in order to bring our Fatherland to the victory of socialist construction. And for all of us there is no joy equal to being able to stand under the banner of the party and striving to hit this great target.

Our nation has adequate material and spiritual conditions to successfully build a new system, a new economy, and a new man.

Our 50 million people, who have written the most glorious pages of history and taken our country to the heights of the period, have rights and are worthy of the right to enjoy a good life. Celebrating the birth of the Socialist Republic of Vietnam and greeting the first leaders of our socialist State, we see justifiable pride and unlimited confidence in the brilliant future of our beloved Fatherland rising up.

As Le Duan* said at the Sixth National Assembly of the Socialist Republic of Vietnam, First Session:

"We will certainly build a grander and more beautiful Fatherland these 10 days. We will certainly transform our country into a unified socialist country having a modern industry and agriculture, a strong national defense, a progressive culture and science, a civilized and happy way of life, and a worthy position in the world. We have adequate conditions for accomplishing this.

"Our present slogan of action is 'all for production, all for socialist construction, and all for a prosperous Fatherland and the happiness of the people.'

"For our socialist Fatherland and for the eternal independence, freedom, and

*Le Duan: Ho Chi Minh's successor as Vietnamese Communist chief—Ed.

happiness of our generation and future generations, all the people must bravely advance."

Long live the brave and great Vietnamese people.
Long live the Socialist Republic of Vietnam.

Ultra-Radicalism in Cambodia

The Communist victory in Vietnam was closely followed by the overthrow of the American-sponsored Lon Nol government of neighboring Cambodia by the Communist guerrillas known as the Khmer Rouge, led by Pol Pot and Khieu Samphan. The Khmer Rouge horrified outside observers by liquidating most of the urban and educated elements of the Cambodian population in the name of a purist agrarian equalitarianism originally encouraged by the Chinese Cultural Revolution and articulated by Pol Pot in an unpublished speech to the Khmer Rouge leadership. This experiment in violent utopianism was largely stamped out by the Vietnamese invasion of December, 1978, and the installation of the more conventional, pro-Soviet and anti-Chinese Communist government of Heng Samrin (which captured the Pol Pot documents).

Why must we move so swiftly?

Because enemies attack and torment us. From the east and the west they persist in pounding and worrying us; this is their strategy, to the east and to the west. If we are slow and weak, the contemptible people to the west will mistreat us also. If, on the other hand, we are strong and courageous for one, two, three or four years, the contemptible people to the east and the contemptible people to the west will be unable to do anything to us. If the livelihood of our people doesn't improve every year, our enemies shall certainly exploit us. This is an important aspect of our rationale. No matter how much we may hate the enemies, no matter how much we may want to defend the country, they will persist with a vengeance and penetrate our territory, if we are weak. If they do so, we'll remain in a defensive position rather than in a position to strike back.

But if we are strong, the contemptible people to the west will be unable to invade us; the contemptible people to the east will be unable to invade us too, and we will be in a position to strike back. Our capacity to strike back will stem from our being strong inside the country. . . .

Our socialism is characterized by its speed. Our methods are socialist methods; ours is a socialism fully conscious of every aspect. Compared to other countries, in terms of method, we are extremely fast.

Economics are connected with political methods. If political methods provide no contrary motion, no pulling back and forth, our economic methods can be swift. But if our political methods are individualistic, we will be drawn into a confusingly diverse economy. For example: to make a system of dikes, if we work as individualists, what can we accomplish? In a socialist system, if individualism is the basis, what can be accomplished? If it can be accomplished, only very little can be accom-

FROM: Pol Pot, "Preliminary Explanation before Reading the Plan, by the Party Secretary," August 1976, in David P. Chandler, Ben Kiernan, and Chanthou Boua, eds. & translators, *Pol Pot Plans the Future: Confidential Documents from Democratic Kampuchea, 1976–1977* (New Haven: Yale University Southeast Asia Studies, 1988, pp. 126–129, 138, 150–151, 156–160). Reprinted by permission.

plished. But if we have a firm collective system, canals can be dug swiftly, networks of canals can be built swiftly because nothing is pulling in a contrary direction. Political method, therefore, constitutes the determining factor. It pushes along and accomplishes production. If individualism is the basis, accomplishing objectives isn't easy. . . .

. . . Perform like combatants! We will choose anyone who can serve. Those who will not serve, will be given special work to perform. Problems must be solved according to the revolutionary movement of the people. The important issue is how the line will seep into people and be properly applied. If it is not yet clear, it must be clarified, drawing on experiences until it is seen to fit. . . .

. . . Which form of industry should we follow?

From the outset, some countries place their confidence in heavy industry. Heavy industry serves light industry and also serves agriculture. Some countries characteristically make these arrangements. But in our case, if we established heavy industries first—large steel mills, chemical factories, and primary industries, could we accomplish this or not? Particularly, in terms of capital, we have limits. Even in this Four-Year Plan, we have limits. We place a large proportion of capital into agriculture. If some capital is left over, should we use it to serve heavy industry? If we invested in heavy industry, we would do so at the expense of the peoples' livelihood.

Standing on these principles, we will develop light industry first and heavy industry later. The step toward light industry is the second, at this stage. We shall advance both kinds of industry together, but we should think first in terms of light industry, which serves the livelihood of the people and allows them to gain time. There's no need to buy from abroad. If we don't move forward in this fashion, we'll have to buy from abroad forever. We have sufficient capital for light industry, but not enough for heavy industry, and so we should advance light industry first. . . .

We've raised this problem because the outside world is always arguing about it. The Soviets have a good deal of heavy industry. Soviet light industry lags behind and doesn't serve the people's livelihood or agriculture sufficiently. At the end of 1975 and the beginning of 1976, the Soviets were short sixty million tons of foodstuffs.

The Soviets have moved from heavy industry to light industry to agriculture. We plan to move from agriculture to light industry to heavy industry. Is this line correct or not? We must be united on this issue. . . .

The goal of our collectivism is to raise the living standards of the people quickly and rapidly, including improved housing and eating their fill. But an important point which must be discussed in a systematic way is whether we are to improve the people's living standards in the direction of individualism or in the direction of collectivism. This problem is related to the problem of socialism. Accordingly, our plan is to raise the living standards of the people quickly, in the direction of collectivism. How should we proceed? If we proceed wrongly, we proceed in the direction of individualism. Drawing on the experience of other countries, we see that this poses many serious problems. Our livelihood must improve, but it will do so along collectivist lines.

There are two types of socialist countries. All of them profess socialism. But looking at socialist countries that have had their evolutions already and examining their ways of living, we see that there is collectivism, but not in ways of living, which remain individualistic in many cases. For example, they still have monthly salaries, they still have money to spend. In this way, every person thinks only of saving money to spend on food to eat his fill, to buy clothing, and so on. Some countries are aware of this and are engaged in battling individualism. Other countries, however, haven't become aware of the problem, and they are all moving in the direction of individualism, little by little. Investigating this, we see that they compete, but only for money. These contradictions lead to corruption in the factories, and competition on the collectives. Individualism continues to grow. Every individual thinks only of having a large salary, only of acquiring large amounts of money. Standing on these observations, we will not follow this path at all. We will follow the collectivistic path to socialism. If we do this, imperialism can't enter our country. If we are individualists, imperialism could enter easily. Thus, eating will be collectivized, and also clothing, welfare, and houses will be divided up on a collective basis. Food and dessert will be taken collectively. For this reason, food must be tasty, so that no one can criticize the notion of collectivism, saying that the food and dessert made collectively taste bad. The problem of the people cooking the food must be solved. People should not be allowed to take turns cooking. A core of competent people must be built up to prepare the food. This is a real problem connected with people's livelihood, but what is even more important is its relationship to politics. If it is difficult to arrange things in a collective way, the situation will deteriorate toward individualism. We must train good cooks. If they make tasty food, people will trust them and their stomachs will be full. If we move falsely on this issue and behave in a confused manner, we will walk the capitalist road. . . .

People's Villages

New villages must proceed in accordance with the plan. There must be a map and drawings and a plan for constructing the village, which must be followed rapidly, step by step.

We have the capacity to do it. But we must have a plan before setting out to make new villages. In the meantime, don't tear up the old ones. First make new villages, then tear down old houses. It should take ten years to remake all the villages. In ten years, their fields will be a deep green color. . . .

Edible materials belonging to the people

Rations range from three cans a day to two cans, to one can-and-a-half. There's a possibility that from 1978 on, people will have three cans a day, or at the very least two cans. This is an average. We have made these estimates using old figures which concerned two kinds of food. But, can we manage or not?

Fish must be raised everywhere so that every region will be able to raise fish. As for vegetables there are those that grow wild and those that we cultivate. This problem can be solved.

Desserts will be available in 1977 once every three days. If we compare this with earlier times this is plenty. In 1978 we will have dessert once a day, as in 1980. But can we accomplish this?

It's clear that we must accomplish this. We have nothing to do apart from serving the people. We have the capacity to solve this problem fully.

Resources for work and leisure

Should people rest, or not? According to our observations, working without any rest at all is bad for the health. There's not enough food for people to work all the time; and leisure increases one's strength. If a person doesn't rest, he gets very ill. It is a strategic objective to increase the strength of the people. Therefore, leisure must be considered to be basic. The schedule of free time shall be one day off out of ten and in a year from ten to fifteen days off for travel and study. Women will have two months' maternity leave. In these times they will perform very light tasks.

Places for supporting babies, children and old people

The first objectives are political; the second objectives have to do with production—mothers must not get too entangled with their children; there should be time (for the mothers) to go and work. Third, we must instill the doctrine of collectivism in our young people. Collectivism has rules and policies: socialism must be awakened from a very young age.

As for old people, it is the duty of our revolution to take care of them.

In terms of social policy and health, if we can proceed along these lines, the living standard of the people will rise, our policies will grow stronger, and our influence overseas will increase. . . .

. . . We want to set in motion our own system of schooling: primary and middle school for three years. Higher education is not to be continuous with this, but related to technical experience. The whole educational experience shall occupy nine years, but in this period people won't study every day, on every occasion, or on every hour. Every day there will be time for study, and time for production. Our goals won't allow us to abandon production. Our program is different from programs in effect throughout the world—in its essence, its timing, and its qualities, as well as in its methods of learning. But if we study in this way, will we gain knowledge or not? According to our observations, we study in order to serve the goals of the revolution. If we study and learn subject 1, it's to serve the movement directly; studying and learning subject 2 is to serve the revolution directly.

The first requirement after we learn letters and numbers is to learn technology. Our peasants aren't particularly literate, but they can study technical subjects and make progress.

Experimental technology is also of importance—such as technology involving rubber. Young people who know how to read and write, and who know some numbers, can study this technology.

To summarize, technical studies emerge from work and practice. Practice in turn teaches us technology. We stand on this in order to develop a firm policy, and so as not to allow other Parties to come in with ideas and dominate our independence. In the technology of oil, our male and female combatants have mastery. They benefit from their work experience and profit from it to gain knowledge.

In military matters, people who pilot our helicopters can't read a great deal. But by cultivating good political consciousness, we all can learn swiftly and we can exceed the plan's requirements. Formerly to be a pilot required a high school education—twelve to fourteen years. Nowadays, it's clear that political consciousness is the decisive factor. It shows us our line is correct. If we chose "culture," it would lead to a life and death disaster for the Party. This demonstrates our line. . . .

The Struggle for Independence in Angola

The military coup in Portugal in 1974 that overthrew the dictatorship long headed by António Salazar also opened the way to independence for the African colonies where nationalist guerrillas had been fighting Portuguese forces since the 1960's. In Angola, as independence approached in the fall of 1975, fighting broke out between the Soviet-backed MPLA (Popular Movement for the Liberation of Angola) and the Western-backed factions FNLA (National Front for the Liberation of Angola) and UNITA (National Union for the Total Independence of Angola). With Soviet aid and the assistance of Cuban troops, MPLA led by Agostinho Neto prevailed over its rivals and established an Angolan government with a militant anti-imperialist program.

The form of independence that Angola will have—on which the most varied opinions are being expressed in international lobbies—could well set an example for Africa and the world at large.

Our independence will not be tailored by African countries tied to capitalism. Neither will we accept an independence prepared in Europe by France, in America by the United States, or one devised in Africa by Zaire. The independence which we will achieve within the next 5 weeks shall be the fruit of many sacrifices, privations and of the loss of some of the best sons Angola has produced. For this reason, its independence will have to be exemplary.

It is therefore imperative and paramount that imperialism is isolated from all the international organizations to which it is affiliated.

It is imperative and paramount that a bloc is created within the ranks of the OAU [Organization of African Unity] that is impermeable to imperialist infiltration. The support which some African countries, admitted to the OAU as members, have been giving to organizations of bandits as in the case of UPA [Union of the Angolan Peoples] and FNLA-UNITA, will be a factor which determines whether the OAU is a progressive or a reactionary body.

Just as African countries, like Zaire and others, lend their support to the unjust struggle of the lackeys from the UPA-FNLA-UNITA and, in the debates of the OAU, warmly advocate the continued presence of those bandits in Angola, so also the just struggle of the Angolan peoples, guided by their vanguard the MPLA, has merited the support and understanding from progressive countries like Tanzania, Mozambique, Guinea-Bissau, Congo and others.

If one of the OAU's objectives is to give support to the just liberation struggles of the African peoples, then the Angolans will never be able to understand the acceptance which well-known puppet parties, like UNITA-FNLA, enjoy in the midst of the OAU.

The MPLA is the people and the people are the MPLA. The nations who are the friends of the Angolan people should regard the MPLA as the only and undisputable vanguard of the Angolan people. It is only by doing this that they will be

FROM: Radio Luanda, Statement on Independence and Imperialism, October 9, 1975 (English translation in Joint Publications Research Service, Washington, #66002, pp. 8–9).

able to separate the wheat from the chaff and support more openly the Angolan people, on the eve of their assuming responsibility for their own country.

Pragmatism in China

China's epoch of almost two decades of ultra-radicalism came to an abrupt end after the death of Mao Tse-tung in September, 1976, and the arrest of the "Gang of Four" headed by his wife, Chiang Ch'ing, the following month. Mao's chosen successor Hua Kuo-feng was pushed aside by the pragmatic faction of Teng Hsiao-p'ing, now Deputy Prime Minister after years in eclipse, who endorsed the programs of modernizing the economy with emphasis on decentralized initiative and consumer living standards. Great enthusiasm for such reforms was manifested in the posters that individuals were allowed to put up at "Democracy Wall" in Peking, but the movement went too far for the authorities, and the provocative author of the "Fifth Modernization" was convicted of counter-revolutionary activity and imprisoned until 1993. Nevertheless the party leadership proceeded with its reforms, and in 1981 issued a sweeping reconsideration of the mistakes made by the Communist regime during Mao's leadership.

a) The Fall of the Gang of Four

Red flags are flying over the mountains and rivers, everywhere in the motherland, and the faces of our 800 million people glow with joy. Hundreds of millions of people in all parts of our country have held mammoth demonstrations in the last few days. One million armymen and civilians yesterday met in a grand rally in Peking, the capital. They warmly celebrated Comrade Hua Kuo-feng's assuming the posts of Chairman of the Central Committee of the Communist Party of China and Chairman of the Military Commission of the C.P.C. Central Committee, hailed the great victory in smashing the plot of the anti-Party clique of Wang Hung-wen, Chang Ch'un-ch'iao, Chiang Ch'ing and Yao Wen-yuan to usurp Party and state power, and denounced with great indignation the towering crimes of the "gang of four." The whole Party, the whole army and the people of all nationalities throughout the country are determined to rally most closely round the Party Central Committee headed by Chairman Hua Kuo-feng, carry out Chairman Mao's behests, and carry the proletarian revolutionary cause through to the end.

Comrade Hua Kuo-feng was selected by the great leader Chairman Mao himself to be his successor. Chairman Mao proposed Comrade Hua Kuo-feng for the posts of First Vice-Chairman of the Central Committee of the Communist Party of China and Premier of the State Council in April 1976. Then, on April 30, Chairman Mao wrote to Comrade Hua Kuo-feng in his own handwriting "With you in charge, I'm at ease." In accordance with the arrangements Chairman Mao had made before he passed away, the October 7, 1976 resolution of the Central Committee of the Communist Party of China appointed Comrade Hua Kuo-feng Chairman of the Central Committee of the Communist Party of China and Chairman of the Military Commission of the C.P.C. Central Committee. This represents the common aspiration of the whole Party, the whole army and the people of the whole country and was a great victory in smashing the plot of the "gang

FROM: "Great Historic Victory," editorial in Renmin Ribao, October 25, 1976 (English translation in *Peking Review*, no. 44, October 29, 1976, pp. 14–16).

of four" to usurp Party and state power. It was a joyous event of immense historic significance. Comrade Hua Kuo-feng, in whom Chairman Mao had boundless faith and whom the people throughout the country deeply love, is now the leader of our Party, and our Party and state have a reliable helmsman to continue their victorious advance along Chairman Mao's proletarian revolutionary line.

The Party Central Committee headed by Comrade Hua Kuo-feng crushed the plot of the "gang of four" for a counter-revolutionary restoration and got rid of a big evil in our Party. Wang-Chang-Chiang-Yao had long formed a cabal, the "gang of four," engaged in factional activities to split the Party. The great leader Chairman Mao was aware of this long ago and severely criticized and tried to educate them again and again. . . .

Toward Chairman Mao's criticism and education, the "gang of four" took the attitude of counter-revolutionary double-dealers who comply in public but oppose in private. Not only did they not show the slightest sign of repentance, but on the contrary they went from bad to worse, further and further down the wrong path. During the period when Chairman Mao was seriously ill and after he passed away, they became more frantic in attacking the Party and speeded up their attempts to usurp the supreme leadership of the Party and state. We faced a grave danger of the Party turning revisionist and the state changing its political colour. At this critical moment in the Chinese revolution, the Party Central Committee headed by Comrade Hua Kuo-feng, representing the fundamental interests and common aspiration of the whole Party, the whole army and the people of the whole country and with the boldness and vision of the proletariat, adopted resolute measures against the "gang of four" anti-Party clique, smashed their plot to usurp Party and state power, and saved the revolution and the Party. Thus the proletariat won a decisive victory in counter-attacking the onslaught by the bourgeoisie.

The "gang of four," a bane to the country and the people, committed heinous crimes. They completely betrayed the basic principles of "three do's and three don'ts" that Chairman Mao had earnestly taught, wantonly tampered with Marxism-Leninism-Mao Tse-tung Thought, tampered with Chairman Mao's directives, opposed Chairman Mao's proletarian revolutionary line on a whole series of domestic and international questions, and practised revisionism under the signboard of Marxism. They carried out criminal activities to split the Party, forming a factional group, going their own way, establishing their own system inside the Party, doing as they wished, lording it over others, and placing themselves above Chairman Mao and the Party Central Committee. . . . They worshipped things foreign and fawned on foreigners, maintained illicit foreign relations, betrayed important Party and state secrets, and unscrupulously practised capitulationism and national betrayal. Resorting to various manoeuvres, they pursued a counter-revolutionary revisionist line, an ultra-Right line. Chairman Mao pointed out: **"You are making the socialist revolution, and yet don't know where the bourgeoisie is. It is right in the Communist Party—those in power taking the capitalist road. The capitalist-roaders are still on the capitalist road."** Wang Hung-wen, Chang Chun-chiao, Chiang Ching and Yao Wen-yuan are typical representatives of the bourgeoisie inside the Party, unrepentant capitalist-roaders still travelling on the capitalist road and a gang of bourgeois conspirators and careerists. . . .

While acclaiming our Party's great historic victory, the whole Party, the whole army and the people of all nationalities throughout the country, under the leadership of the Party Central Committee headed by Chairman Hua Kuo-feng, are determined to hold high the great red banner of Marxism-Leninism-Mao Tse-tung Thought, persist in taking class struggle as the key link, adhere to the Party's basic line and persevere in continuing the revolution under the dictatorship of the proletariat. We must thoroughly expose the vile crimes of the Wang-Chang-Chiang-Yao anti-Party clique, penetratingly criticize their counter-revolutionary revisionist line and eradicate its pernicious influence. It is imperative to draw a strict distinction between the two different types of contradictions and handle them correctly, earnestly implement Chairman Mao's principles **"Learn from past mistakes to avoid future ones and cure the sickness to save the patient"** and **"Help more people by educating them and narrow the target of attack,"** so as to unite with all those that can be united with. We should continue to criticize Teng Hsiao-p'ing and repulse the Right deviationist attempt to reverse correct verdicts. We should enthusiastically support socialist new things, consciously restrict bourgeois right and consolidate and develop the achievements of the Great Proletarian Cultural Revolution. We should **grasp revolution, promote production and other work and preparedness against war,** go all out, aim high and achieve greater, faster, better and more economical results in building socialism and continue to develop the excellent situation.

Having eliminated the "four pests," our Party has become even more united, even stronger and even more vigorous, and the dictatorship of the proletariat in our country is more consolidated. The masses of the people are in high spirits and militant everywhere in our motherland, orioles sing and swallows dart. Before us arises **"a political situation in which there are both centralism and democracy, both discipline and freedom, both unity of will and personal ease of mind and liveliness."** Since we have such a great Party, army and people, no difficulty whatsoever can stop our triumphant advance. Under the leadership of the Party Central Committee headed by Chairman Hua Kuo-feng, we are able to continue our advance in the socialist revolution in accordance with Chairman Mao's line and policies and, in accordance with the grand plan Chairman Mao mapped out, accomplish the comprehensive modernization of agriculture, industry, national defence and science and technology and build China into a powerful socialist country before the end of the century, so as to make a greater contribution to humanity and work for the final realization of communism.

b) The Four Modernizations and the Economic Readjustment

. . . In the early years after the founding of the People's Republic, especially after the socialist transformation was in the main completed, Comrade Mao Tse-tung instructed the whole party time and again to shift the focus of our work to the field of the economy and the technical revolution. Under the leadership of Comrade Mao Tse-tung and Comrade Chou En-lai, our party did a great deal for

FROM: Communiqué of the Third Plenum of the Central Committee of the CCP, December 22, 1978 (English translation in Foreign Broadcast Information Service, Washington, FBIS-CHI-78-248, December 26, 1978, pp. E4–E13; hereafter cited as FBIS).

socialist modernization and scored important achievements. But the work was later interrupted and sabotaged by Lin Piao* and the gang of four. Besides, we had some shortcomings and mistakes in our leading work because we lacked experience in socialist construction, and this also hampered the transition in the focus of our party's work. Since the nation-wide mass movement to expose and criticize Lin Piao and the gang of four has fundamentally come to a successful conclusion, though in a small number of places and departments the movement is less developed and still needs some time to catch up and so cannot end simultaneously, on the whole there is every condition needed for that transition.

Therefore the plenary session unanimously endorsed the policy decision put forward by Comrade Hua Kuo-feng on behalf of the Political Bureau of the Central Committee that, to meet the developments at home and abroad, now is an appropriate time to take the decision to close the large-scale nation-wide mass movement to expose and criticize Lin Piao and the gang of four and to shift the emphasis of our party's work and the attention of the whole people of our country to socialist modernization. This is of major significance for fulfillment of the three-year and eight-year programmes for the development of the national economy and the outline for twenty-three years for the modernizations of agriculture, industry, national defence, and science and technology, and for the consolidation of the dictatorship of the proletariat in our country. The general task put forward by our party for the new period reflects the demands of history and the people's aspirations and represents their fundamental interests. Whether or not we can carry this general task to completion, speed socialist modernization and on the basis of a rapid growth in production improve the people's living standards significantly and strengthen national defence—this is a major issue which is of paramount concern to all our people and of great significance to the cause of world peace and progress. Carrying out the four modernizations requires great growth in the productive forces, which in turn requires diverse changes in those aspects of the relations of production and the superstructure not in harmony with the growth of the productive forces, and requires changes in all methods of management, actions and thinking which stand in the way of such growth. Socialist modernization is therefore a profound and extensive revolution. There is still in our country today a small handful of counter-revolutionary elements and criminals who hate our socialist modernization and try to undermine it. We must not relax our class struggle against them, nor can we weaken the dictatorship of the proletariat. But as Comrade Mao Tse-tung pointed out, the large-scale turbulent class struggles of a mass character have in the main come to an end. . . .

The session points out that one of the serious shortcomings in the structure of economic management in our country is the over-concentration of authority, and it is necessary boldly to shift it under guidance from the leadership to lower levels so that the local authorities and industrial and agricultural enterprises will have greater power of decision in management under the guidance of unified state planning; big efforts should be made to simplify bodies at various levels charged with economic administration and transfer most of their functions to such enterprises as specialized companies or complexes; it is necessary to act firmly in line with eco-

---

*Lin Piao: General Mao's deputy during the Cultural Revolution; killed in a plane crash while fleeing after an alleged coup attempt in 1972—Ed.

nomic law, attach importance to the role of the law of value, consciously combine ideological and political work with economic methods and give full play to the enthusiasm of cadres and workers for production; it is necessary, under the centralized leadership of the party, to tackle conscientiously the failure to make a distinction between the party, the government and the enterprise, and to put a stop to the substitution of party for government and the substitution of government for enterprise administration, to institute a division of responsibilities among different levels, types of work and individuals, increase the authority and responsibility of administrative bodies and managerial personnel, reduce the number of meetings and amount of paperwork to raise work efficiency, and conscientiously adopt the practices of examination, reward and punishment, promotion and demotion. These measures will bring into play the initiative, enthusiasm and creativeness of four levels, the central departments, the local authorities, the enterprises and the workers, and invigorate all branches and links of the socialist economy. . . .

The plenary session holds that the whole party should concentrate its main energy and efforts on advancing agriculture as fast as possible because agriculture, the foundation of the national economy, has been seriously damaged in recent years and remains very weak on the whole. The rapid development of the national economy as a whole and the steady improvement in the living standards of the people of the whole country depends on the vigorous restoration and speeding up of farm production, on resolutely and fully implementing the policy of simultaneous development of farming, forestry, animal husbandry, side-occupations and fisheries, the policy of taking grain as the key link and ensuring an all-round development, the policy of adaptation to local conditions and appropriate concentration of certain crops in certain areas, and gradual modernization of farm work. This requires first of all releasing the socialist enthusiasm of our country's several hundred million peasants, paying full attention to their material well-being economically and giving effective protection to their democratic rights politically. Taking this as the guideline, the plenary session set forth a series of policies and economic measures aimed at raising present agricultural production. The most important are as follows: The right of ownership by the people's communes, production brigades and production teams and their power of decision must be protected effectively by the laws of the state: it is not permitted to commandeer the manpower, funds, products and material of any production team; the economic organizations at various levels of the people's commune must conscientiously implement the socialist principle of "to each according to his work," work out payment in accordance with the amount and quality of work done, and overcome egalitarianism; small plots of land for private use by commune members, their domestic side-occupations, and village fairs are necessary adjuncts of the socialist economy, and must not be interfered with; the people's communes must resolutely implement the system of three levels of ownership with the production team as the basic accounting unit, and this should remain unchanged. . . . After the purchase price of farm produce is raised, the urban workers must be guaranteed against a fall in their living standards. The market price of all food grain will remain unchanged, and the selling price of other farm products needed for daily life must also be kept stable; if some prices have to be raised, appropriate subsidies will be given to the consumers.

The plenary session also discussed the strengthening of education in agricultural science, the drafting of regional programmes for developing agriculture, forestry and animal husbandry, the establishment of modern farming, forestry, livestock-breeding and fishing centres, the active expansion of rural industry and side-occupations run by people's communes and production brigades, and other important questions, and decided upon relevant measures.

The plenary session points out that it is imperative to improve the livelihood of the people in town and country step by step on the basis of the growth of production. The bureaucratic attitude of paying no attention at all to urgent problems in the people's livelihood must be resolutely opposed. On the other hand, since our economy is still very backward at present, it is impossible to improve the people's livelihood very rapidly and it is essential to keep the people informed on the relevant state of affairs and to intensify education in the revolutionary ideas of self-reliance and hard struggle among the youth and other sectors of the people, and leading comrades at all levels must make themselves exemplars in this regard. . . .

The session held a serious discussion on the question of democracy and the legal system. It holds that socialist modernization requires centralized leadership and strict implementation of various rules and regulations and observance of labour discipline. Bourgeois factionalism and anarchism must be firmly opposed. But the correct concentration of ideas is possible only when there is full democracy. Since for a period in the past democratic centralism was not carried out in the true sense, centralism being divorced from democracy and there being too little democracy, it is necessary to lay particular emphasis on democracy at present, and on the dialectical relationship between democracy and centralism, so as to make the mass line the foundation of the party's centralized leadership and the effective direction of the organizations of production. . . .

The session emphatically points out that the great feats performed by Comrade Mao Tse-tung in protracted revolutionary struggle are indelible. Without his outstanding leadership and without Mao Tse-tung Thought, it is most likely that the Chinese revolution would not have been victorious up to the present. The Chinese people would still be living under the reactionary rule of imperialism, feudalism and bureaucrat-capitalism and our party would still be struggling in the dark. Comrade Mao Tse-tung was a great Marxist. He always adopted a scientific attitude of dividing one into two toward everyone, including himself. It would not be Marxist to demand that a revolutionary leader be free of all shortcomings and errors. It also would not conform to Comrade Mao Tse-tung's consistent evaluation of himself. The lofty task of the party Central Committee on the theoretical front is to lead and educate the whole party and the people of the whole country to recognize Comrade Mao Tse-tung's great feats in a historical and scientific perspective, comprehensively and correctly grasp the scientific system of Mao Tse-tung Thought and integrate the universal principles of Marxism-Leninism-Mao Tse-tung Thought with the concrete practice of socialist modernization and develop it under the new historical conditions.

The session holds that the Great Cultural Revolution should also be viewed historically, scientifically and in a down-to-earth way. Comrade Mao Tse-tung initiated this great revolution primarily in the light of the fact that the Soviet Union had turned revisionist and for the purpose of opposing revisionism and preventing its occurrence.

As for the shortcomings and mistakes in the actual course of the revolution, they should be summed up at the appropriate time as experience and lessons so as to unify the views of the whole party and the people of the whole country. . . .

c) The Wall Poster Movement

After the arrest of the Gang of Four, people eagerly hoped that Vice-Chairman Deng,* the so-called "restorer of capitalism," would once again appear as a great towering banner. Finally, Vice-Chairman Deng did return to his post on the Central Committee. The people were indeed excited. . . . However, to the people's regret, the hated old political system has not changed, and even any talk about the much hoped for democracy and freedom is forbidden. People's living conditions remain the same and the "increased wages" are far behind the soaring commodity prices. . . .

When Vice-Chairman Deng put forward the slogan "Be practical," people's enthusiasm was like surging waves. Time and again he was helped by the people to come to power. The people expected him to review the past and lead them to a realistic future with a "seeking truth from facts" approach.

However, some people have warned us: Marxism-Leninism-Mao Zedong Thought is the foundation of all foundations; Chairman Mao was the Great Savior of the people; "Without the Communist Party, there would be no new China"; "Without Chairman Mao there would be no new China"; and anyone disagreeing with these will come to no good end. "Some people" even warned us: Chinese people need dictatorship. His superiority over feudal emperors precisely shows his greatness. Chinese people need no democracy unless it is "democracy under collective leadership," without which democracy is not worth a dime. It is up to you to believe or to doubt it, but the prisons (from which so many have recently been released) were convincing "proof."

However, someone has now given you a way out. Take the Four Modernizations as the key link and follow the principle of stability and unity and be brave (?) to serve the revolution (?) as an old ox does. Then you will find your way to paradise, namely, the prosperity of communism and the Four Modernizations. Some well-intentioned people have given us this advice. "When you cannot think straight, try hard to study Marxism-Leninism-Mao Zedong Thought!" The reason why you cannot think straight is your lack of understanding which reflects on the level of your ideological accomplishment. You should be obedient, otherwise the leadership of your unit cannot forgive you! And on and on.

I advise everyone not to believe such political swindlers anymore. Knowing that we are being deceived, we should implicitly believe in ourselves. We have been tempered in the Cultural Revolution and cannot be that ignorant now. Let us find out for ourselves what should be done.

According to the definition of the Marxist ancestors, socialism means that the people, or the proletariat, are their own masters. Let me ask the Chinese workers and peasants: With the meager wages you get every month, whose master and what kind of master can you be? Sad to relate, you are "mastered" by somebody else even in the matter of matrimony. Socialism guarantees the producers' rights to the surplus production from their labor over what is needed as a service to the society. But this service is limitless. So are you not getting only that miserable little wage "necessary for maintaining the labor force for production"? Socialism guarantees

FROM: Wei Jingsheng, "The Fifth Modernization," January, 1979 (English translation in James D. Seymour, *The Fifth Modernization: China's Human Rights Movement, 1978–1979*, Pine Plains, N.Y., Coleman, 1980, pp. 47–50, 52–54). Reprinted by permission of the publisher.

*Deng Xiaoping (Teng Hsiao-P'ing in the old transliteration)—Ed.

many rights, such as the right of a citizen to receive education, to use his ability to the best advantage, and so forth. But none of these rights can be seen in our daily life. What we can see is only "the dictatorship of the proletariat" and "a variation of Russian autocracy"—Chinese socialist autocracy. Is this kind of socialist road what people want? Can it be claimed that autocracy means the people's happiness? Is this the socialist road depicted by Marx and hoped for by the people? Obviously not. Then what is it? Funny as it may sound, it is like the feudal socialism mentioned in the "Manifesto," or a feudal monarchy disguised as socialism. We have heard that Soviet Russia has been promoted from social feudalism to social imperialism. Must Chinese people take the same road? . . .

What is democracy? True democracy means the holding of power by the laboring masses. Are laborers unqualified to hold power? Yugoslavia has taken this road and proved to us that even without dictatorial rulers, big or small, the people can work even better.

What is true democracy? It means the right of the people to choose their own representatives to work according to their will and in their interests. Only this can be called democracy. Furthermore, the people must also have the power to replace their representatives anytime so that these representatives cannot go on deceiving others in the name of the people. This is the kind of democracy enjoyed by people in European and American countries. In accordance with their will, they could run such people as Nixon, de Gaulle, and Tanaka out of office. They can reinstate them if they want, and nobody can interfere with their democratic rights. In China, however, if a person even comments on the already dead Great Helmsman Mao Zedong or the Great Man without peers in history, jail will be ready for him with open door and various unpredictable calamities may befall him. What a vast difference will it be if we compare the socialist system of centralized democracy with the system of capitalist "exploiting class!" . . .

We want to be masters of our own destiny. We need no gods or emperors. We do not believe in the existence of any savior. We want to be masters of the world and not instruments used by autocrats to carry out their wild ambitions. We want a modern lifestyle and democracy for the people. Freedom and happiness are our sole objectives in accomplishing modernization. Without this fifth modernization all others are merely another promise. . . .

To accomplish modernization, Chinese people should first practice democracy and modernize China's social system. Democracy is by no means the *result* of social development as claimed by Lenin. Aside from being the inevitable outcome of the development of productive forces and the relations of production up to a certain stage, it is also the *condition* for the existence of productive forces and the relations of production, not only up to that certain stage but also at much higher stages of development. Without this condition, the society will become stagnant and economic growth will encounter insurmountable obstacles. Therefore, judging from past history, a democratic social system is the major premise or the prerequisite for all developments—or modernizations. Without this major premise or prerequisite, it would be impossible not only to continue further development but also to preserve the fruits of the present stage of development. The experiences of our great motherland over the past thirty years have provided the best evidence. . . .

. . . The biggest reactionary is always the biggest opponent of democracy. As clearly shown in the history of Germany, the Soviet Union, and "New China," the strongest opponent of democracy has been the biggest and most dangerous enemy of social peace and prosperity. From the history of these countries, we can also clearly see that the spearheads of all struggles by people for happiness and by societies for prosperity were directed against the enemies of democracy—the autocratic fascists. From the history of the same countries again, we can see that victory for democracy has always brought along with it the most favorable conditions and the greatest speed for social development. On this point, American history has supplied the most forceful evidence.

d) De-Maoization

After the basic completion of socialist transformation, our Party led the entire people in shifting our work to all-round, large-scale socialist construction. In the ten years preceding the "cultural revolution" we achieved very big successes despite serious setbacks. . . .

All the successes in these ten years were achieved under the collective leadership of the Central Committee of the Party headed by Comrade Mao Zedong [Mao Tse-tung]. Likewise, responsibility for the errors committed in the work of this period rested with the same collective leadership. Although Comrade Mao Zedong must be held chiefly responsible, we cannot lay the blame for all those errors on him alone. During this period, his theoretical and practical mistakes concerning class struggle in a socialist society became increasingly serious, his personal arbitrariness gradually undermined democratic centralism in Party life and the personality cult grew graver and graver. The Central Committee of the Party failed to rectify these mistakes in good time. Careerists like Lin Biao [Lin Piao], Jiang Qing [Chiang Ch'ing] and Kang Sheng,* harbouring ulterior motives, made use of these errors and inflated them. This led to the inauguration of the "cultural revolution."

The "cultural revolution," which lasted from May 1966 to October 1976, was responsible for the most severe setback and the heaviest losses suffered by the Party, the state and the people since the founding of the People's Republic. It was initiated and led by Comrade Mao Zedong. His principal theses were that many representatives of the bourgeoisie and counter-revolutionary revisionists had sneaked into the Party, the government, the army and cultural circles, and leadership in a fairly large majority of organizations and departments was no longer in the hands of Marxists and the people; that Party persons in power taking the capitalist road had formed a bourgeois headquarters inside the Central Committee which pursued a revisionist political and organizational line and had agents in all provinces, municipalities and autonomous regions, as well as in all central departments; that since the forms of struggle adopted in the past had not been able to solve this problem, the power usurped by the capitalist-roaders could be recaptured only by carrying out a great cultural revolution, by openly and fully mobilizing the broad masses from the bottom up to expose these sinister phenomena; and that the cul-

FROM: Resolution of the Central Committee, "On Certain Questions in the History of Our Party since the Founding of the People's Republic of China," June 27, 1981 (English translation in *Resolution on CPC History [1949-81]*, Beijing, Foreign Languages Press, 1981, pp. 24, 31-33, 35, 37-41, 44-47, 56-57, 73-74).

*Kang Sheng: Mao's secret police chief until his death in 1975—Ed.

tural revolution was in fact a great political revolution in which one class would overthrow another, a revolution that would have to be waged time and again. . . .

Nominally, the "cultural revolution" was conducted by directly relying on the masses. In fact, it was divorced both from the Party organizations and from the masses. After the movement started, Party organizations at different levels were attacked and became partially or wholly paralysed, the Party's leading cadres at various levels were subjected to criticism and struggle, inner-Party life came to a standstill, and many activists and large numbers of the basic masses whom the Party has long relied on were rejected. . . .

Comrade Mao Zedong's personal leadership characterized by "Left" errors took the place of the collective leadership of the Central Committee, and the cult of Comrade Mao Zedong was frenziedly pushed to an extreme. Lin Biao, Jiang Qing, Kang Sheng, Zhang Chunqiao [Chang Ch'un-ch'ao] and others, acting chiefly in the name of the "Cultural Revolution Group," exploited the situation to incite people to "overthrow everything and wage full-scale civil war." . . .

In 1970–71 the counterrevolutionary Lin Biao clique plotted to capture supreme power and attempted an armed counterrevolutionary coup d'état. Such was the outcome of the "cultural revolution" which overturned a series of fundamental Party principles. Objectively, it announced the failure of the theories and practices of the "cultural revolution." Comrades Mao Zedong and Zhou Enlai [Chou En-lai] ingeniously thwarted the plotted coup. Supported by Comrade Mao Zedong, Comrade Zhou Enlai took charge of the day-to-day work of the Central Committee and things began to improve in all fields. During the criticism and repudiation of Lin Biao in 1972, he correctly proposed criticism of the ultra-Left trend of thought. In fact, this was an extension of the correct proposals put forward around February 1967 by many leading comrades of the Central Committee who had called for the correction of the errors of the "cultural revolution." Comrade Mao Zedong, however, erroneously held that the task was still to oppose the "ultra-Right." . . .

In 1975, when Comrade Zhou Enlai was seriously ill, Comrade Deng Xiaoping, with the support of Comrade Mao Zedong, took charge of the day-to-day work of the Central Committee. He convened an enlarged meeting of the Military Commission of the Central Committee and several other important meetings with a view to solving problems in industry, agriculture, transport and science and technology, and began to straighten out the work in many fields so that the situation took an obvious turn for the better. However, Comrade Mao Zedong could not bear to accept systematic correction of the errors of the "cultural revolution" by Comrade Deng Xiaoping and triggered the movement to "criticize Deng and counter the Right deviationist trend to reverse correct verdicts," once again plunging the nation into turmoil. In January of that year [1976], Comrade Zhou Enlai passed away. Comrade Zhou Enlai was utterly devoted to the Party and the people and stuck to his post till his dying day. He found himself in an extremely difficult situation throughout the "cultural revolution." He always kept the general interest in mind, bore the heavy burden of office without complaint, racking his brains and untiringly endeavouring to keep the normal work of the Party and the state going, to minimize the damage caused by the "cultural revolution" and to protect many Party and non-Party cadres. He waged all forms of struggle to counter sabotage by the counter-revolutionary Lin Biao and Jiang Qing cliques. His death left the whole Party and people in the most profound grief. In April of the same year, a powerful movement of protest signalled by the Tian An Men Incident* swept the whole country, a movement to mourn for the late Premier Zhou Enlai and oppose the Gang of Four. In essence, the movement was a demonstration of support for the Party's correct leadership as represented by Comrade Deng Xiaoping. It laid the ground for massive popular support for the subsequent overthrow of the counterrevolutionary Jiang Qing clique. The Political Bureau of the Central Committee and Comrade Mao Zedong wrongly assessed the nature of the Tian An Men Incident and dismissed Comrade Deng Xiaoping from all his posts inside and outside the Party. As soon as Comrade Mao Zedong passed away in September 1976, the counterrevolutionary Jiang Qing clique stepped up its plot to seize supreme Party and state leadership. Early in October of the same year, the Political Bureau of the Central Committee, executing the will of the Party and the people, resolutely smashed the clique and brought the catastrophic "cultural revolution" to an end. This was a great victory won by the entire Party, army and people after prolonged struggle. Hua Guofeng [Hua Kuo-feng], Ye Jianying, Li Xiannian and other comrades played a vital part in the struggle to crush the clique.

Chief responsibility for the grave "Left" error of the "cultural revolution," an error comprehensive in magnitude and protracted in duration, does indeed lie with Comrade Mao Zedong. But after all it was the error of a great proletarian revolutionary. Comrade Mao Zedong paid constant attention to overcoming shortcomings in the life of the Party and state. In his later years, however, far from making a correct analysis of many problems, he confused right and wrong and the people with the enemy during the "cultural revolution." While making serious mistakes, he repeatedly urged the whole Party to study the works of Marx, Engels and Lenin conscientiously and imagined that his theory and practice were Marxist and that they were essential for the consolidation of the dictatorship of the proletariat. Herein lies his tragedy. While persisting in the comprehensive error of the "cultural revolution," he checked and rectified some of its specific mistakes, protected some leading Party cadres and non-Party public figures and enabled some leading cadres to return to important leading posts. He led the struggle to smash the counterrevolutionary Lin Biao clique. He made major criticisms and exposures of Jiang Qing, Zhang Chunqiao and others, frustrating their sinister ambition to seize supreme leadership. All this was crucial to the subsequent and relatively painless overthrow of the Gang of Four by our Party. . . .

The history of the socialist movement is not long and that of the socialist countries even shorter. Some of the laws governing the development of socialist society are relatively clear, but many more remain to be explored. Our Party had long existed in circumstances of war and fierce class struggle. It was not fully prepared, either ideologically or in terms of scientific study, for the swift advent of the newborn socialist society and for socialist construction on a national scale. The scientific works of Marx, Engels, Lenin and Stalin are our guide to action, but can in no way provide ready-made answers to the problems we may encounter in our socialist cause. . . . Subjective thinking and practice divorced from reality seemed to have a "theoretical basis" in the writings of Marx, Engels, Lenin and Stalin because certain ideas and arguments set forth in them were misunderstood or dogmatically

*Suppression of a demonstration to honor Zhou Enlai at Tiananmen Square in Beijing—Ed.

interpreted. For instance, it was thought that equal right, which reflects the exchange of equal amounts of labour and is applicable to the distribution of the means of consumption in socialist society, or "bourgeois right" as it was designated by Marx, should be restricted and criticized, and so the principle of "to each according to his work" and that of material interest should be restricted and criticized; that small production would continue to engender capitalism and the bourgeoisie daily and hourly on a large scale even after the basic completion of socialist transformation, and so a series of "Left" economic policies and policies on class struggle in urban and rural areas were formulated; and that all ideological differences inside the Party were reflections of class struggle in society, and so frequent and acute inner-Party struggles were conducted. All this led us to regard the error in broadening the scope of class struggle as an act in defence of the purity of Marxism. Furthermore, Soviet leaders started a polemic between China and the Soviet Union, and turned the arguments between the two Parties on matters of principle into a conflict between the two nations, bringing enormous pressure to bear upon China politically, economically and militarily. So we were forced to wage a just struggle against the big-nation chauvinism of the Soviet Union. In these circumstances, a campaign to prevent and combat revisionism inside the country was launched, which spread the error of broadening the scope of class struggle in the Party, so that normal differences among comrades inside the Party came to be regarded as manifestations of the revisionist line or of the struggle between the two lines. This resulted in growing tension in inner-Party relations. Thus it became difficult for the Party to resist certain "Left" views put forward by Comrade Mao Zedong and others, and the development of these views led to the outbreak of the protracted "cultural revolution." . . .

. . . It remains difficult to eliminate the evil ideological and political influence of centuries of feudal autocracy. And for various historical reasons, we failed to institutionalize and legalize inner-Party democracy and democracy in the political and social life of the country, or we drew up the relevant laws but they lacked due authority. This meant that conditions were present for the over-concentration of Party power in individuals and for the development of arbitrary individual rule and the personality cult in the Party. Thus, it was hard for the Party and state to prevent the initiation of the "cultural revolution" or check its development. . . .

Comrade Mao Zedong was a great Marxist and a great proletarian revolutionary, strategist and theorist. It is true that he made gross mistakes during the "cultural revolution," but, if we judge his activities as a whole, his contributions to the Chinese revolution far outweigh his mistakes. His merits are primary and his errors secondary. . . .

Making revolution in a large Eastern semi-colonial, semi-feudal country is bound to meet with many special, complicated problems which cannot be solved by reciting the general principles of Marxism-Leninism or by copying foreign experience in every detail. The erroneous tendency of making Marxism a dogma and deifying Comintern resolutions and the experience of the Soviet Union prevailed in the international Communist movement and in our Party mainly in the late 1920s and early 1930s, and this tendency pushed the Chinese revolution to the brink of total failure. It was in the course of combating this wrong tendency and making a profound summary of our historical experience in this respect that Mao Zedong Thought took shape and developed. It was systematized and extended in a variety of fields and reached maturity in the latter part of the Agrarian Revolutionary War and the War of Resistance Against Japan, and it was further developed during the War of Liberation and after the founding of the People's Republic of China. Mao Zedong Thought is Marxism-Leninism applied and developed in China; it constitutes a correct theory, a body of correct principles and a summary of the experiences that have been confirmed in the practice of the Chinese revolution, a crystallization of the collective wisdom of the Chinese Communist Party. Many outstanding leaders of our Party made important contributions to the formation and development of Mao Zedong Thought, and they are synthesized in the scientific works of Comrade Mao Zedong. . . .

The objective of our Party's struggle in the new historical period is to turn China step by step into a powerful socialist country with modern agriculture, industry, national defence and science and technology, and with a high level of democracy and culture. We must also accomplish the great cause of reunification of the country by getting Taiwan to return to the embrace of the motherland. The fundamental aim of summing up the historical experience of the thirty-two years since the founding of the People's Republic is to accomplish the great objective of building a powerful and modern socialist country by further rallying the will and strength of the whole Party, the whole army and the whole people on the basis of upholding the four fundamental principles, namely, upholding the socialist road, the people's democratic dictatorship (i.e., the dictatorship of the proletariat), the leadership of the Communist Party, and Marxism-Leninism and Mao Zedong Thought. These four principles constitute the common political basis of the unity of the whole Party and the unity of the whole people as well as the basic guarantee for the realization of socialist modernization. Any word or deed which deviates from these four principles is wrong. Any word or deed which denies or undermines these four principles cannot be tolerated.

The Chinese-American Rapprochement

Two decades of bitter hostility between Communist China and the United States began to yield to a rapprochement while the Cultural Revolution was winding down. After the episode of "ping pong diplomacy" in 1971, unofficial diplomatic missions were established in the respective capitals, and in December, 1978, the United States accorded *de jure* recognition to Peking. Deng Xiaoping travelled to Washington in January, 1979, to cement the new trans-Pacific détente and warn of the Soviet threat.

The significance of the normalization of Sino-U.S. relations extends far beyond bilateral relations. Amicable co-operation between two major countries on opposite shores of the Pacific is undoubtedly an important factor working for peace in this area and in the world as a whole. . . .

The people of the world have the urgent task of redoubling their efforts to maintain world peace, security and stability, and our two countries are duty-bound to work together and make our due contribution to that end. . . .

Sino-U.S. relations have arrived at a fresh beginning, and the world situation is at a new turning point. China and the United States are great countries, and the

FROM: Deng Xiaoping, Speeches in Washington, January 29 and 30, 1979 (English translation in *Beijing Review*, February 9, 1979, pp. 8–11).

Chinese and American peoples are two great peoples. Friendly co-operation between our two peoples is bound to exert a positive and far-reaching influence on the way the world situation evolves. . . .

For thirty years, our two nations were estranged and opposed to each other. This abnormal state of affairs is over at last. At such a time we cherish, in particular, the memory of the late Chairman Mao Zedong and Premier Zhou Enlai who blazed the trail for the normalization of Sino-U.S. relations. Naturally, we think also of the efforts made by former President Nixon, former President Ford, Dr. Kissinger, many U.S. Senators and Congressmen, and friends in all walks of life. We think highly of the valuable contributions of President Carter, Secretary of State Cyrus Vance and Dr. Brzezinski to the ultimate normalization of our relations.

Our two countries have different social systems and ideologies, but both Governments are aware that the interests of our peoples and of world peace require that we view our bilateral relations in the context of the overall international situation and with a long-term strategic perspective. This was the reason why the two sides easily reached agreement on normalization.

Moreover, in the joint communiqué on the establishment of diplomatic relations our two sides solemnly committed themselves that neither should seek hegemony and each was opposed to efforts by any other country or group of countries to establish such hegemony. This commitment restrains ourselves and adds to our sense of responsibility for world peace and stability.

We are confident that the amicable cooperation between the Chinese and American peoples is not only in the interests of our two countries' development, but will also become a strong factor working for the preservation of world peace and the promotion of human progress. . . .

The world today is far from tranquil. In Africa, the Middle East, and in West and Southeast Asia, the independence and security of many third world countries have been threatened or infringed upon. . . .

With the full backing of the Soviet Union, Viet Nam is brazenly subjecting Democratic Kampuchea to a massive armed aggression. Europe, too, is overshadowed by the threat of war. It is very evident that hegemonist expansion is the main source of turmoil in all parts of the world. . . .

The zealous pushing of a global strategy for world domination by the hegemonists cannot but increase the danger of a new world war. It has become an urgent task of all countries and people who cherish independence and peace to combat hegemonism. . . .

The Chinese people suffered amply from the miseries of war. We do not wish to fight a war unless it is forced upon us. We are firmly against a new world war. One of the objects of China's foreign policy is to delay its outbreak.

We want peace—a genuine peace in which the people of each country may develop and progress as they wish, free from aggression, interference and bullying—not a false peace dictated by hegemonism. We are in favour of detente—a genuine detente which truly reduces the danger of war and safeguards the security of all nations—not a false detente used by some countries as a cover under which they carry on military buildup in preparation for wars of aggression and expansion. . . .

We know that many friends are concerned over the future of Taiwan. Reunifying the motherland is the common wish of the entire Chinese people. . . . I believe the American people, who had the bitter experience of a divided nation more than a century ago, can understand the national wish of the Chinese people for reunification. The way to resolve the question of bringing Taiwan back to the embrace of the motherland is China's internal affair. . . . We wish from the bottom of our hearts to resolve this question in a peaceful way, for that will be advantageous to our country and to our nation. This has been stated clearly in the Message to Compatriots in Taiwan by the Standing Committee of the National People's Congress. I should say that after the normalization of relations between China and the United States the chances for a peaceful solution have become greater. Naturally, things do not depend on our wishes alone, we have to see how they develop.

The Iranian Revolution and the Tudeh Party

When revolution toppled the Shah of Iran in January, 1979, and put power in the hands of the Islamic fundamentalist Ayatollah Khomeini, the Soviet-controlled Tudeh or People's Party of Iran attempted to hitch itself to the new movement and steer it in a pro-Soviet direction. The party's exiled First Secretary Kianouri expressed these hopes soon after Khomeini's takeover. However, Khomeini's government remained almost as much anti-Soviet as anti-American, and the Tudeh failed to achieve legal recognition. Exactly four years after the revolution, Kianouri and other Tudeh leaders were arrested on charges of spying for the Soviet bloc, and in June, 1983, Kianouri was executed.

The importance of the people's revolution in Iran, which culminated in the victorious uprising of February 10 and 11, 1979, lies not only in the fact that it has changed the face of Iranian society and has overthrown the hated despotic monarchy. A heavy blow has been dealt at U.S. imperialism, which had been using Iran as its gendarme in the Middle East. That is why the consequences of the Iranian revolution will inevitably make themselves felt beyond the boundaries of our country and even of our region.

The truly popular character of our revolution is its key feature. Only a thin stratum of big capitalists and landowners and a handful of politicians, who tried to rescue the regime, remained on the side of the barricades. The regime was attacked by literally the whole people: the working class, the urban middle sections, the peasantry and the national bourgeoisie.

All these classes and sections rallied round the slogans of the revolution: overthrow of the monarchy and establishment of an Islamic democratic republic (and the program put forward by the religious leaders is precisely democratic); eradication of the power of imperialism in the political, military, economic and cultural fields; Iran's withdrawal from the military pacts set up by imperialism, expulsion of U.S. military advisers, and cancellation of the Shah's colossal military orders; release of the country's main resource—oil—from the grip of the international consortium; punishment of the Shah and his gang of henchmen, expropriation of the whole property of the Shah, his family and all those who betrayed the people; release of political prisoners.

The people's struggle for these goals continued for a whole year, and this was a process in which the Iranian revolution took shape, gained in strength and grew. . . .

FROM: Nourredin Kianouri, "Start of a New Stage of the People's Revolution," February 20, 1979 (*World Marxist Review*, XXII:4, April, 1979, pp. 105–11). Reprinted by permission of Progress Books.

Over the past 25 years, the Shah and the imperialists plundered the Iranian people on an unprecedented scale, and every flare-up of dissatisfaction among the masses was suppressed with equal ferocity by SAVAK, the secret police set up by the secret services of the United States and Israel. But each act terrorism fueled the *people's hatred for its oppressors, and its explosive force grew.

Despite the country's large earnings from oil, the level of exploitation of the working class was exceptionally high, and the workers ever more frequently resorted to strikes, to which the government responded with barbarous reprisals. There was also growing dissatisfaction among the peasants. The Shah's policy dislocated and destroyed Iran's agriculture. The much-advertised benefits of the "White Revolution" proved to be false, the peasants' living conditions worsened and millions of rural people were ruined. In the past two or three years, more and more peasants fled to the towns, where they swelled the ranks of the unemployed.

The economic policy pursued by the Shah, who put more and more money into the arms race, resulted in the grave economic crisis of the past few years. . . . In Iran there was a combination of political, economic and social oppression, and this determined the nature of the revolution. But the religious tenor of the popular movement was yet another key feature, and there are objective and subjective reasons for this.

First, Shia, a branch of Islam which is prevalent in Iran, has traditional ties with the popular and revolutionary movement. The patriotic Shiite clergy have repeatedly taken part in fighting foreign invaders, and had an active role to play, for instance, in the 1906–1911 revolution.

Second, historically, Shiite social doctrine has features which now objectively tend to acquire a positive significance.

Third, over the past 25 years, while the despotic regime hounded the underground revolutionary groups and the prison cells were filled with Shah opponents, who died under SAVAK torture, the mosques provided the only refuge the Shah did not dare openly to attack. Patriotic Islamic groups were able to maintain contacts with the people and to spread anti-dictatorial and anti-imperialist demands, which met with a broad response among the people. . . .

. . . On the whole, the working class has fine traditions of democratic and revolutionary struggle, and the young generation is adopting these traditions from the older generation educated by our party. The political consciousness of the Iranian working class was greatly influenced by the international situation, the changing balance of world forces in favor of socialism and the role of the Soviet Union and the whole socialist community in supporting the heroic struggle of the peoples of Vietnam, and also of Angola, Mozambique and other countries.

The class maturity of our industrial proletariat was expressed in the unanimous and all-embracing strike movement under revolutionary political slogans. The oil workers were the vanguard contingent of this movement. . . .

Characteristically, the massive and resolute influx of soldiers into the revolution began when the people fearlessly faced the bullets and demonstrated both their strength and the depth of their despair and wrath. The savagery of the regime and of the top army clique loyal to the Shah helped the soldiers to see the light, and they refused to shoot at their brothers. This shattered what seemed to be the Shah's most reliable support.

Meanwhile, the people quickly saw through the game of the Shah and the reactionaries supporting him, and began to arm. In a letter to Ayatollah Khomeini in early January 1979 and in a call issued by the Central Committee on January 13, our party urged the people to prepare for armed resistance and for the civil war which the regime wanted to start. Other revolutionary forces also supported the slogan of preparing for armed resistance.

Subsequent events showed how correct and timely that slogan was. Under the wing of the Bakhtiar government, the United States, acting through General Huyser, who was sent to Iran, was preparing the military units which remained loyal to the Shah, notably the Imperial Guard, for a coup. They hoped to carry out a sudden strike, put an end to the national democratic movement, and to eliminate Ayatollah Khomeini and its other leaders. At the same time, Bakhtiar carried on negotiations with the top army clique in search of a compromise.

But the people were prepared for such a turn of events. And when the Shah's Guard tried to stage a coup on February 10, the response came in the form of an uprising in the Air Force. This sparked off the general armed uprising which decided the issue of power in a revolutionary manner.

The victory of the February 10-11 uprising marked the end of the first stage of the revolution. It resulted in a partial attainment of the goals of the revolutionary movement: overthrow of the monarchy; a heavy blow at imperialist rule in the country; transfer of political power from the Shah and the old ruling classes to a front of democratic national forces. . . .

Finally, let me emphasize the following important circumstance: despite the 25 years of strident pro-American and anti-Soviet propaganda, the mass movement assumed a most pronounced anti-American character. At the same time, there was not a single instance of anti-Soviet or anti-socialist acts. This was also the result of the tremendous significance of the changes in the world balance of forces in favor of socialism and democracy.

A new stage of struggle has now begun in Iran. At issue are the chief, strategic tasks of the democratic national revolution: Iran's liberation from the economic power of imperialism, and destruction of the whole politico-economic basis of the old regime. The struggle at this stage will, understandably, not involve all of the forces which had acted earlier. The most rightist wing of the national-liberation movement will try to move closer to the reactionary elements which have been left from the old regime and to prevent any deepening of the popular and democratic content of the revolution. This bloc will oppose any radical socio-economic transformations and the elimination of the economic power of the ruling class: the big bourgeoisie allied with imperialism, the big landowners, the profiteers and the bankers.

By contrast, the truly popular forces and their vanguard—the working class—will seek to orient the revolutionary movement upon such transformations for the benefit of the working people and the middle sections of town and country.

In this situation, our party is an organic part of the democratic national-liberation movement. It is a party of the working class which has the longest and soundest revolutionary traditions in Iran, and is the only party which has worked out a concrete program for the progressive development of Iranian society on a scientific basis.

The PPI, conscious of its role in Iran's political life, will continue to do its utmost consistently to act as a working-class party, to build up and strengthen its

organizations throughout the country, and to rouse the working class to independent struggle for the interests of all the working people. Our goal is to establish a
united revolutionary front of popular forces on the basis of a common program,
and to do everything to have the broadest masses in our country actually benefit
from the Iranian people's selfless struggle.

Grenada—The "New Jewel Movement"

In April 1979 the government of the formerly British Caribbean island of Grenada was
overthrown by a Marxist organization under the leadership of Maurice Bishop. Increasingly
apparent ties of Grenada with Cuba and the Soviet Union, followed by the overthrow and
execution of Bishop at the hands of his most radical associates, prompted intervention by the
United States and the liquidation of the "New Jewel" regime in October 1983. Voluminous
documents were captured by the American forces, including a revealing confidential speech
by Bishop to his party in September 1982 on the Marxist-Leninist aims and strategy of his
movement.

. . . The Grenada Revolution is a national-democratic, anti-imperialist Revolution, involving the alliance of many classes including sections of the small bourgeoisie but under the leadership and with the dominant role being played by the
working people and particularly the working class, through their vanguard Party
the NJM. . . .

. . . We cannot proceed straight away to the building of socialism but must
first pass through a stage where we lay the basis, where we create the conditions,
including the socio-economic and political conditions, for the building of socialism
and the creation of the socialist revolution, that is, for the full coming to power of
the working class. In other words, comrades, what we are into now (this national
democratic stage) really means two things. What we are speaking about now is not
socialist construction, not the socialist revolution, we are speaking about the
national democratic revolution, we are speaking about socialist orientation. So the
important things to contradistinguish here are socialist construction the second
stage versus socialist orientation the first stage, which is the stage we are in at this
time. . . .

In terms of the political aspect, the essence of that political aspect is the dictatorship of the working people, dictatorship of rule of the working people—that is
the essence. This essence implies a change in the balance of forces that presently
exists, a change in the balance of forces that will usually be involved in the anti-
imperialist struggle of the national liberation movements. In other words, in your
Angolas, Mozambiques, etc., what you would normally find happening is that
there is a class alliance involved in the fight to end colonialism. And that class
alliance will involve the bourgeoisie, the petty-bourgeoisie and the proletariat (the
working class)—all three. . . .

. . . Laws are made in this country when Cabinet agrees and when I sign a
document on behalf of Cabinet. And then that is what everybody in the country—

FROM: "Line of March for the Party," speech by Maurice Bishop to a general meeting of the
party, September 13, 1982, "confidential"; in Michael Ledeen and Herbert Romerstein, eds.,
Grenada Documents: an Overview and Selection (photocopied edition from U.S. National Archives,
released by the Department of State and the Department of Defense, Washington, 1984, pp. 1–10,
1–11, 1–15, 1–25, 1–28, 1–33, 1–35–36, 1–49).

like it or don't like it—has to follow. Or consider how people get detained in this country. We don't go and call for no votes. You get detained when I sign an order after discussing it with the National Security Committee of the Party or with a higher Party body. Once I sign it—like it or don't like it—its up the hill for them.

It is also important to note, comrades, that while we are in an alliance with sections of the bourgeoisie and upper petty-bourgeoisie, they are not part of our dictatorship. They are not part of our rule and control—they are not part of it. We bring them in for what we want to bring them in for. They are not part of our dictatorship because when they try to hold public meetings and we don't want that, the masses shut down the meeting. When we want to hold Zonal Councils and we don't want them there, we keep them out. When they want to put out newspaper and we don't want that, we close it down. When they want freedom of expression to attack the Government or to link up with the CIA and we don't want that, we crush them and jail them. They are not part of the dictatorship. In fact, if the truth is told, they have been repressed by the dictatorship. They have lost some of the rights they used to have. Now it is the working people who have these rights, not the bourgeoisie. . . .

. . . It is the Party that has to be at the head of this process, acting as representatives of the working people and in particular the working class. That is the only way it can be because the working class does not have the ideological development or experience to build socialism on its own. The Party has to be there to ensure that the necessary steps and measures are taken. And it is our primary responsibility to prepare and train the working class for what their historic mission will be later on down the road. That is why the Party has to be built and built rapidly, through bringing in the first sons and daughters of the working class.

And finally, comrades, the need always for firmness and inflexibility on political questions that affect the building of socialism. On the economic front, you can have a lot of flexibility; on the political front the flexibility must be very little. We have to be firm because we are walking a real tight rope. On the one hand, you have to give encouragements and incentives and build the confidence of the bourgeoisie. But on the other hand, when they step out of line, we still have to crush them. So it's that kind of tight-rope that has to be walked. . . .

. . . Our primary task must be to sink the ideas of Marxism/Leninism amongst the working people so that their own ideological level can advance and they can begin to better understand what we are trying to do and why their class consciousness can be raised in this way. . . .

Develop proletarian internationalism. As representatives of the working class in Grenada, we have to ensure that our working class and the working people always demonstrate maximum solidarity with all international working class struggles. That is a fundamental responsibility.

Develop equal and friendly relations with all governments in the world, except the fascist military dictatorship and apartheid types. That is why comrades, we have been making trips to different countries in Latin America like Mexico, Venezuela, Ecuador, Panama and so on. That is why in a few days time we leave for France to another state visit. We must develop relations with all different kinds of countries—some of them revolutionary—democratic, some of them social-democratic, some of them, like in the case of many in CARICOM, straight pro-capitalist and pro-imperialist in outlook.

Build rapidly our links with the Socialist World, especially the Soviet Union. And here I should hardly need to say more; we have just come back from an important visit to the land of Lenin, the Soviets in the last two days have arrived, nine of them including the Ambassador and their Embassy is about to be opened and so on. So these links and relations are building reasonably satisfactory. . . .

We believe, comrades, that this line of march will equip us to go into the field and to move rapidly to ensure that this first stage of the path we are on—the socialist orientation stage—is rapidly built. We believe that we have correctly defined the new tasks required to handle the new situation that has developed. We believe that as Party, individually and collectively, we must now develop ourselves into becoming more professional, more disciplined, more Leninist so that we would be able to meet the demands of this period. We also believe firmly that the path we have chosen is the ONLY correct one. We believe that this path would *certainly* bring us to our second major historical objective to seeing socialism, of seeing socialist construction achieved in our country, thus ensuring that the working class in Grenada would assume their rightful role and become fully emancipated for the first time.

> LONG LIVE THE NEW JEWEL MOVEMENT!
> LONG LIVE THE MEMBERS, CANDIDATE MEMBERS AND APPLICANTS OF
>   OUR PARTY!
> LONG LIVE THE REVOLUTIONARY HISTORY OF OUR PARTY!
> LONG LIVE THE WORKING CLASS OF GRENADA!
> LONG LIVE THE INTERNATIONAL WORKING CLASS!
> LONG LIVE PROLETARIAN INTERNATIONALISM!
> LONG LIVE THE GRENADA REVOLUTION!
> FORWARD FROM SOCIALIST ORIENTATION TO SOCIALIST CONSTRUCTION!
>   FORWARD EVER! BACKWARD NEVER!

Nicaragua—The Sandinistas

After years of guerrilla warfare the dictatorship of Anastasio Somoza Debayle in Nicaragua was overthrown in July 1979 by the Sandinista National Liberation Front (FSLN). The Sandinistas soon manifested the Marxist-Leninist sympathies articulated by their late leader Carlos Fonseca Amador (along with a critique of the orthodox Communists) prior to his murder by the Somoza regime in 1976. Nicaragua's swing into the Soviet orbit was affirmed when the Sandinista president Daniel Ortega Saavedra went to Moscow in 1982.

a) Fonseca on Guerrilla Revolution (1969)

The people of Nicaragua have been suffering under the yoke of a reactionary clique imposed by Yankee imperialism virtually since 1932, the year in which Anastasio Somoza G. was named commander in chief of the so-called National Guard (GN), a post that had previously been filled by Yankee officials. This clique has reduced Nicaragua to the status of a neocolony—exploited by the Yankee monopolies and the local capitalist class. . . .

FROM: Carlos Fonseca Amador, "Nicaragua: Zero Hour," *Tricontinental* (Havana), no. 14, 1969, reprinted by the FSLN, 1979 (English translation in *Sandinistas Speak*, New York, Pathfinder Press, 1982, pp. 22, 27-28, 31, 35-36, 39-41). Reprinted by permission.

1927. José María Moncada, a representative of the Liberal bourgeoisie and military head of the people's army that has been fighting the government imposed by the North American intervention, commits a betrayal and enters into agreement with the representative of the State Department, Henry L. Stimson, who years later would become secretary of war in the Truman government. While Stimson occupied this post, the barbaric atomic bombing of Hiroshima and Nagasaki took place.

Augusto César Sandino, head of a column of the people's army, refuses to accept the Moncada agreement and rises up in arms against the North American occupation and the traitors who support it. The Army for the Defense of National Sovereignty, headed by Sandino, carries out more than 500 clashes with the occupation forces. This makes it impossible for the Yankee occupiers to defeat the Nicaraguan patriots militarily, but before leaving the country at the beginning of 1933, they leave behind them a reactionary force called the National Guard.

1934. On February 21 of that year, Augusto César Sandino is murdered. Anastasio Somoza G. [Garcia], commander in chief of the National Guard, orders this crime carried out after receiving instructions from the Yankee Ambassador Arthur Bliss Lane. The murder is carried out during the days when Augusto César Sandino and his comrades were preparing to fight against the antipopular direction in which the country was being led. Having received guarantees that his life would be respected, Sandino decided to take part in talks in order to dispel the slanderous charge that he was not interested in peace. . . .

. . . One of the factors that contributed to the weakness of the Marxist sector originated in the conditions in which the Nicaraguan Socialist Party (the traditional Communist organization in Nicaragua) was formed. That organization was formed in June 1944, when the Second World War was still not over, and in a period when the views of Earl Browder were in full force. Browder, the general secretary of the Communist Party of the United States, proposed conciliation with the capitalist class and with North American imperialism in Latin America. . . .

The Nicaraguan Socialist Party was organized in a meeting whose objective was to proclaim support to Somoza's government. . . .

It was correct in that period [1963–66] to pass over to rebuilding the insurrectional organization and accumulating new forces with which to relaunch the armed struggle, but this goal naturally demanded an uninterrupted maintenance of a series of insurrectional-type tasks: accumulating material resources, training combatants, carrying out certain armed actions appropriate to the strategic defensive stage, etc.

This deviation in tactics was also expressed in the ideology that the Sandinista Front adopted. Although it raised the banner of anti-imperialism and the emancipation of the exploited classes, the Front vacillated in putting forward a clearly Marxist-Leninist ideology. The attitude that the traditional Marxist-Leninist sector had maintained in the Nicaraguan people's struggle contributed to this vacillation. As has been stated, this sector in practice has openly played the game of the Somozaist clique. This factor, together with the ideological backwardness prevailing in the revolutionary sector of the country, led to vacillation in adopting an ideology that on the national level was rooted in compromise. It can be said that at that time there was a lack of clear understanding that it was only a question of time before the youth and people of Nicaragua would begin to distinguish between the false Marxists and the true Marxists.

Consequently, in the years 1964 and 1965, practically all the emphasis was put on open work, which included legal work among the masses. Clandestine tasks were carried out, above all in the countryside, but the main emphasis of the work during that time was legal. Reality showed that legal work carried out in that manner did not serve to accumulate forces and that the progress achieved was minimal. Neither can it be overlooked that the legal work through the now-disappeared Republican Mobilization group, the student movement, and peasant movement suffered from lack of discipline, audacity, and organization.

One must also conclude that revolutionary work (whether it be public, legal, or clandestine), cannot be advanced in an accelerated way if the armed revolutionary force is lacking. It was the lack of such a force that determined the extreme limitations of the legal work carried out in the years 1964–65.

Our experience shows that the armed revolutionary force (urban and rural) is the motor force of the revolutionary movement in Nicaragua. The armed struggle is the only thing that can inspire the revolutionary combatant in Nicaragua to carry out the tasks decided on by the revolutionary leadership, whether they be armed or of any other revolutionary character.

Parenthetically, during the years 1964 and 1965 important contact with the peasant sector was developed. Comrades of urban extraction permanently established themselves in areas situated on both ends of the northern region of the country, and made trips to learn the peasants' problems firsthand and organize the revolutionary struggle in the countryside. . . .

Under Nicaraguan conditions, as well as in most countries of Latin America, the center of action of the revolutionary war has to be the countryside. However, the cities must also play a role of particular importance, given that in the first stage of the war the city has to supply the countryside with the most developed cadres to lead the political and military detachment. In general, the revolutionary elements from the cities have a greater ability to develop themselves in the first stage. These elements are composed of the revolutionary sector of workers, students, and a certain layer of the petty bourgeoisie.

One must take into account the habits that the capitalist parties and their faithful servants have imposed on the popular masses through their electoral policy. These parties have conditioned broad sectors of the people to participate in the hustle and bustle of electoral rigamarole. This circumstance must be taken into account to fully understand why many sectors of the population, despite their sympathy with the revolutionary armed struggle, cannot demonstrate that sympathy through action. This forces us to consider the need to fully train a broad number of persons from among the population to have the material capacity to support the armed struggle. To seek out the people is not sufficient; they have to be trained to participate in the revolutionary war. . . .

. . . At the current time it is necessary for us to strongly emphasize that our major objective is the socialist revolution, a revolution that aims to defeat Yankee imperialism and its local agents, false oppositionists, and false revolutionaries. This propaganda, with the firm backing of armed action, will permit the Front to win the support of a sector of the popular masses that is conscious of the profound nature of the struggle we are carrying out. . . .

Relating to the situation of the Nicaraguan Socialist Party, it can be stated that the changes that have taken place in that political organization's leadership are purely changes in form. The old leadership builds illusions regarding the Conservative sector, and calls for building a political front in which these stubborn agents of imperialism participate. The so-called new leadership currently justifies having participated in the electoral farce of 1967, supporting the pseudo-oppositional candidacy of the Conservative politician Fernando Aguero. Like the old leadership, the so-called new leadership keeps talking about the armed struggle, while in practice it concentrates its energies on petty legal work.

The above statements do not contradict the possibility of developing a certain unity with the anti-Somozaist sector in general. But this is unity at the base, with the most honest sectors of the various anti-Somozaist tendencies. This is all the more possible due to the increase in the prestige of the Sandinista National Liberation Front and the discrediting and splintering of the leadership of the capitalist parties and the like.

The Sandinista National Liberation Front understands how hard the guerrilla road is. But it is not prepared to retreat. We know that we are confronting a bloody, reactionary armed force like the National Guard, the ferocious GN, which maintains intact the practices of cruelty that were inculcated in it by its creator, the U.S. Marines. Bombardment of villages, cutting of children's throats, violation of women, burning huts with peasants inside of them, mutilation as a torture—these were the study courses that the U.S. professors of civilization taught the GN during the period of the guerrilla resistance (1927–1932) led by Augusto César Sandino.

The frustration that followed the period of the Sandinista resistance does not have to be repeated today. Now the times are different. The current days are not like those in which Sandino and his guerrilla brothers battled alone against the Yankee empire. Today revolutionaries of all the subjugated countries are rising up or preparing to go into the battle against the empire of the dollar. At the apex of this battle is indominatable Vietnam, which with its example of heroism, is repulsing the aggression of the blond beasts.

b) Joint Soviet-Nicaraguan Communiqué (1982)

At the invitation of the CPSU Central Committee, the President of the USSR Supreme Soviet and the Soviet government, a state delegation from the Republic of Nicaragua, headed by Commander of the Revolution Daniel Ortega Saavedra, member of the National Leadership of the Sandinist National Liberation Front (FSLN) and Coordinator of the Executive Council of the Government of National Reconstruction, was in the Soviet Union on an official friendly visit from May 4 to 9, 1982. . . .

The two sides emphasized the importance of the ties between the CPSU and the FSLN and expressed satisfaction with the level of cooperation between the two parties and a desire to continue to broaden and deepen these relations.

The successful development of trade, economic, scientific, technical and cultural ties between the Soviet Union and the Republic of Nicaragua was noted, and the desire of both countries for the further development of mutually advantageous cooperation was emphasized.

An intergovernmental agreement on the further development of economic and technical cooperation was signed during the visit, as well as protocols envisaging

FROM: *Pravda*, May 10, 1982 (English translation in CDSP, XXXIV:18, June 2, 1982, p. 13).

deliveries of machinery and equipment from the USSR to Nicaragua and the provision of assistance in the development of hydroelectric engineering, the mining industry, agriculture, communications and other branches of the Nicaraguan economy. . . .

D. Ortega noted the great importance of the Soviet Union's experience in developing a socialist economy and culture and in implementing a nationalities policy. . . .

The Soviet side expressed resolute solidarity with the efforts of the heroic Nicaraguan people aimed at attaining the goals they have set, understanding of the difficult tasks that confront Nicaragua, and wishes for success in accomplishing them. The inalienable right of the Nicaraguan people to decide the fate of their country themselves, in an atmosphere free of outside pressure and threats, was emphasized.

D. Ortega expressed gratitude to the Soviet people for this solidarity and support.

An exchange of opinions on international questions disclosed that the two sides share common views on highly important problems of the present international situation. It was characterized as complicated and as cause for serious concern. The reason for this is the growing aggressiveness of the forces of imperialism and reaction, headed by the United States of America, and their attempts to undermine the process of detente, to escalate the arms race and to kindle enmity and distrust among the peoples. . . .

In the Western Hemisphere, as in other regions, imperialism and its accomplices, in an effort to suppress the people's legitimate striving for independence and independent development, are deliberately whipping up tension and resorting to provocations and subversive actions.

The two sides resolutely demanded an end to US threats against Nicaragua, Cuba and other states in Central America and the Caribbean Basin. They condemned American interference in El Salvador and the support of the United States of America for the antipopular regime in that country, called for a political solution of the problem through negotiations, and declared their solidarity with the patriotic, democratic and revolutionary forces of Latin America. . . .

The Soviet side expressed its full support for the Nicaraguan government's concrete peace proposals aimed at easing tension and normalizing the situation in Central America. The Soviet Union and the Republic of Nicaragua gave a high appraisal of the initiatives in this direction advanced by the President of Mexico. . . .

The Nicaraguan side voiced its full support for the Soviet peace proposals, including support for the immediate resumption of talks between the USSR and the US on strategic arms limitation. . . .

The two sides condemned the imperialist policy of economic sanctions, trade and economic blockades and other discriminatory measures, which disrupt normal ties and cooperation between states. . . .

The two sides expressed profound satisfaction with the talks, which took place in an atmosphere of cordiality and complete mutual understanding, and noted that the results of the visit of the Nicaraguan state delegation are a new and important contribution to the strengthening and development of relations of friendship and cooperation between the Soviet Union and the Republic of Nicaragua.

On behalf of the National Leadership of the Sandinist National Liberation Front and the Executive Council of the Government of National Reconstruction of the Republic of Nicaragua, D. Ortega invited L. I. Brezhnev, General Secretary of the CPSU Central Committee and Chairman of the Presidium of the USSR Supreme Soviet, to pay an official friendly visit to Nicaragua. The invitation was accepted with gratitude.

Revolution and Intervention in Afghanistan

The most internationally disturbing of all the Soviet ventures of the 1970's occurred, ironically, in an adjacent area of traditional Russian influence—Afghanistan—where a new revolutionary experiment was in danger of collapsing. Following the overthrow of the monarchy in 1973 and the installation of the Khalq ("Masses") faction of the People's Democratic Party in 1978, guerrilla revolts broke out among traditionalist tribesmen. The seizure of power in mid-1979 by the extremist Hafizullah Amin made matters worse. In December the Soviet Union intervened to put down the rebels, ostensibly at the invitation of the Afghan government; in fact Amin was executed and replaced by the Soviet-controlled leader of the Parcham ("Banner") faction, Babrak Karmal. Soviet forces numbering some 100,000 remained in Afghanistan to support the new government against the American-armed guerrillas.

Karmal's Address

Long-suffering compatriots, soldiers, officers, workers, young people, intellectuals, peasants virtuous clergymen, believers, honest Moslems, both Sunnites and Shiites, heroic men and women of our country, craftsmen, merchants, representatives of national capital, the glorious tribes, the nationalities of Afghanistan—Pashtuns, Tajiks, Hazaras, Uzbeks, Turkomans, Baluchis, Nuristanis—and other compatriots, who up to now have been subjected to intolerable violence and torture from the bloody apparatus of Hafizullah Amin and his henchmen, those agents of American imperialism! United in the name of the freedom, honor and conscience of the homeland!

At last, after cruel suffering and torment, the day of freedom and rebirth has come for all the fraternal peoples of Afghanistan. Today the torture machine of Amin and his henchmen, savage butchers, usurpers and murderers of tens of thousands of our compatriots—fathers, mothers, brothers, sisters, sons and daughters, children and old people—has been broken. This bloodthirsty machine has fallen completely to pieces, to the last bloody cog. Today real freedom has been attained for all the peoples of Afghanistan under the genuine national and liberation banner of the great April [1978] revolution. The great April revolution, accomplished through the indestructible will of the heroic Afghan people, with the assistance of the victorious uprising of the revolutionary army of Afghanistan, in a broad front with all the country's national and democratic elements and forces under the leadership of a single united party—the People's Democratic Party of Afghanistan—has entered a new stage. The bastions of the despotism of the bloody dynasty of Amin and his supporters—those watchdogs of the sirdars of Nadir Shah, Zahir Shah and Daud Shah, the hirelings of world imperialism, headed by American imperialism—have been destroyed. Not one stone of these bastions remains. The last remnants of the citadel of national and social oppression in our beloved homeland are crumbling.

The Central Committee of the United People's Democratic Party and the Revolutionary Council of the Democratic Republic of Afghanistan proclaim for all to hear—with full confidence and faith in the rightness of their cause, with a sense of

FROM: Radio Kabul, December 27 and 28, 1979, and *Prauda*, December 28 and 29, 1979 (English translations in CDSP, XXXI:52, January 23, 1980, pp. 1-3).

national pride and patriotic conscience—a genuinely people's power, congratulate all compatriots on this event, and declare that the protection of the achievements of the great April revolution and the protection of the homeland and its national independence and sovereignty are not only the sacred duty of the party and our revolutionary state but also the sacred duty of all the people of Afghanistan.

Compatriots, heroic friends and comrades! It is with pure and patriotic intentions that we have raised again the banner of a national holy war, the banner of the great April revolution! Our holy war is a great and just war of the Afghan people for true democratic justice, for respect for the sacred Islamic religion, for respect for our family, people's and national traditions, for implementation of the objectives of the glorious April revolution, for its development, for peace and freedom, for independence and democracy, progress and well-being, equality and fraternity, justice and happiness for all the fraternal peoples of Afghanistan. This war of ours is for a rightful cause.

Dear compatriots! Wherever you may be, fight, by joint efforts, bravely and selflessly, against internal and external enemies—the enemies of the conscience and honor of the nation and homeland—and boldly and valiantly defend your fighting party and Revolutionary Council.

Compatriots! Forward along the path leading to the complete destruction of the usurpers, imposters, exploiters and wreckers!

Death to the bloodthirsty oppressors, Nadirs and Amins!

Death to black reaction, to greedy imperialism!

Friends and comrades! Under the banner of the great April revolution, forward along the path leading to the complete unity of all national and progressive forces, to the final victory of the national-democratic, antifeudal and anti-imperialist revolution and the creation of a proud, free and independent new Afghanistan!

No matter what means the bloody enemies of our freedom and independence resort to, our people will be victorious!

Appeal by the Government of Afghanistan for Soviet Aid

The DRA government, taking into account the continuing and broadening interference and provocations by external enemies of Afghanistan and with a view to protecting the gains of the April revolution, territorial integrity and national independence and maintaining peace and security, and proceeding from the Dec. 5, 1978, Treaty of Friendship, Good-Neighborliness and Cooperation, has asked the USSR for urgent political, moral and economic assistance, including military assistance, which the government of the Democratic Republic of Afghanistan had earlier repeatedly requested from the government of the Soviet Union.

The government of the Soviet Union has satisfied the Afghan side's request.

TASS on the Coup

A meeting of the Politburo of the Central Committee of the People's Democratic Party of Afghanistan took place today, Radio Kabul reports. Babrak Karmal was unanimously elected General Secretary of the Central Committee.

The Politburo of the PDPA Central Committee considered and approved the main directions of the DRA's domestic and foreign policy.

The radio also broadcast a report on the formation of a Presidium of the Revolutionary Council. Babrak Karmal is now Chairman of the Revolutionary Council, and Asadollah Sarwari and Sultan Ali Keshtmand are Vice-Chairmen.

Other members of the Presidium of the Revolutionary Council are Noor Ahmed Noor, Gen. Abdul Kadir, Lieut. Col. Ghul Aga and Lieut. Col. Aslam Watanjar.

The radio said that the Revolutionary Court sentenced H. Amin to death for crimes against the noble people of Afghanistan, crimes as a result of which many compatriots were killed, including civilian and military members of the party, representatives of the Moslem clergy, intellectuals, workers and peasants.

The sentence has been carried out.

The formation of a new government of the Democratic Republic of Afghanistan, headed by Babrak Karmal, Chairman of the Revolutionary Council and Prime Minister, was announced. . . .

Brezhnev Congratulates Karmal

I cordially congratulate you on your election as General Secretary of the Central Committee of the People's Democratic Party of Afghanistan and to the highest state posts in the Democratic Republic of Afghanistan.

On behalf of the Soviet leadership and on my own behalf, I wish you great success in all of your multifaceted activities for the good of the friendly Afghan people. I am confident that in the present conditions the Afghan people will be able to defend the gains of the April revolution and the sovereignty, independence and national dignity of the new Afghanistan.

Poland—The Rise and Fall of Solidarity

The farthest-reaching movement of internal change yet to befall a Communist country occurred in Poland in 1980–81, when a strike movement originating in the Gdansk shipyards mushroomed into a nation-wide non-Communist labor organization, "Solidarity." For months the usual police-state controls were suspended, while Solidarity under the leadership of Lech Walesa undertook to analyze the nation's problems and their possible solutions. Meanwhile the Communist Party ousted its former leader Edward Gierek (successor to Gomulka at the time of the workers' riots of 1970) and the interim leader Stanislas Kania. The new chief, General Wojciech Jaruzelski, caught between escalating demands by Solidarity and the growing threat of forcible Soviet intervention, sought to avert the latter by invoking martial law to dissolve Solidarity and restore the dictatorship of the Communist Party.

a) Solidarity's Program

Basic Values

Our labor union was set up just six months ago as a result of the workers' struggle backed by the entire country. Today we are a great social force totaling many millions of members. Thanks to all that, the entire labor world in Poland is at last able to take dignified and effective action for the sake of its common causes.

We were born of the protest against wrongs, humiliation, and injustice. We are an independent, self-governing labor union of the working people from all regions and all trades. We defend the rights, dignity, and interests of the entire labor world.

FROM: Center for Social and Labor Tasks, Report to the National Consultative Commission of Solidarity, "The Directions of the Operations of Solidarity, the Independent Self-Governing Labor Union, in the Current Situation of the Country" (February, 1981; English translation by Radio Free Europe Research, RAD BR/210, July 22, 1981, pp. 3–5, 7–11, 15, 25–26).

We want to mold life in our country in keeping with the ideals of patriotism, social justice, and civil democracy. As a labor union we do not intend to take over the job of the state apparatus of power. What we want to do is to represent the working people's interests before the apparatus, and that is why we will defend the rights of man, the citizen, and the worker. At the same time, we shirk no responsibility for our nation's and state's fates.

1. *The nation's best traditions, Christianity's ethical principles, democracy's political mandate, and socialist social thought*—these are the four main sources of our inspiration.

We are deeply attached to the heritage of Poland's whole culture, which is merged with European culture and has strong links with Catholicism, but which contains various religious and philosophical traditions. The ties with the generations of Poles who fought for national freedom and social justice and who handed over to us traditions of tolerance, brotherhood, and civil responsibility for the republic and of equality before the law are alive in us. That is why there is room among us for everyone regardless of his world outlook, nationality, or political convictions.

2. The idea of uniting working people imparts great importance to the qualities produced by common efforts. Those qualities are represented by *Solidarity*—a term that we have adopted as the name of our labor union—and by *good fellowship and the ability to make sacrifices* and to do everything for the labor union community and for broader social interests. *The idea of the working people's brotherhood* in their common front against exploitation, no matter what slogans are used to disguise such exploitation, should also be this sort of virtue.

3. Defending the working people, which is our basic labor union job, is based on the principle of observing *social justice.* We will seek to make sure that this principle is the basis of running the state and its institutions and offices, and that it governs all solutions relating to social policy and to the organization of communal life.

We base social justice on the principle of the natural *dignity of the person of man, of the working man, and of his toil.* It is our wish that the principle of man's dignity permeate everything about our union and serve as the foundation on which relations in the new society are built.

The principle of social justice and of man's dignity makes it obvious that in their most essential nature *all people are equal.* That is why we will seek *social equality.*

We recognize the principle that one should be paid according to the quality, quantity, difficulty, and risk of one's work ("*to each according to his work*"), and we will seek to level off unjustified disproportions in that regard. However, *the principle of meeting the social minimum has precedence over the aforementioned principle.* Meeting the social minimum means satisfying not only elementary needs in food, clothing, and housing, but also all those social and cultural needs that make it possible to lead a dignified life in order to develop one's personality. Fighting for just wages for work, we will require ourselves to be honest in professional work and to observe high ethics in performance, reliability, and effective work results. Shoddy work, turning out defective products, and common "trash" detract from the dignity of the worker and harm society.

The principle of equality makes it obvious that total *democracy* must be observed in public life. Only under a truly democratic system will we be able effectively to fight for our labor union and workers' interests. Only under such a system will it be possible to fulfill the principle of genuine *participation by the working people in the country's social and public life*. That is why we will seek to expand the forms of social participation in public decision-making and in reviewing what the authorities do.

4. Our labor union proceedings require us to observe the *civil liberties* recorded in the Constitution of the Polish People's Republic, liberties such as *the right to profess one's own views, freedom of speech and the press, the rights to honest information, to assembly, and to free association*. We will defend people who are subjected to repression for those liberties, and we will regard such repression as a violation of the law. For those reasons we will also demand the elimination of curbs on the right to form associations, of curbs that stem from censorship, and especially of those that are not connected with overriding public interests but result from manipulation in order to defend the current interests of the governing teams.

5. Our labor union observes the *traditions of the workers' movement* and invigorates the features of those traditions that strengthen our ideals of social justice, democracy, freedom, and independence. We will enrich those traditions with the memories of the 1956 actions taken by the Poznan workers and with the bloody sacrifices of the workers in the coastal areas in 1970 and of the Radom and Ursus workers in 1976.

May Day is a special symbol. We must impart a new meaning and a new form to May Day, because it is our day—the day of the working people, not of the state employer. We will make it a day when those who stand on the dais and those who march are not divided: it will be a day of festive meetings among united and equal working people.

6. We recognize *national values* as a valuable and vital part of our collective consciousness, and we take the view that the Poles' patriotism is an irreplaceable platform for social integration and generosity for the sake of the fatherland. We take the view that national values form the basic bond of our society in the contemporary world and constitute the final justification of our independence and sovereignty. The social protest in the form of a strike last summer was also directed against efforts to eliminate our national values from our social consciousness. That protest is one of the sources of our union.

7. Our labor union is an *organization with a plurality of outlooks on the world* and is open to believers of all faiths and to nonbelievers. Nevertheless, an overwhelming majority of our union members—like the majority of our nation—have been brought up in the Christian religion. *Christian inspiration* has been one of the foundations of the ideological merits that are included in our program. The cross hanging side by side with the white eagle in many union rooms reminds our members of their moral origins and fills them with faith in the justice of our cause. We will continue that stream of inspiration, while never giving up the lay nature of our organization. . . .

Economic Issues

Our country's profound economic crisis manifests itself primarily by the enormous, increasing disproportion between supply (of goods and services) and demand. This crisis affects all spheres of the economy. It did not arise in the past few months or past few years: it has been developing gradually for decades. It is a crisis caused by a profound degeneration of the productive system, which is unable to meed demand insofar as the quantity and range of goods are concerned. This crisis bears directly on society's standard of living, on working conditions, and on the working people's real income. While the crisis intensifies, the working people's already low wages are losing their real value. . . .

The structural disproportions of the economy are the result of a long-term economic policy conducted in a voluntaristic way by a narrow group of people from institutions who are not subject to social control. In addition, the concentration of decisions in the main centers of command, the lack of cost accounting, and the price chaos have made any control by society impossible. Such a state of affairs amounts to total economic arbitrariness and irresponsibility. As a result economically harmful decisions were made and gigantic investments were initiated without the necessary justification and without providing the necessary conditions (transportation, energy, cooperation). Under the voluntaristic policy, private farmers were subjected to special discrimination: It was made especially difficult for them to obtain scarce capital goods and the necessary prices. Attempts have been made to compensate for the inefficiency of the system and economic policy by contracting ever larger foreign loans. Capitalist bankers were supposed to finance the economic incompetence of the centrally planned state economy, but loans have to be repaid together with interest, which is possible only if the economy functions properly. Such a mode of compensation could not therefore be used for long. On the contrary, it became an additional factor in the breakdown of the economy. The end results of that method of compensation are an enormous debt of over 24,000 million dollars, not counting short-term loans and the prospect of further debts. . . .

The most profound reasons for the present crisis must be sought in the system itself. All economic decision-making has been monopolized by the main centers of command, which issue orders to the individual enterprises: What they have to produce, how much, and how. This is called *running the economy through a command and distribution system*. In such a situation the enterprises have no freedom to fix production programs and to choose production methods, which means that it is useless for many enterprises to practice cost accounting. Nor do the central planners practice cost accounting themselves because they lack the necessary information in the form of correct prices. Such a situation is made worse by the enterprises' effort to boost outlays to the maximum extent, because they are interested in fulfilling their plans in terms of value, which is done by increasing costs, *inter alia*. Finally, the increasing concentration of decision-making has been responsible for the total failure to exploit the mechanism of motivating individuals and teams. All that together has brought about large-scale waste of human labor and of material resources. It is enough to say that we have to use far more raw materials, energy, transportation, and labor to produce one unit of national income than is the case in the French or West German economies. . . .

The economic reform should shape in a new way the structure and functioning of the central planning done by the main centers of command, the socialized enterprises, and the other elements of the economic system.

Central planning should be deprived of its prescriptive and command characteristics, which means that it must not transfer its tasks to enterprises by means of commands and prohibitions. Tasks for enterprises should be defined with the help of economic instructions (such as prices, taxes, etc.). . . .

Socialized enterprises should be granted independence in the sphere of adopting a production program and of determining production methods.

For that reason, the central distribution of raw materials and other means of production should be restricted and purposefully eliminated. The work of the enterprise should be based on self-financing, that is, on meeting one's own expenses with one's own income. Enterprises should be evaluated not for their plan fulfillment but for their economic results. An enterprise should be able to use its profits freely, including allocating them for investments and particularly for the rational maintenance of its installations. The way in which an enterprise functions, its degree of independence, and the way public management operates in it depend on the scale and nature of the enterprise. To enable an enterprise to work properly under the new system, the market should be demonopolized and producers should be permitted, to some degree, to compete. . . .

Making the socialized enterprises independent makes it possible and even necessary to *establish authentic workers' self-government*. Our union considers that the formation of workers' self-governing bodies in socialized enterprises is an indispensable element of the economic reform. Self-governing bodies in an enterprise should have powers enabling them effectively to control the operations of the enterprise and should therefore have the right to manage the enterprise property, should draw up policy for production and sales, the methods of production, and investment policy. They should also have a decisive say in the division of the enterprise's profits. Detailed solutions may depend, among other things, on the size and specific feature of an enterprise. The participation of workers' self-governing bodies is particularly necessary in the appointment and dismissal of directors (appointment, advising, or offering the job competitively). The problem of workers' self-government should be broadly discussed in the union. . . .

The costs of the programs for restoring equilibrium should primarily be borne by the most prosperous groups, particularly by people enjoying privileges linked with the exertion of power. The union should advocate such a policy calmly but firmly, because in the 1970s social inequalities increased markedly and the privileges enjoyed by people exerting power expanded on an even larger scale. At the same time, that is precisely the group of people responsible for the present state of our country. The preservation of privileges for people exercising power is socially dangerous and under the existing circumstances also profoundly immoral. People exercising power, isolated by privilege from the realities of life for the rank and file citizen and alienated from society, are unable to understand society's problems. . . .

Conclusion

Solidarity is the main guarantee for the process of renewal. There is no other social force in Poland that would be able to replace Solidarity in that job. Following the path of renewal, we must be determined and ready to make sacrifices. Either Solidarity transforms its social environment, or the present system will impose its norms and goals, will paralyze our efforts, and in the end, will swallow us up, annihilating our hopes for a rebirth.

There is no turning back from the path we have chosen. We can only go forward toward the complete renewal of the country.

b) Martial Law

Citizens of the Polish People's Republic, I address you today as a soldier, as the chief of the Polish Government. I address you on the most important matters.

FROM: Radio Address by Gen. Jaruzelski, December 13, 1981 (English translation in *The New York Times*, December 14, 1981).

Our country is on the edge of the abyss. Achievements of many generations, raised from the ashes, are collapsing into ruin. State structures no longer function. New blows are struck each day at our flickering economy. Living conditions are burdening people more and more.

Through each place of work, many Polish people's homes, there is a line of painful division. The atmosphere of unending conflict, misunderstanding and hatred sows mental devastation and damages the tradition of tolerance.

Strikes, strike alerts, protest actions have become standard. Even students are dragged into it.

Last night, many public institutions were occupied. There are calls for physical debate with "Reds," with people of different opinions. There are more and more examples of terror, threats, moral lynching and direct assaults. Crimes, robberies and break-ins are spreading like a wave through the country. Fortunes of millions are being made by the sharks of the economic background.

Chaos and demoralization have reached the level of defeat. The nation has reached the borderline of mental endurance, many people are desperate. Now, not days but hours separate us from a nationwide catastrophe. Honesty demands a question: Must it come to that? . . .

We have to declare today, when we know the forthcoming day of mass political demonstrations, including the ones in the center of Warsaw called in connection with the anniversary of the December events—that tragedy cannot be repeated. It must not. We cannot let these demonstrations be a spark causing a fire in the country.

The self-preservation instinct of the nation must be taken into account. We must bind the hands of adventurers before they push the country into civil war. Citizens of Poland, heavy is the burden of responsibility which lies upon me at this very dramatic moment in Polish history. But it is my duty to take it, because it concerns the future of Poland for which my generation fought on all the fronts of the Second World War and gave the best years of their lives.

I declare that today the army Council of National Salvation has been constituted, and the Council of State obeying the Polish Constitution declared a state of emergency at midnight on the territory of Poland.

I want everybody to understand my motives and aims for action. We do not aim at a military takeover, a military dictatorship. The nation is strong and wise enough to develop a democratic system of socialist government. And in such a system, military forces could stay where their place is. None of Poland's problems can be solved by force.

The army Council of National Salvation is not a substitute for the constitutional government. Its only task is to protect law in the country, to guarantee re-establishment of order and discipline. That is the way to start coming out of the crisis, to save the country from collapsing. The committee for the country's defense nominated army military commissars on every level of state administration and in certain economic units.

They are granted a law for supervising the activity of the state administrative organs from the ministry down to the local government level. The declaration of the military Council of National Salvation and other decrees published today define the terms and standards of public order for the duration of the state of emergency. The army military council would be disbanded when law governs the country and when the conditions for the functioning of civilian administration and representative bodies are created. As the situation stabilizes itself gradually, the limits on freedom in public life will be overruled. But nobody can count on weakness or indecision.

In the name of national interests, a group of people threatening the safety of the country has been interned. The extremists of Solidarity are included in this group as well as other members of illegal organizations.

On the demand of the military council, several people responsible for pushing the country into the crisis during the 1970's and abusing the posts for personal profit have been interned. Among them are Edward Gierek,* Piotr Jaroszewicz† . . . and others. The full list will be published. We will consequently clean Polish life from evil no matter where it arises.

Despite all the failures and mistakes we made, the party is still the leading and creative force in the process of changes to fulfill its mission sufficiently and cooperate with our allies. To achieve this it must lean on honest, modest and brave people, on those who deserve the name of fighter for social justice in every environment. This will decide the party's authority in society.

This is its perspective. We shall clean up the everlasting sources of our ideals from deformations and deviations. We shall protect universal values of socialism, enriching it with our national elements and tradition. This way the socialist ideals will come closer to the majority of the population, nonparty members, the younger generation and the healthy workers trend in Solidarity, which will move away from the prophets of confrontation by its own strength and its own interest. . . .

Poles, brothers and sisters: I address all of you as a soldier who remembers well the cruelty of war. Let's not allow a drop of Polish blood to flow in this tormented country which has experienced so many defeats and suffering. Let's restrain the phantom of civil war, let's not erect barricades where a bridge is needed. . . .

I turn to all citizens. The hour of hard trial has come. We must meet this challenge, prove that we are worthy of Poland.

Fellow countrymen, before the whole world I want to repeat these immortal words: Poland is not yet lost as long as we live.

Nuclear War and Deterrence

With the breakdown of détente and the acceleration of the arms race with the United States in the late seventies and early eighties, Soviet statements stressed the nation's power to deter a nuclear war but if necessary to fight and win under those conditions, while abjuring the first use of nuclear weapons.

a) Ogarkov on Nuclear War

Soviet military strategy views a future world war, if the imperialists manage to unleash it, as a decisive clash between two opposed world socio-economic systems—socialist and capitalist. It is supposed that in such a war simultaneously or consecu-

---

*Gierek: First Secretary of the United Workers (Communist) Party, 1970-1980—Ed.

†Jaroszewicz: Prime Minister, 1970-1980—Ed.

FROM: Marshal N. V. Ogarkov, "Military Strategy," *Soviet Military Encyclopedia*, Vol. 7 (Moscow, Voyenizdat, 1979), pp. 564-65 (excerpts translated in Harriet F. Scott and Wilham F. Scott, eds., *The Soviet Art of War*, Boulder, Colo., Westview, 1982, pp. 246-49). Copyright © 1982 by Westview Press, Boulder, Colo. Reprinted by permission of Westview Press.

tively the majority of the states in the world may become involved. It will be a global opposition of multimillion coalitional armed forces unprecedented in scale and violence and will be waged without compromise, for the most decisive political and strategic goals. In its course all the military, economic, and spiritual forces of the combatant states, coalitions and social systems will be fully used.

Soviet military strategy recognizes that world war might begin and for a certain length of time be waged with the use of just conventional weapons. However, widening military actions may lead to its escalation into general nuclear war in which nuclear weapons, primarily of strategic designation, will be the main means of waging it. At the base of Soviet military strategy lies the position that the Soviet Union, proceeding from the principles of its politics, will not use this weapon first. And it in principle is against the use of weapons of mass destruction. But any possible aggressor must clearly recognize that in the event of a nuclear rocket attack on the Soviet Union or on other countries of the social community it will receive a crushing retaliatory blow.

It is taken into consideration that with modern means of destruction world nuclear war might be comparatively short. However, taking into account the great military and economic potentials of possible coalitions of belligerent states, it is not excluded that it might be protracted also. Soviet military strategy proceeds from the fact that if nuclear war is forced on the Soviet Union then the Soviet people and their Armed Forces must be ready for the most severe and long ordeals. The Soviet Union and fraternal socialist states in this event will have, in comparison with imperialist states, definite advantages, conditioned by the just goals of the war and the advanced character of its social and state structure. This creates for them objective possibilities for achieving victory. However, for the realization of these possibilities, it is necessary to prepare the country and the armed forces thoroughly and in good time.

Soviet military strategy takes into account also the possibility of local wars arising, the political nature of which will be determined according to the classic positions and Leninist theses on just and unjust wars. While supporting national-liberation wars, the Soviet Union decisively opposes the unleashing by imperialists of local wars, taking into account not only their reactionary nature but also the great danger connected with the possibility of their escalation into world war.

In evaluating the strategic content of war, Soviet military strategy considers war to be a complicated system of interrelated major simultaneous and consecutive strategic operations, including operations in continental TVD's [Theaters of Military Action]. The common goal of each such operation will be one particular military-political goal of the war connected with assuring the defense and retention of important regions of its territory, and, if necessary, also destroying actual enemy strategic groupings. For such operations, the scale—conditioned by the possibilities of the sides, the range of the means of destruction, the ability to support troops (forces) materially—and also the actual conditions of the TVD, will be characteristic indicators.

In the framework of strategic operations in continental TVDs might be conducted: initial and subsequent operations of fronts; in coastal areas also initial and subsequent operations of fleets; air, antiair, air-landing, sea-landing, combined landing and other operations; and also the delivery of nuclear rocket and aviation strikes. Other kinds of strategic operations also might be conducted. Contemporary operations will be characterized by growing size, a fierce struggle to seize and hold the strategic initiative, highly maneuverable actions of groups of armed forces in separate directions in conditions of a lack of a solid front, deep, mutual penetration of the sides, and rapid and accurate changes of operational-strategic circumstances. The achievement of the goal of all these operations, as also the achievement of victory in war as a whole, is possible only with the combined efforts of all services of the armed forces and service branches. Taking this into consideration, one of the most important principles of Soviet military strategy is considered to be the organization and support of close, constant cooperation in war and strategic operations.

Soviet military strategy considers that the conduct of modern war demands the availability of multimillion mass armies. Since maintaining them in peacetime is practically impossible and is not called for by the needs of the country's defense, corresponding mobilization deployment of the Armed Forces is envisaged. In connection with the possibility of a surprise attack by an aggressor, a special place in Soviet military strategy is given to assuring the combat readiness of the Armed Forces which is examined in the broad plan: ". . . In the combat readiness of the troops, as in a focus, are concentrated enormous efforts and material expenditures of the people on equipping the army, consciousness, combat training and discipline of all servicemen, the art of the command staff to control troops and much more. This in the final count is the crown of combat mastery of troops in peacetime and the key to victory in war." (L. I. Brezhnev, *Leninskim Kursom* [Following Lenin's Course], Moscow: Politizdat, 1970, p. 49.)

While considering the offensive as the basic kind of strategic action, Soviet military strategy at the same time recognizes the important role of defense in war, the necessity and possibility of its organization and conduct on a strategic scale for the purpose of frustrating or repulsing an enemy attack, holding (defending) certain territory, winning time to concentrate the necessary forces by economy of forces in some directions and the creation of superiority over the enemy in other directions. In doing this it is considered that defense on any scale must be active, must create conditions for going over to the offensive (counteroffensive) for the purpose of the complete destruction of the enemy.

As a necessary condition for achieving victory in war and success in strategic operations Soviet military strategy considers the all-around support of actions of the armed forces and firm centralized control over them. In Soviet military strategy has been accumulated great experience in strategic leadership. This experience, with a calculation of new demands, will be used in resolving tasks standing before it. Soviet military strategy is the same for all the services of the Armed Forces; its positions are common both for waging war as a whole, as well as for conducting strategic operations taking into account the actual conditions of circumstances in different TVDs.

Troop (force) control in contemporary circumstances on the one hand is becoming more and more complicated, the volume of work to be done by organs of strategic leadership is constantly growing, and on the other hand, the time to accomplish this is getting shorter. In connection with this, the demand for steadiness, flexibility, operativeness and concealment of control in conditions of active enemy radioelectronic countermeasures is growing.

b) Brezhnev On No First Use

On behalf of the Soviet Union, on behalf of the 269 million Soviet people, I am addressing the General Assembly of the United Nations, which has convened for its second special session devoted to disarmament. This session is faced with great and responsible tasks. Its agenda includes a number of items of paramount importance.

But if we are to single out what is the most important, the most urgent, what now animates people in all corners of the globe, what preoccupies the minds of statesmen and public figures in many countries of the world, this is concern for halting the endless buildup of ever more destuctive types of weapons; insuring a break-through in improving international relations, and preventing a nuclear disaster.

Concern for peace is the dominant feature of the Soviet Union's policy. We are convinced that no contradictions between states or groups of states, no differences in social systems, ways of life or ideologies, and no transient interests can eclipse the fundamental need common to all peoples, the need to safeguard peace and avert a nuclear war.

Today, as never before, purposeful considered action is required of all states in order to achieve this lofty goal. Guided by the desire to do all in its power to deliver the peoples from the threat of nuclear devastation and ultimately to exclude its very possibility from the life of mankind, the Soviet state solemnly declares the Union of Soviet Socialist Republics assumes an obligation not to be the first to use nuclear weapons.

This obligation shall become effective immediately at the moment it is made public from the rostrum of the United Nations General Assembly.

Why is it that the Soviet Union is taking this step in conditions where the nuclear powers participating in the NATO grouping, including the United States, make no secret of the fact that not only does their military doctrine not rule out the possibility of the first use of nuclear weapons, it is actually based on this dangerous premise?

In taking this decision, the Soviet Union proceeds from the indisputable fact which plays a determining role in the present-day international situation that, should a nuclear war start, it could mean the destruction of human civilization and perhaps the end of life itself on earth.

Consequently, the supreme duty of leaders of states, conscious of their responsibility for the destinies of the world, is to exert every effort to insure that nuclear weapons are never used. The peoples of the world have the right to expect that the decision of the Soviet Union will be followed by reciprocal steps on the part of the other nuclear states.

If the other nuclear powers assume an equally precise and clear obligation not to be the first to use nuclear weapons, that would be tantamount in practice to a ban on the use of nuclear weapons altogether, which is espoused by the overwhelming majority of the countries in the world.

In the conduct of its policy, the Soviet Union will naturally continue to take into account how the other nuclear powers act; whether they heed the voice of reason and follow our good example or push the world downhill.

FROM: Brezhnev, Statement addressed to the General Assembly of the United Nations, June 15, 1982 (*The New York Times*, June 16, 1982).

It is also the objective of the Soviet Union's initiative to raise the degree of trust in relations between states. And that is particularly important in the present-day international situation, where trust has been gravely crippled by the efforts of those who are trying to upset the obtaining balance of forces to gain military superiority over the Soviet Union and its allies, and to wreck all the positive elements which the policy of détente brings.

The military-political stereotypes inherited from the times of the one-time monopoly on the atom bomb have become outdated. The realities of today require a fundamentally different approach to questions of war and peace. The present move of the Soviet Union makes it easier to take a different look at the entire complex of problems related to the limitation and reduction of armaments, especially nuclear arms, and furthers the cause of disarmament as a whole.

The vast achievements scored by human creative and technological genius permit the peoples to open a new chapter in their history. Even now, boundless opportunities exist to approach the solution of such human problems of global magnitude as the struggle against hunger, disease, poverty and many others. But that requires scientific and technological progress to be used exclusively to serve peoples' peaceful aspirations.

The Soviet Union is assuming an obligation not to be the first to use nuclear weapons, being confident in the power of sound judgement and believing in mankind's ability to avoid self-annihilation and to insure peace and progress for the present and coming generations.

I would like further to invite the attention of the representatives of states attending the special session of the U.N. General Assembly to the following question: In the search for measures which would actually halt the arms race, many political and public figures of various countries have recently turned to the idea of a freeze; in other words, stopping a further buildup of nuclear potentials.

The considerations advanced in this connection are not all in the same vein; still, on the whole, we believe they go in the right direction. We see in them the reflection of peoples' profound concern for their destinies. To use a figure of speech, people are voting for preserving the supreme value in the world, which is human life.

The idea of mutual freeze of nuclear arsenals as a first step towards their reduction and eventually complete elimination is close to the Soviet point of view. Moreover, our country has been the initiator of concrete proposals aimed at stopping the nuclear arms race in its quantitative and qualitative aspects.

And, finally, still another issue which the U.N. General Assembly, in our view, cannot disregard: Despite the obvious danger incident to nuclear weapons, it is not to be forgotten that there are other means of mass destruction in the arsenals of states, including chemical weapons. The fact, however unthinkable, is that a few kilograms of poisonous agents from the tens of thousands of tons which are operational in the armies of certain countries, are sufficient to kill several million people. And, in addition, new programs are being launched for the production of still more sophisticated lethal types of chemical weapons.

Everything should be done for the elimination of chemical weapons from the face of the earth. The Soviet Union is a convinced champion of this approach. We are prepared to agree, without delay, on the complete prohibition of chemical weapons and the destruction of these stockpiles.

On the whole, the Soviet Union is in favor of moving ahead in all areas where opportunities exist for limiting and radically reducing armaments—be it nuclear weapons, other types of mass-destruction weapon, or conventional armaments. There is no type of weapon which the Soviet Union would not be prepared to limit or ban on the basis of reciprocity.

I would like to express the confidence that the special session of the General Assembly of the United Nations devoted to disarmament will provide an effective impetus to a cessation of the arms race and transition to practical measures for real disarmament. In this way, it would justify the hopes which the peoples are pinning on such a representative forum. I wish the participants in the session fruitful work, for the benefit of the peoples and the benefit of universal peace.

Soviet Globalism

By the early 1980's, exploiting ferment in the Third World and challenging the United States in all categories, the Soviet leadership had embraced a program of global reach. A key to the extension of Soviet influence was the establishment of pro-Soviet dictatorships by "vanguard parties" embracing the essentials of Communist belief even though they lacked a real working-class base. These developments were backed up by the promise of Soviet force to aid any "progressive" regime anywhere in the world threatened by "imperialistic" intervention.

a) Vanguard Parties

The distinctive feature of the present stage of the world revolutionary process is the broadening and deepening of the struggle of the peoples of Asia, Africa and Latin America against imperialism and internal reaction, and for democratic reforms and socialism. The ranks of governments of socialist orientation that emerged in the 1960's in Asia and Africa (the Algerian People's Democratic Republic, The People's Revolutionary Republic of Guinea, the People's Democratic Republic of Yemen, the People's Republic of the Congo, the United Republic of Tanzania, etc.) were augmented in the 1970's by the People's Republic of Angola, the Democratic Republic of Afghanistan, the People's Republic of Benin, the Republic of Guinea-Bissau, the People's Republic of Mozambique, Socialist Ethiopia, etc. With the emergence of these governments in Asia and Africa there was formed a broad zone of countries of socialist orientation with a population of around 150 million persons and a territory of more than 12 million square kilometers. In Latin America, Nicaragua and Grenada entered on the path of social progress in the 1970's, and the revolutionary struggle of the people of Salvador and a number of other countries of this continent is developing.

In the development of the revolutionary process in Asia, Africa, and certain countries in Latin America an important role is played by revolutionary democracy. Revolutionary-democratic forces, groups, and parties are in power as a practical matter in all governments of socialist orientation; they are an important factor reflecting the anti-imperialist and anti-capitalist tendencies of society in many recently liberated countries, and actively participate in current national-liberation

FROM: Yu. V. Irkhin, "Vanguard Revolutionary Parties of the Working People in Recently Liberated Countries," *Voprosy Istorii* (Questions of History), #4, 1982, pp. 55–64, 67 (editor's translation).

movements and often head them up. The distinctive feature of the development of revolutionary-democratic forces in Asia, Africa, and Latin America in the 1970's and the beginning of the 1980's is the fact that they are assuming anti-imperialist and anti-capitalist positions more consistently than before; in a number of countries they are proceeding to the creation of revolutionary parties based on the principles of scientific socialism; and they are strengthening their cooperation with the Communist movement and the countries of the socialist commonwealth. . . .

The historical possibility of forming revolutionary parties in backward and dependent countries and their transformation into parties of a Marxist-Leninist type was first put forth and demonstrated by V. I. Lenin. In his report to the commission on national and colonial questions at the Second Congress of the Comintern and in his theses on the report, Lenin pointed to the possibility of the emergence in backward countries of "elements of future proletarian parties," who are called upon to combine scientific theory with the elemental pull of the toiling masses toward socialism. More than once he noted that revolutionary parties in backward countries have to accomplish a great amount of work on the path of transforming themselves into Communist parties; he warned them against leftist deviations. . . .

In Soviet and foreign Marxist historical science the term "vanguard revolutionary parties of the working people" is understood as "parties of a transitional type"—moving from the revolutionary-democratic to the Marxist-Leninist. Vanguard parties have a number of classical features and marks in common with parties of the Marxist-Leninist type. They recognize Marxism-Leninism as their ideological foundation, and base their activity on the principles of democratic centralism; they fill out their ranks by way of individual selection of the best representatives of the working class, peasantry, and other working strata of the population. The features indicated here define the vanguard character of these parties, which are in their own way forerunners of parties of the Marxist-Leninist type. The difference of vanguard revolutionary-democratic parties of the working people from parties of the Marxist-Leninist type lies in the fact that their members have not yet mastered scientific communism or applied it in practice fully, the proportion of the working class in them is small (especially of cadres), their primary organizations are insufficiently strong or active in production and in the army, and in certain important spheres of the economy and social life they are by and large absent. Therefore vanguard parties are essentially inferior to Communist parties in the level of theoretical maturity of their cadres, the degree of their revolutionary influence on the working people, and their ideological-political and organizational experience. Their social base consists of non-proletarian strata of working people, a working class that is still taking shape, and the intelligentsia. . . .

Only a vanguard party, armed with Marxism-Leninism, called on to be a directing, moving force and guarantor of the socialist orientation, can assume a really scientific level in leading the process of struggle for the socialist perspective in these countries, education of the broad popular masses on the basis of the principles of scientific communism, development of the democratic initiative of the working people, and the enhancement of their role in public life. The experience of Ghana, Mali, Egypt, etc.* testifies to the fact that without such a party it is impossible to fulfill completely the tasks of the national-democratic revolution or to guarantee the stability of revolutionary-democratic regimes. . . .

*All of which entered into alliances with the Soviet Union and later broke them off—Ed.

Historical experience shows that the process of forming parties of the vanguard type in countries of socialist orientation can take different forms and proceed by different paths. The first direction is the formation of vanguard parties in those countries of socialist orientation that already have revolutionary-democratic organizations or groups. In this case the left wing of the revolutionary democracy, in creating a vanguard party, can utilize the experience and some of the cadres of the revolutionary-democratic party. The Congolese Party of Labor, for example, was founded in 1969 by M. Nguabi, the leader of the left wing of a mass party, the National Revolutionary Movement, which was active in the Congo from 1964 to 1968.* In Angola and Mozambique in 1977 a transformation was made of party-movements into vanguard parties.

The second direction is the formation of vanguard parties in those countries where revolutionary-democratic parties were previously lacking. In this case revolutionary or military-revolutionary democrats rely basically on their own forces as they begin to form vanguard parties; this is what happened in Benin, where the military-revolutionary government headed by M. Kerekou that came to power in 1972 formed the Party of the People's Revolution of Benin in 1975. The First Extraordinary Congress of the PPRB in 1976 adopted the party program and confirmed a course of development of the country on the basis of the principles of scientific socialism. In Ethiopia the progressive wing of the ruling military-revolutionary democracy, heading up the process of forming a vanguard party, is meanwhile seeking to collaborate with those political organizations or their representatives who support the course of the government.

The third form of creating a vanguard party is the convergence of positions and then unification of Marxist and revolutionary-democratic organizations on a platform of scientific socialism. In the People's Democratic Republic of Yemen [South Yemen] in 1975 a merger took place of the Political Organization—National Front, the People's Democratic Union, and the Party of the People's Vanguard, into the United Political Organization—National Front, on the basis of which the Yemen Socialist Party was created in 1978. In principle other paths are also possible for forming vanguard parties. . . .

Bourgeois historians and political scientists assert that in the recently liberated countries the necessary social base—above all a proletariat—is lacking for the creation of vanguard and Communist parties. However, analysis of the numbers of the working class, its proportion in the social structure of the countries of socialist orientation, and its role in the vanguard parties leads to the opposite conclusion. . . . Consequently, the working class in the countries of socialist orientation can without doubt serve as, and actually is, the most important social basis for the formation of vanguard parties. . . .

The development of relations with the Communist parties has invaluable significance for the strengthening of the vanguard parties. In the 1970's a series of joint international conferences and symposia on theory was held, at which there was exchange of experience and opinions between Communist and revolutionary-democratic parties. A tendency can be seen of strengthening ties between the CPSU and vanguard parties in the recently liberated countries. Recently delegations of the Yemen Socialist Party, the MPLA-PT,† FRELIMO [Mozambique], the

*Referring to the former French Congo (Brazzaville), not the Belgian Congo, now Zaire—Ed.

†Popular Movement for the Liberation of Angola—Party of Labor; see p. 270—Ed.

People's Democratic Party of Afghanistan, the Congolese Party of Labor, the Sandinista National Liberation Front, and the Organizing Committee for the Party of the Workers of Ethiopia have visited the USSR. In turn, the Central Committee of the CPSU at the invitation of vanguard parties has sent party delegations to the corresponding countries. In the course of these visits plans were signed for collaboration of the USSR with a majority of the vanguard parties, for exchange of parliamentary delegations, and for cooperation in the area of economics, science and culture. . . .

b) The Projection of Military Power

The need to have a powerful Navy corresponding both to the geographical position of our country and to its political importance as a great world power has already long been understood, as we have said above. However, this question became particularly acute in the postwar years, when as a result of the alignment of forces in the world arena, the U.S.S.R. and other Socialist countries found themselves surrounded on all sides by a hostile coalition of maritime states posing the serious threat of a nuclear-missile attack from the direction of the sea.

At the same time the imperialists, headed by the U.S.A., having created a situation for the Socialist countries in which they were surrounded from the direction of the sea, did not experience a similar danger. Could the Soviet Union reconcile itself to such a situation? Could it agree to an age-long domination of the seas and oceans by the traditional Western sea powers, especially under the conditions when vast areas of the oceans had become launching pads for nuclear-missile weaponry? Of course not!

The Communist Party and the Soviet government fully appreciated both the threat to our country which is arising from the oceans, and the need to deter the aggressive aspirations of the enemy through the construction of a new, ocean-going Navy. And this need is being answered.

While continuing a policy of peaceful coexistence between different social systems and of prevention of a new world war, our Party and government are taking serious steps to ensure the security of the Socialist countries. The chief measure was the building up of powerful modern Armed Forces, including the Navy, capable of opposing any enemy plots, also including those in the oceanic sectors, where the mere presence of our Fleet presents a potential aggressor with the need to solve those same problems himself which he had hoped to create for our Armed Forces.

The need to build a powerful ocean-going Navy, which stemmed from the situation which arose on the oceans in the postwar period, from the policy of the U.S.S.R., and from her military doctrine, was backed up and is being backed up by the vast capabilities of the military-economic potential of the Soviet state and by the achievements of our science and technology.

In speaking of the military-economic potential of our country, it should be noted that it possesses vast, practically inexhaustable energy, raw material, and fuel resources. The high, stable rate of growth of the economic power of the U.S.S.R., observed throughout its entire history, confirms the stability, planned nature, and harmoniousness of the process of development of the Soviet state.

FROM: Fleet Admiral S. G. Gorshkov, "Some Problems in Mastering the World Ocean," *Morskoi Sbornik* (Naval Symposium), 1972–73 (English translation in Gorshkov, *Red Star Rising at Sea*, Annapolis, Md., U.S. Naval Institute, 1974, pp. 128–31, 134–35).

The utilization of the achievements of science and industry together with the introduction of scientific methods in determining the more valuable mix of weapons and equipment characteristics, taking into account economic factors, has made it possible for naval development to approximate the Navy's vital needs to the maximum degree, without copying naval construction in the Western countries and following our own national path which best corresponds to the specific tasks facing the Navy and the conditions for carrying them out.

The operational combat qualities of the new weaponry, of the means for depicting the situation, and of power plants, have been an important precondition determining the development of the Soviet Navy. Here, nuclear weaponry, which has permitted the Navy's submarine forces to become a part of the country's strategic nuclear forces, should be considered the decisive factor. . . .

Military geographical conditions, which even today the imperialists strive to utilize primarily in order to surround the Socialist countries with a ring of their naval and air bases and also with groupings of naval forces, have always had an important influence on naval development. In peacetime, the imperialists have deployed these groupings in combat patrol areas ready to deliver a surprise attack against land objectives located on the territory of the Soviet Union and of the countries of the Socialist community. According to the testimony of the Americans themselves, the U.S.A. alone has 3,429 military bases, and supply and administrative points manned by 1.7 million men in various countries outside its national borders. . . .

As is well known, through the will of the CPSU Central Committee a course has been charted in our country toward the construction of an ocean-going Navy whose base consists of nuclear-powered submarines of various types. It is precisely these forces, combining in themselves the latest achievements of scientific-technical progress, which are characterized by such qualities as great endurance and high combat capabilities.

However, a modern navy, whose mission is to conduct combat operations against a strong enemy, cannot be only an undersea navy. The underestimation of the need to support submarine operations with aircraft and surface ships cost the German high command dearly in the last two wars. In particular, we have already pointed out above that one of the reasons for the failure of the "unlimited submarine war" prosecuted by the Germans was the absence of such support for the submarines, which forced them to operate alone without the support of other forces.

Therefore, we, while giving priority to the development of submarine forces, believe that we have a need not only for submarines, but also for various types of surface ships. The latter, in addition to giving combat stability to the submarines, are intended to accomplish a wide range of missions both in peacetime and in war. The diversity of the tasks confronting us has evoked the need to build numerous types of surface ships with a specific armament for each of them. It is characteristic that the attempts which have been made in many countries to build general-purpose combatants to carry out all (or many) missions have been successful. Therefore surface ships continue to remain the most numerous (with respect to type) of naval forces.

The foreign and domestic preconditions cited above which determined the development of the Navy in the postwar period have had a considerable effect on the formation of views on its role in modern warfare. Thus, in connection with the equipping of the Navy with strategic nuclear weapons, the Navy is objectively acquiring the capability not only of participating in the crushing of the enemy's military economic potential, but also in becoming a most important factor in deterring his nuclear attack.

In this connection, missile-carrying submarines, owing to their great survivability in comparison with land-based launch installations, are an even more effective means of deterrence. They represent a constant threat to an aggressor who, by comprehending the inevitability of nuclear retaliation from the direction of the oceans, can be faced with the necessity of renouncing the unleashing of a nuclear war.

Only our powerful Armed Forces capable of blocking the unrestrained expansionism displayed today all over the world by imperialism can deter its aggressiveness. In addition, of course, to the Strategic Missile Troops, it is the Navy which is this kind of force, capable in peacetime of visibly demonstrating to the peoples of friendly and hostile countries not only the power of military equipment and the perfection of the naval ships, embodying the technical and economic might of the state, but also its readiness to use this force in defense of state interests of our nation or for the security of the Socialist countries. . . .

Under today's conditions the basic mission of navies of the great powers in a world-wide nuclear war is their participation in the attacks of the country's strategic nuclear forces, the blunting of the nuclear attacks by the enemy navy from the direction of the oceans, and participation in the operations conducted by ground forces in the continental theaters of military operations. In this instance, navies will perform a large number of complex and major missions.

Important missions in protecting the interests of the Soviet state and the countries of the Socialist community confront the Navy in peacetime too.

This latter point is particularly important because local wars, which imperialism is waging practically uninterruptedly, invariably remain within the sphere of imperialist policy. Today these wars can be regarded as a special form of the manifestation of the "flexible response" strategy. By seizing individual areas of the globe and interfering in the internal affairs of countries, the imperialists are striving to gain new advantageous strategic positions in the world arena which they need for the struggle with Socialism and in order to facilitate carrying out missions in the struggle with the developing national freedom movement. Therefore local wars can be regarded as a manifestation of the more determined imperialist method for acting against the movement for national independence and progress. Under certain circumstances such actions carry with them the threat of escalation into a world war.

The constant upgrading of its readiness for immediate combat operations in the most complex situation is a most important precondition determining the development of the Navy. At the present time, when in a matter of minutes it is possible to reach major strategic targets and even to accomplish particular missions of the war in certain areas, the need is objectively arising to maintain the highest readiness for naval forces and weaponry. This is a consequence of the effect of the development of naval equipment and weaponry and also of the conditions in which navies have to carry out missions. . . .

In order to ensure the defense of a country and the accomplishment of military-political missions, states have always strived to have armed forces appropriate to these aims, including naval forces, and to maintain them at a modern level. Within the armed forces of a country navies fulfill an important role as one of the instruments of state policy in peacetime, and are a powerful means of achieving the political goals of an armed struggle in wartime.

History shows that the creation of major navies is feasible only for maritime states having the necessary resources and a developed economy at their disposal. In this connection, a policy taking into account the country's need for sea power is an important factor determining the nature of naval construction, promoting the mobilization of its capabilities for the indicated goal, and is an indispensible condition of the development of sea power.

An analysis of the alignment of forces in the international arena today and the sharp increase in the capabilities of modern navies to have a decisive effect on all fronts of an armed struggle provide the basis to assert that the absolute and relative importance of naval warfare in the overall course of a war has indisputedly grown.

It has been essential in all stages of its history, for our state—a great continental world power—to have a mighty Navy as an indispensible integral part of the armed forces. Today our armed forces have a fully modern Navy equipped with everything necessary for the successful performance of all missions levied upon it on the expanses of the World Ocean.

We must once more stress the fundamental difference in the goals for which the naval forces of the imperialist states, on one hand, and those of the Soviet Union, on the other, have been built and exist. While the navies of the imperialist states are an instrument of aggression and neocolonialism, the Soviet Navy is a powerful factor in the creation of favorable conditions for the building of socialism and communism, for the active defense of peace, and for strengthening international security.

The Central Committee of the Communist Party and the Soviet government, in bringing to life the precepts of V. I. Lenin on strengthening the defense of the country, are displaying unwavering attention to boosting the defensive might of the state, to strengthening its armed forces, to increasing its sea power, and to the harmonious, balanced development of the forces of an ocean-going Navy meeting today's needs, and capable of carrying out the tasks confronting them. L. I. Brezhnev firmly and confidently stated this at the 24th CPSU Congress: "Everything that the people have created must be reliably protected. It is imperative to strengthen the Soviet state—this means strengthening its *Armed Forces*, and increasing the defensive capability of our Motherland in every way. And so long as we live in an unsettled world, this task will remain one of the most primary tasks."

Soviet navymen consider their highest duty to be the maintenance of a high state of readiness of all naval forces to carry out tasks of defending the state from the direction of the sea, and in every way to improve skills of employing combat equipment under any climatic and weather conditions. All of this must support the protection of the state interests of the Motherland and be a reliable shield from enemy attacks from the sea and a real warning of the inevitability of retaliation for aggression.

The concern of the Communist Party and the Soviet people for the valiant armed forces of the country, including the Navy, serves as a true guarantee of the fact that the Soviet Union will also in the future remain not only one of the strongest continental powers, but also a mighty sea power, a faithful guardian of peace in the world.

The Andropov Era—Nadir of East-West Relations

Yuri Andropov's brief tenure as Soviet leader saw the peak of confrontational tension between the USSR and the USA. Relations were particularly aggravated when on September 1, 1983, Soviet air defenses shot down Korean Air Lines flight 007 en route from Anchorage, Alaska, to Seoul, South Korea. In retrospect all parties agree that navigational error by the Koreans and mistaken identification by the Soviets were responsible, but at the time the USA alleged a deliberate crime and the Soviets, already nervous about falling behind in the nuclear arms race, countered with charges of a CIA provocation and a vast American threat to peace.

The Soviet leadership deems it necessary to make known to the Soviet people, to other peoples and all those who are responsible for shaping the policy of states its assessment of the course pursued in international affairs by the present United States Administration.

Briefly, it is a militarist course that poses a grave threat to peace. Its essence is to try and assure for the United States a dominant position in the world without reckoning with the interests of other states and peoples.

Precisely these aims are served by the unprecedented buildup of the United States' military potential, large-scale programs of manufacturing weapons of all types—nuclear, chemical and conventional. Now it plans to spread the unrestricted arms race into outer space as well.

The American military presence is being expanded under pretexts of all sorts for thousands of kilometers from United States territory. Strongholds are being set up for direct armed interference in the affairs of other states and for use of American weapons against any country that rejects Washington's dictate. As a result, tensions have grown worldwide—in Europe, Asia, Africa, the Middle East and Central America. . . .

The sophisticated provocation masterminded by the United States special services with the use of a South Korean plane is an example of extreme adventurism in politics. We have elucidated the factual aspect of the action in a thorough and authentic way. The guilt of its organizers, no matter how hard they may dodge and what false versions they may put forward, has been proved.

The Soviet leadership expressed regret over the loss of human life resulting from that unprecedented, criminal subversion. It is on the conscience of those who would like to assume the right not to reckon with the sovereignty of states and the inviolability of borders, who masterminded and carried out the provocation, who literally on the following day hastily pushed through Congress colossal military spending and are now rubbing their hands with pleasure. . . .

In their striving to justify in some way their dangerous, inhuman policies, the same people pile heaps of slander on the Soviet Union, on socialism as a social system, with the tone being set by the President of the United States himself. One must say bluntly—it is an unattractive sight when, with a view to smearing the Soviet people, leaders of such a country as the United States resort to what almost amounts to obscenities alternating with hypocritical preaching about morals and humanism.

The world knows well the worth of such moralizing. In Vietnam, morality, as

FROM: Yuri V. Andropov, Statement, *Pravda* and *Izvestiya*, September 29, 1983 (English translation by TASS, *The New York Times*, September 29, 1983).

understood by the leaders in Washington, was brought home with napalm and toxic agents; in Lebanon, it is being hammered in by salvos of naval guns; in El Salvador, this morality is being imposed by genocide. And the list of crimes can be continued. We thus have grounds for mentioning the moral aspects of United States policy, both by recalling history and by talking about the present time. . . .

But those who are blinded by anti-Communism are probably not able to ponder this. Starting with a scare about the "Soviet military threat," they have now proclaimed a "crusade" against socialism as a social system. Attempts are being made to convince people that there is no room for socialism in the world. They do not specify that they mean the world according to Washington.

Wishes and possibilities are far from being the same thing. No one will ever be able to reverse the course of history. The U.S.S.R. and other socialist countries will live and develop according to their laws, the laws of the most advanced social system.

The Soviet state has successfully overcome many trials, including crucial ones, during the six and a half decades of its existence. Those who encroached on the integrity of our state, its independence and our system found themselves on the garbage heap of history. It is high time that everyone to whom this applies understood that we shall be able to insure the security of our country, the security of our friends and allies under any circumstances.

The Soviet people can rest assured that our country's defense capability is being maintained at such a level that it would not be advisable for anyone to stage a trial of strength. . . .

We proceed from the premise that mankind is not doomed to destruction. The arms race can and must be terminated. Mankind deserves a better fate than living in a conflict-torn world, suffocating under the burden of deadly weapons.

By advancing far-reaching proposals on limitations and reductions of nuclear armaments, both strategic and medium-range in Europe, we have shown our concern not only for the security of the U.S.S.R. and the other states of the socialist community, but also for the security of all other countries.

As to the policy of the United States, its growing militarization is manifest, among other things, in its unwillingness to conduct serious talks of any kind, to come to agreement on questions of curbing the arms race.

The Soviet-American talks on the burning problem—the reduction of nuclear armaments in Europe—have been going on for two years now. The position of the Soviet side is directed at finding mutually acceptable solutions on a fair, just basis, solutions that do not infringe on anyone's legitimate interests. At the same time, these two years made it clear that our partners in the talks at Geneva are not at all there to reach an accord. Their task is different—to play for time and then start the deployment in Western Europe of Pershing 2 ballistic missiles and long-range cruise missiles. They do not even try to conceal this. . . .

No one should mistake the Soviet Union's good will and desire to come to agreement for a sign of weakness. The Soviet Union will be able to make an appropriate response to any attempt to disrupt the existing military-strategic balance, and its words and deeds will not be at variance.

However, we are basically opposed to competition in the production and stockpiling of arms of mass annihilation. This is not our path. It cannot lead to a solution of any problem facing mankind, i.e. economic development of states, conservation of the environment, creation of at least elementary conditions for life, nourishment, health and education. . . .

Mankind has not yet lost, nor can it ever lose its reason. This is manifested with great vigor by the scope of the antimissile, antiwar movement being mounted in Europe and on other continents, a movement that draws people of different social, political and religious affiliations.

All those who are raising their voices against the senseless arms race and in defense of peace can be sure that the policy of the Soviet Union and of the other socialist countries is directed at precisely these aims. The U.S.S.R. wishes to live in peace with all countries, including the United States. It does not nurture aggressive plans, does not impose the arms race on anyone, does not impose its social system on anyone.

Our aspirations and strivings are being implemented in concrete proposals directed at effecting a decisive turn for the better in the world situation. The Soviet Union will continue to do everything possible to uphold peace on earth.

CHAPTER EIGHT

The Collapse of International Communism, 1985–1991

After seventy-plus years of anti-capitalist defiance and the construction of a vast machine of vast military and political power, the international Communist enterprise passed into oblivion, with no bang and scarcely a whimper. Simultaneously with his internal reforms in the Soviet Union, Mikhail Gorbachev recognized that his country was losing in its military and economic competition with the West. He saw the folly of superpower confrontation based on nuclear weapons, and pushed quickly to bring the Cold War to an end.

Gorbachev's reform example, and his unwillingness to rely any longer on subversion or force to project Soviet power abroad, spelled the doom of the Communist satellite regimes in Eastern Europe and the collapse or disorientation of pro-Soviet movements in the Third World, on which the Brezhnev leadership had banked to equalize the Soviet Union's international competition with the USA. Nationalism was the main force to fill the vacuum left by Communism; it tore the Soviet Union apart and plunged Yugoslavia into civil war. Where the Communists had come to power on their own outside Europe, notably in China, hardline regimes remained for the time being, with the choice of isolation or pragmatic adjustment to the world economy. Russia, shorn of the non-Russian Soviet republics, hoped to rejoin "civilization" and secure the benefits of its charity. The old polarity of Communist and anti-Communist that had defined so much of the twentieth century yielded to other, familiar and unfamiliar forms of crisis that began to write a new chapter in world history.

The End of the Cold War

The end of the Cold War was above all the outcome of Gorbachev's personal initiatives between 1985 and 1989, prompted by recognition of the Soviet Union's economic weakness vis-à-vis the West, by genuine fear of nuclear war, and by a realization that he was losing the arms race despite the monumental price paid by the Soviet peoples. Despite past ideological polemics, the USA responded immediately to Gorbachev's overtures. Gorbachev and President Reagan held their first summit meeting in November, 1985, and followed it with annual summits climaxed by the meeting of Gorbachev and President Bush at Malta in December 1989 when the Cold War was declared at an end. This momentum continued until the ultimate conclusion of the first nuclear arms reduction treaty in 1991.

a) Gorbachev's "New Thinking"

In the summer of 1987 Gorbachev composed a book-length statement of his reform aims and their international implications, dismissing the traditional Marxist view of the Commu-nist-capitalist struggle and calling for international cooperation to avert nuclear war.

. . . We say with full responsibility, casting away the false considerations of "prestige," that all of us in the present-day world are coming to depend more and more on one another and are becoming increasingly necessary to one another. And since such realities exist in the world and since we know that we in this world are, on the whole, now linked by the same destiny, that we live on the same planet, use its resources and see that they are not limitless and need to be saved, and nature and the environment need to be conserved, then such a reality holds for all of us. The necessity of effective, fair, international procedures and mechanisms which would ensure rational utilization of our planet's resources as the property of all mankind becomes ever more pressing.

And here we see our interdependence, the integrity of the world, the imperative need for pooling the efforts of humanity for the sake of its self-preservation, for its benefit today, tomorrow and for all time.

Last but not least, there is one more reality which we must recognize. Having entered the nuclear age when the energy of the atom is used for military purposes, mankind has lost its immortality. In the past, there were wars, frightful wars which took millions upon millions of human lives, turned cities and villages into ruins and ashes and destroyed entire nations and cultures. But the continuation of humankind was not threatened. By contrast, now, if a nuclear war breaks out, every living thing will be wiped off the face of the Earth. . . .

. . . All of us face the need to learn to live at peace in this world, to work out a new mode of thinking, for conditions today are quite different from what they were even three or four decades ago.

The time is ripe for abandoning views on foreign policy which are influenced by an imperial standpoint. Neither the Soviet Union nor the United States is able to force its will on others. It is possible to suppress, compel, bribe, break or blast, but only for a certain period. From the point of view of long-term, big-time politics, no one will be able to subordinate others. That is why only one thing—relations of equality—remains. All of us must realize this. Along with the above-said realities of nuclear weapons, ecology, the scientific and technological revolution, and infor-matics, this also obliges us to respect one another and everybody. . . .

Having adopted at the 27th Congress the concept of a contradictory but inter-connected, interdependent and, essentially, integral world, we began to build our foreign policy on this foundation. Yes, we remain different as far as our social sys-tem, ideological and religious views and way of life are concerned. To be sure, dis-tinctions will remain. But should we duel because of them? Would it not be more correct to step over the things that divide us for the sake of the interests of all mankind, for the sake of life on Earth? We have made our choice, asserting a new political outlook both by binding statements and by specific actions and deeds.

FROM: Mikhail Gorbachev, *Perestroika: New Thinking for Our Country and the World*, New York, Harper & Row, 1987, pp. 137–141, 146–149. Reprinted by permission of the HarperCollins Publishers, Inc.

People are tired of tension and confrontation. They prefer a search for a more secure and reliable world, a world in which everyone would preserve their own philosophic, political and ideological views and their way of life.

We are looking at what is taking place with open eyes. We see that stereotypes persist and that the old outlooks have struck deep roots, nourishing militarism and imperial ambitions according to which other countries are regarded as targets for one's political and other activities and are deprived of the right to independent choice and independent foreign policy. . . .

The fundamental principle of the new political outlook is very simple: *nuclear war cannot be a means of achieving political, economic, ideological or any other goals.* This conclusion is truly revolutionary, for it means discarding the traditional notions of war and peace. It is the political function of war that has always been a justification for war, a "rational" explanation. Nuclear war is senseless; it is irrational. There would be neither winners nor losers in a global nuclear conflict: world civilization would inevitably perish. It is a suicide, rather than a war in the conventional sense of the word.

But military technology has developed to such an extent that even a non-nuclear war would now be comparable with a nuclear war in its destructive effect. That is why it is logical to include in our category of nuclear wars this "variant" of an armed clash between major powers as well.

Thereby, an altogether different situation has emerged. A way of thinking and a way of acting, based on the use of force in world politics, have formed over centuries, even millennia. It seems they have taken root as something unshakable. Today, they have lost all reasonable grounds. Clausewitz's dictum that war is the continuation of policy only by different means, which was classical in his time, has grown hopelessly out of date. It now belongs to the libraries. For the first time in history, basing international politics on moral and ethical norms that are common to all humankind, as well as humanizing interstate relations, has become a vital requirement. . . .

The backbone of the new way of thinking is the recognition of the priority of human values, or, to be more precise, of humankind's survival.

It may seem strange to some people that the Communists should place such a strong emphasis on human interests and values. Indeed, a class-motivated approach to all phenomena of social life is the ABC of Marxism. Today, too, such an approach fully meets the realities of a class-based society, a society with opposing class interests, as well as the realities of international life which are also permeated by the opposition. And up to the most recent time class struggle remained the pivot of social development, and still remains as such in class-divided countries. Correspondingly, Marxist philosophy was dominated—as regards the main questions of social life—by a class-motivated approach. Humanitarian notions were viewed as a function and the end result of the struggle of the working class—the last class which, ridding itself, rids the entire society of class antagonisms.

But now, with the emergence of weapons of mass, that is, universal destruction, there appeared an objective limit for class confrontation in the international arena: the threat of universal destruction. For the first time ever there emerged a real, not speculative and remote, common human interest—to save humanity from disaster. . . .

In developing our philosophy of peace, we have taken a new look at the interdependence of war and revolution. In the past, war often served to detonate revolution. One may recall the Paris Commune which came as an echo of the Franco-Prussian war, or the 1905 Russian Revolution triggered by the Russo-Japanese war. The First World War provoked a real revolutionary storm which culminated in the October Revolution in our country. The Second World War evoked a fresh wave of revolutions in Eastern Europe and Asia, as well as a powerful anti-colonial revolution.

All this served to reinforce the Marxist-Leninist logic that imperialism inevitably generates major armed confrontations, while the latter naturally create a "critical mass" of social discontent and a revolutionary situation in a number of countries. Hence a forecast which was long adhered to in our country: a third world war, if unleashed by imperialism, would lead to new social upheavals which would finish off the capitalist system for good, and this would spell global peace.

But when the conditions radically changed so that the only result of nuclear war could be universal destruction, we drew a conclusion about the disappearance of the cause-and-effect relationship between war and revolution. The prospects of social progress "coincided" with the prospects of the prevention of nuclear war. . . .

Economic, political and ideological competition between capitalist and socialist countries is inevitable. However, it can and must be kept within a framework of peaceful competition which necessarily envisages cooperation. It is up to history to judge the merits of each particular system. It will sort out everything. Let every nation decide which system and which ideology is better. Let this be decided by peaceful competition, let each system prove its ability to meet man's needs and interests. The states and peoples of the Earth are very different, and it is actually good that they are so. This is an incentive for competition. This understanding, of a dialectical unity of opposites, fits into the concept of peaceful co-existence. . . .

We see how strong the positions of the aggressive and militarist part of the ruling class are in the leading capitalist countries. Their main support comes from the powerful military-industrial complex whose interests are rooted in the very nature of the capitalist system and which extracts huge profits from arms production at the tax-payers' expense. And to make the people believe that all that money is not being spent in vain, they must be convinced of the existence of an "external enemy" which wishes to encroach upon their well-being and "national interests" in general. Hence the reckless and irresponsible power politics. How can this total reliance on strength be possible in our nuclear age when the existing stocks of weapons are so huge that even a minor part of these weapons can easily annihilate mankind? This is exactly what we call a mentality of the notorious "Cold War." . . .

. . . We are sincerely prepared for disarmament, but only on a fair basis of equal security, and for cooperation along a very broad front. However, bearing in mind the bitter lessons of the past, we cannot take major unilateral steps for fear that they may serve as a temptation for the advocates of "global national interests." In our opinion, the most important thing to do now is to set the mechanism of humankind's self-preservation into motion and to bolster the potential of peace, reason and good will.

b) The Malta Summit

In December 1989 Gorbachev held his first summit meeting with the new American president, George Bush, aboard ship in the harbor of Valetta, Malta. The meeting was distinguished by the nearest thing to a formal declaration of the end of the Cold War, as Gorbachev implicitly ratified the collapse of the Communist governments in Eastern Europe.

Ladies and gentlemen, comrades, there are many symbolic things about this meeting, and one of them—it has never been in the history that the leaders of our two countries hold a joint press conference. This is also an important symbol. I share the view voiced by President Bush that we are satisfied, in general, with the results of the meeting. . . .

. . . I would say that in all directions of the political dialog of our discussion, including bilateral relations, we not only confirmed the consistency of our political course, the continuity of our political course—and I should say it—although we had an informal meeting, we met only for the first time with President Bush in his capacity, and the confirmation of the continuity of the course is an important element. . . .

I assured the President of the United States that the Soviet Union would never start hot war against the United States of America, and we would like our relations to develop in such a way that they would open greater possibilities for cooperation. Naturally, the President and I had a wide discussion—rather, we sought the answer to the question where we stand now. We stated, both of us, that the world leaves one epoch of cold war and enters another epoch. This is just the beginning. We're just at the very beginning of our long road to a long-lasting peaceful period. . . .

. . . We have reaffirmed once again to the President that we have ceased arms shipment to Central America. We also reaffirmed our position that we're sympathetic with the political process that is going on there regarding the settlement of the situation. We are in favor of free elections, with the representatives of the United Nations and other Latin American countries, to determine the fate of Nicaragua. We understand the concerns of the United States. We listened carefully to the arguments by President Bush, in this respect, and we assured him that our position of principle is that we are in favor of a political settlement of the situation in Central America. . . .

. . . Regarding Helsinki II. I think that we have found during this meeting, we have come to a common understanding of the extreme importance of the CSCE process and have noted the positive results of the CSCE process, the results that have made it possible to proceed with deep changes in Europe and in the world as well, as Europe has a great influence on the world due to certain reasons. Both the President and myself are in favor of developing the CSCE process in accordance with the new requirements that are required by our times so that we would think of and build a new Europe on the basis of common elements among the European countries. We reaffirmed that this is a common affair for all the European countries that signed the Helsinki Act, including the whole EC [European Community]. And this element was present everywhere whenever we discussed Europe and

FROM: Remarks of Soviet Chairman Mikhail Gorbachev at a Question-and-Answer Session with Reporters in Malta, December 3, 1989 (English translation in *Public Papers of the Presidents of the United States, George Bush, 1989*, Washington, Government Printing Office, 1990, book II, pp. 1626-1628, 1630-1634).

other parts of the world with the active and constructive participation of the United States and Canada. Thus, we are in favor of the process gaining in strength and in force.

The transformation of the CSCE-Helsinki institutions at this stage should be such that their nature would change, or rather would be adequate to the current changes. Take, for example, NATO and the Warsaw Pact. They should not remain military alliances, but rather military-political alliances, and later on just political alliances, so that their nature would change in accordance with the changes on the continent.

We are also entitled to expect that when the Common Market and the CMEC would also change in respect of greater openness, with the active participation in economic processes of the United States. . . .

Q. I'm from the group of Czechoslovak journalists. President Gorbachev, did you assure President Bush that the changes in Eastern Europe are irreversible and that the Soviet Union has forsaken the right to intervene there militarily? And President Bush, similarly, as a result of this meeting, are you now more trusting that the Soviets have indeed renounced the Brezhnev doctrine?

The Chairman. I wouldn't like you to consider me here or to regard me as a full-fledged representative of all European countries. This wouldn't be true. We are a part of Eastern Europe, of Europe. We interact with our allies in all areas, and our ties are deep. However, every nation is an independent entity in world politics, and every people has the right to choose its own destiny, the destiny of its own state. And I can only explain my own attitude.

I believe that those changes, both in the Soviet Union and in the countries of Eastern Europe, have been prepared by the course of the historic evolution itself. No one can avoid this evolutionary process; and those problems should be resolved on a new basis, taking into account the experience and the potential of those countries, opening up possibilities for utilizing anything positive that has been accumulated by mankind. And I believe that we should welcome the thrust of those processes because they are related to the desire of the people to make those societies more democratic, more humane, and to face the world. Therefore, I'm encouraged by the thrust of those processes, and I believe that this is highly assisted by other countries.

I also see deep, profound changes in other countries, including Western European countries, and this is also very important because this is a reciprocal movement so that the people will become more close around the continent, and preserving at the same time the identity of one's own people. This is very important for us to understand. . . .

. . . The reality is such that we have today's Europe with two German states, the Federal Republic of Germany and the German Democratic Republic, which are both members of the United Nations and sovereign states.

This was the decision of history. And I always revert to this subject, or thesis, which saves me. Indeed, in order to remain realists, we should say that history itself decides the processes and fates on the European continent and also the fates of those two states. I think this is a common understanding shared by anyone. And any artificial acceleration of the process would only exacerbate and make it more difficult to change in many European countries those changes that are now taking place now in Europe. Thus, we wouldn't serve that process by an artificial accelera-

tion or prompting of the processes that are going on in those two countries. . . .
. . . Today's meeting boosts our contacts to a higher level. I'm satisfied with the discussions and meetings we had, including our two private discussions. I share the view of the President that personal contacts are a very important element in the relations between leaders of state, the more so we are talking about the leaders of such countries as the United States and the Soviet Union. And I welcome those personal relations.

And the President was quite correct in saying that this didn't mean that we would sacrifice our long-held positions at the expense of our personal ties or that we forget our responsibility. I think our personal contacts help us implement our responsibilities and help us better interact in the interests of our two nations and in the interests of the entire would community. And I, myself, would like to thank the President for cooperation for this meeting, for the cooperation in a very important joint Soviet-U.S. endeavor. And our share is 50–50.

c) The START Treaty

Arms control negotiations between the USSR and the USA made little progress with the worsening of relations in the late 1970s and early 1980s. The new Reagan administration in Washington rejected the proposed sequel to the SALT I Treaty in favor of a "Strategic Arms Reduction Treaty," finally agreed to in July 1991, after the Bush administration overcame its initial reservations, and just before the hard-line coup attempt in Moscow. Bush and Gorbachev signed the document in Moscow at the latter's last summit meeting.

The Treaty

The United States of America and the Union of Soviet Socialist Republics, hereinafter referred to as the Parties,

Conscious that nuclear war would have devastating consequences for all humanity, that it cannot be won and must never be fought,

Convinced that the measures for the reduction and limitation of strategic offensive arms and the other obligations set forth in this Treaty will help to reduce the risk of outbreak of nuclear war and strengthen international peace and security,

Recognizing that the interests of the Parties and the interests of international security require the strengthening of strategic stability,

Mindful of their undertakings with regard to strategic offensive arms in Article VI of the Treaty on the Non-Proliferation of Nuclear Weapons of July 1, 1968; Article XI of the Treaty on the Limitation of Anti-Ballistic Missile Systems of May 26, 1972; and the Washington Summit Joint Statement of June 1, 1990,

Have agreed as follows:

ARTICLE I

Each Party shall reduce and limit its strategic offensive arms in accordance with the provisions of this Treaty, and shall carry out the other obligations set forth in this Treaty and its Annexes, Protocols, and Memorandum of Understanding.

FROM: Treaty Between the United States of America and the Union of Soviet Socialist Republics on the Reduction and Limitation of Strategic Offensive Arms, in *Dispatch* (U.S. Department of State), Vol. II, Supplement no. 5, October 1991, pp. 1, 11, 15; M. S. Gorbachev, address at the START Treaty signing ceremony, Moscow Central Television, July 31, 1991 (English translation in FBIS-SOV-91-148, August, 1, 1991, p. 12).

ARTICLE II

1. Each Party shall reduce and limit its ICBMs and ICBM launchers, SLBMs and SLBM launchers, heavy bombers, ICBM warheads, SLBM warheads, and heavy bomber armaments, so that seven years after entry into force of this Treaty and thereafter, the aggregate numbers, as counted in accordance with Article III of this Treaty, do not exceed:

(a) 1600, for deployed ICBMs and their associated launchers, deployed SLBMs and their associated launchers, and deployed heavy bombers, including 154 for deployed heavy ICBMs and their associated launchers;

(b) 6000, for warheads attributed to deployed ICBMs, deployed SLBMs, and deployed heavy bombers, including:

(i) 4900, for warheads attributed to deployed ICBMs and deployed SLBMs;

(ii) 1100, for warheads attributed to deployed ICBMs on mobile launchers of ICBMs;

(iii) 1540, for warheads attributed to deployed heavy ICBMs.

2. Each Party shall implement the reductions pursuant to paragraph 1 of this Article in three phases, so that its strategic offensive arms do not exceed:

(a) by the end of the first phase, that is, no later than 36 months after entry into force of this Treaty, and thereafter, the following aggregate numbers:

(i) 2100, for deployed ICBMs and their associated launchers, deployed SLBMs and their associated launchers, and deployed heavy bombers;

(ii) 9150, for warheads attributed to deployed ICBMs, deployed SLBMs, and deployed heavy bombers;

(iii) 8050, for warheads attributed to deployed ICBMs and deployed SLBMs;

(b) by the end of the second phase, that is, no later than 60 months after entry into force of this Treaty, and thereafter, the following aggregate numbers:

(i) 1900, for deployed ICBMs and their associated launchers, deployed SLBMs and their associated launchers, and deployed heavy bombers;

(ii) 7950, for warheads attributed to deployed ICBMs, deployed SLBMs, and deployed heavy bombers;

(iii) 6750, for warheads attributed to deployed ICBMs and deployed SLBMs;

(c) by the end of the third phase, that is, no later than 84 months after entry into force of this Treaty: the aggregate numbers provided for in paragraph 1 of this Article.

3. Each Party shall limit the aggregate throw-weight of its deployed ICBMs and deployed SLBMs so that seven years after entry into force of this Treaty and thereafter such aggregate throw-weight does not exceed 3600 metric tons. . . .

ARTICLE IX

1. For the purpose of ensuring verification of compliance with the provisions of this Treaty, each Party shall use national technical means of verification at its disposal in a manner consistent with generally recognized principles of international law.

2. Each Party undertakes not to interfere with the national technical means of verification of the other Party operating in accordance with paragraph 1 of this Article.

3. Each Party undertakes not to use concealment measures that impede verification, by national technical means of verification, of compliance with the provisions

of this Treaty. In this connection, the obligation not to use concealment measures includes the obligation not to use them at test ranges, including measures that result in the concealment of ICBMs, SLBMs, mobile launchers of ICBMs, or the association between ICBMs or SLBMs and their launchers during testing. The obligation not to use concealment measures shall not apply to cover or concealment practices at ICBM bases and deployment areas, or to the use of environmental shelters for strategic offensive arms.

4. To aid verification, each ICBM for mobile launchers of ICBMs shall have a unique identifier as provided for in the Inspection Protocol. . . .

ARTICLE XV

To promote the objectives and implementation of the provisions of this Treaty, the Parties hereby establish the Joint Compliance and Inspection Commission. The Parties agree that, if either Party so requests, they shall meet within the framework of the Joint Compliance and Inspection Commission to:

(a) resolve questions relating to compliance with the obligations assumed;

(b) agree upon such additional measures as may be necessary to improve the viability and effectiveness of this Treaty; and

(c) resolve questions related to the application of relevant provisions of this Treaty to a new kind of strategic offensive arm, after notification has been provided in accordance with paragraph 16 of Section VII of the Notification Protocol. . . .

Gorbachev's Address

Mr. President, ladies and gentlemen, comrades, in several minutes I and the President of the United States are to append our signatures to the treaty on reducing strategic offensive arms. It is a result, a result of many years of efforts which, apart from enormous work and patience, required that statesmen, diplomats, and servicemen have the will and boldness; that they break with the deeply rooted images of each other, and that they have trust. It is also the beginning of a voluntary reduction of nuclear arsenals of the Soviet Union and the United States, unprecedented as far as its scale and goals are concerned. It is an event of worldwide importance, because we are giving such momentum to the dismantling of the infrastructure of fear that used to hold sway over the world that it will be difficult to put a halt to it.

A far from simple process of ratification of the new treaty is ahead for both countries. There will be criticism, too. There will be talk of unilateral concessions here in Moscow, while in Washington there will be talk of concessions made to the Soviet Union. Others will say that the new treaty fails to justify all hopes for a peace dividend, since not inconsiderable resources will be required to have the missiles destroyed. And if the missiles are not destroyed, critics will say that they have become obsolete, and that they must be replaced with new ones and this will cost even more. One can also expect vigorous criticism from those who would like faster and further-reaching steps toward being rid completely of nuclear weapons. In a word, the treaty will have to be defended.

I am convinced that what we have done at present is the optimum possible, and what is necessary for further progress. Colossal work has been done, and unique experience of cooperation in a most complex sphere has been amassed.

It is important that there is a growing understanding of the absurdity of arming oneself beyond all measures at a time when the world has moved toward an era of economic interdependence, and the information revolution is making the integrity of the world ever more apparent.

Politicians are forced to take into account, however, that on the way to this era great efforts will be needed for removing the dangers which have been inherited from the past and those appearing anew, and for overcoming obstacles of a material, intellectual and psychological order.

Normal human thinking must take the place of militarized political thinking, which is deeply rooted in the public conscience. This will take time. A new conceptual basis for security is to help the matter. Doctrines for waging wars must give way to a concept of the forestalling and prevention of wars. Plans for the utter defeat of a notional enemy must be replaced by joint projects for strategic stability and defense sufficiency. The document before us is a moral achievement and marks a major breakthrough in the thinking and behavior of our countries. The future goal is to use this breakthrough fully and to establish the irreversibility of the disarmament process.

Let us do justice to what has been achieved and express gratitude to those who made the mental and nervous effort and who invested a lot of skills working on the treaty. Let us embark on tackling new tasks for the sake of our and worldwide security.

Mr. President, we can congratulate each other, and we can congratulate the Soviet and American people and the entire world community on the conclusion of such an agreement. Thank you. [applause]

d) Shevardnadze on the Burden of Militarism

Gorbachev's foreign minister, the former Georgian party boss Eduard Shevardnadze, went beyond his chief in his critique of the Soviet regime, and resigned in December 1990 with a warning about new dictatorship. He then published a trenchant account of his political Odyssey, emphasizing the price the old system paid for its super-power status.

We became a superpower largely because of our military might. But the bloated size and unrestrained escalation of this military might was reducing us to the level of a third-rate country, unleashing processes that pushed us to the brink of catastrophe. Our military expenditures as a percentage of gross national product were two and a half times greater than those of the United States. Although we take pride in achieving military parity with the Americans, we could not even dream of equaling them in the manufacture of disposable syringes, food products, and basic necessities. The catastrophic shortages of these goods hardly strengthen our security or serve our national interest. We have captured first place in the world weapons trade (28 percent of the entire sales total), and have made the Kalashnikov submachine gun the hallmark of our advanced technology. But we occupy about sixtieth place in standard of living, thirty-second place in average life expectancy, and fiftieth in infant mortality.

FROM: Eduard Shevardnadze, *The Future Belongs to Freedom*, pp. 54-56, 58-59. Reprinted with the permission of The Free Press, a Division of Macmillan, Inc. from *The Future Belongs to Freedom* by Eduard Shevardnadze, translated by Catherine A. Fitzpatrick. Copyright © 1991 by Eduard Shevardnadze. *Budushchee prinadlezhit svobode.* English translation, Copyright © 1991 by The Free Press, a Division of Macmillan, Inc. Published by permission of Rowohlt Verlag, Berlin/Hamburg, Germany, © 1991.

What kind of national security is this? It is not just immoral but politically dangerous to equate national security with tanks and nuclear warheads, while leaving out such "trivia" as human life and welfare.

It is not true that issues of national security and protection of national interests have been overlooked by Soviet diplomacy, the foreign policy establishment, or the Foreign Minister. At the outset, we questioned why the security of such a powerful military state had become so vulnerable in terms of economy, scientific-technological potential, the government of the republics, and the citizen, and his spiritual and material welfare. Why had all these factors been relegated to an auxiliary role, pressed into the service of military power?

Traditional, centuries-old notions of national security as the defense of the country from external military threat have been shaken by profound structural and qualitative shifts in human civilization, the result of the growing role of science and technology and the increasing political, economic, social, and informational interdependence of the world. States that rely mostly on military means of protection cannot consider themselves safe. They are in a no-win position, for the source of political influence in the world and the protection of national interest increasingly depend on economic, technological, and financial factors, whereas enormous arsenals of weapons cannot provide rational answers to the challenges of the day. These weapons cannot be used without risking the destruction of one's own country, its neighbors, and half the world.

In trying to trace how, when, and why the Soviet Union was compelled to stockpile nuclear arms, one must conclude that we were always trying to catch up to the Americans. Of course, given the conditions at the end of the 1940s and beginning of the 1950s, the Soviet Union was compelled to develop its own nuclear potential. But in allowing ourselves to be dragged into the arms race—both nuclear and conventional—and infatuated with volume and quantity, we responded with excessive zeal, when it would have been possible to give asymmetrical, quantitatively less, but qualitatively better "answers."

Along with their losses and wounds, our long-suffering Soviet people emerged from World War II with a sense of pride in themselves and their country for having saved the world from fascism. Later they were willing to sacrifice everything for the sake of strengthening the country's defense. And their sacrifices were accepted without the slightest thought given to the fact that a country of socially and politically humiliated people cannot gain security. In such a country, a human being is only the means for obtaining security (we might ask: whose?), not the object of that security.

In overcoming the inertia of customary notions, we discovered that the possession of a bloated nuclear arsenal undermined rather than augmented national defense, draining resources from the effort to ensure a high technical level of peaceful production, education, and health, and maximum satisfaction of the population's needs. It became abundantly clear to us that any foreign policy programs, plans, and actions, including methods of achieving national security, must be strictly measured against real national priorities, with the long-range interests of the citizen in mind.

There is no question that over the decades the U.S.S.R. has created an enormous technological, intellectual, and economic potential. But how is it being used? How do factors of "national might" like size of territory, natural resources, intellectual potential, and state and national institutes of learning work—if they are working at all?

Vast expanses have been turned into ecological disaster areas under pressure from irrational centralism. What about natural resources? Avaricious exploitation—"fulfilling the plan at any price"—has exhausted national resources and has not even compensated with a qualitative growth in the economy. Having earned a "quick and easy" 180 billion dollars on oil, the Soviet Union derived no economic benefit at all, nor any improvement in the material status of its citizens. The morale of the society and the stability of national and state institutions were maintained by a mendacious "propaganda of success," the suppression of dissent, and the encouragement to fear internal and external enemies, with threats of punishment and revenge for wrong behavior. . . .

. . . The "image of the enemy," which we had so much difficulty overcoming, was fashioned to contrast with the true character of the Soviet people, but it was alien to their friendliness, bravery, wisdom, and self-sacrifice. Belief in the Soviet people's creative, peace-loving nature was undermined by reprisals against "dissidents," statements like "we'll bury you," wrongful actions (to put it mildly) with regard to our friends, and the preaching of peaceful coexistence as a specific form of class struggle.

Foreign policy was made in the name of the people—behind their backs. It had always claimed to be in the national interest. But was it really? Did the paranoid obsession with military security, which led to the massive deployment of RSD-10 (SS20) missiles, benefit the people? Did the habit of "slamming the door," formed in the 1950s, which became a stereotype of behavior in the early 1980s, when we walked out of the Geneva talks and thus accelerated the creation of a hostile second strategic front in Europe? Did the self-defeating policy of pseudo-support for developing nations, mainly through guns and armaments? Was the sending of our troops to Afghanistan for the welfare of the people? Alas, questions of this type could be continued at length. . . .

Let us have a look at the political and economic cost of the cold war. The last two decades of ideological confrontation with the West, by some estimates, added 700 billion rubles to the cost of military defense, in excess of what it cost to achieve military parity with the United States and the West.

By worshipping the idols of pseudo-ideology, we impoverished our whole country. Unrealistic, essentially confrontational doctrines and an entrenched bureaucratic-command system for making the most important foreign policy decisions have proved to be unbearably costly. Now we are being called to account supposedly because the philosophy of the new thinking has come into clear conflict with the interests of national security. I am prepared to accept this argument, but with one slight amendment: It is in clear conflict with the superpower philosophy and psychology.

We could, of course, eliminate the conflict by sacrificing the new thinking, but then we would doom the country to a final break with world civilization, with all the attendant consequences.

I want the critics of the new thinking to name the price they are willing to pay for this "back-tracking" in terms of the only possible standard, the one we scorned in the past and, by doing so, turned ourselves from victors into losers. I mean the standard of human life.

The Fall of Communism in Eastern Europe

Reform in the Soviet Union and Gorbachev's withdrawal from Cold War confrontation with the West set the stage for the extraordinary series of governmental changes in Eastern Europe in the year 1989, by sapping the will of the East European Communists to hold out against popular opposition. Change began with step-by-step democratization in Poland and Hungary, the more reform-oriented Communist regimes; continued with the abrupt collapse of the hard-line regimes in East Germany and Czechoslovakia; and concluded with the violent overthrow of the oppressive, personalistic dictatorship of Nicolae Ceauşescu in Romania. The bit-by-bit crumbling of Yugoslavia followed in the succeeding months.

In 1991 the de facto collapse of the Communist alliance in Eastern Europe was formally acknowledged with the dissolution of the Warsaw Treaty organization.

a) Poland—The Compromise with Solidarity

In the climate of reform set by perestroika in the USSR, the Solidarity labor movement under Lech Wałęsa resumed its oppositional efforts in Poland, especially by strikes. In the "round table" talks of the winter and spring of 1989 between the government and the opposition, the Communists were forced to give up their one-party dictatorship and agree to free elections to the Senate and partially free elections to the Sejm (the lower house of parliament). In the June elections Solidarity swept all seats that were open and set the stage for the first post-Communist cabinet under Tadeusz Mazowiecki. The Communist president General Wojciech Jaruzelski resigned the following year and Wałęsa was elected to replace him.

After years of the economic crisis and political conflicts, Poland is facing a great threat but also a great chance. The threat of the deepening crisis is real but there is however a chance to overcome it through the radical reform of the state and the simultaneous restructuring of the economic system. In defence against the crisis and in actions in favour of the reforms, Poles can and should reach an agreement.

A political compromise of various forces will help materialize the common target: the independent, sovereign, secured by equal alliances, democratic and economically strong Poland.

The foundation for the agreement are the principles of the future political system stemming from the inalienable right of citizens to live in a state that fully implements [the] nation's sovereignty. This means:

—Political pluralism that finds its reflection above all in the right to freely set up associations, within the democratic constitutional order, of political, social and labour character,

—the freedom of speech, this including the creating of real possibilities of access to all mass media to different political forces,

—the democratic course of appointing all representative bodies of the state authority so that the voters be the ones to decide who is to wield power,

—independence of courts and their statutory right to control other bodies set up to guard the law-abidingness and public order,

—a territorial self-government strong through its rights and chosen in free elections.

FROM: "Round Table Stance on Political Reforms," summary in English by the Polish Press Agency, April 5, 1989 (in FBIS-EEU-89-065, April 6, 1989, pp. 26-28).

The sides stated that such rules should map out the further political evolution and declared their support for them.

An important stage in the political evolution are changes made already now: the implementation of the principle of trade union and social pluralism (including the legal activities of NSZZ [Independent Self-Governing Trade Union] Solidarność, NSZZ Solidarność and Private Farmers, and the legalisation of NZS [Independent Students Union]), the recognition of the opposition's right to legal activities, the new law on associations, the beginning of reforms in the law and courts of law, expansion of the freedom of expresson, and a considerable democratisation of the elections to represent[ative] organs. This year's elections will choose the Sejm and Senate in which various political forces will share decisions concerning the future of the state.

This is the beginning of the road to parliamentary democracy. The task of the parliament elected in this year's election is to produce a new, democratic constitution and a new democratic election law. The sides will do all they can to have the next parliament fully determined by the will of the electorate.

Poland is a common home of all citizens. We agree that all the national minorities living in Poland have full rights. We are aware of the responsibility for maintaining and developing the links with all compatriots and persons of Polish lineage residing abroad in the East and West alike.

The basis for bringing democracy in the structures of all levels of the state will be provided by the separation of power into the legislature, executive, and judicature.

We disagree on many questions. We speak of that openly in the agreement being signed at the round table. We have, however, a common willingness to act in a way that will give Poland a democratic and efficient organisation of the state life, prevent the attempts to hamper and reverse the democratic changes.

The elections to the Sejm and Senate in 1989 will be held according to the following procedure:

All procedures of screening candidates which are not part of the elections are cancelled. The number of candidates for each deputy['s] mandate and candidates for senators is unrestricted depending solely on the number of correctly made nominations.

The right to nominate candidates is given not only to the PUWP (Polish United Workers Party), UPP (United Peasants Party), DP (Democratic Party), PAX (Catholic Association), UCHS [Social-Christian Party] but also to every independent group of 3,000 or more citizens. . . .

The freedom of the elections to the 10th Sejm will be limited by the allocation of mandates agreed upon at the round table. The deal concerning the allocation of mandates applies only to the election for the 10th Sejm. It says that 60 per cent of mandates goes to the coalition of the PUWP, UPP, and DP, 5 percent to the PAX, PZKS, and UCHS (Catholic groups). Non-party candidates nominated by independent groups of citizens will compete for 35 percent of the total number of mandates. Part of the coalition's mandates will be given to persons on the nationwide list including up to 10 per cent of the seats in the future Sejm.

The freedom of Senate elections is not restricted by any agreement concerning the allocation of mandates. . . .

The reform of state institutions covers the Sejm, Senate, office of president and courts.

The Sejm remains the supreme authority of legislative power. The Senate, merged with the Sejm into the National Assembly, will elect [the] president of the first term of office by an absolute majority. The candidate for the president may be forwarded by one-fourth of deputies and senators.

The Senate, chosen through the nation's sovereign will, will perform an essential control particularly in the field of human rights and law-abidingness as well as socio-economic life.

The president's term of office will last six years. The president will have vast powers in the field of representation of the state and executive power. The president may refuse to sign a law and return it to the Sejm together with a substantiated motion for re-examination. The Sejm may overrule presidential veto with two-thirds of votes. The presidential acts of essential significance (acts of high public authority), with the exception of implementing acts [of] powers applying to foreign and defense policy of the state, will require countersignature (confirmation) of the chairman of the Council of Ministers.

The president may introduce a three-month state of emergency in the case of a threat to the state's security or a natural calamity. It may be extended for another three months only one time, by an agreed resolution of the Sejm and the Senate. The Sejm and the Senate cannot be dissolved during the state of emergency, nor can the Constitution and the electoral law be changed.

The president may dissolve the Sejm if it fails to appoint a government in the course of 3 months, or pass a long-term socio-economic development plan, and if a Sejm law hits out at the president's constitutional prerogatives. After dissolving the parliament the president declares new elections.

Independence of the judiciary will be guarded by the national council of the judiciary. . . .

b) Hungary—The Last Stand of Reformed Communism

Reformers led by Politburo member Imre Poszgay took control of the Hungarian Communist ("Socialist Workers") Party in the spring of 1989, adopted a program of democratization, and agreed in the "Trilateral Political Coordination Talks" with the political opposition and trade unions in the summer of 1989 to end the one-party dictatorship. As the hard-liners split off, the party changed its name to "Hungarian Socialist Party," but it had to go into opposition when anti-Communist and nationalist forces prevailed in the free elections of March 1990.

The Reform Manifesto

"The reform forces of the HSWP [Hungarian Socialist Workers Party] that have existed for decades, have gained the upper hand and opened the way for a peaceful transition from state socialism to democratic socialism," says the introductory

FROM: Draft Manifesto of the Hungarian Socialist Workers Party, summarized and quoted by Budapest radio, August 18 & 19, 1989 (in English; FBIS-EEU-89-163, August 24, 1989, pp. 32–35); Report on Coordination Agreement, Budapest Radio, September 18, 1989 (in English; FBIS-EEU-89-180, September 19, 1989, pp. 39–40); Reszö Nyers [Communist Minister of the Economy], Statement on the Trilateral Political Coordination Talks, Budapest Television, September 18, 1989 (English translation in FBIS-EEU-89-181, September 20, 1989, pp. 27–28).

statement of the HSWP draft manifesto published in the Saturday issue of the Hungarian newspaper "Nepszabadsag".

The text, which is about 20 pages long, says, "the main purpose of the HSWP is a peaceful and gradual transition to democratic socialism, to bring about a society of self-governing communities that allows the free development of individuals and their societies."

"Hungary will become a constitutional state based on a multi-party system in which the source of power is the will of the people manifested at free elections.

The HSWP wants to establish a "socialist welfare state," which "has a just social system built on the results of an efficient market economy."

A change of models became necessary because, "the situation in Hungary has become critical owing to state socialism." . . . Therefore, the HSWP dissociates itself from all versions of Stalinism, but, at the same time, feels responsible for the crisis, and consequently considers it its duty to take a part in overcoming it. The HSWP calls for sacrifices, and at the same time provides safeguards that they will not be in vain: "With the establishment of a multi-party system, social control and openness, the party itself has created the institutions for calling it to account to control how it keeps its promises," the document stresses.

The document says the essence of the transition to democratic socialism can be summarized as follows: The establishment of the institutions of a democratic and constitutional state, a balanced distribution of power, in which the main share goes to a parliament controlled by public opinion, the president of the Republic, and the constitutional court, and in which local self-governing communities are given total autonomy, a multi-party system, the protection of ethnic, religious and other minorities, openness and a political system functioning in a clear-cut way and easy to control.

The HSWP feels the socialist character of this system would lie in the free development of communities and individuals, social justice and equity, an equality of chances and solidarity, the firm system of social security, independent action and participative democracy, as well as social control over every level of the political system.

The primary aspect of the reform endeavours is a reform of the party itself, which involves changing its name as well. The HSWP intends to turn into a socialist party and enter into competition with the other parties under the constitution; it will acknowledge the common will of the nation as it is manifested at the elections, but at the same time, strives to obtain a major governmental influence. . . .

The economic role of the state should be reshaped so that it would fulfil the same function as in all the developed countries of the world, namely that of encouraging the market, fending off its harmful effects, supporting the introduction of new technology, etc.

The draft calls it socially useful that new types of income are appearing in addition to those earned by work, such as capital, entrepreneurial profits, innovation fees, fees for brokers and middlemen, etc. It acknowledges that the minority who are willing to take a risk and are the power behind development should receive larger incomes in return for their successful efforts. It underlines, however, that no stratum should be allowed permanently and fatally to lag behind the average groups of society even during the period of rapid transformation.

The draft regards education and the development of science as basic conditions for progress. There should be an immediate and radical turn-around in the material and moral recognition of intellectual work and that done by the professional classes. The state monopoly over the foundation and running of educational institutions should be terminated at every level of the educational system, and professional autonomy, academic freedom and self-government should be guaranteed. . . .

The renewing party is committed to left-wing socialist and humanist ideas, and wishes to unite communist and social democratic values. It is aware that no historical example exists for the transition from dictatorical socialism to a democratic socialism that is based on a market economy. This goal cannot be reached by copying foreign models and the application of abstract ideologies. A break should be made with models that are alien to life, that are forced onto society from above and outside. . . .

The aim of the HSWP is for NATO and the Warsaw Treaty to become unnecessary and dissolvable simultaneously in this century. The party holds the internal reform of the Warsaw Treaty, its democratization, and the intensification of the defence nature of its military doctrine to be necessary. Its conviction is that affiliation to an alliance system cannot be the basis of interference into the internal affairs of states. . . . It supports the idea that all foreign troops be withdrawn from the areas of the European states. This would include the pull-out—as part of the disarmament process—of the Soviet troops stationed in Hungary. . . .

"Following the bloody tragedy of the World War II, we began to form the new-type democracy in a relatively favourable atmosphere until 1947. The representational-parliamentary system, and the direct, territorial self-government developed in a liberated manner. When all is said, democratic socialism was outlined in the picture of the future presented to the nation by the socialist forces."

"However, the cold war, the sharp opposition of the great powers with each other, the deterioration of the world political climate ended this highly promising development." . . . "The party essentially ceased to exist as a political movement. The institutionalized violence was accompanied by a personality cult and the repoliticization of all areas of life."

"From 1953, the reform tendency that professes the original democratic targets of the party, that expresses the actual demands of society, that represents the national interests, is visibly and with unbroken continuity present in the Hungarian Communist movement with the government programme of Imre Nagy. From that time on, the true history of the party is the history of the internal fight against Stalinism."

"A popular uprising broke out in October 23, 1956 to sweep away Stalinism in Hungary, to renew socialism."

"The Hungarian Socialist Workers' Party was set up on October 31, 1956, under the leadership of János Kádár and Imre Nagy, and declared the satisfaction of the just popular demands as an indispensable condition of democratic socialist renewal."

"However, contrary to its statement made on October 30, the Soviet leadership decided on military intervention, and crushed the uprising. The HSWP wing led by János Kádár accepted the task of consolidation, against the threatening danger of the restoration of the Rakosi-Gerö group."

"Imre Nagy . . . accepted a martyr's death. . . . János Kádár was forced to make grave compromises. . . . He had to accept the monolithic political system, and centralized plan economy. What is more, he also had to temporarily give up the reforms prepared after November 4. In return for this, however, he tried to realize all that was possible from the 1956 efforts of the HSWP in the power space of the Soviet intervention, with cautious, gradual and partial modifications, a change in political style."

"The new policy was highlighted by the announcement of the comprehensive reform of the economic mechanism and the agricultural cooperative practice in the 1960's and 1970's. However, the Hungarian experiment remained isolated, and economic relations between the socialist countries made it impossible to consistently enforce our goals. The unchanged nature in the essence of the political system led to regression from time to time. However, the 15-20 year stage of the Kádár policy brought, even with its contradictions, a prosperity unparalleled in the recent history of Hungarian society." . . . "From the mid-1970's the HSWP became the prisoner of the rapidly outdated economic structure and the rigid power relations. The economic leadership replied to the growing difficulties first by reducing investments, and then the growth of the living standard." . . .

"It became clear for the reform forces of the party that it is impossible to solve the vital problems of the nation without the internal renewal of the HSWP and the transformation of the system of political institutions. The fact that [a] turn occurred in the policy of the Communist Party of the Soviet Union in 1985, and reform processes emerged also in several other socialist countries, greatly promoted these efforts." . . .

The Trilateral Agreement

An agreement was signed on Monday at the plenary session of the political coordination talks. The document was signed by representatives of the Hungarian Socialist Workers' Party, and—of the nine organizations that belong to the Opposition Roundtable—by the Endre Bajcsy-Zsilinszky Society, the Independent Smallholders' Party, the Christian Democratic People's Party, the Hungarian Democratic Forum, the Social Democratic Party of Hungary, and the Hungarian People's Party, as well as the social organizations and movements constituting the third side.

The sides declared that in accordance with the principles set down in the basic agreement, the talks serve to create the political and legal conditions of the peaceful transition, to establish the democratic constitutional state based on a multiparty system, and to seek the road that leads out from the social and economic crisis.

As a result of the talks, six bills related to the essential, cordial issues of peaceful transition are to be forwarded to the prime minister, for [the] government to submit these to National Assembly. The bills concern the amendment of the constitution, the court of the constitution, the operation and management of parties, the election of MPs to parliament, the amendment of the penal code, and the amendment of the criminal proceedings law.

The drafts contain alternative solutions. The Opposition Roundtable is to make public its differing opinion in the form of a statement.

The agreement includes the statement that peaceful transition is to last until the statutory session of the new National Assembly to come about through free elections, and the demand that participants of the trilateral coordination talks enjoy political and personal immunity.

The sides hold it necessary to reduce the pressures on [the] National assembly and its members, in other words, MPs should be spared from unjustified recalling and appeals for resignation.

A multi-party political system cannot fundamentally imply greater financial burdens on society than the one-party structure.

Under the agreement, the principle of impartiality should be fully enforced in the work of the national information institutions. In this interest, the impartial information committee is to be set up from personalities to be delegated by the organizations of the three sides. . . .

The Reform Communists on the Agreement

. . . As a result of 3 months' hard consultations, we have reached the end of a stage. With our signature we can strengthen the political consensus that has come into being on the principles and regulations serving the peaceful transition. This is a joint achievement, which is witness to the three sides' constructiveness, their intention to reach agreement and their self-discipline. I am of the view that we have made a big stride toward a political system in which the political will springs from the citizen, and this will is realized by institutions built on society's creditable initiatives coming from below. The national building of democracy will be a work which we shall create shoulder to shoulder by joint effort.

Since May 1988 the MSZMP [Hungarian Socialist Workers Party, i.e., the Communists] has been progressing unwaveringly on the path of reforms. It has set as its target the realization of democratic socialism. We are living through fateful times. Our decisions will determine the future of the nation. To avoid deepening the crisis demands a change of political model, a constitutional state, the institutions of a modern parliamentary democracy. This system, with regard to our common conduct, can be built only on patience and on mutual understanding. Let us heed the warning of Lajos Kossuth*: let us not argue about what we have been: let us unite upon what we should become.

Taking into consideration also the political experiences of our recent historical past, the MSZMP considers democracy, the principle of people's sovereignty, to be a value that cannot be replaced by anything else. We, however, also think and act in practice. We must keep it in view that the change of political model has to be realized by retaining the country's governability. We are all responsible also for seeing to it that the economy's ability to function should be maintained even amidst the considerable changes.

Only one way out of the economic crisis is on offer: a radical speed-up of the economic reform process, the increasingly effective involvement of external resources, including in the form of operating capital. One of the indispensable conditions for this, however, is the stability of our domestic political life. A self-lacerating country burdened with party conflicts cannot expect the governments of the developed countries to see it as an attractive partner, or international financial circles to consider it to be a promising area for investments. . . .

When our negotiating delegation signed the document on the preliminary agreements, our party was guided not by the method of handing over power, but

*Kossuth—leader of the unsuccessful Hungarian revolt against Austrian rule, 1848-49—Ed.

by the objective of transforming the exercise of power. I would like to remind you that it was our party itself which started the dismantling of the party-state, and it considered the creation of constitutional statehood to be its main task. It is our conviction that the development of legal institutions which also by European standards is reckoned to be modern, serve alike political stability, peaceful transition, and the new national consensus.

We do not consider the assertion of people's sovereignty, the creation of democracy, to be closed with the development of multiparty parliamentarism. While we commit ourselves on the side of representational democracy based on the multiparty system, we also take a stance that the citizens' organization of a nonpolitical purpose should also expand and strengthen, and that autonomous communities should widely develop. . . .

It is in the country's interest that we hold free elections as soon as possible. This, however, also makes it necessary that the parties' operation, their economic management, should happen within legal guarantees, settled legal frameworks. The practice of the developed bourgeois democracies warns us not to curb the parties' operation where that does not run counter to the demands of constitutional statehood. Also for this reason, the MSZMP, as first and foremost the party of the workers, insists that no state regulations or laws should prohibit free organization at workplaces.

The MSZMP ascribes great significance to the institution of President of the Republic. We are of the view that it is in the common national interest that the presidential election should take place this year. Such a solution would have a calming effect on the country's ever more vexed public opinion before the complexities of a parliamentary election of multiple chances, an eventual multiparty government. But rationality dictates this even if I think of the tasks connected with the maintaining and improving of the country's international relations. Within a foreseeable time, therefore, parliamentary elections will take place in Hungary.

On behalf of our negotiating delegation I would again like to reaffirm: Our party undertakes to be measured by means of democratic elections. Only the free expression of society's will can bring into being a new parliament which, with the knowledge of its responsibility felt for the nation's fate, and also knowing that it has the population's support behind it, can do its legislative work.

The MSZMP, depending on the results of the election, is ready to share governmental responsibility with other parties. It is unavoidable that in the current situation, the political forces have an interest, rather, in separating themselves from one another, in shaping their own political profile and in making this known. In spite of this, in the coming months, we ought to endeavor that, in spite of egotistical party interests, the joint sense of responsibility and joint work prevail in the political landscape.

We are facing decisive months. To no small extent it also depends on those sitting in this hall whether we shall be able to take advantage of this unparalleled historical opportunity, whether we shall create a democratic constitutional state that facilitates modernization. At present, our left-wing, socialist reform party, which is undergoing rebirth, is mobilizing its forces to make use of this historical opportunity, and it calls on every Hungarian citizen who feels responsibility for his homeland's fate to support this. . . .

c) The Collapse of East Germany

East Germany's hardline Communist government faced a crisis when Gorbachev's visit for its fortieth anniversary on October 7, 1989, encouraged the democratic "New Forum" opposition and triggered a wave of pro-democracy demonstrations. Lacking Soviet backing, the East German authorities hesitated to use force, while the opening of travel to the West through reformist Hungary invited a torrent of refugees to flee. The Berlin government tried to save itself by opening the Berlin Wall, but opposition nevertheless snowballed, and the Communists surrendered to the coalition government that soon negotiated reunification with West Germany. Meanwhile reform Communists tried to restructure their party on social-democratic lines, to little avail.

New Forum

In our country there is a clear breakdown in communication between state and society. This is confirmed by widespread disaffection and retreat into the private sphere or mass exodus. Refugee movements on this scale are usually caused by want, starvation and violence. That clearly cannot be true of the GDR.

The damaged relationship between state and society paralyses the creative forces of our society and prevents solutions being found to the problems we face at local and global level. We squander our energies in bad-tempered passivity when we have more important things to do for our lives, our country and humanity. The reconciliation of interests between groups and social divisions in state and the economy is not working properly. In addition, public communication about the situation and personal interests is repressed. In private, everyone readily offers a diagnosis and discusses the most important measures to be taken, but their wishes and efforts differ widely and are neither weighed up rationally nor assessed for their practicability. On the one hand we want a broader choice of goods and a better supply; on the other we see the social and environmental costs of these measures and call for an end to unrestrained growth. We want scope for economic initiative without this degenerating into a rat-race. We want to hold on to what has been successful while creating space for renewal so that we can live less wasteful and environmentally destructive lives. We want ordered relations but not state diktat. We want free, confident people who also act with a sense of community. We want to be protected against violence without having to face a society of henchmen and informers. Idlers and armchair heroes should be driven from their privileged positions without placing the socially weak and defenceless at a disadvantage. We want an effective health system for all, but no one should be allowed to feign illness at the expense of others. We want to export and participate in international trade without becoming either the debtor or servant of the leading industrial nations or the exploiter and creditor of the economically weaker ones.

If we are to recognise all these contradictions, listen to and assess opinions and arguments and distinguish general from particular interests, we need a *democratic dialogue* about the role of the rule of law, the economy and culture. We must care-

FROM: "Awakening 89," New Forum Manifesto, September 9, 1989 (English translation Copyright © by Gert Glaessner 1992. From *The Unification Process in Germany*. By Glaessner, Gert-Joachim. Reprinted with permission of St. Martin's Press, Incorporated. Pages 137–38. Also reprinted by permission of Pinter Publishers, London, England). German Democratic Republic, New Travel Regulations, November 9, 1989 (English translation in FBIS-EEU-89-217, November 13, 1989, p. 27); Programme of the Party of Democratic Socialism, Feburary 25, 1990 (English translation in Glaessner, pp. 153–154).

fully consider and debate these questions publicly, *together*, the *length and breadth of the country*. The readiness and will to achieve this will depend on our ability to find a way out of the present critical situation in the foreseeable future. In the circumstances of current social developments we need
—the participation of more people in the process of social reform,
—the pooling of the many individual and group efforts.
To this end we hereby found a *political platform* for the whole of the GDR which will enable people from all professions, backgrounds, parties and groups to play a role in the discussion and resolution of social problems which is vital to this country. We choose to give this overarching initiative the name NEW FORUM.

We shall place the activities of NEW FORUM on a legal basis in accordance with the basic right enshrined in Article 29 of the Constitution of the GDR to articulate our political interest by common action as an association. We shall register the creation of such an association with the responsible organs of state of the GDR in accordance with the Constitutional Order of 6 November 1975 (*Legal Gazette I*, No. 44, p. 723).

Any effort to give NEW FORUM expression and a voice is based on the quest for justice, democracy, peace and the protection of our natural world. It is this impulse we wish to see fulfilled in all areas in the coming transformation of society. We appeal to all the citizens of the GDR eager to participate in a transformation of society to join NEW FORUM. The time is ripe.

Opening The Berlin Wall

. . . The GDR council of Ministers has decided that until a relevant legal regulation of the People's Chamber comes into force the following rules for private trips and permanent emigration from the GDR abroad are in force with immediate effect:

1. Private journeys abroad can be applied for without meeting preconditions (reasons for journeys and degree of kindred). Permission will be given promptly. Reasons for rejection will only be applied in particularly exceptional cases.

2. The responsible passport and registration departments of the district offices of the People's Police in the GDR are instructed to issue visas for permanent emigration without delay and without the still valid conditions for permanent emigration having to exist. The application for permanent emigration is, as before, also possible at the departments for internal affairs.

3. Permanent emigration can take place via all GDR border crossing points to the FRG and Berlin (West).

4. The temporary issuing of permission at the foreign missions of the GDR and permanent emigration with the GDR personal identity card via third countries thus lapses.

The Party of Democratic Socialism

Our values
The values our party is committed to are:

1. *Individuality*. This includes the free development of thought and feeling, the abilities and talents of everybody, the implementation of individual aspirations and endeavours, rich social relations with other people, and independence in judgement and action of each individual.

2. *Solidarity.* We want to develop and shape solidarity among the working people, the generations, the sexes, the people, nations and nationalities.

3. *Justice.* Everybody, each social and national group, each democratic political force shall have the same chances and the same rights to represent their interests in society.

4. *Meaningful work and leisure time.* This presupposes efficient working conditions, gradual reduction and flexibility of working time in the interest of the employees and a work content which promotes the personality of the worker. There must be more possibilities to make creative use of leisure time according to one's wishes and so find the rest, relaxation, and stimulation necessary for the well-being and development of mankind.

5. *Freedom, democracy, and human rights.* Respect for the dignity and freedom of each individual is indispensable to life in a democratic society. For us, the human rights in their unity and universality are the decisive yardstick for all actions in society.

6. *Preservation of the natural foundations of life.* The existence of each individual depends on this. For this reason, economy and ecology must be connected with each other in a new way in the overall social reproduction process as well as on an international scale. Needs and life-style must be oriented to a healthy and attractive environment so as to preserve it for future generations.

7. *National and international peace.* A political life marked by non-violence, tolerance, mutual respect of all social groups, of sexes, generations, and nationalities, by dialogue and creative debates, love and peace, humanism, anti-Fascism, international friendship and by respect for other cultures is indispensable to the safeguarding of peace in our society and in all nations.

Our aims
We pursue a left-wing, socialist policy and stand for
—freedom for everybody to develop;
—a modern state under the rule of law, where individual and political as well as social, cultural, and collective human rights are put into practice;
—a market economy with a high degree of social and ecological security, equal chances and personal freedom for all members of society;
—real social equality for men and women and a new way of their living together;
—a society which provides warmth, protection and assistance for children, senior citizens, handicapped, and all people with special needs;
—unbureaucratic structures and self-determined development for communities;
—broad possibilities for the political, professional and cultural development of young people;
—a society with a culture where the individual can develop, where science, education, culture and sports develop freely and are accessible to all people;
—peace, general and complete disarmament, cosmopolitan attitudes, friendship and solidarity with all nations, for a just international economic order and for the respect of the right to self-determination for all peoples.
To realise these aims we strive for a democratic socialism together with other left-wing and democratic forces.
Democratic socialism means to fight for a peaceful, humane society marked by

solidarity, where everybody can freely develop alongside everybody else and all enjoy equal participation in economic, political, intellectual and cultural life.

Democratic socialism is not yet a completed system nor is it a social system which will soon exist on German soil. It is a road, a permanent task and challenge.

d) Czechoslovakia—The "Velvet Revolution"

After the breakup of Communist rule in East Germany the days of the Communist regime in Czechoslovakia, the last hardline holdout in Central Europe, were numbered. A series of student demonstrations in Prague culminated on November 17, 1989, in a vicious police attack on the marchers. This triggered a nationwide wave of revulsion mobilized by the new umbrella opposition group Civic Forum under the playwright Václav Havel, and the authority of the government evaporated. The die-hards under General Secretary Miloš Jakeš quit; the Communist Party surrendered its monopoly of power; and on December 10 the former deputy prime minister Marian Čalfa formed a coalition cabinet (just as he was leaving the Communist Party himself). Shortly afterwards the National Assembly elected Havel president. This largely non-violent transition set the stage for free elections, an ardently anti-Communist government, and the ultimate separation of the Czech Republic and Slovakia.

Civic Forum

Our country has found itself in a deep moral, spiritual, ecological, social, economic, and political crisis. This crisis is testimony to the ineffectiveness of the hitherto existing political and economic system. All mechanisms essential for society to react to changing domestic and foreign conditions have been discarded. The self-evident principle that whoever has power must also accept responsibility has not been respected for many decades. All three fundamental powers in the state—the legislative, the executive, and the judicial—have merged into the hands of a narrow, ruling group consisting almost exclusively of Communist party members. The foundations of the legal state have thereby been destroyed.

The Communist party monopoly in filling all important posts has created a system of subjection that has paralyzed the whole of society. People are thereby condemned to the role of mere executors of the orders handed down from on high. They are denied political, civil, and human rights. The centralized management of the economy operating under the command system has been a conspicuous failure. The promised restructuring of the economic mechanism has been slow, inconsistently applied, and not accompanied by appropriate political changes.

These problems will not be changed by replacing those persons in positions of power or by the retirement of a handful of politicians from public life.

Citizens Forum is striving for the following objectives:

1. *The Law.* The Czechoslovak republic must be a legal, democratic state in the spirit and traditions of Czechoslovak statehood and of internationally valid principles expressed above all in the international treaty on civil and political rights.

A new constitution must be worked out in this spirit, in which the relations between citizens and the state must be more precisely regulated. Only a newly elected constituent assembly can pass such a constitution. The exercise of civil

FROM: "What We Want: the Program and Principles of Civic Forum," November 26, 1989 (English translation in Bernard Wheaton and Zdeněk Kavan, *The Velvet Revolution: Czechoslovakia, 1988–1991,* Boulder, Colo., Westview Press, 1992, pp. 206–208, reprinted by permission of the publisher); News Conference of Federal Premier Marian Čalfa, Prague Television, December 10, 1989 (English translation in FBIS-EEU-89-236, December 11, 1989, pp. 28–29, 31–33).

rights and freedoms will be reliably ensured by a developed system of legal guarantees. The independent judiciary will also include constitutional and administrative courts.

The whole Czechoslovak legal system will gradually be brought into agreement with these principles and become binding on all citizens and also on the organs and officials of state.

We insist that the wrongs done in the past occasioned by politically motivated persecution be put right.

2. *The Political System.* We demand fundamental, consistent, and permanent changes in the political system of our society. We must remake or renew democratic institutions and mechanisms that make possible the real participation of all citizens in the administration of public affairs and at the same time provide effective barriers against the abuse of economic and political power. All existing and newly emerging political parties and other social and political associations must therefore have equal conditions for participation in free elections at all levels of government. This assumes, however, that the Communist party abandon its constitutionally guaranteed leading role in our society and likewise its monopoly of the means of communication. Nothing prevents it from doing so tomorrow.

Czechoslovakia, though remaining a federation, will be a union of both nations and all nationalities with equal rights.

3. *Foreign Policy.* We must take steps so that our country regains an honorable place in Europe and the world. We are a part of Central Europe, and hence we wish to maintain good relations with all our neighbors.

We count on becoming part of the process of European integration. We would also prefer to give priority to the idea of the Common European Home over that of the Warsaw Pact and Comecon. Maintaining our sovereignty as a state, we nevertheless wish to revise agreements that were inspired by the unreasonable ambitions of the leading representatives of the state.

4. *The Economy.* We must abandon the previous system of economic management. It takes away all appetite for work, squanders its results, devastates natural resources, destroys the environment, and deepens the wholesale backwardness of Czechoslovakia. We are convinced that it is not possible to improve this method of management by piecemeal reforms.

We wish to create a market undeformed by bureaucratic intervention. Its successful functioning is conditioned by the monopoly positions of today's great concerns and by the formation of genuine competition. This can only emerge on the basis of the parallel existence of different kinds of ownership with equal rights and with the gradual opening of our economy to the world.

The state naturally will maintain a series of indispensable functions. It will guarantee general conditions of enterprise, the same for all, and introduce a macroeconomic policy of regulation to control inflation, the growth of our foreign debt, and impending unemployment. Only the state can guarantee the essential minimum of public and social services and the protection of the environment.

5. *Social Justice.* It is essential that conditions emerge in society for the development and application of everybody's abilities. The same conditions and chances should be extended to everybody.

Czechoslovakia must become a socially just society in which the people receive help in old age, in sickness, and in times of hardship. However, a growing national economy is the essential prerequisite for such a society.

The church, the community, firms, and the most varied state and voluntary organizations can contribute to the origin of a diverse network of social services. This will thereby extend opportunities for the application of the precious sense of human solidarity, responsibility, and love for your neighbor. These humane principles are essential, particularly today, for our national fellowship.

6. *The Environment.* All of us must seek a way to the renewal of the harmony between human and nature. We will strive for a gradual rectification of the damage we have done to the environment in the last decades. . . .

7. *Culture.* Culture cannot simply be a matter for artists, scientists, and teachers but must be a way of life for the whole of civil society. It must free itself from the shackles of whatever ideology and overcome the artificial division from world culture. . . .

Let a democratic school system be organized on humanist principles without a state monopoly of education. Society must value teachers in all kinds of schools and must give them space to apply their own personalities. It is necessary to return historical rights to the universities, which once guaranteed them their independence and academic freedom, not only for the faculty but also for the students.

We regard the education of our society as the most valuable national asset. Upbringing and education must lead to independent thought and morally responsible behavior.

This is what we want. Today our program is short. We are, however, working on its finalization. Citizens Forum is an open association of citizens. We therefore appeal to everybody who can contribute to this work to take part.

Calfa's News Conference

Ladies and gentlemen, I would like to inform you that today at 1300, the president of the Czechoslovak Socialist Republic appointed the federal government in [its] new composition. The forming of this government was preceded by very complex talks among all major political forces of Czechoslovak society. These talks culminated yesterday by a principle agreement at the table—which was not round, because we did not manage to quickly find one of necessary size—but it fulfilled the political function which we imagine under the conception of a roundtable. The result is a government of national understanding. The president appointed me as its chairman. . . .

Allow me, ladies and gentlemen, to inform you briefly of the principal tasks the government is facing:

First, the new federal government must, within the framework of its constitutional powers, do everything to prepare for free and democratic elections. Only such elections will justly measure the real distribution of political forces and will enable the formation of state bodies fully representing the people's will.

To achieve this objective, it is necessary to adopt a number of legislative measures in the field of human rights, electoral, assembly, association, press, and similar laws.

Second, the government has an irreplacable role in managing the national economy. We shall continue our efforts to radically reform the economy, which would lead society out of stagnation. The prerequisite is a stable functioning of production, trade, and services and the maintenance of social guarantees for the population. A task of particular importance is the finalization of a well-thought out and realistic program to achieve economic balance, including guarantees for anti-inflationary development, and the purposeful conduct of structural changes. In my view these are the two main tasks of our government.

Right from the beginning we are devoting great attention to the problems of the State Security corps. Our public must be absolutely certain that the entire Security Corps activity is under the control of the government. . . .

Ladies and gentlemen! Czechoslovakia has lived through difficult days. Today we are able to say that the traditional high political culture of our peoples has been demonstrated. We found a way out of the crisis. The agreements between the main political forces, which were concluded yesterday, impose upon us many obligations. I believe that all participants in these talks, especially those who became members of the federal government today, are aware, just as I am, of the moral and political obligations to society which proceed from these agreements. The government of national understanding has undertaken an uneasy role. We shall be able to fulfil it only if we rise above narrow party and personal interests and when we put all our efforts towards benefitting the Republic and benefitting our people. . . .

. . . We are prepared to open up, to open up broadly to mutual cooperation in the economic sphere. Not only this: We want to open up to the world and want to call on all our citizens who have emigrated abroad in any wave of emigration, to return to Czechoslovakia, to visit Czechoslovakia, to invite them and tell them that our country's doors are open to them, and that we shall be glad to see them here. . . .

As far as the events of 17 November are concerned, and court proceedings—if there is a minister in the government in charge of this issue? As I said: An investigation of these events is under way, and the inquiry is carried out by the investigation system, which is not linked to the executive power and therefore not to the government. It is under the control of the Federal Assembly, with the participation of students and representatives of Civic Forum. If this investigation leads to the conclusion that somebody committed a crime—according to my view as well as according to this state's law—then such a person should be tried and an independent court should determine an appropriate sentence. There is nobody in the government in charge of this issue. I draw your attention once more to the fact that those in question are the systems independent of the government. . . .

Why does the CPCZ [Communist Party of Czechoslovakia] have the most weight in the government? I would reply that we adopted a conclusion that the government should consist of people who are capable of carrying out the work of the government in the new conditions, and that is why the Civic Forum representatives also proposed CPCZ members for the government. So it is not a matter of a polarization of forces in the government according to membership of the CPCZ or not. The government should consist of people who should genuinely carry out a new, reformist, humane, and genuinely populist policy. That is the spirit in which we have worked and intend to work in the future, too.

e) Rumania: The December Uprising

Following the Communists' abdication of rule in most of Eastern Europe, a popular uprising broke out in December 1989 against the most repressive—though anti-Soviet—regime

FROM: Communiqués of the National Salvation Front, Bucharest Radio, December 22 and 24, 1989 (English translations in FBIS-EEU-89-246, December 26, 1989, pp. 65–67).

in the region, the dictatorship of Nicolae Ceauşescu in Rumania. Ceauşescu and his wife, attempting to flee, were captured and summarily tried and shot, while a self-styled "National Salvation Front" dominated by anti-Ceauşescu Communists under Ion Iliescu seized power and proclaimed a new democratic era.

NSF Communique of December 22

Citizens, we are living in historic times. The Ceauşescu clan, which has led the country to disaster, was removed from power. All of us know and admit that the victory in which the whole country rejoices is the outcome of the spirit of sacrifice of the broad masses of all nationalities, particularly of our wonderful youth, who, with their blood, restored to us the feeling of national dignity. This is also the great merit of those who for years on end have jeopardized their lives by protesting against the tyranny.

A new page is being opened in Romania's political and economic history. At this turning point, we decided to organize ourselves into the National Salvation Front, which itself relies on the Romanian Army and encompasses all of the country's healthy forces, regardless of nationality, and all organizations and groups who bravely rose to defend freedom and dignity in the years of totalitarian tyranny. The goal of the National Salvation Front is to establish democracy, liberty, and the Romanian people's dignity.

As of this moment, all power structures of the Ceauşescu clan have been dissolved. The government has been dismissed. The State Council and its institutions are ceasing their activity, all state power has been assumed by the Council of the National Salvation Front. The Higher Military Council, which coordinates all of the activity of the Army and the Ministry of Interior units, will be subordinated to the Council of the National Salvation Front. . . .

As a program, the Front proposes the following:

1. To abandon the leading role of a single party and to establish a democratic and pluralistic system of government. [applause from the people in the studio]

2. To organize free elections in April.

3. To separate the legislative, executive, and judiciary powers in the state and to elect all political leaders for one or two mandates [terms], at the most. Nobody should claim power for life.

The Council of the National Salvation Front suggests that in the future the country should be called Romania.* [cheers, applause, chants of "Romania"]

A drafting committee of the new constitution will start to operate at once.

4. To restructure the whole national economy in accordance with the criteria of profitability and efficiency. To eliminate the administrative, bureaucratic methods of centralized economic management and to promote free initiative and competence in the management of all economic sectors.

5. To restructure agriculture and to assist the small scale peasant production. To halt the destruction of villages.

6. To reorganize Romanian education in accordance with the current requirements. To reorganize the educational structure on democratic and humanistic bases. To eliminate ideological dogmas that have caused so much damage to the Romanian people, and to promote genuine values of humanity. To eliminate lies and imposture and to establish criteria of competence and justice in all areas of

*I.e., no longer the "Socialist Republic of Romania"—Ed.

activity. To base the development of the national culture on a new foundation. To take the press, radio, and television from the hands of a despotic family and turn it over to the hands of the people.

7. To observe the rights and freedoms of national minorities and to ensure their full equality with those of the Romanians.

8. To reorganize all of the country's trade, proceeding on the basis of the requirements of primarily satisfying all of the daily needs of Romania's population. In this respect we will end the export of agricultural and foodstuffs, we will reduce the export of oil products, and we will give priority to satisfying the heating and electric power needs of the people.

9. The whole foreign policy of the country should serve the promotion of good-neighborliness, friendship, and peace in the world and should be integrated in the process of building a united Europe, a common home of all the people of this continent. We will observe Romania's international commitments; primarily those to the Warsaw Pact.

10. To promote a domestic and foreign policy subordinated to the needs and the interests of developing the human being. To ensure complete observance of human rights and freedoms, including the right to free movement.

11. By organizing ourselves within this front, we are firmly determined to do our utmost in order to reestablish a civil society in Romania and to guarantee the triumph of democracy, freedom, and dignity of all citizens of the country. . . .

NSF Communique of December 24

The overthrow of the odious dictatorship of the Ceauşescu clan has added a last page to the bloody chronicle of the years of suffering endured by the Romanian people.

Déclassé and irresponsible elements which remained faithful to the tyrant have tried to continue the terrorist practices of the former regime by resorting to provocations, attacks against civilians, indiscriminately killing unarmed people, attacking public institutions, industrial enterprises, military targets, trade outlets, hospitals, and housing quarters.

The Romanian people have, once again, affirmed their tremendous moral energy unleashed by their desire for freedom.

The Army has done its duty and so has a major part of the workers in the Ministry of Interior.

The revolution has won.

To completely restore the situation and to ensure the tranquility needed for a normal life in our free society, the Council of the National Salvation Front has decided to adopt extraordinary measures, which are imperative under the current circumstances. . . .

The bodies of the new structures of democracy must urgently begin their activity of restoring the country by firmly setting themselves up and becoming immediately subordinated to the Council and adopting, together with it, the measures of a political, social, administrative, and economic order; all measures of which are absolutely necessary in the first stages of the reconstruction work.

May the first free New Year bring to Romania, along with the joy of liberation, tranquility and calm which will permit us to assume all the responsibilities of the nation which is affirming its dignity.

The national consensus, the cooperation of the creative forces of our country and of all social categories, of any nationality, constitute a vital condition and the guarantee for fulfilling the basic targets of the revolutionary process in Romania.
The Council of the National Salvation Front.

f) Yugoslavia—From Federalism to Civil War

Far in advance of the rest of the Communist world for many years in introducing political and economic reform, Yugoslavia was ironically the last country in Eastern Europe (apart from Albania) to reject formally the Communist monopoly of power. This was accomplished in January 1990 at the badly divided Fourteenth (and last) Congress of the League of Communists of Yugoslavia. Reform came too late, however, to contain the forces of ethnic separatism gathering within Yugoslavia's federal structure and unleashed by democratization. The Slovene Communists walked out of the very congress that promised reform, and within a year and a half Slovenia, Croatia, Bosnia-Herzegovina, and Macedonia had declared independence, engulfing the former Yugoslavia in a brutal civil war.

Socialism in the world has been faced with the obsolesence of the present model of social reproduction. Authoritarian socialism has come to an end. It is being swept aside by democratic reforms and the laws of market goods production which change production relations at their root.

Yugoslavia has embarked on a radical social reform. Let us create a new order with the attributes of democratic socialism.

Our aims are a society of freedom and democracy, self-management, material wealth, social justice, and solidarity. Our society should move toward the ever increasing rights of the person and citizen—toward a citizens' republic—but also toward greater social fairness and security. With this democracy and motivation in the market economy, it will become an efficient society according to the criteria of the protection of the person and economic, scientific-technological, and cultural progress. . . .

Our society should be founded on the inalienable freedoms and rights of the individual.

There is no other higher historical, state, or class aim above the dignity of the person, nor is there a right or freedom older than the person's individual rights and freedoms. State authority should not encroach on these freedoms; it is obliged only to protect them.

Let us develop political, social, and civil forms of the free activity of the person and their associations. Let us stop the imposed collectivism of the class, the nation, and party and any political violence over the free individuality of the person. Let us liberate people's creativity and spontaneity. . . .

The LCY has taken a stand toward the freedom to express opinions regardless of political beliefs, the freedom to gather and associate, the freedom of political and trade union association, public information, and all other civil freedoms that are guaranteed by the modern democratic world.

The setting up of associations, movements, and parties [stranka] depends on the

FROM: "Proposed Declaration of the Extraordinary Fourteenth Congress of the League of Communists of Yugoslavia: For a New Project of Democratic Socialism and a Federal Yugoslavia," *Politika*, January 24, 1990 (English translation in FBIS-EEU-90-021, January 31, 1990, pp. 79–84).

will of citizens, and the Constitution must guarantee them the freedom of elections. . . .

Under conditions of the freedom of citizens' association, the League of Communists [LC] will fight for the democratic socialist nature of such an association which it represents itself and for cooperation between all equal political entities that are oriented in this way. The LC will fight for its political legitimacy as one of the equal political entities at elections and through other forms of direct expression of the citizens' political will.

With political pluralism we acquire a new quality of life, a new way of achieving power at free elections, and its temporal limitation to an electoral period.

We are fighting for the right to self-management as one of the most important rights in our system. This should be realized as the individual right of every person to free self-organization and self-realization in all spheres of life and particularly as an economic and social right on the basis of labor and means (the right to self-management, to joint decision making, or participation in enterprises) and as a right to self-management for citizens within local and regional frameworks and within the dimensions of the whole community. We will break with an unrealistic normative projection of the self-management system. We will develop self-management as motivation for the creative freedom of the individual and for productive labor and as a way of direct self-liberation of the person and citizen from all types of monopoly.

In the further affirmation of socialist self-management, we will also expand opportunities in relations of entrepreneurship because both are constructed on the foundation of a creative, free, and motivated person. . . .

The LCY stresses the legitimacy of national interests and supports their full affirmation and realization in institutions of the society and the state, but it condemns and rejects nationalist exclusivity and chauvinism because they undermine national equality in Yugoslavia. We will struggle in a decisive and principled way against any violation of national integrity and against the undermining of the common interests of Yugoslavia's peoples and nationalities.

Our aim is a harmonious common life in national equality, in the spread of national cultures, in diversity, in solidarity and reciprocity, and in trust and respect among peoples. We will consistently support the equal position and rights of the nationalities in Yugoslavia and their full integrity. . . .

The first condition of our social reform is to rid the political system of anyone's monopoly, even that of the LCY. We will thus release those political forces which endeavor to disable any form of bureaucracy and particularly to eliminate them for the sake of economic prosperity, ecological equilibrium, democratic and cultural blossoming, social justice, and security for themselves and all people.

Let us change as soon as possible the system of monopolistic economic and political rule which established a "political class" of bureaucrats and pushed us into an autarky according to the logic of self-perpetuation and prevented us from keeping pace with economic, technological, political, and social changes in Europe and the world. Let us change all that so that tomorrow is not too late for socialism in Yugoslavia.

It is necessary to establish state authority on the principles of a law-governed state, the autonomy of a civil society, and the economic and social functions of a modern state. . . .

The federal structure based on AVNOJ [Anti-Fascist Council of National Liberation of Yugoslavia] principles is the foundation of a socialist Yugoslavia. Our society's democratic reform also requires radical democratization of the federation.

The modern Yugoslav federation can exist and develop only as a community of voluntarily associated and equal peoples and nationalities and as a federal state of their socialist republics and citizens created by the free will of peoples on the basis of inalienable rights to self-determination—which also include the right to secession. . . .

The federation's constituent subjects are the federal units and citizens of Yugoslavia with their inalienable national sovereignty. These subjects contain the federal state's source of power and sovereignty, and the organs of the state are responsible to them.

The new constitution should apply these principles in organizing the federal state and defining relations with republics and provinces. The federal units need to be independent and efficient as integral parts of the federal constitutional order. This will make possible successful national development and the development of every federal unit, as well as the consolidation of the Yugoslav community on the basis of these units' responsibility for their own development and the country's development. We reject all ideas and attempts to change this position of the republics in the direction of the unitarization or state-legal disintegration of the Yugoslav federation. . . .

Our aim is economically efficient, market-based, but also ecologically and socially responsible economic operations.

The reformed economic order will mark a break with the so-called consensus economy which destroys the effect of market laws. Adherence to the market of all factors of production and the state's modern role will facilitate a quicker move toward material and spiritual prosperity and the qualitative maintenance and development of all areas of life and society's institutions. . . .

We advocate total freedom of artistic and other creative powers of the human spirit. We consider the creation of material conditions and an inspirational social climate for such creativity a measure of our humanist orientation.

We will strive for equal general conditions for conducting business operations in enterprises with all types of ownership, for social property that will reproduce and increase itself as social capital, for a rational management of social property in different forms, under the conditions characterized by competing types of ownership, for different types of ownership to mutually link and permeate one another, and for the process of socialization and privatization to develop itself according to the market's economic laws; we will strive for such production relations as will facilitate a high level of development of production forces through the market competition of all types of ownership.

Social property must have an owner in the economic and legal sense in order to be property. We cannot and will not resolve this issue according to the administrative but rather according to the market logic which also implies the possibility of stock-ownership, collective ownership, and similar methods of socializing production, that is, the socialization of the currently apparent social as well as private property and the right to appropriate the results of social production. We are starting a complex process of transforming social ownership. We are in favor of every individual having the right to be the owner of property, by himself or with others, with the guarantee that nobody can deprive him of this property arbitrarily.

The LC strives for state and public ownership wherever they are the most appropriate for the nature of activity and the purpose of things and where the public interests are prevalent and where the primary objective is not to make a profit or where making profit is not possible. These types of ownership require effective mechanisms of social control and different forms of participation in management.

The meaning and fate of human life increasingly depend on the environment's protection and preservation. This protection has become an existential, biological, economic, political, legal, and cultural question of every modern society, including ours. This is why this issue is among the primary program objectives of the LCY. The world must apply its joint efforts to stop the destruction of nature so that it does not slide into the abyss of self-destruction forever. This danger represents a fabric that binds not only Yugoslav society, but also European and world societies, because it requires global action. Socialism is facing a new opportunity—an initiative for ecological movements.

Yugoslavia must develop much more rapidly if it is to pull itself out of undevelopment, but in doing so it must join the modern world which is looking for a way to balance quantitative progress with as good a life as possible, a life in which ecology will occupy the prime position. Man's right to a healthy environment is one of the most important individual rights which every society and its organs of power must protect. . . .

The LCY should transform itself as soon as possible into a modern, unified, democratic, and political organization with a renewed socialist program. . . . The Yugoslav Communists will work under the conditions of a pluralist political organization in society as an equal political organization in democratic interaction with other political subjects and in a democratic alliance with socialist oriented organizations, associations, and movements of citizens.

The LC needs new political ideas and new programs for socialism in Yugoslavia, it needs public political initiatives in the democratic pluralist ambience, and especially in the electoral and assembly life, for the realization of these programs. Only such a LC can succeed in the new project of socialism.

g) Dissolution of the Warsaw Pact

The fall of Communist rule in East Europe and Soviet acquiescence in this sweeping change made the old Warsaw Pact security ties among the Communist bloc in practice a dead letter. In 1991 reality was recognized juridically by agreements between the Soviet Union and its former satellites formally terminating the Warsaw treaty alliance and Comecon, the Council for Mutual Economic Assistance.

Pravda on the Pact

The Warsaw Treaty—the military and political alliance of Bulgaria, Hungary, Poland, Romania, the USSR and Czechoslovakia—is becoming a part of history. We are bidding farewell to its military structures. These structures will be dissolved before April 1. . . .

History will give everyone his just deserts.

FROM: Editorial, "Now it's NATO's Turn," *Pravda*, February 18, 1991 (English translation in CDSP, XLIII:7, March 20, 1991, p.22); Protocol Ending the Validity of the Treaty on Friendship, Cooperation, and Mutual Assistance Signed in Warsaw on 14 May 1955 and the Protocol Extending its Validity, Signed in Warsaw on 26 April 1985, July 1, 1991 (English translation in FBIS-SOV-91-128, 3 July 1991, p. 4).

It wasn't our headquarters that devised plans for the nuclear destruction of the USSR and its allies—such as "Charioteer," "Trojan," "Dropshot," "Bravo," "Off Tackle," and whatever else they were called. And what dogged efforts were made to weave a network of military blocs along the immediate and distant approaches to our countries' borders. In signing the Treaty on Friendship, Cooperation and Mutual Assistance on May 14, 1955, in Warsaw, we were responding to the West, in order to keep the cold war from developing into a "hot" one.

What did the Warsaw Pact give us? The short answer is this: During the stormy years of postwar upheaval, when the world was split apart, when politicians had yet to adapt themselves to the new ways and new borders, and when the forces of revenge were drying out their powder and cleaning their ammunition, the Warsaw Pact dependably ensured the inviolability of the borders of our country and its allies and the opportunity to engage in peaceful labor.

Europeans have not known war for 46 years. Impartial analysts cannot help but credit the Warsaw Pact with this. More than once it initiated constructive ideas aimed at detente, arms limitation and the development of all-European cooperation.

And so the Warsaw Pact is parting with its military structure. One can't help thinking: Doesn't this mean the collapse of our doctrine? Isn't it capitulation in the face of a stronger rival, a sign of our weakness? Some people think just that. But the underlying reasons for the move lie elsewhere—in the defeat of the cold war, in the new conditions emerging in Europe, in the radical changes in the East European countries, and in the successes of the new political thinking. . . .

The Treaty

The states which are contracting parties to the Treaty or Friendship, Cooperation and Mutual Assistance which was signed in Warsaw on 14 May, 1955,

—taking into consideration the profound changes which are taking place in Europe, and which mean an end to confrontation and the split in the continent;

—intending in view of the new situation to develop energetically relations among themselves on a bilateral and, depending on the degree of interest, a multilateral basis;

—noting the significance of the joint declaration of the 22 states which signed the Treaty on Conventional Forces in Europe and stated that they are no longer enemies, and will build new relations of partnership and cooperation;

—having decided to promote a gradual shift toward all-European security structures on the basis of agreements achieved at the Paris CSCE summit in November 1990;

—have agreed on the following:

ARTICLE I

The Treaty on Friendship, Cooperation and Mutual Assistance signed in Warsaw on 14 May 1955 (henceforth Warsaw Treaty), and the protocol on extending the validity of the Treaty on Friendship, Cooperation and Mutual Assistance signed on 26 April 1985 in Warsaw cease to be valid on the day the current protocol comes into force.

ARTICLE 2

The parties to the current protocol state that they have no claims at all on each other's property as a result of the Warsaw Treaty. . . .

[Signed] For the Union of Soviet Socialist Republics.
G. I. Yanayev,
vice president of the Union of Soviet Socialist Republics;

[Signed] For the Republic of Bulgaria,
Zhelyu Zhelev,
President of the Republic of Bulgaria;

[Signed] For the Hungarian Republic,
Jozsef Antall,
prime minister of the Hungarian Republic;

[Signed] For the Polish Republic,
Lech Walesa,
president of the Polish Republic;

[Signed] For Romania,
Ion Iliescu,
president of Romania;

[Signed] For the Czech and Slovak Federal Republic,
Václav Havel,
president of the Czech and Slovak Federal Republic.

The End of International Revolution

Casting aside the doctrinaire Marxist-Leninist rationale of Soviet policy as a struggle of the proletarian state against its bourgeois enemies, Gorbachev pragmatically reassessed the Soviet Union's overseas commitments to Third World revolutionaries, and found them both economically and politically unsustainable. Simultaneously with his abandonment of the Communist bloc in Eastern Europe, he sought face-saving withdrawals from the numerous "regional conflicts" around the world, notably in Afghanistan, Central America, and Africa. Meanwhile most Western Communists shed their revolutionary allegiance, and like the most powerful party in Europe, the Italian, sought a new identity as democratic socialists.

a) The Rejection of Revolutionary Politics

Backing up Gorbachev's aim of ending the Cold War, and contending that Lenin never supported world revolution, the authoritative scholar Viacheslav Dashichev articulated the rationale for Soviet withdrawal from foreign revolutionary involvements, as a provocation to the capitalist world and as a detriment to Soviet national interests and the quest for peace.

The realities of the nuclear age and of the scientific and technological revolution call for new thinking and new approaches to the accomplishment of foreign-policy tasks. . . .
. . . In books and articles about our foreign policy you will not find a single mention of any mistakes or miscalculations. Everything that has been done is por-

FROM: Viacheslav Dashichev, "The Search for New East-West Relations—On the Soviet State's Foreign-Policy Priorities, "*Literaturnaya Gazeta*, May 18, 1988 (English translation in CDSP, XL:24, July 13, 1988, pp. 1, 3–5).

trayed as infallible. Of course, Soviet foreign policy has great prestige. It has always been marked by an anti-imperialist thrust, and it has been aimed at ensuring the security of the USSR and its allies and at supporting the international workers' movement and the national-liberation struggle throughout the world. But has everything been done correctly? Can one seriously believe that, having committed major errors in domestic development, we have managed for all these 70 years to avoid them in the international arena? Such a thing just doesn't happen. To err is human. It is important to know one's mistakes and to be able to learn from them. . . .

After World War II, the military-political situation in Europe changed drastically. . . . A united front of Western powers against the USSR came into being. An anti-Soviet coalition unprecedented in its makeup and in its might (with nuclear weapons and delivery vehicles) was formed.

Was this delimitation inevitable? Probably so. The imperialist centers of power saw the growth of world socialism as a direct threat to their interests and resorted to the concepts of "containment," "rollback" and "deterrence." The priority given to these concepts in the arms race that got under way after World War II is obvious. But, while knowing a great deal about the West's unseemly behavior, we are inclined to this day to assess our position at various stages as unambiguously correct, as the only correct position. However, tendencies operated in Soviet foreign policy too that could be perceived as hegemonistic and were perceived as such.

Let us recall V. I. Lenin. Like K. Marx and F. Engels before him, he was a resolute opponent of "making other peoples happy." He mercilessly criticized the ultraleftist plans (advanced after October by the Trotskyists) for the forcible spreading of revolution to Western Europe, Afghanistan, India and other countries, pointing out bluntly that "no decree to the effect that all countries ought to live according to the Bolshevik revolutionary calendar has been issued, and if one were issued, it would not be carried out."

These principles were not at variance with deeds. The dangerous illusions of "world revolution" were overcome. Conditions were created for peaceful coexistence with the capitalist countries. . . .

The hegemonistic, great-power ambitions of Stalinism, becoming deeply rooted in foreign policy, repeatedly jeopardized the political equilibrium among states, especially the East-West equilibrium. In the process, the interests of expanding the social revolution relegated to the background the task of preventing the threat of war. . . .

How has the opposing side perceived—and how does it still perceive today, out of inertia—the USSR's policies and objectives? In the eyes of the overwhelming majority of the Western public, the Soviet Union is a dangerous power whose leadership is striving by military means to liquidate the bourgeois democracies and to establish a Soviet-type Communist system throughout the world.

The thesis about Soviet expansionism has served as the basic cementing material for uniting the states of the other social system against the USSR. The NATO countries' ruling circles have regarded all progressive social processes almost exclusively through the prism of further changes in the global political equilibrium in the Soviet Union's favor. This has very much impeded the activity of progressive forces in the capitalist zone and in the developing world, and massive repression has been brought down against them.

Washington has vigorously exploited the "Soviet military threat" in order to ensure for itself a dominant influence in Western Europe, to advance its hegemonistic interests in various regions of the world, and to create a broad network of military-strategic bases. Ill-considered actions on our part have given US expansionist circles the pretext they have sought for acts of aggression against many peoples, for deploying mighty armed forces and creating more and more new types of lethal weapons. How about the dangerous extremism and adventurism of American policy? They, too, have lived parasitically on the "Soviet threat."

By the early 1970s, the Soviet Union had reached a level in its nuclear-missile forces that made a global nuclear conflict unacceptable for the US. A period of détente between East and West began. Western politicians turned their gaze to peaceful means of achieving anti-Soviet political goals. Special hopes were pinned on an economic weakening of the Soviet Union and on the inefficiency of its economy. This promised the West an erosion of the USSR's international positions and a narrowing of its sphere of influence. Pursuing such a policy required a break with the cold war, the elimination of rough edges in relations with the USSR, and the reaching of compromises on a broad range of questions.

Détente gave the Soviet Union an opportunity, too. The possibility appeared of minimizing confrontation with the West and thereby averting the process of a buildup in the forces of the "anticoalition." Additional resources could have been directed into the accomplishment of domestic tasks and into the political and social development and democratization of the country, and its economy could have been shifted onto a path of intensive development.

For the US and its allies, it soon became clear, détente was acceptable only if the international-political and military-strategic status quo was maintained. As the West saw it, however, the Soviet leadership actively took advantage of détente to build up its military forces, striving for military parity with the US and with all the opposing powers combined—a fact unprecedented in history. The US, paralyzed by the Vietnam catastrophe, was pained by the expansion of Soviet influence in Africa, the Middle East and other regions.

In the West, all this was interpreted as a further increase in the Soviet threat. The extreme right-wing political circles that came to power in the US and other NATO countries turned abruptly from détente to confrontation. The Soviet Union found itself faced with unprecedented new pressure from imperialism.

In Western eyes, the expansion of the sphere of Soviet influence reached critical dimensions with the introduction of Soviet troops into Afghanistan. In earlier times, this could have served as an occasion for unleashing a war. But the threat of nuclear destruction kept the West from resorting to a frontal military clash with the USSR. The "anticoalition" turned to other means of pressure. Chief among them was a massive race in the latest armaments, one that even the West's powerful economy had difficulty sustaining. The spiritual and material resources of the capitalist world were united against the Soviet Union. A "crusade" against the USSR was declared.

The "feedback" effect put the Soviet Union in an extremely grave condition in the areas of foreign policy and the economy. The world's great powers—the US, Britain, France, the FRG, Italy, Japan, Canada, China—were ranged against it. Countering their many times superior potential was dangerously beyond the USSR's capability.

Could such a great exacerbation of tension in the USSR's relations with the West in the late 1970s and early 1980s have been avoided?

Yes, certainly. It is our conviction that the crisis was caused mainly by errors and the incompetent approach of the Brezhnev leadership to the accomplishment of foreign-policy tasks.

The overall goals were formulated quite correctly: peace, security, disarmament, cooperation, noninterference in internal affairs, peaceful coexistence. But there were clearly not enough purposeful, competent, scientifically substantiated and carefully considered actions. We erred in our assessment of the global situation in the world and of the alignment of forces, and we did not undertake any serious efforts to regulate fundamental political contradictions with the West. Despite our political, military (through supplying weapons and advisers) and diplomatic involvement in regional conflicts, we ignored their impact on the easing of tension between the USSR and the West and on the entire system of relations between them.

Clear-cut notions about the Soviet Union's true national-state interests were lacking. Those interests by no means included the pursuit of essentially petty, pro forma gains connected with top-level coups in certain developing countries. Our true interest was in ensuring a favorable international atmosphere for profound transformations in the Soviet Union's economy and in its social and political system. But at the time, it was thought that no transformations were needed. . . .

The uncreative nature of decisions led to a situation in which our foreign policy became exceptionally cost-intensive. The Reagan Administration imposed a colossal increase in military spending on us. Those expenditures grew in the US from $122 billion in 1979 to $284 billion in 1985. To maintain military parity, we tried to keep up with the US in these colossal, unproductive outlays, amounting to more than $1 trillion over a five-year period. . . .

. . . The main problem is whether a political modus vivendi can be reached between the USSR and the Western powers, and whether they can achieve a high level of mutual trust. It is here, in the political and ideological sphere, that the key to disarmament lies. A further "feedback" effect and the strength or weakening of the "anticoalition" opposing the USSR will depend on this sphere.

The USSR and the Western powers should renounce total confrontation, not interfere in the internal affairs of one another or of third countries, set up wide-ranging peaceful cooperation, refrain from putting pressure on the other side's sore spots, not harm its interests, and seek no unilateral advantages. . . .

. . . Since 1945, the Soviet Union has played the role of military guarantor of the expansion of the sphere of socialism in the world. As a result, it has been drawn into an extremely acute confrontation with the main forces of imperialism. Nuclear missiles have made this confrontation exceptionally dangerous and risky.

Socialism has now become an invincible force. Therefore, it is vitally important—from the standpoint not only of the preservation of peace but also of the further development of world socialism—that the center of gravity in the struggle for social progress again be shifted away from the sphere of interstate relations between the USSR and the West to the sphere of the domestic social and political development of the Soviet Union, the socialist countries, and the states of the West and the third world. Whereas in 1917 it turned out to be possible to break the chains of imperialism without outside help in a single country—Russia—today immeasurably better conditions exist for the advance toward socialism on a national basis. The Soviet Union can and should influence world social progress exclusively through its economic, political, scientific and cultural successes. This is a basic Leninist principle concerning the role and tasks of the Soviet state in the international community. . . .

. . . Our foreign-policy activity has assigned overriding importance to a principle that develops Leninist ideas: The interests of saving human civilization from nuclear destruction stand higher than any class, ideological, material, personal or other interests.

b) Soviet Withdrawal from Afghanistan

Eight years of inconclusive counter-insurgency warfare in Afghanistan damaged Soviet relations both with the Western powers and with the Third World, and contributed to disaffection at home. In 1988 Gorbachev decided to accept international mediation and end this involvement, the only acknowledged case of Soviet forces sent into combat since World War II. The Communist Afgan government of Najibullah finally fell to the nationalist guerrillas in the spring of 1992, without Russian interference.

Gorbachev's Policy Statement

The military conflict in Afghanistan has been going on for a long time now. It is one of the most severe and most painful regional conflicts. Now, from all indications, definite prerequisites have been created for its political settlement. In this connection, the Soviet leadership deems it necessary to express its views and to completely clarify its position.

The next round of talks between Afghanistan and Pakistan, through the personal representative of the UN Secretary-General, will take place in Geneva in the near future. There is a significant chance that the coming round will be the final one.

At present, the drafting of documents covering all aspects of a settlement has almost been completed at the Geneva talks. Among these documents are Afghan-Pakistani agreements on noninterference in each other's internal affairs and on the return of Afghan refugees from Pakistan; international guarantees of noninterference in the internal affairs of the Republic of Afghanistan; and a document on the interrelationship of all elements of a political settlement. There is also an accord on creating a verification mechanism. . . .

Seeking to promote a rapid and successful conclusion of the Afghan-Pakistani talks in Geneva, the governments of the USSR and the Republic of Afghanistan have agreed to set a specific date for beginning the withdrawal of Soviet troops— May 15, 1988—and to complete their withdrawal over a period of 10 months. This date has been set based on the assumption that the agreements on a settlement will be signed no later than March 15, 1988, and, accordingly, that they will all go into effect simultaneously two months later. If the agreements are signed before March 15, the troop withdrawal will, accordingly, begin earlier. . . .

FROM: M. S. Gorbachev, Statement on Afghanistan, *Pravda* and *Izvestiya*, February 9, 1988 (English translation in CDSP, XL:6, March 9, 1988, pp. 1–3); Joint Soviet-Afghan Statement, *Pravda*, April 8, 1988 (English translation, ibid., XL:14, May 4, 1988, pp. 10–11); US-USSR Declaration on International Guarantees, *Department of State Bulletin*, June 1988, p. 57.

Any armed conflict, including an internal one, is capable of poisoning the atmosphere in an entire region and of creating a situation of uneasiness and alarm for the neighbors of the country involved, not to mention the sufferings of and casualties among the people of the country itself. That is why we are opposed to all armed conflicts. We know that the Afghan leadership holds the same position.

As is known, all this led the Afghan leadership, headed by President Najibullah, to a profound rethinking of its political course, a process that resulted in a patriotic and realistic policy of national reconciliation. We are talking about a very bold and courageous action: It is not merely a call to end armed clashes but a proposal to create a coalition government and to share power with the opposition, including those who are waging an armed struggle against the government, and even with those who are abroad directing the actions of the rebels and supplying them with weapons and combat equipment obtained from foreign states. This has been proposed by a government that is invested with constitutional authority and wields real power in the country.

The policy of national reconciliation is an expression of new political thinking on the Afghan side. It shows not weakness but the strength of spirit, wisdom and dignity of free, honest and responsible political leaders who are concerned about their country's present and future.

The success of the policy of national reconciliation has already made it possible to begin the withdrawal of Soviet troops from parts of Afghan territory. At present, there are no Soviet troops in 13 Afghan provinces, because armed clashes there have stopped. It is completely possible to say that the sooner peace is established on Afghan soil, the easier it will be for Soviet troops to leave.

The policy of national reconciliation has provided a political platform for all those who want peace in Afghanistan. What kind of peace? The kind that the Afghan people want. The proud, freedom-loving and valiant Afghan people, whose history of struggle for freedom and independence goes back many centuries, have been, are and will be the masters of their country, which is based, as President Najibullah has said, on the principles of multiple parties in the political field and multiple structures in the economic field.

The Afghans themselves will determine the ultimate status of their country among other states. Most often, it is said that the future, peaceful Afghanistan will be an independent, nonaligned and neutral state. Well, we will be nothing but happy to have such a neighbor on our southern borders. . . .

Now about our boys, our fighting men in Afghanistan. They have honestly fulfilled and are continuing to fulfill their duty, in the process showing selflessness and heroism.

Our people deeply respect those who performed their military service in Afghanistan. The state provides them with priority opportunities to obtain a good education and interesting, suitable work.

The memory of those who died the death of the brave in Afghanistan is sacred to us. Party and Soviet agencies are obliged to see to it that the families of the dead and their relatives and loved ones are surrounded with concern, attention and kindness. . . .

If the arms race, which we are so insistently seeking to halt—and with some success—is mankind's insane rush to the abyss, then regional conflicts are bleeding wounds capable of causing spots of gangrene on the body of mankind.

The earth is literally pockmarked with danger spots of this kind. Each of them means pain not only for the peoples directly involved but for everyone, whether in Afghanistan, in the Middle East, in connection with the Iran-Iraq war, in southern Africa, in Kampuchea or in Central America.

Who gains from these conflicts? No one, except arms merchants and various reactionary, expansionist circles who are accustomed to taking advantage of and turning a profit on the misfortunes of peoples.

Carrying through a political settlement in Afghanistan to conclusion will be an important break in the chain of regional conflicts.

Soviet-Afghan Statement.

On April 7, 1988, M. S. Gorbachev, General Secretary of the CPSU Central Committee, met in Tashkent with Najibullah, President of the Republic of Afghanistan and General Secretary of the Central Committee of the People's Democratic Party of Afghanistan. . . .

As a result of the meeting, M. S. Gorbachev and Najibullah arrived at a common opinion with respect to the following:

First. The Soviet Union and the Republic of Afghanistan will act in accordance with the statements published on Feb. 8, 1988. These statements gave a new impetus to the process of a political settlement of the extremely complex regional conflict and made it possible to put the talks on the plane of a practical solution.

Second. The General Secretary of the CPSU Central Committee and the President of the Republic of Afghanistan believe that, as a result of the constructive interaction of all those who are involved in the settlement, the last obstacles to the conclusion of the agreements have now been removed, and they favor their signing without delay.

At the same time, both sides duly appreciate the role of the UN Secretary-General and his personal representative, D. Cordovez.

The President of the Republic of Afghanistan welcomes the readiness of the USSR and the US to be guarantors of the agreements reached in Geneva.

Third. The Soviet Union and Afghanistan reaffirm that, if the aforementioned agreements are signed at the earliest possible date, the accord reached between Afghanistan and the Soviet Union to the effect that Soviet troops will be withdrawn in the period established by these agreements, beginning on May 15, 1988, will remain in force.

Fourth. The policy of national reconciliation makes it possible to settle the situation around Afghanistan, to end the war and fratricide, to establish peace throughout the country, and to form a coalition government with the participation of all forces representing Afghan society, including those which at present are confronting one another.

Fifth. The Afghans themselves, and no one else, will determine the final status of their country among other states. The Soviet Union reaffirms its support for President Najibullah's statement about Afghanistan as an independent, nonaligned, neutral state. In doing so, it proceeds from the premise that this country's territory or any part thereof will never be used for purposes hostile to its neighbors, with respect to which Afghanistan will continue a policy of good-neighborliness and cooperation. This applies equally to the Soviet Union, the Chinese People's Republic, the Republic of India, the Islamic Republic of Pakistan and the Islamic Republic of Iran. The Soviet side supports the statement by the President of Afghanistan to the effect that the internal structure of Afghanistan will be based on the multiparty principle in the political field and the multisector principle in the economic field.

US-Soviet Declaration

The Governments of the United States of America and of the Union of Soviet Socialist Republics,

Expressing support that the Republic of Afghanistan and the Islamic Republic of Pakistan have concluded a negotiated political settlement designed to normalize relations and promote good-neighbourliness between the two countries as well as to strengthen international peace and security in the region;

Wishing in turn to contribute to the achievement of the objectives that the Republic of Afghanistan and the Islamic Republic of Pakistan have set themselves, and with a view to ensuring respect for their sovereignty, independence, territorial integrity and non-alignment;

Undertake to invariably refrain from any form of interference and intervention in the internal affairs of the Republic of Afghanistan and the Islamic Republic of Pakistan and to respect the commitments contained in the bilateral Agreement between the Republic of Afghanistan and the Islamic Republic of Pakistan on the Principles of Mutual Relations, in particular on Non-Interference and Non-Intervention;

Urge all States to act likewise. . . .

c) Nicaragua—Defeat of the Sandinistas

Under international pressure the Sandinista regime in Nicaragua acceded to free elections in February 1990, and lost to the liberal bloc led by Violeta Chamorro. The Sandinistas were allowed to operate as a legal opposition, and undertook to reformulate their program to sustain the aims of the revolution while complying with democratic principles.

The FSLN led the Nicaraguan people in a long struggle to overthrow the dictatorship and started the country's democratization and national reconstruction.

The FSLN made great efforts to achieve the aims of its historic program with the support and participation of broad segments of society, but from the very first years was forced to confront the economic blockade and political-ideological, diplomatic, and military aggression of the U.S. government, which used Somoza supporters and allies and the country's most reactionary sectors as a tool.

Imperialist aggression and economic exhaustion prevented the FSLN from carrying out its historic program and from capitalizing on the results of the far-reaching changes begun in 1979. Society had reached the limits of its endurance and the war seemed never-ending. The majority of the people understood that the war would continue if the FSLN remained in government. This, together with the FSLN's mistakes, was used by the local right wing and imperialists and led to the electoral defeat of FSLN. . . .

The FSLN's historic program was what united all honest Nicaraguans in the

FROM: "Principles and Program of the FSLN," adopted at the First Congress of the FSLN, July 21, 1990 (English translation in Vanessa Castro and Gary Prevost, eds., *The 1990 Elections in Nicaragua and Their Aftermath*, Lanham, Md., Rowman and Littlefield, 1992, pp. 180–183, 187, 190, 200–201). Reprinted by permission of the publisher.

merciless struggle against the Somoza dictatorship. The Sandinista Front hereby reaffirms the democratic, revolutionary, and popular principles that inspired it:

a. The FSLN takes up Sandino's standard, defends national sovereignty and independence, Latin Americanism, and solidarity with the peoples of the world, and struggles against any form of imperialist intervention that infringes on independence.

b. As a revolutionary party, it defends the interests of the poor majority and, rooted in the people, struggles for the freedom and social progress of the humblest sectors of the people.

c. It defends the social, political, and economic gains already achieved and struggles with the aim of carrying out and perfecting the changes society needs to achieve social justice, the equitable distribution of national wealth, real democratization, and progress towards a society free from exploitation and oppression.

d. Political pluralism, a mixed economy, and nonalignment are essential parts of the FSLN's revolutionary platform.

e. The FSLN identifies with and is supportive of the just causes of all the peoples of the world fighting against all forms of exploitation and domination.

f. The FSLN is guided by the immortal example of Carlos Fonseca and all its heroes and martyrs.

The current historical juncture presents the Sandinistas with new battles and new challenges. The election defeat revealed the erosion of the overwhelming support and popularity the FSLN had initially enjoyed. For this reason, a priority is to recover popular consensus.

Since April 1990, the branches of government have been infiltrated with capitalist and reactionary groups opposed to the people's interests and those of the FSLN. From the outset, these groups have tried to get rid of the revolutionary gains and spaces of power accumulated over 10 years of Sandinista administration. They push forward laws and administrative and political actions that seek to dismantle the social and democratic changes achieved.

The Sandinista Front is the revolutionary party that brings together the most outstanding fighters for national independence, democracy, peace and the social progress of Nicaragua.

As a revolutionary party, the FSLN must root itself in the poor majority in the struggle to defend revolutionary achievements and the democratic changes which have taken place in society.

After 10 years of far-reaching change, Nicaraguan society has become pluralist. Now economic and political power are distributed among numerous institutional and civil groups.

The FSLN recognizes this reality as a basic condition for the functioning of a genuine democracy. We propose to strengthen this by promoting and developing the skills and capacity of the poor majority to exercise political power in defense of their interests and in favor of an economic, social, and political model that benefits them.

Elections are the means by which to take government power. The FSLN, however, does not limit itself to attempting to win an electoral contest every six years. As a revolutionary party, and recognizing that in democratic society there are different ways to exercise power, it will always use different means to achieve the people's aspirations, whether or not it is in government. . . .

. . . The agrarian reform should be—through the distribution of land—a solid basis for economic democracy. We will struggle to create a land bank with national lands, the controlled opening of the agricultural frontier, and the confiscation of the idle lands of large landholders. This will meet the demands of the peasants; the demobilized and discharged members of the armed forces and the Ministry of Government; the mothers of heroes and martyrs, and the demobilized Contra, at the same time as it promotes the rational use of land so as not to harm our nation's ecological balance.

[We propose] to recognize the right acquired by the workers to become owners in the privatization process. The FSLN demands that the government support the workers with financing and technical resources in this process. The FSLN will struggle so that the privatization of public enterprises does not mean handing over key sectors of the economy to foreign capital.

. . . Foreign investment should be subordinated to the interests and laws of the nation and serve the country's economic and social development plans. Within this framework, the conditions should be created to encourage foreign investment as part of the alternative for reactivating and remodeling the productive sector and promoting industrial reconversion. . . .

The past five years have seen international political and social changes of global importance. These changes inevitably affect the way in which the small countries and peoples of the Third World confront their serious economic, political, and social problems, as well as their possibilities for doing so. The collapse of the socialist bloc, the emergence of geoeconomic blocs built around the European Community and Japan, the military predominance and relative economic decline of the United States, the sharpening of the economic crisis in the Third World in general and Latin America in particular, have seriously obstructed independent paths to development. Therefore, we believe the economic integration of the countries of Latin America is the best alternative.

This poses the reality of an unjust international order with a dividing line between the countries that daily produce, accumulate, and consume in the north and those of the south, whose hardships, needs, and hunger increase every day. . . .

. . . The FSLN struggles

a. so that the freedom of worship of any religion be ensured and effectively respected, as stipulated in the Constitution;

b. so that all its cadres and members show complete respect for the people's religious traditions and feelings. We will fight all signs of disrespect of religious feelings among Sandinistas and towards the population; and

c. for the improvement of relations of cooperation with the churches with aim of working for reconciliation, peace, and social well being.

The FSLN acknowledges the commitment of many Christians who, led by their faith, have struggled for social change and justice for the majority, trying to make a reality of the preferential option for the poor professed by the Latin American Christians. . . .

The FSLN will struggle for

a. the defense of the freedom of expression and the right of all citizens, journalists and communicators to communicate;

b. the democratization of the ownership of the media to prevent them from becoming the instruments of power of large national and foreign economic groups;

c. support and respect for the autonomy of the revolutionary media: the state media outlets should be guided by strictly professional, pluralist, and nonpartisan criteria; we will struggle so that the granting of state advertising is not ruled by political interests;

d. the people's participation in the strengthening of all democratic spaces that exist in the media. The media should promote the debate of ideas and the solution of conflicts through peaceful means;

e. the defense of the rule of law, the Constitution, democratic rights, popular and national interests, and the values of national culture by the mass media; and

f. the FSLN will support all initiatives to raise the professional level of journalism; the exercise of a critical, investigative, truthful, and responsible journalism, and promote respect for the professional dignity of the journalists.

d) Angola: Attempted Compromise

One of the most heated points in the Soviet Union's drive for influence in the Third World in the Brezhnev period was Angola, where Cuban troops were brought in to fight for the Communist-oriented government of the MPLA (Popular Movement for the Liberation of Angola) against the rival rebel movement of UNITA (Union for the Total Independence of Angola) and their South African allies. With Soviet and American encouragement an agreement was reached in the spring of 1991 providing for the withdrawal of foreign froces and a multiparty government based on free elections. However, UNITA, under the leadership of Jonas Savimbi, after losing the election to José Eduardo dos Santos of the MPLA, opted to continue guerrilla resistance.

Principles of the Lisbon Agreement

1. The recognition by UNITA of the Angolan state, President José Eduardo dos Santos, and government until general elections are held.

2. As the cease-fire comes into effect, UNITA will acquire the right to freely carry out and take part in political activities under the terms of the revised constitution and relevant laws on the creation of a multiparty democracy.

3. The Angolan Government will hold talks with all political forces with a view to learning about their views on the proposed constitutional changes. Accordingly, the Angolan Government will work with all parties to draft laws which will speed up the electoral process.

4. Free and fair elections to choose a new government will be held after the registration of voters, and under the supervision of international observers who will remain in Angola until they confirm that the elections were free and fair, and that the results were officially announced. On the signing of a cease-fire accord, the sides will set the timetable under which elections will be held. The specific date of elections will be set after consultations with all Angolan political forces.

5. Respect for human rights and fundamental freedoms, including the right to free association.

6. The process of creating a single national army will begin once the cease-fire comes into effect, and will be completed by the time elections are held in terms of an agreement to be finalized between the government of the People's Republic of Angola and UNITA. The neutrality of the national Army during elections will be

FROM: Summary of the Accord of Principles for Peace in Angola, May 1, 1991, and May Day Speech by President José dos Santos, May 1, 1991, Luanda National Radio, May 1 and 3, 1991 (English translations in FBIS-AFR-91-086, May 3, 1991, pp. 7–8).

guaranteed by the Angolan sides within the framework of the joint political and military commission, and with the assistance of the international monitoring team.

7. Declaration of a nationwide cease-fire in line with a relevant accord to be signed between the government of the People's Republic of Angola and UNITA.

Dos Santos' Speech

. . . As you know, for several years now we have been searching for a political solution to Angola's internal conflict. We began by dealing with a number of external factors which aggravated Angola's internal situation. After a number of talks and negotiations, we reached an agreement in New York which helped reduce outside influence in Angola's domestic problems.

Therefore, we began to search for internal peace. We went to Gbadolite and managed to reach agreement; however, the accord did not last long. We then began new contacts and embarked on fresh initiatives, and since April 1990 we have been holding direct talks with UNITA (National Union for the Total Independence of Angola) in Portugal.

Today I can announce to Angolan workers, who have strongly stated their desire for peace, that we have reached a political understanding. The first documents on a general political accord will be signed this afternoon. This does not mean that the war will end at once, but subsequent steps will be taken so that hostilities can end this month.

However, one must be careful. The fact that we have reached a political accord means that from now on we have more responsibility for creating conditions to effectively implement what has been agreed upon. First, this demands a great deal of vigilance. Second, there ought to be a great deal of understanding and tolerance. Third, we should always be ready to prevent our adversaries from achieving through force of arms what they have not been able to achieve so far. Therefore, I have come here to tell you, comrades, that peace is near. Therefore, let us continue making efforts and struggling so that peace may in fact be a reality this month.

Workers have also said that they want bread. We all want bread. There is little bread and water. I think, however, that we ought to secure peace first. It would be great if we could attain peace, bread, water, and other things, but let us center our efforts on attaining peace. Once peace is achieved the immediate task ahead of us will be for us to roll up our sleeves and work. Those who do not work cannot eat bread. . . .

. . . Despite the difficult conditions that our country faces, Angolan workers believe in the policy pursued by our party and in the strength of our government, and they trust that we will achieve peace. Thereafter we will mobilize all Angolans regardless of their political views to carry out other tasks which will permit us to have bread, water, housing, and better living conditions. . . .

e) Abjuring the Revolutionary Tradition— the Communist Party of Italy

In January 1991, after a long evolution away from dogmatic Marxism-Leninism and dependence on the Soviet Union, and after a heated internal debate, the Italian Communist Party heeded the urging of its leader, Achille Occhetto, to transform itself into the "Democratic

FROM: Achille Occhetto, "Declaration of Intent," presented to the leadership of the PCI, October 10, 1990, *L'Unità*, October 11, 1990 (Editor's translation).

Party of the Left" with a purely reformist program. Die-hard Marxists split off as the "Communist Reestablishment" (Rifondazione Comunista).

The object of the present declaration of intent is to offer some basic ideological and political reasons that impel us to support the birth of a new party of the Left; to spell out its necessity and historical function; to specify the elements of conceptual and analytical rupture and those of continuity with our Communist tradition; to furnish the directions and the essential reference points that underly our proposal to bring to life a new political formation. . . .

The fundamental contradictions of our epoch—between the necessity of development broadened to the whole of humanity, and the need to defend nature and the ecological equilibrium of the planet; between the internationalization of the processes of production, and the centralization of the seats of decision and control; between the new supranational forms of political, social, and cultural expression, and the emergence of particularism and conflict on national, ethnic, and religious lines—all these contradictions can be resolved only by a politics that is prepared to carry out a qualitative transformation in the model of development and to establish a new world economic and social order.

Such a politics constitutes today the essential object of a new worldwide Left and defines the watershed between conservatives and progressives. . . .

It is clear that in every field, modernity, if it is not accompanied and guided by a higher vision of civilization, of relations among men, between men and women, and of their relationship to nature, will not lead to progress but to a real crisis of civilization. The task of a new Left is to point out the possibility of salvation for the human species, not confining itself to promoting certain fundamental values and principles, but by pointing out the way that leads to the construction of a new economic and social order. . . .

By now everyone recognizes that in 1989 world history changed. The historical process from which the world Communist movement drew its origin, the revolutionary breakthrough of October, the societies which have emerged from this breakthrough, have entered a phase of organic crisis. The failure of that model of social organization is irreversible. The breakthrough of 1917 opened the way for a great process of human emancipation, as the working classes and the popular masses came to autonomous and independent consciousness. It opened the way for the liberation of so many people under colonial regimes, and provided a reference point for the hopes of immense masses of the oppressed and marginalized in every corner of the earth.

The whole world has felt this historic experience and has been transformed by it. It created the concept of a different kind of power, i.e., a different social and governmental setup—a kind of concept, however, that has led to the suppression of the market and the dictatorship of the party in the name of the proletariat, and has failed specifically in regard to the tasks of transforming and governing society.

The international Communist movement—which cannot be simplistically identified with communist ideals of human liberation—thus did not succeed in providing an answer to the problems that evoked it. The crisis and the failure in the experience of so-called "real socialism" have shown that there is an inseparable relationship between the affirmation of democratic guaranties and liberties, and the possibility of accomplishing a change in the social relationships of production in the direction of a socialization of the economy and of power. . . .

. . . Lack of democracy has limited the socialist experiment. The various forms of bureaucratic state socialism have thus ended up in negating the ideals of socialism and in causing inestimable damage to all the forces who, like us, want to keep open the path to the renewal of society. The squandering of the ideological patrimony that had been enhanced by the great political and moral victory of the European Resistance caused its most general significance as a fight for liberty to be obscured.

The prospect of human liberation contained in the ideals of communism has been more and more gravely contradicted and obfuscated. In the countries of the East the words communism and socialism have ended up by losing their attractiveness, to the extent that in the collective consciousness they are identified with the experience of authoritarian regimes. The countries of the Third and Fourth worlds are no longer able to find new reference points. All this has gravely weakened the entire Left on a world scale. What is clear is that the historic failure of those regimes, not their inevitable and liberationist collapse, is what weakened the Left.

The historic crisis of the experience connected with the international Communist movement has caused and is causing radical changes in the international equilibrium. The positive liberation from authoritarianism in the countries of the East does not in itself reopen the way towards a democratic and humane socialism. . . .

. . . A new Left, compared to all the previous historical experience of the Communist and socialist workers' movement, must take a new position regarding power. The proposition of the dictatorship of the proletariat that has been embodied in the authoritarian regimes of "real socialism" has not only failed, but has caused, as is obvious, monstrous tragedies. Even the social-democratic proposition of the mere exercise of governmental power for the purpose of more equal redistribution finds itself facing structural knots of supranational scope and of such an extent that renders strategies of "national reformism" impractical. . . .

. . . A new Left on a global scale must work everywhere for peace and for unity, for the democratization of all international relations, and for concentrating the great energy and technological potential of the whole world in solving the problems of the South, of hunger, of poverty, of sickness, to take on projects of broad scope, grand propositions of sympathetic action and development cooperation between the North and South of the world. . . .

. . . To such an end the safeguard of international legality must be entrusted to a world government and not to the unilateral action of great and small powers. Just for this reason it is very important politically and historically that the UN is today at the center of efforts to find a solution to the crisis in the Gulf. A new international order demands a more active and significant role for the UN, a reform of this organization, the construction of a solid international democracy, able to involve both large and small countries, the global North and South. . . .

The great ideal objective of the European Left and of the new party of the Left in Italy, must be to unite two values that in the course of this century have become separated: liberty and equality. In the East, under the regimes of real socialism, the lack of liberty has prevented the affirmation of equality; in the West, the lack of equality has not allowed liberty to be expressed fully and universally. The pluralistic democracies remain unfilled regarding the three fundamental principles of 1789: equality, liberty, and fraternity. . . .

At the outset of the workers' movement a common perspective was established, with which comparison remains open although profound changes have intervened in the human world. Such perspectives were singled out by Marx and Engels, in the Manifesto of the Communist Party of 1848, when they spoke of the creation of "an association in which the free development of each is the condition for the free development of all." This perspective, in its libertarian principle, retained and still retains the heritage of the liberal and democratic revolutions, and is enriched today by the greatest non-violent revolution of contemporary history, that of women. To remain faithful to this perspective today demands a profound renewal, an ideological and programmatic redefinition on the part of all the political traditions of the Left. . . .

In the Marxist tradition and in the varieties of historical experience arising from it, the great socialist theme of the reappropriation of social wealth still seems unsolved. It is therefore crucial to work out a program of economic democracy, specifying the instruments through which workers and citizens may enjoy in new forms the wealth that has been produced, or participate in the control and management of the process of accumulation, of their jobs, of the ends to which this process should be directed.

The growth of great multinational concentrations poses the question of the need for new forms of control, regulation, and democratic guidance of the economy at the supranational level. The Left does not fight against the internationalization of the economy, but poses the problem of its democratic regulation. . . .

The new party of the Left must . . . take on the task of constructing, in detail and in practice, a new relationship between the function of the market and the need for conscious management of production and social development. To induce the market to operate in such a way as will correspond to essential social ends is a crucial task of the Left, that only the Left can accomplish. The problem is the reverse of the proposition that has guided international Communism: not to abolish the market in order to establish socialism, but to use and govern the market to realize gradually a society of free and equal people. Therefore, a new relationship between the state and the market is now central. . . .

Solidarity, cooperation, the aim for labor that is freer and more humanized, justice, nonviolence, diversity are values that must constantly be tested in a coherent relation with our basic program and in practice. The new party of the Left carries within itself diversity, not as deviation, not as an idea of schism and fragmentation, but as a fruitful and active factor in building unity. This requirement, equivalent to a basic break with the old conceptions of the seizure of power, of the party, and of the state, can no longer be expressed in the form of the "mass party of a new type" squaring with the system of democratic centralism. Overcoming democratic centralism represents the sharpest discontinuity not only with the tradition of international Communism but also with that of Italian Communism. This discontinuity alone is in itself sufficient to transform the Communist Party radically from what it had been historically. . . . The explicit presence of diverse components, legitimately organized, is a guarantee against ideological ossification and above all against the use of ideology as a permanent justification of the policies of ruling groups. Only in this framework can we today make Gramsci's idea of the collective intellect come true. . . .

. . . An entirely secular conception of politics, one that is conscious of the limits of politics itself, recognizes fully the autonomous significance, the unsuppressible, irreducible value of the religious quest, conscience, and experience. The new party thus opens itself to the competition of diverse ideas and policies. . . .

Still, really solid participation in forming the new party requires that the diverse paths that join to give life to a new political formation should enter into a relationship of positive recognition of the values and needs that have been historically inscribed in the ideological perspective of Italian Communism and its democratic inspiration.

This has to do with those communist ideals, contradicted by the historical experience of international Communism, which refer to the idea of liberation and the liberated society, to the critique of the supremacy of the production of goods over every other aspect of social life and activity, to the project of a real humanization of man's needs, that develop the critique of alienated labor and consumption and of the state as a machine apart. . . .

I propose, therefore, that at its Twentieth Congress the Italian Communist Party should promote and ratify the creation of a new party.

I propose that the name of the new party should come out of the two great ideas that define the basic coordinates of the forces of renewal on the world scale.

The idea of democracy as the path to socialism. The idea of a renewed Left; of a Left that in Italy takes on the task of working to conduct to a higher synthesis, without losing them, the ideals and the experience of Italian Communism, of liberal and Socialist reformism, of social and democratic Catholicism; of a Left that opens itself to meet all the currents and forces of global renewal and that thus contributes to the realization of the great cause of the liberation of mankind.

I therefore propose that the name of the new party should be: Democratic Party of the Left. . . .

Thus, in a new form, the great objective for which we are fighting is summed up: socialism.

f) The End of Soviet Aid Programs

Following the collapse of Communist rule in Eastern Europe and the abandonment of its overseas revolutionary gambits, the Soviet Union reconsidered and rejected its whole policy of spending on foreign aid for ideological and strategic purposes.

Izvestiya's Comment

The debate over our aid to foreign states has grown more lively in the past few months. And now comes the first victory of those who want to reduce it: The USSR Supreme Soviet resolution [adopted on June 13—Trans.] on the concept of our transition to a regulated market economy instructs the USSR Council of Ministers to work on cutting back the amount of aid we give.

I'd like to congratulate the Deputies on an important step toward glasnost and on the fact that they have come closer to solving the external problems that complicate our internal ones. At the same time, however, one can only regret the fact that the question has been posed so narrowly and deals only with the volume of aid. For the problem is not one of volume; that is a consequence. The essence of the problem lies elsewhere—namely, in the thrust and objectives of our aid. From this

FROM: Yelena Arefyeva, "Charity or Still Ideology?" *Izvestiya*, July 24, 1990 (English translation, CDSP, XLII:31, September 5, 1990, pp. 6–7); Decree of the President of the USSR, "On Changes in the Soviet Union's Foreign Economic Practice," *Pravda* and *Izvestiya*, July 25, 1990 (English translation, ibid., p. 7).

standpoint, the diverting of resources from the national economy fails to stand up to any criticism. And precisely on account of its openly prerestructuring character, it prompts just one desire—to reduce it.

In other words, we should be talking about a full review of our aid policy, which would in turn lead to a reduction. At any rate, provided we base our reasoning not on ideology, as in the past, but on humanitarian considerations and sober economic calculation. . . .

Normal universal human logic will suggest where and how we should show humanitarian concern, in the process helping both ourselves and others. And then it will turn out that taking humanitarian considerations into account is cheaper and, moreover, more effective for a partner than paying for ideology. It will become apparent that the byword of those who oppose cutbacks in aid—"we must be charitable"—conceals an intention to continue paying a tax on our blind submission to ideology.

With this slogan, they urge us to be charitable—though not to our own people, of course. In the process, the notion of charity becomes the object of double and even triple speculation.

The discussion surrounding Cuba is typical. It seems we are beholden to Cuba—for its charity toward our Afghanistan veterans and the children of Chernobyl, whom it is prepared to take in and treat. Yet it is clear that Cuba has developed its excellent health care system not without the credits we have given it. Moreover, attempts are made to prove the necessity of being charitable toward that faraway country through the highly dubious manipulation of economic indices. It turns out that we even benefit from our own charity—something unprecedented in international aid practice.

But the basic scope of this speculation extends even further: While emphasizing humanitarian considerations, the proponents of this kind of aid never mention the real gain, a gain programmed into this aid in past years. I am referring to the ideological and military-strategic gain, which undermines potential partners' trust in us. . . . I think the Americans are fully justified when they ask: Just where is our new political thinking? Where is the real confirmation of our new defense doctrine? And isn't it in order to preserve confrontation that we maintain close military ties with Cuba, ties supplemented with an infusion of economic resources? . . .

This is the kind of aid—aid that is determined by the former ideological objectives of the "struggle between two systems" or is subordinate to obsolete military objectives—that undoubtedly must be reduced. On all continents, not just in Latin America. And along with purely military aid, of course, which is becoming our disgrace. . . . It would be good to voluntarily give up our regrettable lead among exporters of arms to the third world. . . .

Outright aid accounts for one-fifth to one-sixth of all [our aid] expenditures, not counting the vast military assistance we provide. The problem is one of ensuring that our remaining outlays are not outright gifts as well. After all, some of these outlays are adding to already hopeless debts. . . . If we are to recover these debts, we must provide credits not to ideological allies, but on the basis of economic realities. . . .

Gorbachev's Decree

In connection with the transition to a market economy and the policy of openness and broader participation in world economic ties, and taking into real consideration the social, economic and political changes occurring in the CMEA member-countries and in the world as a whole, I resolve:

1. The USSR Council of Ministers is to ensure a changeover, as of Jan. 1, 1991, to the settlement of accounts at world prices in freely convertible currency in economic relations with the other CMEA member-countries. It is to submit draft laws and other acts necessary for the legal substantiation of this changeover to the USSR Supreme Soviet.

2. In implementing measures to further expand economic cooperation with developing countries, it is to base this cooperation on the principles of mutual benefit and mutual interest, guided by international norms and practice. It is to proceed from the premise that economic aid must be provided with due regard for our country's real capabilities.

3. The USSR Council of Ministers and the Union-republic Councils of Ministers, making maximum use of new forms of economic interaction with foreign countries, are to ensure the creation of conditions for the broad participation of enterprises and associations of enterprises in foreign economic ties, with a view to expanding export potential and enhancing the effectiveness of economic and scientific-technical cooperation.

M. Gorbachev
President of the Union of Soviet Socialist Republics.
The Kremlin, Moscow, July 24, 1990.

The Hard Line in China

For a time in the later 1980s the ferment in the Soviet Union and Eastern Europe seemed to be drawing China in the direction of reform. A massive student pro-democracy movement culminated in the occupation of Tiananmen Square in the heart of Beijing, only to end in the bloody suppression of the protesters after Deng Xiaoping (aged but still the real boss) dropped the reformers from the leadership and affirmed the tough approach of his premier, Li Peng. Nevertheless, though affirming Communist rule the Chinese leadership moved successfully ahead with its program to relax economic controls and promote development.

a) The Tiananmen Massacre

In the spring of 1989 a mounting wave of student demonstrations, appealing to the tradition of the democratic "May Fourth Movement" of 1919, virtually immobilized the Chinese leadership for over a month. Finally Deng Xiaoping and Li Peng ordered military intervention at Tiananmen Square and elsewhere, resulting in hundreds of deaths and thousands of arrests. Deng endeavored to justify this repression as a move to protect the masses from bourgeois reaction.

New May Fourth Manifesto

Fellow students, fellow countrymen:

Seventy years ago today, a large group of illustrious students assembled in front

FROM: Wuer Kaixi, "New May Fourth Manifesto," read at Tiananmen Square, May 4, 1989 (English translation in Han Minzhu, ed., *Cries for Democracy: Writings and Speeches from the 1989 Chinese Democracy Movement*, Copyright © 1990 by Princeton University Press, pp. 133–37. Reprinted by permission of Princeton University Press. Deng Xiaoping, Speech to Martial Law Units, June 9, 1989, Beijing radio, June 27, 1989 (English translation in FBIS-CHI-89-122), June 27, 1989, pp. 8–10.

of Tiananmen, and a new chapter in the history of China was opened. Today, we are once again assembled here, not only to commemorate that monumental day but more importantly, to carry forward the May Fourth spirit of science and democracy. Today, in front of the symbol of the Chinese nation, Tiananmen, we can proudly proclaim to all the people in our nation that we are worthy of the pioneers of seventy years ago.

For over one hundred years, the pioneers of the Chinese people have been searching for a path to modernize an ancient and beleaguered China. Following the Paris Peace Conference, they did not collapse in the face of imperialist oppression, but marched boldly forward. Waving the banners of science and democracy, they launched the mighty May Fourth Movement. May Fourth and the subsequent New Democratic Revolution were the first steps in the patriotic democracy movement of Chinese students. From this point on, Chinese history entered a completely new phase. Due to the socioeconomic conditions in China and the shortcomings of intellectuals, the May Fourth ideals of science and democracy have not been realized. Seventy years of history have taught us that democracy and science cannot be established in one fell swoop and that impatience and despair are of no avail. In the context of China's economy and culture, the Marxism espoused by the Chinese Communist Party cannot avoid being influenced by remnants of feudal ideology. Thus, while New China has steadily advanced toward modernization, it has greatly neglected building a democracy. Although it has emphasized the role of science, it has not valued the spirit of science—democracy. At present, our country is plagued with problems such as a bloated government bureaucracy, serious corruption, the devaluation of intellectual work, and inflation, all of which severely impede us from intensifying the reforms and carrying out modernization. This illustrates that if the spirit of science and democracy, and their actual processes, do not exist, numerous and varied feudal elements and remnants of the old system, which are fundamentally antagonistic to large-scale socialist production, will reemerge in society, and modernization will be impossible. For this reason, carrying on the May Fourth spirit, hastening the reform of the political system, protecting human rights, and strengthening rule by law have become urgent tasks of modernization that we must undertake.

Fellow students, fellow countrymen, a democratic spirit is precisely the absorption of the collective wisdom of the people, the true development of each individual's ability, and the protection of each individual's interests; a scientific spirit is precisely respect for individual nature, and the building of the country on the basis of science. Now more than ever, we need to review the experiences and lessons of all student movements since May Fourth, to make science and rationalism a system, a process. . . .

. . . To this end, we urge the government to accelerate the pace of political reform, to guarantee the rights of the people vested in the law, to implement a press law, to permit privately run newspapers, to eradicate corruption, to hasten the establishment of an honest and democratic government, to value education, to respect intellectual work, and to save the nation through science. Our views are not in conflict with those of the government. We only have one goal: the modernization of China.

. . . Our present tasks are: first, to take the lead in carrying out experiments in democratic reform at the birthplace of the student movement—the university campus, democratizing and systematizing campus life; second, to participate actively in politics, to persist in our request for a dialogue with the government, to push democratic reforms of our political system, to oppose graft and corruption, and to work for a press law. We recognize that these short-term objectives are only the first steps in democratic reform; they are tiny, unsteady steps. But we must struggle for these first steps, we must cheer for these first steps.

Fellow students, fellow countrymen, prosperity for our nation is the ultimate objective of our patriotic student movement. Democracy, science, freedom, human rights, and rule by law are the ideals that we hundreds of thousands of university students share in this struggle. Our ancient, thousand-year civilization is waiting, our great people, one billion strong, are watching. What qualms can we possibly have? What is there to fear? Fellow students, fellow countrymen, here at richly symbolic Tiananmen, let us once again search together and struggle together for democracy, for science, for freedom, for human rights, and for rule by law.

Let our cries awaken our young Republic!

Deng Xiaoping's Response

This storm was bound to come sooner or later. This is determined by the major international climate and China's own minor climate. It was bound to happen and is independent of man's will. It was just a matter of time and scale. It is more to our advantage that this happened today. What is most advantageous to us is that we have a large group of veteran comrades who are still alive. They have experienced many storms and they know what is at stake. They support the use of resolute action to counter the rebellion. Although some comrades may not understand this for a while, they will eventually understand this and support the decision of the Central Committee.

The April 26 *Renmin ribao* [People's Daily] editorial ascertained the nature of the problem as that of turmoil. The word turmoil is appropriate. This is the very word to which some people object and which they want to change. What has happened shows that this judgment was correct. It was also inevitable that the situation would further develop into a counterrevolutionary rebellion.

We still have a group of veteran comrades who are alive. We also have core cadres who took part in the revolution at various times, and in the army as well. Therefore, the fact that the incident broke out today has made it easier to handle.

The main difficulty in handling this incident has been that we have never experienced such a situation before, where a handful of bad people mixed with so many young students and onlookers. For a while we could not distinguish them, and as a result, it was difficult for us to be certain of the correct action that we should take. If we had not had the support of so many veteran party comrades, it would have been difficult even to ascertain the nature of the incident.

Some comrades do not understand the nature of the problem. They think it is simply a question of how to treat the masses. Actually, what we face is not simply ordinary people who are unable to distinguish between right and wrong. We also face a rebellious clique and a large number of the dregs of society, who want to topple our country and overthrow our party. . . . Their goal is to establish a totally Western-dependent bourgeois republic. The people want to combat corruption. This, of course, we accept. We should also take the so-called anticorruption slogans raised by people with ulterior motives as good advice and accept them accordingly. Of course, these slogans are just a front: The heart of these slogans is to topple the Communist Party and overthrow the socialist system.

In the course of quelling this rebellion, many of our comrades were injured or even sacrificed their lives. Their weapons were also taken from them. Why was this? It also was because bad people mingled with the good, which made it difficult to take the drastic measures we should take.

Handling this matter amounted to a very severe political test for our army, and what happened shows that our PLA passed muster. . . . The army is still the People's Army and . . . it is qualified to be so characterized. This army still maintains the traditions of our old Red Army. What they crossed this time was in the true sense of the expression a political barrier, a threshold of life and death. This was not easy. This shows that the People's Army is truly a great wall of iron and steel of the party and state. This shows that no matter how heavy our losses, the army, under the leadership of the party, will always remain the defender of the country, the defender of socialism, and the defender of the public interest. They are a most lovable people. At the same time, we should never forget how cruel our enemies are. We should have not one bit of forgiveness for them. . . .

We have already accomplished our first goal, doubling the GNP. We plan to take twelve years to attain our second goal of again doubling the GNP. In the next fifty years we hope to reach the level of a moderately developed nation. A 2 to 2.9 percent annual growth rate is sufficient. This is our strategic goal. . . .

. . . There is nothing wrong with the four cardinal principles.* If there is anything amiss, it is that these principles have not been thoroughly implemented: They have not been used as the basic concept to educate the people, educate the students, and educate all the cadres and Communist Party members.

The nature of the current incident is basically the confrontation between the four cardinal principles and bourgeois liberalization. It is not that we have not talked about such things as the four cardinal principles, work on political concepts, opposition to bourgeois liberalization, and opposition to spiritual pollution. What we have not had is continuity in these talks, and there has been no action—or even that there has been hardly any talk.

What is wrong does not lie in the four cardinal principles themselves, but in wavering in upholding these principles, and in very poor work in persisting with political work and education.

In my CPCCC [Communist Party of China Central Committee] talk on New Year's Day in 1980, I talked about four guarantees, one of which was the enterprising spirit in hard struggle and plain living. Hard struggle and plain living are our traditions. From now on we should firmly grasp education in plain living, and we should grasp it for the next sixty to seventy years. The more developed our country becomes,. the more important it is to grasp the enterprising spirit in plain living. Promoting the enterprising spirit in plain living will also be helpful toward overcoming corruption.

After the founding of the People's Republic, we promoted the enterprising spirit in plain living. Later on, when life became a little better, we promoted spending more, leading to waste everywhere. This, together with lapses in theoretical

---

*I.e., socialism, dictatorship of the proletariat, leadership by the Communist Party, and affirmation of Marxism-Leninism-Maoism—Ed.

work and an incomplete legal system, resulted in breaches of the law and corruption.

I once told foreigners that our worst omission of the past ten years was in education. What I meant was political education, and this does not apply to schools and young students alone, but to the masses as a whole. We have not said much about plain living and enterprising spirit, about the country China is now and how it is going to turn out. This has been our biggest omission.

Is our basic concept of reform and openness wrong? No. Without reform and openness, how could we have what we have today? There has been a fairly good rise in the people's standard of living in the past ten years, and it may be said that we have moved one stage further. The positive results of ten years of reforms and opening to the outside world must be properly assessed, even though such issues as inflation emerged. Naturally, in carrying out our reform and opening our country to the outside world, bad influences from the West are bound to enter our country, but we have never underestimated such influences. . . .

. . . We must continue to persist in integrating a planned economy with a market economy. There cannot be any change in this policy. In practical work we can place more emphasis on planning in the adjustment period. At other times, there can be a little more market regulation, so as to allow more flexibility. The future policy should still be an integration of a planned economy and a market economy.

What is important is that we should never change China into a closed country. There is not [now?] even a good flow of information. Nowadays, do we not talk about the importance of information? Certainly, it is important. If one who is involved in management doesn't have information, he is no better than a man whose nose is blocked and whose ears and eyes are shut. We should never again go back to the old days of trampling the economy to death. . . .

America has criticized us for suppressing students. In handling its internal student strikes and unrest, didn't America mobilize police and troops, arrest people, and shed blood? They are suppressing students and the people, but we are quelling a counterrevolutionary rebellion. What qualifications do they have to criticize us? From now on, we should pay attention when handling such problems. As soon as a trend emerges, we should not allow it to spread. . . .

b) Authoritarian Reform

Though he repelled the challenge of political reform, Deng Xiaoping nevertheless held to the basic economic strategy he had followed since the early 1980s, of encouraging individual agriculture and small enterprise while retaining the Communist Party's political monopoly and the machinery of central state planning. After some zigzagging, the party leadership reaffirmed this line late in 1990, and China went on to enjoy an economic boom contrasting with the collapse suffered by the Soviet economy in the wake of political reform.

. . . Since China opened up a new situation of socialist modernization construction in the 1980's, we have undergone severe political tests while facing many contradictions and problems in economic and social development; some destabiliz-

FROM: Proposals Adopted by the Seventh Plenary Session of the Thirteenth Chinese Communist Party Central Committee, December 30, 1990, Beijing Radio, January 28, 1991 (English translation in FBIS-CHI-91-019, January 29, 1991, pp. 14–19, 27–34).

ing factors have existed despite the overall situation in the country which is characterized by stability and unity. Internationally, in the next decade, we will be able to
continue to win a favorable external environment for China's modernization drive
amid rapid political changes and fierce economic competition in the world. Success
or failure in our efforts in the 1990's to consolidate and develop achievements of
the 1980's, further promote economic growth and social progress, and usher
China into the 21st century with even greater pride will have a direct bearing on
the rise or fall of socialism in China and the destiny of the Chinese nation. . . .

The first-step strategic objective—that is, doubling the gross national product
of 1980 and providing enough for the people to eat and wear—basically has been
achieved. Basic requirements for realizing the second-step strategic objective in the
next decade are as follows:

—On the basis of greatly improving economic efficiency and optimizing the
economic structure, the gross national product of 1980 will be quadrupled by the
end of this century in terms of constant price. To achieve this objective, the gross
national product will be required to grow at an annual rate of about six percent,
which is a relatively high growth rate in the world.

—The people's living standards will improve from just having enough to eat and
wear to a state of leading a fairly comfortable life, with more ample means of sub-
sistence, the rationalization of consumption structures, significant improvement in
the conditions of dwellings, a more colorful cultural life, and continuous improvement of health and social services.

—Efforts will be made to expand educational undertakings, promote scientific
and technological progress, improve economic management, readjust the economic
structure, and give priority to key construction projects so as to lay the material
and technological foundation for China's sustained economic and social development in the early 21st century.

—An economic structure and operating mechanism initially will be established
to meet the growth needs of the socialist planned commodity economy, based on
public ownership and combining the planned economy with market regulation.

—The building of socialist spiritual civilization will be raised to a new high and
socialist democracy and the legal system [will] be further improved. . . .

. . . Economic and social life in both rural and urban areas, and in both coastal
and inland regions in China has shown unprecedented vitality in the 1980's. Our
national economic strength has been enhanced remarkably, and a profound change
has taken place in the situation of our society. The socialist system gradually is
being brought to perfection, and the political situation of stability and unity is
being consolidated and enhanced continuously. The great achievements in the
1980's have further firmed the confidence of the Communist Party of China and
the Chinese people in wholeheartedly undertaking socialist modernization and have
enhanced their courage and perseverence in overcoming difficulties.

Upholding the road of building socialism with Chinese characteristics is the
fundamental guarantee for realizing the second-stage strategic goal. On Comrade
Deng Xiaoping's initiative, . . . our party has reached the scientific conclusion
that China is in the primary stage of socialism, and has formulated the basic line of
making economic development the central task, . . . in accordance with the principle of integrating the universal truth of Marxism with China's concrete practice

and on the basis of thoroughly summing up historical and current practical experiences. . . .

. . . The promotion of rich socialist culture and ethics is a fundamental task of building socialism with Chinese characteristics. Without socialist culture and ethics, there would be no guarantee of the orientation and motive force for social-ist modernization. In the face of a complicated international situation and Herculean tasks in reform and development at home, it is all the more necessary for us to make great efforts to promote socialist culture and ethics, strengthen ideological and political work, struggle against bourgeois liberalization, and broaden and deepen education in patriotism, collectivism, and socialism. . . .

. . . After more than two years of efforts, we have achieved marked results in improving the economic environment and rectifying the economic order; total social demand and supply are growing in balance, inflation is under control; agri-culture has seen rich harvests for two consecutive years; industrial production is turning upward step by step; and the economic order is being straightened out with initial successes. The improvement of the economic environment and the rec-tification of the economic order on the one hand and carrying out in-depth reform on the other are in unison and promote each other. While we are improving the economic environment and rectifying the economic order, reform not only does not bog down but also is being continuously carried out and deepened. However, irrational structures in economic life, poor economic results, failing systems and relationships, and other contradictions accumulated for years, and problems in the deep structure await fundamental solutions. . . .

We should initially establish a new economic structure in the coming decade. Reform is the process by which the socialist system improves and develops itself. In a general sense, the socialist system, from its birth to the stage of relative maturity, inevitably requires the readjustment and reform of the relations of production and the superstructure in order to suit the development of productive forces. . . .

It is the basic direction of deepening economic restructuring to set up an eco-nomic operating mechanism that combines the planned economy with market reg-ulation in line with the requirements for developing a socialist planned commodity economy. . . .

The main tasks in deepening the reform of the economic structure are as follows:

—To persist in an ownership structure embracing diverse economic sectors with public ownership as the main body to form an ownership structure that suits the present level of our country's productive forces.

—To establish a vigorous management system, operating mechanism, and self-control mechanism for state-owned enterprises and explore diversified ways for the effective materialization of the public sector of the economy.

—To strengthen the construction of the market system and the market organi-zations and gradually establish a unified national market system under the guidance and administration of the government. . . .

. . . The aim is to establish and perfect the mechanism for setting prices at reasonable levels and the structure for managing prices, and to gradually put under state control the price of a small number of important commodities and services affecting national welfare and the people's livelihood. The prices of other common commodities and services will be determined through market mechanisms. During the Eighth Five-Year Plan, we must further reduce the scope by which prices are fixed by the state, and expand the portion covered by market mechanisms. . . .

. . . The stress of planning should be put on the forecasting, planning, guiding, regulation, and control of economic activities in the entire society and on maintaining the overall balance of the economy and the harmony of major proportions and structures. We should improve the forms and methods of planning management according to the principle of combining planned economy with regulation through the market and the objective conditions for economic development in different periods, and persist in and improve the system for overall balancing of the national economy. We should rationally readjust the scopes of mandatory and guidance planning and regulation through the market, conscientiously apply the law of value and the principles of supply and demand, gradually use economic policies and levers as the principal means for managing and regulating economic activities, and make planning decisions and exercise management in a more scientific and efficient way. . . .

[We should] accelerate the building of an economic law system and bring about the regularization and systematization of economic control. During the Eighth Five-Year Plan period, we should gradually establish a relatively complete economic law structure, so that various economic activities may follow the law. Steps should be taken to accelerate the pace of formulating such basic economic laws as the "planning law," "budget law," "banking law," "investment law," "corporate law," "pricing law," "market law," "labor law," "wage law," and "auditing law," and work on strengthening economic supervision and economic jurisdiction should proceed in a down-to-earth manner. . . .

. . . Giving full play to the advantages and favorable conditions of coastal regions in the course of opening to the outside world will have a major strategic significance in accelerating economic development and in promoting the invigoration and prosperity of the nation's economy. . . .

The execution of the 10-year program and the Eighth Five-Year Plan will make China richer, stronger, and more prosperous, and will contribute to world peace and development. China has always pursued an independent foreign policy of peace, and advocated the Five Principles of Peaceful Coexistence in the handling of relations between nations. China's development needs a peaceful international environment and a constant expansion of friendly contacts and sincere cooperation with countries around the world. We believe that in the course of implementing the 10-year program and the Eighth Five-Year Plan, economic and technological exchanges between China and the rest of the world will become more dynamic, on the basis of equality and mutual benefits. The various forms of friendly cooperation already in existence will consolidate and develop further.

[We will] continue to press ahead with the cause of reunifying the motherland. Along with the return of Hong Kong and Macao to the motherland, China will actively press ahead to bring about direct mail, trade, and traffic across the strait in the 1990's. Under the principle of "one country, two systems," we will step up exchanges, improve understanding, welcome investment on the mainland by Taiwan businessmen, and promote the reunification of the motherland. This is the sacred mission bestowed upon us by history. . . .

It is necessary to strengthen and improve the leadership of the Communist

Party of China. The Communist Party of China is the force at the core in leading people of all nationalities of our country to proceed in the building of socialist modernization and in the cause of reform and opening to the outside world. The smooth implementation of the 10-year program and the Eighth Five-Year Plan calls for further strengthening and improving the party's leadership. All members of the Communist Party, especially the party's leading cadres, must conscientiously study Marxism-Leninism and Mao Zedong Thought while serving the people whole-heartedly. It is necessary to continue to carry forward and develop the fine tradition of combining theory with practice, maintaining close ties with the masses, and unfolding criticism and self-criticism; adhere to the principle of democratic central-ism; keep to the working method of "from the masses and to the masses"; maintain the flesh-and-blood ties with the masses; and strengthen the party's inner cohesion and fighting power. . . .

The CPC Central Committee issues the following call: All members of the Communist Party and Communist Youth League; workers, peasants, and intellec-tuals of all nationalities of our country; the broad masses of cadres and soldiers of the People's Armed Forces; all patriotic people of democratic parties, mass organi-zations and non-party personnel; and all people who love their motherland—you shall unite even more closely, work with one heart, quietly put your shoulder to the wheel, struggle hard for the successful accomplishment of the 10-year program and the Eighth Five-Year Plan, and create a better future with your own wisdom, talent, and hard working hands!

Cuba—Castro Holds Out

Fidel Castro's regime, ruling Cuba since 1959 but heavily dependent on Soviet support, nevertheless resisted the movement for reform elsewhere in the Communist world. Like China, Castro had to address pragmatically the economic needs of his country in the hope of surviving abandonment by the Soviet Union, while he continued to defy the USA.

. . . Our political system and our democracy have absolutely nothing to envy of any country on earth. I believe our democracy is highly meritorious, because it is located 90 miles from the United States and because the sword of Damocles has dangled over our heads for so long. . . .

I strongly believe that men do not need excessive power. Men who have great responsibilities within the government and the state require limited power.

That power must be limited by the party first of all. It must be limited by gov-ernment institutions. This will prevent the election of an individual who has power over everything around him and who answers to absolutely no one. . . .

I have another strong conviction regarding our countries and Cuba in particular, and that is my belief in the tremendous convenience of the single party system. I have strong convictions about this. I have thought about all these problems many times in my revolutionary life, because the multiparty system is an instrument of imperialism to keep societies fragmented and divided into 1,000 pieces. It turns societies into societies that are unable to solve their problems. . . .

FROM: Fidel Castro, Speech at the Closing Session of the National Assembly of the People's Government, December 27, 1991, Havana radio and television, December 29, 1991 (English translation in FBIS-LAT-92-001, pp. 8–11, 13–16, 18–19).

. . . Bolívar was for Latin American unity and a central government with much authority. He knew there were many dividing factors in those Spanish colonies and he strongly defended the idea of a single republic with a strong central authority. Bolívar was not for a parliamentary government because during that long war— that tremendous struggle to unify all those societies—he saw that unity and strong authority were essential. We could say that Bolívar was also in favor of single party government. He was a constant critic of factions and parties. . . .

Latin America will soon have spent 200 years struggling for independence and what does it have? What does it have? Latin America, the America born from Spain, the Spanish and Portuguese colonies, could have been much more powerful than the United States is today. If Latin America had united, the United States would have been unable to snatch away more than half of Mexico. If Latin America had united, Puerto Rico would be part of that Latin America today. There would be no Panama Canal owned by the Yankees [and] that Republic would not have been colonized for so long. Central America would not have been subjected to tyrannic and bloodthirsty governments for dozens of years, governments that have written the history for almost a century-and-a-half in our America. Had Latin America become united like the forefathers wanted—particularly José de Miranda, the fore-runner of this idea—or like Bolívar wanted, today, possibly, Latin America would be the most powerful nation on earth, without a doubt, because of its territory, population, and natural resources. What are we? . . . We could have been every-thing, but we are nothing. . . .

The CIA became the master. The CIA became the highest level professor of all torturers. The CIA made torture a science. It implemented all tactics as to how to make people disappear and do horrible things. It taught all governments how to torture. . . .

. . . One hundred years ago, Jose Martí, the greatest thinker of this continent, the greatest political thinker, without any doubt whatsoever, clearly saw that there was a need to lead the war in a set way, based on history. He saw that there was a need for solid unity. He saw that a party was needed to lead the revolution.

I do not recall seeing anything else by Martí, any reference to the multiparty sys-tem. He said the multiparty system caused the country's fragmentation. . . .

I am firmly convinced that one party is and must be—for a long historical period, no one can predict how long—the form of political organization in our society. . . .

Imperialists want a multiparty system, politicking, market economy, return to capitalism, and all that. This is why we do what we do, based on our principles and to improve our system. I believe that to have taken this step is to improve our sys-tem, which establishes the direct participation of the population in the election of deputies. But we have to do this without politicking. . . .

This is the most difficult period in Cuba's history. It is not just the most difficult period of the revolution, but the most difficult in Cuba's history. . . . The enemy is busy trying to make 1992 a difficult year for us, as difficult as possible. It will try to prevent us from having any market for our products. It will try to prevent us from getting fuel, not even for cash. The enemy is busy, busy everywhere. The enemy is busy in Moscow. Now, the enemy moves around in Moscow. There are many people of the worm pit in Moscow. They are trying to influence the authorities there, making offers, and doing things. They are trying to hurt our economic ties with whatever is left of the USSR. . . .

To give you an idea, I just have to say that at the beginning of 1991, commercial agreements already experienced a big drop in the sugar price. It dropped by $300 in 1991.

In spite of all this, there were a series of agreements and industrial objectives under construction and some credits.

According to this year's agreements we should have received $3.763 billion in merchandise. As of 21 December, we have received $1.673 billion. Traditional imports from the USSR dropped by more than $1 billion and what was left dropped by $2.1 billion. So, if Soviet imports were once $5 billion, now they amount to $1.673 billion. Can you think of a more drastic reduction? Can you think of something more drastic?

To all this we must add the disappearance of trade with the socialist sphere—what we lost when the socialist area ceased to exist, without considering the USSR. We have been suffering since 1990. To all this we must add the Yankees, who are more daring and influential than ever. They are tightening the screws as much as they can. The imperialists and their agents are busy everywhere. This is why I said yesterday: Do you know the USSR disappeared? All those things seemed completely inconceivable. As I have told you on other occasions, it seemed strange when I mentioned that possibility, almost two-and-a-half years ago. It is a very sad reality, but it is a reality. The USSR does not exist. . . .

It might get a little worse, but it is impossible to expect more harm. Now it is our time, because we are not like those common roosters that fly away, speaking in a country style, such as in Pepe's times, we are fighting cocks and fighting cocks do not jump the fence. They do not flee a fight. They fight until the end. We are not a lineage that surrenders, we are another type of people. . . . What could be said about us, spiritual and moral heirs of entire generations that have fallen in the long struggle to have a fatherland, a fatherland with dignity, a fatherland with pride; not that trash, that type of a fatherland we had for more than 50 years because of the Yankees. . . .

. . . In no circumstances, however difficult they may be, however extremely difficult they may be, should a fighter's morale, a revolutionary's morale drop. I see here some comrades who remind me of feats performed by our comrades in many places at various times. . . .

We also had times like the famous Bay of Pigs. All the best, most intelligent calculations by the Pentagon, about air total superiority, the OAS prepared, the government prepared, and even so we did not give them a single minute to carry out their plans. We did not stop fighting them. We fought for 68 straight hours, and they were liquidated.

Then there was the October missile crisis, and no one here vacillated when the crisis occurred. I do not remember seeing a single comrade vacillate or become demoralized. We could have disappeared from the map, because at any time something could have exploded. We did not know what might happen, if they might bomb our bases, if someone might fire a rocket. There was a real danger of an atomic, nuclear war. I did not see a single citizen of this country become demoralized or intimidated. We were very indignant when our allies did us the favor of negotiating over there without saying a word to us, and they pledged to withdraw the missiles. We were very indignant, but we did not vacillate.

. . . From the time Reagan became U.S. President . . . we reached the conviction that the defense of this country depended on our own skin and heart, and no one became demoralized.

We began to develop all the ideas of the all-people's war, which were our old ideas, our ideas from the Sierra Maestra, our ideas from the early years of the revolution. We began to rectify, because some doctrines in the military sphere had also done us harm. They made us depart a little from the ideas we had had at the beginning of the revolution, the concepts of the all-people's war. Who was going to argue with the Soviets . . . ? Who knew more than them about military matters? They knew a lot more than us, and they might have known about strategic war, although I am not very sure about that now, after seeing the mistakes they have made. . . .

I saw them make very serious mistakes during the October missile crisis. I saw them make very serious military mistakes. But, well, they have mastered the cosmos, you know how many missiles they have, what accuracy, what range. Who could argue with them? But one day we realized, and we have to thank Reagan especially for this, when he came with his increased threats, when we reached the conviction that in the event of a war or Yankee attack, we were the only ones who would defend ourselves. . . .

. . . We reached the conclusion that the USSR, the former USSR, when it was in the fullness of its power, and had who knows how many missiles and other things. . . , we reached the conclusion that we could not count on the USSR to defend this country if there was a Yankee invasion, other than with laments and declarations of solidarity and protests.

. . . It is different with the all-people's war. That war would never end. . . . They can occupy the whole country, and the day they occupy the whole country they will be worse off than the day they disembarked. Because that day they would have to fight against millions of people, even against adolescents, all mixed up together. The time they mix together with us is when they will be worst off. A division can be annihilated, but you cannot annihilate a people that fights. This has been shown in all wars throughout history. . . .

I said two-and-a-half years ago that if one day we woke up to the news that the USSR no longer existed, we would continue to defend the revolution and socialism. They knew what I was saying, and they were not worried. Everything that has happened in that country with so much history and glory, so many merits, so many services it has provided to humanity, is very bitter. We clearly saw the consequences of everything that was happening, the consequences it would have for us, and that the revolution and the country were going to be left in a difficult, very difficult situation. . . .

The problems in the world are there to be seen. We will see how problems of Third World countries will worsen. We will see how there will be fierce competition between the great economic blocs in the world. We will see how poverty will increase in a great part of the world. At that time, we will be coming out of our most difficult time. That is the way these events will take place. Awareness plays a very important role in this struggle; ideology plays a decisive role. . . .

We should never give up ground in ideology. We should never give up ground in combativity and fighting spirit. Never allow anyone to do so. Remember that in every man there is always a little bit of pride. Life has taught us this, especially in war, even when we saw men make mistakes. There have even been cases of men who were frightened and later showed impressive, reckless courage. We need to know how to incite the pride of each human being. Do not worry, because when it seems that there is nothing left in a revolutionary, there will always be a bit of pride, and you can do a lot with that little bit of pride. . . .

Let us never forget that this was the country which did the most generous international missions. This was the country that offered hundreds of thousands of men. Every time there was an internationalist mission hundreds of thousands would volunteer. Look at what kind of spirit our people were educated in! They are willing to fulfill their duty no matter how difficult the mission might be. . . .

There are those who are talking over there about dividing up the country among themselves, or they are dividing it up over there—sugar mills, lands, houses, schools—those who dream of taking everything once again and assigning an owner to everything, a private owner to everything. It is clear that none of us can ever resign ourselves to thinking about that. It is clear that this will not happen while there is even a single one of us, a revolutionary, a man or woman of pride, alive. . . .

That horde of reactionary people would not want the smallest symbol of the revolution to remain in the country. What would they turn our schools into? Into cabarets or brothels? . . . What would they do with the women of this country? What would they do with our proletariat or working class? What would they do with those who fought during these 30 years defending the revolution in the party, the youth organization, the Federation of University Students, the Committees for the Defense of the Revolution, the labor unions, the farmers associations? What would they do? What would they do with the remains of our dead?

Because we already know what they would do with the nation's symbols; they would vilely hand them over to our enemies. They would give our nation, our land, our waters, our natural resources, and the blood and sweat of our people to the empire. They would give our land to the empire. . . .

The world expects us to be capable of resisting. The revolutionary movement and the revolutionaries of the world expect that of us. Our ideas expect that of us; our flags expect that of us. We are a symbol today, and we are playing a role that we did not seek but that came to us. We must carry it out. We are a hope. We are a bastion of Latin American independence, as the declaration which was approved here today said. We are a bastion of the just causes of this world.

. . . Those who have pride and know how to defend their ideas to the end are saluted with admiration, with hats off. That is why I am expressing here my conviction that this generation of Cubans, and those who come afterwards, and those who came before us, will be respected and admired. They will always have to recognize that we were able to fight in the most incredibly difficult conditions, that we were willing to give everything to defend everything that we hold sacred, that we were able to give everything for victory. Because if we act as we should act, if we conduct ourselves as we should conduct ourselves, and as I am sure we will, victory is the only possible end result.

Let it never be said of any of us present, of those who make up this ANPP, or even of our guests, let it never be said that a single one of us wavered. [applause]

Let it never be said that a single one became demoralized. Let it never be said that a single one sold out. Let it never be said of any of us who are witnesses to this historic moment we are experiencing, let it never be said that we were not capable of fighting and that we were not capable of dying for the nation, for the revolution, and for socialism. [applause]

Socialism or death, fatherland or death, we will win. . . . [applause]

Russia's Quest for Acceptance

After six years of reform leading to economic and ethnic crisis at home and the collapse of Communist influence abroad, Gorbachev's government was ready to abandon its superpower status and its revolutionary pretensions, even before the failed coup and the breakup of the Soviet Union in 1991 formally put an end to Soviet Communism. The successor government of Boris Yeltsin in the Russian Federation continued Gorbachev's efforts to secure Western aid and to assure the outside world that Russia would be a cooperative member of the international community.

a) A Plea for Western Aid

Economic difficulties at home heightened the Soviet Union's readiness to end Cold War confrontations and become a part of the world economy, with the hope of Western aid to see it through the crisis of perestroika. Grigory Yavlinsky, an economic advisor both to Gorbachev and to Yeltsin, negotiated with the Group of Seven major industrial powers, and in conjunction with the American political scientist Graham Allison proposed a "grand bargain" of Soviet reform and Western aid.

. . . For the USSR today, integration into the world is a top-priority issue, an urgent one and, in the current situation, also a step that we are forced to take, chiefly because of the state that the country's economy is in. . . .

Today all the preconditions exist for the emergence of conditions favorable to the initiation of a qualitatively new policy of cooperation between the USSR and the world's leading countries.

Lately there have been signs of an improvement in the political situation in the country. The retreat from confrontation includes the "nine plus one" agreement [between Gorbachev and the heads of nine republics], the end of the miners' strikes and many other things. In addition, society is "digesting" the price increase and adapting to the new economic situation.

But the equilibrium is unstable and could be "blown" by social and interethnic problems if the initial agreements and declarations are not followed by joint practical actions, if we do not move on to a policy of results. . . .

The consultations that have been held in recent weeks indicate a fairly high degree of readiness on the part of certain Western countries to cooperate in the event that our side takes the necessary steps. Let us note that situations favorable to pursuing a policy of cooperation and large-scale programs, both inside and outside

FROM: Grigory Yavlinsky, Mikhail Zadornov, and Aleksei Mikhailov, "Program for an Organized Return to the World Economy," *Izvestiya*, May 20, 1991 (English translation in CDSP, XLIII:20, June 19, 1991, pp. 1, 3–5).

the country, do not arise often. For instance, after the agreements between Gorbachev and Yeltsin in July-September 1990, there was a relatively long period of open confrontation before the main political forces in the country moved closer together again. Do we have the right to let slip, once again, a suitable moment for beginning to act?

Carrying out economic reforms in cooperation with the most developed countries will give us a chance, an opportunity for an "organized return" to the world economy and, more broadly, the world community. Conditions will be created enabling us to make use of the whole of human experience in overcoming our backwardness.

Economic cooperation will provide the impetus for stepping up contacts between people in all areas—science, culture, business. Friendly ties with citizens of other countries will be established. Opportunities will increase for replacing hopelessly outdated technologies in many branches of the economy—and that will mean an increase in the output of goods, the easing of environmental problems and an improvement in working conditions. It will be significantly easier to find solutions to problems that arise in the course of the reforms themselves.

The economic reforms will have to be carried out during a deep slump, and they will require significant resources. The retraining of unemployed people will involve substantial expenditures. To make the ruble convertible we need certain reserves of foreign exchange, and we do not have them today. Finally, colossal sums will be needed for the structural transformation of the economy—many sectors will have to be rebuilt virtually from scratch.

We will have to find the bulk of the money for this in our own country—by getting rid of inefficient production facilities, overcoming mismanagement and huge losses, etc. But at the most critical period—the lowest point of the slump, with massive unemployment and inflation—direct support in the form of resources from developed countries would provide a very important helping hand. . . .

It is impossible to "fence oneself off" from our country and let events develop on their own. This is not only because the USSR occupies one-sixth of the world's land area. There is also our huge nuclear potential. There are our stockpiles of chemical and bacteriological weapons, our dozens of nuclear power plants and other industrial facilities. In the event of an escalation of violence in our country, it will be impossible to forget about all this—the lesson of Chernobyl is far too vivid.

The economy of the USSR is a part of the world economy, albeit a relatively isolated one. It is here that the traditional sources of raw materials and traditional markets for the countries of Eastern Europe, which are also living through difficult times, are located. Hundreds of firms in developed countries are geared toward filling Soviet orders. If an uncontrollable crisis in the USSR coincides with a general slump in the world economy and with some sort of major international conflict, there will be no avoiding a serious destabilization of the world economic order. . . .

One thing is clear—the world community, and the developed countries above all, will have to participate in one way or another in solving the Soviet Union's problems. And if that is so, the question of cost arises.

The developed countries have an interest in keeping their expenditures on support for reforms in the USSR to a minimum—that is natural. But after all, the sooner a program of cooperation gets under way, the less money and effort it will require from our partners. As long as a large part of our economic potential remains, as long as state institutions are operating, and as long as the economic slump can still be gotten under control, support from outside will be very important, but it will nevertheless be a supplement to our own efforts. But with every passing year, and recently, literally with every passing month, the ratio between the Soviet economy's own possibilities and resources and the outside support needed to overcome the crisis has been shifting toward the latter. The cost of the negative consequences of an uncontrollable turn of events in the USSR and the destruction of the country's economic potential will unquestionably be many times higher for the entire world than the expenditures that a cooperation program will require.

Therefore, it is time to think seriously about what kind of program of cooperation there can be between the developed countries and the Soviet Union.

A Program for Cooperation.—Clearly, this should not be a purely economic plan, although support for specifically economic reforms will be an important part of our joint actions. It should also reflect the problems of arms limitation and disarmament, cooperation in settling international conflicts, and humanitarian cooperation—all of this should rise to a new level.

As for economic cooperation proper, it should not just be help in the form of foodstuffs, consumer goods and hard currency, as is usually supposed. We envision it as a joint program of action designed to extend over three to five years, including stages with specific goals and reciprocal obligations. On our side, decisive actions aimed at creating a mixed economy are needed: a reduction of state spending and elimination of the budget deficit; devaluation of the ruble and a gradual transition toward making it convertible; the privatization and demonopolization of state property. A structural transformation of the economy in favor of its consumer sector and a modernization of technologies will be needed.

Only an economic policy of this kind will offer hope of getting out of the crisis and realizing returns from the money invested.

The forms of cooperation with foreign partners can be varied:

—technical support for the reforms (joint drafting of economic legislation, the sharing of know-how, consultations and work by foreign specialists, expert evaluations);

—the training of personnel;

—work on settling problems related to the country's foreign debt;

—the granting of most-favored-nation status to the USSR, participation in international economic organizations and the lifting of various restrictions;

—investments in accordance with agreed-upon priorities—humanitarian aid in the most difficult period. . . .

Won't we lose our independence? It's true that our customary notion of independence based on isolation from the world will have to be revised. For a long time we took pride in our "exclusiveness," until we began to understand that the gap in development between the USSR and the rest of the world was not shrinking but growing. And our economic isolation has in fact resulted in such dependence on imports that the lack of foreign exchange threatens to paralyze many branches of industry this year.

As for our partners in the West, they, in turn, will evidently have to give up their customary notions of what is advantageous to them, as summed up in the formula, "The worse for the USSR, the better." It is clear that a Union carrying out the present policy is no longer an adversary. . . .

b) The Rejection of Imperial Ambition

As the Soviet Union dissolved into its constituent republics in 1991, President Boris Yeltsin of the Russian Federation forswore old Communist expansionist aspirations along with his rejection of Communist politics and economics. With the downfall of the Union and the Communist Party, Russia remained a major power, but only one among several, with no more than conventional national aims and interests.

Izvestiya's Comment

For the first time in modern history, Russia is acting on its own and independently of the Soviet Union, as the largest of the 11 new states of the still-unfledged Commonwealth with its unclear future. . . .

If history is understood to mean epochal changes, then the Russian President's visit to the UN is without a doubt truly historic. Throughout the postwar period, Moscow's top leaders graced the UN skyscraper on the East River with their presence only three times. Only three times, including Yeltsin's visit. Hence the tectonic shifts separating these events are all the more apparent.

In 1960, Nikita Khrushchev spent almost three weeks at the UN and, making blustering speeches and even pounding his shoe on the table at a General Assembly session, proclaimed confrontation between the two systems and the inevitable triumph of socialism over capitalism. He was convinced that the third world would also take a noncapitalist course, and he called on third-world countries to join in an alliance to put an end to Western domination of the UN by means of the "troika principle," under which the UN would have not one but three secretaries-general, each representing a different group of states—the socialist countries, the capitalist countries and the developing countries.

Mikhail Gorbachev, speaking at the UN in December 1988 (only recently!), preferred not to recall his distant predecessor. He preached not confrontation and class hatred, but universal human values, the removal of ideology from international relations, total repudiation of the use of force and, most importantly, the principle of freedom of choice. In fact, Gorbachev's UN speech, like the new thinking as a whole, confirmed the gradual start of the historic retreat of the CPSU and the USSR under the twin pressures of supermilitarization and economic degradation, brought on by the inefficiency of the totalitarian-bureaucratic system. Like Khrushchev, however, Gorbachev went to the UN as leader of the Soviet Communists, still drawing his legitimacy from the precepts of the October Revolution and the Bolsheviks, unaware that he was fated to be the last in the memorable series of General Secretaries.

There is no great valor in having 20-20 hindsight. But on rereading Gorbachev's UN speech now, one can't help but be struck by how blind he proved to be with respect to the near-term outlook. He was a captive of Marxist historical optimism and out of touch with the truth when he asserted that, armed with the theory and practice of perestroika, he was moving forward. He never imagined that exactly one year later, the principle of freedom of choice would lead to the collapse of the "socialist commonwealth" and subsequently to the breakup of the Soviet

FROM: Stanislav Kondrashev, "Boris Yeltsin's Western Itinerary," *Izvestiya*, January 28, 1992 (English translation in CDSP, XLIV:5, March 4, 1992, pp. 15–16); Boris N. Yeltsin, Speech to the UN Security Council, January 31, 1992 (English translation in *UN Security Council Provisional Verbatim Record*, January 31, 1992, pp. 42–48).

Union itself. Nevertheless, we should give him credit for remaining faithful to the principle he had proclaimed. . . .

And now comes only the third visit to the UN in over 30 years. And the man at the helm in Moscow, the one with his finger on the most important button, is no longer a Communist, no longer a Socialist, but a reformer, populist and pragmatist, one who, for the first time in Russian history, was democratically elected to the office of President by popular vote. The country has not completely broken with the past, but it is already post-Soviet, postcommunist and postsocialist.

Back in the summer of 1990, after breaking with the CPSU, Yeltsin continued Gorbachev's work in international affairs, but he went further and acted much more decisively: The ideological barriers between Russia and the West were torn down (at least as far as declared principles are concerned), and we accepted the West's democratic values, including the primacy of the human being over the state and a market economy with private ownership instead of state ownership. We are also prepared to remove all barriers blocking Russia's incorporation into the world economy, but this cannot be done in a day or even a year. For the barriers were erected not so much by flawed legislation as by backwardness, an inability to work, corruption and dependence, established as a way of life in the previous era.

During the years of perestroika, the USSR, in its relations with the West, went from inherent confrontation, interspersed with brief periods of détente, to partnership—partnership that was tested in arms reduction treaties, in efforts to reach an Afghan settlement and in the creation of the anti-Iraq coalition. Closing the book on the Soviet period, Russia is now proclaiming, in its concept of relations with the West, that we are natural allies. . . .

Russia's strength today still lies in something it doesn't need that much—even though the price we paid for it is all our current misfortunes—namely, military and armed strength. Russia's gaping weakness lies in something in which other states are strongest—the weakness of an economy that produces for the consumer and promotes a high standard of living for its people. How can we exchange the surplus unnecessary strength for the strength we really need and rid ourselves of permanent weakness?

In the first stage of our incipient reform, the most important thing is to survive without an explosion. Russia will give up its terrifying strength, but it would very much like to obtain assistance in overcoming its weakness—this, it seems, will be the essence of Boris Yeltsin's message on all legs of his upcoming Western trip. And the essence of the proposed deal will be this: reliable control over and rapid reductions (much more rapid than hitherto undertaken) in the nuclear arsenal and other excessive weaponry, in exchange for comprehensive aid in shifting the Russian economy toward a market system.

In broader terms, the question arises of Russia's identity, without which it cannot live in harmony with itself or the world. Inordinate power arrayed in the clothing of Marxist-Leninist messianism is what gave the Soviet Union its own, albeit sullen, identity. But whether we like it or not, that really was an identity, and not just a mask worn by a Russia subjected to a cruel experiment. Now Russia is going through the critical phase of losing its Soviet identity. A new identity will be acquired when the period of weakness has passed and a respectable, civilized concept of strength arises, and when the economy starts working in a new way: After all, amid poverty and ruin it is impossible to assume a worthy place among other countries, and impossible to pursue a fitting foreign policy, something that, in peacetime, is first and foremost a projection of economic strength and rests on a sound economic foundation (consider the relations of the US, the European Community and Japan). Then and only then will we rightfully regard others, on an equal basis, as our natural allies, respecting the German, the Japanese, and the American, and differing from them just as they differ from one another by virtue of their unique national characteristics. And rightfully taking pride in being Russians and citizens of the Russian Federation.

The President of Russia is leaving on his first tour of Western capitals—and of history too, as he presents to the civilized world his country's troubled, promising and far from fully defined features.

Yeltsin's UN Speech

This summit meeting of the Security Council, the first of its kind on the political Olympus of the contemporary world, is a historic and unprecedented event. The end of the twentieth century is a time of great promise and new anxieties. The age-old search for truth and the attempt to discern what the future has in store for humanity seem to be getting a kind of second wind. Perhaps for the first time ever there is now a real chance to put an end to despotism and to dismantle the totalitarian order, whatever shape it may take. I trust that after all the unthinkable tragedies and tremendous losses it has suffered, mankind will reject this legacy; it will not allow the twenty-first century to bring new suffering and privation to our children and grandchildren.

The process of profound change is already under way in various spheres of life, and above all in the economic sphere. It is a problem that concerns not just individual nations or States, but the whole of mankind. After all, it is an economy mutilated by ideological diktat and built in defiance of all common sense that forms the principal material base of totalitarianism. A profound awareness of this causal relationship has led the Russian leadership to embark upon a most difficult course of economic reform. We have taken that risk in a country where an all-out war was waged against economic interests for many decades.

I am grateful to the world community for its support of our efforts and for understanding that the future not only of the people of Russia but of the entire planet largely depends on whether or not these reforms are successful. I am also grateful to the people of Russia for their courage and steadfastness. They should take a great deal of credit for the fact that the world community is moving ever farther away from the totalitarian past.

Democracy is one of the major achievements of human civilization. All times and all countries have known people who have risen up selflessly in its defence. The people of Russia defended democracy at the walls of our Moscow White House. Now we must accomplish the most difficult task—that is, the creation of legal, political and socio-economic guarantees to make democratic changes irreversible.

All of us [are] weighed down by a tremendous burden of mutual mistrust. It is no secret that a most profound abyss has separated the two States that until recently were referred to as the super-Powers. This abyss must be bridged. That is the wish of our nations and the commitment of the Presidents of the United States of America and the Russian Federation. . . .

. . . Russia believes that the time has come to reduce considerably the presence of means of destruction on our planet. I am convinced that together we are capable of making the principle of minimum defence sufficiency a fundamental law of the existence of contemporary States. . . .

We are ready to participate actively in building and putting in place a pan-European collective security system—in particular during the Vienna talks and the upcoming post-Helsinki-II talks on security and cooperation in Europe.

Russia regards the United States and the West not as mere partners but rather as allies. This is a basic prerequisite for, I would say, a revolution in peaceful cooperation between progressive nations. We reject any subordination of foreign policy to pure ideology or ideological doctrines. Our principles are clear and simple: primacy of democracy, human rights and freedoms, legal and moral standards. . . .

A special role in establishing a new international climate in the world belongs to the United Nations. This Organization has stood the test of time and managed, even in the ice age of confrontation, to preserve the nascent norms of civilized internatioal cohabitation contained in its Charter.

We welcome the United Nations increased efforts to strengthen global and regional stability and to build a new democratic world order based on the equality of all States, big or small.

Russia is prepared to continue partnership between the permanent members of the Security Council. The current climate in the activities of this body is conducive to cooperative and constructive work.

For us, the peace-making experience of the United Nations is particularly valuable.

The new Russian diplomacy will contribute in every possible way to the final settlement of conflicts in various regions of the world that have been unblocked with the assistance of the United Nations. We are ready to become more fully engaged in these efforts. . . .

We are prepared to play a practical role in United Nations peace-keeping operations and contribute to their logistical support.

My country firmly supports steps to consolidate the rule of law throughout the world. It is necessary to enhance the prestige of the International Court of Justice as an effective instrument for the peaceful settlement of international disputes. . . .

It is a historical irony that the Russian Federation, a State with centuries-long experience in foreign policy and diplomacy, has only just appeared on the political map of the world. I am confident that the world community will find in Russia, as an equal participant in international relations and as a permanent member of the Security Council, a firm and steadfast champion of freedom, democracy and humanism.

Last year's events have confirmed that the nations of the world have now come of age and are capable of adopting responsible and meaningful decisions.

This was vividly demonstrated by the developments in the [Persian] Gulf, when our joint efforts resulted in the just punishment of the aggressor [Iraq], and by the defeat of the coup in Moscow last August.

Difficult work lies ahead for us all to consolidate the positive trends in the evolution of today's world and to make them irreversible. It is only on this basis that we can ensure a decent and prosperous life for our nations and every individual. Russia is prepared to do all it can to achieve this goal.

In conclusion, permit me to wish Mr. Boutros-Ghali every success in his important post of Secretary-General of the United Nations.

UNIVERSITY PRESS OF NEW ENGLAND publishes books under its own imprint and is the publisher for Brandeis University Press, Brown University Press, University of Connecticut, Dartmouth College, Middlebury College Press, University of New Hampshire, University of Rhode Island, Tufts University, University of Vermont, Wesleyan University Press, and Salzburg Seminar.

LIBRARY OF CONGRESS CATALOGING-IN-PUBLICATION DATA

A Documentary history of communism and the world : from revolution to
collapse / edited, with introduction, notes, and original
translations by Robert V. Daniels.—"Third, revised and updated
edition"—Preface (1994 edition)
    p. cm.
    Rev. and updated ed. of: A Documentary history of communism.
    ISBN 0-87451-678-1 (pbk.)
    1. Communism—Soviet Union—History. 2. Communism—History.
  I. Daniels, Robert Vincent. II. Documentary history of communism.
HX313.D64   1994
320.5'32'09—dc20   93-46972

∞